Journeys

A History of Canada

Journeys

A History of Canada

R. Douglas Francis
University of Calgary

Richard Jones

Donald B. Smith
University of Calgary

THOMSON
★
NELSON

Australia   Canada   Mexico   Singapore   Spain   United Kingdom   United States

THOMSON

NELSON

Journeys: A History of Canada

by R. Douglas Francis, Richard Jones, and Donald B. Smith

Associate Vice-President, Editorial Director:
Evelyn Veitch

Publisher, Social Sciences & Humanities:
Chris Carson

Marketing Manager:
Lenore Taylor

Senior Developmental Editor:
Rebecca Rea

Photo Researcher and Permissions Coordinator:
Cindy Howard

Production Editor:
Lara Caplan

Copy Editor:
Shirley Corriveau

Proofreader:
Gail Marsden

Indexer:
Jin Tan

Senior Production Coordinator:
Helen Locsin

Creative Director:
Angela Cluer

Interior Design Modifications:
Katherine Strain

Cover Design:
Peter Papayanakis

Cover Image:
Glenbow Archives, Calgary, Canada / NA-2685-61; National Archives of Canada / C-30193

Compositors:
Zenaida Diores

Printer:
Transcontinental

Library and Archives Canada Cataloguing in Publication

Francis, R. D. (R. Douglas), 1944–

Journeys : a history of Canada / R. Douglas Francis, Richard Jones, Donald B. Smith.

Includes bibliographical references and index.
ISBN 0-17-622436-X

1. Canada—History—Textbooks.
I. Jones, Richard, 1943– II. Smith, Donald B., 1946– III. Title.

FC165.F73 2005   971   C2004-906194-1

To Barbara, Lilianne, and Nancy

PREFACE

THE NATURE OF HISTORY

The word "history" refers to both the events of the past and the historian's study of them. While many naturally assume that what the historian tells us about past events is definitive, students of history realize that no conclusive or final study of any event in the past is possible. Historians constantly search for a deeper and richer understanding of, and new perspectives on, past events. That is why history is always being revised and rewritten.

The rewriting of history occurs for many reasons. New evidence, for example, constantly emerges through the discovery of new sources or documents. The work of scholars in other humanities and social science disciplines — such as archaeology and anthropology for Native history, or demography, sociology, and geography for social history — leads to new insights. As well, new perspectives result from historians asking new questions. When, for example, historians were preoccupied with the study of political figures and events, this perspective dictated the sources they consulted and the questions they asked of those sources. When a new generation of historians desired to learn more about the lives of "ordinary people" or of social events, they located different sources, and asked new questions of traditional ones. Today, the study of history has expanded significantly to include a host of subdisciplines: such as women's, ethnic, Native, working-class, intellectual, military, and cultural history, to mention only a few. Such a multiplicity of approaches enriches our understanding of the past.

Adding complexity to the study of history today, besides the unearthing of new sources and the emergence of new varied types of history, are new theoretical approaches. Theories of relativism, Marxism, feminism, and, more recently, post-modernism, force historians to question the nature of history, the role of the historian, and, in some cases, even the ability to write history if seen as some kind of objective study of the past. Still, historians continue to study the past in the belief that it provides knowledge essential for understanding the present, and for providing a perspective on the future. The current debates over the nature of history have influenced and shaped the writing of history within Canada and elsewhere.

THE NATURE OF THIS TEXT

Journeys presents Canada's past from the beginnings to the present. The text reflects and incorporates the new trends in historical writing. First, we include the most recent and up-to-date research by Canadian historians. In a format and style that is clear and engaging for students interested in studying Canada's history, we present as comprehensive and rich a study of Canada's past as possible in a one-volume text. Secondly, we introduce students to the new types of history broadly defined as the "new social history" and the "new cultural history," while also providing them with the more traditional political and economic accounts. Thirdly, we include the historical development and contribution of the Aboriginal people, French-speaking and English-speaking Canadians, recent immigrants, women, and minority groups, realizing that together they make up Canada's rich past. As well, we include the history of each of the country's regions, while keeping Canada as the focal point. Finally, short, up-to-date annotated bibliographies appear at the end of each chapter to identify the major historical writings on the events covered in the chapter.

To review Canadian historians' lively debate on important events, issues, or trends in historical writing, *Journeys* provides a series of boxed inserts entitled "Where Historians Disagree" that highlight differing views. These debate boxes remind students that the writing of Canadian history is an ongoing process. To show that history is the action of individuals, we include "Historical Portraits" that highlight the life of well-known, and not-so-well-known, persons who made their mark in history. Individuals seldom act alone, however, but are part of a community. Thus, in *Journeys*, "Community Portraits" appear to demonstrate the contribution of selected communities to Canada's history.

In terms of format, *Journeys* is divided into thematic sections, each one introduced by a brief overview of themes highlighted in the chapters within the section. Each chapter treats a major topic or period and begins with a "Time Line" listing the key events discussed. *Journeys* follows a chronological approach to help students understand how events developed through time. As well, headings and subheadings throughout the chapters assist in organizing the material. At the end of each chapter a section entitled "Linking to the Past" directs students to additional information for selected topics on the World Wide Web.

In terms of content, *Journeys* tells the story of Canada from its origins with the Native peoples and the coming of the Norse, the Portuguese, the Spanish, the Basques, and particularly the French and the British who eventually established permanent European settlements. It notes the pockets of settlements that occurred in Atlantic Canada, the St. Lawrence River valley, the Great Lakes, the Red River, and the Pacific coast, and accounts the history prior to the formation of Canada in 1867. Then after 1867, *Journeys* shows how Canada came to take the transcontinental form it did, and how the various groups within its boundaries united together. We focus on various regional, ethnic, and social tensions as well as including references to more harmonious events.

We hope that *Journeys* provides students of Canadian history with a knowledge of Canada's past, a desire to explore that past in greater depth in more specialized courses in Canadian history, and an appreciation of the multi-layered, vibrant, and exciting nature of the writing of Canadian history in keeping with the discipline of history as a whole.

Students seeking more extensive bibliographical information are encouraged to consult R. Douglas Francis, Richard Jones, and Donald B. Smith, *Origins: Canadian History to Confederation* 5th ed. (Toronto: Nelson, 2004) and *Destinies: Canadian History since Confederation* 5th ed. (Toronto: Nelson, 2004). Important annotated bibliographical guides to the study of Canadian history include M. Brook Taylor, ed., *Canadian History: A Reader's Guide*, vol. 1, *Beginnings to Confederation* (Toronto: University of Toronto Press, 1994); Doug Owram, ed., *Canadian History: A Reader's Guide*, vol. 2, *Confederation to the Present* (Toronto: University of Toronto Press, 1994); Carl Berger, ed., *Contemporary Approaches to Canadian History* (Toronto: Copp Clark Pitman, 1987); and John Schultz, ed., *Writing about Canada: A Handbook for Modern Canadian History* (Scarborough, ON: Prentice-Hall, 1990). An invaluable bibliography (without annotation) is Paul Aubin and Louis-Marie Côté's *Bibliographie de l'histoire du Québec et du Canada/Bibliography of the History of Quebec and Canada*, published (in several volumes) by the Institut québécois de recherche sur la culture in Quebec City. Easy to use, it contains more than 100 000 titles, all published between 1946 and 1985. Current bibliographies of the most recent publications are listed in every issue of the *Canadian Historical Review* and the *Revue d'histoire de l'Amérique française*. An invaluable reference work for Canadian history has become available, *The Oxford Companion to Canadian History*, ed. Gerald Hallowell (Don Mills, Ontario: Oxford University Press, 2004).

ACKNOWLEDGEMENTS

The authors wish to acknowledge the many Canadian historians who assisted them in the preparation of the five editions of *Origins: Canadian History to Confederation* and *Destinies: Canadian History since Confederation,* from which material for *Journeys: A History of Canada* has been taken.

At Nelson, we benefited enormously from a dedicated and enthusiastic editorial team. In particular, we wish to thank Chris Carson, Publisher, Social Sciences & Humanities; Rebecca Rea, Senior Developmental Editor; Lara Caplan, Production Editor; Shirley Corriveau, Copy Editor; and Gail Marsden, Proofreader. It was our pleasure to work with each of them.

We also wish to thank our wives, Barbara Grant, Lilianne Plamondon, and Nancy Townshend, for sharing our enthusiasm for the project.

CONTENTS

PART TWO ∽ THE CANADAS, 1760–1864

CHAPTER 9

THE NORTHWEST TO THE 1860s   196

PART FOUR ✐ BUILDING THE NEW DOMINION, 1867–1914

➤ CHAPTER 15

URBAN AND INDUSTRIAL CANADA   322

➤ CHAPTER 16

SOCIAL REFORM AND CULTURE:
1890–1914   344

PART FIVE ∼ THE IMPACT OF TWO WORLD WARS AND THE GREAT DEPRESSION, 1914–1945

LIST OF MAPS

Journeys

A History of Canada

THE FIRST PEOPLES

TIME LINE

**70 000–
14 000
years ago—** A land bridge between North America and Siberia, known as Beringia, exists

**c. 15 000
years ago—** The glaciers begin to melt and to retreat

**c. 12 000
years ago—** A human settlement exists in the southernmost portion of the Americas, Monte Verde, Chile

**10 000
years ago—** Humans live throughout large sections of what is now Canada

**5000
years ago—** The glacial ice recedes to approximately its present northern position, and the climate becomes similar to today's

**3500–
2000
years ago—** Civilizations develop in Mexico, Central America, and Peru

**1500
years ago—** The First Nations of southern Ontario begin to grow corn, resulting in the development of societies based on agriculture

**500
years ago—** A variety of peoples reside within what is now Canada, with more than 50 languages, belonging to 11 linguistic families (1 Inuit and 10 First Nations)

The first question of Canadian history remains unanswered: What was the place of origin of the first inhabitants of what would become Canada? First Nations elders believe that their ancestors emerged from this continent, while most archaeologists contend that early humans migrated to the Americas across the land bridge that then spanned the Bering Strait. They disagree, however, as to when this migration first occurred, although consensus exists that the original inhabitants of North America lived on this continent at least 10 000 years before the Europeans' arrival.

ORIGIN OF THE FIRST PEOPLES OF NORTH AMERICA

Many First Nations elders accept as a spiritual truth — one revealed in sacred myths, dreams, and visions — that their ancestors originated in North America. This spiritual belief offers an insight into the First Peoples' vision of their cultures and their rights to the land. Young Blackfoot-speaking children in present-day southern Alberta and Montana, for example, learn many stories about Napi or "Old Man," the creator of the world. Other First Nations have their own explanations of the earth's beginnings, but the Blackfoot's is one of the most descriptive and complete.

In the beginning, water covered the entire world. One day, the curious Napi decided to find out what lay below. He sent a duck, then an otter and a badger, but they all dived in vain. Then Napi asked a muskrat to plunge into the depths. He was gone so long that Napi feared he had drowned. At last the muskrat surfaced, holding a ball of mud. The Old Man took this lump and blew on it until it was transformed into the earth. Napi then piled up rocks to make mountains, dug out river and lake beds and filled them with water, and covered the plains with grass. He made all the birds and animals and, finally, people. He taught the men and women how to hunt and how to live. His work completed, the Old Man climbed a mountain and disappeared. Some say Napi's home is in the Rocky Mountains at the head of the Alberta river that bears his name — The Oldman.[1]

Modern scientists base their theories exclusively on observable data in the natural world. On the basis of archaeological and geological evidence, archaeologists argue that humans did not evolve independently in the Americas but migrated from Siberia.[2] A few archaeologists propose that other migrations occurred by sea, principally to South America from across the Pacific.

Archaeologists believe that *Homo habilis*, the first direct ancestor of modern-day human beings, appeared nearly 2 million years ago in Africa. A more advanced form, *Homo erectus*, followed, approximately 1.5 million years ago, in Asia, Africa, and Europe. About 100 000 years ago, *Homo sapiens neanderthalensis*, or Neanderthal man, emerged. (Canadian archaeologist Robert McGhee has written, "Only within the past 100 000 years have there existed people, who if appropriately clothed and barbered, could walk down a city street without being suspected of having escaped from a zoo."[3]) Physical evidence of hominid bones, dating back up to 40 000 years, have been found in Africa, Asia, and Europe, but not in the Americas. Physical and genetic data link Aboriginal peoples in the Americas to Asian populations. Thus, archaeologists conclude that the human species originated outside the Americas.

Most archaeologists, including some who are members of contemporary First Nations, believe that the early inhabitants of North America crossed from Siberia during the last Ice Age, when sea levels dropped and the continental shelf became exposed. This land bridge, known as Beringia, existed from 70 000 to 14 000 years ago. At one point, the expanse of open grassland and tundra was more than 2000 km wide. Beringia served as a highway for animals passing back and forth between Asia and the Americas. To date no evidence has been found of an ice-free corridor that may have existed along the eastern slope of the Rocky Mountains, thus providing the animals — and, later, humans — with a pathway southward. But an ice-free coastal corridor may have been present. Thus, human hunters, after crossing Beringia, may have travelled by water between the unglaciated pockets of land. Whether by foot or boat or a combination of the two, humans gradually advanced southward throughout North, Central, and South America, eventually crossing more than 15 000 km from Alaska to Patagonia, at the tip of South America. Canada's high Arctic was the last region to be populated, roughly 4000 years ago, as the ice retreated.

The possibility of human migration across the South Pacific from Polynesia to South America is regarded by most archaeologists as unlikely due to unfavourable ocean current and wind patterns, as well as an absence of adjacent islands.

ARCHAEOLOGICAL HYPOTHESES

Scientists disagree as to when the migration from Siberia occurred. Supporters of the more controversial claims contend that humans possibly entered the Americas as early as approximately 100 000 years ago, although no incontrovertible evidence of such an early arrival exists. Most archaeologists place the earliest migration in a much more recent time span. They refer to sites, such as that at Monte Verde in Chile, that show evidence of human occupation more than 12 000 years ago. (This, of course, indicates a human occupation of North America at least several thousand years earlier, if one accepts the northern migration route.) Most archaeologists accept as evidence only those artifacts found in sealed deposits with organic matter that can be radiocarbon-dated. In addition, they require evidence of distinctively styled artifacts. One example is the "fluted point," a stone projectile point with one or more flutes, or hollowed-out channels, that allowed for the attachment of the point to a wooden or bone shaft.

By the "conservative" criteria, there are four Canadian sites — at Debert, Nova Scotia; Vermilion Lakes, Banff National Park; Charlie Lake Cave, north of Fort St. John, British Columbia; and Wally's Beach (St. Mary's Reservoir) in southwestern Alberta — that confirm the presence of humans in Canada at least 10 000 years ago.

About 10 000 years ago a drastic change in climate occurred in the northern hemisphere. For reasons still not fully understood, the great ice sheets (more than 3 km thick) that once covered 97 percent of Canada began to melt. The run-off raised the sea level, causing the Beringian Plain to disappear and the Bering Strait to form.

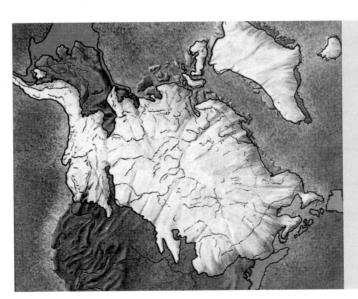

Canada between approximately 80 000 and 20 000 years ago. At this time, almost all of Canada was buried beneath a kilometre or more of glacial ice. A large ice-free area known as Beringia connected Siberia and Alaska. Animals and human hunters moved between the Old World and the New across this arctic landscape.

Canada about 12 000 years ago. At this time, the rapidly retreating glaciers were fringed by large lakes of glacial meltwater. The ancient beaches of some of these lakes reveal the remains of camps occupied by First Nations peoples who moved north to occupy the land that is now Canada.

Canada today.

Source: © Canadian Museum of Civilization, illustrator Gilles Archambault, 1989, image nos. 598-10739, 598-10741, 598-10742.

The absence of ice sheets in formerly glaciated territories meant that wind and rainfall patterns shifted. Forests replaced grasslands, and deserts developed. Some animals now became extinct, especially large grazing animals such as mammoths (giant elephants), American camels, and a very large race of bison that foraged on the grasslands.

CIVILIZATIONS OF THE AMERICAS

About 5000 years ago, the ice receded to approximately its present northern position and the climate became similar to today's. The Bering Strait attained its present width of approximately 80 km, and land animals could no longer cross between Siberia and Alaska. People still made that journey, but no longer from Asia's inland centres; they were sea-mammal hunters and fishers who traded across the strait. The First Nations grew largely as a result of natural population increase, rather than migration.

Adapted their behaviour to suit the environ- ment.

The First Nations population of the Americas underwent major economic and social change over thousands of years. From 3500 to 2000 years ago, the peak of technological and social complexity was achieved in present-day Mexico, Central America, and the Andes of Peru, where permanent communities had the highest population densities on the two continents. In central and southern Mexico, a series of great classical civilizations developed. The dominant one, the Aztec, emerged about 800 years ago. Agriculture (corn, beans, and squash) and rich sea resources formed the basis of these civilizations. Centres with temples and other large structures such as plazas, chiefs' houses, and highways, all constructed with carved and painted stone, appeared as well. Tenochtitlan, the capital of the Aztecs, now located under the present-day Mexico City, became one of the biggest metropolises in the world about 500 years ago, with an estimated population between 150 000 and 300 000 inhabitants.

These civilizations developed without the aid of Europe's domesticated animals — horses, oxen, and donkeys. They had discovered the wheel (wheeled toys have been found in various parts of Mexico), but without animals for transport (other than the dog and, in the Andes, the llama) they had no use for it. They also lacked sufficient supplies of usable copper and tin, to allow for the replacement of stone tools. The Peruvians made a few tools from metal that had washed down in the streams, but in Mexico and Central America only stone tools existed.

-stone tools of various types
• Projectile points
-spearheads, darts, arrowheads
-show great craftmanship + utility.
-stone tools can be re-sharpened + re-used reformed into new tools.

• Evidence of trade system.

Despite the absence of the wheel and of metal tools, the Native peoples of the Americas became well advanced in science and arts. The Maya in Central America, whose civilization flourished between 1700 and 1100 years ago, developed a sophisticated system of mathematics, applying the concept of zero 500 years before the Hindus did. The Maya, being knowledgeable about astronomy, developed a 365-day annual calendar and plotted the cycle of the planet Venus. They calculated eclipses and recorded their calculations in a writing system that was both pictographic and phonetic. In the Andes, the Incas between 800 and 500 years ago developed irrigation systems, built bridges and roads, erected stone walls using enormous rocks cut to fit so tightly that a knife blade could not be pushed between two blocks, and did metalwork of the highest quality in gold and silver. First Nations farmers developed more than 100 species of plants that are routinely farmed today, including two of the world's basic food crops: corn (maize) and potatoes (the other two are wheat and rice).

cereal crops, potatoes, squash

THE MOUND BUILDERS

About 2000 years ago, immediately south of the Great Lakes, farming and a sedentary way of life replaced gathering and hunting in the Ohio and later the Mississippi valleys. The "Mound Builders" of the Ohio River valley (the Hopewell culture) constructed gigantic sculptured earthworks — some nearly 25 m high — in geometric designs, sometimes in the shape of humans, birds, or serpents.

Archaeologists have located thousands of mounds used as burial sites and have excavated several earthen-walled enclosures, including one fortification with a circumference of more than 5 km, enclosing the equivalent of 50 modern city blocks. The Ohio peoples had an extensive trading network. Archaeologists have found, among the artifacts in the burial mounds, large ceremonial blades chipped from obsidian (a volcanic glass) from deposits in what is now Yellowstone National Park in Wyoming; embossed breastplates, ornaments, and weapons made from copper nuggets from the Great Lakes; decorative objects cut from mica sheets from the southern Appalachians; and ornaments made from shells and shark and alligator teeth from the Gulf of Mexico.

The Mound Builders' civilization evolved slowly, reaching its peak roughly 2000 years ago. The Ohio mounds may have been the model for the Great Serpent burial mound, near present-day Peterborough, Ontario. Approximately 2000 years ago, the local people built the earth-works, 400 m long, 15 m across, and rising half a metre to a metre above the surface.

About 1500 years ago, the Mound Builders' culture declined, perhaps as a result of attacks by other nations or of severe changes in climate that undermined agriculture. A similar civilization farther west, around present-day St. Louis, also based on several agricultural crops (corn, beans, squashes, and pumpkins), replaced that of the Mound Builders. It extended over most of the Mississippi watershed, from Wisconsin to Louisiana and from Oklahoma to Tennessee. In the Mississippi Valley cities like Cahokia, which flourished in the present-day St. Louis area, had populations as large as 20 000 people. From 1300 to 800 years ago, this Mississippian civilization of central North America influenced the less technologically advanced Aboriginal nations to the east and north. Indeed, its example led the Iroquoian-speaking peoples of the lower Great Lakes and the St. Lawrence valley to adopt agricultural techniques similar to those of the Mound Builders and the Mississippians.

POPULATION GROWTH

Agriculture could support a larger population than hunting and gathering. The cultivation of as little as 1 percent of the land, in fact, could greatly increase the food supply. Recent estimates of the Aboriginal population of the Americas in the mid-fifteenth century indicate numbers as high as 100 million people, or approximately one-sixth of the human race at that time. The population north of Mexico may have reached 10 million before European contact. Native populations reached such numbers because they lived in a relatively disease-free zone. The Iroquoians, for instance, in present-day southern Ontario and southwestern Quebec, domesticated high-yield cereals and tubers, which allowed them to feed a large population. Approximately half a million people (the most widely accepted estimate) lived within the boundaries of present-day Canada. Roughly half of them lived along the Pacific coast, with its abundant and easily available resources, and in present-day southern Ontario and Quebec, where the Iroquoians practised farming.

The Europeans reduced the Native populations dramatically by unintentionally exposing them to diseases new to the Americas. The Native population lacked defences against such contagious diseases as smallpox and measles. Environmental historian Alfred Crosby has written that "the initial appearance of these diseases is as certain to have set off deadly epidemics as dropping lighted matches into tinder is certain to cause fires."[4] Aboriginal healers had never before encountered these epidemic diseases. They could not combat them, nor could the Europeans, until the twentieth century — long after the Native population had been repeatedly devastated. After European contact, death rates in some areas of the Americas reached as high as 90–95 percent. By the early twentieth century, the entire First Nations population in Canada and the United States had been reduced to less than 1 million, or one-tenth of the estimated population at the time of European contact. Historian Olive P. Dickason has noted that in the seventeenth century, "the lands that appeared 'vacant' to the new arrivals were either hunting areas or else had been recently depopulated because of introduced epidemics."[5]

CLASSIFYING THE FIRST NATIONS

The First Nations population has been classified according to three distinct categories: linguistic, national, and cultural. None is satisfactory. A linguistic division in Canada reveals twelve separate indigenous language units. One is Eskimo–Aleut, the language spoken by the Inuit; the other eleven are First Nations linguistic groups. Seven of them (Salishan, Tsimshian, Haidan, Wakashan, Tlingit, Kutenaian, and Athapaskan) are found in British Columbia. The Siouan speakers are found on the prairies and in the foothills of the Rockies. The Iroquoian speakers live in eastern Canada. The Algonquian (or Algonkian) linguistic family, the largest group, extends from the Atlantic coast to the Rockies. The Athapaskan language group can be found throughout Yukon and the Northwest Territories and the northern sections of the four western provinces. As nearly as can be determined, the First Nations spoke about 50 different languages.

This linguistic classification unfortunately leads to the linking together of widely disparate groups that had little in common, except language. The language of one could differ as much from another as English from German or Portuguese from Romanian. Within the same linguistic family, groups often had different ways of life. The Mi'kmaq of the Maritimes and the Blackfoot of the Prairies, for instance, although separated by 4000 km, are joined together in the Algonquian linguistic family. But they lived entirely different lives, totally unaware of each other's existence. Conversely, the Haidas of the Queen Charlotte Islands culturally resembled their mainland neighbours, the Tsimshians, in everything except their completely unrelated language.

To classify Canada's original inhabitants by political categories also poses problems. Nations — that is, groups of people bound together by a common culture and language and acting as a unit in relations with their neighbours — certainly existed. But among some groups, the ties between the various bands were not strong. The more remote bands diverged considerably in dialect and, in some cases, had so thoroughly assimilated the customs of alien peoples around them that they lost all sense of political unity with their distant relatives.

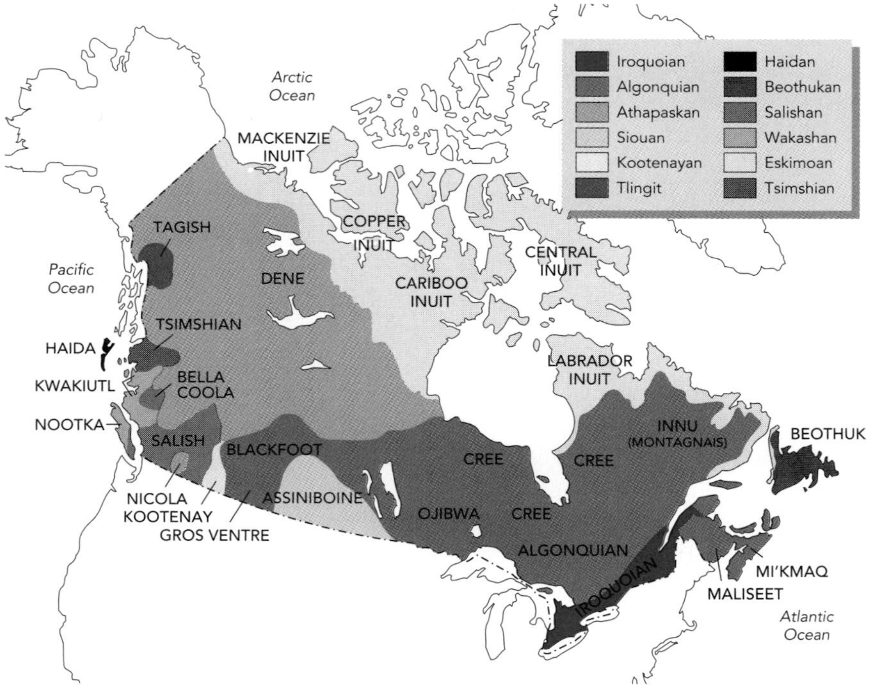

[margin note: — National ≠ a political approach]

Aboriginal language families within the boundaries of present-day Canada: an approximate guide for the period from the sixteenth to the eighteenth centuries.

Source: Adapted from P.G. Cornell, J. Hamelin, F. Ouellet, and M. Trudel, *Canada: Unity in Diversity* (Toronto: Holt, Rinehart and Winston, 1967), p. 14.

NATIVE CULTURE AREAS

similar cultures emerge from adaptation to a common environment.

A better classification of Native North Americans is that by cultural areas because it recognizes how climate and regional resources influence the development of societies and technologies. According to this classification, Native societies in Canada consisted of six culture areas: Northwest Coast, Plateau, Plains, Subarctic, Arctic, and Northeast. The cultural areas tend to coincide with ecological zones. None of these cultural areas stopped at what is now the Canada–U.S. border.

Gradually each band fitted itself to a culture area. They adapted to new environmental conditions, especially climate change. Over time, Native societies dynamically changed. As archaeologist Robert McGhee has written: "Native North American cultures were not fixed in ancient traditions, any more than were those of Old World peoples, and were remarkably flexible to

Aboriginal culture areas. Rather than being an authoritative representation of actual territories at any one time, this map should be regarded as a rough guide to contiguous groups that had or have similar cultures and histories.

Source: Based on *Handbook of North American Indians*, vol. 4, *History of Indian–White Relations* (Washington: Smithsonian Institution, 1988).

change in response to new ideas or circumstances."[6] The First Nations developed extensive trading networks. The peoples of northern North America belonged to a larger world than their own communities. The peoples of Aboriginal Canada were not isolated, but part of a hemisphere-wide civilization.

THE NORTHWEST COAST

Archaeologists believe that the ancestors of the Native peoples of the Pacific coast had resided there for thousands of years before European contact. The linguistic complexity of the coastal region, with its nineteen distinct languages, suggests that it is an "old area," and thus the most likely starting point for migrations of successive groups to the east and south.

Yet, despite the diversity of languages and cultures, the Northwest Coast peoples' ways of life resembled each others in many aspects. Evidence exists of wide-scale adaptation to a similar environment. All along the coast, groups shared knowledge and techniques. A widespread pattern of trade existed.

The coastal inhabitants relied on the abundant fish for their livelihood: herring, smelt, oolichan (candle-fish), halibut, and several species of cod. Salmon, which they speared, netted, and trapped in large quantities, then sun-dried or smoked, became their basic, year-round staple. In addition, they hunted sea mammals, such as whales, seals, sea lions, porpoises, and sea otters. Such an abundant food supply made the Pacific coast region the most densely populated area in Canada.

The Northwest Coast peoples used the giant cedars and firs of the coastal rain forest to build houses and to make dugout canoes and woodwork, such as carved boxes, bowls, dishes, and ladles. They lived the year round in villages located in sheltered island coves or on channels near the mouths of rivers. Each village was self-contained, but on occasion, particularly in times of war, several settlements joined together. Their communal activities included the potlatch, a large ceremonial feast, which they used to mourn the dead, to celebrate the investiture of new chiefs, or to mark the completion of a new house.

A hierarchical social structure based on wealth and heredity evolved on the Northwest Coast, with chiefs, nobles, and commoners. Social grading existed within each class. Below the commoners were slaves, who in some villages apparently made up a third of the population. Historian Olive P. Dickason observed that slaves "were usually prisoners of war, but sometimes individuals who had lost status because of debt; one could also be born into slavery, one of the few regions in North America where this happened. In any event, slaves had no rights of any kind and could be put to death at the will of their masters."[7]

THE PLATEAU

The Plateau culture area, the smallest of the six regions, takes in the Coast Range and the Rocky Mountains in the south–central interior of British Columbia. It extends southward through western Montana, Idaho, and eastern Washington and Oregon. The Canadian portion of the Plateau area is a region noted for its hot, dry summers and cold winters. In Canada the Plateau cultural area includes the Kutenai (or Kootenay) in the east, the Interior Salish in the west, and the Athapaskan-speaking groups to the north. These nations depended on salmon, and thus their populations were concentrated downriver, where the fish were most abundant. Their Northwest Coast neighbours influenced them greatly. But, after the arrival of the horse in Plateau society in the early eighteenth century, they had more contact with the Plains people. In dress, customs, and religion, the Plateau people came to resemble, in many ways, those on the Plains.

THE PLAINS

East of the Plateau region lies the Plains (or Great Plains) culture area, the broad central region of North America west of the Mississippi and Red River valleys and east of the Rockies. The open grasslands, with tall grass in the east and short grass in the west, extend on a north–south axis from northern Alberta and Saskatchewan and western Manitoba to Texas. The region has a continental climate — hot, dry summers and cold winters.

Throughout the buffalo era, the northern Plains attracted Native communities from all directions. They learned to live successfully and with relative security in a harsh land in pursuit of the vast buffalo herds. Often several local bands belonging to different First Nations formed a single encampment. Mixing, merging, and amalgamation were common. Relations between Native communities spanned the spectrum from peaceful to hostile.

In the eighteenth century, First Nations belonging to three linguistic families lived on the Canadian Plains: the Algonquian, the Athapaskan, and the Siouan. As the Plains became a crossroads for many First Nations, a sign language developed to allow people to communicate. These Plains Native peoples specialized in the communal hunt of the buffalo, or bison, an animal that was central to their way of life. They ate its flesh and used the hide to make teepee covers, clothing, and robes. From the thick hide of the buffalo's neck they made shields, from the horns they fashioned spoons and drinking cups, and from the sinew they created thread and bow string. On the treeless Great Plains, dried buffalo dung provided fuel.

[margin note: thread, bow string, shields, drinking cups and spoons.]

Natives hunted the buffalo on foot in small nomadic bands of roughly 50 to 100 people. Finding the buffalo required knowledge of their migratory habits. Large herds existed in abundance, but one could go for days or weeks without seeing a single animal. Hunting also required considerable skill in approaching the animals because neither the lance nor the bow was effective against them except at close range. Buffalo also could run at speeds of over 50 km per hour, making it impossible for hunters on foot to run them down.

Over the millennia, the Plains people developed increasingly effective subsistence strategies. The drive became the best way of harvesting the herds. The Plains Native peoples lured the buffalo into corrals or pounds of poles and brush in small valleys where they could ambush them. Where the land was uneven, as in the foothills to the west, the ambush frequently took the form of a jump, where the hunters stampeded the animals over a cliff or steep cutbank.

One such location is Head-Smashed-In Buffalo Jump, a UNESCO World Heritage Site in the Oldman River valley, 130 km south of Calgary in southwestern Alberta. Used for at least 6000 and possibly for 9000 years, it is one of the oldest, largest, and best preserved of all the buffalo jumps in North America. Evidence remains of several of the drive paths, marked by rock piles about a metre in diameter and a third of a metre high, stretching back, in one case, as far as 8 km from the cliff.

The arrival of the horse on the northern prairie in the early eighteenth century provides perhaps the most dramatic example of the ability of Plains people to adapt to new situations, to take advantage of new opportunities. The horse originally existed in the Americas, but then it disappeared, until reintroduced by the Spaniards into Mexico in the sixteenth century. Quickly the horse replaced the dog as the chief transporter of goods. The Plains peoples adopted the dog travois (two trailing poles on which was attached a platform or net for holding a load) for use with the horse. Their horse-drawn travois carried a load of 150 kg, in contrast to 35 kg pulled by a dog travois. As well, a horse could travel 20 km a day — twice as far as a dog. With the horse, the Plains peoples could take more than just the basic necessities as they moved from one hunting camp to another and could keep extra suits of clothing, additional buffalo robes for winter, and more dried provisions. The horse transformed the buffalo hunt. Mounted hunters simply surrounded a buffalo herd, without having to drive it into an enclosure or over a cliff.

THE SUBARCTIC

To the north lies the Subarctic culture area, a sparsely populated region. A low-lying region covered with coniferous trees, it extends across the Canadian Shield, from the Labrador coast to the mouth of the Yukon River, covering over a quarter of present-day Canada. Its northern boundary is below the tree line. The winters are long and harsh, but the forests provide shelter for its human inhabitants. Members of two linguistic families lived in the Subarctic: in the west, the Athapaskan-speaking groups, or "Dene" (pronounced "de-ne" or "de-nay" and meaning "the people"); and in the east, the Subarctic Algonquians.

In the summer, the Subarctic peoples lived in communal encampments of several hunting bands (about 100 people) situated at good fishing sites. In the autumn they divided into individual hunting bands of approximately 25 people, closely related either by family ties or by marriage, to hunt for food. A senior male directed the group and, in consultation with the other men, decided where and when they would hunt and camp. Many Dene and Algonquians relied on the moose, whose importance to them was comparable to that of the buffalo to the Plains peoples. On account of the thin distribution of game animals over vast areas of the boreal forest, the Subarctic human population remained among the lowest in the world.

The Subarctic peoples have left numerous rock painting sites across northern Canada.

Manitoba Museum of Man and Nature.

THE ARCTIC

Immediately north of the Subarctic, above the tree line, lies the Arctic culture area. Today, this area includes much of Alaska, all of the Canadian North above the tree line, and Greenland. The region has one of the world's harshest climates. For about eight months of the year it remains snow-covered and its seas frozen.

Today, the various Inuit groups speak related languages, which suggests that these languages derived from a single ancestral tongue. Their languages also have similarities to those of the Chukchi, Koryak, and Itel'men peoples of northeastern Siberia. Racially as well, the Inuit resemble First Nations. This suggests that the Inuit originated in Asia.

About 4000 years ago, humans developed skills and technologies to hunt and fish which enabled them to survive winters on the treeless tundra of Arctic Canada. They constructed dog sleds, snow houses, and soapstone lamps. They killed sea mammals with harpoons attached to retrieving lines, and used barbed stone spears to fish and hunt birds. They also used the bow and arrow expertly. Although fewer species of animals exist in this region, they are relatively larger. In certain areas, migration and the availability of food lead to dense seasonal concentrations of many mammals, such as caribou, walrus, and seals.

By 1000 years ago, an Alaskan people, the Thule — the direct ancestors of the modern Inuit — had entered the central Arctic. Four hundred years later, a sparse Thule population occupied most of Arctic Canada north of the tree line. In the relatively mild weather conditions at the time of their arrival, they adapted their rich maritime hunting culture to the Canadian Arctic. After perfecting the techniques of hunting on the open seas, they could take even large sea mammals, like the bowhead whale. The colder climate of the sixteenth century onward made this life untenable and they developed the well-known classic Inuit culture. Modern Canadian and Greenlandic Inuit are descended from them.

THE NORTHEAST

The Northeast (or Eastern Woodlands) culture area extended roughly from the Atlantic to the Great Lakes, and north to the Subarctic. The Northeast Native peoples hunted a variety of large game, particularly deer, as well as smaller game. They also fished and gathered edible wild plants and roots. Dramatic changes followed when hunters in southern Ontario adopted the bow and arrow from the Ohio region, about 1500 years ago. Climate and soil conditions south of the Canadian Shield allowed some nations to grow corn, beans, and squash. Two linguistic families lived in the Northeast: the Algonquians, a migratory people primarily dependent on hunting and fishing; and the Iroquoians, a semi-nomadic and agricultural people. The Algonquians occupied the northern part of the region, while the Iroquoians inhabited much of present-day southern Ontario and neighbouring New York State.

THE ALGONQUIANS   Migratory

The Algonquian-speaking peoples were widespread on the eve of European contact. The Mi'kmaq (Micmac) lived in the Maritimes, and the closely related Maliseet (Malecite) in what is now western New Brunswick. North of the St. Lawrence and east of the St. Maurice River dwelt the Montagnais (Innu). The Algonquins (Algonkins), the group that gave its name to the Algonquian linguistic family, lived in the Ottawa valley. (Note that the tribal name ends in "-quin" and that of the linguistic family in "-quian.") Still farther west lived the Nipissings on Lake Nipissing, the Ottawas (Odawa) on Manitoulin Island in Lake Huron, and the Ojibwas (Ojibways, Chippewas) around Lake Superior. The Beothuk, now extinct, lived in Newfoundland. They might have been Algonquian speakers, but the evidence is inconclusive.

Although many Algonquian groups grew crops, those north of the Great Lakes chiefly hunted and fished. During the winter they broke up into family groups to hunt deer, elk, bear, beaver, and other animals. In the early spring they met at maple groves to gather and boil the tree sap. In the summer, the women undertook agricultural work, while the men fished. During the fall they gathered wild rice, and, farther south, harvested corn.

Several winter hunting groups joined together for summer fishing. According to anthropologist Bruce Trigger, each fishing band had its own name, territory, and leader. The leader, however, had relatively little power or authority.[8] The men of these male-centred hunting groups usually married women from neighbouring bands, thus maintaining friendly ties. Adjacent bands, sharing a common language and customs, constituted a local community. Their unity was more cultural than political, since the band constituted the only clearly defined political unit. They traded extensively with their neighbours.

THE IROQUOIANS   *Semi-nomadic*

Initially, the Northeast peoples were hunters and gatherers, but gradually many in the area south of the Canadian Shield became Aboriginal farmers. Crops that originated in Mexico and Central America played an important role in the development of Iroquoian culture. About 1500 years ago, corn spread northward via the Ohio and Illinois areas to southern Ontario. It adapted to the shorter growing season and the more rigorous climate. Tobacco probably entered eastern *Agricultural* Canada 2500 years ago, and beans about 1000 years ago. Beans, high in protein, partially freed the Iroquoians from having to supplement their corn diet with animal protein. This new food supply contributed to rapid population growth. The new reliance on horticulture initiated a series of changes in their communities.   *Allowed for large settlements + formation of communities*
—up to 1500 inhabitants

Where Social Scientists Disagree

How Much Power Did Women Have in Northern Iroquoian Society?

The question of women's authority in Iroquois society has long fascinated scholars. Ethnologists a century ago noted that the Iroquois organized their societies on different lines than did the patrilineal western Europeans. The American ethnologists Lucien Carr,[1] and J.N.B. Hewitt,[2] himself of Iroquois background (Tuscarora), concluded that Iroquois women controlled their societies.

In the mid-twentieth century scholars returned to this topic, re-examining the same material but arriving at different conclusions. Anthropologist Cara E. Richards, for instance, argued that Iroquois women enjoyed little real power in the seventeenth century.[3] It was only in the eighteenth and nineteenth centuries, when population losses and other postcontact pressures necessitated a change to the early-seventeenth-century power structure, that women's power and influence prevailed.

In her book *Chain Her by One Foot: The Subjugation of Women in Seventeenth-Century New France*, Canadian sociologist Karen Anderson took a middle position arguing that before Huron contact with the French, equality existed between males and females. The Jesuit fathers, however, upset this balance by imposing Christianity and European standards on male–female relations. By 1650, Anderson notes, "Women, especially, had been profoundly changed, accepting the domination of their husbands and fathers." Elsewhere she emphasizes, "What is astonishing is how quickly women's status was changed once Christianity was established."[4]

Controversy also centred on the sources that Anderson and others used: the Jesuit annual reports or *Relations*, published from the early seventeenth century to the 1670s, and Jesuit writings in the early eighteenth century. Anthropologist Judith K. Brown points out that "the *Relations* cover an extended period of time and are anecdotal rather than descriptive. They are the work of many authors, whose prime purpose was to describe not the customs they found, but their own missionary activities."[5]

In the 1970s, the Iroquoianist William N. Fenton and French-language specialist Elizabeth L. Moore made available an English translation of the early-eighteenth-century ethnological classic *Moeurs des sauvages amériquains, Comparées aux moeurs des premiers temps* (1724) by Joseph-François Lafitau. While Lafitau's remarks on male–female relations apply to only one Iroquois community near Montreal, at a specific period of time, the 1710s, it is invaluable. The Jesuit missionary lived for nearly six years (1712–17) with the Christianized Iroquois converts at Sault St. Louis (later known as Caughnawaga or Kahnawake). He based his study on his own observations, information from another Jesuit who had worked in New France for over half a century, and on the Jesuit *Relations*. Lafitau summarized the status of Iroquois women in this manner: "Nothing is more real [...] than the women's superiority. It is they who really maintain the tribe, the nobility of blood, the genealogical tree, the order of generations and conservation of the families. In them resides all the real authority: the lands, fields and all their harvest belong to them; they are the soul of the councils, the arbiters of peace and war; they hold the taxes and the public treasure; it is to them that the slaves are entrusted; they arrange the marriages; the children are under their authority; and the order of succession is founded on their blood."[6]

Anthropologist Elisabeth Tooker added a fresh new geographical dimension to this topic in her 1984 essay, "Women in Iroquois Society." She emphasized the importance of the two different domains of Iroquois societies: the clearing — the domain of females; and the forest — that of males: "As the women did all the agricultural work of planting, tending, and harvesting of crops, the whole clearing (village and fields) also was regarded as the domain of women. The land beyond the clearing, the forest, was the domain of men."[7]

Over a hundred years after it began, the debate over the balance of power between Iroquois men and women in the seventeenth century continues.

[handwritten margin note: – The clearing/ the forest]

---

[1] Lucien Carr, "On the Social and Political Position of Women among the Huron–Iroquois Tribes," *16th and 17th Annual Reports of the Trustees of the Peabody Museum*, 3, 3–4 (1884): 211; reprinted in William Guy Spittal, ed., *Iroquois Women: An Anthology* (Ohsweken, ON: Iroqrafts, 1990), p. 13.

[2] J.N.B. Hewitt, "Status of Women in Iroquois Polity before 1784," *Annual Report of the Board of Regents of the Smithsonian Institute for the year ending June 30, 1932*, p. 487; reprinted in Spittal, ed., *Iroquois Women*, p. 67.

[3] Cara E. Richards, "Matriarchy or Mistake: The Role of Iroquois Women through Time," in V.F. Kay, ed., *Cultural Stability and Cultural Change, Proceedings of the 1957 Annual Spring Meeting of the American Ethnological Society*, reprinted in Spittal, ed., *Iroquois Women*, pp. 149–59. (The quote appears on p. 153.)

[4] Karen Anderson, *Chain Her by One Foot: The Subjugation of Women in Seventeenth-Century New France* (London and New York: Routledge, 1991), pp. 52 and 162.

[5] Judith K. Brown, "Economic Organization and the Position of Women Among the Iroquois," *Ethnohistory*, 17, 3–4 (1970); 165, footnote 5, reprinted in Spittal, ed., *Iroquois Women*, p. 196.

[6] Joseph-François Lafitau, trans., *Customs of the American Indians Compared with the Customs of Primitive Times*, 2 vols. (Toronto: Champlain Society, 1974 and 1977), vol. 1, p. 69.

[7] Elisabeth Tooker, "Women in Iroquois Society," in *Extending the Rafters: Interdisciplinary Approaches to Iroquoian Studies* (Albany: State University of New York Press, 1984), pp. 109–23; reprinted in Wendy Mitchinson et al., eds., *Canadian Women: A Reader* (Toronto: Harcourt Brace, 1996), p. 28.

At first, small-scale gardening supplemented hunting and fishing, but later the opposite was true. By the time of European contact the Iroquoian farming nations of the lower Great Lakes depended on their crops for up to four-fifths of their food. Every 10 to 15 years, they moved their village sites as the soil and firewood became depleted. Iroquoian women assumed the tasks of planting, cultivating, and harvesting the crops, thus freeing the men for clearing the land for farming, and for hunting, fishing, trading, and warfare.

With the development of horticulture, community organization changed. Larger settlements appeared. Native confederacies formed. Two Iroquoian confederacies existed in the Great Lakes area at the time of European contact: the Huron, an alliance of four or five nations; and the Five (later Six) Nations or Iroquois. The territory of the Five Nations, or as they called themselves, the League of Hodenosaunee (People of the Longhouse), south of Lake Ontario, was more extensive than the lands of the Huron, south of Georgian Bay on Lake Huron. The languages of the Five Nations (from east to west, Mohawk, Oneida, Onondaga, Cayuga, and Seneca) were more distinct from each other than those of the Huron nations. Each member nation had its own council, which met in the group's largest village. The national councils sent representatives to the League, or Confederacy Council, which governed the confederacies. By the mid-1530s, another group of Iroquoians — neither Huron nor Iroquois — occupied the St. Lawrence River valley: the St. Lawrence Iroquoians.

At the moment of European contact the Iroquoian peoples lived in stockaded villages of up to 1500 inhabitants. From ten to thirty families belonging to the same clan lived together in "longhouses," some the size of half a football field in length, and consisting of a framework of saplings, often arched in a barrel shape, covered with sheets of bark. The Iroquoians divided the longhouses into apartments, occupied by closely related families. A corridor ran down the middle of the house, and families on each side shared fireplaces.

The core of any household consisted of a number of females descended from a common ancestor. When a man married, he moved to his wife's home, where authority was invested in an elderly woman. In Iroquoian society the older women had real social and political power. The matrons of the appropriate families elected the chiefs, who were men; these women could also vote out of office any chief who displeased them.

At the time of European contact, First Nations groups lived in six culture areas that parallel Canada's major environmental areas: the Northwest Coast, the Plateau, the Plains, the Subarctic, the Arctic, and the Northeast. Linguistic diversity also existed, with more than 50 different languages being spoken in six culture areas. On the

Caroline Parker, a Seneca woman, around 1850, wearing beaded clothing she made herself.

Courtesy of the Southwest Museum, Los Angeles, Photo # N.24963.

eve of European contact, the Aboriginal peoples had achieved full occupation and use of North America. Those living in the northern portion of the continent later to be known as Canada belonged to a hemisphere-wide civilization.

In each cultural area, nature and the availability of natural resources largely dictated the lifestyle of the particular groups. Immensely resourceful and adaptable each community in northern North America gradually fitted itself to the land, and beyond. First Nations communities often traded across linguistic and cultural boundaries. These exchanges sealed political and social relationships. In some cases, hostile groups went to war against each other. Individuals considered themselves part of their family, their band, and their nation, but, on the eve of contact with Newcomers from across the North Atlantic, did not look upon all Aboriginal groups as one.

INITIAL EUROPEAN CONTACT WITH ABORIGINAL CANADA

The original inhabitants of present-day Atlantic and Arctic Canada witnessed the arrival of the first Europeans—the Norse—a thousand years ago, and that of the English, Portuguese, French, Spanish, and Basques five centuries later. Unfortunately, little contemporary information has survived about how the First Nations and Inuit perceived the first Europeans they met. The information that does exist attests to the Native peoples' amazement at the range and abundance of material goods that the newcomers possessed. The Hurons of the Great Lakes called the French "Agnonha," Iron People.

These northern First Nations people had not been isolated from events to the south. They belonged to a hemisphere-wide civilization. For millennia trade routes had carried goods and ideas across the continent. The northern peoples in what is now Canada were remarkably adaptable to change.

The First Nations retained their superbly crafted bark canoes, snowshoes, toboggans, and bark-covered wigwams, because they were superior to what the Europeans could offer. They willingly traded, however, many animal skins in exchange for the Europeans' metal tools and weapons. The newcomers' steel axes lightened the labour of gathering firewood. Their copper cooking pots were not fragile like pottery vessels or perishable like wooden boxes and birchbark kettles. Steel knives proved more durable than stone knives. Steel awls and needles made sewing and the working of hides and leather much easier.

European trade goods entered the extensive Native trading networks, and interior groups obtained them long before they ever saw a European. As they had for millenia the First Nations adapted quickly to new opportunities. Archaeology has confirmed, for example, the presence, by the early sixteenth century, of European trade goods among the Seneca south of Lake Ontario, an Iroquoian nation located hundreds of kilometres from the Atlantic.

If the Native peoples of North America initially regarded the European newcomers with awe (interpreting their possession of metal objects as evidence of some great supernatural power), the amazement quickly passed. They became more critical and demanding in their commercial dealings. Missionary reports from the early seventeenth century reveal that First Nations soon noted the slowness of the French in mastering Native languages and in learning to use canoes, snowshoes, and everything else that seemed to the First Nations to be commonplace. They had no idea either of the number of Newcomers to arrive in the centuries to follow, or, the impact of new infectious diseases the Newcomers inadvertently introduced to the Americas. The epidemics, against which they had no natural immunity, would reduce the Aboriginal populations to a fraction of their total number.

NOTES

1. This paraphrasing of the Blackfoot origin story is based on the account given in John Ewers, *The Blackfeet* (Norman: University of Oklahoma Press, 1958), pp. 3–4.
2. Alice Kehoe discusses this subject in her book *North American Indians: A Comprehensive Account*, 2nd ed. (Englewood Cliffs, NJ: Prentice-Hall, 1992), pp. 2–3; and also in her *America Before the European Invasions* (London: Pearson Education, 2002), pp. 9, 20.
3. Robert McGhee, *Ancient Canada* (Ottawa: Canadian Museum of Civilization/Libre Expression, 1989), p. 12.
4. Alfred W. Crosby, "Virgin Soil Epidemics as a Factor in the Aboriginal Depopulation in America," *William and Mary Quarterly*, 3rd series, 33 (1976): 290.
5. Olive P. Dickason, *Canada's First Nations: A History of the Founding Peoples from Earliest Times* (Toronto: McClelland & Stewart, 1992), p. 43.
6. Robert McGhee, "Canada YIK: The First Millennium," *The Beaver*, December 1999/January 2000, p. 10.
7. Dickason, *Canada's First Nations*, p. 67.
8. Bruce G. Trigger, *The Indians and the Heroic Age of New France* (Ottawa: Canadian Historical Association, 1977), p. 6.

LINKING TO THE PAST

Aboriginal Canada: Antiquity
http://www.ucalgary.ca/applied_history/tutor/firstnations/antiquity.html

An overview of the First Nations within the present-day boundaries of Canada before European contact.

A History of the Native People of Canada
http://www.civilisations.ca/archeo/hnpc/npint00e.html

A study of the history of the Native peoples in present-day Canada from 12 000 years ago to European contact, based upon archaeological evidence.

Native Civilizations
http://www.ucalgary.ca/applied_history/tutor/firstnations/civilisations.html

An introduction to regional, cultural, and linguistic approaches to classifying the First Nations in Canada, complete with maps, images, and links to other sites of interest.

An Iroquoian Longhouse in RealSpace VR
http://www.thinedge.com/longh-rs.htm

Explore the inside of a longhouse in 3-D (you will need Java and Live Picture Viewer to view this page).

BIBLIOGRAPHY

Three valuable overviews by anthropologists are Alice B. Kehoe, *North American Indians: A Comprehensive Account*, 2nd ed. (Englewood Cliffs, NJ: Prentice-Hall, 1992); R. Bruce Morrison and C. Roderick Wilson, eds., *Native Peoples: The Canadian Experience*, 3rd ed. (Don Mills, Ontario: Oxford University Press, 2004); and Alan D. McMillan, *Native Peoples and Cultures of Canada: An Anthropological Overview*, 2nd ed. (Vancouver: Douglas & McIntyre, 1995). While Diamond Jenness's study *The Indians of Canada* (Ottawa: King's Printer, 1932) should still be consulted, by far the best survey is Olive P. Dickason, *Canada's First Nations: A History of the Founding Peoples from Earliest Times*, 3rd ed. (Don Mills, Ontario: Oxford University Press, 2002). Useful overviews include Arthur J. Ray, *I Have Lived Here Since the World Began: An Illustrated History of Canada's Native People* (Toronto: Key Porter Books, 1996); and Bruce G. Trigger and Wilcomb E. Washburn, eds., *The Cambridge History of the Native Peoples of the Americas: Volume 1, North America* (Port Chester, NY: Cambridge University Press, 1996).

Alice Kehoe provides a splendid account of the development of human cultures in North America in *America Before the European Invasions* (London: Pearson Education Limited, 2002). A valuable popular account of the archaeological record is Robert McGhee's *Ancient Canada* (Ottawa: Canadian Museum of Civilization/Libre Expression, 1989). His short article, "Canada Y1K: The First Millennium," *The Beaver*, December 1999/ January 2000, pp. 9–17, also is very helpful. A speculative work, by a non-specialist, is Elaine Dewar's *Bones: Discovering the First Americans* (Toronto: Random House, 2001).

Henry F. Dobyns, *Native American Historical Demography: A Critical Bibliography* (Bloomington: Indiana University Press, 1976) provides demographic information. For details on the impact of disease consult Alfred W. Crosby, "Virgin Soil Epidemics as a Factor in the Aboriginal Depopulation in America," *William and Mary Quarterly*, 3rd series, 33 (1976): 289–99, and his *Ecological Imperialism: The Biological Expansion of Europe, 900–1900* (Cambridge: Cambridge University Press, 1986). Recently David Helge challenged Dobyns's estimates on the magnitude of the demographic decline in *Numbers from Nowhere: The American Indian Contact Population Debate* (Norman: University of Oklahoma Press, 1998).

Short reviews of Native culture areas appear in Morrison and Wilson, *Native Peoples*; Kehoe, *North American Indians*; and McMillan, *Native Peoples and Cultures of Canada*. Very helpful are the well-researched essays included in Paul Robert Magocsi, ed., *Canada's Aboriginal Peoples. A Short Introduction* (Toronto: University of Toronto Press, 2002). Six volumes in the series *Handbook of North American Indians* (Washington, DC: Smithsonian Institution) are invaluable: vol. 1, David Dumas, ed., *Arctic* (1985); vol. 6, June Helm, ed., *Subarctic* (1981); vol. 7, Wayne Suttles, ed., *Northwest Coast* (1990); vol. 12, Deward E. Walker, ed., *Plateau* (1998); vol. 13, Raymond J. Demaillie, ed., *Plains* (2001); and vol. 15, Bruce G. Trigger, ed., *Northeast* (1978). Useful studies of Native languages are Michael K. Foster's "Canada's First Languages," *Language and Society* 7 (Winter–Spring 1982): 7–16, and his entry "Native People, Languages" in *The Canadian Encyclopedia*, 2nd ed., vol. 3 (Edmonton: Hurtig, 1988), 1453–56. To date the best historical study of the relationships between the First Nations and their environments is Shepard Krech III, *The Ecological Indian. Myth and History* (New York: W.W. Norton, 1999).

The early maps in R. Cole Harris, ed., *Historical Atlas of Canada*, vol. 1, From the Beginning to 1800 (Toronto: University of Toronto Press, 1987), are based on the most recent archaeological discoveries. This atlas contains a wealth of new information about the first inhabitants of present-day Canada. The most up-to-date summary of our current understanding is Dickason's *Canada's First Nations*. A survey of developments in Ontario appears in Edward S. Rogers and Donald B. Smith, eds., *Aboriginal Ontario: Historical Perspectives on the First Nations* (Toronto: Dundurn Press, 1994); and in Peter A. Baskerville's chapter, "Change and Exchange: 9000 b.c.e.–1500 c.e.," in his *Ontario, Image, Identity, and Power* (Don Mills, Ontario: Oxford University Press, 2002), pp. 1–11. Good overviews of how First Nations groups embraced change include: Bruce G. Trigger's *Natives and Newcomers: Canada's "Heroic Age" Reconsidered* (Kingston and Montreal: McGill-Queen's University Press, 1985); and Theodore Binnema's *Common and Contested Ground. A Human and Environmental History of the Northwestern Plains* (Norman: University of Oklahoma Press, 2001). For bibliographical information consult Shepard Krech III, *Native Canadian Anthropology and History: A Select Bibliography*, rev. ed. (Winnipeg: Rupert's Land Research Centre, University of Winnipeg, 1994).

PART ONE

EARLY EUROPEAN SETTLEMENT
TO 1760

When western Europeans first crossed the North Atlantic in the fifteenth and sixteenth centuries they entered a world that was remarkably different from that of Europe. The First Nations' ancestors had occupied what would become known as Canada for over 10 000 years. The two groups — First Nations and Europeans — interacted sometimes peacefully, more often through conflict, as they both sought to use the vast natural resources to their own advantage. Fish and furs brought the Europeans back annually, eventually leading the French to establish permanent settlements in what they called New France. French settlements prevailed in Acadia (the present-day Maritimes) and in Canada, or the St. Lawrence valley. New France was large, but in comparison with the colony of New England to the south, founded about the same time, the population remained quite small, numbering only 65 000 people at the time of the Conquest in 1760, almost 150 years after Champlain founded Quebec in 1608.

New France inherited French institutions, such as the French administrative and judicial systems, but because of differing geography and historical circumstances, they were modified to meet North American circumstances. Conflict with the Iroquois and English helped to forge a common identity among the French settlers. By the mid-eighteenth century, the contours of the Canadian and Acadian identities were evident. The British conquest in 1760 ended the French regime in North America, but not the French fact in the St. Lawrence valley or in the Maritimes.

EARLY EUROPEAN SETTLEMENT AND THE BEGINNING OF NEW FRANCE

TIME LINE

1001 — Leif Eiriksson leads an expedition to northeastern North America from Greenland but within a decade the attempts to establish permanent Norse settlements fail

1497 — Giovanni Caboto (John Cabot), an Italian navigator in the English service, lands in northeastern North America

1534 — Jacques Cartier, on his first of three voyages for the king of France, enters the Gulf of St. Lawrence

1608 — Champlain builds a fortified trading post at Quebec

1609 — For the first time Champlain and the French clash with the Iroquois or Five Nations initiating a nearly century-long conflict

1642 — Ville-Marie, later known as Montreal, is founded

1649 — The fall of Huronia, the Iroquois defeat the Hurons in a quick military campaign

1667 — Truce between the French and the Iroquois League of Five Nations, the beginning of two decades of peace

The strange boat amazed the Aboriginal hunters along the Labrador and Newfoundland coast. They believed that the world ended beyond the horizon and that they were the only inhabitants. Never before had anyone seen such a sight emerging from the edge of the world. Upon the small sea monster's back arose a tall leafless tree from which hung a gigantic white blanket. Around the tree stood ugly beings with facial hair and skin the colour of the underbelly of a fish. The year was about a 1000 years ago, and the newcomers were the Norse. After an interval of nearly five centuries, other Europeans followed in quick succession: the English, the Portuguese, the French, the Spanish, and the Basques.

The absence of written source materials makes the narration of the Europeans' arrival a formidable task. No written accounts by the original inhabitants are available. Only a few Norse oral sagas, or adventure stories, that were passed on orally from generation to generation for about 300 years before being written down, and the occasional European explorer's journal, exist for the period before 1600. Morris Bishop, a biographer of Samuel de Champlain, the founder of Quebec in 1608, put it best when he wrote, "In reading history one must always be impressed by the fact that our knowledge is only a collection of scraps and fragments that we put together into a pleasing design, and often the discovery of one new fragment would cause us to alter utterly the whole design."[1]

THE ARRIVAL OF THE NORSE

From the ninth to the twelfth centuries, Scandinavia led the European sea powers with a commercial empire extending from Russia in the east to Sicily in the south and Normandy in the west. The Norse occupied small coastal areas on the southwestern coast of Greenland, as part of their voyages from the European mainland and Iceland. In the year 1001, Leifr (or Leif) Eiriksson assembled a crew of 35 and set out to explore the lands southwest of Greenland. He reached an attractive location with a moderate climate, which he named "Vinland" (Wineland) for its plentiful "wineberries" (probably wild red currants, gooseberries, or mountain cranberries). Scholars have placed Vinland at different locations between Labrador and Florida. In 1960, Helge Ingstad and his archaeologist wife, Anne Stine Ingstad, located the first known site of European settlement in North America, L'Anse aux Meadows, on the northeastern tip of the Great Northern Peninsula of Newfoundland. Today L'Anse aux Meadows, the only authenticated Viking site in northeastern North America, is designated a World Heritage Site by UNESCO.

For nearly 500 years, the Norse occupied Greenland. Their economy was based on raising stock, hunting, and fishing. They travelled to the west for timber from "Vinland," trading with the Inuit along the Greenlandic coast, and on Baffin and Ellesmere Islands. Hostile relations with the Native peoples, however, prevented permanent settlement.

The Greenland settlements prospered in the twelfth century, when an estimated 2000–4000 people, and perhaps as many as 6000, lived there. Then, in the thirteenth century, Greenland's climate became colder, which threatened agriculture. Furthermore, the settlements' prosperity, precariously built on the walrus-ivory trade, declined when the Portuguese imported African elephant ivory. As well, the Black Death of 1349 struck Norway and Iceland severely. The epidemic of bubonic plague killed one third of the population — a loss that cost the Norse their command of the seas. Thereafter, the annual ship that brought vital supplies from Norway no longer appeared. By 1450, the Greenlandic settlements had disappeared.

THE EUROPEAN EXPANSION IN THE FIFTEENTH CENTURY

The Portuguese replaced the Scandinavians as the leading European sea power by the fifteenth century, as a result of their fast and efficient sea-going vessels known as caravels (their long,

[Margin notes, left side, handwritten:]
Motives driving European explorers
—sea route to far east
• trade
—wealth
• capitalism
• extravagance
• conflict
—National advantage
• rise of modern nation-state
• attempts to outdo each other
• mercantilism
—religious zeal
—sense of adventure
—new food sources

narrow ships with two masts). No doubt curiosity and the desire to find a "New World," a better land than that in which they lived, led the Portuguese — and later the Spanish, French, English, and Dutch — to expand beyond Europe. Economic motives also played an important role. The Turks' capture in 1453 of Constantinople, the key city in Europe's trade with the Orient, caused a desperate search by the Europeans to find a new route to "the Indies," as China, Japan, Indonesia, and India were then collectively called, for spices and the riches of eastern and south Asia. As well, they came to convert the "heathen" to Christianity.

THE ENGLISH CROSS THE NORTH ATLANTIC

[Margin note, handwritten:]
1st presence of British in North America.

When news of Columbus's first two Atlantic voyages to "Asia" in 1492 and 1493 reached England, King Henry VII sponsored his own expedition. In 1496, he chose John Cabot (Giovanni Caboto), an experienced Italian mariner, to lead it. The merchants of the English port of Bristol, anxious to secure direct access to the east, sponsored the expedition.

[Margin note, handwritten:]
Great banks rich w fish/cod.
—becomes Canada's 1st great business.

Cabot set sail in late May 1497. On June 24 he reached land, probably the eastern coast of Newfoundland. Here he planted the flags of England and his native Venice and claimed the territory for Henry VII. He discovered the nearby sea swarmed with fish by letting down and drawing up baskets weighted with stones, thus locating the great continental shelf of Newfoundland. These shallow areas, called "banks," are favourite breeding places of cod. Cabot also entered the Gulf of St. Lawrence, believing it to be a direct route to China and India.

Encouraged by this information, Henry VII sponsored a second voyage. In May 1498, Cabot sailed again from Bristol with five ships. Shortly out of port, one vessel turned back in distress to Ireland, but the other four were lost. Cabot's disappearance, followed shortly afterwards by the death of Henry VII, caused English interest in the search for a Northwest Passage to lapse temporarily. Nevertheless, John Cabot's first voyage announced England's interest in the Americas. The voyage also brought to Western Europe's attention the Grand Banks fishery. Possibly, Bristol fishers had fished the Grand Banks since the 1480s, but now their secret was out. Fishing — the first great European business in North America — had begun.

THE PORTUGUESE IN THE NORTH ATLANTIC

www

Soon after Cabot came the Portuguese. Despite the dangers of navigating the uncharted North Atlantic, they annually fished the Grand Banks and the coastal waters of Newfoundland. Around 1520, the Portuguese made one attempt at permanent settlement, probably on the eastern coast of Cape Breton Island. After a year or so, difficulties arose with the local First Nations, and the settlement — the first European settlement since the Norse — died out. After their colony's failure the Portuguese returned, not to settle, but to continue to fish the Grand Banks.

FRENCH INTEREST IN THE NORTH ATLANTIC IN THE SIXTEENTH CENTURY

Of all European powers in the early sixteenth century, France was perhaps the best situated to dominate northeastern North America. It had twice the population of Portugal and Spain together, and six times that of England. It also had more ocean-facing territory, at least as many seaports as England, and far greater wealth. Yet, due to its involvement in European conflicts, France did not become involved in North Atlantic exploration until 1524.

[Margin note, handwritten:]
Start of French interest in N.A.

The French selected an Italian navigator, Giovanni da Verrazzano, as the commander of their expedition in 1524. He searched the North American coast, from the Carolinas to Gaspé, for a westerly route to Asia. Despite his failure to find such a passage, France acquired a better

[Handwritten note at bottom:]
Explored coast from Cape Breton to Florida.

understanding of the eastern North American coastline. Afterward France did not follow up Verrazzano's expedition. At war against the Hapsburgs (the rulers of Austria, the Low Countries, and Spain), they did not reach out to explore.

THE FIRST OF JACQUES CARTIER'S THREE VOYAGES, 1534

Jacques Cartier, a mariner from the wealthy port of Saint-Malo in Brittany, northwestern France, ten years later led a second French expedition, in search of a passage to China and India. Cartier entered the Gulf of St. Lawrence and landed at present-day Prince Edward Island. Next, he sailed north to Chaleur Bay, which divides Quebec from New Brunswick, and met Mi'kmaq traders. Cartier's journal contains the first reference since the Norse sagas to a trading exchange between Native peoples and Europeans — initiated by the Natives. They "set up a great clamour and made frequent signs to us to come on shore, holding up to us some furs on sticks," a clear indication that they had already participated in a previous exchange, or exchanges.

As the French moved north to Gaspé they encountered Iroquoians who had come from the interior to fish. Unaccustomed to trading with Europeans, they had brought no furs with them. The French first gave the Iroquoians "knives, glass beads, combs, and other trinkets of small value" to win their friendship, then kidnapped two sons of the chief, Donnacona. They took them back to France to learn French, so that they could serve as guides on the next voyage.

It was standard practice among early Europeans in the Americas to capture the inhabitants and take them back to Europe as proof of having reached the new lands. Often, the First Nations did not survive the voyage across the Atlantic; those who did often died in Europe, unable to fight off illnesses that did not exist in the Americas and to which they had not developed immunities. In this instance, Taignoagny and Domagaya, Donnacona's sons, lived and assisted Cartier in his next expedition.

CARTIER'S WINTERING OVER IN "CANADA," 1535–1536

In 1535, Cartier returned with three ships and sailed up the St. Lawrence to the Native village of Stadacona (present-day Quebec), the home of his guides. The French mariner recorded a word that they used to refer to their home: "They call a town, *Canada*."[2] En route, Cartier gave the name "St. Lawrence" to a cove at which the French stopped, after the Christian martyr whose feast day it was (August 10). The entire gulf and the great river later obtained the same name.

The Iroquoians at Stadacona initially saw the French as powerful and valuable trading partners. But, by travelling upriver without Donnacona's permission, Cartier interfered with the Stadaconans' trading rights. In addition, the French who had been left behind built a small fort during Cartier's absence — an act that infringed on the Stadaconans' land rights, which the French did not recognize.

The winter, much longer and colder in Canada than in France, proved a nightmare for the French. To add to the sailors' problems, scurvy, a disease caused by insufficient vitamin C in the diet, broke out. Twenty-five men (one-quarter of Cartier's crew) died before the French learned the Native cure for the disease: boiling the bark and leaves of the *annedda* (white cedar) to make a brew with a high content of ascorbic acid (vitamin C).

Despite the Stadaconans' help, Cartier remained antagonistic to Donnacona and his people. Anxious to obtain more information about the lands to the west, particularly the rich "kingdom of the Saguenay" that Taignoagny and Domagaya had spoken of, the French mariner kidnapped them, Donnacona, and three of his principal supporters. The French believed this fabulous land to be a second Mexico, rich in gold and silver. (In reality, the stories of the Saguenay probably referred to copper deposits around Lake Superior.) After promising to return his hostages the

[handwritten annotations: "established French claim for Canada." and "hostile relationship w First Nations"]

following year, Cartier left in the spring of 1536. Four children presented to Cartier by Donnacona and the chief of a neighbouring village went along as well. The ten First Nations captives never saw "Canada" again.

Cartier entered Saint-Malo in July 1536, after an absence of 14 months. Although the French sea captain had not discovered great wealth, he had nonetheless made some important contributions: he proved that Newfoundland was an island, charted much of the Gulf of St. Lawrence, and recorded in his journal the existence of a great river flowing from deep in the interior.

THE CARTIER-ROBERVAL EXPEDITION, 1541–1543

War between France and Spain delayed Cartier's third voyage to "Canada" until 1541. This time, he left with 150 French settlers to found a colony and locate the famed "kingdom of the Saguenay." Very little information has survived regarding the settlement that winter, but it was later reported that First Nations killed at least 35 settlers. By the spring, Cartier had had enough and returned to France. As initially planned, Cartier's superior, Jean-François de La Rocque de Roberval, would come in 1542, to reinforce the initial settlement. He did, but Cartier was gone. Roberval and his 200 settlers spent a terrible winter at the site of Cartier's encampment. An inscription on a French map of 1550 explains the reasons for Roberval's departure the following summer: "It was impossible to trade with the people of that country because of their austerity, the intemperate climate of said country, and the slight profit."

During the French Wars of Religion (1562–1598), France left Canada to its Native inhabitants. French fishers, whalers, and traders continued to come in great numbers to northeastern North America, but France did not attempt colonization again for another half-century. The harsh climate, hostile relations with the Native peoples, and the failure to find gold combined to give the French a poor image of Canada.

EUROPEAN FISHERS AND TRADERS' ACTIVITIES IN THE SIXTEENTH CENTURY

European fishers maintained contact with Newfoundland. Between March and October of each year, large fishing fleets — Portuguese, Basque, French, and English — gathered there. They supplied the markets of western Europe and the Mediterranean with the "beef of the sea" (cod). The Newfoundland fishery had become big business by the mid-sixteenth century. With an estimated 10 000 individuals visiting annually, it provided a livelihood for twice as many fishers as did the fisheries of the Gulf of Mexico and the Caribbean combined, where the great Spanish fleets sailed.

The success of the Newfoundland cod fishery initially depended on the harvesting of salt left by the evaporation of seawater. This salt was better than the mineral variety for curing fish because it was more uniform in quality. France, Spain, and Portugal produced an abundance of "solar salt," but England, not as blessed with sunshine, did not. This hurt England in the age of the "green fishery," the term sailors used to describe a method of salting fish immediately upon catching them, then transporting them back to Europe for drying. To compensate for the lack of solar salt, the English developed "dry fishing" — drying their lightly salted fish before returning home. The sun-cured codfish lasted indefinitely if kept dry, and could be reconstituted by soaking it in water.

Estimates of the number of English ships involved in Newfoundland expeditions around the year 1600 vary from 250 to 400, and the number of men from 6000 to 10 000. These expeditions made good England's claims to the Avalon Peninsula on Newfoundland's east coast, the

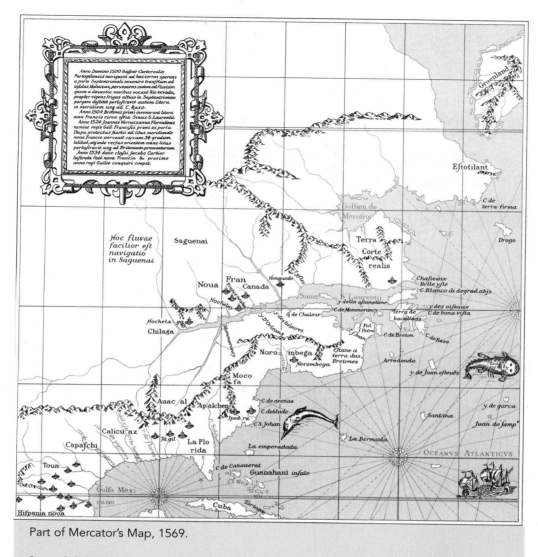

Part of Mercator's Map, 1569.

Source: D.G.G. Kerr, ed., *A Historical Atlas of Canada* (Toronto: Thomas Nelson & Sons, 1961), p. 11.

location of the best English fishing and processing sites. Just to the west, in the region of the Strait of Belle Isle, which separates Newfoundland and Labrador, the Basques were active.

The Basque Whaling Stations

Basque whalers, from their homeland in the border region of France and Spain, joined the cod fishers in the early sixteenth century and carried out whaling in the Strait of Belle Isle. Europe's first commercial whalers came prepared to set up a long-distance fishery. The south coast of Labrador became the first region of northeastern North America to undergo extensive exploitation by Europeans. Whaling stations flourished there for half a century. Sixteenth-century Europeans treasured whale oil as a fuel for lamps, an all-purpose lubricant, an additive to drugs, and a major ingredient of scores of products, such as soap and pitch. At its peak, the fishery employed about 2000 men, who remained in Newfoundland–Labrador waters for six months each season, from June until January.

Community Portrait

The Basque Whaling Community of Red Bay, Labrador, 1550–1600

Disappear due to depletion of whale stocks, Spanish war with Britain.

In the mid-1970s, Selma Barkham, a researcher employed by the Public Archives (now the National Archives) of Canada, discovered a forgotten chapter of Canadian history. While it had long been known that Basque whalers had hunted off the Labrador coast, the extent of their operations, and the location of their whaling stations, was not known. While examining wills, lawsuits, mortgages, and insurance policies in Basque archives in Spain, Barkham came across a wealth of information on the whale fishery in the Strait of Belle Isle, separating Labrador from the northern tip of Newfoundland. The Strait was excellent for whale hunting, as it acted as a funnel through which migrating whales passed in great numbers.

Barkham made a preliminary investigation of the southern Labrador coast with James Tuck, an archaeologist from Memorial University of Newfoundland, and several other scientists in the summer of 1977. All down the coastline they found evidence that the Basques had been in the region. At several locations they found red patches on the beaches, the remains of the imported red roof tile used by the Basque whalers for their buildings. Tuck returned in the summer of 1978 to excavate the most promising site, on Saddle Island in Red Bay, one of the finest harbours in the Strait of Belle Isle. On the harbour side of the island he found fragments of old stone walls stained with a black material, later identified as burnt whale oil.

The archaeologist had discovered the remains of the ovens where whale blubber was tried (boiled down) into oil. During future visits to Saddle Island, Tuck and his team located additional evidence of Basque activity. They found the remains of houses and of the workshops where the coopers (barrel-makers) constructed the barrels to ship whale oil.

In 1978, Robert Grenier, head of marine archaeology for Parks Canada, began underwater investigations that greatly complemented Barkham's archival research and Tuck's archaeological work on Saddle Island. He discovered the well-preserved remains of a sunken Basque ship only thirty metres offshore of the Saddle Island station. It had gone down in a squall with a load of nearly 1000 barrels of whale oil. Subsequent investigations in the icy waters led to the location of the ship's compass, anchor, rudder, and loaded swivel gun. In 1979, the Historic Sites and Monuments Board of Canada designated the forgotten Basque whaling station of Red Bay a place of national historic interest.

Red Bay appears to have been the Basque whalers' favourite whaling station. Normally about ten galleons arrived in Red Bay every summer in the late sixteenth century. Depending on a ship's tonnage, crews ranged from 50 to 120 men. During the whaling season, the men harpooned whales from small open whale boats. Once killed, the dead whales were towed back to the galleon left moored in the harbour. After the men removed large strips or slabs of blubber, they hauled it ashore. At the whaling station they rendered it into whale oil in huge ovens or tryworks, containing several ovens, sheltered by roofs of red tile brought to Red Bay for that purpose.

The graves located at Red Bay reveal that the tradespeople were sturdy and relatively young. Basque males of all ages, some as young as 11 or 12, joined the whaling expeditions. The captains hired in the late winter and early spring. They did not allow females to join their crews. Each crew member had to produce, at personal expense, essential items, such as clothing, suitable for great variations in climate. The

Basque crews earned shares in the season's catch rather than fixed salaries. Constant upward mobility allowed individuals to climb the shipboard hierarchy and, with special training, to become harpooners or pilots themselves. For food the ships brought large amounts of cider, wine, and ship's biscuit. At Red Bay the men enjoyed a diet based largely on cod and salmon, with an occasional piece of caribou or a wild duck.

Between mid-June and early July the whaling ships left for Labrador. An average Atlantic crossing in the sixteenth century normally took a month. Basque whalers commonly stayed in Labrador well into the winter, returning to Spain by the end of January, by which time the Strait of Belle Isle had normally frozen over. Their residency in

An artist's reconstruction of Basque galleons riding at anchor in Red Bay, Labrador, the largest whaling port on the Strait of Belle Isle. Smoke billows forth from the massive stone tryworks built by the Basques to render blubber into whale oil. Painting by Richard Schlecht.

"Discovery in Labrador: A 16th-Century Basque Whaling Port and Its Sunken Fleet," *National Geographic*, 168, 1 (July 1985): 42–43. Richard Schlecht.

Labrador in winter required solid buildings, hence the Basques imported large amounts of Iberian tile for the construction of their buildings.

The whaling effort at stations such as Red Bay proved so effective that it led to a massive depletion in northwestern Atlantic whale stocks. Another factor that helped to put an end to the Basque Labrador whale fishery by the end of the sixteenth century was the ill-fated Spanish Armada of 1588, the attempted Spanish naval invasion of Britain, a disaster that claimed many Basque ships and sailors' lives. One written source indicates that perhaps another contributing factor was Native resistance, particularly by the Inuit, to the Basque presence on the southern Labrador coast. In any event, the Basque whaling community at Red Bay vanished shortly after the beginning of the seventeenth century.

Further Reading

Selma Barkham, "The Basques: Filling a gap in our history between Jacques Cartier and Champlain," *Canadian Geographical Journal*, 96, 1, (Feb./March, 1978): 8–19.

Robert McGhee, "Chapter 10. The Grand Bay," *Canada Rediscovered* (Ottawa: Canadian Museum of Civilization, 1991): 141–153.

Jean-Pierre Proulx, *Basque Whaling in Labrador in the 16th Century* (Ottawa: National Historic Sites, Parks Services, 1993).

James A. Tuck and Robert Grenier, *Red Bay, Labrador. World Whaling Capital, a.d. 1550–1600* (St. John's, Newfoundland: Atlantic Archaeology Ltd., 1989).

ENGLISH ACTIVITY IN THE NORTH ATLANTIC AND ARCTIC

England sponsored a number of expeditions north of Newfoundland in the late sixteenth and early seventeenth centuries. In 1576, Martin Frobisher, 37 years old and a mariner of great repute, sailed northerly in search of a Northwest Passage to India and China. Off southern Baffin Island, Frobisher encountered Inuit, who came to trade meat and furs for metal objects and clothing. The Inuit showed that they were no strangers to European ships by doing gymnastic exercises in the ship's rigging. They indicated that they wanted to trade. Evidently they had already encountered vessels of the Newfoundland fishing fleet and had probably traded with the fishers, from whom they obtained iron. Frobisher himself discovered this when, in a skirmish with the Inuit, he was struck by an iron-tipped arrow.

Frobisher failed to find a passage to the Orient, either on this first journey or on two subsequent voyages in 1577 and 1578. Ten years later, John Davis followed up on Frobisher's work in three successive summers (1585–87), but without success. The necessary maritime technology for the penetration of the Arctic Archipelago simply did not exist in the late sixteenth century. It was as impossible a goal for that age as a landing on the moon would have been for the nineteenth century.

THE RISE OF THE FUR TRADE

Jacques Cartier's three voyages established a French claim to the Gulf of St. Lawrence, but international recognition of France's claim would come only with successful occupation. It was the fur trade in the early 1580s that led to France's return, and to its permanent occupation of the St. Lawrence valley. In the Gulf of St. Lawrence and along the Atlantic coastline, the fur trade began as a by-product of the fishing industry. Fur coats, muffs, wraps, gloves, fur-trimmed garments, and most important, wide-brimmed beaver hats all commanded high prices. Fur proved an ideal product for the European traders. By returning each year to the same locality, the French established good trading relationships with the local First Nations. In the 1580s, French merchants sent out ships commissioned solely to trade for furs.

Initially, the First Nations did not perceive the fur trade as posing any danger to their independence. By the early seventeenth century, however, the Algonquians on the Atlantic coast had lost much of their self-sufficiency and become reliant on the Europeans. The fur trade transformed coastal groups from hunters and fishers into trappers. Prior to European contact, the Mi'kmaq spent more than half the year living on the coast, since the sea supplied as much as 90 percent of their diet. Now they spent long periods each year hunting inland for fur-bearing animals. This change in their traditional activities affected their winter diet. They no longer accumulated their usual summer food stores and instead relied partly on the dried foods they received in trade.

Tadoussac, at the mouth of the Saguenay River, became France's principal trading centre on the Gulf of St. Lawrence. Pre-existing trading networks led from there to Hudson Bay and the Great Lakes. In the mid-1580s, as many as 20 vessels at a time called at Tadoussac in the summer.

SAMUEL DE CHAMPLAIN

Much had changed in the St. Lawrence valley since Cartier's journeys. On the official French expedition to the St. Lawrence valley in 1603 Samuel de Champlain, who kept the journal of the voyage, saw large numbers of Algonquian-speaking groups, at Tadoussac and small groups at several encampments along the St. Lawrence, but the Iroquoian-speaking peoples of the St. Lawrence valley had mysteriously left.

Unfortunately, we have only hypotheses, and no complete accounts, of the St. Lawrence valley from the time of Cartier's voyages in the mid-sixteenth century to Champlain's visit in 1603. Canadian economic historian Harold Innis believed that eastern Algonquian nations drove out the St. Lawrence Iroquoians.[3] They had obtained iron weapons before the St. Lawrence Iroquoians, which gave them a technological advantage in warfare.

In the 1970s, Bruce Trigger, an anthropologist who has done extensive research on the ethnohistory of northeastern North America, advanced another theory.[4] Trigger speculates that the landlocked New York Iroquois wanted European trade goods, but found them difficult to obtain from either the Saint Lawrence Iroquoians or the Algonquians. Consequently, the Iroquois raided and dispersed their neighbours, the St. Lawrence Iroquoians, some of whom may have moved west to join the Hurons on Georgian Bay on Lake Huron. Archaeologists, Trigger states, have established that European goods reached all of the New York Iroquois groups by 1600. These, he surmises, must have been largely obtained as booty from the St. Lawrence Iroquoians. Although both explanations for the disappearance of the St. Lawrence Iroquoians are plausible, the data are lacking to reach any definite conclusions. It is also possible that European diseases, inadvertently introduced by Cartier and the French, wiped out these people.

THE FRENCH IN ACADIA

Today we take for granted that Quebec was the natural site for France's first permanent settlement in present-day Canada. In reality, however, the French initially rejected this location. From 1604 to 1607 they searched elsewhere for the best place to establish a colony. They sailed south to the present-day Maritime provinces, a region with a climate milder than that of the

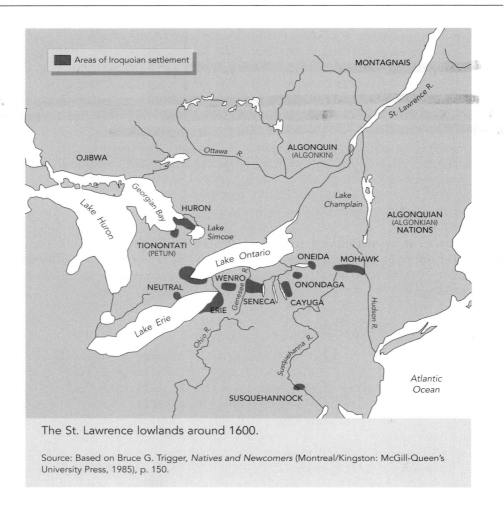

The St. Lawrence lowlands around 1600.

Source: Based on Bruce G. Trigger, *Natives and Newcomers* (Montreal/Kingston: McGill-Queen's University Press, 1985), p. 150.

St. Lawrence region and one potentially rich in minerals. They also searched for a more southerly location for the colony in the hope that they might still find a route to Asia.

Their first winter on a small island near the mouth of the St. Croix River, now on the border between Maine and New Brunswick, proved catastrophic, roughly half of the expedition of 79 died of scurvy. After their second summer exploring the coastline, the French stayed the winter of 1605/06 on the south coast of what is now Nova Scotia. Their colony at Port-Royal became the first European agricultural settlement in what is now Canada. The French continued to explore the coastline the following summer and then wintered again at Port-Royal, but decided not to stay. After three years of considerable expenditures, unsuccessfully searching for mineral resources and the Northwest Passage, the French realized the area's limitations. The expedition could not enforce its fur-trade monopoly along the winding and indented coasts of the Maritimes. Ironically, the very year that the French left Acadia (the name given to the area of what is now Maine, New Brunswick, Nova Scotia, and Prince Edward Island), the English established their first permanent settlement at Jamestown in Virginia.

The French did return to Acadia, but only in the early 1630s made a serious attempt to establish a French colony there. Many of the settlers came from the west coast of France, near the Atlantic port of La Rochelle. Labourers skilled in harvesting salt joined the contingent of several hundred colonists. In Acadia, rather than clear the forested upland areas, they built dikes to reclaim the fertile marshland that the Bay of Fundy's strong tides flooded twice daily. To ensure the effective drainage of the diked marshlands, the Acadians also constructed a system of drainage ditches, combined with an *aboîteau* (a hinged valve in the dike itself), which allowed fresh water to run off the marshes at low tide and at the same time prevented salt water from flowing onto the diked farmland when the tide rose. For two to four years, the Acadians let snow and rain wash away the salt from the tidal marshes. At the end of that period they planted crops on the fertile, stone-free plains. As they reclaimed land from the sea, and encroached very little on Native territory, the First Nations welcomed them. After the 1630s further emigration from France was quite limited, but the Acadian colony thrived in the mid-seventeenth century, and increased in number, thanks to natural increase.

The Founding of Quebec

In 1608 Samuel de Champlain, who had been a member of the Acadian expedition, returned to the St. Lawrence valley, to find a location where the French could control access to the interior and prevent competition from other traders. This time Champlain served as the leader of the expedition. At the point where the St. Lawrence narrows before widening out again, and in the shadow of a towering cliff, Champlain constructed a *habitation*, a collection of wooden buildings built in the form of a quadrangle and surrounded by a stockade and moats. He called it Quebec — Kebec being the Algonquian word for "strait" or "narrow passage." Champlain's *habitation* became the heart of the first permanent and continuous French settlement in Canada.

Acadians repairing a dike in the early eighteenth century. This re-creation by Azor Vienneau is based on archaeological and historical evidence.

History Collection/Nova Scotia Museum, Halifax/NSM 87.120.2.

[margin note: Location was chosen to give French control over trade & access to the interior.]

In hindsight, one might ask why the Native peoples welcomed the French occupation of Quebec. Like other Europeans, the French did not recognize the First Nations' rights to the land. They officially claimed the St. Lawrence valley for France on the basis of Jacques Cartier's "discovery" of it. And, as a Christian nation, the newcomers assumed they had the right to occupy non-Christians' lands. In fact, they soon began to provide land to colonists. In 1627, for instance, they simply granted all of North America then not occupied by a Christian prince to the newly created Company of One Hundred Associates.

The First Nations of northeastern North America regarded the land as theirs. Each Algonquian band around Tadoussac and Quebec, for example, occupied a specific territory; the boundaries were well known and usually well defined by recognizable geographical features. Fortunately for the French, however, they had entered a war zone. The Algonquians welcomed the French traders because they saw them as potential allies who possessed muskets. They could use help against the Iroquois raiders. The trading post at Quebec also ensured that they could obtain badly needed iron goods, at advantageous rates. *[handwritten: He hoped that the First Nations would settle, farm, become Christian & intermarry with the French eventually creating a single ppl.]*

[margin note: trade for iron goods]

EARLY FRENCH–NATIVE RELATIONS

No sooner had the French established Quebec and concluded an alliance with the Algonquians than they asked Champlain to join their war parties against the Iroquois. As the French depended on these nations for furs, they complied. In 1609, Champlain and the French joined

Indian Preparing Birch Bark Map for Professor Hind, by Henry Youle Hind, 1861–62. A scene from a mid-nineteenth-century expedition across what is now northern Quebec and Labrador. For more than three centuries, Europeans relied on the Native peoples for geographical information about the Americas.

J. Ross Robertson Collection/Toronto Reference Library/T31956.

the Algonquians and some Hurons, their Iroquoian-speaking allies in the interior, in an attack on the Iroquois to the southwest. The French firearms so frightened the Iroquois that they lost the battle at the lake the French named Lake Champlain. The French and their Native allies again defeated an Iroquois war party near the mouth of the Richelieu River the next summer.

The Franco–Algonquian alliance proved invaluable to the French. They taught them how to adapt to winter and supplied them with invaluable geographical information about the interior. The French learned the value of birchbark canoes, and when the waterways froze, of toboggans and snowshoes. As well, they relied on the First Nations for food.

In 1610, Champlain arranged an exchange with the Hurons. He sent Étienne Brûlé, a young Frenchman, to live with them. In return, Champlain took Savignon, brother of a Huron headman and roughly the same age as Brûlé, into his custody. Brûlé became the first of the coureurs de bois (literally, "runners of the woods"), the individuals who lived with the First Nations and reinforced their economic and political alliance with the Algonquians and Hurons.

From Brûlé and Savignon the French learned about the Huron Confederacy, an alliance of several Iroquoian-speaking nations with a population of up to 30 000 on Lake Huron. The Hurons' trading area extended as far west as Lake Superior and as far north as James Bay. Huron, in fact, was the trading language of the entire Upper Great Lakes.

Champlain made his last journey into the interior in the summer of 1615, for the purpose of strengthening the Franco–Huron alliance. While in Huronia, Champlain concluded treaties in friendship with individual Huron leaders, affirming French support in their wars — provided that the Hurons continued to trade with the French. By joining a large war party of Hurons and Algonquians against the Iroquois, he convinced the Hurons of his support. Henceforth, the French could live securely as guests among their Huron allies. By the 1620s, the Hurons supplied from one-half to two-thirds of the furs obtained by the French.

THE COMPANY OF ONE HUNDRED ASSOCIATES

New France grew slowly. During the winter of 1620–21, no more than 60 people lived at Quebec. Thanks to the co-operation of the Native peoples, the fur trade required few Europeans. Furthermore, no incentive existed for Europeans to settle and farm in the northern colony. To whom would farmers have sold their produce? No market existed. In contrast, the English colony of Virginia, with its tobacco-based economy, had 2000 inhabitants by 1627, or twenty times New France's population. Even the newly established Dutch colony of New Netherlands in the Hudson River valley had 200 settlers by 1625.

In 1627, the French government, observing the success of other European settlements in America, decided to end New France's total dependency on furs. Cardinal Richelieu, Louis XIII's prime minister, sponsored a new company called the Compagnie des Cent-Associés ("Company of One Hundred Associates"), which obtained working capital from 100 investors to develop and exploit New France's resources and to encourage Roman Catholic missionary activity. In return for its trade monopoly, the company promised to bring out 4000 settlers, all French and Roman Catholic, within 15 years and to promote missions to the First Nations.

Unfortunately for New France, the project began at the worst possible time: war had just broken out between France and England. In 1627 the English seized Tadoussac and captured, off the shores of the Gaspé, the French ships that were bringing 400 settlers to New France. In 1629, the English attacked Quebec itself. Cut off from France and their provisions long exhausted, Champlain and his starving garrison surrendered in July 1629. Champlain and the garrison left Quebec. For three years, the St. Lawrence remained closed to the French, which meant heavy losses for the One Hundred Associates, from which it never really recovered. Only

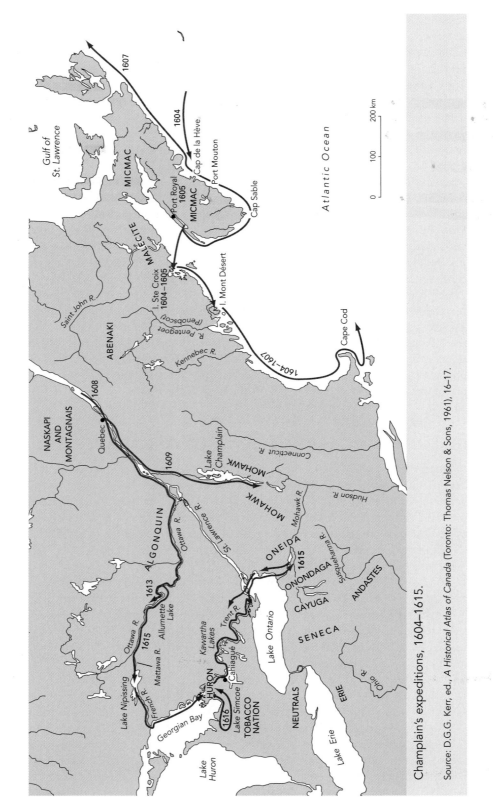

Champlain's expeditions, 1604–1615.

Source: D.G.G. Kerr, ed., *A Historical Atlas of Canada* (Toronto: Thomas Nelson & Sons, 1961), 16–17.

in 1632 did the English leave Quebec. Champlain returned to New France and undertook one last initiative: he founded a fur-trading post above Quebec in 1634 at Trois-Rivières.

Champlain deserves full credit for establishing New France, their Laurentian colony in northeastern North America. The French leader served, in effect if not in title, as New France's governor. Through his numerous alliances with the Algonquians and Hurons, managed by young French coureurs de bois, he kept the tiny trading post of Quebec alive. Rightly, he is considered "the founder of New France." With the founder's death on Christmas Day, 1635, the effective leadership of the fur-trading colony passed into the hands of the religious orders, particularly the Jesuits.

THE CONTRIBUTIONS OF THE FRENCH RELIGIOUS ORDERS

In the sixteenth century, France had been rent by civil strife between Catholics and Protestants, or Huguenots. The Catholic majority in France fought back. The Roman Catholic church launched a "Counter-Reformation," first to root out the corruption in the Catholic church, and then to win back those lost to the Protestant heretics. The Society of Jesus (commonly known as the Jesuits), the papacy's most expert missionaries, led the struggle. Other groups, such as the Ursulines, a female teaching order, followed them. Both the Jesuits and the Ursulines extended their mission to convert non-Christians throughout the world.

Champlain wanted the neighbouring Algonquians on the St. Lawrence to convert to Christianity, form settlements, and farm, as the French did. Ultimately he hoped that the French and the Christianized First Nations would amalgamate, through intermarriage, into a single people. The first French missionaries assigned the task of transforming the Native peoples into a French people were the Récollets, a branch of the Franciscan Friars. At first they believed the task would be relatively easy, but quickly learned that the First Nations had no desire to assimilate into French society. Their seminary soon closed for lack of students and funds.

THE JESUIT ORDER AND THE URSULINES

In an attempt to solve their financial problems, the Récollets sought to collaborate with the Jesuits, a wealthy and powerful order founded by Ignatius Loyola a century earlier. From 1625 to 1629, the Jesuits assisted the Récollets in establishing missions in New France. This highly disciplined order, renowned for its ability to attract able candidates, often of high rank, was also known for its willingness to take on the most dangerous tasks. Thanks to their *Relations*, or annual reports back to France, we know a great deal about their activities in New France.

In 1632, Cardinal Richelieu gave the Jesuits a monopoly over the Canadian mission field. Their work then began in earnest. Yet when they opened a school for Native children, they [boarding school] encountered the same problems as the Récollets had. Enlisting Native students was difficult because their parents often refused to let the children go. The priests had to give presents to the parents in order to gain students for the seminary. Many students ran away, and others became ill and died. The deaths increased the parents' resistance to their children's schooling, as did the French custom of physically punishing children, a practice foreign to the Natives' approach to child rearing. [Founded by Marie-Madeline de Chauvigny de la Peltrie]

The arrival of the Ursuline nuns in Quebec in 1639 marked the beginning of their outreach to the First Nations. The Jesuits invited them to Christianize and to "civilize" the young Native girls. But the Ursulines, despite determined efforts on their part, had little success. In 1668 [Extensive letters describe activities.] Marie de l'Incarnation, founder of the Ursuline Order in New France, wrote, "We have observed that of a hundred that have passed through our hands we have scarcely civilized one. We find

[Read last 2 slides]

docility and intelligence in these girls but, when we are least expecting it, they clamber over our wall and go off to run with their kinsmen in the woods, finding more to please them there than in all the amenities of our French houses."[5]

THE JESUITS BRING INDENTURED WORKERS TO NEW FRANCE

The church, in effect, became the second industry of the colony. The Jesuits, Ursulines, and the Hospital nuns came in number to serve the Native peoples and in turn brought out *engagés*, or indentured workers, on three-year contracts, to help them. These newcomers created a market for agricultural produce in the colony. Upon being discharged, many left to return to France, rather than stay on in a land that had little to offer in terms of security or creature comforts, with its formidable winters, heavily forested land to clear, and shortage of marriageable women. But some *engagés* stayed and began to farm.

THE FOUNDING OF MONTREAL

The Société de Notre-Dame de Montreal, a group of fervent French Roman Catholics, planned a mission settlement remote and independent from the main settlement at Quebec. It believed that once it had built a church, a school, and a hospital, the First Nations would come, and accept Christianity. The organizers chose the island of Montreal, at the crossroads of the Ottawa and the St. Lawrence rivers, a location that could be easily reached by the Algonquian-speaking nations. Paul de Chomedey de Maisonneuve, a 33-year-old career soldier, led the first forty settlers to establish what they hoped would become a model Christian community. Go they did, and in mid-May 1642 they founded Ville-Marie, the future Montreal.

The first settlers farmed on the grassy areas where villages of the Laurentian Iroquoians once stood. The only sizable influx of new settlers, 100 in all, arrived in 1653. Despite an initial burst of enthusiasm, the outpost grew slowly, and chronic underpopulation remained a problem until the late 1660s. Two factors prevented the colony's expansion: the Société's quick loss of enthusiasm for its missionary enterprise, and the repeated raids by the Iroquois, who resented the founding of a French village in their northern hunting grounds. It took a large dose of courage to settle in the centre of the battle zone. In 1663 the Sulpicians, another French religious order, took over the direction of the settlement and became the seigneurs of the island of Montreal.

NEW FRANCE IN THE MID-1640S

In 1645 — a decade after Champlain's death — the French colony in the valley of the St. Lawrence remained quite marginal. It contained only 600 residents and a few hundred *engagés*. Clerical intervention in the 1630s had helped, but the colony's population still remained smaller than a single large Iroquoian village.

THE MISSIONARIES' ARRIVAL IN HURONIA

At the time of French–First Nations contact in the seventeenth century, the Hurons and the Iroquois were at war. A desire for war honours and prestige contributed to the hostility. Participation in a war party, if successful, raised a man's standing in his clan and village. It increased his chances of an advantageous marriage and his hopes of one day becoming a village leader. Moreover, the necessity of avenging the dead led to more warfare, since the Iroquois and the Hurons believed the souls of the dead would not rest in peace until they had been avenged. This led to an escalation of the feud between the two hostile groups.

European beachheads in America, 1650.

Source: Paul W. Bennett et al. *Canada: A North American Nation*, 2nd Edition. (Toronto: McGraw-Hill Ryerson, 1995), p. 69.

With the arrival of the Europeans, economic motives joined those of prestige and the blood feud as causes of Native warfare. Both the Iroquois and the Hurons needed a steady supply of furs to buy European trade goods. By the 1620s, the Hurons had become the principal economic partners of the French, exchanging furs for corn and European goods with the neighbouring Algonquians, who, in turn, traded as far north as James Bay and along the shores of Lakes Michigan and Superior. As elsewhere on the continent, the fur trade and the goods that it

A rare photo of an Iroquois trail, taken a century ago in the territory of the Seneca, near Conesus Lake, New York. Generally, the paths followed the ridges, where the forest was not so thick.

National Anthropological Archives/Smithsonian Institution/947A.

brought enriched Huron culture. The Hurons began to decorate their pottery with more elaborate patterns and to use iron knives to make more intricate bone carvings.

THE JESUITS AND THE HURONS

After establishing an economic alliance with the Hurons, the French obtained permission to send Roman Catholic priests to Huronia, first Récollet missionaries in 1615 and then Jesuit fathers in 1627. As a condition for renewing the Franco–Huron alliance after the English ended their occupation of Quebec in 1632, the French insisted that the Hurons allow Jesuits to live in Huronia. Reluctantly, the Hurons agreed. In 1634, Jean de Brébeuf and two companions reopened the Huron mission. Dressed in black gowns, wearing broad-brimmed black hats, and with iron chains and black beads hanging from their belts, the "Black Robes" went from village to village to spread the Christian gospel. The Hurons met them with apprehension and a growing fear, particularly after the outbreak of European diseases.

The Jesuit order put great effort into building up its mission. They mastered the Huron language and then communicated their ideas to the would-be converts. They also used non-verbal methods: pictures of holy subjects or of the sufferings of lost souls; religious statues; coloured beads as prizes for successful memorization; ceremonies, chants, and processions on holy days and on such occasions as baptisms, marriages, and funerals. They decorated the churches with crosses, bells, and candles, creating a colourful visual display.

CULTURAL DIFFERENCES BETWEEN THE HURONS AND THE FRENCH

In this initial period the Jesuits made some progress, but the gulf between the two societies remained vast. For the Hurons, the meaning of existence was to maintain harmony with nature. They did not consider humans superior to other entities in the natural world, but rather equal partners. Their sacred stories explained their perception of the universe: the relationship between humanity and the earth, between people and animals, between the sun and the moon, between sickness and health. Christianity differed from the Hurons' religion in viewing the world as provisional and preparatory to the afterlife. John Webster Grant, the Canadian religious historian, wrote that if the First Nations religious symbol was the circle, the Christian's "might well be an arrow running from the creation of the world through God's redeeming acts in history to the final apocalypse."[6]

To gain an audience among the Hurons, the Jesuits emphasized the similarities between the Hurons' faith and their own. They pointed out that both believed in a supernatural power that influenced their lives, one that the Hurons located in the sun or sky and the Jesuits in heaven. Both Huron shamans and Roman Catholic priests encouraged personal contact with the supernatural. At puberty, every young Huron man was expected, through fasting and a vision quest, to find his own guardian spirit. The Jesuits also encouraged spiritual quests and valued fasts and vigils. The common reliance on prayer revealed a shared conviction that divine power controlled warfare, caused rain or drought, and gave health or disease. Finally, both Jesuits and Hurons

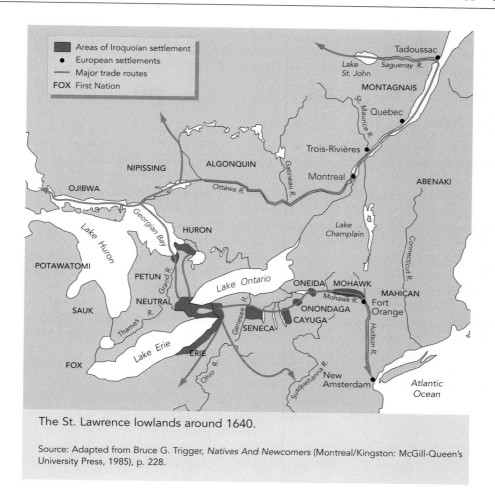

The St. Lawrence lowlands around 1640.

Source: Adapted from Bruce G. Trigger, *Natives And Newcomers* (Montreal/Kingston: McGill-Queen's University Press, 1985), p. 228.

accepted the idea of an afterlife; for the Hurons it was a pleasant place where life continued essentially as on earth, and for Christians it was heaven.

These common elements aside, the two religions had enormous differences. The Christian insistence that only one deity ruled the universe conflicted with the Hurons' belief in many supernatural beings. Furthermore, the Hurons had nothing remotely close to the Jesuits' concepts of the Trinity and the Incarnation. Marriage was another controversial issue. The Jesuits found the Hurons' sexual behaviour aberrant. Among the Hurons, divorce was easy and frequent, in contrast with the Jesuits' ideal of the indissolubility of marriage. Since Huron children by custom belonged to the mother, divorce did not endanger family stability. The Hurons also failed to see lifetime marriage as superior to their own custom. Moreover, they could not understand the Jesuits' practice of celibacy and sexual self-denial.

The two cultures also disagreed on issues of human sinfulness and the need for salvation. Although the Hurons distinguished between good and evil, they had no concept similar to the missionaries' idea of universal guilt, of a fundamental inadequacy in human nature. Like most Native North Americans, the Hurons believed that almost all people would experience the same pleasant afterlife, regardless of how they had lived on earth. For the Jesuits, there was both a heaven and a hell. The only way to escape hell was through Christianity. This concept of a place of torment proved very difficult to convey to the Hurons.

The Jesuits tried to convince the Hurons of the worthiness of biblical standards. They insisted that the Hurons curtail easy divorce, marry for life, and end their undue reliance on dreams. To the Hurons, the missionaries threatened to subvert the very customs and beliefs essential to successful hunting, good health, and survival.

NEW EPIDEMICS STRIKE HURONIA

The French brought with them more than European trade goods and a Christian missionary message. Unknowingly, they brought European diseases that devastated the Hurons and their neighbours. By 1639 smallpox raged throughout Huronia, killing more than half the Huron population and reducing their numbers to 10 000. Since old people and children died in the greatest numbers, the Hurons lost much of their traditional religious knowledge, which tended to be the preserve of the elderly, and suffered a shortage of warriors in the next decade with the deaths of so many children.

By the late 1630s, the Hurons concluded that the Jesuits were sorcerers who brought disease. The Hurons recognized three major sources of illness: natural causes, unfulfilled desires of a person's soul (alleviated by a form of dream-fulfilment), and witchcraft. Not surprisingly, the Hurons blamed the new diseases on their visitors, since the Jesuits alone seemed immune to the diseases. The Jesuits' celibacy also suggested that the "white shamans" nurtured great supernatural power for the purposes of witchcraft. Furthermore, they seemed to cause death by their rituals: after they touched sick babies with drops of water, many died.

As the epidemics spread, the Hurons' fear of the Jesuits increased. They denied the Jesuits entry into their longhouses and villages. The Hurons harassed and threatened the Jesuits. On at least two occasions, in 1637 and 1640, general Huron councils discussed the death penalty for the missionaries or at least the possibility of forcing "the sorcerers" to return to Quebec. Yet they pursued neither course of action. Many of the leading chiefs realized that the Hurons depended on the French for European hardware and dry goods and that now they could not live without them. Thus, trading relations with the French forced the Hurons to tolerate the missionaries.

HURON CHRISTIAN CONVERTS

In the early 1640s, conversions increased. Several factors contributed to this. No doubt the Jesuits' repeated explanations of the two faiths' common themes helped, and the Jesuits' unquestioned bravery during the Iroquois attacks influenced others to convert. Simple economics also influenced many Huron traders. French traders and government officials accorded Native Christians far greater honour and gave them additional presents at Quebec and Trois-Rivières. Another incentive to convert came from the French policy of selling guns only to First Nations people who were baptized. By 1646, the Christian Huron community numbered 500 and was growing.

THE FINAL STRUGGLE BETWEEN THE HURONS AND THE IROQUOIS

At the time when disease had weakened them and their internal cohesion had been reduced by the growth of a Christian faction, the Hurons faced their greatest military threat from the Iroquois. An Iroquois invitation to the Hurons to join the Five Nations Confederacy had been refused. Furthermore, the Iroquois looked for new sources of furs. The Huron country bordered the fur-rich areas around the upper Great Lakes that the western Iroquois wanted to exploit. They coveted the hunting grounds of southern Ontario.

Guns made the Iroquois a formidable foe. By 1639, they obtained firearms from English traders in the Connecticut valley and then directly from Dutch traders on the upper Hudson River. The longer and heavier Dutch guns were superior to those that the French sold to their Christian converts. Thus equipped, the Iroquois could raid the nations to the north much more easily than before.

Where Historians Disagree
Why the Hurons Accepted Christianity

In the 1640s an extraordinary event occurred; large numbers of Hurons in good health accepted Christianity. Before 1639, the Jesuits' attempts to Christianize the Hurons met with limited success mostly with individuals who were on the point of death, yet by 1648 they had converted several thousand people. Had it not been for the Iroquois defeat of the Hurons in 1649–50 and their subsequent dispersal, the Jesuits' dream of establishing a Roman Catholic Huronia might have been realized. The massive conversion of Hurons to Christianity in the last years of Huronia has recently aroused new interest among historians.

The impact of disease offers one explanation for the Hurons' sudden receptiveness to Christianity. From 1635 to 1640, a series of epidemics carried away more than half the population. The Hurons lost many of their most skilful leaders and craftspeople, and this had the effect of increasing their dependence on trade with the French. Anthropologist Bruce G. Trigger, in his article "The French Presence in Huronia," identified the economic motives, among other factors, that led many Hurons to convert. They sought, through conversion, "to receive preferential treatment in their dealings with traders and officials in New France," and in particular, to be able to secure guns, which were given only to converts. In fact, as Trigger points out, "in 1648, when only

15 percent of the Hurons were Christian, half of the men in the Huron [trading] fleet were either converts or were preparing for baptism."[1]

Trigger's secular explanation of the Jesuits' success in his later two-volume work[2] greatly annoyed historian Lucien Campeau, a Jesuit. Referring to Trigger's work as "malheureusement biaisée et peu exacte sous l'aspect historique" [unfortunately biased and not very historically accurate], Campeau wrote a full account of his order's work among the Hurons in order to prove that the Hurons understood the Christian message as it was preached to them and that this message was the primary reason for their conversion.[3] In reply, Trigger pointed out that Campeau had failed to examine the most recent ethnohistorical research in preparing his study. Moreover, he was too ready to accept, uncritically and at face value, the Jesuits' account of their mission work. "What we have here is splendid hagiography but very old-fashioned historiography."[4]

Biography can be useful in humanizing historical controversies such as this by putting a human face on the discussions. Yet, in the case of the Hurons, the would-be biographer faces incredible obstacles. As Trigger has written, "For the majority of Indians whose names have been preserved, only a few isolated events are recorded and even a skeletal life history of such individuals remains beyond our grasp."[5] Fortunately, however, Trigger was able to use the Jesuit *Relations* to provide an account of the Christian convert Joseph Chihoatenhwa.[6] Expanding upon Trigger's sketch, John Steckley, an anthropologist and student of the Huron language, has completed a short biography.[7] In Chihoatenhwa's case, economic factors apparently played very little part in his decision to accept Christianity, as he traded with the neighbouring Petuns and not with the French. Steckley argues, as does Trigger, that Joseph Chihoatenhwa converted in 1637 for reasons deep within his First Nations culture. "As a Christian, Chihoatenhwa did have, or believed he had,

a source of power on which he could draw, a spiritual source not unlike that upon which a pre-contact Huron shaman could rely.... The priest appeared to have an effective medicine when no other was forthcoming; a preventative or cure which Chihoatenhwa accepted much [as] he would have in earlier times accepted the curing vision or dream of a powerful shaman."[8]

Historians, anthropologists, and ethnohistorians radically differ about the causes of the Hurons' conversion to Christianity, but all agree on the importance of the phenomenon and on the richness of the Jesuits' descriptions of their efforts to convert the Hurons.

[1] Bruce G. Trigger, "The French Presence in Huronia," *Canadian Historical Review* 49 [1968]: 134, reprinted in R. Douglas Francis and Donald B. Smith, eds., *Readings in Canadian History: Pre-Confederation*, 6th ed. [Toronto: Nelson Thomson Learning, 2000), p. 35.
[2] Bruce G. Trigger, *The Children of Aataentsic: A History of the Huron People to 1660*, 2 vols. (Montreal/Kingston: McGill-Queen's University Press, 1976).
[3] Lucien Campeau, *La Mission des Jésuites chez les Hurons*, 1634–1650 (Montreal:Éditions Bellarmin, 1987), p. 18.
[4] Bruce G. Trigger, "Review of La Mission des Jésuites chez les Hurons, 1634–1650 by Lucien Campeau," *Canadian Historical Review* 69 (1988): 102.
[5] Trigger, *The Children of Aataentsic*, vol. 1, p. 22.
[6] Ibid., vol. 2, pp. 550–51, 565–67, 594–95, 598–601.
[7] One of the three biographies included in John Steckley's *Untold Tales: Three 17th Century Huron* (Ajax, ON: R.A. Kerton, 1981).
[8] Steckley, *Untold Tales*, pp. 9–10.

Bruce Trigger estimates that in 1648 the Iroquois had more than 500 guns, while the Hurons probably had no more than 120.[7] These guns were crude, awkward to handle, and in many ways little better than the bow and arrow, but their thunderous noise and their ability to inflict mortal wounds made them a source of terror. They also increased their owners' self-confidence.

The Fall of Huronia and its Impact on the French Colony

In mid-March 1649, a large Iroquois army struck a small Huron village, killing or capturing all but 10 of the 400 inhabitants. They then used the village as a base camp to destroy other settlements. Over the course of the campaign, several hundred Hurons died or were captured. The Iroquois took prisoner and tortured to death Fathers Jean de Brébeuf and Gabriel Lalemant. The attacks threw the surviving settlements into chaos. The Hurons, seeing their position as untenable, burned their villages and deserted them. Hunger and contagious diseases claimed many Huron refugees, who spent the winter on Christian Island, in Georgian Bay. A small number of survivors eventually accompanied the Jesuits to Quebec, where the order established a fortified mission for them on Île d'Orléans, just east of the town. Others joined the Algonquians to the north. In the next few years, a number of Hurons voluntarily joined the Iroquois. The Hurons' dispersal marked the end of Huronia.

The fall of Huronia led to Iroquois attacks on other Iroquoian-speaking peoples. The urgency behind this warfare appears to be a result of the severe depopulation from epidemics after the mid-1630s. Economic motives played a part, but the demand for captives to replace the deceased relatives was equally important. The Five Nations' subsequent victories over the Hurons' neighbours to the west, the Petuns, and to the south, the Neutrals, greatly disrupted the fur trade.

In the long run, however, the dispersal of the Hurons helped New France's economy. Because the Hurons could no longer supply food to the northern Algonquians, the latter became a new market for the colony's farmers. By 1653, the French coureurs de bois had also replaced the vanquished Huron intermediaries in the fur trade. They went inland to live with the Algonquians of the upper Great Lakes, or the "Ottawa," as the French called them, and to take their furs to New France.

RENEWED IROQUOIS ATTACKS ON NEW FRANCE

The early 1650s were difficult years for the colony. The Iroquois's use of guerrilla war tactics, their avoidance of open combat in favour of ambush, and the speed and unexpectedness of their attacks demoralized many colonists in the three tiny French settlements. Only with the outbreak of war between the Iroquois and the Eries to the west did New France obtain a 5-year truce with the Iroquois in the mid-1650s. However, fighting resumed in 1658. Fortunately for the French, their population had increased by this time: the population had tripled, from 1050 permanent French residents in 1651 to nearly 3300 by 1662, thanks largely to new farming opportunities. From their Algonquian allies they also began to master guerilla warfare tactics.

Security finally came for the habitants when, in 1663, King Louis XIV elevated the tiny colony to a royal province of France. He dispatched two years later the Carignan-Salières regiment, over 1000 strong. In 1666, the French made two overland attacks on the Iroquois in present-day New York State. The Iroquois, who were also then involved in a war with the Susquehannock (Iroquoian-speaking First Nations living in present-day Pennsylvania), made peace with the French in 1667. Twenty years of peace followed, during which the colony greatly advanced. It took lasting form in the years of Royal Government.

Early contact between Europeans and the First Nations in northeastern North America had led to the development of the fur trade. The Europeans dealt with, to use the description of archaeologist Robert McGhee, "the most easterly representatives of a hemispheric civilization that had achieved full occupation and use of the American continents."[8] At the beginning of the seventeenth century, the European presence in what is now Eastern Canada remained marginal. The establishment in the early seventeenth century of French settlement in the St. Lawrence valley, and a French presence in Acadia, did allow for further advances by the French. The impact of new diseases wrecked havoc amongst the First Nations, weakening them at the moment of greater French expansion.

NOTES

1. Morris Bishop, *Champlain: The Life of Fortitude* (Toronto: McClelland & Stewart, 1963 [1948]), p. 26.

2. H.P. Biggar, ed., *The Voyages of Jacques Cartier* (Ottawa: King's Printer, 1924), p. 245. For an important discussion of other possible origins of the word "Canada" see Olive P. Dickason, "Appendix 1: Origin of the Name 'Canada,'" in *The Myth of the Savage and the Beginnings of French Colonialism in the Americas* (Edmonton: University of Alberta Press, 1984), pp. 279–80.

3. Harold Innis, *The Fur Trade in Canada: An Introduction to Canadian Economic History* (Revised ed., Toronto: University of Toronto Press, 1956), p. 15.

4. Bruce G. Trigger, *Natives and Newcomers. Canada's 'Heroic Age' Reconsidered* (Kingston and Montreal: McGill-Queen's University Press, 1985), pp. 144–148.

5. Marie de l'Incarnation, *Word from New France. The Selected Letters of Marie de l'Incarnation.* Translated and edited by Joyce Marshall (Toronto: Oxford University Press, 1967), p. 341.

6. John Webster Grant, *Moon of Wintertime: Missionaries and the Indians of Canada in Encounter since 1534* (Toronto: University of Toronto Press, 1984), p. 24.

7. Trigger, *Natives and Newcomers*, 262.

8. Robert McGhee, "Canada Y1K: The First Millennium," *The Beaver*, December 1999/January 2000, p. 17.

LINKING TO THE PAST

Early Exploration and Settlement of Newfoundland and Labrador
http://www.heritage.nf.ca/exploration/early_ex.html

An account of exploration and early settlement from the arrival of the Norse to John Cabot's voyages; includes information on geographical knowledge and navigation methods.

Leif Eiriksson
http://viking.no/e/people/leif/e-leiv.htm

An overview of the lives and adventures of Eric the Red, Leif Eiriksson, and Thorvaldr, Leif's brother.

Later Exploration and Settlement of Newfoundland and Labrador
http://www.heritage.nf.ca/exploration/later_ex.html

An overview of exploration after Cabot, including contributions of Portuguese, English, and French explorers, as well as an illustrated section on cartography.

Jacques Cartier's Voyages
http://www.civilization.ca/vmnf/explor/carti_e1.html

An account of Jacques Cartier's voyages and colonization efforts.

Living in Canada in the Time of Champlain, 1600–1635
http://www.civilization.ca/vmnf/expos/champlain/indexeng.htm

A virtual exhibition featuring Champlain's voyages, as well as commerce, warfare, farming, and other aspects of life in New France during this period.

Huron and Iroquois History

http://www.tolatsga.org/hur.html and http://www.tolatsga.org/iro.html

These pages from the First Nations Histories site feature a wealth of information on these two confederacies, including detailed accounts of the wars between them, and of the influence that French settlers and French trade had on their relations.

BIBLIOGRAPHY

Well-written summaries of the early European explorers' accounts include Samuel Eliot Morison, *The European Discovery of America: The Northern Voyages, a.d. 500–1600* (New York: Oxford University Press, 1971); Daniel J. Boorstin, *The Discoverers: A History of Man's Search to Know His World and Himself* (New York: Random House, 1983); and Robert McGhee, *Canada Rediscovered* (Ottawa: Canadian Museum of Civilization/Libre Expression, 1991). The primary texts are available in David Quinn, ed., *New American World: A Documentary History of North America to 1615*, 5 vols. (New York: Arno Press, 1979). Michael Bliss briefly reviews economic aspects in *Northern Enterprise: Five Centuries of Canadian Business* (Toronto: McClelland & Stewart, 1987). The *Dictionary of Canadian Biography*, vol. 1, *1000–1700* (Toronto: University of Toronto Press, 1966), contains biographical portraits. It is now available online: www.biographi.ca. Ralph T. Pastore provides a bibliographical guide to the secondary literature in his essay "Beginnings to 1600," in M. Brook Taylor, ed., *Canadian History: A Reader's Guide*, vol. 1, *Beginnings to Confederation* (Toronto: University of Toronto Press, 1994), pp. 3–32.

Marcel Trudel provides an overview of the period in *The Beginnings of New France, 1524–1663* (Toronto: McClelland & Stewart, 1973). A shorter summary appears in W.J. Eccles, *The Canada Frontier, 1534–1760* (Toronto: Holt, Rinehart and Winston, 1969). His later work, *France in America*, rev. ed. (Markham, ON: Fitzhenry & Whiteside, 1990 [1972]), also contains information on the early French colonies in the Caribbean as well as New France and Acadia. Two well-written biographies of Champlain are available: Morris Bishop, *Champlain: The Life of Fortitude* (Toronto: McClelland & Stewart, 1963 [1948]); and Samuel Eliot Morison, *Samuel de Champlain: Father of New France* (Boston: Little, Brown, 1972). Bibliographical guides include Jacques Rouillard, ed., *Guide d'histoire du Québec du régime français à nos jours: Bibliographie commentée* (Montreal: Éditions du Méridien, 1991); and Thomas Wien, "Canada and the Pays d'en haut, 1600–1760," in M. Brook Taylor, ed., *Canadian History: A Reader's Guide*, vol. 1, *Beginnings to Confederation* (Toronto: University of Toronto Press, 1994), pp. 33–75.

For First Nations affairs, Bruce G. Trigger's *The Children of Aataentsic: A History of the Huron People to 1660*, 2 vols. (Montreal/Kingston: McGill-Queen's University Press, 1976), and his *Natives and Newcomers: Canada's "Heroic Age" Reconsidered* (Montreal/Kingston: McGill-Queen's University Press, 1985). Denys Delâge's *Bitter Feast: Amerindians and Europeans in Northeastern North America, 1600–64*, trans. Jane Brierley (Vancouver: University of British Columbia Press, 1993), also provides a complete overview. An older study, A.G. Bailey's *The Conflict of European and Eastern Algonkian Cultures, 1504–1700* (Toronto: University of Toronto Press, 1969 [1937]), is still valuable. Arthur J. Ray, *Indians in the Fur Trade* (Toronto: University of Toronto Press, 1974), covers the economic aspects of early Native–European contact. An excellent overview of early French–First Nation relations is the chapter, "The Native People and the Beginnings of New France," in John A. Dickinson and Brian Young's *A Short History of Quebec*, 3rd ed. (Montreal/Kingston: McGill-Queen's University Press, 2003), pp. 3–27.

For excellent maps of early European exploration see: R. Cole Harris, ed., *Historical Atlas of Canada*, vol. 1, *From the Beginning to 1800* (Toronto: University of Toronto Press, 1987); and Derek Hayes, *Historical Atlas of Canada. Canada's History Illustrated with Original Maps* (Vancouver: Douglas and McIntyre, 2002).

NEW FRANCE AND ACADIA, 1663–1760

TIME LINE

1663 – Louis XIV makes New France a royal province under his direct control

1682 – The first term of office of the Comte de Frontenac, the best-known governor of New France; he also served from 1689–1698

1686 – The number of French settlers in present-day Nova Scotia grows to 800

c. 1700 – The ratio between males and females in New France becomes evenly balanced

1713 – In the Treaty of Utrecht, France cedes Acadia to England; the beginning of 30 years of peace in the St. Lawrence valley

1720 – France begins the construction of its fortress Louisbourg on Île Royale (Cape Breton Island)

1755 – The expulsion of the Acadians begins

1760 – Of the 67 000 European inhabitants in the St. Lawrence valley, 10 percent lived in the Trois-Rivières district, with the remainder divided equally between the Quebec and Montreal regions

In 1661, Louis XIV became king of France. He created an absolute monarchy in which all authority descended from him (*L'état c'est moi*," he said in his famous phrase). The "Sun King," as he became known, ruled France for the next half-century, until his death in 1715. The new monarch sought to create a dynamic French presence in North America by making New France a *province de France*, a colony directly under his personal rule. Jean-Baptiste Colbert, the minister of the marine, or use the modern term, minister of colonies, worked to strengthen the colony's economic infrastructure. He also introduced new political institutions that would last nearly a century. The French colony in the St. Lawrence valley truly took form in the period of Royal Government. In contrast, however, the colony of Acadia received little attention.

The French used the name "Acadia" to distinguish the eastern or maritime part of New France from the valley of the St. Lawrence, which they called Canada. Under French rule, Canada and Acadia remained separate colonies. Just where Acadia ended and Canada began was never clearly defined, but certainly Acadia included present-day Maine, New Brunswick, Nova Scotia, and Prince Edward Island. Acadia had the misfortune of being located in a war zone between the English- and French-dominated areas.

THE FIRST HALF-CENTURY OF ROYAL GOVERNMENT IN CANADA

Colbert dreamed of making Canada into a much more self-reliant, defensible colony, with a prosperous agricultural base and its own basic domestic industries. The minister wanted it to become a "compact colony," one centred in the St. Lawrence valley, without unnecessary forts and outposts on the periphery. He also opposed western expansion. Colbert's first objective was to strengthen the colony militarily. In the mid-1660s, he dispatched regular troops to New France, the Carignan-Salières regiment. When the Iroquois made peace in 1667, Colbert's program to transform the St. Lawrence valley into a profitable and well-populated colony began.

THE REFORM OF THE SEIGNEURIAL SYSTEM

In fashioning the French colony in the St. Lawrence valley, the minister of the marine reformed the system of land holdings. French immigrants to the colony were familiar with it because it formed the basis of land tenure in France. Peasant settlers, or *censitaires*, depended on seigneurs, or lords (or, more appropriately, squires or gentry), in turn themselves vassals of the king. Title to all the land rested with the king, who granted fiefs, or estates, as he saw fit. The soil belonged to the seigneur, but the mineral or subsoil rights and all oak trees on the property belonged to the monarch. Landowners who acquired large domains and who did nothing to improve them lost their lands to more energetic seigneurs.

In 1627, the Company of One Hundred Associates gained legal and seigneurial rights over the territory of New France. The company in turn granted to favoured individuals — usually nobles or religious bodies such as the Jesuits, the Ursulines, or the Sulpicians — large tracts of land, called "seigneuries," along the St. Lawrence between Quebec and Montreal. In return for their rectangular estates fronting on the river and usually extending into the foothills behind, the seigneurs undertook to bring out the *censitaires* (or habitants, to employ Canadian usage), who in turn paid them rent and dues.

Under royal government, the intendant, among his other administrative duties, granted seigneuries and supervised the seigneurial system. On his arrival in 1665, Jean Talon, the first intendant of New France, implemented Colbert's plan. He made actual occupancy a condition of all future grants. Talon and his immediate successors also kept the size of the seigneuries relatively small to prevent the rise of a class of large landowners who might challenge royal authority. Nearly 200 seigneuries were open for settlement by 1715, most of them along the St. Lawrence from Montréal to below Quebec.

THE OBLIGATIONS OF THE SEIGNEURS AND THE *CENSITAIRES*

Both the seigneurs and the *censitaires* had obligations to fulfil under the seigneurial system. The seigneurs had to clear some of their seigneury, maintain a manor house, and reside there or have a responsible person living there throughout the year. They had to make land grants of up to 80 ha to any genuine settlers who applied. Finally, on part of their land, they had to establish a flour mill for the use of their *censitaires*. Some seigneurs also maintained a court of law to settle minor disputes.

The *censitaires*, or habitants, also had responsibilities. They had to build their own house, clear their land, and pay their seigneur the *cens* (a small cash payment) and *rentes* (another money payment). Together, these two charges amounted to less than one-tenth of a *censitaire's* annual income. They had to take their wheat to the seigneurial mill, paying the seigneur one sack of flour out of every fourteen for this privilege. In a few seigneuries, the seigneur had the *droit de corvée* (right to forced labour), usually three days per year, determined in the contract with the *censitaire*. As well, the *censitaires* were required by the Crown to work without pay for a day or two a year, doing general maintenance work on any seigneurial roads or bridges. In return for their grant of land, the habitants must maintain the portion of road that passed through their farms. If they met these requirements, the habitants became virtual owners of their land, which they could pass on to their children. If they sold their land outside their families, however, they must pay the seigneur a portion of the money they obtained, somewhat like a real-estate sales tax.

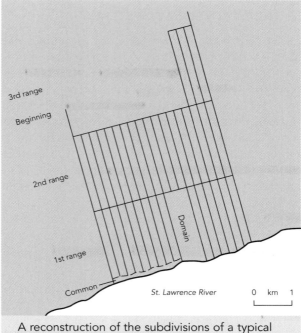

A reconstruction of the subdivisions of a typical seigneury in New France.

Under Royal Government, the settlers became part of a well-organized social unit and gained title to a tract of land. In time, the seigneur built a manor house, a church, and a mill on the seigneury. Many seigneurs in pioneer times lived and worked as their habitants did, and this blunted the social distinctions that had prevailed in France between lord and peasant. Later social distinctions did become important as the seigneuries became heavily settled and the opportunity for social mobility declined.

THE GROWTH OF SETTLEMENT

To help populate the seigneuries, Colbert and Jean Talon worked to correct a social imbalance in the colony: the abundance of eligible bachelors and shortage of French women. In Montreal in 1663, for example, there was only one marriageable woman for every eight eligible men. Colbert sought French women to immigrate to the colony who were strong enough for work in the fields and who had a good moral character. At first the French Crown selected orphanage girls, but when they proved not to be rugged enough, it recruited young, healthy country girls. A number of the *filles du roi* ("daughters of the king") were not much older than sixteen. The king provided substantial dowries — "the king's gift" — usually consisting of clothing or household supplies. The state sent out nearly 800 *filles du roi* between 1663 and 1673.

Where Historians Disagree
ꙮ The Nature of the Seigneurial System in New France

French-Canadian historians have debated the nature of the seigneurial system in New France for more than a quarter of a century. Earlier historians, such as François-Xavier Garneau, held that the system was neither harsh nor oppressive. According to them, the institutions that France established in the St. Lawrence valley, including the seigneurial system, had been purified in the new setting, their negative aspects removed by the French Crown. In 1899, historian Benjamin Sulte suggested that the seigneur in New France was not an exploiter but a "colonization agent."[1] This traditionalist interpretation of New France as an open, egalitarian society dominated in Quebec until the mid-twentieth century.

A new, critical view of the seigneurial system emerged in the 1960s and 1970s. In 1974, Louise Dechêne published a meticu-lous local study of the Montreal area that pointed to the oppressive nature of the seigneurial system in the late seventeenth century.[2] She thus sided with fellow historian Fernand Ouellet, who, in his numerous writings from the 1960s to the 1980s, argued that in the eighteenth century New France was a class-bound society. Both Dechêne and Ouellet maintained that seigneurial practices in the St. Lawrence valley conformed to French patterns. In some cases, the customs in Canada were more outdated than those in France. As Ouellet wrote in 1981, "In brief, the ancien régime society that had developed in the St. Lawrence valley, far from being a modernized or purified version of that of the mother country, was in a sense more archaic."[3]

Anglophone historians are equally divided on the seigneurial system. R. Cole

Harris, for instance, agrees with traditionalist French-Canadian historians. He questions the interpretation that farmers in New France occupied a position comparable to that of peasants in rural France during the last two centuries of pre-revolutionary France. "Rural Canada provided relative opportunity (cheaper land and higher wages) for ordinary people, and relative disincentive (higher labour costs, land of little value, and weak markets) for a landed elite."[4] Harris argues that the rural population of New France was independent and self-reliant, and that it had opportunities for upward mobility. To a certain extent, the late W.J. Eccles, the leading anglophone historian on New France, in the 1970s and 1980s, sided with the traditionalists. He wrote, "The seigneurs were little more than land settlement agents and their financial rewards were not great."[5]

Historian Allan Greer, in a monograph,[6] has challenged the traditionalists' viewpoint. Greer contends, "exploitation, domination, and the clash of interests were characteristics of rural Canada since the early years of the French regime."[7] More recently, he elaborated further: "By the end of the French regime, a substantial proportion of the surplus production, that is, of the grain not needed to keep family members alive, was being siphoned off by the colony's seigneurs. All in all, seigneurial exactions did tear a significant chunk out of the habitant household economy."[8]

[1] Benjamin Sulte, "Le système seigneurial," in *Mélanges historiques*, vol. 1 (Montréal, 1918), p. 80; cited in Serge Jaumain et Matteo Sanfilippo, "Le Régime seigneurial en Nouvelle-France: Un débat historiographique," *The Register* 5,2 (Autumn 1984): 227.

[2] Louise Dechêne, *Habitants et marchands de Montréal au XVIIe Siècle* (Paris: Les Edition Plons, 1974).

[3] Fernand Ouellet, "The Formation of a New Society in the St. Lawrence Valley: From Classless Society to Class Conflict," in Jacques A. Barbier, ed. and trans., *Economy, Class and Nation in Quebec: Interpretive Essays* (Toronto: Copp Clark Pitman, 1991), p. 33; originally published in French in the *Canadian Historical Review* 62, 4 (1981): 407–50.

[4] R. Cole Harris, in the new preface to *The Seigneurial System in Early Canada: A Geographical Study*, 2nd ed. (Montreal/Kingston: McGill-Queen's University Press, 1984), p. xix).

[5] W.J. Eccles, *The Canadian Frontier 1534–1760* (Toronto: Holt, Rinehart and Winston, 1969), p. 68.

[6] Allan Greer, *Peasant, Lord, and Merchant: Rural Society in Three Quebec Parishes, 1740–1840* (Toronto: University of Toronto Press, 1985).

[7] Ibid, p. xiv.

[8] Allan Greer, *The People of New France* (Toronto: University of Toronto Press, 1997), p. 38.

The girls, kept under supervision in one place, chose their husbands themselves, usually within two weeks after arrival. A young man in search of a wife had to declare his possessions and means of livelihood to the "directress" in charge of the girls. To encourage marriage, the government fined bachelors and denied them trading rights. Thus, men sought brides, and women had a good deal of choice. Usually they first wanted to know whether the suitor had a farm.

Even if the young man had built a home, a difficult life awaited these women, whose marriage contract bound them for life. They faced relentless work in clearing and maintaining their new family farms, for women in New France toiled in the fields alongside the men. The severity of Canadian winters also came as a shock to the young French women. In northern France, snow covered the ground for a few days, at most. In New France, it remained for over four months — then there was the extreme cold, the freezing of lakes and rivers.

Fortunately, though, by the time the *filles du roi* arrived, the French settlers had learned to adjust to winter conditions. They now slaughtered animals at the onset of winter and hung the

FRENCH IMMIGRANTS BY SEX AND DECADE, 1608–1759

PERIOD	MEN	WOMEN	TOTAL
Before 1630	15	6	21
1630–1639	88	51	139
1640–1649	141	86	227
1650–1659	403	239	642
1660–1669	1075	623	1698
1670–1679	429	369	798
1680–1689	486	56	542
1690–1699	490	32	522
1700–1709	283	24	307
1710–1719	293	18	311
1720–1729	420	14	434
1730–1739	483	16	499
1740–1749	576	16	592
1750–1759	1699	52	1751
Unknown	27	17	44
TOTAL	6908	1619	8527

Source: R. Cole Harris, ed., *Historical Atlas of Canada*, vol. 1, *From the Beginning to 1800* (Toronto: University of Toronto Press, 1987), plate 45. Reprinted by permission of the University of Toronto Press Incorporated.

meat in icy cellars. By eating fresh meat and the past season's vegetables through the winter, they escaped scurvy. They also learned to construct houses in ways that improved heat retention and heating efficiency, by digging cellars first and by putting fireplaces in the centre of the houses. In addition, they built roofs with steep angles that readily shed the snow. In the late seventeenth century, the settler introduced another improvement: iron fireboxes that produced four times more heat than conventional fireplaces. They built larger barns to store fodder for the winter and to keep domestic animals inside during the coldest weather.

To make the settlers' lives easier, Colbert sent livestock to Canada at the Crown's expense. The first horses arrived in 1665. The First Nations, who had never seen such animals, called them the "moose of France." Horses thrived in the colony. The habitants developed a particular fondness for them, and by the eighteenth century even the poorest settler tried to keep one. By the 1720s, there was one horse for every five settlers.

In the first years of Royal Government the Crown sent several thousand men, mostly indentured labourers, and women to Canada. Many died from disease, either on the voyage or in the colony itself. A number returned to France. Nonetheless, New France's population grew rapidly from roughly 3000 in 1663 to almost 10 000 a decade later. Most settled along the St. Lawrence River from below Quebec to Montreal, and they cleared more land east of Montreal along the Richelieu River.

THE SETTLEMENT OF THE ST. LAWRENCE VALLEY

Throughout the French regime, the St. Lawrence River remained the colony's main thoroughfare, both in summer by canoe or small boat and in winter by sleigh over the ice. Frontage along the water highway was always most sought after. In addition, the settlers wanted to be close to one another, within hailing distance of their neighbours, in the event of Iroquois attacks. Around Quebec, the shores of the St. Lawrence already looked like one sprawling, unending village street, with the habitants' whitewashed farmhouses huddled closely together. The narrow farms extending back from the river were often twenty times as long as they were wide.

The French state achieved significant population growth in the colony from 1663 to 1672. The women sent out in Colbert's great wave of immigrants married and produced large families. In the late seventeenth century, the state encouraged births by offering what might be viewed as Canada's first baby bonuses. Couples with ten or more living children received a substantial gift of money. The sexes became evenly balanced in New France. By 1700, women were an average age of 22 when they were married, an age seven years higher than it had been 40 years earlier! Their spouses tended by 1700 to be older; the males averaged 28 years of age. Despite disasters, such as the smallpox epidemic of 1701, which killed 1000 people, New France's rapid population increase continued: It doubled every 25 years, almost entirely as a result of the high birth rate rather than immigration. The fact that women married earlier than their European counterparts effectively gave them more child-bearing years.

In the colony's early years, women gave birth to eight or nine children on average (after 1700, the figure dropped to seven). One out of every five children, however, died before the age of one; hence the average "completed" family in the eighteenth century consisted of 5.65 children per couple. Midwives delivered babies at home. A new mother might have a woman friend stay for a week or so after the birth, and her own mother usually stayed with her for at least a month.

COLBERT'S ADMINISTRATIVE REFORMS

To mark New France's new status as a royal colony, Colbert established administrative structures identical to those already existing in the provinces of France. At the top was the king, Louis XIV. He, however, delegated enormous powers to his ministers, particularly to Colbert. In effect, the government of New France resided with the minister of the marine, assisted by his *commis*, or secretary (the equivalent of a twentieth-century deputy minister in Canada). The colony was administered by the Sovereign Council, that was headed by a governor and an intendant, both appointed by the king.

In the political structure of Royal Government the governor general held supreme authority. Almost without exception, he was a noble and a soldier. He ensured that the other officials discharged their responsibilities honestly and efficiently. He had undisputed control over military and diplomatic affairs. Probably the most celebrated occupant of the post in the late seventeenth century was the Comte de Frontenac (1672–82 and 1689–98), who spent much of his time dealing with the First Nations and with the English colonies.

The intendant — the official responsible for justice, public order, and finance — was the second-ranking official in the colonial hierarchy. A skilled administrator with a good educational background and, usually, extensive legal training, he ran most of the daily affairs of New France. He managed the budgets of both the army and the colony. The intendant headed the police and looked after road construction and maintenance. He was also responsible for the construction and maintenance of fortifications.

The bishop played a role in the political life of the colony, even though the powers of the office were significantly reduced after 1663. When the Sovereign Council was first established, the bishop ranked directly behind the governor. Thus, the first bishop, François de Laval, initially shared with the governor the responsibility of selecting the other council members from among the leading colonists. But after Laval clashed with the governor, he lost this right.

THE POLITICAL ADMINISTRATION OF NEW FRANCE

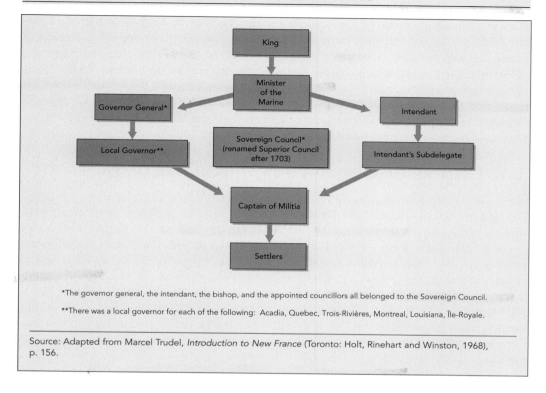

*The governor general, the intendant, the bishop, and the appointed councillors all belonged to the Sovereign Council.

**There was a local governor for each of the following: Acadia, Quebec, Trois-Rivières, Montreal, Louisiana, Île-Royale.

Source: Adapted from Marcel Trudel, *Introduction to New France* (Toronto: Holt, Rinehart and Winston, 1968), p. 156.

Thereafter, the bishop's influence declined, and his attendance at the council became infrequent. The Crown respected the social and religious role of the church, but opposed any political authority it might claim. The minister of the marine instructed the governor and the intendant to subordinate the church to the authority of the state. After 1663, the king nominated the bishop and contributed 40 percent of the colonial church's finances in order to control the church.

The Sovereign Council, after 1703 known as the Superior Council, both made laws and heard criminal and civil cases. The members of the tribunal sat around a large table, with the governor, bishop, and intendant at the head — the governor in the centre, the bishop on the governor's right, and the intendant on the governor's left. As the amount of litigation in the colony increased, the council restricted itself to legal functions, and the intendant enacted legislation. In 1664 the law for the area around Paris, the so-called Custom of Paris (*coutume de Paris*), officially became the colony's legal code. Today's Civil Code in Quebec evolved from this "law of Canada."

Colbert also established the office of captain of militia. In 1669, the intendant organized the entire male population between the ages of 16 and 60 into militia units. He formed a company in each parish and appointed a captain from among the most respected habitants to command it. The office carried with it no salary, but it brought considerable status and prestige; the captains became the most influential men in their communities. In addition to drilling the militia, supervising their equipment, and leading them in battle, the captains acted locally as the intendant's agents, communicating his regulations and ordinances to the habitants and seeing that they were carried out. They also directed the *corvées* for work on bridges and roads. During a *corvée*, even the local seigneur came under the militia captain's command. This new office thus prevented the seigneurs from becoming too powerful.

Colbert made no provision for local self-government. New France had no municipal governments, nor mayors or town councils. Furthermore, people could not call a meeting or arrange a public assembly. Government came from above, not from below. Even the magistrates of the Sovereign Council were appointed and paid stipends, and were, therefore, dependent on the governor and the intendant. The only elected office in the late seventeenth century (and for the remainder of the French regime) was that of church warden. Yet, a little flexibility did exist. Occasionally the governor and the intendant consulted the public on issues of general interest. They called together seventeen assemblies between 1672 and 1700.

THE FAILURE OF COLBERT'S PLAN FOR A "COMPACT COLONY"

Having set up a new administrative structure, Colbert sought capable men to fill the senior posts so as to establish a self-reliant colony, or "a compact colony," in the St. Lawrence valley. Intendant Jean Talon, a man of about 40 who had been an intendant in France as well, began investigating New France's economic possibilities — discovering what the soil would grow, surveying the forests, and sponsoring expeditions to search for minerals. He also tried to develop a shipbuilding industry in the colony. The Crown sent skilled ship carpenters, tarmakers, blacksmiths, and foundry workers, as well as the necessary supplies. Three ships were built, but the industry never became profitable. The imported skilled workers demanded high wages; iron had to be imported; and the industry required heavy capital outlays. In the end, ships cost much more to build in Canada than in France, and the program was curtailed.

New France also failed to develop a large overseas trade with the West Indies. Ships out of New France could sail south only in the summer months — the hurricane season in southern waters. They had to run the gauntlet of English vessels in wartime. As well, the Canadians had to compete with New England mariners, who could sell wheat and fish at lower prices year round. For these reasons, then, New France failed to secure a foothold in the West Indies market.

Of the industries in New France, fishing offered the greatest promise. Colbert subsidized the necessary equipment. But Canadian fishers faced several disadvantages, the foremost being the failure to establish salt works in the colony. This meant a reliance on France for a supply of salt. In addition, French merchants in France sent their ships directly to the Grand Banks, and they returned directly to France without ever landing in New France and purchasing Canadian fish.

One of Talon's enterprises that did succeed was a brewery at Quebec. Cheap beer brewed in the colony proved popular. Unfortunately for Colbert's hopes, everything Canada produced, except for furs and beer, could be obtained more cheaply elsewhere. When Jean Talon left the colony in 1672, the industries he had promoted died. The Crown allocated no more funds because France had begun a costly war with the Dutch. New France had to depend solely on the fur trade, which remained its main economic activity.

ECONOMIC DEVELOPMENT AFTER THE TREATY OF UTRECHT

In 1713, the British and French signed the Treaty of Utrecht, which ended a period of roughly two decades of continuous warfare in northeastern North America. The welcome peace inaugurated a 30-year truce. This "30 years of peace" finally enabled New France to consolidate itself economically and socially. This time the French government successfully supported economic initiatives in New France. The number of flour mills in the colony increased by 50 percent between 1719 and 1734. The fishing industry also grew, with fish and seal oil becoming export products. Tanneries were established at Quebec, Lévis, and Montreal.

The Crown also improved transportation. In 1737, the intendant completed the "Chemin du Roi" (King's Highway), which connected Montreal and Quebec for the first time. It greatly facilitated travel. A return trip by water from Montreal to Quebec might take several weeks, while the trip by coach over the King's Highway could be completed in as little as nine days. The highway opened up new lands north of the St. Lawrence to settlement. It would also become the colony's lifeline in the summer of 1759, when the British fleet gained control of the St. Lawrence.

Private citizens also worked to develop the colony's industrial resources. Beginning in the 1720s, local contractors established small shipyards along the St. Lawrence. The intendant assisted in establishing state-owned shipyards where workers were employed in sail-making, rope manufacturing, tar works, foundries, sawmills, and tool and machinery making. He also encouraged the building of large ships, even though Canada's resources were better suited for small ones. In the 1740s, for example, the royal shipyard at Quebec constructed nine warships. The labour costs were too high, however, and in the 1750s the shipyard cut back to only five naval vessels.

In 1729, François Poulin de Francheville established Canada's first heavy industry, the St. Maurice Forges, or ironworks, 15 km north of Trois-Rivières. But by 1741, as a result of serious technical errors and lax administration, the company declared bankruptcy. The Crown, which had given large subsidies, now took control. Production under royal administration fluctuated greatly from year to year, but for a few years profits were reported. The ironworks employed about 100 workers, who produced sizable quantities of cooking pots, pans, and soup ladles, as well as cannons and cannonballs. They also made the first Canadian stoves.

By 1700, agriculture replaced the fur trade as the leading economic activity in New France, with three out of four Canadian families involved in farming. This greatly changed the colony's economic structure. Between 1706 and 1739, the Canadian population increased 250 percent and the amount of land under cultivation increased 430 percent. Wheat accounted for about three-quarters of the cultivated farmland, so the colony became self-sufficient in wheat and flour. (Wheat, in fact, made up one-third of the colony's exports by the 1730s.) The habitants also grew peas, oats, rye, barley, buckwheat, and maize. Surprisingly, the vegetable that in the early nineteenth century became the staple food of the habitants' diet was not grown in the colony: the English introduced the potato to the St. Lawrence valley after 1760.

Market conditions limited the production of produce and the growth of livestock. The towns of New France were not large, and many town dwellers kept their own gardens and livestock. But, in the eighteenth century, an increase in the population and the opening of an export market improved the situation. Flour, biscuits, and peas were exported regularly to the new French fortress at Louisbourg on Île Royale (now Cape Breton Island) as well as to the French West Indies.

The unlimited supply of land and the high productivity of the new soil discouraged farmers from applying the intensive agricultural methods then commonly used in France, where land was scarce and expensive. When the good land became exhausted, the farmers cleared more with no concern for conservation. They avoided elaborate crop rotations, heavy manuring, and selective breeding of their cattle.

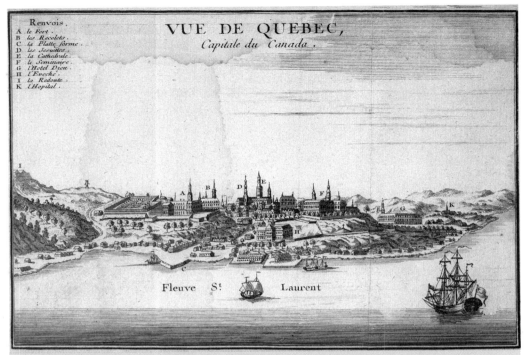

View of Quebec, about 1730. Note the Fort, "A"; the Cathedral, "E"; the Hotel Dieu, "G"; and the Bishop's Residence, "H."

National Archives of Canada/C-43730.

THE SOCIETY OF NEW FRANCE IN THE EIGHTEENTH CENTURY

During the eighteenth century, about one-quarter of New France's inhabitants resided in towns. At the end of the French regime, in 1760, nearly 8000 people lived in Quebec, with Montreal having only one-half of Quebec City's population. Quebec was the seaport and administrative capital, Montreal was a secondary town on the westernmost edge of French settlement. Trois-Rivières remained a small service centre with fewer than 1000 inhabitants.

From the St. Lawrence, the church spires, the religious communities' residences, the governors' and intendants' homes, the stone warehouses along the waterfront, all gave the towns of New France an impressive look. But appearances were deceiving. Well into the eighteenth century, pigs rooted among the refuse citizens dumped in the narrow streets. On a few streets open sewers carried garbage down to the river during heavy rains and the uncobbled streets became quagmires. There was no street lighting.

Royal officials and military officers dominated life in Quebec, Montreal, and Trois-Rivières. In terms of social ranking, these senior administrators stood at the top. The metropolitan French predominated in the Sovereign Council and held the top positions in the civil-service hierarchy. At the local level Canadian-born judges dominated.

The military formed a vital part of the community, especially considering that the St. Lawrence valley had enjoyed only 50 years of complete freedom from war in the course of New France's 150-year existence. Every year, the Crown spent large sums for the maintenance of about 1500 regular French soldiers in New France, many of whom were stationed in the towns. Most of the soldiers were billeted in private homes. Within the army, tension arose between the French and the Canadian-born officers. Canadian leaders enjoyed greater popularity with the Canadian troops than did the metropolitan French officers. Unlike the French soldiers, Canadian troops had adapted to, and preferred, a different type of warfare — what in the twentieth century would be called guerrilla warfare.

The metropolitan French controlled the biggest commercial operations connected with the profitable wholesale trade. They had the necessary funds and contacts to obtain adequate supplies in France. These French merchants provided most of the imported manufactured goods at Louisbourg and at Quebec. French Canadians dominated in smaller-scale trading. In the eighteenth century, scores of small partnerships participated in the fur trade. The companies usually consisted of three or four partners who obtained a three-year lease on the trade at a particular fur-trading post, and shared in the profits or losses according to the percentage of the capital they had invested. The partners obtained trade goods from the large Montreal merchants, usually on credit at 30 percent interest. These Montreal merchants in turn marketed the furs through their agents at home in France.

Women in eighteenth-century New France frequently ran small businesses that sold cloth, clothes, furs, brandy, and utensils. During their husbands' absences in the interior, the fur traders' wives and daughters often looked after their stores and accounts. A number of widowed merchants' wives continued their husbands' businesses. Throughout New France, married women shared in the work of their husbands. At busy times of the year, they helped in the fields. In the urban areas, artisans' and merchants' wives assisted their spouses. Both rural and urban women often kept the family accounts and managed the servants (if there were any) or the apprentices, in the case of artisans.

The colony had about 2000 trades workers by the 1740s. The most numerous in the construction industry were carpenters and masons; in transportation, navigators and carters; and in the food industry, bakers and butchers. As a rule, crafts workers owned all their own tools and worked in small workshops attached to their homes. The French authorities often accused Canadian workers of being headstrong and insubordinate; their self-confidence and independence were frowned upon by the administrators from Old France, where the average person had little, if any, personal freedom or opportunity for personal advancement.

A French-Canadian couple in their Sunday clothes.

Ville de Montréal. Gestion de documents et des archives.

THE HABITANTS AND THEIR WAY OF LIFE

The habitants comprised the largest group in the colony. By the 1740s, the oldest seigneuries had two (in some cases, three) rows of farms stretching back from the river. The habitants' lots, or *rotures*, were rectangular in shape and generally had a ratio of width to length of one to ten.

The habitants paid no direct taxes, apart from the occasional tax for local improvements, whereas in France the peasants paid between one-third and one-half of their income in taxes. In addition, the habitants paid only half the rate for the church tithe that was required at the time in northern France.

The majority of the habitants apparently ate well. They enjoyed almost daily pork and game, particularly venison and wild hare. Gradually, though, wild game came to be relied on less and less as it became harder to obtain near the settled areas. The pig remained a mainstay of the habitants' diet because it was inexpensive to keep (it would eat anything from acorns to kitchen scraps) and because, as the old folk saying in both France and New France put it, "You can eat everything but the squeal." Fish formed part of the core diet of the French settlers, as did buckwheat, a hardy cereal used to make bread, pancakes, and porridges. Maple syrup was used for sweetening.

Vegetables from the garden, particularly peas and fèves (the large tough-fibred beans from Normandy that were brought to the St. Lawrence valley), were favourites. Dried peas and beans could be stored for years and then made into tasty soups. And because legumes absorbed the flavour of either smoked or salted pork fat well, the habitants frequently used pork in their recipes for pea soup and baked beans.

The *Canadiens* also enjoyed such fruits as apples, plums, and cherries. Apple trees, brought from the northwest of France, thrived in the cool, moist Canadian climate. Wild fruits, especially raspberries, red and black currants, and cranberries, were to be had for the picking.

As for beverages, wealthy habitants could obtain expensive tea and coffee from the traders. Milk, in contrast, was cheap and plentiful. Cider was drunk at all meals. The well-to-do could afford wine imported from France, while the habitants drank the cheaper beer brewed in the colony or, indeed, beer that they brewed themselves.

Farmers in New France detested being called "peasants." As the Finnish visitor Pehr Kalm noted in 1749, "The gentlemen and ladies, as well as the poorest peasants and their wives, are called Monsieur and Madame." The habitants had more personal freedom than did their counterparts in France. The royal officials in New France repeatedly complained that the independent-minded Canadians always pleased themselves and paid little attention to the administrators' directives.

THE CHURCH IN NEW FRANCE

During the years of royal government, and particularly during the years of the great migration from France in the late 1660s and early 1670s, the church suffered from an acute shortage of priests. As late as 1683, the intendant reported that three-quarters or more of the habitants heard mass only four times a year. This problem remained until well into the nineteenth century.

The frequent *ordonnances* of the intendant directed to the inhabitants of the parishes with priests provide proof of the independence of many *Canadiens* from the clergy. The ordinances prohibited walking out of church as soon as the priest began his sermon, standing in the lobby arguing, brawling during the service, and even bringing dogs into church.

The clergy did, however, enjoy the respect of the community for what today would be called social services. During the early history of New France, the clergy were actively involved in teaching, nursing, and other charitable work. In 1760, the nearly 100 diocesan or parish priests in the colony were assisted by 30 Sulpicians (a religious order that had begun work in the colony in 1657), 25 Jesuits, 24 Récollets (who had returned in 1670), and more than 200 nuns belonging to six religious communities. The clerically administered social institutions endured, in many cases, into the twentieth century.

EDUCATION AND SOCIAL WELFARE

The church controlled schooling in the colony, and all the religious communities assumed some responsibility for education. Urban dwellers benefited most from the schools, as most schools were located in the major towns. The Quebec Seminary ran the Petit Séminaire, the most important elementary school in the colony. The Jesuit College at Quebec provided male students with a postsecondary education equivalent to that which could be obtained in a provincial town in France. The Congrégation de Notre-Dame and the Ursuline order established elementary schools for girls in the larger centres.

The church also provided welfare services and maintained charitable institutions. To help pay for these institutional services and for their hospitals, the church held initially about one-tenth of the seigneurial lands in the St. Lawrence valley, and by the 1750s about one-quarter of the land. In 1760, more than one-third of New France's population lived on church seigneuries, providing the clergy with substantial revenue.

The seminary in Quebec trained Canadian priests at its theological college. During the eighteenth century, Canadians increasingly staffed the parishes in New France. By 1760, Canada had about 100 parishes, most of them run by diocesan clergy, about four-fifths of whom were Canadian. Tensions, however, existed between the Canadian-born clergy at the lower levels of the church's administration and the French-born clergy who dominated at the top.

THE FIRST NATIONS POPULATION

In many regards New France was a multicultural society, with a considerable First Nations population and an African community. The Native presence was greatest in the Montreal area where, from the 1670s to the 1710s, the "mission" First Nations outnumbered the French settlers. Several thousand First Nations people lived in four major *réductions*, or missions, in the St. Lawrence valley in the late seventeenth and early eighteenth centuries: the Hurons at Lorette, near Quebec; the Abenakis from present-day Maine at Saint-François, east of Montreal; and the Iroquois at Sault St. Louis (Kahnawake), and the Lake of Two Mountains (Kanesatake or Oka), both west of Montreal. The Catholic missionaries did not insist on Native amalgamation with French civilization. As long as Aboriginal customs did not conflict with Christianity, they were accepted.

These First Nations communities acted as a buffer against Iroquois and English invaders. But their existence had an unanticipated side-effect. It speeded up the expanding contraband fur trade between New France and the American colonies, in which both the Roman Catholic Iroquois and the Abenakis participated. The "mission" First Nations did not consider themselves subjects of French law. As the French needed the resident First Nations for protection and assistance in their raids against the English, they could not antagonize them by rigorously enforcing French laws.

FIRST NATIONS AND AFRICAN SLAVES

A slave class existed in Canada to help meet an acute labour shortage. From the late 1680s, Native slaves from the upper Mississippi valley began arriving in New France on a regular basis. Other First Nations sold these *panis*, or Pawnees (the name of a single nation, was used despite the fact that the slaves were taken from many other groups as well), to the French. Africans captured during raids on the English colonies or brought in from the French West Indies also increased the number of slaves in the colony. The few African slaves were sold at an average price twice as high as that received for the more numerous Native captives, because Africans had greater resistance to disease than did the First Nations. Montreal, the centre of New France's fur trade, had the largest number of slaves in the colony — several hundred by the mid-eighteenth century.

The Canadians traded slaves like cattle, at the marketplace and at auctions. Three-quarters of the slaves lived in towns, where they worked mainly as domestic servants. The governors owned slaves: Rigaud de Vaudreuil, governor from 1703 to 1725, owned 11 slaves, while the Marquis de Beauharnois, in office from 1726 to 1746, owned 27. But the biggest slave owners were merchants, traders, and the clergy. First Nations and African slaves also worked at the convents and hospitals operated by nuns in Quebec and Montreal.

While no exact census of New France's slave population exists, local records reveal that approximately 3600 slaves lived in the colony from its origin to 1759; of these, about two-thirds were First Nations, and one-third were African. They lived short lives: for Native slaves, the average age at death was about 18, and for Africans, 25.

THE RISE OF A *CANADIEN* IDENTITY

By the early eighteenth century, the colonists called themselves "Canadiens." Some families had already resided in Canada for two or three generations. A new French people, self-confident and increasingly conscious of their separation from the French in France, emerged. As well, the regional dialects of France eventually died out in the St. Lawrence valley, as the newcomers from various areas of France intermingled, settling together in one area and speaking a common French language. They spoke canadien–français, a language with its own distinct expressions to describe Canadian realities — for example, "poudrerie" (drifting or powdering of snow), "cabane à sucre" (a cabin used at maple sugar time), and First Nations words such as canoë and toboggan.By the mid-eighteenth century, the Acadians (the majority of whom lived under British rule, after the Treaty of Utrecht of 1713 ceded mainland Nova Scotia to England) had also become a people distinct from both the Canadians and the French.

THE RISE OF AN *ACADIEN* IDENTITY

In Acadia the descendants of the immigrants of 1632 intermarried and developed a tightly knit community. The population doubled every 20 years, a faster rate than in New France. By 1670, the colony had a population of about 500. The absence of war, famine, or epidemics (such as typhoid, smallpox, and cholera) contributed to the rapid population increase.

Blood ties, common beliefs, and a system of mutual aid and solidarity united these first Europeans in Acadia. They developed their own speech patterns in an amalgam of various French dialects — with some English and a few First Nation words — that merged and adapted into a single new language that reflected the Acadians' distinctive way of life and their need for a special vocabulary to describe it.

Although Port-Royal was Acadia's largest settlement, there were other small outlying communities on the Bay of Fundy and along the eastern coastline of present-day Nova Scotia. With the addition of about 40 families brought out after 1671, the population grew to more than 800 by 1686.

By the end of the seventeenth century, the Acadians had established themselves in the region's fertile marshlands. Wheat and peas became their principal field crops. Every farm included a plot of vegetables. Most farms had a small orchard of cherry, pear, and apple trees. Most farmers had cattle and sheep. Their pigs roamed freely in the forest behind their houses. The Acadians produced small agricultural surpluses to trade for items they did not make or grow themselves. They traded mainly with New England, rather than Canada or France.

In Acadian society, the family and the church, rather than the seigneurial system that dominated Canadian society, became the most powerful institutions. In the St. Lawrence valley the intendant enforced the seigenurial system, but in Acadia no such official existed. Acadia was much more egalitarian than Canada with its clearly stratified society.

The inhabitants often sought the advice of their priests, who acted as unofficial judges in the disputes that arose among them. But the clergy did not rule the settlements. As in New France in the late seventeenth and eighteenth centuries, the Acadian clergy had limited authority over the populace.

RELATIONS WITH THE NATIVE PEOPLES

 At first the Acadians maintained good relations with the Mi'kmaq, in part because they used the tidal flats, lands of little interest to the First Nations. Unlike the New England settlers, who antagonized the Native peoples by seizing their lands and clearing away the forests, the Acadians initially posed little threat. Indeed, a few Acadian men married Native women. But, as the Acadian population increased, it began to compete with the Mi'kmaq for the same natural resources.

ACADIA BECOMES NOVA SCOTIA

 New England wanted political as well as economic control over Acadia. When war broke out in Europe in 1689, the New Englanders seized Port Royal, and held on to Acadia for seven years until 1697, when France regained the colony. With the outbreak of war in Europe in 1702, Acadia again became easy prey for seafaring raiders from New England. The Acadians held their own with little help from France, until 1710. With the fall of Port Royal in mid-October the colony again fell into English hands. Finally the Treaty of Utrecht in 1713 put to rest the question of ownership of the peninsula. Acadia became Nova Scotia. France did retain Île Royale

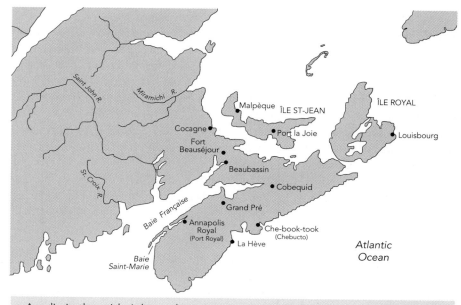

Acadia in the mid-eighteenth century.

(Cape Breton Island), where it began in 1720 to build a fortified town to protect the Gulf of St. Lawrence. They called their new fortress Louisbourg.

Anxious to establish a strong colony there, the French tried to attract the Acadians. The Acadian community did send representatives to inspect the lands on Cape Breton, but the delegates reported negatively on the rocky soil. Few Acadians liked the idea of having to leave their rich farmlands and comfortable houses to pioneer once again. From the English vantage point, French immigration to Cape Breton would only reinforce the French presence there and weaken Nova Scotia, which would lose successful farmers and their livestock. The British also feared that the Acadians might destroy their homesteads and the restraining dikes as they left.

The English administrators of Nova Scotia did insist that the Acadians become British subjects by swearing an oath of allegiance. The Acadians insisted on remaining neutral. As a border people between two rival empires, the Acadians wanted to proceed cautiously. In particular, they feared reprisals from the Mi'kmaq, firm allies of the French, if they appeared to ally themselves with the British.

Finally, in 1717, the Acadians worked out the terms on which they would remain under British government: they would have the right to practise their Catholic faith and the right to maintain neutrality in future wars against France. In 1730 the British agreed to their terms, and required in return only that the Acadians take this mild oath:

> I sincerely promise and swear on my faith as a Christian that I will be utterly loyal, and will truly obey His Majesty King George the second, whom I recognize as the sovereign lord of Acadia or Nova Scotia. May God so help me.

NOVA SCOTIA, BETWEEN THE TREATY OF UTRECHT AND THE EXPULSION OF THE ACADIANS

After the Treaty of Utrecht the Acadians prospered. Their high birth rate and longevity led to a phenomenal population increase. In 1711, there were approximately 2500 Acadians; in 1750, more than 10 000; and in 1755, more than 13 000 (Louisbourg excluded). The Acadian population spread into settlements along the present-day New Brunswick shoreline, as well as Île Saint-Jean (Prince Edward Island) and even into areas of present-day Nova Scotia that had been surveyed and reserved for future English immigration. Then, in 1744, war broke out between England and France once again. The conflict lasted four years, and during it the English captured Louisbourg. But the peace treaty of 1748 restored the status quo. The English returned Louisbourg to France, an act that angered the New Englanders who, at great expense and loss of life, had captured it.

England consequently felt obliged to fortify Nova Scotia, to make it a proper counterbalance to Louisbourg. Now they sought to make the Acadians into completely trustworthy subjects, and to populate Nova Scotia with Protestant settlers.

The new governor, Edward Cornwallis, transported 2000 colonists to the port the Mi'kmaqs knew as "Che-book-took" (at the biggest harbour), a name the English rendered as "Chebucto." Cornwallis renamed it Halifax, after the Earl of Halifax, the president of the English Board of Trade and Plantations, which was a committee of Crown appointees in London who handled the administration of Britain's North American colonies until 1768.

In 1750–51, the British also brought in approximately 1500 "foreign Protestants," largely Germans, whom they settled at Lunenburg on the south shore of the peninsula, within easy reach of Halifax. Lunenburg became the first British settlement in Nova Scotia outside Halifax, the new seat of government. Cornwallis introduced British institutions and laws to Nova Scotia, and fortified the new settlement to equal the strength of Louisbourg. These measures, together with the construction of roads to the Acadian settlements and the introduction of a large English garrison, completely changed the balance of power in the colony. Simultaneously, the French strengthened their position in what is now New Brunswick.

THE FIRST NATIONS AND THE ENGLISH

The French had maintained their alliance with the Mi'kmaq and Maliseet (from present-day western New Brunswick) in the hope of using them against the English. The Mi'kmaq needed little encouragement, since they were resentful of English encroachments on their hunting grounds. In addition, unlike the French, the British had refused to give them annual gifts in return for the use of their land. The English seldom took the Mi'kmaqs into account when the question of land ownership arose. As far as they were concerned, France had ceded its title to the land with the Treaty of Utrecht in 1713, and it belonged to Britain.

Years of Mi'kmaq raids and harassment followed the Treaty of Utrecht, with many of the attacks against the British taking place at sea. (The Mi'kmaqs had purchased European longboats after their first contact with French fishers.) They captured dozens of English trading and fishing boats in the course of these attacks. With the outbreak of war between England and France in 1744, the Mi'kmaq raids against the British in Nova Scotia reached a new level of intensity. In wartime the French paid the First Nations for English scalps, just as the English paid for the scalps of Native enemies and of any Acadian French fighting beside them.

BRITAIN'S GROWING ANXIETY ABOUT THE ACADIANS

As frontier incidents and Mi'kmaq raids increased, Cornwallis became ever more doubtful of the Acadians' loyalty to Britain in the event of another war. In 1749 the governor commanded them to swear an oath of unconditional allegiance to Britain or risk deportation. But when the Acadian delegates replied negatively to Cornwallis's ultimatum, he did not expel them. This convinced the majority of the Acadians that he had, like other English governors before him, accepted their "neutral" status.

When Charles Lawrence became lieutenant governor of Nova Scotia in 1753, the Acadians expected the situation to remain the same. This time, however, they were wrong. First and foremost, Colonel Lawrence was a soldier. Like most soldiers, he knew only allies and enemies, not "neutrals." To him, the Acadians posed a definite threat in the event of another full-scale war between France and Britain.

THE EXPULSION OF THE ACADIANS

The outbreak of war in North America in 1754 and a serious British military defeat outside Fort Duquesne in the Ohio country in 1755 totally altered the military situation. Governor Lawrence now fully turned his attention to the Acadian question.

In July, Lawrence ordered representatives of the Acadians to appear before the Halifax Council, which advised the governor. The council, dominated by military officers, insisted on an ironclad oath from the Acadians that they would support Britain in the event of war. (The council may have had ulterior motives in setting such strict terms: some of the twelve council members were perhaps eyeing the Acadians' rich lands along the Bay of Fundy; there were profits to be made in the evacuations, as well as in the resettlement of New Englanders in Nova Scotia.)

On July 23, two days before the first Acadian delegates from the villages arrived, the news of General Braddock's catastrophic defeat near Fort Duquesne reached Halifax. Casualties approached 40 percent, and the British commander himself had been killed. Nova Scotia's need for the Acadians to make a declaration of unequivocal allegiance to Britain, to recognize themselves as unconditional subjects of the British Crown, became all the more urgent.

The Acadian delegates pointed out that they had always been loyal to George II and agreed to present all their firearms to the English as proof of their loyalty. They were prepared to abide by the oath they had sworn earlier, but not to take a new one. They asked to be considered as a neutral people, pointing out that between 1713 and 1755 they had never fought for France. Throughout the discussion, none of the delegates foresaw the catastrophe impending if they refused to swear the required oath. They underestimated the determination of Lawrence's council.

The final confrontation came on July 28. After hearing the delegates one last time, the council reached a decision. It endorsed the deportation of all Acadians under British jurisdiction who had refused to take the unqualified oath. Now, in the general hysteria after Braddock's defeat, the British were prepared to remove them. The Acadians' fate passed into the hands of 2000 hostile, anti-Catholic New England militiamen working under the instructions of Lieutenant Governor Lawrence.

THE DEPORTATION BEGINS

The deportation began immediately after the council's decision. Lawrence attempted initially to prepare carefully for the evacuation, providing adequate cabin space on the ships and ample provisions for the duration of the journey. But, in the end, the evacuation was brutal and poorly planned. The English first herded the Acadians together at their settlements, then dispersed most of them among the Thirteen Colonies and sent some to England. Lawrence's troops burned houses and barns to deprive those who escaped of shelter. Within hours, the work of more than a century of toil had become ashes.

THE DESTRUCTION OF ACADIAN SOCIETY

The expulsion destroyed Acadian society. It broke up communities and dispersed closely knit families. An estimated 2000 Acadians fled to Île Saint-Jean (Prince Edward Island). The refugees outnumbered the original Acadian residents on the island three to one. The exodus brought confusion to Île Saint-Jean. Many Acadian refugees came with only the clothes on their backs. Starvation was widespread as the islanders had enjoyed only one good harvest over the previous five years. But, despite the hardships, the Acadian refugees felt that this life was preferable to that of banishment from the Maritimes. After the fall of Louisbourg in 1758, however, the British landed on the island and began to deport all the Acadians they could capture.

Many died, victims of malnutrition and exposure in the deportations from the Maritimes. Storms at sea, a shortage of food and drinking water, and poor sanitary conditions meant that many ships lost more than one-third of their Acadian passengers. The expulsions continued for seven years, until 1762. Approximately 7000 were deported in 1755, alone. By the time the policy ended in 1762, the British had exiled perhaps another 3000 Acadians.

The British military occasionally sent ships from the same village to different destination points. Inevitably, family members were separated. Massachusetts, New York, Pennsylvania, Maryland, Virginia, the Carolinas, and Georgia all received Acadians. For the most part, the Americans provided support and tried to settle the exiles in various small towns and villages, but these efforts proved to be largely unsuccessful. Despite all prohibitions to the contrary, the Acadians, footsore and half-clad, wandered from town to town, looking for family and friends. They remained outsiders in the communities where they were settled. Their mortality rate in the

Where Historians Disagree

The Expulsion of the Acadians: Was It Necessary?

Canadian historians have long discussed the necessity and the degree of cruelty of the British expulsion of the Acadians in 1755. The controversy owes as much to the complexity of the question and the contradictions in the evidence as to differing perspectives. As historian Naomi Griffiths wrote: "Acadian history 1710–1755 provides endless questions of fact and interpretation, problems about what actually happened and whether it was brought about intentionally or not.... As the years lead on to 1755, the problems which divide historians multiply, and the events of the expulsion itself have been so diversely treated that one sometimes wonders whether the authors are writing about the same events."[1] Some condemn the English; others believe the Acadians themselves were to blame for their misfortunes. A third group contends that interference from Quebec and Louisbourg resulted in the tragedy.

The argument that the deportation was necessary was still being made in the 1950s. As late as 1956, popular historian Joseph Lister Rutledge summarized this position: "If ever a conquered people were treated with consideration by their captors, it was the Acadians.... The net result was generous and understanding treatment for people who represented a very stubborn breed indeed. This conquered people retained their land and freedom and the assurance of the exercise of their religion. The loyalty oath required of them was generous to a fault."[2]

Several English-language writers have argued that the expulsion should be seen solely as a military operation necessary for Nova Scotia's defence. Archibald McKellar MacMechan, professor of English at Dalhousie University, for instance, wrote as follows in 1913: "Before passing judgement on the men who conceived and executed this removal of an entire population, it should be remembered that they acted as did Louis XIV in expelling the Huguenots from France and the United States in expelling the tories. All were precautionary measures dictated by the need of national self-preservation; and they were regarded by those who took them as imperative in a dangerous crisis. Lawrence acted like the commander of a fort expecting a siege, who levels trees and houses outside the walls in order to afford the enemy no shelter and to give the garrison a clear field of fire."[3]

Most French-language historians have rejected the arguments advanced in defence of the expulsion. In the 1920s, French historian Émile Lauvrière noted of Governor Lawrence's actions, "only a criminal soul could devise such a plot in all its details."[4] French-Canadian writer and Roman Catholic priest Henri Beaudé (who wrote under the pseudonym of Henri d'Arles) considered the deportation order entirely undeserved and "conceived in hate, a prejudice of race and religion."[5]

While not overlooking the cruelty of the expulsion, two English-language historians have tried to understand more fully the British decision to evict an entire people. In 1979, Naomi Griffiths wrote that the imposition in 1755 of a "declaration of unequivocal allegiance to British interests" was "reasonable enough" because war with France had begun.[6] Historian Stephen E. Patterson has commented as well on the circumstances, or the context, in which the deportation occurred: "It took place in a time of war, a bitter war between inveterate enemies for whom possession of Nova Scotia had become symbolic of their power and prestige in the international world."[7]

A recent resolution, passed unanimously in June 2002 in the Quebec National Assembly, proves, however, that intense feelings remain on this issue. The Quebec legislators expressed their support for the Acadian people in Canada's demand, "that the British Crown officially recognize the historical wrongdoing in the deportation of their ancestors."[8] In mid-December 2003, the governor general of Canada officially acknowledged the Acadian expulsion in a royal proclamation. It acknowledged the wrongs done to the Acadians during the expulsion. It also stated that, beginning in 2005, and then annually thereafter, July 28 would become a commemorative day to mark the deportation.

[1] Naomi Griffiths, ed., *The Acadian Deportation: Deliberate Perfidy or Cruel Necessity?* (Toronto: Copp Clark, 1969), p. 3.

[2] Joseph Lister Rutledge, *Century of Conflict* (Toronto: Doubleday, 1956), p. 409. *Century of Conflict* was published in the popular *Canadian History Series*, edited by Thomas B. Costain.

[3] Archibald McKellar MacMechan, in A. Shortt and A.G. Doughty, eds., *Canada and Its Provinces*, vol. 13. (Toronto: Glasgow Brook, 1914), p. 98.

[4] N.E.S. Griffiths, "The Acadians," in the *Dictionary of Canadian Biography*, vol. 4, *1771–1800* (Toronto: University of Toronto Press, 1979), p. xxvi.

[5] Henri d'Arles [Henri Beaudé] *La déportation des Acadiens* (Montreal: Bibliothèque de l'Action française, 1918), pp. 21–26, translated and quoted in Griffiths, *The Acadian Deportation*, p. 156.

[6] Griffiths, "The Acadians," p. xxvi.

[7] Stephen E. Patterson, "1744–1763: Colonial Wars and Aboriginal Peoples," chapter seven of Phillip A. Buckner and John G. Reid, eds., *The Atlantic Region to Confederation: A History* (Toronto: University of Toronto Press, 1994), p. 145.

[8] Rhéal Séguin, "Britain made a mistake with Acadians, Quebec says," *The Globe and Mail*, June 14, 2002.

American colonies was high. An estimated one-third of those deported died from diseases that had been practically unknown to them before 1755 — smallpox, typhoid, and yellow fever.

Eventually, after the British permitted the Acadians to resettle in Nova Scotia, a steady stream returned, an estimated 3000. But since New Englanders now owned their farms they could not regain their land. The majority of the returned Acadians went to present-day New Brunswick where there was vacant land. Buffeted about for a generation from 1755 to the late 1780s a number of Acadians settled in Louisiana. Today it is home to more than a million descendants of the Acadians. As the Acadians spread across the Louisiana bayous and prairies their neighbours shortened the French name "Acadien" to "Cadien," and eventually to "Cajun."

By 1754, the St. Lawrence valley colony had truly become a New France, a new community in Canada. Particularly from the mid-seventeenth century onward, the French had become *Canadiens*, with an outlook that separated them more and more from the metropolitan French. Despite their common French origins and shared Roman Catholic faith emerging cultural differences also existed between the Acadians and the Canadians. The Acadians had become a people distinct from both the Canadians and the French by the mid-eighteenth century, but the events of 1755 made them a people in exile. It is tragic that the first European immigrant group to establish itself successfully in the present-day Maritime provinces received such treatment. The horrors of the deportation of the Acadians strengthened the resolve of the Canadiens in the late 1750s to resist the British invaders in the St. Lawrence valley, who, if victorious, might also attempt to expel them.

LINKING TO THE PAST

Virtual Museum of New France
http://www.civilization.ca/vmnf/vmnfe.asp

Extensive information is included on the exploration of and life in New France during the seventeenth and eighteenth centuries. Look at "People" to learn all about those who lived in New France: habitants, *filles du roi*, voyageurs, coureurs de bois, and more.

Tracing the History of New France
http://www.archives.ca/05/0517_e.html

Topics discussed include land, First Nations, administration, seigneurial regime, economy, population, religion, and wars. Play the interactive game to test your knowledge of New France.

The Black Community in the History of Quebec and Canada
http://www.qesn.meq.gouv.qc.ca/mpages/unit1/u1p3.htm

This site offers a brief look at the introduction of black slaves into Canada, some decrees related to slavery.

Musée Acadien de l'Université de Moncton
http://www.umoncton.ca/maum

Permanent online exhibit offers a concise discussion of Acadian history illustrated with images from the museum's collection.

Mi'kmaq Portraits Collection
http://museum.gov.ns.ca/mikmaq

This site features hundreds of images related to the Mi'kmaq from the 1500s to the present.

Nova Scotia: Acadian Historical Atlas
http://collections.ic.gc.ca/neo-ecossaise

The atlas contains modern and historical maps of regions of Nova Scotia, along with a list of people who lived there before the deportation.

BIBLIOGRAPHY

Allan Greer provides a good introduction to the social history of New France in *The People of New France* (Toronto: University of Toronto Press, 1997); also consult John A. Dickinson and Brian Young, *A Short History of Quebec*, 3rd ed. (Montreal/Kingston: McGill-Queen's University Press, 2003), pp. 3–104. More detailed treatments include W.J. Eccles, *Canada Under Louis XIV, 1663–1701* (Toronto: McClelland & Stewart, 1964); and Dale Miquelon, *New France, 1701–1744* (Toronto: McClelland & Stewart, 1987). Other works include W.J. Eccles, *The Canadian Frontier, 1534–1760* (Toronto: Holt, Rinehart and Winston, 1969), and his *France in America*, rev. ed. (Markham, ON: Fitzhenry & Whiteside, 1990). A number of important articles by W.J. Eccles have been reprinted in his *Essays on New France* (Toronto: Oxford University Press, 1987). Peter N. Moogk's *La Nouvelle France: The Making of French-Canada—A Cultural History* (East Lansing, Michigan: Michigan State University Press, 2000), a series of exploratory articles on various aspects of French-Canadian culture before 1760, is invaluable. For the activities of women in New France consult Micheline Dumont et al., *Quebec Women: A History* (Toronto: Women's Press, 1987); and "Women in New France," Chapter 2 of Alison Prentice et al., *Canadian Women: A History* (Toronto: Harcourt Brace, 1996), pp. 33–57. Jan Noel's *Women in New France* (Ottawa: Canadian Historical Association, 1998), contains an up-to-date bibliography.

Biographies of prominent individuals in Canada and Acadia appear in the *Dictionary of Canadian Biography*, vols. 1–4 (Toronto: University of Toronto Press, 1966, 1969, 1974, 1979). It is now also available online: www.biographi.ca. Two valuable bibliographies on New France's and Acadia's history, particularly their social and economic pasts, are Thomas Wien's essay on Canada in M. Brook Taylor, ed., *Canadian History: A Reader's Guide*, vol. 1, *Beginnings to Confederation* (Toronto: University of Toronto Press, 1994), pp. 33–75; and, in the same volume, Barry Moody's on Acadia, pp. 76–111.For valuable maps of the St. Lawrence colony consult R. Cole Harris, ed., *Historical Atlas of Canada*, vol. 1, *From the Beginning to 1800* (Toronto: University of Toronto Press, 1987). Naomi Griffiths has written two good summaries of Acadian history: *The Acadians: Creation of a People* (Toronto: McGraw-Hill Ryerson, 1973); and *The Contexts of Acadian History, 1686–1784* (Montreal/ Kingston: McGill-Queen's University Press, 1992). Jean Daigle's account, "Acadia, 1604–1763: An Historical Synthesis" in Jean Daigle, ed., *The Acadians of the Maritimes* (Moncton: Centre d'études acadiennes, 1982), pp. 17–46, is very useful. Various opinions on the issue of the expulsion appear in Naomi Griffiths, ed., *The Acadian Deportation: Deliberate Perfidy or Cruel Necessity?* (Toronto: Copp Clark, 1969). T.G. Barnes provides a good historiographical review in his "Historiography of the Acadians' *Grand Dérangement*, 1775," *Quebec Studies* 7 (1988): 74–86.

Maps of Acadian marshland settlement and of the Acadian deportation and return appear in R. Cole Harris, ed., *Historical Atlas of Canada*, vol. 1, *From the Beginning to 1800* (Toronto: University of Toronto Press, 1987). For a complete overview of Acadia in the seventeenth and eighteenth centuries consult the early chapters of Phillip A. Buckner and John G. Reid, eds., *The Atlantic Region to Confederation: A History* (Toronto: University of Toronto Press, 1994).

STRUGGLE FOR A CONTINENT

TIME LINE

1670 – Establishment of the Hudson's Bay Company

1689–
1697 – War between England and France

1701 – Great Peace with the Iroquois

1701–
1713 – War between England and France resumes

1713 – Signing of the Treaty of Utrecht; France gives up her claim to Hudson Bay and Newfoundland, and cedes "Acadia" to England

1756 – Beginning of the Seven Years' War

1759 – Wolfe's victory on the Plains of Abraham, leading to the fall of Quebec

1760 – The British conquer New France and establish a military government until the signing of the peace treaty in 1763, which ends the war

At approximately the same time that the French settled Quebec, England established its first colonies in North America: Virginia in 1607, Newfoundland in 1610, and Massachusetts in 1620. Others followed on the Atlantic seaboard, and in 1664 the Dutch colony of New Netherlands passed into English hands and was renamed New York. The English also sponsored expeditions into Hudson Bay. Henry Hudson in 1610–11 first located the immense body of water the size of the Mediterranean Sea. A little more than half a century later, an English company established a string of fur-trading posts around Hudson Bay. Conflict between England and France arose in the late 1680s, when the two empires confronted each other in the North American interior. The struggle continued, with several interludes of peace, until 1760, when the French forces capitulated at Montreal.

THE ENGLISH CHALLENGE FROM THE NORTH

 English interest in finding the Northwest Passage revived in the early seventeenth century. In June 1610, Henry Hudson entered an ice-bound strait previously noted (in the 1570s and 1580s) by English Arctic explorers Martin Frobisher and John Davis. Both the strait and the inland sea into which it led were later named after him. Although Hudson and his men spent a terrible winter on the east coast of James Bay, they continued their search for the Northwest Passage the following spring. Hudson's crew mutinied and seized him, his son, and seven others, and set them adrift. Nothing is known of Henry Hudson's fate.

Other English expeditions followed until 1631, when it became clear that, even if the Northwest Passage existed, it would not be a commercially viable trade route. Since both the Dutch and the English had already begun to make the longer but less hazardous journey around Africa to India and China, the lure of the Northwest Passage diminished.

Ironically, two renegade French traders, Pierre-Esprit Radisson and Médard Chouart Des Groseilliers (Mr. Radishes and Mr. Gooseberry, as the English called them), who had found no support in New France for their plan to expand their operations into the rich fur country south of Hudson Bay and James Bay, directed the English to that area. In 1668, a group of English merchants under the patronage of Prince Rupert, a cousin of King Charles II, sponsored Groseilliers' expedition, which was to winter on Hudson Bay and return with a cargo of fur. The enterprise proved so successful that in 1670 Charles II gave the Hudson's Bay Company exclusive trading rights and property ownership to "Rupert's Land," all the lands within the area drained by the rivers flowing into Hudson and James Bays (nearly half the area of Canada today).

FRENCH EXPANSION TO THE NORTH AND WEST

The English now threatened New France's fur trade from two sides: New York and Hudson Bay. The collapse of the French trading system with the Hurons in 1649 had left a vacuum and greatly facilitated the English dominance of Hudson Bay. In response, the French in the early 1670s sent overland expeditions to Hudson Bay, Lake Superior, and the Mississippi River.

Frontenac, who became governor in 1672, openly promoted further westward expansion into the Mississippi valley. His ally was René-Robert Cavelier de La Salle, a daring and ambitious fur trader, who in 1682 reached the Mississippi delta. He raised the royal arms of France and claimed all the land drained by the Mississippi River and its tributaries for the king of France. He named the huge valley Louisiana, after Louis XIV. La Salle attempted to found a colony in Louisiana, but his efforts ended in failure — and his assassination in 1687 — although the French established a successful settlement 20 years later.

In the mid-1670s, Montreal traders built Michilimackinac at the junction of Lakes Michigan and Huron, which became the starting point for the fur trade along the upper Mississippi River and beyond Lake Superior. Soon the French built trading posts from the Ohio River to Lake Superior and north to Hudson Bay. A mixed First Nations and French (Métis) population arose at these western posts, particularly at the larger centres like Michilimackinac, and later Green Bay and Detroit. First Nations, Métis, and Canadians lived as neighbours. They shared cultural traits and developed a new trade language, accommodating words and expressions from Native languages and from French. Historian Richard White describes the new culture as "the middle ground."[1]

THE FIRST ROUND OF CONFLICT WITH THE ENGLISH COLONIES, 1689–1713

Frontenac's successors faced an increasingly difficult military situation in the 1680s. After the French ended their truce with the Iroquois in the mid-1680s, the Five Nations, with the encouragement of the English, resumed their raids on New France. Few in number and scattered over a vast area, the French realized the importance of co-operation with their Algonquian allies. The coureurs de bois now became the colony's greatest strength, as they linked New France with its Native allies in the interior.

The Iroquois raid in 1689 on Lachine, a settlement just west of Montreal, sent in retaliation for earlier French attacks, led to a new round of conflict between the French and the Iroquois,

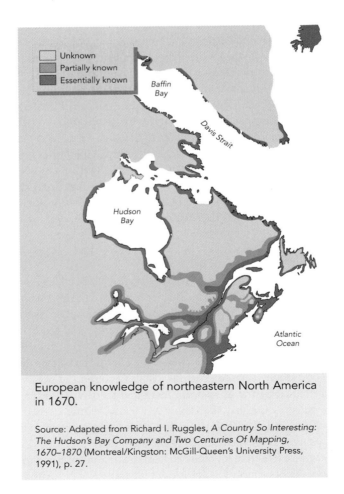

European knowledge of northeastern North America in 1670.

Source: Adapted from Richard I. Ruggles, *A Country So Interesting: The Hudson's Bay Company and Two Centuries Of Mapping, 1670–1870* (Montreal/Kingston: McGill-Queen's University Press, 1991), p. 27.

and their allies, the English colonies. Sent back to New France as governor in 1689, Frontenac launched French-Canadian and First Nations guerrilla raids against the English settlements. At Schenectady, New York, and Salmon Falls, New Hampshire, the French and Native raiding parties broke into homes. They scalped men, women, and children and took (in the raids between the 1690s and 1713, and then again between 1744 and the fall of New France in 1760) hundreds of prisoners. They brought them back to the Native communities or to the French settlements in the St. Lawrence valley. While many eventually returned to New England, others (particularly those taken as young children) refused to leave, and remained with their new Native or French-Canadian families.

THE GREAT PEACE WITH THE IROQUOIS, 1701

A major break in the unity of the League of the Iroquois came in the late seventeenth century. The presence of Jesuit priests in their villages during the truce weakened the Iroquois, especially from 1668 to 1686. The priests attracted war captives, who had previously encountered missionaries and others, to move from the Iroquois villages in present-day New York State to their mission on the island of Montreal (later moved to the Lake of Two Mountains, to Oka, in 1717), and to Sault St. Louis (Caughnawaga, now Kahnawake) southwest of Montreal. By 1700, an estimated two-thirds of the Mohawks, the most easterly of the Five Nations or Iroquois Confederacy, lived in the Montreal area. In the early 1690s, Iroquois from the Montreal area fought beside the French against the League Iroquois.

The French settlers (by necessity now skilled in the techniques of guerrilla warfare), together with 1500 regular troops sent from France, and mission Iroquois from around Montreal, gained the upper hand against the League Iroquois in the mid-1690s. By 1693, the Five Nations were suffering very heavy losses as a result of both war and disease. In the face of the Algonquians' attacks, they could no longer maintain their forward position on the north shore of Lake Ontario. Their numbers fell from more than 10 000 in the 1640s to less than 9000 at the turn of the century, despite the massive adoptions of other Iroquoians. In 1700 the League Iroquois made an offer to the French, who convened a council with them at Montreal.

The Iroquois south of Lake Ontario made peace with the French and their Algonquian allies in August 1701. First Nation representatives travelled to Montreal for the ratification of the treaty. To ensure that the Iroquois continued to serve as a buffer between the English colonies and New France, the French allowed them to continue to trade some northern furs with the English. (The Christian Iroquois at Kahnawake became the intermediaries in the lucrative Albany–Montreal trade route.) In turn, the Five Nations promised their neutrality in any future colonial war between France and England. The Great Peace ended the Iroquois wars that had menaced New France for decades. But in 1701, the very year that New France's long conflict with the Iroquois ended, war broke out again with England, after a short four-year truce.

FRANCE'S NEW NORTH AMERICAN STRATEGY, 1701

France developed a new North American strategy in 1701 and held to it for the remainder of the French regime. With a glut of furs in France, the fur trade no longer was of any real economic benefit. But rather than retreat from the Great Lakes and the Mississippi valley, the French chose to stay in order to keep the First Nations in the French alliance and thus prevent English expansion into the West. As a result, the French retained their fur-trading empire for strategic rather than economic reasons. No more attention was paid to Colbert's idea of a "compact colony" on the banks of the St. Lawrence. Instead, the French began preparations for a chain of posts linking the Great Lakes to the Gulf of Mexico. Louis XIV also ordered the building of a new settlement, to be named *Détroit* ("the straits"), at the narrows between Lakes Erie and Huron. Detroit would bar English access to the northwest and maintain French control of the upper Great Lakes. With their Native allies, the French planned to contain the English within the coastal strip between the Alleghenies and the Atlantic.

NEW FRANCE IN WARTIME

In the struggle with the English between 1689 and 1713, marked only by four years of peace from 1697 to 1701, New France had three limitations. First, it had a small population in comparison with the English colonies, being outnumbered by nearly twenty to one. A second weakness lay in New France's precarious economy. Only one export industry existed — the heavily subsidized fur trade — and it was extremely vulnerable in wartime when the transport of furs from the interior could be cut off. The relatively small scale of its agriculture, vulnerable to disruption in wartime, constituted its third weakness. Even in good years, the habitants produced only a small surplus. In wartime, they had a deficit, because militia service took farmers off the land. War also meant increased dependence on France for food and war materials at a time when the sea lanes to and from France became exposed to English attack.

The French colony did, however, have a number of strengths. It had effective political leadership. Royal government in 1663 had left New France with a unified command structure in times of war. Subject only to annual review, the governor had complete control over the marshalling of the colony's resources, its negotiations with the Native peoples, and the planning of its war strategy. Nature had provided New France with a second strength: natural defences. The Adirondacks of New York, the Green Mountains of Vermont, and the White Mountains of New Hampshire and Maine all protected the French colony from a direct attack from the south. Two of the three gateways to the St. Lawrence — the river itself (closed half of the year by ice) and the Hudson River–Lake Champlain–Richelieu River waterway — could be sealed. Quebec commanded the St. Lawrence River, and a system of forts existed on the Richelieu River (later complemented by French fortifications at the southern end of Lake Champlain). The western approach from Lake Ontario only remained open. Inadvertently the Iroquois had built up the third strength of the French, by teaching the habitants the techniques of guerrilla warfare. A cadre of tough and versatile French raiders had emerged from the wars with the Iroquois in the Illinois country — individuals who subsequently became Frontenac's most valued troops in his raids against English frontier settlements in New England and New York.

NEW FRANCE'S FIRST NATIONS ALLIES

New France's Native allies constituted her fourth great asset. The French had very close trading (and, hence, military) ties with the Abenakis from Maine, many of whom had sought refuge in Canada at Odanak (St. François) and Bécancour. These Catholic converts now joined the other First Nations groups in the St. Lawrence valley, living beside the French. The "mission" First Nations included the Iroquois near Montreal: at Kahnawake (Caughnawaga), Kanesatake (Oka), and Akwesasne (St. Regis); as well as the Algonquian-speaking peoples at Kanesatake, and the Hurons at Lorette (Wendake) near Quebec. The close French allies, who numbered approximately 4000 individuals in the mid-eighteenth century, helped to protect the St. Lawrence valley. The French "mission" First Nations formed an alliance network known as the Seven Nations of Canada. Anxious not to antagonize these allies, the French left them with a surprising degree of independence. They were, for example, largely excluded from the application of the French legal system.

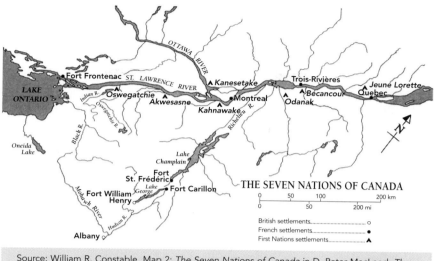

Source: William R. Constable, Map 2: *The Seven Nations of Canada* in D. Peter MacLeod, *The Canadian Iroquois and the Seven Years War* (Toronto: Dundurn Press, 1996).

New France also had alliances with the Great Lakes Algonquians: the Ojibwa, Ottawa, Potawatomi, Miami, and Illinois. Canadian fur traders and fort commanders cultivated the friendship of the Great Lakes Algonquians by giving them gifts and presents. While the English benefited from the Five Nations' support in the 1680s and 1690s, the majority of the Native groups in northeastern North America sided with the French.

DIVISION AMONG THE ENGLISH COLONIES

The French also benefited from divisions within the English colonies. A great deal of friction existed in English America, arising in part from differences in origin and religion. Thus the numerical superiority of the English colonies was more apparent than real. Furthermore, not all the colonies felt threatened by the French, and therefore not all were prepared to fight. The colonies of the Carolinas, Virginia, Maryland, and Pennsylvania, for instance, believed themselves quite safe behind their mountain barriers. New York and Massachusetts shielded Rhode Island and Connecticut. In the north, only two highly populated colonies — Massachusetts and New York — supported the struggle.

Of the two English colonies that fought New France, New York might have proved Canada's match had the colony's non-Native population not been divided in the 1690s between the descendants of the original Dutch colonists and the new English settlers. The Dutch in the north showed little enthusiasm for offensive operations in the name of the English king, and consequently New York posed little threat to New France. Massachusetts, though, did launch a naval attack on Quebec in 1690.

TWO DISASTROUS ENGLISH NAVAL EXPEDITIONS

Two English attempts to seize Quebec by naval attack failed. In 1690 Sir William Phips of Massachusetts took command of a naval expedition of more than 30 vessels with 2300 men. Fortunately for the survival of Canada, Phips's ships took two months to reach Quebec from Boston: en route, smallpox broke out and swept through his ranks. He also faced a determined

French defence force at Quebec. When Phips demanded that Frontenac surrender, the governor informed the invader that he would obtain his reply "from the mouths of my cannon and muskets." Having arrived at Quebec late in the season, and fearing entrapment in the ice during a lengthy siege, Phips withdrew. Frontenac's blistery response had its intended effect. After Phips's retreat grateful residents of Quebec named the newly built parish church at Place Royale, Notre-Dame-de-la-Victoire.

The English failed again to take Quebec 21 years later, at the end of the first round of the Anglo–French struggle for northeastern North America. In 1711, Sir Hovenden Walker organized an armada of some 7500 troops, while an additional 2300 troops worked their way up the Lake Champlain route by land. New France thus faced an invasion force equal to half the total French population of the St. Lawrence valley. Once again, disaster struck the invaders. In fog and gales at the mouth of the St. Lawrence, the English lost ships and nearly 900 men. The Walker expedition turned back. Quebec's thankful citizens rejoiced by renaming the little church in the lower town — this time, Notre-Dame-des-Victoires, in honour of both victories. (A church still stands on this site today.)

THE TREATY OF UTRECHT AND ITS AFTERMATH

The Treaty of Utrecht in 1713 settled the war that had been waged in Europe as well as in northeastern North America. By the end of the struggle, the French in North America had gained ground. They occupied York Factory, the most important Hudson's Bay Company post on Hudson Bay. They retained Detroit and their forts on the Great Lakes. The establishment of Louisiana had consolidated their position in the Mississippi valley. Yet the peace treaty did not reflect these strengths.

At the bargaining table at Utrecht, New France paid for Louis XIV's European losses. France had to make concessions, and the French monarch decided to make them in North America. France ceded all claims to Newfoundland, except for fishing rights on the north shore, and renounced its claims on Hudson Bay. The French recognized British suzerainty over the Iroquois Confederacy and surrendered control over what the English called Nova Scotia, handing the major French Acadian settlements over to the English. Thus, without losing a single major battle, the Canadians were defeated in the Treaty of Utrecht.

MILITARY PREPARATIONS, 1713–1744

France's forfeiture of Acadia and Newfoundland was a serious setback for New France. But the French still held Île Royale (Cape Breton Island), whose cod fishery was worth more to France's economy than the entire fur trade of New France. In an attempt to redress the strategic situa-tion, they began the construction of the military fortress of Louisbourg there in 1720. It also served as the administrative centre for Île Royale and Île St-Jean (Prince Edward Island). Although essentially a garrison town, Louisbourg also became an important fishing port and trading centre among France, Quebec, and the West Indies. As one of the busiest seaports in colonial America — fourth after Boston, New York, and Charleston — it was visited in the 1740s, on average, by 130 to 150 vessels every year. By the 1740s, its year-round population was 2500 to 3000. Soldiers made up about one-quarter of the population in the 1740s, and in the 1750s they constituted nearly one-half.

To protect the major towns in the St. Lawrence valley, Governor Philippe de Rigaud de Vaudreuil built fortifications at Quebec and Montreal. The French also moved to strengthen their military position on the Great Lakes and on Lake Champlain. They built Fort Saint-

Frédéric on Lake Champlain, at the narrows of the lake near its southern end to close off the main invasion route into Canada from New York.

THE WAR AGAINST THE FOX

While strengthening their military position on the Great Lakes, the French became involved in a Native war west of Lake Michigan. The Fox nation, wishing to retain their position as intermediaries in the fur trade, prevented the French from making direct contact with the Dakota (Sioux), the Fox's neighbours and enemies immediately to the west. Friction with the French turned into open warfare from 1714 to 1717. The first campaigns checked the Fox only temporarily, and conflict broke out again in 1728. For the first and only time in the Great Lakes area, the French incited neighbouring nations to kill off the Fox. This annihilation policy, however, proved impossible. In 1737 the French authorities conceded the futility of continued military action and granted the Fox a pardon.

The strength of the French in the interior rested on the "gift diplomacy" they so skillfully practised. Each year at Detroit, Niagara, Michilimackinac, and other posts around the Great Lakes and Lake Winnipeg, the French gave their Native allies gifts of guns, ammunition, and supplies. The First Nations regarded the annual gifts as a form of rent for the use of the land on which the French forts stood and also as a fee for the right to travel across their territory. They controlled their lands and limited the French to the confines of their trading posts, and to their towns and settlements in the St. Lawrence valley.

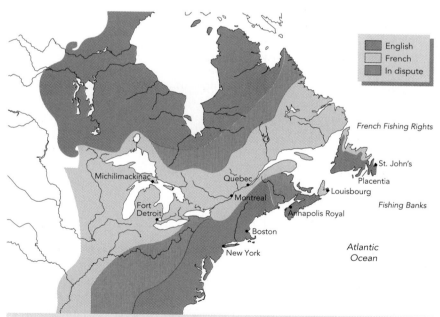

Declared French and English spheres of interest after the Treaty of Utrecht, 1713. Beyond the palisades of the French and English forts, the Native peoples controlled the interior.

Source: Adapted from P.G. Cornell, J. Hamelin, F. Ouellet, and M. Trudel, *Canada: Unity in Diversity* (Toronto: Holt, Rinehart and Winston, 1967), p. 38.

THE SECOND ROUND OF CONFLICT WITH THE ENGLISH COLONIES, 1744–1760

Apart from the war with the Fox to the west and the Mi'kmaq raids against the British in Nova Scotia, peace prevailed in the period 1713–44. This tranquillity ended in 1744 with the outbreak of war in Europe between France and England. The New England business community welcomed the opportunity to attack Île Royale. If it fell, they could secure a monopoly of the North Atlantic fisheries.

Governor William Shirley of Massachusetts organized an expedition of 4000 New Englanders to capture Louisbourg. In spite of the many years spent on construction, the walls on the town's southern and northern flanks remained extremely weak. The French also lacked adequate provisions and munitions. The attackers bombarded the town heavily for nearly seven weeks, reducing it to ruins. When no help came from France, the defenders surrendered.

Louisbourg's fall caused great anxiety in Canada. It revealed the precariousness of France's position in the interior. It also opened the gates of the St. Lawrence, clearing the way to Quebec. Fortunately for New France, England could not mount an invasion of Quebec in 1745, as their control of Scotland was threatened. Only after their defeat of Charles Edward Stuart (Bonnie Prince Charlie) and his insurgent Highlanders at Culloden Moor in April 1746, did they have troops to send elsewhere.

France, realizing the importance of Louisbourg, attempted to retake it in the summer of 1746. The invasion, however, proved to be one of the most unfortunate ever undertaken by the French. Scurvy and smallpox took their toll. Nearly 600 of the 7000 soldiers died and another 1500, stricken with disease, could not fight. The force returned to France without having attained a single one of its objectives.

England's possession of Louisbourg continued to hurt the French. It prevented supplies of ammunition and trade goods, so badly needed for the Native trade, from reaching the interior. This led to the defection of many of France's Great Lakes First Nations allies. Fortunately, hostilities with England ceased in 1748 and the French rushed trade goods to the interior, ending the Natives' hostility.

France now knew that without its leading Atlantic port it would lose the interior of North America, and perhaps the St. Lawrence valley as well. During the peace treaty negotiations at Aix-la-Chapelle in 1748, France therefore sacrificed its conquests in the Netherlands as well as the city of Madras in India in order to regain Louisbourg.

RIVALRY IN THE OHIO COUNTRY

The Treaty of Aix-la-Chapelle in 1748 was no more than a glorified ceasefire. The next clash came in the Ohio country. In 1753 the Marquis Duquesne, the new governor of New France, made French control of the Ohio River, the natural highway to the West, a top military priority. He sent a French military expedition to clear a route from Lake Erie to the forks of the Ohio River. The following year he commanded French soldiers to build Fort Duquesne at the forks of the river.

In early 1754, Virginia's governor sent George Washington, a 22-year-old militia officer, and a number of Native allies to expel the French from the Ohio. Washington's party ambushed a small French detachment in the Ohio country. Washington then withdrew to Fort Necessity, about 100 km from Fort Duquesne. The French retaliated with a force of 500 French, Canadians, and First Nations. They attacked the Virginians and soon overpowered them. The French allowed Washington and the Virginians to return home, but their defeat brought all the wavering Native bands into the French alliance. These skirmishes, in essence, began the Seven Years' War, two years before the first shots were fired in Europe.

NEW FRANCE AT THE OUTSET OF THE SEVEN YEARS' WAR

By the mid-1750s, New France had built up its military strength considerably. The population of Canada tripled after 1713, to more than 55 000 in 1755, thus enlarging the militia. As well, settlers cleared new farmland along the Richelieu River, southeast of Montreal; along the Ottawa River, northwest of Montreal; and along the Chaudière River, south of Quebec, providing additional food for the army. In addition, extensive road building allowed expansion back from the waterfront, thereby facilitating better communication.

Many weaknesses existed, however. First, New France's elongated frontier was a liability; for example, it took a year to exchange letters between Quebec and New Orleans. To protect French interests, the Crown built a string of forts from Louisbourg to Fort Duquesne, but many of these outposts were simply trading posts grown into wooden forts. Second, Canadian control of the interior depended on the precarious support of the Great Lakes First Nations. Third, although the population of New France had increased to more than 55 000, the population of the American colonies now exceeded 1 million. American settlement extended nearly 200 km from the coastline. Fourth, although the 8000 militia of the colony could be called up quickly, few of them knew the guerrilla techniques that their grandfathers and great-grandfathers had mastered. Fifth, the growing friction between the French and the Canadian-born in the army officers' ranks weakened New France.

A sixth weakness of New France lay in its economy. Although agricultural productivity had improved, the colony still could not feed its more than 6000 regular troops, as well as varying numbers of First Nations and militia who had to be supplied in wartime. Another problem existed as well: the need for farm labour to harvest crops made it impossible for the French to go on lengthy offensives.

More troubling than all these shortcomings was the new unity of the American colonies. The co-ordination of strategy under a British commander-in-chief did much to draw the English colonies together. In addition, the colonists wanted to defeat New France in order to end the border raids and to gain access to the rich farmlands of the Ohio valley. The English colonists had a labour-force advantage of roughly twenty to one over the Canadiens. The foodstuffs available to them were enormous. In 1755, the governor of Pennsylvania claimed that his colony alone produced enough food to provide for an army of 100 000.

NEW FRANCE'S SUCCESSES, 1754–1757

In its early years, despite their advantages, the war for North America went badly for the British. In 1755, General Edward Braddock planned a four-pronged offensive aimed at taking four French forts: Duquesne, Niagara, Saint-Frédéric, and Beauséjour (on the Isthmus of Chignecto, between present-day Nova Scotia and New Brunswick). Braddock took command of the assault on Fort Duquesne with a strike force of 1000 regulars and 1500 colonial troops. It took two months for the force to make its long march over the mountains. As they travelled they constructed a road, a technique of war totally foreign to the French and Native allies, who valued speed and the surprise attack. The advance column of 1450 men had high spirits when they finally arrived within 15 km of Fort Duquesne. Then came the ambush at the Monongahela River. The French and their Native allies unleashed a barrage of gunfire at the scarlet-coated regulars and blue-coated Virginians, inflicting 1000 casualties. They killed Braddock and destroyed his army.

Upon receiving news of the defeat at Fort Duquesne, the British postponed their expedition against Fort Niagara. Meanwhile, in their attack on Fort Saint-Frédéric in the Lake Champlain area, they did no better than a draw. The newly appointed Canadian-born governor, the Marquis de Vaudreuil, immediately built Fort Carillon at the northern end of Lake George. Carillon, so named because it was located where the falling waters produced the sound of bells, became New France's first line of defence for the St. Lawrence valley.

The Anglo-Americans scored their only clear-cut success in Acadia. In June 1755, the British took Fort Beauséjour and, with it, French Acadia. On the grounds of military necessity, the British authorized the deportation of the Acadians in late July. They captured and expelled nearly 10 000 Acadians, who numbered approximately one-sixth of the population of New France.

With the exception of their loss of Fort Beauséjour, the French and their Native allies humiliated the larger English colonies and the British army in 1755. Governor Vaudreuil wanted to keep up the momentum. In 1756, he sent out more than 2000 First Nations warriors and Canadians in raids from Fort Duquesne. The Canadian guerrilla bands caused so much terror in Virginia and Maryland that these two colonies stayed out of the war until 1758, fearing that the raids might trigger slave uprisings. The French gained control of the Great Lakes by capturing Fort Oswego, at the eastern end of Lake Ontario, in 1756. The following year Vaudreuil attempted to take Fort William Henry, south of the French stronghold of Carillon (or Ticonderoga, as the English called it). This was a greater challenge, as Fort William Henry — unlike Oswego — lay at the end of a short and easy supply line and could be reinforced speedily from Albany. In addition, grain shortages proved to be severe and persistent in Canada, and the limited provisions would not permit a long siege of the English fort.

A reconstruction by Edwin Willard Deming of General Braddock's defeat by the French and their Native allies at the Battle of Monongahela, 1755.

A final problem surfaced: a growing rift arose between Governor Vaudreuil and the Marquis de Montcalm, the new French military commander in Canada. When Fort William Henry fell, Vaudreuil wanted to march against Fort Edward, the English post on the Hudson River, 25 km to the south, but Montcalm opposed such a strategy. He wanted to concentrate French and Canadian troops in the St. Lawrence valley in order to protect Montreal and Quebec against the next English invasion. The French ministry resolved the dispute in late 1758 by putting Montcalm in command over Vaudreuil in military matters.

Britain Gains the Upper Hand

The entire aspect of the war changed in 1757 with the accession of William Pitt the Elder, the self-styled saviour of the British empire, to the prime ministership of England. He inspired the nation to make a greater effort, and made the American war and the conquest of Canada his major objectives. The British offensive of 1758 aimed at the same four localities as that of 1755, but on this occasion, the results proved quite different.

Several factors explain the improvement in England's fortunes. First, Pitt decided in 1758 to commit large numbers of regular soldiers to America, men reliable under fire in set-piece European-style battles. Second, by 1758 the Royal Navy had effectively blockaded France to prevent "escapes" of French support squadrons to Canada. Finally, Pitt greatly increased Britain's financial commitment to the war. More men, more ships, and more money made a significant difference in British fortunes in 1758 and 1759.

France's Reverses in 1758

The first English objective in 1758 was to retake Louisbourg. On account of the effectiveness of the British blockade on France, Louisbourg lacked the protection of a fleet. The British, with their attack force of approximately 27 000, believed that Louisbourg had to be taken quickly if Quebec was to be captured in the same season. Although outnumbered three to one, however, the defenders held out for seven weeks — just long enough to rule out an expedition against Quebec before winter arrived.

The successful French defence at Carillon also served to prevent an attack on Canada in 1758. Montcalm faced an English army of 15 000 with only 3500 men. Yet, Montcalm won. But the French success had its price. Indirectly, it cost the French both Fort Frontenac on Lake Ontario and Fort Duquesne in present-day Pennsylvania. Since Fort Frontenac, with its small garrison and inadequate walls, could not be defended against an English attack, the French themselves destroyed the important post in August 1758. They also blew up Fort Duquesne and retreated. The English renamed the site "Pittsburgh," after their prime minister.

The largest single explanation for the English success in 1758 was the Royal Navy. It allowed the English colonies to obtain troop reinforcements and supplies, while also blockading New France. In 1759, New France faced odds of nearly three to one in ships, four to one in regular soldiers committed to North America, and ten to one in money.

The Fall of New France

In 1759, Pitt concentrated all his efforts on taking the French colony. With the great resources England had in America, it could attack both Quebec and Carillon in equal strength. New France, by contrast, with its limited resources, had to concentrate its defence forces in the most vital area, Quebec. At the capital, white-haired men and beardless boys turned out to defend their homeland. They feared the fate of the Acadians: deportation. The Franco–Canadian army

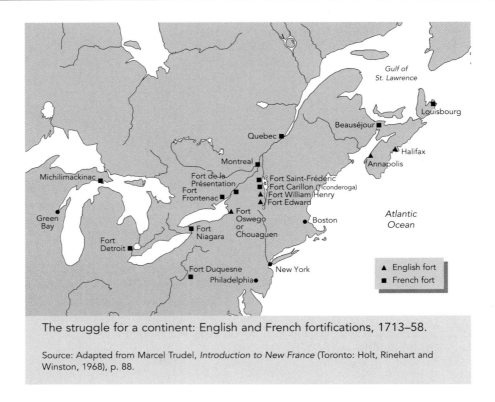

The struggle for a continent: English and French fortifications, 1713–58.

Source: Adapted from Marcel Trudel, *Introduction to New France* (Toronto: Holt, Rinehart and Winston, 1968), p. 88.

at Quebec numbered approximately 15 000 defenders, an impressive force in a colony of only about 60 000.

The defenders at Quebec faced several defensive problems in the summer of 1759. First, the city walls on the western side facing the Plains of Abraham had no gun emplacements, seriously weakening the city's defence. Second, the French made a monumental error: they left undefended the south bank of the river opposite the city. Worse still, under cover of this fire, the Royal Navy could transport its ships up the river beyond Quebec. In effect, the British army could land either above or below Quebec for an assault on the walled town.

All that summer, inland French-held garrisons fell into enemy hands. By the end of June 1759, the British had reoccupied Fort Oswego. Fort Niagara succumbed to a British attack in late July. Rather than see the British take Fort Rouillé, France's small outpost in the area that the First Nations called Toronto, the French burned it to the ground. (An obelisk on the grounds of Toronto's Canadian National Exhibition marks the fort's location.) The French now lost control of Lakes Ontario and Erie, and the Ohio country. In addition, they abandoned Forts Carillon and Saint-Frédéric and retreated northward to the head of Lake Champlain.

JAMES WOLFE AT QUEBEC

James Wolfe, a 32-year-old professional soldier who had performed well at Louisbourg, commanded the British invasion force of some 13 500 men against Quebec. An excellent battalion commander, he had never led an army before. At the time of the attack on Quebec, Wolfe looked ill and indeed was. Frequently in pain, he was often depressed to the state of despair.

The Canadian historian C.P. Stacey aptly called James Wolfe a "Hamlet-figure" — because of his enormous difficulty making up his mind.[2] Only after several weeks of indecision did he

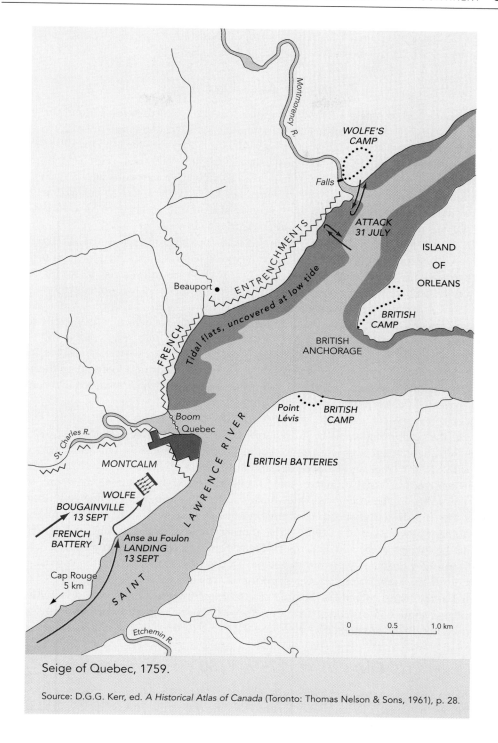

Seige of Quebec, 1759.

Source: D.G.G. Kerr, ed. *A Historical Atlas of Canada* (Toronto: Thomas Nelson & Sons, 1961), p. 28.

decide to strike Montcalm and his forces at Montmorency, just east of Quebec. Wolfe's frontal attack on the French army's entrenchments failed, and the British retreated. The English commander spent the remainder of the summer systematically devastating the parishes around

Quebec. On the south shore of the St. Lawrence, the British destroyed a thousand buildings as well as the French Canadians' harvest.

THE BATTLE OF THE PLAINS OF ABRAHAM

Wolfe knew he had to obtain a foothold on the north shore and then force Montcalm into an open, European-style battle. Fortunately, he found a small cove, Anse au Foulon (now known in English as Wolfe's Cove), from which a narrow path led up the steep, 65 m cliffs. Believing that an invasion force could not climb the heights on the tiny path, the French had left it lightly guarded. Equally surprising, the French had failed to establish a password for a French convoy expected to bring supplies on the night of September 12. As well, Montcalm believed the British attack would come on the other side of the city or at its centre — never at Anse au Foulon to the west. Thus, the British achieved complete surprise.

The French sentries on the shore believed that the boats gliding past them belonged to the French convoy expected that night. (In fact, the convoy had been cancelled.) The British commander placed his few French-speaking officers in the forward vessels; in the dark, they answered the sentries' challenges satisfactorily. A half-hour before dawn on September 13, the British landed. Three waves of landing ships reached the shore in total darkness. The advance party, two abreast, then walked up the steep pathway and, without detection, gained the summit of the cliffs.

A series of risks paid off for Wolfe: the difficult naval landing succeeded and his advance guard of Scottish Highlanders overpowered the French post, securing a foothold on the cliffs. If the French sentries had identified the British in time, they could have sounded the alarm and easily eliminated the advance guard as they climbed the cliffs.

By daybreak, Wolfe had deployed 4500 highly trained British troops on the Plains of Abraham, the grassy field close to the unarmed western walls of the citadel. At this point, Montcalm made a fatal mistake. Instead of waiting for Colonel Louis-Antoine de Bougainville to arrive with his 3000 regulars stationed at Cap Rouge, about 15 km upstream, he attacked. The decisive battle lasted less than half an hour. Wolfe was ready: to ensure accurate and concentrated fire power, he had deployed three-quarters of his men in a single line confronting the French. The British held their fire until the French army was within 40 m of them. Then the British officers gave the order, "Fire." The muskets roared, and a second volley followed, breaking the French attack and causing the French army to retire in disorder. Wolfe, leading a picked force of grenadiers, was shot down and died on the battlefield. In the confusion after Wolfe's death the French army retreated up the St. Lawrence by a circuitous route. Mortally wounded in the battle, Montcalm died the next morning from wounds received in battle. Both sides suffered about 650 casualties. On September 18, Quebec, short of provisions and soldiers and weakly fortified, surrendered.

NEW FRANCE'S FINAL YEAR, 1759–1760

New France's fate was not decided on the Plains of Abraham. The loss of Quebec proved a serious blow to the French, but they still controlled the rest of the St. Lawrence valley and their army remained intact. Ironically, the decisive battle for New France was a naval battle fought at Quiberon Bay, off the coast of France. The Royal Navy's destruction of the French fleet meant that France could not send, even if it wished to do so, a reserve force to save Canada. The success of the French army's offensive against Quebec in the spring of 1760 depended on the dispatch of a French armada, with fresh troops and supplies. But help would not arrive.

A Historical Portrait ☞

☞ The Marquis de Montcalm

Louis-Joseph de Montcalm was born in 1712 at the Château of Candiac in the south of France, near Montpellier. He came of a noble background. The Montcalm family had turned Protestant during the sixteenth century. When the persecution of French Protestants intensified in the mid-1680s, Montcalm's uncle took refuge in the Protestant stronghold of Geneva, Switzerland, while his father converted to Catholicism and thus was permitted to inherit the family's confiscated estates.

At the age of 20, Louis-Joseph began his active military career. In 1736 he married Angélique Talon de Boulay, whose family had powerful connections at court, which, no doubt, helped her husband to obtain his rapid promotions. Before his call to Canada in 1756 he fought in eleven European campaigns and was wounded five times. In the intervals between campaigns he spent much of his time at Candiac, with his wife and children (four of the ten children died in infancy). He truly loved his wife. Just four months before the fateful battle on the Plains of Abraham, he wrote to her: "I think that I should have given up all my honours to be back with you, but the king must be obeyed; the moment when I shall see you again will be the finest of my life. Good-bye, my heart, I believe I love you more than ever."

As the commander of French regular soldiers (troupes de terre) in New France, Montcalm was subordinate to Governor Vaudreuil, who directly controlled the colonial troops (troupes de la marine) and the militia, as well as relations with the First Nations allies. The two men did not get along at all. Montcalm viewed the Canadian-born governor as a civilian playing at war. In turn, Vaudreuil found Montcalm pompous and arrogant. Despite their differences, New France won three great battles from 1756 to 1758: Oswego (1756), William Henry (1757), and Carillon (1758).

Montcalm advocated a cautious strategic policy, whereas the Canadian-born Vaudreuil favoured boldness. The French general wanted all of New France's forces withdrawn from the interior and concentrated in the St. Lawrence valley. But Vaudreuil refused to abandon the outer defence lines.

The threat of a massive British invasion of the St. Lawrence valley in 1759 led the king to intervene. He made Montcalm supreme commander, responsible for all French forces at Quebec, in 1758. The marquis was a brave and experienced soldier, but at the important battle of the Plains of Abraham on September 13, 1759, he made the mistake of rushing forward, without waiting for nearby reinforcements, to fight the British on the Plains. He paid with his life for that serious tactical error. Mortally wounded in the battle, Montcalm died at the age of 47 in the early morning of September 14. He was buried by torchlight that evening, in a shell crater under the floor of the Ursuline chapel. The Church of the Ursulines was the only church in Quebec not completely destroyed by shell-fire.

Before the ice left the rivers in April, the Chevalier de Lévis, Montcalm's successor as French commander, marched his 7000 troops to Quebec. James Murray, the British commander, had experienced a terrible winter, in which scurvy had reduced his garrison to only 4000. Lévis defeated him at Ste. Foy, immediately west of the city (near the site of Université Laval today). This battle proved bloodier than the Plains of Abraham, with about 850 casualties on the French side and nearly 1100 on the English side.

Lévis then proceeded to beseige Quebec. But short of ammunition and supplies, Lévis — and all of New France — prayed for French ships to reach Quebec. Unfortunately for New France, it was English, not French, ships that arrived first at Quebec in mid-May. Lévis had to abandon his plans to retake Quebec. The rest of the year's operations were a foregone conclusion. General Jeffery Amherst, British Commander-in-Chief in America, advanced toward Montreal from the south, with a huge invasion army.

At Montreal that September, Lévis and 2000 troops confronted 17 000 British and American troops. The French capitulated on September 8, 1760, and the British took possession of Montreal. Canada passed into British hands.

Where Historians Disagree
Was Montcalm an Asset or a Liability for New France?

Historians have long debated the abilities of Montcalm as a military leader. Nineteenth-century French-Canadian historians like François-Xavier Garneau and the Abbé J.B.A. Ferland had little use for him. Vaudreuil, the first Canadian-born governor of New France, is their hero, active and energetic — in contrast to the apathetic, defeatist Montcalm. But the late nineteenth century American historian Francis Parkman favoured Montcalm over Vaudreuil, adding to the debate. Then, in the early twentieth century, the French-Canadian historian Thomas Chapais stepped forward to defend the French general. In *Le Marquis de Montcalm*, a full-length biography published in 1911, Chapais argued that Montcalm had energy, courage, and ability. He also loved, not detested, the Canadian people. Up until the 1950s, both French- and English-Canadian historians regarded the book as thorough, objective, and well researched. Montcalm's reputation was intact when Lucien Bouchard, a future sovereignist premier of Quebec, attended secondary school.

Years later Bouchard remembered his history lessons in the 1950s: "There was the battle of Wolfe against Montcalm. That was the big thing. We spent weeks on that. The battle, before the battle, during the battle, after the battle. The sense of loss and sadness and mourning. It was so sad when Montcalm died — we didn't care much about Wolfe."[1]

Chapais's study was eventually challenged. In 1955, Guy Frégault, one of the first university-trained French-Canadian historians, published a lengthy study, in which he questioned the competence of Montcalm.[2] English-Canadian historian W.J. Eccles later supported Frégault in his denunciations of the French general. In his negative sketch of Montcalm,[3] Canadian military historian George F.G. Stanley added balance to the discussion when he wrote: "Criticism of Montcalm, two centuries later, may smack of hindsight — that wonderful advantage possessed by historians over people about whom they write." Stanley, however, then added, "but even Montcalm's contemporaries were similarly critical."[4] The best summary on the subject is probably that of C.P. Stacey, who wrote in his postscript to his *Quebec, 1759: The Siege and the Battle,* "The last word will never be said on the remarkable happenings at Quebec in 1759."[5]

[1] Lucien Bouchard, quoted in Jeffrey Simpson, *Faultlines: Struggling for a Canadian Vision* (Toronto: HarperCollins, 1993), p. 279).
[2] Guy Frégault, *La guerre de la conquête* (Montreal:Fides, 1955); translated by Margaret M. Cameron, as *Canada. The War of the Conquest* (Toronto: Oxford University Press, 1969).
[2] W.J. Eccles, "Louis-Joseph de Montcalm, Marquis de Montcalm," *Dictionary of Canadian Biography,* vol. 3: *1741–1770* (Toronto: University of Toronto Press, 1974), pp. 458–469.
[4] George F.G. Stanley, *New France: The Last Phase 1744–1760* (Toronto: McClelland & Stewart, 1968), p. 233.
[5] C.P. Stacey, *Quebec, 1759: The Siege and the Battle* (Toronto: Macmillan, 1959), p. 167.

In 1760, the imperial conflict for mastery of northeastern North America ended. France lost New France essentially because of the low ranking it assigned the colony. Half a century earlier, at the Treaty of Utrecht, it had traded New France's gains in North America to win back lost territory in Europe. During the Seven Years' War, Europe, the Caribbean, and India remained France's priorities. Compared to England and the Thirteen Colonies, France supplied little assistance to New France in the late 1750s. The flippant line by Voltaire in *Candide* (1759) that the North American conflict was over "a few acres of snow," best summarizes France's attitude.

NOTES

1. See Richard White, *The Middle Ground: Indians, Empires, and Republics in the Great Lakes Region, 1650–1815* (Cambridge: Cambridge University Press, 1991).
2. C.P. Stacey, *Quebec, 1759: The Siege and the Battle* (Toronto: Macmillan, 1959), p. 171.

LINKING TO THE PAST

Henry Hudson
http://www.ianchadwick.com/hudson

An illustrated biography of Henry Hudson, by Ian Chadwick, which includes detailed information about his voyages.

The Fortress of Louisbourg
http://collections.ic.gc.ca/louisbourg

This site offers a virtual tour of the reconstructed fort and recounts the history of Louisbourg, with extensive information on its eighteenth-century inhabitants.

The Seven Years' War
http://www.militaryheritage.com/7yrswar.htm

This site, sponsored by the Discriminating General, a company that specializes in military replicas, includes descriptions of the regiments on both the French and English sides, relevant articles, and sound clips.

Braddock's Defeat

http://www.nationalcenter.org/Braddock%27sDefeat.html

A letter written by George Washington to his mother in July 1755 describing the defeat of General Braddock's forces near Fort Duquesne.

Carillon and the Plains of Abraham

http://www.mohicanpress.com/mo08006.html

This site provides a description of Montcalm's defence at Carillon and the battle on the Plains of Abraham.

BIBLIOGRAPHY

For an overview of French expansion into the interior of North America and New France's conflict with the English colonies see the following works by W.J. Eccles: *The Canadian Frontier, 1534–1760* (Toronto: Holt, Rinehart and Winston, 1969); *France in America*, rev. ed. (Markham, ON: Fitzhenry & Whiteside, 1990); and *Essays on New France* (Toronto: Oxford University Press, 1987). For a bibliographical guide see: Thomas Wien, "Canada and the Pays d'en haut, 1600–1760," in M. Brook Taylor, ed., *Canadian History: A Reader's Guide*, vol. 1, *Beginnings to Confederation* (Toronto: University of Toronto Press, 1994), pp. 33–75.

Excellent volumes on the military events of the late seventeenth and eighteenth centuries include I.K. Steele, *Guerillas and Grenadiers: The Struggle for Canada, 1689–1760* (Toronto: Ryerson Press, 1969), and his more recent book, *Warpaths: Invasions of North America* (New York: Oxford University Press, 1994); George F.G. Stanley, *New France: The Last Phase, 1744–1760* (Toronto: McClelland & Stewart, 1968); C.P. Stacey, *Quebec, 1759: The Siege and the Battle* (Toronto: Macmillan, 1959); and Guy Frégault, *Canada: The War of the Conquest*, trans. Margaret M. Cameron (Toronto: Oxford University Press, 1969). The first four volumes of the *Dictionary of Canadian Biography* (Toronto: University of Toronto Press, 1966–1976) contain important biographical sketches. It is now also available online: www.biographi.ca. Summaries of the two respective armies in the 1750s appear in vol. 3 of the *Dictionary of Canadian Biography*; see the essays by W.J. Eccles, "The French Forces in North America during the Seven Years' War," pp. xv–xxiii; and C.P. Stacey, "The British Forces in North America during the Seven Years' War," pp. xxiv–xxx.

Two overviews of the history of Louisbourg are J.S. McLennan, *Louisbourg from Its Foundation to Its Fall, 1713–58* (Halifax: Book Room, 1990 [1918]); and the short, up-to-date booklet by Terry Crowley, *Louisbourg: Atlantic Fortress and Seaport* (Ottawa: Canadian Historical Association, 1990).

Important books on the Iroquois and the Great Lakes Native peoples include Daniel K. Richter, *The Ordeal of the Longhouse: The Peoples of the Iroquois League in the Era of European Colonization* (Chapel Hill: University of North Carolina Press, 1992); Richard White, *The Middle Ground: Indians, Empires, and Republics in the Great Lakes Region, 1650–1815* (Cambridge: Cambridge University Press, 1991); and Gilles Havard, *The Great Peace of Montreal of 1701. French–Native Diplomacy in the Seventeenth Century* (Montreal/Kingston: McGill-Queen's University Press, 2001). For background on the Native involvement in the Seven Years' War see D. Peter MacLeod, *The Canadian Iroquois and the Seven Years' War* (Toronto: Dundurn Press, 1996).

Valuable maps depicting events of the Seven Years' War and the battles for Quebec, 1759–60, are contained in R. Cole Harris, ed., *Historical Atlas of Canada*, vol. 1, *From the Beginning to 1800* (Toronto: University of Toronto Press, 1987).

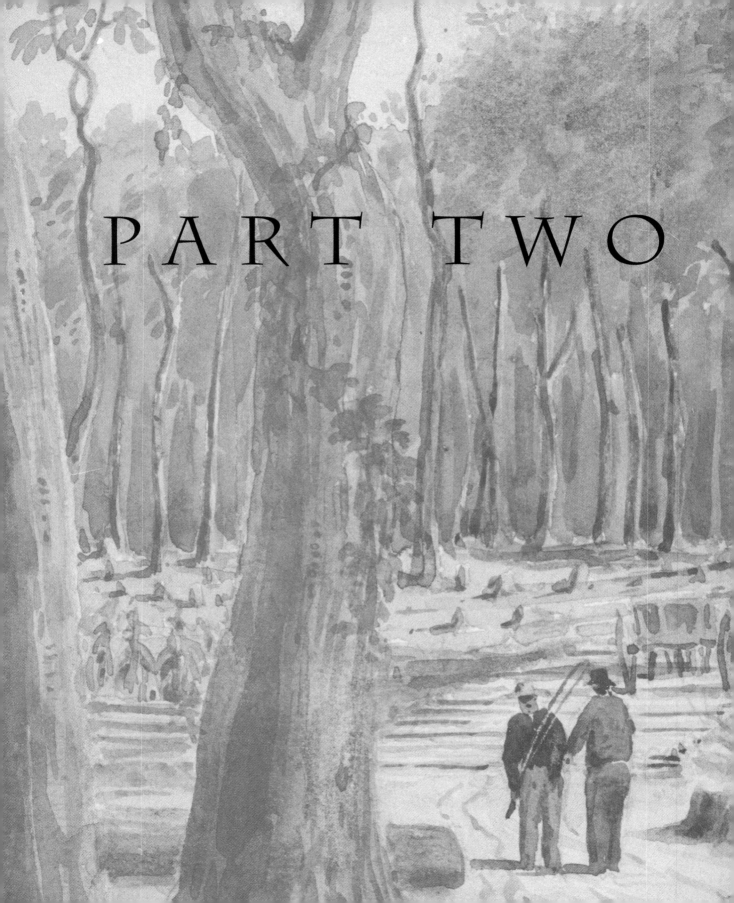

PART TWO

THE CANADAS, 1760–1864

Quebec became Britain's first new colony in 1763. The Conquest had required tremendous adjustment for the French inhabitants as they came under British rule. And yet, in light of the upheaval that occurred, the French inhabitants adjusted well. By 1791, they retained many aspects of their former lifestyle, including their Catholic religion, the seigneurial system, and their language.

The British government shifted its policy toward its newly acquired colony of Quebec three times between 1760 and 1815. In the Proclamation of 1763, the British aimed to assimilate the French. Then in the Quebec Act of 1774, the authorities publicly accepted the "French fact" and recognized French-Canadian institutions. What caused Britain to alter its policy had less to do with the internal dynamics of the colony of Quebec and the reaction of French Canadians to British rule, and more to do with external circumstances. When the hoped-for immigration of New Englanders to Quebec after the Conquest did not occur in significant numbers, the British government realized the advantages of winning over the French-Canadian population. Then in the 1780s the desired immigration from the south of a large Loyalist population made it imperative to make another alteration. The Constitutional Act of 1791 led to the creation of Upper Canada out of the western portion of the Province of Quebec as a new Loyalist homeland.

The first governor of Upper Canada, John Graves Simcoe, aimed to make Upper Canada a "model British colony" in hopes of attracting more Loyalists from the south. Late Loyalists did come, although more often in search of cheap land than from any desire to remain loyal to Britain. On the eve of the War of 1812, probably four-fifths of the population of Upper Canada was of recent American origin, without any Loyalist connections. The American invasion in the War of 1812 helped to promote among a number of the newcomers an identification with their new home, an emotional link with Upper Canada.

Both Canadas experienced a population boom in the period between the end of the War of 1812 and Confederation. In Upper Canada, the population increase occurred as a result of large-scale immigration from the British Isles, thus reinforcing the already British American nature of this inland colony. In Lower Canada, the population growth — especially among the French Canadians — was a result of a high birth rate. Whatever immigration did occur into Lower Canada was English-speaking, thus heightening tension between the two cultural groups. Lower Canada also experienced a large out-migration of French Canadians in the 1850s and 1860s to the United States, mostly to work in the textile industries in the New England states or to farm in the American Midwest.

Population growth in the Canadas coincided with a period of economic prosperity, based on external trade. Until 1849, most of the trade occurred with the mother country through the mercantile system, by which the colonies supplied the raw materials in return for British manufactured goods. Once Britain dismantled its mercantile system in favour of free trade in the late 1840s, the British North American colonies looked increasingly to the United States for markets for their raw materials, especially during the period when the Reciprocity Treaty was in effect between 1854 and 1866.

The two Canadas benefited from increased trade with Britain and the United States through a system of canals and railroads that were in place by the mid-1850s and the 1860s. When this trade pattern was disrupted by the decision of the American government to end the Reciprocity Treaty in 1866, the British North American colonies looked for alternative trade relations among themselves — one of the factors leading to Confederation.

But prosperity in the Canadas was also the result of rapid internal growth, as these colonies experienced the beginnings of industrialization, symbolized by railroads, factories, and manufacturing centres in the growing towns and cities. An emerging middle class, especially in the commercial sector, both directed and benefited the most from the prosperity that industrialization and external trade provided.

Politically, the period begins with the struggle for responsible government. In both the Canadas, the privileged group around the governor opposed the elected members of the Assembly. In Upper Canada, the Rebellion of 1837 was a minor occurrence, but not so in Lower Canada, where it took on a greater intensity.

The British government commissioned Lord Durham to look into the reasons for the rebellions and to suggest solutions to the problems. One of Durham's more contentious recommendations was a union of the Canadas, which took place in 1841. The two colonies of Upper Canada, predominantly English-speaking, and Lower Canada, predominantly French-speaking, had some common interests, but in general were quite distinct. This resulted in tension. What developed was a *modus vivendi*, by which moderate political leaders from the two Canadas worked together to achieve responsible government in 1849.

QUEBEC AND LOWER CANADA, 1760–1840

TIME LINE

1760 – The British proclaim military rule over Quebec, in effect to 1763

1763 – A Royal Proclamation creates a vast "Indian Territory" south of the Great Lakes and establishes governmental institutions for Quebec

1774 – The Quebec Act extends Quebec's boundaries, modifies the structures of the colony's government, and bestows official recognition upon the Roman Catholic church and the seigneurial system

1775 – American armies invade Quebec; but the arrival in 1776 of British reinforcements forces an American retreat

1783 – The Treaty of Paris ends the war between Britain and the United States; peace returns to North America

1791 – The Constitutional Act

The Province of Quebec divided, by executive order, into the separate provinces of Upper and Lower Canada

1837 – Rebellion against the British colonial authorities breaks out in Lower Canada

1839 – In his report, Lord Durham recommends the union of Upper and Lower Canada

With thousands of British troops massed at the gates of Montreal in early September 1760, the Marquis de Vaudreuil, governor general of New France, saw no sense in continuing the struggle. The French capitulated on September 8, 1760. Two weeks later General Amherst, the British commander, proclaimed military rule over Quebec, which remained in effect until 1763. The British Conquest thus became a reality, at least militarily.

The Treaty of Paris, signed in 1763, formally ended the Seven Years' War. The following year, civil rule began. The three military districts of Montreal, Trois-Rivières, and Quebec were united into the Province of Quebec, with James Murray as governor. Britain faced a difficult dilemma. It now administered a large French population in North America whose loyalty would naturally be doubtful in the event of renewed war with France. The new colonial masters therefore hoped that the French population might be quickly assimilated, with the anticipated arrival of large numbers of English-speaking Protestant immigrants. But rather than move north to Quebec, with its harsh climate and "foreign" population, New England migrants headed west to more fertile lands. The assimilationists' program, to be outlined in the Royal Proclamation of 1763, was doomed from the beginning.

PONTIAC'S RESISTANCE AND THE PROCLAMATION OF 1763

With the return of peace, the First Nations question also posed a problem for Britain. Pontiac, an Ottawa chief in the Detroit region, organized a pan-Indian confederacy that mounted a formidable Native resistance to the British. The First Nations resented settler encroachments on

How the French and English forces might have appeared on the day of capitulation at Montreal, September 8, 1760. Canadian artist Adam Sherriff Scott (1887–1980) painted this scene two centuries after the event.

Scott, Adam Sherriff/National Archives of Canada/C-011043.

their lands around the Great Lakes. Dissatisfaction also arose from another source — a fundamental difference in French and English policy toward the Native peoples. The French practised
"gift diplomacy," the custom of making generous annual payments to First Nations people. In
contrast, the English in the Thirteen Colonies preferred treaties or one-time-only purchases for
the First Nations' lands.

In May 1763, Pontiac and his confederacy attacked British garrisons and frontier settlements throughout the upper Mississippi and Ohio River basins. The First Nations of the Upper
Great Lakes captured every British post west of Niagara with the exception of Detroit, killing or
taking captive an estimated 2000 settlers. Several factors finally led the First Nations to make
peace. First, the key fort of Detroit still remained in English hands. Also, by autumn the Native
peoples had to resume their hunting to bring in winter food supplies. Then came word of the
peace treaty between the French and the English, signifying that Pontiac could not expect
French military aid from Louisiana. In addition, old rivalries resurfaced, destroying the unity of
Native alliance. By late 1764, British military expeditions succeeded in quelling lingering Native
opposition.

 The resistance justified British plans, already drawn up, to satisfy Native grievances. The
Proclamation of 1763, issued by the British in October, at the height of the resistance, set aside
a huge reserve west of the Allegheny Mountains. The British agreed not to colonize First Nations
territory without prior purchase by the Crown and the consent of the affected band. Colonial
governors were forbidden to make any land grants to colonists or to survey within the area of
the reserve. London alone was to manage trade relations with the First Nations.

The Royal Proclamation of 1763 became the first legal recognition by the British Crown of
Aboriginal rights. Events soon showed, however, that the policy was unenforceable without a
substantial British military presence in the interior. In defiance of the British government, thousands of land-hungry Americans began to push over the mountains into First Nations' land,
notably the fertile Ohio country.

IMPACT OF THE ROYAL PROCLAMATION OF 1763 ON THE PROVINCE OF QUEBEC

In creating the "Indian Territory," the Royal Proclamation drastically reduced Quebec's territory
to a rough quadrilateral along both sides of the St. Lawrence River, extending from what is today
eastern Ontario to Gaspé. It also provided the new province with governmental institutions,
among them a council to assist the governor.

Other stipulations in the Royal Proclamation referred directly to the *Canadiens*. They gave
good reason to worry about the future: for one thing, as Roman Catholics, the *Canadiens* were
to be excluded from all offices. Elected assemblies were promised, with a view to attracting
English Protestant immigrants from the New England colonies. While awaiting the expected
wave of settlers that would permit the British to remake Quebec into an English colony, those
few English-speakers already living in Quebec could rely on "the enjoyment of the benefit of the
laws of our realm of England." It was left to the colonial governors in Quebec to deal with the
practical realities and to find appropriate compromises.

In practice, French civil law and the role of the Roman Catholic church remained largely
intact in the new province. The fact that very few English-speakers came north forced Governor
Murray to authorize Roman Catholic barristers to practise in the courts. Murray also adopted a
pragmatic attitude toward the Catholic church. He realized that, even with all the support of the
colonial administration, the handful of Protestants in the conquered colony had no chance of
converting the *Canadiens*. He also judged that the church enjoyed considerable influence with
the habitants. By avoiding any open oppression of Roman Catholics and rewarding loyal priests,

the British administration, Murray reasoned, might even be able to rally the church's support. Thus, he made no attempt to close the churches. Instead, he and his officials simply kept a watchful eye on their activities and administration.

The most delicate problem that had to be solved was the replacement of Bishop Pontbriand, who died in 1760. The British government instructed Murray not to re-establish the "Popish hierarchy." But when the New Englanders failed to come north, the governor needed someone with whom he could deal as the leader of French-Canadian society. Murray, an aristocrat, believed that such a leader should come from the church. He was thus ready, in spite of London's directives to the contrary, to accept a "superintendent of the Romish religion." Murray made known his preference for Jean-Olivier Briand, vicar general of the diocese of Quebec, who had shown great respect for British authority. The Quebec cathedral chapter then nominated Briand for the position. In June 1766, six years after Pontbriand's death, the Canadian church at last had a new leader. With a bishop installed, priests could now be ordained.

Co-operation with the British brought the church obvious benefits. Bishop Briand, for example, even obtained an annuity from the governor for his "good behaviour." But the British exacted a high price for their concessions. After all, the governor had effectively chosen the bishop, and this marked a significant limitation of ecclesiastical authority. The governor used the church to communicate with the general population and to keep French Canadians loyal to the government. Priests made government announcements from the pulpits and on church steps.

CANADIEN SOCIETY IN THE AFTERMATH OF THE CONQUEST

Although the time when Britain ruled Quebec was hardly a golden age for French Canadians, their survival was possible. Pressures on the land in the old seigneurial region along the St. Lawrence were not yet intense, and new concessions could be had with relative ease. Nor did the habitants feel threatened by an increase in the "foreign," English-speaking population: excluding soldiers, the barely 500 British in the colony in 1765 hardly posed a threat to the 70 000 *Canadiens*. Moreover, the presence of British troops prevented any serious uprising among the French Canadians, especially at a time when they could not expect any help from France.

In general, both Murray and his successor Guy Carleton, appointed in 1768, showed favour toward the seigneurs, believing that they had great influence with the habitants. Recognizing that the "nobles" had been deprived of "their honours, their privileges, their revenues and their laws," Guy Carleton recommended that the British show them sympathy in return for their loyalty. London agreed, and by 1771 additional royal instructions had been issued to ensure the perpetuation of the seigneurial system.

URBAN LIFE

The degree of satisfaction among urban dwellers is difficult to judge. Even the term "urban" must be put in context. Barely 20 percent of the Province of Quebec's citizens lived in towns, and even the largest of these were tiny communities by today's standards. Quebec, the largest centre, had scarcely more than 7000 inhabitants in 1765; Montreal had barely 5000. Beyond the new borders, the Detroit area contained perhaps another 2000 *Canadiens*.

Although these townspeople had access to certain goods and services that their country cousins lacked, they suffered important disadvantages. Wageworkers, for example, had to contend with the seasonal nature of much of the available employment. Disease and fire also caused untold misery. Epidemics due to contaminated water supplies and poor hygiene took many lives, especially among the old and the very young.

In the urban areas, particularly Quebec, several hundred merchants were involved in a wide variety of commercial pursuits, including the fur trade. Many of these merchants were French-speaking. Some, however, were English-speaking, having arrived after the Conquest from Britain or the American colonies. This group quickly carved out for itself an important place in the local economy; indeed, research shows that British investments in the fur trade as well as in other sectors appear to have surpassed French investments by the early 1770s.

THE QUEBEC ACT

For Britain, security in North America was paramount. The Quebec Act of 1774, which spelled out Britain's new policy, extended Quebec's frontiers into the Ohio region. The British hoped by this means to put an end to the virtual anarchy and ferocious competition among traders that plagued the territory. Quebec's economy depended far more on furs than did New York's, and giving the West to Quebec would thus preserve the economic balance.

The Quebec Act retained the application within Quebec of English criminal law. In civil matters, the act put into law the significant concessions that Governors Murray and Carleton had already made to the seigneurs. In particular, it reintroduced French civil law with regard to property. This was an attempt to resolve the uneasy co-existence of two completely different legal systems. The return of French civil law enraged the English-speaking merchants but pleased the seigneurs. Britain now legally confirmed the existence of the seigneurial system and gave it a much-needed boost through the restoration of seigneurial dues.

Finally, this new constitution for Quebec substantially modified the structures of government in the province. It established an appointive Legislative Council that could make laws with the governor's consent. The governor could suspend or remove councillors. Significantly, these councillors could now be Roman Catholics.

REACTION TO THE QUEBEC ACT

The English merchants, while satisfied with the colony's new boundaries, were furious that Parliament had denied them the elective assembly for which they had so often petitioned. The higher clergy and seigneurs may well have looked upon the Quebec Act as a veritable charter of French-Canadian rights as well as a vindication of their dominant role in society. In addition, the seigneurs were probably pleased that no representative legislative body had been created. As for the habitants, the legal recognition given to the tithe and seigneurial dues was surely disappointing. Nevertheless, restoration of their system of colonization, which enabled the habitants to obtain land without having to purchase it, no doubt pleased them.

Not surprisingly, the extension of Quebec's boundaries embittered the Americans. They viewed it as a measure that effectively continued to seal off the West, which had been officially closed since the Proclamation of 1763. They also bitterly resented the recognition that the Quebec Act bestowed on the colony's despised "papists" by conceding "the free exercise of the religion of the Church of Rome" and by firmly recognizing the right of the Roman Catholic church to collect tithes. The "tyrannical act" figured prominently among the grievances of the Americans when they launched their rebellion in April 1775, three weeks before the Quebec Act was officially proclaimed.

The Quebec Act showed that the British believed the Roman Catholic church and the seigneurial class were powerful and held considerable sway over the *Canadiens*. There was no quick way in which to Anglicize and Protestantize a colony that had attracted but a few hundred English-speaking Protestant immigrants, largely merchants. Not that the British rejected assimilation as their ultimate aim; it was simply not a realistic policy in 1774. A year later, with

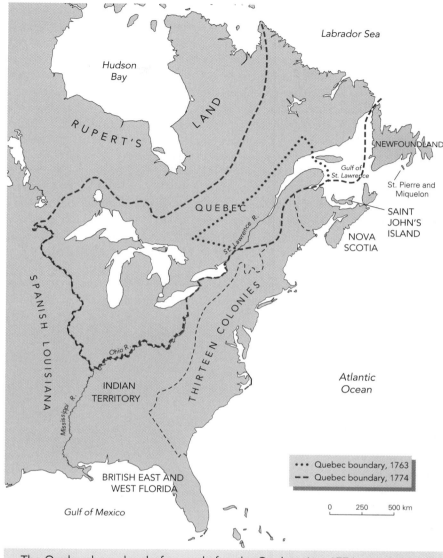

The Quebec boundary before and after the Quebec Act, 1774.

Source: Based on *The Integrated Atlas: History and Geography of Canada and the World* (Toronto: Harcourt Brace, 1996), p. 114.

the outbreak of revolution to the south, it was even less feasible. Eventually, with the arrival of thousands of Loyalists who wished to cast their lot with Britain, the hopes of the assimilationists revived. But for the moment, Quebec's population remained overwhelmingly French-speaking and Roman Catholic.

THE AMERICAN INVASION

From the early 1770s, American radical propaganda denouncing British tyranny, lauding elective institutions, and proclaiming the people's rights and liberties circulated widely in Quebec.

American agents roamed the countryside, appealing to the French Canadians to choose between making the rest of North America their "unalterable friends" or their "inveterate enemies."

The Continental Congress in Philadelphia decided early in the revolutionary war to invade Canada in order to prevent the British from concentrating their forces there and then sweeping down into the Thirteen Colonies. In September 1775, General George Washington's armies advanced into Quebec by way of Lake Champlain and Maine. Both the clergy and the seigneurs upheld the traditional order that the American revolutionaries threatened. They urged the habitants to support the British cause and, indeed, to enlist. Few came forward.

Governor Guy Carleton abandoned Montreal to the invading Americans, but succeeded in defending Quebec against the American assault that came in the early morning of December 31. In May 1776, a fleet of British ships sailed up the St. Lawrence, and the ill-equipped and demoralized Americans hastily departed.

The following year the British conceived a plan to crush the revolt by striking down from Quebec to New York City, thus cutting the rebellious colonies in two. These hopes were dashed when a numerically superior American force surrounded and defeated the British at Saratoga, north of Albany. Thereafter, the British launched no more large-scale expeditions southward from the St. Lawrence.

The alliance of France with the American colonies in February 1778 changed the face of the war. A secret clause of the arrangement stipulated, however, that France would not invade

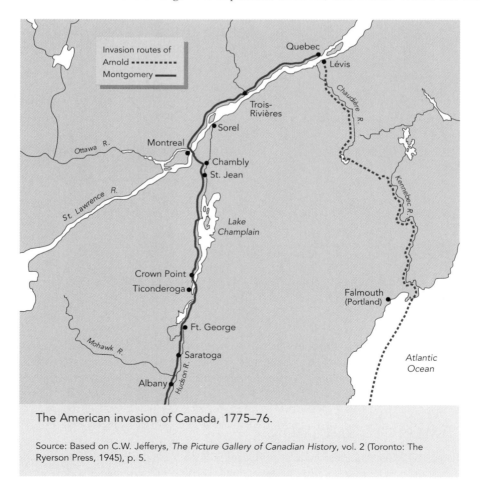

The American invasion of Canada, 1775–76.

Source: Based on C.W. Jefferys, *The Picture Gallery of Canadian History*, vol. 2 (Toronto: The Ryerson Press, 1945), p. 5.

Canada or Acadia; the Americans wanted no restoration of New France. Louis XVI, for his part, wanted to weaken British power by assisting the Thirteen Colonies in gaining their independence, but he did not favour an American conquest of Canada. Indeed, he hoped that a British Canada, by posing a continual threat to the Americans, would ensure the latter's dependence on France. Clearly, neither France nor the United States wished the other to possess Canada.

THE FRENCH CANADIANS' RESPONSE TO THE AMERICAN INVASION

During the American expedition into Canada, some people, often English-speaking merchants, welcomed the invading revolutionaries with enthusiasm. Some habitants, for their part, also seem to have given support to the Americans. No doubt many habitants listened receptively to the Americans' denunciations of tithes and seigneurial rents, both firmly established by the Quebec Act. But linguistically and religiously, the invaders were akin to the conquerors, not the conquered. There was little love lost for the *Bastonnois*, or "people of Boston," as the French Canadians called the Americans. In general, the habitants felt little interest in this struggle, and preferred to keep their neutrality as long as possible. When American fortunes improved and American soldiers were willing to pay good prices in coin for supplies, the habitants sympathized with them. But when the invaders failed to take Quebec and the long winter siege dragged on, and — even worse — when they began to pay for their provisions with paper money or simply not at all, their popularity fell precipitously.

THE AMERICAN REVOLUTION AND THE FIRST NATIONS

Like the *Canadiens*, the Native peoples, particularly the Six Nations, were threatened and cajoled by both sides in the struggle. At the beginning of the American Revolution, the Six Nations Confederacy council declared its neutrality in what it perceived as a "family feud" between the British and their American offspring. Later on, however, the Native peoples could not avoid being drawn into the feud.

Thanks largely to the efforts of Mohawk war chief Joseph Brant, the Mohawks and some Senecas supported the British. The Onondagas and the Cayugas, though, declared their neutrality, while many Oneidas and Tuscaroras, as well as some of the Iroquois in the Montreal area, showed a preference for the Americans. In 1779, however, American troops under General John Sullivan invaded the Six Nations territory, indiscriminately punishing the Iroquois by burning crops and destroying villages. These attacks on the hitherto neutral Onondagas and Cayugas brought them over to the British side. One thousand Iroquois warriors retaliated by burning and pillaging American farms throughout the immense territory between the Ohio and Mohawk rivers.

The cost of the involvement proved heavy: the Iroquois League, now several hundred years old, collapsed, and the Mohawks lost their lands along the Mohawk River in central New York state and elsewhere. Peace came, first in preliminary fashion at the end of 1782 and finally in September 1783 with the Treaty of Paris. The First Nations were not mentioned in the treaty.

Britain's Iroquois allies felt completely betrayed, as they had prevented American control of much of northern New York and Pennsylvania. To appease them the British purchased vast tracts of land from the Mississaugas, as the British called the Ojibwa (Anishinabeg) on the north shore of Lake Ontario. They gave part of this territory, a long narrow strip of land along the Grand River, to the Six Nations. Britain's defeat led 2000 Iroquois to abandon their homelands and migrate to the western section of the Province of Quebec that would become Upper Canada.

Community Portrait

⇐ The Community of Odanak

Often overlooked in discussions of the Native history of the St. Lawrence valley in the eighteenth century are the Algonquian-speaking communities, one of the most prominent being the Abenaki of Odanak. Located on the banks of the St. Francois River, near Sorel, just east of Montreal, "Odanak" means "at the village" in the Algonquian language of the Abenaki. The name "Abenaki" itself is an alteration of "Wabanaki," meaning "and of the dawn," or "country lying to the east." Here today live descendants of the original inhabitants of the northern and central New England states. The community of Odanak was one of four major Roman Catholic mission stations in the St. Lawrence valley, in the French regime, along with Lorette (Hurons) at Quebec, Kahnewake (Iroquois), and Kahnesatake (Iroquois and Algonquian), in the Montreal area. It was a community of great ethnic diversity.

The majority of the Abenaki at Odanak arrived in New France as refugees from Northern New England's Indian Wars. Apparently the Soroki nation originally constituted a majority in the refugee community, founded in the early eighteenth century. But Odanak was swept by smallpox in 1730, and the losses in the raids to the south proved great. Then another important nation, the Abenaki proper, arrived and gained predominance in the community. In total, the members of perhaps as many as twenty Algonquian-speaking First Nations made their way as refugees from the encroaching American settlements to the south. At Odanak they all gradually lost their separate identity. As the majority, the Abenaki proper gave their name to the others in the community.

Abenaki war parties went forth from the St. Francois River against the "Bastoniak" (people from Boston), as the Abenaki called the New England settlers. These loyal French allies served the French to the end of the French regime. Odanak warriors joined other First Nations and the French in the ambush of British General Braddock in 1755, and fought beside the French at Quebec in 1759. In retaliation for their repeated raids on New England settlements, the British made an assault on the "St. Francis Indians" a priority in 1759. Only weeks after their victory on the Plains of Abraham, a company of American frontier rangers led by Major Robert Rogers made a surprise attack on Odanak, during which they burned the village church and all the houses to the ground, and killed Abenakis at random.

In his report to General Amherst, the British Commander, Major Rogers claimed his rangers killed 200 Abenaki, but French sources state that only 30 died. What explains the discrepancy? Anthropologist Gordon Day's investigation of Abenaki oral traditions helped demystify the event. Two hundred years after the horrific raid a vivid oral memory of it remained with several of the eldest members of the community. After evaluating the oral memories with the same degree of care used in documentary analysis, he identified a valuable addition to our knowledge of the raid. At Odanak in the late 1950s he spoke with several elderly people who remembered traditions told to them as children by their grandparents, themselves born in the early nineteenth century. According to these informants, a First Nations person serving with the American forces came to the village the night before the attack to give warning. This allowed the community to move their children, women, and old people into places of safe refuge (hence Rogers' over-estimation of Abenaki losses). The Odanak Abenaki regrouped shortly thereafter and the next year raided an American settlement in New Hampshire. Peace came late that year, and they re-established their village at the same location on the banks of the St. François.

Strangely it was to this same First Nation village that Rev. Eleazar Wheelock sent recruiters in 1774 to obtain students for his Moor's Indian Charity School at Hanover, New Hampshire (today's Dartmouth College). Normally Odanak would have had nothing to do with the detested "Bastoniak," who had occupied the Abenaki homeland. But at the time of their visit an individual then in office as a principal chief proved very sympathetic: Joseph-Louis Gill, "The White Chief of the Abenakis," the son of two New England captives. Gill was of European descent only in a biological sense. In the early eighteenth century the Abenaki had captured two English children, a boy and a girl, from the New England coast. Adopted into Abenaki families at Odanak, and raised as Abenakis and as Catholics, these captives later married at Odanak where they lived their entire lives. Joseph-Louis, the eldest of their seven children, became a chief in the community around 1750. His first wife, an Abenaki woman, died during Rogers's raid; his second wife was French Canadian. During the British regime he met with the British authorities in 1764 to complain of encroachments by settlers in the Odanak area on the Abenakis' hunting territories. Toward the end of his life Gill became prayer leader at Odanak, which meant he was the most important person in the Odanak church after the Catholic missionary.

Although a staunch Roman Catholic, Gill wanted his family to obtain an education, even if the welcoming school was Protestant and in "Bastonki," as the Abenakis called New England. The chief sent four of his relatives to Dartmouth. Although none of the Abenaki young men he sent to the school converted to Protestantism, several Abenaki students from Odanak did, after Chief Gill's death in 1798. These Protestant Abenaki and their converts in the community added an additional layer of complexity to the already multi-ethnic Aboriginal community, made up of descendants of approximately twenty First Nations.

Further Reading

Thomas M. Charland, "Joseph-Louis Gill, known also as Magouaouidombaouit," *Dictionary of Canadian Biography*, vol. 4: *1771–1800* (Toronto: University of Toronto Press, 1979): 293–94.

Gordon M. Day, "Oral Tradition as Complement," *Ethnohistory* 19, 2 (Spring 1972): 99–107.

Gordon M. Day, "Western Abenaki," in Bruce G. Trigger, ed., *Handbook of North American Indians*, vol. 15, *Northeast* (Washington: Smithsonian Institution, 1978), pp. 148–59.

LOYALIST IMMIGRATION

During and after the revolution, thousands of Loyalists, bitterly denounced as un-American by the victorious revolutionaries, fled north across the border. Many came to Quebec from upper New York and New England. The arrival of the Loyalists encouraged those British administrators who wanted to make Quebec into an English-speaking colony. For the first time since the Conquest, a significant contingent of English-speaking immigrants settled in the province. Quebec's population of British origin increased to at least 10 percent of the total non-Native population, estimated at about 160 000 in 1790.

Guy Carleton, now Lord Dorchester, had commanded the evacuation of nearly 30 000 Loyalists from New York City in 1782–83. He had developed a great sympathy for them, and subsequently showed a much more English outlook during his second tour of duty as governor of Quebec from 1786 to 1796. Dorchester himself no longer believed that Quebec was destined to remain predominantly French Canadian "to the end of time."

While the church showed little interest in the colony's constitutional future, the English-speaking merchants discussed it with increasing urgency. They wanted a Legislative Assembly, preferably controlled by the province's tiny English-speaking minority. Many French-Canadian merchants and professionals also desired an Assembly, since the French, as the majority, hoped to control this part of government.

THE CONSTITUTIONAL ACT OF 1791

 The British government drew up the new constitution, the Constitutional Act of 1791. At the same time, the Province of Quebec was divided by executive order into two sections, the provinces of Upper and Lower Canada, with the upper part possessing an English-speaking Loyalist majority.

The Constitutional Act of 1791 established an elective Legislative Assembly in each of the Canadas. Besides giving a voice to the population, this body could raise money through taxes

Thomas Davies (c. 1737–1812), an English military artist, completed this painting of Château-Richer on the Côte de Beaupré, east of Quebec City, in 1787. It offers an excellent view of a mature rural landscape along the St. Lawrence River in the eighteenth century. The wooden enclosures in the river and the tidal marshes are traps for eels.

National Gallery of Canada, Ottawa. Purchased, 1954.

for local expenditures, thus reducing the burden on the imperial treasury. At the same time, wary of what had happened in the American colonies, London moved to place the Assembly under strong executive control that would apply restraint if the people's representatives got out of hand. A lieutenant governor was to be appointed in each province. He would name the members of the Legislative Council, the upper house. The Legislative Council's membership was intended eventually to be hereditary, like that of the British House of Lords. Thus, the "right men" — landowners — would be assured of a place in power. The Executive Council, also composed of appointed officials, would be the governor's personal cabinet. The governor enjoyed extensive veto powers and a measure of financial autonomy, thanks to the revenues from the Crown lands set aside by the Constitutional Act of 1791. Both the appointed executive branch and the elected Assembly possessed considerable powers and frequently used them to thwart each other's will.

On account of property qualifications in England at this time, relatively few people there (less than 3 percent of the population) could vote in elections. Essentially the same qualifications applied in Lower Canada, but because of that colony's very different social structure, the great majority of non-Aboriginal male farmers, or habitants, obtained the right to vote. Still, suffrage was far from universal. Most urban labourers and domestics were disqualified because they neither owned property nor paid sufficient rent. The property qualification eliminated most women from the rolls, although it was only in 1834 that the Assembly of Lower Canada specifically disenfranchised women.

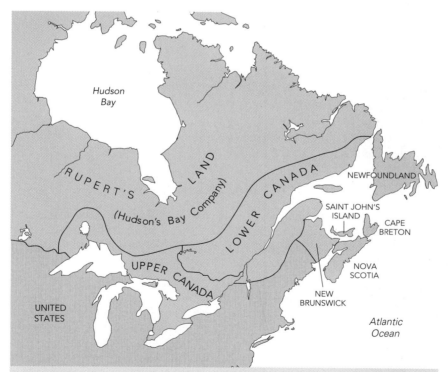

The British colonies in North America, 1791.

Source: Adapted from Ralph Krueger, Ray Corder, and John Koegler, *This Land of Ours: A New Geography of Canada* (Toronto: Harcourt Brace Jovanovich, 1991), p. 130. Used with permission.

After the Proclamation of 1763 and the Quebec Act of 1774, Quebec obtained, with the Constitutional Act of 1791, its third constitution in fewer than 30 years. The American Revolution and the arrival of thousands of Loyalists had made change imperative. Certain Lower Canadian groups, such as the seigneurs, the professionals, and the merchants, thought that they could use the new institutions profitably. Most disappointed as a group were Lower Canada's 10 000 English. The Constitutional Act of 1791 led to their separation from the growing English-speaking population in the new colony of Upper Canada. Moreover, the English-speaking inhabitants of what now became Lower Canada obtained few of the reforms for which they had agitated and did not even succeed in getting the Quebec Act repealed. Nevertheless, regardless of political changes, the English merchants' economic power continued to increase. In the 1790s, in fact, they had reason to be optimistic about the future.

THE ECONOMIC REVOLUTION IN THE EARLY NINETEENTH CENTURY

At the end of the eighteenth century, Quebec entered a period of intense, if uneven, economic growth, as Britain's industrialization and urbanization created new markets for the colony's food-stuffs and resources. The fur-trade era drew to a close, as profits slumped because of declining demand for furs overseas and ruinous competition at home.

The rise of the timber industry offset the decline of the fur trade in Lower Canada. By 1810, wood products accounted for three-quarters of Quebec's exports (and the fur trade only one-tenth). Britain needed wood, especially to build ships. Napoleon's control of northern Europe from 1808 to 1810 cut Great Britain off from its traditional Baltic suppliers. As a result, Britain's imports of timber from Lower Canada and other North American colonies increased significantly. The British government doubled import duties on foreign, but not colonial, timber. This effectively guaranteed a highly profitable monopoly to colonial suppliers.

Other sectors of the economy experienced significant, though less spectacular, growth. Ships were built at nearly 80 localities along the St. Lawrence River. Quebec City had the biggest shipyards, and much of their production went overseas to Britain. Sawmills, candle and soap manufacturers, textile factories, flourmills, and an expanding construction industry contributed to this growth. Banks, beginning with the Bank of Montreal in 1817, were established to supply credit to new enterprises and commercial ventures.

URBAN LIFE IN LOWER CANADA

Lower Canada's rapidly expanding population provided the labour needed for the increased resource exploitation and manufacturing. Thanks largely to a birth rate that stayed slightly above 50 per 1000 throughout the period, as well as to substantial immigration from Britain, the population quintupled, rising from about 160 000 in 1790 to 890 000 in 1851. As early as the 1830s, demographic pressures resulted in increasing numbers of French Canadians emigrating to the United States in search of the land or work they could not find at home.

Lower Canada's two major cities developed rapidly as centres of both wealth and poverty. In the early 1800s, the population of Quebec City grew at an annual rate of more than 5 percent. The Lower Town, around the seaport, was bustling, noisy, and dirty. Fires were frequent throughout the city and took a heavy toll. Montreal also grew quickly. By the late 1830s it had overtaken Quebec, the administrative and ecclesiastical capital, and become British North America's premier city, with a population of 37 000. Citizens of French origin constituted only a minority of its residents. Well over half of the city's anglophones were Irish immigrants, most of them poor labourers who settled in industrial areas near the port. Increasingly, Montrealers

Community Portrait

☚ The St. Maurice Forges, an Early Industrial Community

A few kilometres north of Trois-Rivières, Quebec, the tourist can spend a few pleasant and instructive hours visiting the Forges du Saint-Maurice National Historic Site. Set in rolling countryside along a small stream that drops through a gully to the St. Maurice River just below, it features the large reconstructed Grande Maison, the Master's House, built in 1738, and a modern blast-furnace interpretation centre describing the early development of the iron industry, from 1730 until 1883.

The Forges constituted a remarkable legacy from the era of New France. Already in this early period, the Forges produced large quantities of munitions for the army. After the British conquered New France, they soon realized the importance of the ironworks and made certain that masters and skilled employees continued working and did not return to France. The British also used corvées to force the habitants to cut wood for charcoal.

The Forges attained their maximum development in the first decades of the nineteenth century, using wood charcoal in the process of ore reduction rather than the more modern, more efficient coke-fuelled technology. The ore used was bog ore, found in the form of nodules close to the surface in swampy areas. The Forges employed 400 people directly and also provided work for the surrounding population, who were hired to collect, prepare, and transport raw materials as well as products and goods. Work "campaigns," during which the blast furnace operated without interruption, lasted six to eight months. The pig iron that was produced supplied the

forges where blacksmiths fashioned tools and implements, pots and kettles, stoves, and munitions including cannonballs. From the 1850s, the Forges sold huge quantities of iron to the railway industry.

For most of the company's productive life, the Forges were state-owned, marking the great importance that the French, British, and finally Canadian governments accorded to this industry. Until 1863, the state granted the Forges free access to vast timber and ore resources, a privilege that ensured profitability. When this privilege was withdrawn, and when the plant was forced to pay the real costs of raw materials, it soon collapsed under an increasing load of debt.

Mathew Bell, a Scottish merchant, was master of the Forges from 1793 until 1846, when the government sold the enterprise. The government set very favourable terms for the tenants, who could run the business for their profit. Bell used his influence as a member of the Assembly and then as a legislative councillor to ensure that the Forges disposed of adequate reserves of land for procuring raw materials, including 10 000 cords of wood annually. Bell's monopolistic control of huge tracts of land provoked substantial criticism. The Assembly even accused him in one of the Ninety-two Resolutions in 1834 of having been unduly and illegally favoured by the Executive.

The community that grew up around the Forges had a population of about 400 people, mostly workers and their families. Five generations of workers lived on the site, with fathers often passing on their trade to their sons. Skilled workers and craftsmen lived in houses, while the families of unskilled labourers inhabited more modest tenements. Most workers had kitchen gardens, and kept livestock and poultry. The village boasted a chapel while the Grande Maison contained a well-stocked store.

The St. Maurice Forges constituted the first industrial village in Canada's history, its character defined by its industrial vocation and its population of skilled workers. The community that grew up around the Forges was a precursor of the numerous mining and forestry communities that developed later, particularly in northern regions of Canada.

Further Reading

Michel Bédard, André Bérubé, and Jean Hamelin, "Mathew Bell," *Dictionary of Canadian Biography*, vol. 7 (1836–1850) (Toronto: University of Toronto Press, 1988): 70–75.

Roch Samson, *The Forges du Saint-Maurice: Beginnings of the Iron and Steel Industry in Canada, 1730–1883* (Quebec: Les Presses de l'Université Laval and the Department of Canadian Heritage — Parks Canada, 1998), p. 10.

POPULATION GROWTH IN MONTREAL, HALIFAX, AND TORONTO, 1800–1850

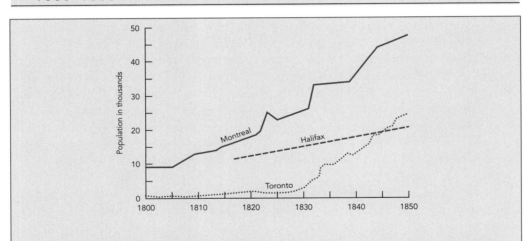

Note Montreal's and Toronto's (after 1830) continuously rising population, in contrast with the almost stationary growth of Halifax.

Source: R. Louis Gentilcore, ed., *Historical Atlas of Canada, vol. 2, The Land Transformed, 1800–1891* (Toronto: University of Toronto Press, 1993), plate 20. Reprinted by permission of the University of Toronto Press Incorporated.

settled in the suburbs. Wealthy British residents built sumptuous residences with gardens on the verdant slopes of Mont Royal.

Communications stimulated Montreal's growth. In 1836, Canada's first railway, linking St. Jean, on the Richelieu River, and hence Lake Champlain, to La Prairie, on the south shore of the St. Lawrence opposite Montreal, was inaugurated. Goods destined to and coming from increasingly prosperous Upper Canada passed through the port of Montreal.

Most workers were unskilled. Many labourers had to spend more than half their earnings simply to feed their families. Prior to the 1830s, there were no unions, and legislation passed in 1802 authorized fines and prison sentences for striking employees. Over one-quarter of the women of Lower Canada appeared to have been in the labour force in 1825, a figure higher than that at the end of the nineteenth century. They toiled in a wide variety of occupations. Many were weavers. Others made soap, candles, and dresses. A census taken in 1825 showed that Montreal had female innkeepers, mercers, blacksmiths, and coachmakers. Some women earned money by taking in boarders, providing meals for them, and washing their laundry. Convents began to train a few women as teachers. Many female labourers found jobs as domestics, work that began at dawn and finished when the family went to bed. By 1820, about one family in five in Quebec City employed at least one servant.

HEALTH CONDITIONS

In the early decades of the nineteenth century, disease posed a serious and constant threat to public health, particularly in the towns, with their filthy living conditions and relatively concentrated populations. In 1832, the first of a series of cholera epidemics provoked a wave of panic among Canadians. The disease, transmitted mainly through contaminated water supplies, had spread from the delta of the Ganges River in India across Europe to Britain. Its attacks were sudden, extremely painful, and very often fatal; death came within 48 hours, a result of complete dehydration of the victim's body. No known cure existed.

The arrival in Canada of large numbers of immigrants, very often indigents from Ireland, caused much concern to the French Canadians living in the St. Lawrence valley. The Irish had been migrating in large numbers to Lower Canada since 1815, although most went on to Upper Canada or to the United States. Some 50 000 arrived in 1831. They were steerage passengers who had spent weeks on the boats, in filthy conditions, and often near starvation. Worried about the threat these immigrants posed to public health, the government of Lower Canada established a quarantine station on Grosse Île, a small island in the upper St. Lawrence River downstream from Quebec.

Conditions in Lower Canadian towns greatly contributed to the spread of infection. Houses were dirty and overcrowded, yards and streets were piled with refuse, and towns had open sewers. People emptied the remains of animal pens and latrines into the streets. Pigs and other animals ran loose. Slaughterhouses, often located in residential districts, dumped their waste into open water. In early spring 1832, the health board of Quebec City tried to force residents to clean up streets, houses, and yards. They were ordered to "scrape, wash and cleanse their premises and carry away all filth." Such regulations proved to be unenforceable in the face of public indifference, if not outright hostility.

Cholera struck Quebec City at the end of the first week in June 1832. Hospitals overflowed with victims, while hundreds more lay in tents on the Plains of Abraham. Many panic-stricken residents fled to rural areas, often carrying the disease with them. To prevent despair, church bells were no longer rung for the dead. Police had to be called to enforce the rapid burial of the deceased. By the end of October, 7500 residents of Quebec and Montreal — more than one-tenth of the population of each city — had died.

RURAL QUEBEC

Nineteen out of twenty French Canadians in the early nineteenth century lived in rural areas, where they practised subsistence farming. Yet rural Quebec also underwent change. Thanks to the good harvests and high wheat prices of the 1790s and early 1800s, many habitants accumulated small surpluses of wheat that they sold to grain merchants for export abroad. For a short time, habitants saw their living conditions improve.

But yields varied enormously, and after 1815, crop failures became more frequent again. The productivity of even the best lands tended to drop after decades of cultivation without fertilization. New lands that had been opened up for colonization, especially those near the Canadian Shield, proved rocky and infertile. Crop diseases and insects posed a constant threat. Historians agree that the 1830s witnessed a rapid deterioration of economic conditions, with famine reported in 1837.

THE CHURCH

During this period, two groups vied to obtain influence and prestige among the habitants: the Roman Catholic church, implacably hostile to republican and liberal ideals; and a new professional elite composed of notaries, lawyers, and doctors. The professionals endorsed increasingly nationalistic ideas, particularly on political issues, and tended to be critical of the church; their forum was the colony's Assembly.

At the turn of the nineteenth century, the church's position in Lower Canada was far from assured. In spite of what has been written by clerical historians about the habitants' profound religiosity, Quebec was not a theocratic society, and the clergy were neither very influential nor dominant. Contemporary accounts detail the spread of religious indifference and even of anti-clericalism, particularly among the bourgeoisie.

To increase its influence within French-Canadian society, the church needed more clergy. Indeed, at this time, it faced a veritable crisis: the number of priests declined from about 200 in 1760 to only 150 in 1790 and then increased to somewhat more than 300 by the time of the rebellion — but the population had grown from 70 000 to 500 000 in the same period. During his tenure as bishop of Quebec from 1806 to 1825, Monseigneur Joseph-Octave Plessis encouraged the establishment of classical colleges and succeeded in increasing the number of vocations.

The church's major triumph in these years was the achievement of independence from government dictates. Until the 1830s, the government interfered with the nomination of bishops, although with decreasing success. By 1840, ecclesiastical nominations became purely a church concern.

Church leaders were skilful diplomats who exploited every opportunity to assert the church's independence while at the same time giving the government full co-operation and assuring British authorities of their unbending loyalty. International events afforded the church new opportunities to demonstrate its loyalty. The clergy had vigorously opposed the "anti-Christian" French Revolution that broke out with the storming of the Bastille prison in Paris on July 14, 1789. Horrified by the Reign of Terror that soon set in (which included Louis XVI among its victims), Canadian prelates issued strong condemnations. Then, while Napoleon's military campaigns provoked new suspicions of all things French, the War of 1812 gave the church a welcome opportunity to preach loyalty through pastoral letters and sermons. Led by the clergy, loyal French Canadians praised the exploits of Charles-Michel de Salaberry and his militia, who forced a numerically far superior American force to retreat at the battle of Châteauguay in 1813.

The rise of the church in the early years of the nineteenth century took place partly at the expense of the colonial government, and partly at the expense of the new professional elite. The professional class was the church's only serious rival in the struggle for support and influence among the French-speaking population. The Rebellion of 1837 brought this conflict to a head and decided its outcome in the church's favour. By 1840 French Canada's clerical elite was poised to enter a golden age that would last for more than a century.

THE PROFESSIONAL ELITE

Many of the members of the new professional class were sons of small farmers. Politics became an outlet for this group's ambitions. Espousing liberal, democratic, and, ultimately, republican ideals, the group sought government reform through enlarging the powers of the lower house and curtailing those of the executive. These professionals were well aware of Lower Canada's colonial status and of French Canadians' lesser role in the economy and in government. They associated the interests of French Canada with those of their own class. Not surprisingly, they framed their declarations of battle in the name of the French-Canadian nation.

This new middle class aspired to replace the seigneurs and, to a degree, compete with the clergy as leaders of French Canada. Many of its members viewed the seigneurs as exploiting the habitants when they raised seigneurial *rentes*. The French-speaking seigneurs also appeared as collaborators who bowed to the British to gain lucrative appointments and pensions. Many notaries and lawyers also condemned the church for its support of Britain. Some were openly anti-clerical, espousing the ideals of the French Revolution and American democracy. The professionals defended traditional agriculture and denounced the threat of commercial capitalism, but, as political radicals, they called for greater autonomy for the colony and some even favoured rebellion.

Understandably, the French-speaking professionals who formed the backbone of the Parti canadien had increasingly hostile relations with the British merchants. The merchants wanted to control Lower Canada's political institutions in order to introduce new laws to promote economic growth, commerce, and transportation. Some even demanded the abolition of the seigneurial system. Naturally, they accused the Assembly's French-speaking majority of systematically blocking necessary change. One solution they put forth was the union of the two Canadas, a measure intended to reduce the influence of the French.

ASSEMBLY VERSUS GOVERNOR

The Rebellion of 1837 marked the failure of the Constitutional Act as a system of government for Lower Canada. Actually, the act's weaknesses had been apparent for at least a generation. Since the turn of the century, the increasingly French and Parti canadien–dominated Assembly had sought to strengthen the elective part of government and to weaken the all-powerful executive, whose members were appointed in London and Quebec.

The causes of the Rebellion of 1837 in Lower Canada were more complex than those in Upper Canada's rebellion because of the colony's ethnic division. In part, this struggle pitted the English against the French, since Lower Canada's tiny English-speaking minority dominated the Executive Council and the Assembly represented the province's French-speaking majority. Yet the deterioration of French–English relations in the colony and the increasingly violent rhetoric on both sides did not prevent a small group of English-speaking Quebeckers from supporting the Patriotes, such as brothers Wolfred and Robert Nelson. Both supporters of reform, they endorsed Patriote demands for an executive that would be responsible to the Assembly.

In an effort to strengthen its role in government, the Assembly sought greater control of the colony's finances. The question of provincial revenues had produced a deadlock in relations between the Assembly and the governor by the 1820s. Louis-Joseph Papineau led the attack. Foremost among the leaders of the Parti canadien (called the Parti patriote after 1826), Papineau entered the Assembly in 1809 and became its speaker in 1815. He had many contradictions. As a seigneur himself, Papineau defended the values of tradition, nation, and family. Yet his education and political career had acquainted him with liberal thought. As the political crisis deepened after 1830, Papineau's early esteem for British institutions evolved into admiration for republicanism and American-style democracy. Liberal in his religious views, he nevertheless viewed the Roman Catholic church as an important national institution, and he attended mass to set an example for his tenants.

On the financial issue the British Parliament adopted what it hoped would be perceived as a compromise solution. It gave the Assembly control of all expenditures on the condition that it agree to pay the civil list each year — that is, to pay for the civil administration of the colony, including the salaries of civil servants. But the mood among the Patriotes was uncompromising. In 1834 they drew up the Ninety-two Resolutions, in part a denunciation of the composition of the appointed Legislative Council and of its tendency to block legislation adopted by the elected Assembly.

In March 1837 the English government issued the Ten Resolutions which announced an end to conciliation. This series of resolutions constituted a refusal by the Colonial Office of all of the Assembly's Ninety-two Resolutions. They authorized the government of Lower Canada, if necessary, to pay its administrative costs from the tax revenues without the Assembly's approval. There would be no elective Legislative Council, thus preserving the English-speaking minority's political influence. The Executive Council, representing wealth and enterprise, would, as before, continue to be responsible to the governor alone, not to the Assembly. Papineau and his party thus failed to gain control over the executive's powers.

THE LOWER CANADIAN REBELLIONS, 1837–1838

 When they received news of Russell's resolutions, the Patriotes altered their tactics, since Britain apparently would not yield. Throughout the tense days of summer and autumn 1837, the Patriote leaders worked on organization. They staged assemblies and collected funds. At a public assembly at St. Charles on the Richelieu River east of Montreal, attended by perhaps 4000 people, Patriote orators called for revolt. The meeting adopted resolutions that included a declaration of independence.

When the government issued warrants for their arrest, the principal Patriote leaders, Papineau included, fled to the countryside south of Montreal. After an initial skirmish at St. Denis on November 23, which the Patriotes won, the British troops momentarily withdrew, awaited their second column, and then advanced. The fierce combat that ensued on November 25 at neighbouring St. Charles, in which Patriote forces were led by Wolfred Nelson, was catastrophic for the rebels. Between 50 and 150 Patriotes were killed, while the British lost only three men. Poorly armed civilians proved no match for well-trained British regulars led by professional officers. Prisoners were then rounded up and sent to jail in Montreal. Throughout the St. Denis and St. Charles area, British troops also torched 20 houses and barns, adding to the atmosphere of terror.

Having pacified the Richelieu valley, Sir John Colborne, the former governor of Upper Canada who had just become commander-in-chief of all British troops in the Canadas, turned his attention to the area north of Montreal. News of the Patriotes' defeat at St. Charles only hardened Dr. Jean-Olivier Chénier, the local resistance leader, in his determination to "die fighting rather than surrender."

When Colborne approached St. Eustache in December 1837, Chénier and a number of his followers took refuge in the church and other buildings. Some 70 Patriotes, including Chénier, died by gunfire or were burned to death. In total, 250 men died in battle in Lower Canada, in

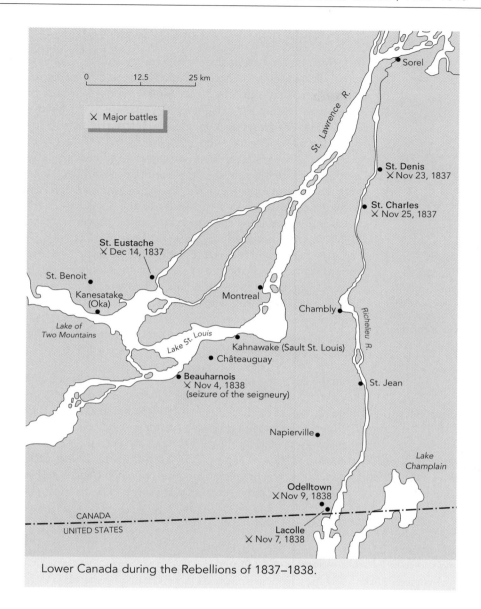

Lower Canada during the Rebellions of 1837–1838.

the Richelieu valley, and at St. Eustache, in late November and December 1837. The victory won, the British imprisoned the rebel leaders they could catch and initiated a policy of home burning throughout the St. Eustache district.

By the time news of the insurrection reached London, just before Christmas, many of the rebel leaders had found asylum in the United States, where they attempted to muster support and regroup. Indeed, in February 1838, Robert Nelson led an incursion across the border. As provisional president of Lower Canada, he declared Canada's independence from Britain before fleeing back to safety on the American side. In November 1838 the British easily turned back Patriote raids from across the American border, ending the Rebellions.

A reconstruction by Henri Julien of the hanging of five Patriotes on January 18, 1839: Joseph-Jacques Robert, François-Xavier Hamelin, Pierre-Théophile Décoigne, and Ambroise and Charles Sanguinet. The British, during the rule of the Special Council, executed 12 Patriotes and sent 58 to the penal colonies in Australia for their part in the 1838 uprising.

National Archives of Canada/C-20295.

CONSEQUENCES OF THE REBELLIONS

To govern Lower Canada after it had suspended the colony's constitution, Britain set up a Special Council composed of members of the English-speaking minority and a few strongly loyalist French Canadians. During the rebellions, it suspended civil liberties and legal rights. Then it set up a police force in Montreal as well as a rural police force to pacify the habitants.

For the longer term, London chose to address the Canadian problem by forming a royal commission under Lord Durham to visit both Lower and Upper Canada. Durham's concerns for economic development made him sympathetic to the Canadian and British merchants' views. They emphasized the ethnic aspect of the conflict. In his report, submitted in 1839, Durham drew attention to the "deadly animosity" between French and English: "I found two nations warring in the bosom of a single state; I found a struggle, not of principles, but of races." A union of the two Canadas would yield a slight English majority, which immigration would further reinforce. Durham voiced his solution: union with Upper Canada. This would assure the assimilation of the French, solving forever the challenge of ethnic conflict in Lower Canada.

From the Conquest to 1791 Quebec obtained three constitutions: the Royal Proclamation of 1763, the Quebec Act of 1774, and the Constitutional Act of 1791. The turmoil of the Rebellions of 1837/38 led to a fourth: the Act of Union of 1840. The colony of Lower Canada lost its own government and was to be joined to Upper Canada in a union that the great majority of the French Canadians did not want. The avowed purpose of joining the two Canadas, as expressed by Lord Durham, British parliamentarians, and Lower Canadian merchants, was to break the power of French Canada and eventually to assimilate it. The advocates of the Union of the Canadas proved to be poor prophets.

LINKING TO THE PAST

The Treaty of Paris, 1763
http://www.yale.edu/lawweb/avalon/paris763.htm
The full text is given of the 1763 Treaty of Paris. Articles IV to VII are of particular relevance.

The Royal Proclamation of 1763
http://www.solon.org/Constitutions/Canada/English/PreConfederation/rp_1763.html
The site contains the full text of the Royal Proclamation of 1763.

The Quebec Act, 1774
http://www.solon.org/Constitutions/Canada/English/PreConfederation/qa_1774.html
The full text of the 1774 Quebec Act appears on this site.

Revolution Rejected: Canada and the American Revolution
http://www.warmuseum.ca/cwm/expo/index_e.html
Historical background, images of artifacts, and a quiz related to the American Revolution as it affected Canada.

Constitutional Act of 1791
http://www.uni.ca/1791_ca.html

The full text of the Act appears. For a summary of its implications, go to http://www.nlc-bnc.ca/2/18/h18-2088-e.html

Forges du Saint-Maurice National Historic Site
http://parkscanada.gc.ca/lhn-nhs/qc/saintmaurice/index_e.asp

An illustrated history of the Forges du Saint-Maurice covering the period from 1670 to the present, plus an online tour and a picture gallery.

Towards Confederation: Lower Canada (1791–1842)
http://www.nlc-bnc.ca/confed/lowercan/elowrcan.htm

An overview of the Lower Canada rebellions, with links to information on James Craig, Louis-Joseph Papineau, Lord Durham, the newspapers *The Quebec Mercury* and *Le Canadien*, and the British American Land Company.

BIBLIOGRAPHY

Although first published more than half a century ago, A.L. Burt, *The Old Province of Quebec* (Toronto: McClelland & Stewart, 1968 [1933]) remains the standard general work on the post-Conquest decades. Hilda Neatby incorporated new research into her book *Quebec: The Revolutionary Age, 1760–1791* (Toronto: McClelland & Stewart, 1966). An excellent study of the framing of British policy toward Quebec is Philip Lawson, *The Imperial Challenge: Quebec and Britain in the Age of the American Revolution* (Montreal/Kingston: McGill-Queen's University Press, 1989). James H. Lambert provides bibliographical references for the period from 1760 to 1867 in "Quebec/Lower Canada," in M. Brook Taylor, ed., *Canadian History: A Reader's Guide*, vol. 1, *Beginnings to Confederation* (Toronto: University of Toronto Press, 1994), pp. 112–83.

A brief synthesis of the rebellions is available in English in Jean-Paul Bernard, *The Rebellions of 1837 and 1838 in Lower Canada* (Ottawa: Canadian Historical Association, 1996, Historical Booklet 55). Allan Greer challenges earlier analyses of the events of 1837 and their origins in *The Patriots and the People: The Rebellion of 1837 in Rural Lower Canada* (Toronto: University of Toronto Press, 1993). Joseph Schull, *Rebellion: The Rising in French Canada, 1837* (Toronto: Macmillan, 1971) is an older, popular treatment. Jacques Monet, *The Last Cannon Shot: A Study of French Canadian Nationalism, 1837–1850* (Toronto: University of Toronto Press, 1969) contains useful material on both the rebellion and its aftermath.

Fernand Ouellet reviews economic aspects of the period in *Economic and Social History of Quebec, 1760-1850* (Toronto:Macmillan, 1980); and *Lower Canada, 1791–1840: Social Change and Nationalism* (Toronto: McClelland & Stewart, 1979). Ronald Rudin provides a short review of Quebec's embryonic English-speaking community in *The Forgotten Quebecers: A History of English-Speaking Quebec, 1759–1980* (Quebec: Institut québécois de recherche sur la culture, 1985). For material pertaining to women in Lower Canada in the early nineteenth century see Micheline Dumont et al., *Quebec Women: A History* (Toronto: Women's Press, 1987), 31–59. The major individuals of these years all have biographies in various volumes of the *Dictionary of Canadian Biography*. It is now also available online: www.biographi.ca.

The following books and articles provide a good introduction to the Native history of the period: Francis Jennings, *Empire of Fortune: Crowns, Colonies and Tribes in the Seven Years War in America* (New York: W.W. Norton, 1988); Howard H. Peckham, *Pontiac and the Indian Uprising* (Chicago: University of Chicago Press, 1961 [1947]); Richard White, *The Middle Ground: Indians, Empires and Republics in the Great Lakes Region, 1650–1815* (Cambridge: Cambridge University Press, 1991).

Useful maps of the St. Lawrence valley in the late eighteenth and early nineteenth centuries appear in the first two volumes of the *Historical Atlas of Canada*, vol. 1, R. Cole Harris, ed., *From the Beginning to 1800* (Toronto: University of Toronto Press, 1987); and vol. 2, R. Louis Gentilcore, ed., *The Land Transformed, 1800–1891* (Toronto: University of Toronto Press, 1993).

UPPER CANADA, 1791–1840

TIME LINE

1791 – The Constitutional Act of 1791 is followed by the division of the Province of Quebec into Upper and Lower Canada

1792 – John Graves Simcoe arrives as the first lieutenant governor of Upper Canada

1812–
1814 – The War of 1812

1813 – Tecumseh, the great First Nations leader, dies at the battle of Moraviantown

1824 – William Lyon Mackenzie begins his newspaper, *The Colonial Advocate*, at Queenston, Upper Canada

1829 – Welland Canal open for navigation between Lake Ontario and Lake Erie

1837–
1838 – William Lyon Mackenzie leads an unsuccessful rebellion against British rule

Battle of the Windmill near Prescott, Upper Canada

In 1774, the Province of Quebec included the territory north of the Great Lakes and immediately south of the Canadian Shield. The only European settlement of any size was located on the outskirts of present-day Windsor, where French-Canadian farmers who supplied Fort Detroit, just across the river, had settled farms. The remainder of the whole western portion of the Province of Quebec remained one continuous forest.

The American Revolution led to the creation of Britain's first inland colony in 1791. John Graves Simcoe, commander of the Queen's Rangers (a Loyalist corps) in the revolution became the first lieutenant governor of Upper Canada. He spent four years constructing the framework for a colony intended to be the ideal home for Loyalists. In the end, Americans in search of cheap land, not Loyalists, formed the majority of the settlers, outnumbering the Loyalists four to one at the beginning of the War of 1812. Yet, thanks to a strong British and First Nation military resistance the northern colony avoided American conquest.

From 1815 to 1840 Upper Canada's population quadrupled, from less than 100 000 to more than 400 000. Immigration accounted for much of this increase. Some of the new immigrants came from the United States, but most arrived from the British Isles: northern Irish Protestants, southern Irish Roman Catholics; Lowland and Highland Scots; Welsh and English. The newcomers settled the land; established and refined political, social, and educational institutions; contributed to the colony's economic growth; and participated in its political movements. The British immigrants, with the exception of some Catholic Irish, worked to develop a sense of loyalty to Britain. These newcomers brought British customs and attitudes that eventually mixed, in the years to follow, with those of the settlers already there to create a unique Upper Canadian character.

THE ANISHINABEG AND LOYALIST SETTLEMENT

The Proclamation of 1763 had recognized the Great Lakes area as First Nations country; hence, the Native peoples had to surrender that land to the Crown before Loyalist settlement could proceed. Until the early 1780s, three nations lived in what is now southern Ontario: the Ojibwas (Chippewas), the Ottawas (Odawas), and the Algonquins — the three Algonquian nations who called themselves the "Anishinabeg," meaning true human beings.

 Sir Frederick Haldimand, the governor of Quebec from 1778 to 1784, arranged for the purchase of the land from the Mississaugas, as the British called the Ojibwa along the north shore of Lake Ontario. Why did the Mississaugas make agreements with the British? First, they did so because they relied on the traders' European goods and on the gifts that the English had given them annually since the suppression of Pontiac's resistance. Second, it appears that they did not believe they were selling the land once and for all. The Native pattern of land ownership and use differed from that of the British. Among the Great Lakes Algonquians, an individual family could use a recognized hunting ground, fishing place, or maple sugar bush, but as soon as the family ceased to go there, it reverted to the collective ownership of the entire band. Most likely, the Anishinabeg regarded the initial agreement as one with tenants for the use of the land as long as they practised good behaviour. Third, the Mississaugas had a small population of about 1000, divided into a dozen or more separate bands along the 500 km of lakefront. They could have resisted their British and Iroquois allies only with great difficulty. Thus, weakly organized, reliant on European trade goods, and believing that they would receive presents in perpetuity for the use of their land, the Mississaugas agreed to the proposals.

A Historical Portrait 🖋

🖝 David Ramsay

In the 1790s David Ramsay, fur trader, revolutionary war soldier, guide — and Indian-killer — was one of the best-known individuals in Upper Canada. The colonial administrators and the Loyalist settlers respected him. In contrast, Joseph Brant, the Mohawk leader, regarded him as an "unworthy rascal." A number of the Mississaugas tolerated him — although he once killed and scalped eight Anishinabeg, including a woman and two children — because he provided a link with the dominant settler society. That the Mississaugas had to rely on this dangerous, unstable man, simply because he knew their language, shows their isolation from the British officials, and from the incoming settlers.

What little is known about Ramsay's early life comes from a land petition that he submitted to Governor Simcoe and from notes made by a British traveller, Captain Patrick Campbell, whom Ramsay guided in 1792 from Niagara to New York. Taking great interest in his fellow Scot's adventures, Captain Campbell stayed up with him one whole night to record his story, which he accepted completely because, as he wrote in his *Travels in North America*, "His honesty and fidelity is so well known, that he is entrusted with sums of money to any amount without requiring any token or receipt for the same." Ramsay claimed that he came from the town of Leven, Fifeshire, Scotland. As a young man he joined the crew of the British warship *Prince of Orange*, serving in the sieges of Louisbourg in 1758 and Quebec in 1759. After the Seven Years' War, he entered the Great Lakes fur trade, operating out of Schenectady, New York.

The details of Ramsay's life confirm that he might have been a psychopath. He spent the winter of 1771–72 on the north shore of Lake Erie with his 17-year-old brother, who had just arrived from Scotland. Ramsay alleged that he had been forced, in self-defence, to kill several Native people who, in a drunken state, attacked them. Sir William Johnson, the Indian Superintendent for the northern colonies had a different account. Johnson argued that Ramsay deserved "Capital punishment." He dismissed Ramsay's argument of self-defence because, "the Indians, whenever they meditate mischief, carefully avoid Liquor." But Johnson also realized that a jury would acquit him. As he wrote to an Indian Department assistant: "I don't think he will Suffer, had he killed a Hundred." Johnson was correct. In September 1773, a Montreal jury released Ramsay for "want of Evidence." Ramsay's brother, the only eyewitness of the killings present at the trial, supported his brother's story of self-defence. No Mississaugas were present.

After his military service with the Royal Navy on the Atlantic coast during the American Revolution, Ramsay went back to live among the First Nations people whose relatives he had killed a decade earlier. He learned to dress like them, to live like them, and to speak their language. Why he did so remains a mystery, especially as his dislike of them in no way appears to have diminished. He told Campbell, for example, in describing the killings of 1771–72: "After killing the first Indians, I cut lead, and chewed above thirty balls, and above three pound of Goose shot, for I thought it a pity to shoot an Indian with a smooth ball." Although in the late 1780s and early 1790s he received death threats from some Mississaugas, he remained among them.

Why did the Mississaugas tolerate him? First, they did so probably because Ramsay followed their custom. He "covered the graves" of the murdered, paying a certain number of gifts to the relatives of those that he had killed. Secondly, and more important, a number of Mississaugas saw him as a valuable ally, perhaps their only ally. This "eccentric white man," as the Mississauga Methodist minister Peter Jones later described him, forwarded their grievances to the government. In a petition sent in their name to Governor Simcoe in the winter of 1793, for instance, Ramsay outlined the settlers' encroachments on their hunting territories and fishing grounds.

David Ramsay claimed that the Mississaugas in 1789 gave him a large tract of land at the mouth of the Twelve Mile (Bronte) Creek, between present-day Hamilton and Toronto as a gift. He stated that he and his heirs would allow the Mississaugas to use the land, to hunt and fish, and to plant orchards there, "forever as they now are or until they are half white. (But no black mixture allowed to inherit the above land)." The government never recognized the gift, but it did give Ramsay two substantial land grants elsewhere in Upper Canada, that were together roughly 500 ha in size. Ramsay died in New York City in 1810.

LOYALIST SETTLEMENTS

In 1785, approximately 7500 Loyalists (5500 non-Native and 2000 Iroquois Loyalists) lived in what is now present-day southern Ontario. By 1791, the number had risen to perhaps 30 000. New settlements had been established throughout the area that extended north from the St. Lawrence up the Ottawa River to the Rideau River. They were spread over 15 km around the Bay of Quinte and formed a narrow strip along the Lake Ontario shore from the Bay of Quinte to York (now Toronto), where farms extended 25 km up Yonge Street. Settlers, mostly from rural New York and Pennsylvania, now occupied the narrow strip of good land below the escarpment around the Niagara peninsula and part way up the Lake Erie shoreline. From the concessions along the front of the Detroit River, settlement began to move along the south shore of Lake St. Clair, and into the lower Thames River valley.

The early Upper Canadian Loyalists came from many ethnic backgrounds, but most came from the same economic and social level — a humble one. Not until the wave of immigration from New Brunswick in the 1790s did Upper Canada receive what might be termed a Loyalist elite, composed of families such as the Robinsons, the Jarvises, and the Ryersons.

THE CONSTITUTIONAL ACT OF 1791

The Constitutional Act of 1791 brought the colony of Upper Canada into existence. It provided for freehold tenure and free land. (Settlers paid only the fees for issuing and recording land titles.) The legislation also set aside the equivalent of one-seventh of all lands granted in the future for "the Support and Maintenance of a Protestant Clergy." Unfortunately, the act failed to make explicit just what constituted the "Protestant Clergy" — the Church of England only, as it was the established, or state-recognized national church in England — or the Church of Scotland and other Protestant denominations as well? This caused confusion and controversy. Initially, for instance, the provincial government interpreted the phrase to refer only to the Church of England. In addition, the British government set aside another seventh of all lands as

On a Bush Farm near Chatham, Upper Canada, 1838, by Philip John Bainbrigge. Side by side, pioneer men and women shared in clearing the land, constructing log houses, and planting, tending, and harvesting the crops.

National Archives of Canada/C-11811.

Crown reserves; the revenues from the sale or rental of these lands were to be used to fund the colonial government.

A "TRULY BRITISH" COLONY

John Graves Simcoe, an energetic and enthusiastic military officer in the revolutionary war, then in his late thirties, became Upper Canada's first lieutenant governor. He wanted to make Upper Canada a centre of British power in North America. To him, "democracy" and "republicanism" were wicked words. Believing that many in the new republic to the south remained actively loyal to England, he attempted to win Americans back to their old allegiance. He was convinced that a new colony with "a free, honourable British Government" would remind Americans of what they had lost in leaving the empire and of the benefits of returning to it.

The governor wanted to create a hierarchical society like that which existed in England. He firmly believed in the established Church of England. In his model British colony, the Anglican Church alone would enjoy the right of performing marriages. Reluctantly Simcoe agreed that justices of the peace in remote areas might conduct marriage ceremonies, provided they followed the Anglican ritual. Only in 1798 was the right to solemnize marriages extended to Lutheran, Calvinist, and Church of Scotland ministers. Methodists remained excluded until 1831. The Upper Canadian administration regarded the Methodists, particularly the Methodists from the United States, with great suspicion, because they remained affiliated with the American parent church until 1828. The American Methodists had formed an independent Methodist church in the United States immediately after the American Revolution, separating themselves from their British co-religionists.

Simcoe placed the new colony on a firm military footing. The British government allowed him to raise an infantry corps of 425 officers and men, the Queen's Rangers (the name of his old Loyalist regiment in the revolution) to protect Upper Canada. The first governor contributed to the establishment of a road system in the colony. In 1793 he ordered the construction of a military road from Burlington Bay to the Thames River, which he named Dundas Street after Henry Dundas, then the secretary of state in the English cabinet. Simcoe believed that a second military road should be built from York to Lake Simcoe, to ensure rapid communication with the upper lakes. It was begun in 1796. The governor called this road Yonge Street after Sir George Yonge, the British secretary of war.

Initially Simcoe established his headquarters at Newark (now Niagara-on-the-Lake), only later changing it to York (Toronto). Then he called for elections to the Legislative Assembly. The legislature created a judicial system. William Osgoode, a well-regarded English lawyer, became chief justice, with responsibility for the Court of King's Bench, the new superior court of civil and criminal jurisdiction. Within each district Simcoe created surrogate courts and a provincial court of probate. At a lower level, meetings for the courts of quarter sessions were organized. The justices of the peace presided over these and performed as well a wide range of administrative and judicial duties. At the township level the justices of the peace enjoyed considerable power. Township officials in Upper Canada were appointed, not elected as they were in New England.

THE SLAVERY QUESTION

While the majority of African-American Loyalists and slaves went to Nova Scotia after the revolution, some slaves, perhaps as many as 500, were brought to Upper Canada. Slavery, however, did not prosper in a northern area such as Upper Canada. Crops such as cotton, which required a cheap, plentiful labour force, were ruled out by the short Canadian growing season. Furthermore, owners had to feed, clothe, and house slaves throughout a long and unproductive winter. Finally, many Upper Canadians, including Simcoe, found slavery abhorrent.

Under the governor's direction, the Assembly adopted a bill in 1793 that abolished slavery but freed not one single slave. It stated that slaves already in Upper Canada had to remain slaves until death, but all children born after the act's passage would become free at the age of 25. Furthermore, no additional slaves could be brought to Upper Canada. After 1793, slavery steadily declined in the colony.

Simcoe left Upper Canada in mid-1796. While serving as governor, he experienced many disappointments. While he may have considered the colony as something approaching the centre of the universe, the British government did not. It turned down his expensive schemes to build up Upper Canada economically and militarily. His proposal to create a provincial university also received little support, as did his attempt to establish the Church of England in the colony under a bishop's tutelage. In addition, he failed in his attempt to promote a hierarchical society in Upper Canada, based on large land grants. Nevertheless, he did succeed in placing the colony on a firm military footing, in establishing a legal framework for Upper Canada, and organizing its early transportation system.

LOYALIST WOMEN IN EARLY UPPER CANADA

During the American Revolution, female Loyalists displayed exceptional courage. They took charge of their families and farms during their husbands' absences. Many had been harassed or persecuted. The insurgents had stolen their property and seized their homes, and in some cases jailed them. They had travelled, in many cases, with very young children through difficult

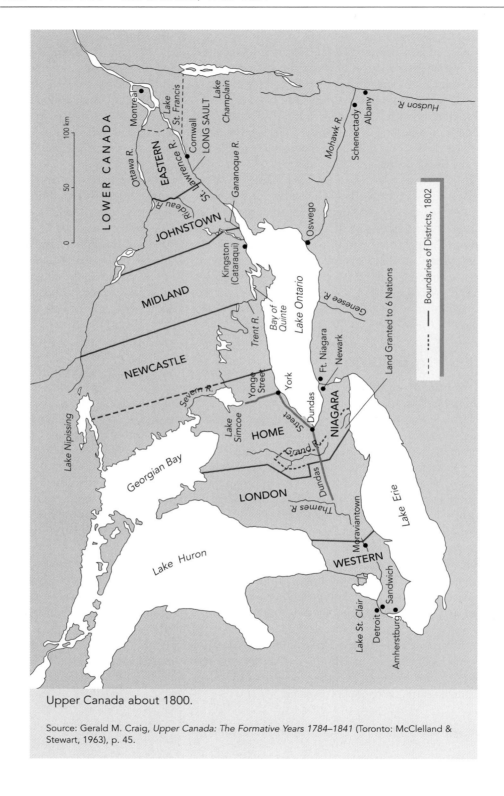

Upper Canada about 1800.

Source: Gerald M. Craig, *Upper Canada: The Formative Years 1784–1841* (Toronto: McClelland & Stewart, 1963), p. 45.

wilderness to British refugee camps. Even here their struggles did not end. As historian Janice Potter writes, once behind British lines, "They had to fit once again into a patriarchal power structure in which their inferiority and dependence were assumed."[1] Men remained the decision-makers, the women and children being expected to follow their directions. A married woman had no legal identity separate from that of her husband. Some Loyalist women did submit claims for compensation to Britain after the war. Without fail, however, the all-male adjudicators of Loyalist claims awarded much more, proportionally, to men than to women.

THE FIRST NATIONS: A DISPLACED PEOPLE

By 1796, the Native peoples understood that the land treaties meant the denial of a right of way across cleared fields, and if they camped on the settlers' lands, the farmers shot their dogs. The elders told the young people, such as Kahkewaquonaby (Sacred Feathers, known in English as Peter Jones), that when the British first came, they "asked for a small piece of land on which they might pitch their tents; the request was cheerfully granted. By and by they begged for more, and more was given them. In this way they have continued to ask, or have obtained by force or fraud, the fairest portions of our territory." Between 1805 and 1818, the Crown successfully pressured the Mississaugas to sell their last remaining tract, between Toronto and the head of the lake (present-day Hamilton). In two separate agreements, the British acquired the desired land.

Other tragedies followed for the First Nations. Between the 1790s and the 1820s, smallpox, tuberculosis, and measles killed almost two-thirds of the Mississaugas at the western end of the lake. The band's population in that area dropped to 200 in the 1820s, down from more than 500 a generation earlier. The Iroquois also experienced difficult times in the 1790s and 1800s, as land sales eliminated much of their reserve on the Grand River. Chief Joseph Brant had welcomed settlers to the Grand River to teach European agricultural techniques. Not all his followers agreed. Many objected to the presence of the outsiders who, by 1798, controlled two-thirds of the Six Nations' original grant on the Grand River.

THE GROWTH OF SETTLEMENT

Upper Canada's non-Native population continued to grow in the 1790s and in the decade following, not at the phenomenal rate of the 1820s and 1830s, but still substantially. Many were "late Loyalists," or individuals of non-Loyalist backgrounds who came in search of cheap land. Among the immigrants to Upper Canada were members of religious sects commonly called the "Plain Folk," because they believed in a pure religion and plain dress. They included Quakers, Mennonites, and Dunkards (a small group of Baptists who practised adult baptism by "dunking" the individual in water). By 1812, settlers lived on all the vacant townships along the north shore of Lake Ontario and on several townships on Lake Erie as well. Although few roads existed, the waterways allowed for the dispersal of settlement along an 800 km front in a period of less than 20 years.

On the eve of the War of 1812, the population of Upper Canada reached 75 000. Scattered along the St. Lawrence River and Lakes Ontario, Erie, and St. Clair, the settled areas rarely extended more than a few kilometres into the interior. The work of establishing farms and clearing new land took much of the settlers' time. The newcomers from the United States outnumbered the Loyalists and the British immigrants four to one. Like the Acadians of Nova Scotia a century earlier, these Americans lived in a British colony without really belonging to it. The War of 1812 led to enormous pressures on them to choose sides.

Old Fort Erie with the Migrations of the Wild-Pigeon in Spring, April 12, 1804, by Edward Walsh (1766–1832). In her diary entry for November 1, 1793, Elizabeth Simcoe commented that passenger pigeons were so numerous in Upper Canada in the spring and autumn that, at times, they darkened the entire sky. The pioneers put a stop to that. On both sides of the border, settlers trapped, clubbed, and shot the pigeons by the millions. The last recorded sighting of passenger pigeons in Ontario was in 1902. The last passenger pigeon in North America died in 1914 in a zoo in Cincinnati, Ohio.

Courtesy of Royal Ontario Museum, Toronto/952.218 © ROM.

THE WAR OF 1812

Many Great Lakes First Nations already knew the side they would support in any future Anglo-American conflict. In the first decade of the nineteenth century, Tecumseh, a Shawnee chief, and his brother, a religious leader, assembled a formidable Native confederacy. In 1811, Tecumseh was at open war with the Americans. Many Ohioans, Tennesseeans, and Kentuckians suspected — incorrectly — that the British continued to encourage and finance the First Nations raids. Many aggressive and intensely patriotic Americans judged it time to attack the British in the Canadas. At the same time, American "war hawks," anxious to begin a war with Britain, argued that the United States could use the opportunity to seize Upper Canada.

Two direct provocations by Britain led many Americans, including President James Madison, to support the pro-war group. In 1812, Napoleon's Continental System, which forbade trade with Great Britain on the part of France, her allies, and neutrals, closed all of western Europe, except Portugal, to British goods. Britain retaliated by imposing a naval blockade on France, preventing all ships, including American vessels, from trading with France. Officially neutral in the struggle, the Americans called for freedom of the seas. What right had England to board American ships on the high seas and prevent them from trading with countries on the continent? Madison considered this act the first provocation.

Without regard for neutral rights, British cruisers stopped and searched American ships on the North Atlantic. The British looked for British deserters who had gone over to American vessels to obtain higher wages, better food, and better working conditions. The Royal Navy seized thousands of sailors, alleging that they were British deserters. If a man produced his easily obtained certificate of American naturalization, the English ignored it, as their government did not recognize the right of a British subject to transfer allegiance to another country. "Free Trade and Sailors' Rights" became the cry of many Americans.

Forced, as he put it, to choose between war and degradation, Madison sent a message of war to Congress on June 1, 1812. Congress agreed and declared war against Britain.

Throughout the first year of the war, the Americans believed that Upper Canada's American population would welcome them as liberators. Had not the majority of Upper Canada's population only recently arrived from the United States? Thomas Jefferson assured Americans that the conquest of Upper Canada would be a "mere matter of marching." This proved not to be the case at all.

Major General Isaac Brock, who had fought in the French wars in Europe and had then been stationed in North America, deserves much of the credit for Upper Canada's success in 1812. Before the war, Brock had built up the province's fortifications, trained the provincial militia, and maintained good relations with the Native peoples. As soon as war broke out, he took the offensive.

The First Nations' military contribution helps to explain Brock's success. For the Great Lakes First Nations, war did not break out in 1812; they had fought American frontiersmen for generations. Welcoming the outbreak of the second Anglo–American War in 1812, Tecumseh and hundreds of warriors joined the British in Upper Canada. At the outset, they assisted a small British force to take Michilimackinac, the leading fur-trading post in the Upper Great Lakes. Then they helped to cut the Americans' communication lines to Detroit, effectively winning that fort for the British. The fall of Detroit led to the embarrassing loss of all American territory west of Lake Erie.

Brock's unexpected victory at Detroit in August restored confidence among the loyal population that Upper Canada could be defended. He proved it again in October at Queenston Heights, but this time at the cost of his life: he was hit as he led a charge up the face of the heights. The attack, however, succeeded after 500 Iroquois joined 1000 British regulars and 600 Upper Canadian militia in retaking the strategic heights. The British victors captured 900 American prisoners. Having lost one army at Detroit, the Americans lost another on the Niagara frontier.

THE CAMPAIGNS OF 1813 AND 1814

The Upper Canadians' worst moment in the war came in the spring and summer of 1813, when the gains of 1812 were reversed. The Americans twice briefly occupied York and launched a second invasion of the Niagara peninsula, forcing the British to withdraw to Burlington Heights at the head of the lake (present-day Hamilton). Desertions from the militia grew, and even two members of the Upper Canada Legislative Assembly joined the Americans. Only a surprise attack by British regular troops at Stoney Creek, immediately south of Burlington Heights, dislodged the Americans and saved Upper Canada. A second battle followed at Beaver Dams, where Iroquois from the Montreal area and from the Six Nations territory at the Grand River ambushed the Americans. The attackers benefited from vital information about the location of the American troops received from Laura Secord, a 37-year-old settler, who overheard American officers discussing their invasion plans. Slipping through the American cordon, she took a

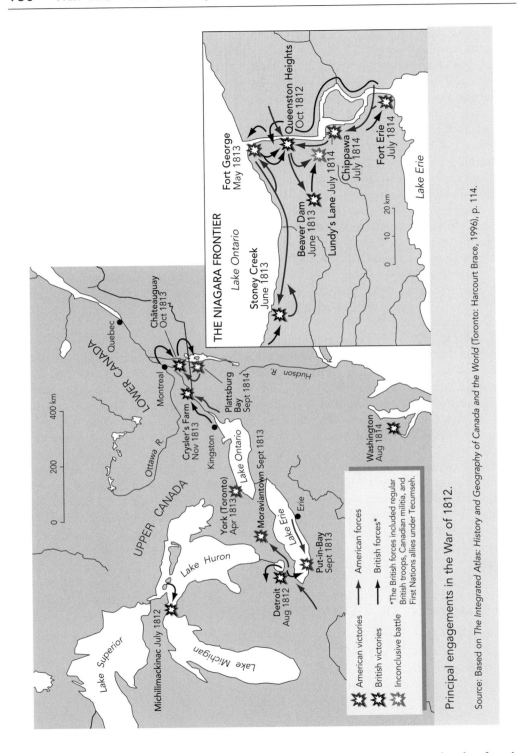

THE NIAGARA FRONTIER

Fort George May 1813
Queenston Heights Oct 1812
Beaver Dam June 1813
Lundy's Lane July 1814
Chippawa July 1814
Fort Erie July 1814
Stoney Creek June 1813
Lake Ontario
Lake Erie

0   10   20 km

LOWER CANADA
Quebec
Châteauguay Oct 1813
Montreal
Crysler's Farm Nov 1813
Plattsburg Bay Sept 1814
Kingston
Lake Ontario
Hudson R.
Ottawa R.
Washington Aug 1814
UPPER CANADA
York (Toronto) Apr 1813
Moraviantown Sept 1813
Lake Huron
Lake Erie
Erie
Put-in-Bay Sept 1813
Detroit Aug 1812
Lake Superior
Michilimackinac July 1812
Lake Michigan

0   200   400 km

American victories
British victories
Inconclusive battle

→ American forces
↑ British forces*

*The British forces included regular British troops, Canadian militia, and First Nations allies under Tecumseh.

Principal engagements in the War of 1812.

Source: Based on *The Integrated Atlas: History and Geography of Canada and the World* (Toronto: Harcourt Brace, 1996), p. 114.

roundabout route to the British–First Nations camp with this information. Shortly after the Iroquois victory at Beaver Dams, the American invaders withdrew from the peninsula.

While their Niagara campaign in 1813 ended in failure, the Americans, that same year, proved successful in the Detroit sector of the conflict. The Americans' fortunes revived after their naval forces obtained control of Lake Erie. The British then withdrew from Detroit. At Moraviantown, on the Thames River, the Americans defeated the British regulars, the Upper Canadian militia, and the First Nations. The Americans held on to southwestern Upper Canada until the end of the war. That fall, their two-pronged attack on Montreal ended in defeat at Crysler's Farm in eastern Upper Canada, and at Châteauguay in Lower Canada.

Tecumseh was killed at Moraviantown on October 5, 1813. With his death, his confederacy collapsed. The link between the British and the Native peoples of the American Midwest was broken. Never again in the lower Great Lakes area did the First Nations constitute a serious military threat.

After Moraviantown, the battle lines consolidated for the remainder of the war. On July 25, 1814, the British defeated the Americans' last great attempt to capture Upper Canada, at Lundy's Lane in the Niagara peninsula. Lundy's Lane was the site of the bloodiest battle of the War of 1812. The six-hour battle lasted until darkness, and each side lost over 800 men. Although each side claimed victory, at the end of the battle the Americans had failed to dislodge the British. They withdrew, ending their final offensive in Upper Canada. The peace treaty was signed on December 24, 1814.

UPPER CANADA IMMEDIATELY AFTER THE WAR OF 1812

 The War of 1812 did not change the boundaries of Upper Canada. The peace treaty essentially confirmed the status quo. But, in one respect, the war had a very profound effect on Upper Canada: the unsuccessful and destructive attacks of 1812–14 engendered anti-American sentiments among a number of non-Loyalist settlers. Ironically, the American invasion contributed to the work that Simcoe had begun — the promotion of a loyalty to Upper Canada.

After 1815, growing numbers of British settlers arrived in the colony. The end of the Napoleonic Wars best explains the migration. Peace brought economic depression and unemployment to Great Britain. It curtailed the army's demand for manpower, and, at the same time, made overseas travel less dangerous. Postwar Britain encouraged emigration. From the government's perspective, it reduced the population pressure in Britain, provided relief from social unrest, and facilitated expansion and control of its empire. The British government in the late 1810s and early 1820s assisted the exodus with generous aid, similar to that first given the Loyalists.

In the mid-1820s, however, the British government stopped aiding emigrants, as private charitable associations and landowners, anxious to rid their estates of impoverished tenants, now provided at least minimal assistance. Many immigrants were also willing to come on their own, without government assistance, to escape a desperate situation. This was especially true of the victims of the Irish potato famine in the 1830s and 1840s.

Upper Canadian landowners, such as Colonel Thomas Talbot, also assisted immigrants in the hope of profiting from government incentives for settlement and land development. Talbot eventually accumulated an estate of nearly 30 000 ha, making him one of the largest landholders in Upper Canada. In return, he contributed to the transformation of more than 200 000 ha of forest into 3000 farm lots in southwestern Upper Canada. His extensive road system made his lands more accessible and hence more valuable.

In 1826, the British government itself created the Canada Company, the first large-scale Canadian land company. The Canada Company purchased over 400 000 hectares of land, consisting of Crown reserves and the huge Huron Tract (the latter in southwestern Upper Canada on the shores of Lake Huron). The Company founded the towns of Goderich, in the Huron Tract, and the town of Guelph in another of its parcels of land east of the Tract.

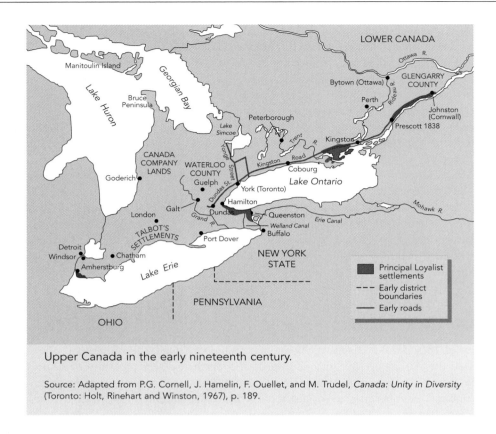

Upper Canada in the early nineteenth century.

Source: Adapted from P.G. Cornell, J. Hamelin, F. Ouellet, and M. Trudel, *Canada: Unity in Diversity* (Toronto: Holt, Rinehart and Winston, 1967), p. 189.

THE NATIVE PEOPLES

The land for the immigrants came from the First Nations peoples, who, by 1815, were already outnumbered ten to one by non-Natives. After the War of 1812, the First Nations in Upper Canada made seven major land surrenders, opening up much of present-day southern Ontario for settlement. In 1818, the government of Upper Canada changed the method of purchasing the land, offering to make annual payments or annuities in perpetuity, an arrangement that was preferable for the government to a simple one-time payment. Although by this time the First Nations realized that these land-sale agreements were final and irreversible, they lacked the strength in numbers to resist the proposed cessions. In addition, settled areas now divided the bands from one another, a situation which deterred a united response. Finally, groups like the Mississaugas were influenced by the government's oral promise to help them adjust to farming — a promise not fulfilled, in the case of the Mississaugas at the western end of Lake Ontario, until the mid-1820s.

First Nations migrated north to settle in Upper Canada. They came to escape the American government's removal policy, which dictated that Natives east of the Mississippi must move west of the river. Several thousand Anishinabeg took up residence in Upper Canada in the 1830s and 1840s. Most of the Oneida, one of the Iroquois nations remaining in New York state after the American Revolution, also migrated around 1840 and purchased land on the Thames River west of London. Apart from Governor Francis Bond Head's unsuccessful attempt in 1836–37 to relocate the Anishinabeg of southern Ontario (the Ojibwas, Odawas [Ottawas], and Potawatomis) to Manitoulin Island — a proposal they vigorously opposed — the government of Upper Canada allowed the First Nations to remain on their reserved lands, or reserves. Here they were encouraged to farm in the hopes that they would be acculturated and ultimately assimilated into the dominant society.

COLONIAL OLIGARCHY: THE FAMILY COMPACT

During the years 1815–40, a small, tightly knit elite popularly known as the "Family Compact" ruled Upper Canada. Through political patronage they appointed like-minded people to the local centres, thus creating, or recognizing already-existing, smaller oligarchies throughout the province.

At the centre of the Family Compact stood John Strachan, cleric and educator, as a leading adviser to the governors of Upper Canada. Around Strachan gathered a group of whom many were his former pupils. Members of this "old boys' network" had strikingly similar backgrounds and views. About half of the Family Compact consisted of descendants of the original Loyalist families. The other half included British immigrants who, like Strachan, had come in the early years of the colony.

Their role in the defence of the province during the War of 1812 heightened their British patriotism. They believed, first, that Upper Canada's strength came from its imperial connection. Secondly, they wanted power to remain in the hands of the governor and his appointed advisers. Thirdly, they wanted the established Church of England to give a "moral underpinning to society." Finally, this elite believed in the economic progress of the province — to be directed by themselves — through commerce, canal building, settlement schemes, and banks.

The Mississauga village on the Credit River during the winter of 1826–27. The houses, just built, were dressed log cottages with two rooms, of the type erected as a second house by settlers who had been on their farms for 5 to 10 years. Two families occupied each home, and each family had its own room. Originally, 20 of these two-family houses were built.

Egerton Ryerson, *The Story of My Life*, edited by J. George Hodgins (Toronto: William Briggs, 1883), p. 59.

RELIGIOUS DISPUTES

The first challenge to the Anglicans' ecclesiastical monopoly came from the Presbyterians. As the established Church of Scotland, this major Protestant denomination demanded a share of the clergy reserves, which consisted of one-seventh of the land in each township for the support of a "Protestant clergy." In 1829, the Colonial Office authorized their inclusion. The Executive Council denied the Methodists the same right. Since Methodism had come into Upper Canada from the United States, Family Compact members suspected it of having radical republican sympathies. Thus, the Methodists had to fight for a portion of the clergy reserves.

The Methodists counterattacked through Egerton Ryerson, a 23-year-old preacher of Loyalist background, who wrote a thundering reply in 1826. Raised in a prominent Anglican family but converted to Methodism, Ryerson upheld the educated quality of the itinerant preachers, denied that Methodists held republican views, and challenged the legality of Strachan's position that the Church of England was the established church in the province. So began the public career of Egerton Ryerson. For a half-century he would maintain a position of prominence in education and politics in Upper Canada.

Other Protestant denominations and religious sects appeared in the province. Baptists, Quakers, Dunkards, Millerites, Campbellites, Christian Universalists, Mormons, and German-speaking Amish created greater religious pluralism. With the arrival of substantial numbers of Irish Catholics, the Roman Catholic Church also strengthened its position.

WOMEN IN UPPER CANADA

Women played an integral role in British North American society in the early to mid-nineteenth century, although their importance was seldom acknowledged publicly. Their responsibilities consisted mainly of childbearing, childrearing, and social assistance to others, as well as "domestic employment," which included such tasks in the home as cooking, cleaning, sewing, knitting, spinning, and weaving, in addition to outdoor work, such as taking care of the poultry and the barnyard, the vegetable garden, and fruit growing — thereby freeing the men and boys to work in the fields. When her husband was away, a farm wife often assumed complete responsibility for outdoor work. Beyond the immediate family obligations, some women took in sewing or laundry, or boarders, or were seamstresses, keepers of inns or taverns in their homes, or schoolteachers within their homes.

Women were regulated and restricted by rules, traditions, customs, and laws made by male social elites, church leaders, government officials, and legal authorities. The concept of "domesticity" was taking hold in upper-middle-class families in the early to mid-nineteenth century. It was premised on the belief in a differentiation between women and men in work and lifestyle, with women restricted essentially to the private sphere of the home and family and men to the public sphere of the workplace.

British common law defined women as subordinate to their husbands, fathers, and even brothers. In the eyes of the law, husband and wife constituted one person — the husband. That meant a wife did not have the legal right to sign a "contract" or to run her own business without her husband's permission. A married woman did have the right of a dowry, a lifetime interest in one-third of her husband's property. But even when and where the law was operative, it only applied upon the death of the husband, and not in instances of separation or marriage breakdown. As well, it could be overridden, since the husband had the right to dispose of the family property to whomever he chose as heir, which in most cases was a son, or even a grandson or son-in-law over a wife or a daughter. Divorce was possible but difficult, since in Upper Canada it required a special act of the legislature.

Christian law criminalized abortion and forbade infanticide. The murder of a child was punishable by death, although the ruling was seldom applied. It was considered "criminal" to conceal the birth of a "bastard," a child born out of wedlock. As noted in *Canadian Women: A History*, all of the laws "affecting sexuality, marriage, and motherhood might be regarded as evidence of new kinds of intrusions into women's lives, as male lawgivers attempted to reinforce or reinterpret traditional male control over, as well as their protection of, women in a changing world."[2]

Despite such restrictions, some women played active roles in education and religion. Some became schoolteachers in tax-supported schools. By 1851, women constituted almost one-fifth of "common" school teachers in Upper Canada. They were most often in rural schools, where few male teachers were available, or in districts where financial restraints necessitated hiring a female teacher, since she could be hired for "half the price." Women were also active in the Sunday school movement and in missionary societies, both of which played a social and educational role. Women were still refused entry into medical and law schools, and into the ministry. A few women did preach and prophesy, especially in the evangelical religious denominations, but even here they could not become ministers because this would imply gender equality. The one possible exception consisted of Quaker women, considered separated from, but equal to men.

Some women were able to exercise their vote in general elections in the early nineteenth century in Upper Canada. But in 1849, a Reform government passed a law excluding women from the franchise in both the Canadas. Still, in the first half of the nineteenth century, politicians' wives played an active role "behind the scenes." Isabel Mackenzie, for example, fought as hard against the Tory elite as her husband, William Lyon Mackenzie, did. Women were also involved in distributing and signing petitions for political change. Women in Upper Canada exercised considerable social power, even if they lacked official authority.

ECONOMIC GROWTH AND CONSERVATION

The mass immigration of 1815–40 contributed to economic growth. During this period, Upper Canada became a thriving, complex, and viable society based on an exchange economy, both export and domestic, and financed by both capital and credit. The expansion rested to a large extent on wheat farming, although timber rivalled wheat as the major export staple of Upper Canada. In the Ottawa valley, with its rich forests of pine and oak and the region's easy access to the St. Lawrence, lumbering, not farming, became the primary industry. The timber trade was a by-product of farming, since settlers had to clear the forests before being able to farm the land.

The early settlers transformed the landscape of Upper Canada ecologically. In general, they had little interest in conservation or in the long-term management of land. They sought only to maximize short-term profits. Thus, they came to see the forests as a monolith to push back.

In the name of "progress," settlers and woodsmen cut down trees at an astonishing rate. A contemporary witness, journalist William Smith, noted the determination by which settlers cleared the Oak Ridges Morraine, north of Toronto: "the universal Canadian practice has been followed in clearing the land, that of sweeping away everything capable of bearing a green leaf. The new settlers look upon trees as enemies."

While such activity did result in a host of productive farms that greatly boosted the economy of Upper Canada, "progress" came at a price: the loss of a large segment of the eastern woodland forests and the plants and animals that lived in these wooded areas. Animals, from bears and deer to the passenger pigeon and the vole, were in retreat. So too were other species of birds and animals, as well as insects. Some areas cleared were at the headwaters of rivers, resulting in soil erosion that caused tonnes of silt to pour into streams that flowed into Lake Ontario. Thus, the water ecology was adversely affected, along with the fish and aquatic animals. Atlantic salmon, for example, lost their spawning grounds, and by the mid-nineteenth century no longer migrated in vast numbers up the St. Lawrence River. The last Atlantic salmon were caught in Ontario in the 1890s. (A century later, in 1988, the Ontario Ministry of Natural Resources began reintroducing the fish to Lake Ontario.)

By the 1850s, over one-third of the forested areas of southern Ontario had been destroyed. Within the next generation, three-quarters were gone, and by 1914 and the outbreak of World War I, over 90 percent.

TRANSPORTATION

Wheat and timber required transportation networks. Native trails soon became roads, giving greater accessibility. The settlers built road systems in the Huron Tract beside Lake Huron, in the Talbot settlement south of London, in the Ottawa valley and the Kingston area. Around

The Road between York and Kingston, Upper Canada, 1830, a watercolour by James Pattison Cockburn (1779–1847), a British army officer, shows the density of the early Upper Canadian forests.

National Archives of Canada/C-12632.

York, a road system was developed to link the capital to outlying regions dependent on it for trade. Canal-building followed.

The British government paid for Upper Canada's first megaproject: the Rideau Canal, to link Bytown (Ottawa) with Kingston for defence purposes. It was completed and opened for public use in 1832. The construction of the province's second megaproject, a canal bypassing Niagara Falls and linking Lake Ontario to Lake Erie, began at roughly the same time as the Rideau Canal. It opened, however, three years earlier, in 1829. The incentive behind construction of the Welland Canal was strictly commercial.

THE RISE OF A REFORM MOVEMENT

In the 1820s, Upper Canada became strongly polarized into conservative and reform camps. Led by the Family Compact, the conservatives favoured British monarchical association, appointed Legislative and Executive Councils, and a stable and hierarchical society free of any political opposition. Their ideology was premised on a strong central government. Economically, they favoured the construction of canals and the establishment of banks, both of which they believed would advance the commercial well-being of the province. The conservatives obtained strong support from the newly arrived middle- and upper-class British immigrants.

The Reform members of the Assembly opposed conservative policies and called for political change. They tended to be "late Loyalists," or recent poorer British immigrants who favoured an elected Legislative Council, or upper house, and an Executive Council that was responsible to the Assembly rather than to the governor. Economically, the Reformers favoured policies that promoted agriculture. In large measure they represented the farmers of the central and western areas of the province. They often opposed commercial enterprises such as canal building and banks, which they saw as being either expensive or of limited benefit to farmers.

Thus, there developed in the province a situation roughly parallel to that in Lower Canada. One could class many of the conservatives in both provinces as "reactionary" politically but "progressive" economically, and the Reformers as "radical" politically but "reactionary" economically.

THE MOVE TO REBELLION

In the mid-1830s, William Lyon Mackenzie, an important reform leader, gradually shifted to a Republican position. Mackenzie's views were not even representative of the majority of Reformers. A rift occurred by the mid-1830s between a moderate wing led by Robert Baldwin and a radical wing under Mackenzie. The moderates desired to preserve Upper Canada's allegiance to the monarchy and its ties to the British empire, and did not want the American form of elective government that Mackenzie advocated. Instead, they favoured the British plan of responsible government — a government responsible to the Assembly. To the moderate Reform politicians who had spent years trying to dissociate reform from republicanism, Mackenzie was an acute embarrassment.

Mackenzie and his followers underestimated entirely the strength of Upper Canadian conservatism, as well as the moderate Reformers' opposition to rebellion. In his recently created newspaper, *The Constitution*, begun symbolically on July 4, 1836, Mackenzie cited the American Revolution as justification for overthrowing the government. A group of his followers issued a Toronto Declaration closely modelled on the American Declaration of Independence.

Economic and social forces contributed to unrest in the province. In 1836, an economic downturn occurred throughout the western world. In Upper Canada, this recession led to tight bank credit and even a recall of loans, which hit farmers especially hard. Such action intensified

Mackenzie's already deep distrust of banks. News of the uprising of Lower Canadian Patriotes under Louis-Joseph Papineau further encouraged the rebels. By early November, no British soldiers remained in Upper Canada because they had been dispatched to quell trouble in Lower Canada.

THE UPPER CANADIAN REBELLION, 1837

In early December about 500 ill-clad and poorly armed rebels gathered at Montgomery's Tavern on Yonge Street (just north of present-day Eglinton Avenue in Toronto). Government supporters quickly defeated them. Mackenzie's ill-conceived and ill-fated rebellion was over. With a price on his head, he managed to escape to the United States, while some of his followers were captured.

From across the border, the rebel leaders planned further attacks on the government of Upper Canada. Mackenzie found support in the United States among those Americans who saw the rebellion as a Canadian version of the American Revolution — an attempt to end British tyranny. Other Americans saw the uprising as an opportunity for the United States to annex Upper Canada. Some American supporters simply saw participation in a counterattack as an opportunity for looting.

Small, unsuccessful attacks followed along the border. The most serious counterattack occurred at the Battle of the Windmill along the St. Lawrence River near Prescott, in November, in which 200 invaders barricaded themselves in an old windmill until they were forced to surrender. By the end of the Rebellion of 1837/38, the Upper Canadian authorities jailed more than 1000 people on suspicion of treason. Nearly 100 of them were sent to the convict settlements in Australia (more than 70 of these individuals were Americans) and twenty were hanged.

Where Historians Disagree
∼ The Causes of the 1837 Rebellion in Upper Canada

Amateur historians were the first to write about the Rebellion of 1837 in Upper Canada. They were both partisan and emotional in their approach because of their closeness to the incident in both time and circumstance. Charles Lindsey, the son-in-law of William Lyon Mackenzie, the leader of the rebellion, blamed the Family Compact's refusal to compromise for driving the moderate Mackenzie to rebellion. In a two-volume work on the rebellion, journalist-cum-historian J.M. Dent challenged Lindsey's view and depicted a diabolical and extreme Mackenzie who led the colony to an unnecessary struggle.[1] These amateur historians all believed that the cause of the rebellion was political — a classic struggle between "democracy" and "privilege." This was the Liberal interpretation of history that held sway in the late nineteenth and the early twentieth centuries. During the 1920s, when Canada was moving toward autonomy, a liberal-nationalist school of historical writing saw the rebellion as an attempt to gain independence from Britain. The rebellion became an important event on the road from "colony to nation."

In the midst of the economic upheaval of the Great Depression of the 1930s, an economic interpretation of the rebellion appeared. Historian Donald Creighton depicted the rebellion in Upper Canada as a struggle between agrarian interests, represented by Mackenzie and his followers, and commercial interests, which controlled the appointed Executive and Legislative Councils. "The rebellions were," Creighton wrote, "the final expression of that hatred of the rural community for the commercialism of the St. Lawrence."[2] Creighton bolstered his economic argument by pointing out that the rebellions broke out in Upper Canada after a succession of crop failures that had brought farmers to the point of starvation and bankruptcy.

Other historians have argued that economic distress was not really at the root of the rebellion. Historian Colin Read pointed out in *The Rebellion of 1837 in Upper Canada* that "the rebels were, for the most part, well-settled members of a reasonably prosperous agrarian society." He saw "no single cause or grand overriding explanation" for their participation. Short-term economic dislocation played a part, as did more individual motivations based on family loyalties or personal friendships and animosities: "So too did specific political grievances as well as the general reform perception that the world was ordered too much in the interests of the few, too little in the interests of the many."[3] The rebels' ignorance of the military strength of the loyalist militia also was a contributing factor, according to Read.

Intellectual historians depict Mackenzie as a man of ideas, who drew his inspiration and his direction from reform movements in both Britain and the United States, for greater public participation in government. They see the rebellion in Upper Canada as part of the general reform impulse. R.A.

MacKay notes: "Few public men in Canadian history have so represented the spirit of their age as did William Lyon Mackenzie, and particularly during the pre-Rebellion stage of his career... On both sides of the Atlantic the new wine of liberty and democracy was bursting the old bottles of restriction and privilege.... In the 1820's and 1830's William Lyon Mackenzie was the principal purveyor of these wines of liberty to the backwoods colony of Upper Canada."[4]

In the 1960s, social historians questioned whether the rebellion in Upper Canada was a class struggle. Marxist historian Stanley Ryerson interpreted the rebellion as a bourgeois-democratic revolution caused by oppression and led by men who were fighting for the cause of popular liberty. "Workers ... made up nearly half, and farmers over 40 per cent of the victims of oppression: a significant indication of the social forces that were engaged in action."[5] Fellow Marxist historian Leo Johnson saw the roots of the rebellion in an inequitable system of land grants designed at the time of Governor Simcoe to create a landed gentry class at the expense of the ordinary farmer. The rebellion was a fight between two different views of land ownership held by two different classes of people.[6]

Read challenges the image of the Upper Canadian rebellion as a "people's revolution." Using the less-known Duncombe uprising in the London area, Read concludes: "There is no basis for arguing that the rebels comprised a clearly disadvantaged sector of society and hence were driven to arms by economic despair or the prospect of plunder." What did distinguish rebels from loyalists, according to Read, was the large number of rebels who were either American-born or born to American parents and who "may well have retained or adopted the deep American dislike of

Britain and have been more willing to rebel, hoping to sever the provincial ties to Great Britain."[7] This ideological split was the real cause of the rebellion.

The debate continues, with no interpretation emerging as the definitive one. The net result, however, is a richer and deeper understanding of the decade of the 1830s in Upper Canada, out of which the Rebellion of 1837 arose.

[1] J. M. Dent, *The Story of the Upper Canadian Rebellion*, 2 vols. (Toronto: C. Blackett Robinson, 1885).

[2] Donald Creighton, *The Empire of the St. Lawrence: A Study in Commerce and Politics*, [1937]. Reprint with Introduction by Christopher Moore (Toronto: University of Toronto Press, 2002), p. 316.

[3] Colin Read, *The Rebellion of 1837 in Upper Canada* (Ottawa: Canadian Historical Association, 1988), p. 18.

[4] R.A. MacKay, "The Political Ideas of William Lyon Mackenzie," *Canadian Journal of Economics and Political Science*, 3 (1937), p.1.

[5] Stanley Ryerson, *Unequal Union: Confederation and the Roots of Conflict in the Canadas, 1815–1873* (Toronto: Progress Books, 1968), p. 131.

[6] Leo Johnson, "Land Policy, Population Growth and Social Structure in Home District, 1793–1851," *Ontario History*, 63 (1971), 41–60.

[7] Colin Read, *The Rising in Western Upper Canada, 1837–38: The Duncombe Revolt and After* (Toronto: University of Toronto Press, 1982), pp. 207, 208.

LORD DURHAM'S REPORT

The Rebellion of 1837 in Upper Canada was a minor affair from a military standpoint. Simply put, the populace of Upper Canada did not support revolution. But together with the more extensive uprising in Lower Canada, the troubles in Upper Canada convinced Britain of the need to investigate the causes of the unrest. The British cabinet sent out one of its most gifted politicians, Lord Durham, to inquire into the affairs of the colony and report back to the British government. Durham spent only five months in the Canadas, most of the time in Lower Canada. But he made one short visit to Upper Canada.

The Durham Report of 1839 made two very important recommendations: First, it advised that the colonial governor should choose his closest advisers, the members of the Executive Council, from the majority party in the Assembly and abide by the wishes of these elected representatives. Although Durham did not call this "responsible government," it nonetheless came to be known as such. Second, the Report recommended a union of the two Canadas. Durham saw such a union of the Canadas as the nucleus of an eventual amalgamation of all the British North American colonies, which he highly favoured, and as a necessary precursor to the assimilation of the French Canadians. The British government accepted union but rejected responsible government.

 By the terms of the Act of Union of 1840, the capital of the new province of Canada became Kingston. English was recognized as the only official language of the Assembly. The united province assumed Upper Canada's debt. And the Assembly consisted of 84 members — 42 from Upper Canada and 42 from Lower Canada. Upper Canada officially ceased to exist. Instead, the area became known as Canada West, part of a larger union of English and French Canadians.

Simcoe's years in Upper Canada marked the beginning of a new British American colony in the interior of the continent. Thanks largely to British military and First Nation support in the War of 1812 it escaped American conquest in the War of l812. The years 1815 to 1840 witnessed a transformation in Upper Canada. Large-scale immigration, chiefly from the British Isles, added some 300 000 people, greatly extended the areas of settlement, and gave the colony a decidedly Upper Canadian orientation, one that rejected violent political change and endorsed the imperial connection.

NOTES

1.   Janice Potter, "Patriarchy and Paternalism: The Case of the Eastern Ontario Loyalist Women," *Ontario History* 81 (1989): 20.
2.   Alison Prentice et al., *Canadian Women: A History*, 2nd ed. (Toronto: Harcourt Brace, 1996), p. 91.

LINKING TO THE PAST

The Mississaugas of the New Credit First Nation
http://www.newcreditfirstnation.com/past2.htm

An overview of the history of this First Nation from the early 1700s to the present.

The War of 1812 Website
http://www.militaryheritage.com/1812.htm

Links to many historical documents and articles about the War of 1812, as well as book reviews and information about British regiments.

Towards Confederation: Upper Canada (1791–1841)
http://www.nlc-bnc.ca/2/18/h18-2001-e.html

This site provides an overview of the period, including information on the 1837 rebellions. Follow the links for more material on selected topics.

Independence Declaration
http://freenet.victoria.bc.ca/history/etext/mackenzie.independence.declare.html

This site reproduces the text of William Lyon Mackenzie's proclamation to the people on the eve of the Upper Canada Rebellion of 1837.

The Union Act, 1840
http://www.solon.org/Constitutions/Canada/English/PreConfederation/ua_1840.html

The full text of the 1840 Union Act, which united Upper and Lower Canada to create the Dominion of Canada appears.

BIBLIOGRAPHY

The best overview of Upper Canadian society remains Gerald M. Craig, *Upper Canada: The Formative Years, 1784–1841* (Toronto: McClelland & Stewart, 1963). For a guide to the historical literature in general see Bryan D. Palmer, "Upper Canada," in M. Brook Taylor, ed., *Canadian History: A Reader's Guide*, vol. 1, *Beginnings to Confederation* (Toronto: University of Toronto Press, 1994), pp. 184–236. Peter A. Baskerville has written a useful overview of all of Ontario's history, *Ontario. Image, Identity and Power* (Toronto: Oxford University Press, 2001).

For information on the Loyalists who settled in Upper Canada see Bruce Wilson, *As She Began: An Illustrated Introduction to Loyalist Ontario* (Toronto: Dundurn Press, 1981); and Janice Potter-MacKinnon, *While the Women Only Wept: Loyalist Refugee Women in Eastern Ontario* (Montreal/Kingston: McGill-Queen's University Press, 1993). Economic issues are examined in Douglas McCalla's *Planting the Province: The Economic History of Upper Canada, 1784–1870* (Toronto: University of Toronto Press, 1993).

The experience of the Six Nations in early Upper Canada is reviewed in Charles M. Johnston, ed., *The Valley of the Six Nations: A Collection of Documents on the Indian Lands of the Grand River* (Toronto: Champlain Society, 1964). For a discussion of the Ojibwas see Peter S. Schmalz, *The Ojibwa of Southern Ontario* (Toronto: University of Toronto Press, 1990); Donald B. Smith, *Sacred Feathers: The Reverend Peter Jones (Kahkewaquonaby) and the Mississauga Indians* (Toronto: University of Toronto Press, 1987); and Janet Chute, *The Legacy of Shingwaukonse: A Century of Native Leadership* (Toronto: University of Toronto Press, 1998).

A short summary of the War of 1812 appears in Wesley B. Turner, *The War of 1812. The War That Both Sides Won,* 2nd ed. (Toronto:Dundurn, 2000). A fuller overview is Victor Suthren, *The War of 1812* (Toronto:McClelland & Stewart, 1999). Useful studies of the First Nations in the War of 1812 include John Sugden, *Tecumseh: A Life* (New York: Henry Holt, 1997); and Carl Benn, *The Iroquois in the War of 1812* (Toronto: University of Toronto Press, 1998).

Helen Cowan, *British Emigration in British North America: The First Hundred Years*, rev. and enlarged ed. (Toronto: University of Toronto Press, 1961) best describes the experience of immigrating to British North America from Britain. A shorter version is Helen Cowan, *British Immigration Before Confederation* (Ottawa: Canadian Historical Association, 1968). Two books which review the experience of African Canadians in Upper Canada include: Robin Winks's *The Blacks in Canada*, 2nd ed. (Montreal/Kingston: McGill-Queen's University Press, 1997); and Peggy Bristow et al., *"We're Rooted Here and They Can't Pull Us Up": Essays in African Canadian Women's History* (Toronto: University of Toronto Press, 1994).

Carol Wilton has written an important political study, *Popular Politics and Political Culture in Upper Canada, 1800–1850* (Montreal/Kingston: McGill-Queen's University Press, 2000). On the background to the Rebellions of 1837/38, William Kilbourn's biography of William Lyon Mackenzie, *The Firebrand* (Toronto: Clarke Irwin, 1956) is a lively account. Colin Read's *The Rebellion of 1837 in Upper Canada* (Ottawa: Canadian Historical Association, 1988) remains very useful.

For early maps of Upper Canada see R. Louis Gentilcore and C. Grant Head, eds., *Ontario's History in Maps* (Toronto: University of Toronto Press, 1984); and consult R. Louis Gentilcore, ed., *Historical Atlas of Canada*, vol. 2, *The Land Transformed, 1800–1891* (Toronto: University of Toronto Press, 1993). Valuable portraits of early Upper Canadian figures appear in the *Dictionary of Canadian Biography*, vol. 4, *1770–1800*; vol. 5, *1800–1820*; and vol. 6, *1821–1835* (Toronto: University of Toronto Press, 1979, 1985, 1987).

THE UNION OF THE CANADAS

TIME LINE

1840 –	The Union of the Canadas comes into effect
1846 –	Britain establishes free trade
1849 –	Lord Elgin sanctions the Rebellion Losses Bill; English-speaking protesters burn the Parliament building in Montreal
	Manifesto of the Annexation Association published
	The Anglican-affiliated King's College becomes the non-sectarian University of Toronto
1852 –	Toronto Stock Exchange opens
	Université Laval founded in Quebec City
1854 –	Emergence of the Liberal–Conservative alliance led by John A. Macdonald and George-Étienne Cartier
	Treaty of Reciprocity between British North America and the United States
1857 –	"Rep by Pop" becomes the main plank of Reform party's platform
	Ottawa selected as Canada's capital
1859 –	Completion of the Victoria Bridge over the St. Lawrence River at Montreal

The Act of Union adopted by the British Parliament in July 1840 joined the two Canadas, now renamed Canada East and Canada West. The union had a short but stormy life, which ended with the realization of a larger British North American Confederation in 1867.

Although ultimately a failure, the union could boast important successes. The government adopted laws providing for the education of children in both sections of the colony. As railway fever swept the nation's business community in the 1850s, solicitous politicians oversaw a multitude of costly construction projects. The railways transformed the agricultural, commercial, and urban character of the province. After Britain, the world's industrial pioneer, adopted free trade in the mid-1840s, the government fostered increased trade relations with the United States by negotiating a Reciprocity Treaty covering natural products. In 1854, it finally abolished the seigneurial system in Canada East and even found a solution to the contentious clergy reserves question in Canada West. According to political scientist S.J.R. Noel, "The overall record of governmental accomplishment compares favourably with that of any other era, either before or since."[1]

The union years also saw the end of constant feuding between the Legislative Assembly and the governor. Within ten years after the failure of the rebellions, London accepted the principles of responsible government. Henceforth, the governor governed less; his ministers, who were responsible to the Assembly, made decisions in his place. With the coming of responsible government, traditional elites were largely replaced by the new commercial and industrial elites, to whom many of the new brand of politicians were closely allied.

In addition, many English-speaking and some French-speaking Canadian historians argue that, in the Union period, French- and English-speaking politicians found common ground on which to co-operate in solving many major political questions. The need to construct a *modus vivendi* also helped restrain ethnic and religious bigotry.

FRENCH CANADIANS AND UNION

Britain originally intended to use union of the Canadas to punish the French and assure their subjugation, if not their eventual demise, as a linguistic group. Certainly the conditions of union constituted a severe blow for Lower Canada in general and for French Canadians in particular. English became the sole official language of parliamentary documents. The elective Assembly had an equal number of representatives from both halves of the colony, even though in 1841 the population of largely French-speaking Canada East was 40 percent greater than that of English-speaking Canada West.

The Act of Union also made Upper Canada's heavy debt burden the responsibility of the Province of Canada as a whole. Upper Canada could no longer by itself finance costly transportation facilities like roads and canals; only union with the virtually debt-free Lower Canada could strengthen its position. Union would bring in higher revenues because the United Canadas could raise tariffs, a measure that Lower Canada, where most goods from Europe entered, could no longer block. Pleasing Montreal's English-speaking merchants, it would also recognize that the two Canadas formed a common economic bloc.

LORD SYDENHAM

Charles Poulett Thomson, Lord Durham's successor as governor general of Canada in 1839, wanted to put Canada on a sound financial footing to attract development capital. He also hoped that substantial British immigration would diminish the political and economic influence of French Canadians. A masterful strategist, Thomson convinced most political groups in Upper Canada to agree to political union. He did not have to convince Lower Canada, which would have no say in the matter.

The union was officially inaugurated in Montreal on February 10, 1841. Most French Canadians, though, were defiant and bitter. They certainly had no reason to trust the assurances of the anti-French Thomson, now Lord Sydenham. Moreover, the union simply had too many elements that they found objectionable. Unyielding opposition appeared to be the only path open to them.

Well aware of French-Canadian hostility, Sydenham worked to assure the election of a maximum number of English-speaking members in Canada East by gerrymandering riding boundaries to eliminate French votes from certain districts and by staging polls in English localities situated far from French-speaking towns. He also used British troops as well as Irish construction labourers to intimidate French-speaking voters in the open voting (the secret ballot was established only in 1874). Not surprisingly, the governor won a comfortable working majority in United Canada's first legislature. Sydenham was now in a position to be his own prime minister.

Sydenham's heavy-handed tactics actually improved the chances for fruitful collaboration between Reformers in Canada East and Canada West. In Canada West, such prominent Reform leaders as Robert Baldwin assured former patriote Louis-Hippolyte LaFontaine in Canada East that, in return for co-operation in working toward responsible government, they would assist French-Canadian efforts to rid the union of objectionable features such as official English unilingualism. LaFontaine and most other French-Canadian leaders finally concluded that French Canada could obtain more by accepting union than by continuing to oppose it.

THE COMMERCIAL EMPIRE OF THE ST. LAWRENCE

 In 1937, historian Donald Creighton advanced the Laurentian interpretation of Canadian history. He argued that the economic life of British North America was based on "staple" trade, the production and exporting of a few "staple" resources such as fish, furs, timber, and wheat. The American Revolution brought an artificial political boundary along the St. Lawrence and the Great Lakes, dividing the northern portion of the North American continent into two political units. But the political boundary did not immediately become an economic one. Up to the mid-1840s, the British North American commercial bourgeoisie competed successfully against their American counterparts in New York and elsewhere, thanks to the highly favourable mercantile system of trade between the British North American colonies and Britain.

The British desired two staples readily available in the United Canadas: timber and wheat. British shipbuilders needed square-hewed timber, made from Canadian white and red pine, for the masts of sailing ships. Britain also wanted lumber for construction. Wood became British North America's most valuable export commodity, making up nearly two-thirds of the value of the colonies' exports to Britain by the 1840s. But the lumber industry remained vulnerable to fluctuating demand in Britain, reduced tariffs which aided lumber exporters in the Baltic region, and overproduction.

Within the Canadas, a second commodity — wheat — rivalled timber. After 1840, a combination of good weather and increased hectarage due to rapid settlement of the rich farmland of Canada West greatly increased total production. Improved transportation lowered costs and reduced insurance rates. Canada West became one of the chief suppliers of wheat to feed industrial Britain's growing urban population.

TRANSPORTATION

Exporting bulky staples such as wheat and timber required a sophisticated transportation system. Roads were needed to get wheat to urban centres for local marketing or export. By the early 1850s, a comprehensive road system linked Windsor to Montreal, with branches northward to towns on Lake Huron and to Bytown (Ottawa).

More important for transportation was the canal system linking Lake Erie with Montreal and the Atlantic Ocean. During the 1840s, the government widened and deepened existing canals such as the Welland and the Lachine to accommodate larger steamboats. It also built new canals, notably between Montreal and Prescott. The St. Lawrence–Great Lakes route now rivalled the Erie–Hudson River route, and Montreal could compete with New York as the major exporting and importing centre for the North American continent.

THE RISE OF A REFORM COALITION

Major political transformations also took place during the Union's first decade. In the early 1840s, Tories and Reformers stood out within Canada West's broad political spectrum. Basically, Tories vaunted their loyalty to the Crown and to the British connection. In their view, responsible government could only weaken ties with Britain because it challenged the authority of the colonial governor. Tory supporters included business interests, numerous professionals, and the many who benefited from government patronage. Many working-class Irish Protestant immigrants also supported the Tories: in return for Tory largesse, the Orange Order provided, notably in Toronto, the "votes and strong arms needed in the rough and tumble polling process of the day."[2]

Reformist ambitions were given a powerful boost by Lord Durham's endorsement of responsible government in 1839. In order to prove their loyalty, Reformists worked to place their demands within the framework of the British constitution and British traditions. That the Crown act in non-partisan fashion was accepted British practice, they asserted. They also reminded their opponents that party government existed in Britain. Reformists denounced the abuses linked to the government's distribution of patronage, although later, when they took power, they would prove themselves to be equally ardent practitioners in the art of dispensing favours.

An alliance between Reformers and French seemed natural, in view of the traditional political goals of both groups and the growing personal friendship between Baldwin and LaFontaine. It took time to establish this common front, however. Many so-called Reformers did not want to oppose the government, as the French Canadians had done, for fear of compromising the public-works projects promised for their districts by Sydenham. Only after Sydenham's death in 1841 did they return to Baldwin's leadership.

Sir Charles Bagot and Sir Charles Metcalfe, Sydenham's successors as governors, walked a tightrope in attempting to govern the colony without the aid of representatives of the French Canadians, who formed half the united province's population. Yet both were conservatives and strong believers in the British connection, and, in trying to appease the supposedly disloyal and rebellious French, they risked losing support among the English-speaking of both Canadas. In addition, the governors had difficulty persuading the British government to renounce at least any immediate hopes for assimilation of the French.

In 1845, Governor Metcalfe asked the British Parliament to amend the Act of Union to end the proscription of French as an official language. At first, the Colonial Secretary vehemently disagreed: the Act of Union was designed " to promote the amalgamation of the French and English races," he reminded the governor, and to authorize bilingualism would be to abandon this goal.

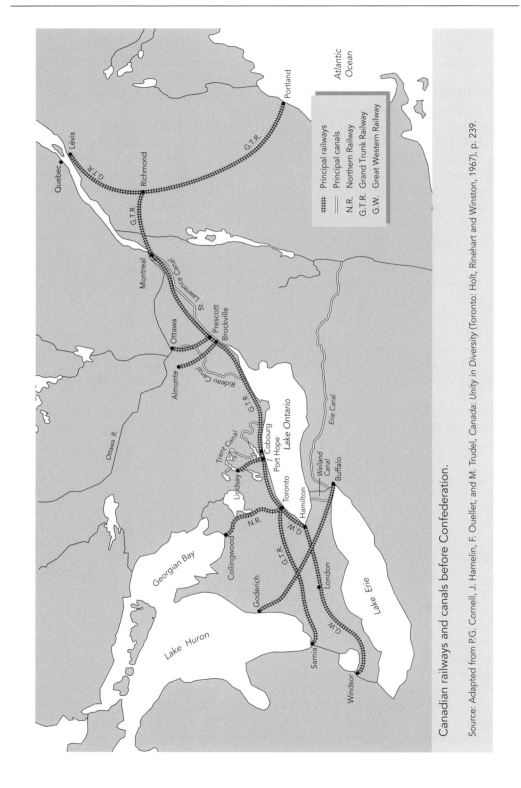

Canadian railways and canals before Confederation.

Source: Adapted from P.G. Cornell, J. Hamelin, F. Ouellet, and M. Trudel, *Canada: Unity in Diversity* (Toronto: Holt, Rinehart and Winston, 1967), p. 239.

Three years later, implicitly agreeing that its linguistic policy was unrealistic, the British government acted to give French official recognition.

THE ARRIVAL OF RESPONSIBLE GOVERNMENT

 The most important single factor in bridging the ethnic gulf during the 1840s was the arduous, but ultimately successful, struggle for responsible government. In 1840, recognition of this principle still appeared far off. The Act of Union concentrated enormous power in the hands of the colonial governor, appointed by London. The governor, in turn, appointed for life the members of the upper house, or Legislative Council. He could also reward his supporters, since he had the right to name a host of public officials. In Parliament he chose his advisers, dismissing and replacing them at will. He also held broad veto powers over bills adopted by the legislature. Yet, over the course of the union's first decade, the governor's powers were radically curtailed.

Responsible government came only after dramatic battles. The Colonial Office urged Canada's governors to avoid concessions lest Canada agitate for independence. But pragmatic governors such as Bagot, a diplomat, understood the necessity, in order to govern, of appointing an Executive Council that would have the support of a majority in the Assembly. Taking into account the growing power of the French bloc, he invited LaFontaine to join his council. When the latter shrewdly demanded that Baldwin, too, have a place, the unhappy Bagot again yielded.

GOVERNING IN THE CANADAS BEFORE AND AFTER RESPONSIBLE GOVERNMENT

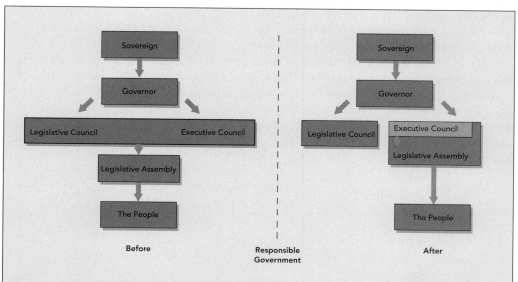

Before responsible government was introduced, the Legislative Assembly had no effective control over the Executive Council, on whose advice the governor relied. With the coming of responsible government, the Executive Council could remain in office only as long as it had the Legislative Assembly's support.

Source: Adapted from P.G. Cornell, M. Hamelin, F. Ouellet, and M. Trudel, *Canada: Unity in Diversity* (Toronto: Holt, Rinehart and Winston, 1967), p. 143.

Colonial administrators expressed the strongest regrets — to which Bagot replied that, had he acted otherwise, "Canada would have again become the theatre of a widespread rebellion, and perhaps the ungrateful separatist or the rejected outcast from British dominion." Despite Bagot's apparent recognition of the principle that he could only choose ministers who commanded the support of a majority of the members of the Assembly, no guarantee existed that the governor might not some day replace his advisers if he disagreed with them. Moreover, Bagot's government, consisting of a wide variety of personalities of various political hues, did not really constitute a ministry. Party government, though undeniably a little closer, had not yet come to the province.

Sir Charles Metcalfe, named governor in 1843, was determined to maintain the British connection. He did not intend to submit to LaFontaine, and he would certainly not commit himself to taking his advice. Not surprisingly, Metcalfe enjoyed little electoral success in Canada East, where LaFontaine had built up an effective political machine.

The moderate regime that governed the colony from 1844 until 1847, led by the eloquent Conservative "Sweet William" Henry Draper as attorney general for Canada West and virtual prime minister, succeeded in adopting several important pieces of legislation. True responsible government still did not exist, however. Although the Executive Council did have the confidence of the Assembly, the governor's powers remained very broad. Moreover, Draper's attempts to build significant French support failed utterly.

LORD ELGIN

The pace of events quickened with the arrival of Lord Elgin, the new governor general, in 1847. By this time Britain had moved toward laissez-faire liberalism and free trade, and saw little need to regulate colonies' trade relations. Indeed, the British government was now convinced that only colonial autonomy could hold the empire together, and it instructed Elgin to accept this principle and to behave in a strictly neutral fashion.

The elections of 1848 produced a strong majority for LaFontaine's group in Canada East and a significant majority for Baldwin's Reform movement in Canada West. The Reformers' victory achieved, Lord Elgin called on LaFontaine and Baldwin to form a government. Henceforth, the governor assented to legislation adopted by Parliament, unless he judged it contrary to the interests of Great Britain. Elgin proved as much in 1849 when he agreed to sign, despite personal reservations, the Rebellion Losses Bill, which compensated those who had lost property during the Rebellions of 1837–38 in Canada East (the question of losses in Canada West had been settled in 1845).

Elgin's action infuriated Montreal's Tories. Denouncing "French domination," a mob invaded Parliament and put it to the torch, then stoned Elgin's carriage, ransacked LaFontaine's house, and rampaged through the town. Canada West experienced considerable unrest, too. The Tories staged protest meetings to denounce the rewarding of "rebels" and "pardoned traitors," and thousands signed petitions demanding Elgin's recall. A Toronto mob burned Baldwin and Lord Elgin in effigy.

In spite of the violence that surrounded its coming, responsible government moved Canada forward along the road to democracy and political autonomy. For that reason, most historians have viewed its coming as a great milestone in Canada's history. The voters, through their elected representatives, would now exercise greater control over government — or at least the property-holding male portion would, for in 1849 the Reformers amended the election law to exclude women from the franchise. In spite of the common-law prohibition against female suffrage, a few women had voted in the past.

This painting by Joseph Légaré depicts the burning of the Canadian Parliament building in Montreal on the night of April 25, 1849. It is believed that rioters, protesting the passage of the Rebellion Losses Bill, smashed the gas mains, then set fire to the escaping gas. Earlier that day, crowds of English-speaking protesters had thrown stones and rotten eggs at Lord Elgin's carriage because the governor-general had sanctioned the bill. The riots lasted two days. Subsequently, it was decided that Montreal would no longer be the seat of government, and the capital alternated between Quebec City and Toronto.

McCord Museum of Canadian History, Montreal, M11588.

Perhaps more relevant to the politicians' daily preoccupations, responsible government also ensured that the leaders of the governing party would control patronage. Political scientist S.J.R. Noel asserts that the British resisted responsible government in part precisely because they "appreciated the central importance of patronage in the political process."[3] Another consequence of responsible government was to ensure a shift of power and influence away from conservative traditional elites and toward the new commercial and industrial classes. Business and politicians co-operated closely. In fact, a great many politicians were businesspeople who came to politics to advance both their personal interests and those of the business community. In this sense, it would be naive to claim that responsible government actually gave power to the common people. Yet business domination was not to go unchallenged, and elections did bring members of a variety of other groups to Parliament.

The achievement of responsible government did not put an end to close co-operation between French- and English-speaking politicians. It did signify the need to build new alliances. In the turbulent early 1850s, when the loosely organized Reform group split into moderate and radical factions, most French-speaking members of the Assembly, representing the moderate

Parti bleu, began to co-operate with Conservatives from Canada West to form governments. This coalition, symbolized by the close association of John A. Macdonald and George-Étienne Cartier, carried over into the post-Confederation period.

FIRST NATIONS IN THE CANADAS

The Act of Union (1841) omitted to make provision for "Indians," or even to provide for the payment of annuities for earlier land surrenders. Nor did the coming of responsible government improve the lot of Canada's Native peoples. Indeed, only in 1860 did the British government finally transfer all authority over "Indian affairs" to the Canadian legislature. Canadian politicians imposed even tighter control over the First Nations population of the Canadas, and Aboriginal people were given little opportunity to administer their remaining lands themselves. The government committed itself to a system of First Nations education, administered by Christian missionaries and based on model farms and industrial or residential schools, in order to bring about the eventual assimilation of the Native population.

Three Indian Chiefs and Peter McLeod Presenting a Petition to Lord Elgin, by Théophile Hamel (1848). On March 12, 1848, three Montagnais (Innu) chiefs from the Saguenay River, with their interpreter, Peter McLeod, met the governor general and presented their grievances. The newcomers had pushed Native peoples further and further into the interior, from Tadoussac, to Chicoutimi, to Lac St. Jean. In Canada East, unlike Canada West, the government did not conclude treaties with the resident First Nations. The British argued that the Royal Proclamation of 1763 had not designated the valley of the St. Lawrence and surrounding area as "Indian Territory."

Private collection/Photo courtesy of the owner.

THE ADVENT OF BRITISH FREE TRADE AND REPERCUSSIONS FOR THE UNITED CANADAS

In 1846, Britain adopted free trade. British factory owners wanted reduced tariffs to enable Britain to compete in a world market. They also sought the repeal of the Corn Laws (protective tariffs on grain), arguing that repeal would mean cheaper food for the industrial working class and hence an opportunity for employers to lower wages. At the same time, Liberal economists increasingly pointed out the costs, economic and military, of keeping colonies.

These free-trade lobbyists convinced Robert Peel's government to repeal the Corn Laws in 1846. Other free-trade measures included the progressive lowering of the timber preference. Then, in 1849, Britain repealed the Navigation Laws, which restricted trade with the colonies to British or colonial vessels.

THE ANNEXATION MOVEMENT

Many members of the commercial elites in the Canadas denounced Britain's move toward free trade because it signified an end to the imperial preferences which gave them, as exporters, an advantage in British markets. Britain's new trade policies helped push large sectors of Canadian commerce into depression. Shipping activity at Montreal declined precipitously. Bankruptcies spread. Some Tories did not hesitate to link their loyalty to economic opportunity. Finding none of the much-vaunted benefits of the British connection, they now campaigned for annexation to the United States.

Montreal became the hotbed of annexationist sentiment. In October 1849, the English-language press published the manifesto of the Annexation Association, signed by 325 citizens, many of them notable businesspeople, such as William Molson and John Redpath. Early in 1850 the formation of the Toronto Annexation Association, supposedly embracing "a large number of the most respectable merchants and inhabitants of this city," was announced. For many Tories, annexation was also a means to escape from so-called "French domination."

FRENCH CANADA AND ANNEXATION

French Canada also displayed some interest in annexation, though obviously for entirely different reasons. Louis-Joseph Papineau and others admired American democratic institutions and hated the Canadian union. Radical young intellectuals belonging to the Institut canadien, a literary and debating society in Montreal, also took up the annexationist cause. The movement, however, had no popular base, and other elites in French Canada vociferously condemned annexation. George-Étienne Cartier echoed conservative sentiment when he warned that American democracy signified "the will of the masses." The Roman Catholic clergy, for its part, feared that annexation would put an end to the liberty that it enjoyed under British rule.

In Canada West, annexationism, though noisy, made little headway. Opponents now suggested alternatives. In July 1849, Tories gathered at Kingston to launch the British-American League, which advocated tariff protection and a union of the British North American colonies. With the revival of prosperity in the early 1850s, annexationist sentiment waned. The Americans' unresponsiveness to annexationist tendencies north of the border hastened the movement's decline.

FROM TRANSATLANTIC TO TRANSCONTINENTAL TRADE

Despite the advent of British free trade, the Canadas neither collapsed nor joined the United States. Commerce soon revived as British North America adjusted to new challenges. Trade increased with the United States, assisted by the growth of railways. Just as the waterways had facilitated east-west trade across the continent and ultimately with Britain, railways best linked the Canadas and the United States for north-south trade. The transition from transatlantic to transcontinental trade had begun.

This transition came swiftly and dramatically. Industrialism in the United States led directly to an initial increase in markets for the Canadian staple products — timber and wheat. The rapidly growing cities of the eastern seaboard and of the American Midwest needed lumber to construct houses and commercial buildings, and wheat to feed a growing population. Grain prices tripled. As a result, agriculture surpassed timber as the major staple of all British North American trade in the 1850s.

The 1850s inaugurated what historian A.R.M. Lower described as "the North American assault on the Canadian forest."[4] As demand for Canadian lumber increased, American lumber firms and sawmill owners established themselves in Canadian forest areas, especially the Ottawa valley.

Equally, Canadian timber found a rising market in Canada West, with its growing immigrant population. Saw and planing mills, sash and shingle factories, and cabinet-making firms arose to serve this local market. Yet Britain still remained the most lucrative market for Canadian timber until into the 1860s.

Farmers in Canada West benefited the most from this increased demand for wheat. Good prices, along with high yields, provided them with capital to increase their hectarage and to diversify their farming. In addition to wheat, they exported wool, meat, eggs, butter, and cheese, especially to the United States. Farmers in Canada East did not fare as well. A shortage of good agricultural land, combined with problems of climate and fertility, meant that they produced little wheat for export. They did export other grains such as oats and barley, along with dairy products in limited quantities.

RECIPROCITY WITH THE UNITED STATES

To expand its lucrative trade with the United States, the Canadas wanted a reciprocal trade agreement. The British government endorsed the idea, as a means of easing tensions and reducing Canadian dependence on the mother country. At first, strong American protectionist sentiment prevented acceptance of the idea. The slavery issue in the United States was also an obstacle. Some northern senators favoured free trade because they now believed it a prelude to annexing the Canadas, which would lead to a preponderance of free states in the Union. Southern senators opposed it for the same reason, until Governor General Lord Elgin convinced them that a prosperous Canada through free trade would be better able to resist annexation to the United States.

Another roadblock to reciprocity concerned Maritime fisheries. Britain and the United States had different interpretations of the territorial waters in British North America from which American fishers were excluded under the Convention of 1818. Neither side wanted an armed conflict, and Britain was willing to use the fisheries issue as a negotiating tool for free trade of colonial natural products in the United States. In the end, Britain threatened to withdraw its patrol boats (which prevented American encroachment), unless Nova Scotia agreed to the treaty.

The Reciprocity Treaty of 1854, approved by the American Senate and ratified by the colonial legislatures, allowed for the free trade of major natural products, such as timber, grain, coal, livestock, and fish, between the British North American colonies and the United States. As well, it gave joint access to coastal fisheries. The agreement ran for a 10-year period commencing in 1855 and was subject to renewal or termination.

THE RAILWAY ERA

Closer economic ties with the United States coincided with the Canadian railway-building era. Increased Canadian–American trade provided the incentive for new rail lines and greater continental economic integration.

The first British North American railway, a 23-km line made of wooden rails that linked Montreal and the Richelieu River, was completed in 1836. But the real era of railway building occurred in the 1850s. By 1856, railways linked all the major urban centres in Canada West. Such expansion came as a result of the combination of popular interest, public and private financial support, and private promotion. One of the negative factors was the environmental impact. As new communities arose, both forests and land came under greater assault. The locomotive contributed greatly to the rapid disappearance of the white pine forests of the Canadas.

Governments eagerly courted railways. These "engines of progress" seemed worth the price even though they required huge expenditures of public funds. Most of the capital for railway building came from Britain and the United States. As the British North American colonies had insufficient credit ratings to borrow vast sums abroad, their governments inevitably became involved in railway financing.

Private companies built four key railway lines in the United Canadas in the 1850s. The St. Lawrence and Atlantic line between Montreal and Portland, Maine, completed in 1853, gave Montreal access to a year-round ice-free port on the Atlantic, and made the city once more competitive with New York in continental trade. The second line, the Great Western Railway, completed in 1855, went from Niagara Falls via Hamilton and London to Windsor. This line sought to capture the trade of the American Midwest by offering a quick route from Chicago through to New York by way of the Canadas. The third major line, the Northern Railway, which ran from Toronto to Collingwood, on Georgian Bay, serviced the rich farmland north of Toronto and opened up the forested area of the Georgian Bay and Muskoka regions. The fourth and most ambitious railway scheme of the decade was the Grand Trunk.

THE GRAND TRUNK RAILWAY

The Grand Trunk Railway originally was to run from Windsor, Canada West, to Halifax, Nova Scotia, thus linking the interior of British North America with an ice-free Atlantic port. When plans to build the Maritime section failed, the company purchased the St. Lawrence and Atlantic line, which ran between Montreal and ice-free Portland, Maine. The scheme proved costly, however, because the track needed major repairs. Equally expensive was the Grand Trunk's decision (taken after it failed in its attempt to purchase the Great Western) to build a competing line through the heart of Canada West from Toronto to Sarnia. As a result, the two railways often ran parallel to each other and serviced the same area.

George-Étienne Cartier, a government minister, proudly guided the Grand Trunk's charter through the Assembly. A prominent member of Montreal's business community, Cartier served as director of a host of banking, insurance, transportation, and mining companies. At the same time, he acted as solicitor for the Grand Trunk Railway and chaired the Legislative Assembly's Railway Committee. Many other politicians were closely linked with the railways and used their

Railway travel in the mid-nineteenth century could be challenging in the winter. A Grand Trunk Railway locomotive with snow-clearing machine, Lévis, Quebec, February 1869.

National Archives of Canada/PA-149764.

positions in government to attempt to assist their companies with tax concessions, loan guarantees, the assumption of bad debts, and outright grants. They exhibited few scruples about combining personal and state interests. None of today's conflict-of-interest legislation existed at that time.

In 1859, the Grand Trunk completed the Victoria Bridge, one of the great engineering feats of the century. This 2700-m bridge spanned the St. Lawrence at Montreal. The railway itself, with 1760 km of track, became the longest in the world. This distinction came at great cost to the Canadian public. From the beginning, the company ran into financial trouble, leading its London bankers to approach the provincial government for help. The government agreed to bail it out. To make matters worse, this trunk line had little success in tapping American markets. In the 1850s and 1860s, the Grand Trunk Railway never made a profit.

Moreover, railways in the 1850s and 1860s were unsafe. One accident in 1854 killed 52 people and injured 48. Railway historian G.R. Stevens noted: " Every railway operation seemed to be conducted in a casual and dangerous manner."[5] In a number of derailments the engine drivers had spotted livestock on the line, but instead of slowing down, they speeded up, trying to knock them off the tracks. Signals were ignored, and maintenance of the roadbed was neglected.

POLITICS IN THE 1850s

After 1850, with responsible government a reality, tensions arose between moderate and radical Reformers in Canada West on such issues as political reform, railway policy, financial affairs, and church–state relations. The radical Reformers, called "Clear Grits" ("grit" being American slang for firmness of character), denounced Montreal business interests, actively promoted agrarian democracy, and, under journalist George Brown's leadership, became vocal champions of "rep by pop," or representation according to population, the implication being that Canada West, with its larger and rapidly increasing population, deserved a greater number of seats — and, therefore, a preponderant influence over government policy — than did francophone Canada East.

At the same time, in Canada East, the Parti rouge gained ground. The *rouges* tended to be somewhat anti-clerical, republican, strongly nationalistic, and highly critical of the close links between government and business. The governing coalition now sought support from conservatives and moderates and as a result, in 1854, the so-called Liberal-Conservative alliance emerged, jointly led by John A. Macdonald and George-Étienne Cartier.

A CAPITAL IS CHOSEN

In the 1850s, politics often seemed divorced from the everyday concerns of common people. The difficulty of choosing a seat of government or a capital for the united province symbolized this apparent detachment. Political, ethnic, and geographical rivalries transformed the issue into one of the most divisive confronting the union. After 1849, with the burning of the Parliament building in Montreal, the seat of government shifted between Toronto and Quebec City. Eventually, the Assembly appealed to Queen Victoria to choose a permanent capital. In 1857, it was announced that Ottawa would become the capital.

URBAN AND COMMERCIAL DEVELOPMENT

The railways promoted commercial development. They attracted foreign investment. They employed thousands of workers to lay and maintain track. New railway-related industries sprang up across the province — engine foundries, car shops, rolling mills, and metalwork shops — that all needed skilled and unskilled workers.

Along with canal building and shipbuilding, railways encouraged the development of a host of secondary industries: flour mills, saw mills, tanneries, boot and shoe factories, textile shops, breweries, distilleries, and wagon and carriage manufacturers. Shipbuilders in Montreal and Quebec City built many of the steamboats that plied the St. Lawrence River and the Great Lakes. Ironworks were established in Hamilton because of the city's easy access to the American coal fields in Pennsylvania. Significant developments in the manufacturing of agricultural implements occurred, especially in Newcastle, Canada West, where Daniel and Hart Massey produced a combined rake, reaper, and mowing machine in 1855, marking the beginning of a lucrative Canadian industry.

This industrial growth led to the creation of a host of towns, especially along the rail lines in Canada West, to service the prosperous agricultural hinterland. Each provided a market centre for local produce and an import centre for manufactured goods. London became the major centre in southwestern Canada West. Hamilton developed as an early industrial city whose port dominated the hinterland to the west and south, extending its influence into the Niagara peninsula.

Toronto enjoyed a central location and good harbour facilities on Lake Ontario. As the railway hub of Canada West, it also serviced a wealthy rural hinterland. Its leading commerce, the import trade, quintupled in value between 1849 and 1856. A new urban mercantile elite appeared in the 1850s. In 1852 the Toronto Stock Exchange opened. By the end of the decade, the city had become the undisputed regional business centre of Canada West.

Montreal remained the largest city and dominant metropolitan centre in British North America. Its location on the St. Lawrence gave it a great advantage over inland Toronto, especially after the canal improvements of the 1840s. The completion of the Grand Trunk Railway provided the city with an ice-free port on the Atlantic at Portland, Maine, and access to the agricultural hinterland of Canada West. Montreal also benefited from the Reciprocity Treaty of 1854, which helped it become a major export centre of Canadian timber and wheat for American markets.

SOCIAL DEVELOPMENTS

Annually, 25 000 to 40 000 immigrants entered the Canadas, especially the western section, whose population surpassed that of Canada East by 1851. Overall, the population of the Canadas nearly doubled to 2 million between 1841 and 1851.

Many new immigrants came from Ireland, fleeing the famine that resulted from the failure of the potato crop. Recent research by historian Donald Akenson shows that the great majority of Irish immigrants farmed on isolated homesteads in rural areas rather than settling in urban ghettos. Furthermore, most were Protestant.

THE "UNDERGROUND RAILWAY"

Between 30 000 and 40 000 African Americans also came to the Canadas by 1861. The passage of the Fugitive Slave Act in the United States in 1850 meant that thousands of presumably free African Americans living in the northern states were liable to be captured and sent back into bondage. Instead, many escaped to the Canadas by way of the Underground Railway — a secret, complex network of free blacks, former slaves, and white American and Canadian abolitionists. The largest number of slave fugitives crossed at Amherstburg, situated at the narrowest point of the Detroit River. Other major "terminals" included Windsor, Hamilton, Toronto, and Kingston.

Community Portrait

⇚ The Orange Community in Toronto's Cabbagetown

Formed by Irish Protestants in Ireland in 1795, the Orange Order spread rapidly throughout Ireland and England. In 1830, the Grand Lodge of British North America was organized. By 1870 Canada had more than a thousand Orange Lodges, many in Toronto. Although the Orange Order's membership was spread across all neighbourhoods, Cabbagetown, or East Toronto, an important destination point for Irish Protestant immigrants, boasted the greatest number of Lodges in the city.

The growth of railways and industries in Toronto created large numbers of jobs. In the 1840s, after immigrants spread along both sides of King Street East, they settled on the vacant land to the north. There the newcomers built squatters' shacks and planted vegetable gardens, hence the district's name, " Cabbagetown."

The largely working-class neighbourhood, close to the adjacent factories and packing houses, soon became the home of a vibrant Orange community. Not only Irish immigrants but also English and Scots assisted the spread of the organization. While the bulk of the membership came from the working class, the Toronto Orange community crossed class lines and had a significant middle-class component.

The Orange Lodge celebrated the British Crown and Protestantism. It opposed Catholic schools and the use of the French language outside Quebec. But in the British Protestant fortress of Victorian Toronto, Irish Catholics, not French Canadians, constituted the resident minority group. As John McAree, a prominent Toronto journalist, wrote in *Cabbagetown Store*, his memoir of Cabbagetown: "Catholics were generally

Twelfth of July Orange parade along King Street in Toronto, 1874.
Toronto Reference Library/T13222.

spoken of as Dogans, a term of contempt... They were considered as foreign as if they had been Italians, and were viewed with suspicion." In mid-nineteenth-century Toronto, Protestants outnumbered Catholics by three to one. Clearly religion, not "race," was the focus of opposition of the Order.

The cohesion of Cabbagetown's Orange community came from a system of secret rituals, an internal hierarchy of five "degrees," and the public celebration of July 12th, the date of William of Orange's ("King Billy's") victory at the Battle of the Boyne. The Catholics' defeat in 1690 led to the Protestant minority's maintenance of its domination of Ireland. In the nineteenth century, and well into the twentieth, Cabbagetowners, on "the Glorious Twelfth," crammed with thousands of other Torontonians along downtown streets to catch a glimpse of "King Billy" on his white horse in the Orangemen's huge parade, their counterpart to the St. Patrick's Day celebrations.

Some sparring did occur between the Orange community of Cabbagetown and the residents of predominantly Catholic Corktown, located south of Queen Street. In the late 1860s, the militant Orange Young Britons arrived to strengthen the Orange community. John McAree describes this group "made up of husky, strutting young men, mechanics and labourers who were extremely provocative. They would parade frequently and always made it a point of invading a neighbourhood east of Parliament Street and south of Queen Street where there was quite a Roman Catholic settlement. These parades always wound up in fist fights and the throwing of stones."

The Orange community in Cabbagetown assisted its members and their families. It served as a social club, and a mutual aid society, which the lower classes could afford to join. Lodge members helped each other in times of sickness. A primitive insurance system existed to cover burial costs and even to provide lump-sum payments to widows. Orangemen also helped fellow members in the community to find work.

Further Reading

J.M.S. Careless, "The Emergence of Cabbagetown in Victorian Toronto," in Robert F. Harney, ed., *Gathering Place: Peoples and Neighbourhoods of Toronto, 1834–1945* (Toronto: Multicultural History Society of Ontario, 1985): 25–45.

Cecil J. Houston and William J. Smyth, *The Sash Canada Wore. A Historical Geography of the Orange Order in Canada* (Toronto: University of Toronto Press, 1980).

Gregory S. Kealey, "The Orange Order in Toronto: Religious Riot and the Working Class," in Michael J. Piva, ed., *A History of Ontario: Selected Readings* (Toronto: Copp Clark Pitman Ltd., 1988): 71–94.

J.V. McAree, *Cabbagetown Store* (Toronto: The Ryerson Press, 1953).

One of the most famous "conductors" — as those who helped lead slaves to freedom were termed — was the former slave Harriet Tubman. In all she made nineteen trips to the South, bringing out at least 300 slaves, and successfully evading all her would-be captors.

MIGRANT MOBILITY IN THE CANADAS

Within Canada West, people moved frequently. In a case study of rural Peel County, just west of Toronto, social historian David Gagan has shown that prior to 1840 the county had ample

Harriet Tubman (far left) with some of her "passengers" from the Underground Railway.

Schomberg Center for Research in Black Culture, the New York Public Library, Astor Lennox and Tilden Foundations/SC-CN-92-0675.

cheap land and a relatively self-sufficient population of farmers.[6] Two decades later, it had become a major wheat exporting region. Young people moved away from the now overpopulated country areas, to newer farming areas within the province, to the growing towns and cities of Canada West, or even to the American Midwest. Those who remained tended to be better off, with larger farms, a higher standard of living, and better-educated children than those who left. Transiency also characterized urban centres. Individuals of all social groups and classes moved frequently, hoping to improve their living conditions.

In Canada East, continued high birth rates increased the population. By the 1840s, however, existing land was depleted, new agricultural land was scarce, seigneuries were subdivided to the point where the habitants could no longer support their families, and unemployment was high in the urban centres. Large numbers of people began to migrate, in search of industrial jobs in New England or of new farmland in the American Midwest.

The departure of French Canadians for the United States alarmed the Roman Catholic clergy, who feared that migrants would lose their language and their religion. In an effort to stem the exodus, the church urged the colonization of regions further north. These efforts enjoyed some success, but emigration continued. In recognition of this fact the church sent many priests to minister to New England's French-speaking communities.

URBAN STRUCTURE IN CANADA WEST

Within the towns and cities of Canada West, a fairly rigid social structure existed. A growing commercial middle class, consisting of merchants, shopkeepers, and artisans, led society, socially and politically, and was joined by a rising male professional class of clergy, lawyers, doctors, and teachers. Middle-class women were expected to stay at home, where they performed domestic duties and reared children.

Below the professional class stood wage labourers, many of them immigrants. This urban proletariat suffered from poor housing, inadequate sanitation, and seasonal unemployment. Most relied on their own resources to survive. The prevailing ethos held that success came to those who worked hard; frustration and failure were the result of a lack of individual initiative. Canada West thus remained a society modelled on the agrarian values of hardy "yeoman farmers" and robust, self-reliant pioneers. Many working-class families hired out their children for additional family income; other families expected young children to take responsibility at home while older children and the parents worked outside the home.

URBAN DEVELOPMENT IN QUEBEC

Only two urban centres claimed the title of "city" in Canada East in the 1850s: Montreal and Quebec City. Quebec was the centre of the timber trade. The majority of its commercial elite were English-speaking families associated with that trade. Many of the city's numerous labourers, who inhabited the city's Lower Town, also worked in the timber industry. Here, in overcrowded and dirty conditions, French-Canadian and Irish workers intermingled. In contrast, the Upper Town, where the English lived, was considered "one of the cleanest cities in the world."

Montreal was the largest and the most industrialized city in British North America. As factories were built in the 1840s and 1850s, employment prospects attracted workers from the countryside. By the 1860s, the French-speaking population once again outnumbered the English-speaking in Montreal. These French Canadians, along with the Irish immigrants, provided cheap labour for the new industries, among them footwear manufacturers, furriers, wood-products manufacturers, distilleries, breweries, tobacco factories, brickyards, and sugar refineries.

The eastern end of the city remained overwhelmingly working class and predominantly French Canadian. Poor sanitation resulted in high mortality rates. The city's west end, however, was decidedly bourgeois and British. The English-Canadian commercial entrepreneurs had begun to build luxurious residences on the slopes of Mount Royal. Historian Paul-André Linteau argues that "social divisions became so visible in Montreal's industrial sector that the city earned the fitting description 'City of wealth and death'."[7]

Poor working-class families in the city often abandoned their children to the Grey Nuns' Foundling Hospital. Many soon died as a result of their weakened condition upon arrival and the lack of pasteurized milk. The Roman Catholic church also looked after the several thousand Irish orphans whose parents died on the Atlantic crossing. Raised as French Canadians, they intermarried with that group.

A WORKING-CLASS CONSCIOUSNESS

Industrialization stimulated the development of a working-class consciousness in the Canadas, as impersonal working conditions, due to the expansion of the factory system, became the norm. From the 1830s, skilled and semi-skilled workers joined together to form local trade unions and self-help organizations to deal with changing conditions. With definite skills to offer employers, they enjoyed far more job security than did labourers. Generally speaking they preferred strikes as a weapon while unskilled workers had recourse to spontaneous rioting.

Labourers organized two early strikes: one on the Lachine Canal in 1843, and the other on the Welland Canal in 1844–45. In both cases, they demanded improved working conditions and higher wages. In 1849, during the protests over free trade, shoemakers in Montreal ravaged a shoe factory and destroyed the sewing machines, in the tradition of the British Luddites, who opposed the mechanization of industry. By the 1860s strikes had generally replaced riots as the main form of labour protest, although they, too, were illegal. (Even trade unions were illegal until 1872.) Police or troops often assisted employers in quelling labour unrest.

The Prohibition Movement

The rise of an urban working class had an impact on the prohibition movement throughout British North America. By the 1850s, there was a noticeable shift in emphasis from temperance — abstinence through self-discipline — to outright prohibition. Social historian Graeme Decarie suggested that this shift in Canada West came about as a result of a perceived threat to traditional rural Protestant middle-class values from the growing urban working class (often made up of Irish Catholics). Prohibition became a means for some middle-class Protestants to reassert their position of power and prominence.[8] Quebec's great "apostle of temperance" was Charles Chiniquy, a lively and eccentric Roman Catholic priest, who persuaded thousands to take the pledge of abstinence. (Sexual escapades and charges of embezzlement later led to Chiniquy's excommunication from the Roman Catholic church.)

Religion

Religion played an important role in Canadian society. In Canada West, in the 1840s, the Church of England was the declared church affiliation of one-fifth of the population. The Presbyterians and Methodists followed closely, and then the Baptists. Roman Catholics, mainly Irish immigrants, comprised 14 percent of the population in 1841.

This shift in focus of churches from rural to urban meant a shift in emphasis from evangelicalism and an emotional approach to religion to an educated clergy and a more rational approach to faith. As well, urban-oriented society required churches to address issues of social reform with regard to such groups as the poor and the sick.

In Canada East, Ignace Bourget, Roman Catholic bishop of Montreal, successfully encouraged French religious orders to come to Quebec to help "Christianize" his diocesans. He also founded new indigenous male and female orders that took responsibility for elementary education, the classical colleges, hospitals, and charitable organizations. Bourget was an advocate of ultramontanism, the belief that the state should be linked to and dominated by the church. To this end, he worked to ensure that education remained under the control of the church instead of coming under state control.

Education and Culture

In the mid-nineteenth century, education entered public debate. Schools multiplied to keep pace with the growing population, and the question of separate schools became a contentious issue in Canada West.

State-supported schools developed in the union period. In Canada West, legislation created the office of superintendent of education to oversee educational matters and established local boards of education with powers to tax inhabitants to build and maintain schools. Opposition to the bill arose among those who argued that public funds should also be used to support separate schools for Roman Catholics, just as they were to support Protestant schools in Quebec. The votes of the French-Canadian members for Canada East gave the supporters of separate schools in Canada West the majority they needed in the Assembly to ensure that such schools received state funding.

At the heart of the separate-school controversy lay the question of the role of education. Roman Catholic leaders believed that education should have a religious component and that religious instruction should be in keeping with the teachings and beliefs of the Roman Catholic church. Opponents of separate schools, such as Egerton Ryerson, who served as superintendent of education for Canada West (Ontario) from 1844 to 1876, and George Brown, the influential political reformer and newspaper editor, argued that education should be free, publicly funded, and non-sectarian. They believed that separate schools perpetuated sectarianism and undermined the common-school system. The debate between these two approaches to education continued throughout the nineteenth century.

Separate and common schools proliferated in the 1850s and 1860s. A Roman Catholic separate-school system came into being, with tax support from parents, who were exempt from paying common-school taxes. In 1863, a final pre-Confederation education bill allowed separate schools to receive a share of both the provincial and municipal grants, and extended separate schools into rural areas. In return for these concessions, separate schools, like their common-school counterparts, submitted to provincial inspection, centralized control of curriculum and textbooks, and government control of all teacher training. This system remained in effect when Canada West entered Confederation as the province of Ontario in 1867.

Common or public schools also came under greater centralized control as a result of Ryerson's efforts. His Common School Act of 1846 established a board of education responsible for assisting the chief superintendent in establishing provincial standards, founded a normal school to train teachers, and made locally elected school boards responsible for operating the schools in their sections. These schools were expected to teach children good moral values — that is, Christian values — as well as to prepare them for work in an expanding commercial economy. Ryerson believed a centralized and highly regulated system could best achieve these goals. Here lay the foundation of the modern Ontario school system.

A similar process of secularism occurred in higher education. In 1849, the government changed the Anglican-affiliated King's College into the non-sectarian University of Toronto. Once King's College had been transformed into the "godless" University of Toronto, John Strachan, Anglican Bishop of Toronto, founded Trinity University. (Later Trinity, the Methodists' Victoria University, and St. Michael's, a Roman Catholic college, all became affiliates of the University of Toronto.)

EDUCATION IN QUEBEC

In Canada East, the Lower Canadian School Act of 1846 provided for two state-aided school systems, one Catholic and one Protestant. Within each Catholic school in Canada East, the local priest had the right to veto the selection of teachers and textbooks, thus leaving only the task of financing the schools to the provincial authorities.

Later, the legislature established a normal school to educate teachers, and set up the Council of Public Instruction to assist the superintendent in making regulations for the normal school, for the organization and administration of common schools, and for the grading of schools and teachers.

At the university level, the English-language McGill University, chartered in 1821, gave instruction in law, medicine, and the arts. Under the guidance of its able principal, William Dawson, McGill later acquired a distinguished reputation, especially in scientific research and medicine. In 1852, Université Laval was founded, having developed out of the Séminaire de Québec, founded by Bishop Laval in 1663. Steeped in the French Catholic tradition, the first French-Canadian university soon gained a position of respect in Canada East, with its courses in theology, civil law, medicine, and the arts.

CULTURE IN THE CANADAS

With the growth of towns and the rise of an urban middle class, the range of cultural activities expanded. In Canada East, François-Xavier Garneau wrote a monumental *Histoire du Canada* as a direct response to Lord Durham's denunciation of French Canadians as a "backward people." Octave Crémazie was the greatest French-Canadian poet of the period, popular for his nostalgic references to the glories of New France. Good-quality newspapers existed, and journalists and public figures gave popular lectures on important topics of the day such as education and nationality. In 1843 newspaper editor Ludger Duvernay organized the Société Saint-Jean-Baptiste de Montréal, a patriotic organization established to promote the interests of French Canada.

Literature in English developed slowly. Poetry became popular during the 1860s. William Kirby described the migration of Loyalists to Niagara in his poem *The U.E.L.*, while Charles Sangster captured the beauty of the Canadian landscape in *The St. Lawrence and the Saguenay*. Other writers included Susanna Moodie and her sister Catharine Parr Traill, both of whom obtained publishers, and a readership, in Britain. Amateur historians wrote in praise of early pioneers. However, no significant publishing industry existed until the late nineteenth century.

In 1855 John McMullen, a journalist, produced the first history of Canada in English. McMullen sought to "infuse a spirit of Canadian nationality into the people generally." Newspapers, among them Toronto's *Globe*, helped cultivate a national feeling among English Canadians.

In the mid-nineteenth century, Canada's urban music life expanded, although few Canadian-born professional musicians could support themselves with only their performances and teaching. Growing prosperity also enlarged the market for artists. Well-known painters included Cornelius Krieghoff and Napoléon Bourassa. By 1860, William Notman of Montreal had already established his reputation as a photographer.

TOURISM AS A FORM OF POPULAR CULTURE

In popular culture, areas of wilderness began to take on special significance as tourist spots, often in juxtaposition to what was meant by their opposite — civilization — in the Victorian mind. As the wilderness began to be "conquered" and thus lost its threatening nature, as Aboriginal people became more "civilized" and declined dramatically in numbers, and as landscape became imbued with a sense of the romantic and sublime, tourism emerged as a "growth industry." Historian Patricia Jasen notes, "The tourist industry was an ally of many forms of economic development in the nineteenth century, such as the growth of railways and steamer companies, and all of these industries were intimately associated with the gospel of expansionism, whereby the fate of the 'unsettled' regions of Canada was identified with the interests of the metropolis."[9] Tourism was, however, the preserve of the upper- and middle-classes. Only they had money and leisure time.

Niagara Falls, above all other tourist attractions, became a special place, attracting as many as 40 000 visitors a year by the late 1840s. From the beginning, Niagara Falls became associated with sexual pleasure, especially as "the Honeymoon Capital of the World." Historian Karen Dubinsky has shown how the "purity" of the Falls, its gendered nature as a female icon, evident in such descriptions of the Falls as "the Queen of the Cataracts," and the fact that the observer of such beauty was usually depicted as a male, "enhanced the spectatorial pleasure of 'doing' Niagara."[10] Already in the mid-nineteenth century, tourist agents realized the importance of identifying natural sites as places of pleasure, especially sexual pleasure.

During the 1840s and 1850s, the United Canadas underwent considerable economic and social change. Canadians adjusted to the end of the mercantile system of trade, to the advent of the railway age, and to rapidly changing social conditions in both rural and urban life. This was an age of transition from a British-oriented to an American-oriented economy and from a pioneer to a commercial society. The shift took decades to complete, but it saw its start in the period 1840 to 1860. Culturally, a French-Canadian identity already existed, but beside it an Upper Canadian or English-Canadian collective identity continued to take shape.

Politically, the coming of responsible government represented a significant milestone in the movement toward democracy and autonomy. For the French, in particular, the dire prophecies of assimilation made at the birth of union did not materialize, though ethnic and religious prejudice remained rampant throughout the era. Chronic political instability helped seal the fate of the union. By 1864, the Canadas were thus once again in the throes of constitutional change.

Notes

1. S.J.R. Noel, *Patrons, Clients, Brokers: Ontario Society and Politics, 1791–1896* (Toronto: University of Toronto Press, 1990), p. 175.
2. Peter Way, "The Canadian Tory Rebellion of 1849 and the Demise of Street Politics in Toronto," *British Journal of Canadian Studies* 10 (1995): 10.
3. Noel, *Patrons, Clients, Brokers*, p. 151.
4. See A.R.M. Lower, *The North American Assault on the Canadian Forest* (Toronto: Ryerson Press, 1938).
5. G.R. Stevens, *Canadian National Railways*, vol. 1 (Toronto: Clarke Irwin, 1960), p. 110.
6. David Gagan, *Hopeful Travellers: Families, Land and Social Change in Mid-Victorian Peel County, Canada West* (Toronto: University of Toronto Press, 1981), pp. 20ff.
7. Paul-André Linteau, "Montreal: City of Pride," *Horizon Canada* 4 (1984): 88.
8. Graeme Decarie, *Prohibition in Canada*, Canada's Visual History Series, vol. 29, Canadian Museum of Civilization, p. 3.
9. Patricia Jasen, *Wild Things: Nature, Culture, and Tourism in Ontario, 1790–1914* (Toronto: University of Toronto Press, 1995), p. 152.
10. Karen Dubinsky, " 'The Pleasure is Exquisite but Violent': The Imaginary Geography of Niagara Falls in the Nineteenth Century," *Journal of Canadian Studies* 29, 2 (Summer 1994): 75.

Linking to the Past

Union and Responsible Government
http://www.canadiana.org/citm/themes/constitution/constitution11_e.hmtl

A description of political developments from the impact of the Durham Report to the introduction of responsible government, with links to original documents and document summaries.

St. Lawrence River
http://greatcanadianrivers.com/rivers/stlawer/stlawer-home.html

Explore the environmental, economic, political, and cultural importance of the St. Lawrence, from the time of Jacques Cartier to the present.

Self-Government and Federal Union (1841–1867)
http://www.canadianheritage.org/books/canada7.htm

A discussion of responsible government, social changes during this period, and the push for a British North American Union.

Grand Trunk Railway
http://www.nlc-bnc.ca/2/18/h18-2997-e.html

A brief history of the railway. For other resources, consult The Ontario Railway History Page at http://web.globalserve.net/~robkath.

George Brown
http://www.nlc-bnc.ca/2/18/h18-2309-e.html

A brief biography of George Brown, with links to other relevant topics.

Fugitives for Freedom: The Black Community in the History of Quebec and Canada
http://www.qesn.meq.gouv.qc.ca/mpages/unit3/u3toc.htm

An overview of the history of the Underground Railway and black settlements in Canada, including brief biographies of Josiah Henson, Harriet Tubman, and others.

BIBLIOGRAPHY

The union years are examined in J.M.S. Careless, *The Union of the Canadas: The Growth of Canadian Institutions, 1841–1857* (Toronto: McClelland & Stewart, 1967); and W.L. Morton, *The Critical Years: The Union of British North America, 1857–1873* (Toronto: University of Toronto Press, 1964). Economic history is examined in Fernand Ouellet, *Economic and Social History of Quebec, 1760–1850* (Toronto: Macmillan, 1980); and Douglas McCalla, *Planting the Province: The Economic History of Upper Canada, 1784–1870* (Toronto: University of Toronto Press, 1993). Donald G. Creighton develops the Laurentian thesis in *The Empire of the St. Lawrence: A Study in Commerce and Politics* [1937]. With a new introduction by Christopher Moore (Toronto: University of Toronto Press, 2002).

On agriculture, see John McCallum, *Unequal Beginnings: Agriculture and Economic Development in Quebec and Ontario until 1870* (Toronto: University of Toronto Press, 1980); and Serge Courville and Normand Séguin, *Rural Life in Nineteenth-Century Quebec* (Ottawa: Canadian Historical Association, 1989). A.R.M. Lower reviews the timber trade in *Great Britain's Woodyard: British America and the Timber Trade, 1763–1867* (Montreal/Kingston: McGill-Queen's University Press, 1973). On railway building in the 1850s see G.P de T. Glazebrook, *A History of Transportation in Canada*, vol. 1 (Toronto: McClelland & Stewart, 1964).

Urban and commercial development is discussed in Jacob Spelt, *Urban Development in South-Central Ontario* (Toronto: McClelland & Stewart, 1972 [1955]); and G. Tulchinsky, *The River Barons: Montreal Businessmen and the Growth of Industry and Transportation, 1837–1853* (Toronto: University of Toronto Press, 1977). R. Cole Harris and John Warkentin, *Canada Before Confederation* (Ottawa: Carleton University Press, 1991 [1974]), provide an overview of social developments in the United Canadas. Books on minority groups include Donald H. Akenson, *The Irish in Ontario: A Study in Rural History* (Montreal/Kingston: McGill-Queen's University Press, 1984); and Robin W. Winks, *The Blacks in Canada*, 2nd ed. (Montreal/Kingston: McGill-Queen's University Press, 1997).

Biographies of political figures include Donald G. Creighton, *John A. Macdonald: The Young Politician* (Toronto: Macmillan, 1956); and J.M.S. Careless, *Brown of the Globe*, 2 vols. (Toronto: Macmillan, 1959 and 1963). On the development of the state see Allan Greer and Ian Radforth, eds., *Colonial Leviathan: State Formation in Mid-Nineteenth-Century Canada* (Toronto: University of Toronto Press, 1992). Works on political culture include Jane Errington, *The Lion, The Eagle, and Upper Canada: A Developing Colonial Ideology* (Montreal/Kingston: McGill-Queen's University Press, 1987); and A.B. McKillop and Paul Romney, eds., *God's Peculiar Peoples: Essays on Political Culture in Nineteenth-Century Canada* (Ottawa: Carleton University Press, 1993). British policy toward Canada is discussed in Phillip Buckner, *The Transition to Responsible Government: British Policy in British North America, 1815–1850* (Westport, CT: Greenwood Press, 1985); and Ged Martin, *Britain and the Origins of Canadian Confederation, 1837–67* (Vancouver: University of British Columbia Press, 1995).

The First Nations' history is reviewed in Daniel Francis, *A History of the Native Peoples of Quebec, 1760–1867* (Ottawa: Department of Indian Affairs and Northern Development, 1983); and Edward S. Rogers and Donald B. Smith, eds., *Aboriginal Ontario: Historical Perspectives on the First Nations* (Toronto: Dundurn Press, 1994). Women's history is covered in Alison Prentice et al., *Canadian Women: A History*, 2nd ed. (Toronto: Harcourt Brace, 1996); and Micheline Dumont et al., *Quebec Women: A History* (Toronto: Women's Press, 1987). On the history of the working class consult Paul Craven, ed., *Labouring Lives: Work and Workers in Nineteenth-Century Ontario* (Toronto: University of Toronto Press, 1995).

Educational questions are treated in J.D. Wilson, R.M. Stamp, and L.P. Audet, *Canadian Education: A History* (Scarborough, ON: Prentice-Hall, 1970). On religion see John Webster Grant, *A Profusion of Spires: Religion in Nineteenth-Century Ontario* (Toronto: University of Toronto Press, 1988). Cultural aspects of the era are reviewed in George Woodcock, *The Century That Made Us: Canada, 1814–1914* (Toronto: Oxford University Press, 1989). Jan Noel examines the temperance movement in *Canada Dry: Temperance Crusades before Confederation* (Toronto: University of Toronto Press, 1995).

Portraits of leading individuals in the Canadas appear in the *Dictionary of Canadian Biography*, now available online at www.biographi.ca. Excellent maps of the Canadas may be found in R. Louis Gentilcore, ed., *Historical Atlas of Canada*, vol. 2, *The Land Transformed, 1800–1891* (Toronto: University of Toronto Press, 1993).

PART THREE

BEYOND THE CANADAS, TO 1864

In Nova Scotia, a dominant English-speaking society emerged after the deportation of the Acadian population in the mid-1750s. A group of New Englanders, known as the Planters, moved north in the post–Conquest era to settle in Nova Scotia. By the beginning of the American Revolution, over 60 percent of Nova Scotia's population consisted of New Englanders. Initially, it seemed that Nova Scotia might join the revolution as the fourteenth American colony in 1775–76; instead, it remained neutral.

When the Loyalists arrived in the immediate post-revolutionary period, most settled in the Saint John River valley. They appealed to the British government for their own government, free from the control of Halifax. Britain complied with the creation of the new colony of New Brunswick in 1784 for the newly arrived Loyalists. Prince Edward Island had enjoyed separate colonial status since 1769. Cape Breton, a separate colony since 1784, would join Nova Scotia in 1820. Newfoundland would only formally be constituted a colony in 1824.

Between 1815 and 1867, distinct British American colonial communities emerged in northeastern North America. In New Brunswick — predominantly Acadian on the north shore and English-speaking in the Saint John River valley — the economy was based on agriculture and lumbering. In Nova Scotia, seaport communities grew along the Bay of Fundy and the Atlantic seaboard. Fishing, shipbuilding, and agriculture in the Annapolis Valley, were the main occupations. Independent communities also developed on Cape Breton Island (which was joined to Nova Scotia in 1820) and Prince Edward Island. The Maritime colonies and Newfoundland pursued an active trade with Britain, the United States, and the West Indies.

In these Maritime colonies, as in the Canadas, conflict erupted between the ruling political elite and the elected members of the Assembly, although it never reached the point of rebellion. But, by the 1850s, each of the Maritime colonies had achieved a form of responsible government.

Newfoundland remained separate and distinct from the other Atlantic colonies. The island's economy was heavily dependent on the cod fisheries of the Grand Banks and on active trade with Britain and the West Indies. The political system evolved slowly in Newfoundland. As late as 1830, no legislature existed and the naval governor had near-dictatorial powers. In 1832, Britain instituted representative government, with an elected Assembly and an appointed Legislative Council, but then suspended it in 1842, due to political deadlock. Representative government was reinstated in 1848 and responsible government implemented in 1855, thus ending direct British rule.

In the Northwest, a community known as the Red River colony emerged at the confluence of the Red and Assiniboine Rivers. It consisted of French Métis (children of French fur traders and First Nations women), the "Country-born" (offspring of British fur traders and First Nations women), and a small number of descendants of the Selkirk settlers who arrived from Britain in the early nineteenth century. The colony's economy was based on a mixture of trade in buffalo hides and small-scale agriculture. Tensions arose within the community in the 1810s when the two rival fur-trading companies, the Hudson's Bay Company and the North West Company, vied for dominance. In 1821, the British government forced them to amalgamate, as the Hudson's Bay Company. The Company attempted to enforce a monopoly of the fur trade, but in the 1840s the Métis resisted, thus strengthening their own identity as a "new nation."

On the north Pacific coast, Britain and the United States competed for control of the area known as Oregon Territory, until they agreed to occupy it jointly. In 1846, the two countries further agreed to extend the boundary from the Rockies along the 49th parallel to the coast, with Britain acquiring all of Vancouver Island.

With the discovery of gold in the Fraser River valley in 1858, Britain created a separate colony on the mainland. In 1866, the mainland colony and Vancouver Island were united into the joint colony of British Columbia, with Victoria as the capital. By the late 1860s, British Columbians had to choose among three future options: remaining a British colony, joining the United States, or becoming part of Canada.

To the north, the land remained in Aboriginal control, visited only by a small number of fur traders and, in the Arctic waters in the mid-1840s and 1850s, by explorers searching for the Northwest Passage.

ATLANTIC CANADA, 1760–1864

TIME LINE

1759–1760 – The Planters from New England begin arriving in great numbers in Nova Scotia

1767 – St John's Island, named Prince Edward Island in 1799, is granted by lottery to British proprietors

1784 – New Brunswick and Cape Breton (to 1820) are established as separate jurisdictions

1824 – Newfoundland is made a regular British colony

1829 – The last known surviving Beothuk, Shawnadithit, dies

1848 – Responsible government is achieved in Nova Scotia, and later in Prince Edward Island (1851), New Brunswick (1854), and Newfoundland (1855)

1854 – The Reciprocity Treaty with the United States is signed

1864 – The governments of New Brunswick, Nova Scotia, and Prince Edward Island agree to meet in Charlottetown to discuss Maritime union

After the British conquest of Canada, the Thirteen Colonies moved toward independence. The United States, however, would not include all of British North America. Nova Scotia, the new colony of Saint John's Island (created in 1769 and renamed Prince Edward Island in 1799), Newfoundland, and the former French colony of Quebec remained part of the British empire.

Britain easily maintained control of the small, isolated colony of Saint John's Island, with its settler population of only 1000 recent British arrivals and Acadians. As for Newfoundland, its Anglo-Irish population looked eastward to Britain rather than southward to the Thirteen Colonies. In contrast, over half of Nova Scotia's approximately 20 000 inhabitants came from New England. They maintained strong economic and cultural ties with their former homeland. Nova Scotia, which then comprised the whole of present-day Nova Scotia and New Brunswick, faced a difficult decision concerning which side to support in the American Revolution. Initially, it looked as if Nova Scotia might become the fourteenth insurgent colony, but it chose to stay in the British empire in 1775–76, and it did so again in the War of 1812.

In the early nineteenth century the population of Atlantic British North America lived widely scattered in isolated coastline communities and forested valleys, with only a few larger centres, such as St. John's, Saint John, Halifax, and Fredericton. Economically, Newfoundland remained dependent on the fisheries. But the full development of the land-based resources in the Maritimes began in the early nineteenth century. On the eve of Confederation, Nova Scotia, New Brunswick, and Prince Edward Island had healthy economies based on agriculture, fish, forest products, and trade with the West Indies.

The half-century following the Napoleonic Wars also witnessed major political developments. By the 1850s, Nova Scotia, New Brunswick, Prince Edward Island, and Newfoundland had achieved responsible government; with the Executive Council (Cabinet) in each colony drawn from the majority party in the Assembly, and responsible to it. Power now passed to the elective branch of government.

NEW ENGLAND'S OUTPOST

With the deportation of the Acadians in 1755 and the capture of Louisbourg in 1758, Americans began moving north. The British authorities wanted to attract loyal Protestant settlers in order to prevent the deported Acadians' return. In crowded, heavily settled southeastern Massachusetts, eastern Connecticut, and Rhode Island, the invitation had great appeal among the poorer farmers. Hundreds of fishers anxious to locate closer to the Grand Banks also came. These New England farmers and fishers became known as the Planters. Between 1759 and 1767, some 8000 Planters from New England settled in Nova Scotia. Most of the immigrants went to the Annapolis valley in peninsular Nova Scotia, to fertile lands previously cleared and diked by the Acadians, and to the area around Cumberland, near present-day Sackville, New Brunswick. A much smaller number entered the Saint John River valley, forming small frontier communities at the mouth of the river and at Maugerville (just south of present-day Fredericton), along the lower Saint John River. On account of the difficult conditions a number of the recent arrivals returned to their homes in New England in the 1760s.

The Planters who remained worked to create a new English-speaking Nova Scotia. But the lack of roads linking the settlements prevented regular communication. As historian George Rawlyk noted, "on the eve of the American Revolution, Nova Scotia was little more than a political expression for a number of widely scattered and isolated communities."[1] Nevertheless, on the eve of the American Revolution, New Englanders constituted about half of Nova Scotia's total population of nearly 20 000.

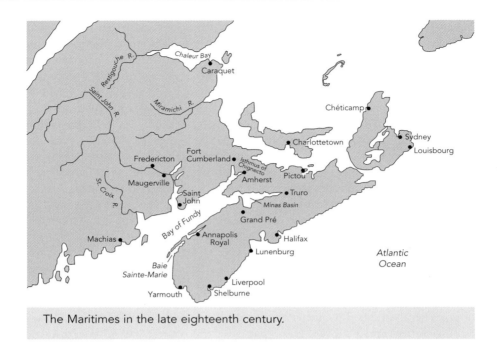

The Maritimes in the late eighteenth century.

Americans were still migrating to the forested lands north of the Bay of Fundy when hundreds of Acadians returned. In 1764, the British government permitted them to settle in Nova Scotia, providing that they dispersed throughout the colony. Many returned not to their farms, which were now occupied by New Englanders, but to the Bay of Chaleur, on the present-day border between Quebec and New Brunswick. The settlement of Caraquet became a focal point for the region. Other Acadians lived on farms along the lower Saint John River.

Several thousand British immigrants came to Nova Scotia in the 1760s and 1770s. They joined the original British residents of Halifax, the 1500 or so Acadians who had returned, and the approximately 1500 "foreign Protestants," largely Germans, who resided south of Halifax in the area around Lunenburg.

NOVA SCOTIA AND THE AMERICAN REVOLUTION

Halifax, as Nova Scotia's only urban centre, became the colony's capital. It housed the military establishment and published the province's only newspaper. The upper level of Halifax society, headed by the governor, included his senior officials, and a group of merchants who had grown rich from army and navy contracts. A handful of smaller merchants and professional people also lived in the colony's capital. The rest of the city's population consisted of poor fishers, carpenters, mechanics, and labourers. Nova Scotia obtained an elected assembly in 1758, but few rural members could afford to take their seats as unpaid legislators. As a result, a small clique of Halifax merchants controlled both the Assembly and the Governor's Council.

The rebellion rhetoric in the Thirteen Colonies in 1775–76 found an audience in rural Nova Scotia. Many New Englanders resented Britain's unfulfilled promises of constitutional rights. At annual town meetings, New England voters elected their officers and decided local issues. But in Nova Scotia in the 1760s, this form of township democracy did not exist; instead, London built a tightly controlled, centralized government structure. The merchant-controlled

Assembly in Halifax, which strongly supported the governor, worked to eliminate local township government. It appointed justices of the peace to administer the local areas and did not allow the election of township officials.

The communities farthest from Halifax showed the greatest enthusiasm for the American cause. The town of Machias, on the vaguely defined border between Nova Scotia and Maine, the Maugerville settlement on the lower Saint John River, and the Chignecto–Cumberland region at the head of the Bay of Fundy became active centres of support for the American Revolution. Jonathan Eddy, a New Englander who farmed in the Chignecto region, took the lead in organizing the revolutionary movement there. His invasion force of about 180 men attacked British-held Fort Cumberland in 1776. But they had no artillery to mount a siege. Few New Englanders on the isthmus openly supported Eddy's small, poorly trained, undisciplined, and badly led army. With the arrival of British reinforcements, Eddy's troops fled in disarray. The British burned the homes and barns of his supporters. The following summer, British naval vessels entered the Bay of Fundy and took control of the area. The Americans' lack of a navy and their failure to win sufficient support among Nova Scotians best explain Britain's success in expelling the revolutionaries.

FIRST NATIONS AND ACADIAN RESPONSES

The British also obtained the neutrality of most of the thousand or so Mi'kmaqs and Maliseets who held the balance of power north of the Bay of Fundy. By now the British had adopted the French techniques of gift diplomacy, giving their Native allies presents of food, medicine, and ammunition. In addition, Britain appeared to be the stronger of the two opponents after it extended its control over the Bay of Fundy and captured the coastline of northern Maine from the Americans. Thanks to the First Nations, the upper Saint John River valley remained in the British zone of influence throughout the war. The Acadians, for their part, had no interest in becoming involved in the civil war between the two English-speaking groups.

GROWING ANTAGONISM TOWARD THE AMERICAN REVOLUTIONARIES

While the American insurgents consolidated their hold on the former Thirteen Colonies, Nova Scotia moved in a different direction. American raids on Nova Scotia made many once-sympathetic Nova Scotians antagonistic to the American revolutionaries. No Nova Scotia port (except Halifax) escaped the raiders, who seized anything they could carry away. These attacks alienated wealthy citizens in Yarmouth, Lunenburg, and Liverpool, and prompted them to launch their own retaliatory attacks against American shipping. By 1781, settlements in the Minas Basin and the Bay of Fundy area, which in 1775–76 had opposed increased taxes for military defence, now willingly accepted militia service and taxes to meet the cost of defending the colony.

HENRY ALLINE AND THE NEW LIGHT MOVEMENT

The unwillingness of many New Englanders in Nova Scotia to support the American Revolution can also be explained by a great religious revival in the colony led by a charismatic young man named Henry Alline. In the late 1770s and early 1780s, a religious gospel rather than a political one monopolized the attention of Nova Scotians.

Born and raised in Rhode Island, Alline belonged to the Congregational church, the church to which most New England immigrants in Nova Scotia adhered. In 1760 his family settled in one of the richest farming areas in the colony — the Minas Basin, near present-day Windsor. The 12-year-old received no further schooling, for no school existed in his township. Nor was there a church. Families maintained their religion through family prayer, Bible reading, and religious discussions at home. But Alline came into contact with an evangelical group that emphasized the need for an intensely emotional conversion experience known as the "New Light."

In 1776, at the age of 28, Alline began his career as an itinerant preacher. Convinced that God had selected him to carry His message, he travelled constantly. The evangelist often rode as far as 80 km a day, bringing religion to rural people. His willingness to preach under all conditions struck a responsive chord among the economically impoverished rural Nova Scotians on their frontier farms. They heard Alline and believed him when he told them that Nova Scotia had become the new centre of Christendom.

Alline's religious revival filled the spiritual vacuum in the new settlements far away from the revolutionary struggle. Very effectively, he spread his message that good Christians should work to secure their spiritual salvation rather than to fight military battles. He convinced many Nova Scotians that they were performing a special role — bringing the world back to God — and that Christ merited their allegiance, not the British or the revolutionaries. As a result, Nova Scotia's "New Light" communities chose political neutrality and worked instead to perfect their spiritual condition.

Alline died of tuberculosis in early February 1784, leaving behind scores of disciples and hundreds of followers. After his death, his manuscript journals were copied and recopied by hand and circulated among his followers until they were published in 1806. Alline's disciples, popularly referred to as Allinites, later became members of the Baptist church and carried on the teachings of the "Apostle of Nova Scotia."

THE NEW ENGLAND LOYALISTS

Throughout the Thirteen Colonies, a substantial number of Americans opposed the American Revolution and wanted to remain loyal to Britain. Historians now estimate that approximately 20 percent of the white American population in 1776 (roughly half a million people) became Loyalists.[2] They were strongest in New York, partly because New York had a strong British aristocracy, and weakest in Connecticut, Massachusetts, and Virginia. Loyalists came from every class, race, occupation, religion, and geographical region. They supported Britain for many diverse reasons, ranging from personal loyalty to the Crown to a fear that the revolution would threaten individual freedoms.

Loyalists who served as colonial office holders had a vested interest in maintaining the status quo. But a high proportion of Loyalists also came from religious and cultural minorities. Not yet having joined mainstream American society, recent immigrants from Europe (Germany, the Netherlands, and the British Isles) and members of religious minorities (such as the French Huguenots, Maryland Roman Catholics, and Quaker pacifists) held on to the British connection for fear that increased American power could result in a loss of their religious freedoms. The First Nations, particularly the Iroquois, looked upon Britain as the lesser of two evils, since Britain wished to slow the advance of the American settlers westward, anxious as it was to avoid the increased expenditures of more wars with the Native peoples. African Americans saw an opportunity to free themselves by joining the British and fleeing their owners.

PERSECUTION OF THE LOYALISTS

Persecution of the Loyalists began as early as 1774, when it became more and more difficult to maintain neutrality in face of the approaching struggle. With the passing of the Declaration of Independence, the local revolutionary committees stepped up their activities against Loyalists. Various states disenfranchised, put in prison, banished, and fined "Tories" and confiscated their

Where Historians Disagree

❧ Why Didn't Nova Scotia Join the American Revolution?

On the eve of the American Revolutionary War in 1775–76, about half of Nova Scotia's 20 000 settlers were New Englanders. The colony appeared to be a northern outpost of New England. Why, then, did it refuse to join the revolution?

Historian Beamish Murdoch offered the first explanation. New England farmers, who had been given land previously owned by the Acadians when they arrived after the Conquest, were, as a result, "full of intense loyalty and affection to the British government."[1] Some 70 years later, in the 1930s, Professor Viola Barnes added an economic motive: Halifax merchants and Governor Francis Legge kept Nova Scotia loyal to the Crown because it was in their best interest to do so. When the Americans boycotted West Indies trade, Halifax merchants saw their opportunity to appropriate the trade themselves. "In short," she wrote, "Nova Scotia remained loyal because the merchant class in control believed the Province profited more than it lost by the connection with the mother country, and because the Governor, with their help, was able to prevent the radicals from stirring the people to revolt."[2]

Other historians now entered the fray. Professor W.B. Kerr challenged Barnes's interpretation. He questioned why Nova Scotia merchants would object to New Englanders carrying a monopoly of their trade, since they were New Englanders themselves. Furthermore, they were free to pursue their own trade if they so desired. Kerr then offered his own explanation, "the almost total want of sympathy among artisans, fishermen, and farmers for the American cause." Furthermore, the Nova Scotia legislature, made up of a majority of New Englanders, expressed their loyalty to the king on the eve of the revolution, acknowledging him to be the "supreme Legislature of the province and it is our indispensable duty to pay a due proportion of the expense of this great Empire."[3] Nova Scotia historian D.C. Harvey added yet another explanation: Nova Scotians "were inclined to submit to the will of the stronger."[4] Simply put, British naval power surpassed that of the rebels.

In 1937, noted historian J.B. Brebner argued that geographical isolation, as well as close economic ties to Britain through mercantile trade, kept Nova Scotia insulated from activities elsewhere on the continent. As he concluded: "Nova Scotia had insulated and neutralized the New England migrants so thoroughly that as Nova Scotians they had henceforth to look eastward to London for direction and help rather than southward to Boston as they had done in the past."[5]

Beginning in the 1940s, historians became interested in religious revivalism as a factor in keeping Nova Scotians neutral. M.W. Armstrong saw the "Great Awakening" (as this revival was called) as "an expression of democratic ideals and spiritual independence" that raised the minds of Nova Scotians above worldly concerns. How could "King George" and the revolution compete with "King Jesus" and redemption, he queried?[6] In 1959, sociologist S.D. Clark applied Frederick Jackson Turner's frontier thesis to an understanding of Nova Scotia's neutrality during the revolution.[7] He saw the New Light religious revival in the outposts of

Nova Scotia as a frontier movement of social protest that strengthened the spirit of local autonomy and resolved their determination to be politically independent of both Britain and its Halifax political agents, and New England.

Professors Gordon Stewart and George Rawlyk introduced their "Missing Decade" thesis. They argued that those New Englanders who migrated to Nova Scotia in the early 1760s missed the rebellious rhetoric that occurred between 1765 and 1775. Therefore they could not identify with their arguments.[8] Rawlyk then went on to explore the role of Henry Alline, the charismatic leader of the religious revival in Nova Scotia, in keeping Nova Scotians neutral. Rawlyk argued that Alline's message to Nova Scotia "Yankees" that they had a divine mission "to lead the world back to God" gave them a purpose above and beyond that of worldly revolution.[9]

More recently, J.M. Bumsted has questioned both the size and the importance of the New England population in Nova Scotia during the American Revolution. He argues that as the war got underway, Nova Scotia "Yankees" who supported the rebel cause returned to New England and therefore played no part in Nova Scotia's decision. As well, the strong British military presence in the colony, and resentment among Nova Scotians at the destructive behaviour of the American rebels within the colony, kept them neutral.[10] The question as to why Nova Scotia did not become the fourteenth state continues to intrigue historians.

---

[1] Beamish Murdoch, *History of Nova Scotia or Acadie*, vol. 2. (Halifax, N.S.: J. Barnes, 1865–67), p. 562.

[2] V.F. Barnes, "Francis Legge, Governor of Loyalist Nova Scotia, 1773–1776," *New England Quarterly*, July 1931, quoted in George A. Rawlyk, ed., *Revolution Rejected, 1775–1776* (Scarborough, ON: Prentice-Hall, 1968), pp. 32–33.

[3] W.B. Kerr, "The Merchants of Nova Scotia and the American Revolution," *Canadian Historical Review* 33 (1932): 22.

[4] D.C. Harvey, "The Struggle for the New England Form of Township Government in Nova Scotia," *Canadian Historical Association Report* (1933): 22.

[5] John Bartlet Brebner, *The Neutral Yankees of Nova Scotia* (Toronto: McClelland & Stewart, 1969), p. 310.

[6] M.W. Armstrong, "Neutrality and Religion in Revolutionary Nova Scotia," *New England Quarterly* (March 1946): 57–58.

[7] S.D. Clark, *Movements of Political Protest in Canada, 1640–1840* (Toronto: University of Toronto Press, 1959).

[8] Gordon Stewart and George Rawlyk, *A People Highly Favoured of God* (Toronto: Macmillan, 1972).

[9] G.A. Rawlyk, *Ravished by the Spirit: Religious Revivals, Baptists, and Henry Alline* (Montreal/Kingston: McGill-Queen's University Press, 1984).

[10] J.M. Bumsted, "1763–1783: Resettlement and Rebellion," in P.A. Buckner and J.G. Reid, eds., *The Atlantic Region to Confederation: A History* (Toronto: University of Toronto Press, 1994), pp. 156–83.

---

property as well. In Loyalist-controlled areas, outrages were also committed against, and restrictions of civil liberties imposed on, those believed to be supporters of the revolution.

The decisive battle of the revolutionary war was fought on October 19, 1781, when Britain's Lord Cornwallis surrendered his army of 7000 at Yorktown, Virginia. As the war now neared its end, the British evacuated southern ports such as Wilmington, Charleston, and Savannah, to which the Loyalists had fled for protection. Persecution reached new levels. Several of the newly independent states subjected the Loyalists to double and triple taxation, and Congress encouraged the states to confiscate their property. Physical violence against Loyalists continued. It became clear that Britain had to do something for them. The British continued to hold New York City and Long Island, and many Loyalists (at one point, 30 000) assembled there, awaiting evacuation.

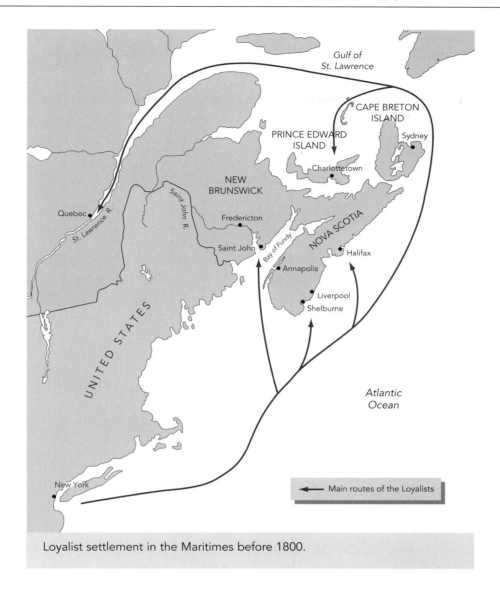

Loyalist settlement in the Maritimes before 1800.

At the peace negotiations, the American commissioners agreed that no further persecutions of Loyalists would take place. But while Congress urged the states to grant restitution and amnesty, it had no power to enforce its requests. Except in one or two states, every clause in the Treaty of Paris relating to the Loyalists was abrogated. When news of the preliminary peace reached the United States in the spring of 1783, the proscriptions, confiscations, and harassment of Loyalists began again.

THE GREAT LOYALIST MIGRATION TO NOVA SCOTIA

The exodus of thousands of Loyalists and their families began even before the peace treaty. Traditionally, the number of exiles has been estimated at 100 000, but this figure is probably inflated. Historians Wallace Brown and Hereward Senior believe that British North America received more than 50 000 white, black, and First Nations Loyalists. The British Isles received approximately 10 000, several thousand went to the British West Indies, and a small number (mainly Germans), returned to the Rhine valley. The overwhelming majority of the Loyalists were of European background, as Brown and Senior note, but approximately 6000 African-American Loyalists migrated to the Maritimes, the West Indies, and Sierra Leone in West Africa. Some 2000 Iroquois also left New York. In all, 70 000 people — approximately the population of New France at the time of the conquest — left the United States.[3]

Both during and after the war, the more influential Loyalists, such as royal officials, wealthy merchants, landowners, professionals, and high military officers, sailed directly for England to press their claims for compensation. The humbler element settled in the remaining British North American colonies.

The Loyalists favoured Nova Scotia over Quebec at a ratio of roughly two to one. Nova Scotia's fisheries, its large tracts of empty land, and the potential trade with the West Indies attracted them. Nova Scotia, too, was the shorter trip by sea. Small groups of Loyalists had been finding their way to Halifax since 1775. The evacuation of New York in 1783, though, led to an unanticipated invasion. The arrival of thousands of Loyalist strengthened Atlantic British North America's ties to the Crown.

THE LOYALISTS' FIRST SETTLEMENTS

About 15 000 Loyalists went to what became New Brunswick in 1784; about the same number to peninsular Nova Scotia, and about a thousand each to Prince Edward Island and Cape Breton, with a few families to Newfoundland. The great migration to the Atlantic colonies more than doubled their population with the arrival of over 30 000 civilian refugees and disbanded soldiers. Arrival proved a mixed blessing. In spite of the British government's promises, the colonists found that few preparations had been made to receive them. At Saint John, for example, no shelter had been prepared, provisions were in short supply, and the land along the river was not surveyed.

THE BLACK LOYALISTS

For the African-American Loyalists great disappointment also awaited them. Among African-Americans' ranks were men and women who had heeded the British proclamation of 1779 that offered freedom to any slaves who left their American masters and rallied to support the Crown. Some blacks had taken part in combat; others had served as spies, guides, nurses, and personal servants. In 1783, some 3000 African-American Loyalists arrived in the Maritimes, having won their freedom during the American Revolution by crossing over to the British lines. The British government might have promised them freedom, but it did not grant them equality. They were given smaller and less fertile grants than the other Loyalists, and substantially fewer provisions and tools. They could not vote, sit in non-segregated sections of churches, or even fish in the Saint John harbour.

Many of the white Loyalists also found economic conditions in Nova Scotia difficult. In one stroke, the colony's population had doubled and the resources of "Nova Scarcity" proved insufficient to meet the demand. Eventually, over half the Loyalists who came to Nova Scotia went elsewhere. Some moved to Upper Canada, others went to England, a number returned to the United States, and, a number of free African-American Loyalists eventually resettled in Sierra

Leone in British West Africa.

THE FOUNDING OF NEW BRUNSWICK

Shortly after the arrival in what is today New Brunswick, elite Loyalists from the St. John River petitioned London to have the section north of the Bay of Fundy removed from Nova Scotia and made a separate Loyalist province. They argued that the distance of the Saint John settlements from Halifax made it difficult to transact business with the capital. No doubt they also realized that the creation of a new colony would provide administrative offices for themselves. In the summer of 1784, Britain created the new colony of New Brunswick. The following year the major settlement at the mouth of the great river was named Saint John. The new capital, approximately 100 km north of Saint John, received the name of Frederick's Town (the "k," "s," and "w" were dropped shortly thereafter), in honour of Frederick Augustus, Duke of York, the second son of George III.

BUILDING A LOYALIST PROVINCE

 The Loyalists gradually built a new society in the Saint John River valley. It was hard work even for the affluent, for New Brunswick had a severe shortage of labour. Slowly a series of largely self-sufficient agricultural communities developed on favourable coastal locations and in the lowland river valleys. The town of Saint John became the major urban centre, with a population of 3500 in 1785. The Acadians' settlements, formed originally by those who had fled to the Miramichi to escape deportation between 1755 and 1758, were located along the eastern and northern shores of New Brunswick.

Ironically, the First Nations, whose allegiance had been critical in retaining western Nova Scotia for the Crown, suffered the most. The Loyalists encroached on their hunting and fishing territories. They helped themselves to Mi'kmaq and Maliseet land, fish, game, and timber. The British confiscated portions of their territories as Crown land without financial compensation. In the Great Lakes area the Royal Proclamation of 1763 protected First Nations land rights, but the British ruled that the Royal Proclamation did not apply in the Maritime colonies. Britain assumed that the French had already dealt in the Maritime area with the issue of Native title, but they had not.

THE LOYALISTS IN PRINCE EDWARD ISLAND

About 800 Loyalists travelled to Saint John's Island, soon to be renamed Prince Edward Island. They formed about one-fifth of the population. In Nova Scotia and New Brunswick, the authorities eventually supplied the Loyalists with free land, government timber, and tools. On Prince Edward Island, however, the hapless newcomers became tenant farmers on land granted to absentee proprietors.

In 1767, the British government had divided the entire island into long belts of land, stretching from north to south. It then proceeded to grant all 67 townships of roughly 8000 ha each to favourites of the Crown. The new landlords had to pay a small annual fee, or quitrent, for their land; they also had to promise to bring over settlers.

To attract Loyalists to their lands, the landowners promised them grants of land with secure titles. But once the settlers had cleared their lands, erected buildings, and planted orchards, the proprietors refused to grant land title to those who wanted to become landowners. Many settlers obtained no redress and left in disgust. Those who remained fought for 75 years for justice. Only in 1860 would a land commission recommend that free grants be made to those who

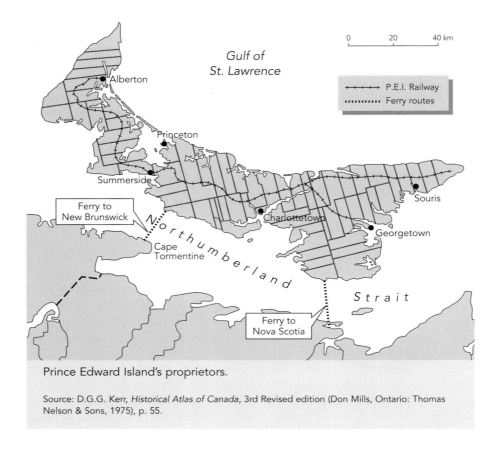

Prince Edward Island's proprietors.

Source: D.G.G. Kerr, *Historical Atlas of Canada*, 3rd Revised edition (Don Mills, Ontario: Thomas Nelson & Sons, 1975), p. 55.

could prove that their ancestors had been attracted to the island by the original promises made to the Loyalists. A final attempt to resolve the land question was made in 1873, in conjunction with Prince Edward Island's entry into Confederation.

THE LOYALISTS ON CAPE BRETON ISLAND

About a thousand Loyalists came to Cape Breton Island. The British government made the island a separate colony. The new capital was named Sydney after the British colonial secretary. But the British government provided little financial support for the colony. London did not even establish an assembly for the island. In 1820 the colonial office, without any consultation with the inhabitants, decided to re-join Cape Breton to Nova Scotia.

The prosperity of the War of 1812 gave the island several good years economically. The major social and economic development, however, came with the arrival of Scottish immigrants from 1802 onward — Catholic Scots from the Hebrides, the coastal islands off the west coast of Scotland, many of whom spoke only Gaelic. The magnificent hills and seacoast reminded them of their homeland. They became fishers and farmers. By the mid-nineteenth century the Scots had become the dominant community on Cape Breton Island, outnumbering the Mi'kmaqs, Acadians, and Loyalist descendants combined.

THE MARITIME ECONOMY FROM THE REVOLUTIONARY WAR TO THE WAR OF 1812

Real economic growth in the Maritimes began only after the outbreak of war between Britain and France in 1793 and, particularly, after the rise of Napoleon in the late 1790s. The British government now spent lavishly on fortifications in Halifax, constructing public and military buildings. Halifax became the strongest fortress outside Europe and the main supply base for the British West Indies.

After the beginning of the Napoleonic Wars, a flourishing timber industry developed in British North America. Britain required a safe supply of masts and spars for building war ships, and it needed timber for construction. The imperial government gave tariff preferences for British American timber. This led to a lumber boom in New Brunswick, the Maritime colony with the greatest timber resources. Wood products would dominate New Brunswick's export economy for the next half-century. Heavily forested New Brunswick, being closer to Britain, was better situated than were the Canadas for this trade.

Inadvertently, the United States also promoted the prosperity of the Maritimes. After France and Britain imposed blockades on each other in 1806, President Thomas Jefferson, in retaliation against both countries' restrictions on neutral trade, prohibited all commerce out of American ports. But the policy backfired, for by closing American ports in 1807, the president ruined New England's trade — and enriched that of the Maritimes.

Since Britain depended on American foodstuffs as much as the United States needed British manufactured goods, Anglo–American trade continued, but now through illegal channels. An active smuggling trade developed, with cargoes being transferred at sea or carried overland across the British–American frontier. In defiance of their government, American ship captains sailed into British ports, making the Maritimes in 1808 into a great clearinghouse for international trade. The Maritime colonies now purchased American produce and goods and then re-exported these materials as if they were their own. Similarly, they sold British manufactured goods to the Americans. This thriving trade continued throughout the War of 1812.

During the entire War of 1812 New England, in effect, was neutral. The legislatures of the New England states had openly condemned the war that had ruined their commerce. As Washington lacked the military capacity to impose its will on New England, its trade with Britain and its Maritime colonies continued. Only naval activity on the high seas reminded Maritimers that they still lived in a war theatre. The occupation by the British in 1814 of part of the coast of present-day Maine allowed more opportunities for commercial profit.

The outbreak of the last and longest of the wars between Britain and France, the Napoleonic Wars (1793–1814), also contributed to the new prosperity on Newfoundland. The price of dried fish rose substantially during the later years of the war because the French had to abandon their Newfoundland fishery. France simply could not protect its fishing fleet in wartime when the country needed to mobilize all of its naval resources to fight England. English vessels also stayed at home. The resident population, and the fisheries, grew. By 1815, residents owned almost the complete fishing fleet and produced the entire yield of saltfish.

During these prosperous years, shipowners, settlers, and St. John's entrepreneurs invested heavily in the fishery, creating a resident Newfoundland fleet. They began sending ships to less crowded parts of the coast, to the northern part of the island, and on to Labrador. Each June, thousands of Newfoundland fishers sailed for Labrador to catch cod. As the Labrador fishery expanded, Britain reattached Labrador to Newfoundland, taking it out of Lower Canada's control in 1809.

ECONOMIC DEVELOPMENTS, 1815–1850

The peace treaty of 1783 granted American citizens fishing privileges in the in-shore waters of the British North American colonies. However, during the negotiations of the Treaty of Ghent, which ended the War of 1812, the British argued that the Americans had abrogated this right by declaring war. Under the Convention of 1818, the Americans lost the privilege of landing and drying their fish in the three Maritime colonies; they retained the right to do so only on unsettled shores in Newfoundland. This helped the British Atlantic fishery. American vessels continued to enter British American harbours to obtain water, purchase wood, or repair damages; but not until the signing of the Reciprocity Treaty in 1854, which instituted free trade in natural products between British North America and the United States, did Americans regain access to the in-shore fisheries.

Newfoundland's maritime economy expanded after the War of 1812. Sailors entered the waters off Newfoundland and Labrador's northern coasts to harvest the seal herds on the ice floes. Mammals and fish provided the bulk of the world's industrial oil in the early nineteenth century, and young seals had an excellent fat for fine-quality oil. Their skins could also be sold in England. The industry grew rapidly. Between 1831 and 1833, the seal fishery averaged between 30 and 40 percent of Newfoundland's total exports. More than 600 000 seals were harvested in 1831 alone. By the 1850s, 13 000 men were employed annually in the seal hunt. It supplemented the production of salt cod.

AGRICULTURE

After the War of 1812 agriculture remained weak in the Maritime colonies. While farming flourished on Prince Edward Island, in Nova Scotia's Annapolis valley, and in New Brunswick's Saint John River valley, it did not fare as well in other areas. Nova Scotia and New Brunswick as a whole continued to depend on American foodstuffs to feed their populations well into the nineteenth century. Commercial farming remained very limited, with only Prince Edward Island, the "Garden of the Gulf," exporting large amounts of farm produce. In the case of Nova Scotia and New Brunswick, the lack of good roads, a scattered population, and the absence of protection against American imports accounted for the limited agricultural exports. Nevertheless farming, more than either logging or fishing, remained the livelihood of a majority of Maritimers. Even a large number of those employed in logging and fishing worked on a part-time basis in agriculture to support their families.

An increase in immigration after 1815 added to the size of the local market and encouraged greater agricultural production. New Brunswick had roughly 75 000 inhabitants in 1824 and almost 200 000 by 1851. During the same period, Nova Scotia's population rose from approximately 100 000 to 275 000. Prince Edward Island's population increased from 23 000 in 1827 to 72 000 in 1855, making it the most densely inhabited colony in British North America, due to its small size.

THE TIMBER INDUSTRY

Forestry became the leading growth industry in the Maritimes after the War of 1812, New Brunswick being known as the "timber colony." As early as 1826, three-quarters of the province's export revenues came from wood products — square timber, lumber, and ships. In the 1840s, New Brunswick survived the gradual reduction of the British preference on colonial timber. British and American demand remained high. By 1865, forest products made up two-thirds of New Brunswick's total exports by value, compared with about 10 percent of Nova Scotia's and Prince Edward Island's exports.

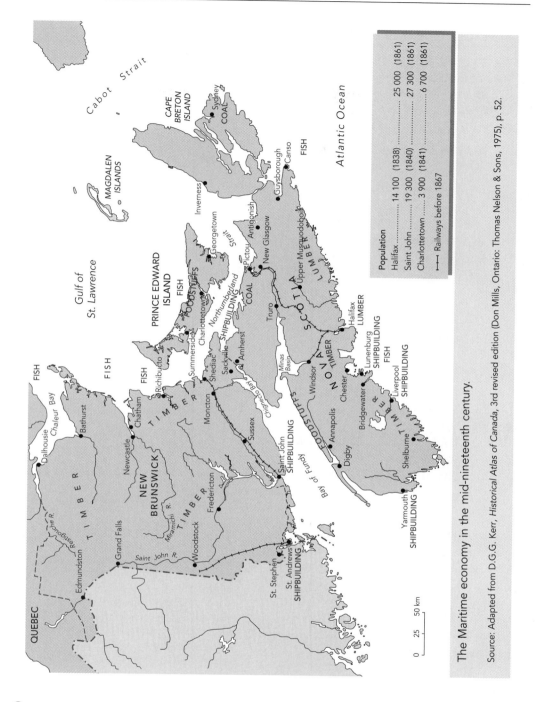

The Maritime economy in the mid-nineteenth century.

Source: Adapted from D.G.G. Kerr, *Historical Atlas of Canada*, 3rd revised edition (Don Mills, Ontario: Thomas Nelson & Sons, 1975), p. 52.

Population	
Halifax	25 000 (1861)
Saint John	27 300 (1861)
Charlottetown	6 700 (1861)
▬▬ Railways before 1867	

(earlier figures noted on map: Halifax 14 100 (1838); Saint John 19 300 (1840); Charlottetown 3 900 (1841))

SHIPBUILDING

Shipbuilding became a major sideline of the timber industry. Square timber, a bulky commodity, had to be shipped in relatively large vessels, and as Britain could not meet the need for such ships in wartime, so the Maritime shipbuilding industry expanded, making it the first major manufacturing industry in the Maritime region. The Maritimes soon supplied many of the new wooden ships used to ferry timber to Britain.

THE GROWTH OF POPULATION IN THE ATLANTIC REGION, 1806–61

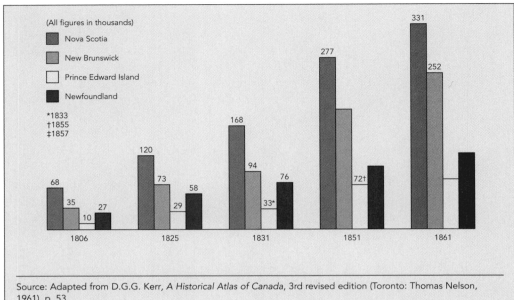

Source: Adapted from D.G.G. Kerr, *A Historical Atlas of Canada*, 3rd revised edition (Toronto: Thomas Nelson, 1961), p. 53.

Where Historians Disagree

The Timber Industry in Early New Brunswick: An Environmental Perspective

Environmental history is a relatively new field in Canadian history. In 1989, historian Ramsay Cook lamented the lack of historical interest in the impact of settlement and industry on the natural environment: "Even the no longer so new social history has largely ignored the environment in the rush for class, gender and ethnicity."[1]

In regard to the forests of New Brunswick, however, environmental concerns have long been raised. As early as 1825, for instance, Peter Fisher raised the alarm in his *Sketches of New Brunswick*, the first historical study published in the province:

The persons principally engaged in shipping the timber have been strangers who have taken no interest in the welfare of the country; but have merely occupied a spot to make what they could in the shortest possible time.... Instead of seeing towns built, farms improved and the country cleared and stocked with the reasonable returns of so great a trade, the forests are stripped and nothing left in prospect, but the gloomy apprehension when the timber is gone, of sinking into insignificance and poverty.[2]

A century later, Arthur R.M. Lower developed this same theme of senseless pillage in three books on Canada's forest industries: *Settlement and the Forest Frontier in Eastern Canada* (1936), *The North*

American Assault on the Canadian Forest (1938), and Great Britain's *Woodyard: British America and the Timber Trade* (1973). He concluded his last book with this statement: "The Canadian forests contributed to the prosperity of the British timber importer and the enrichment of the American lumberman.... [But] it must be concluded that the new colonies got the minimum out of the wreck of their forests."[3]

In *Northern Enterprise*, a study of five centuries of Canadian business, Michael Bliss took issue with Arthur Lower:

> The old idea that the rape of the forests was simply a using up of natural wealth with no compensating benefits is a romantic mockery of the realities and difficulties of colonial development. When A.R.M. Lower wove that theme into his writing about Canadian forest industries, with particular reference to New Brunswick, he was parroting some of the industry's least-informed critics.

Instead Bliss endorsed and cited a New Brunswick contemporary of Peter Fisher, who stated that the timber trade "has brought foreign produce and foreign capital into the Province, and has been the chief source of the money by means of which the country has been opened up and improved; by which its roads, bridges and public buildings have been completed; its rivers and harbours made accessible; its natural resources discovered and made available; its Provincial institutions kept up and its functionaries paid."[4]

Graeme Wynn, who studied the question in depth twenty years ago, takes a middle-of-the-road position. The historical geographer underlines that an export staple was needed to give New Brunswick its economic lift-off. That staple was timber. From 1805 to 1850 the heavy exploitation of the colony's forests transformed the colony from "an undeveloped backwater of 25 000 people to a bustling colony of 190 000." At the same time, Wynn notes the waste and destruction. For example, he commented about early-nineteenth-century sawmilling: "Sawdust dumped into the rivers soon became sodden, sank to the bed of the stream, disturbed the river ecology, and obstructed navigation. In suspension it floated downstream, was deposited on banks and intervals, and drastically reduced fish populations." The debris of bark, slabs, edgings, mill rubbish, and sunken logs was also carried over entire river systems, he noted.

In the end Wynn withholds judgement, claiming the need for further research before definitive statements could be made. With regard to Lower's books, he sees them as "reconnaissance surveys rather than final charts ... early interpretations need to be re-examined as more information becomes available."[5]

William Cronon's *Changes in the Land: Colonists and the Ecology of New England*[6] might be a good model for a follow-up study, as it combines a thorough documentary search with in-depth biological knowledge. A good beginning for New Brunswick is Gilbert Allardyce's 1972 article on Alma Parish in Albert County, New Brunswick.[7] At the beginning of the nineteenth century the parish's forests and fishlife appeared inexhaustible. By 1850, however, sawmill dams blockaded the rivers and prevented the passage of salmon toward their headwater spawning grounds all along the Fundy coast. Still, lumbering aggressively increased, which meant more sawdust. Timber killed fishing. When the lumber became exhausted in the early twentieth century, Alma Parish was left with nothing to support settlement, as it had little fertile land for farming. Today Alma Parish forms Fundy National Park. In any assessment of the impact of the nineteenth-century timber industry on New Brunswick, both the long-term and short-term consequences need to be considered.

1 Ramsay Cook, "Review of The Natural History of Canada," *Canadian Historical Review*, 60 (1989): 386.
2 Peter Fisher, *Sketches of New Brunswick* (Saint John: Chubb and Sears, 1825), p. 72; reprinted in Arthur R.M. Lower, *Great Britain's Woodyard: British America and the Timber Trade, 1763–1867* (Montreal/Kingston: McGill-Queen's University Press, 1973), p.33.
3 Lower, *Great Britain's Woodyard*, p. 250.
4 Michael Bliss, *Northern Enterprise*, (Toronto: McClelland & Stewart, 1987), p. 136.
5 Graeme Wynn, *Timber Colony: A Historical Geography of Early Nineteenth Century New Brunswick* (Toronto: University of Toronto Press, 1981), pp. 24, 33, 93, and 174.
6 William Cronon, *Changes in the Land: Indians, Colonists and the Ecology of New England* (New York: Hill and Wang, 1983).
7 Gilbert Allardyce, "'The Vexed Question of Sawdust': River Pollution in Nineteenth Century New Brunswick," *Dalhousie Review*, 52, 2 (Summer 1972): 177–90.

Generally Maritime shipbuilders built broad-beamed vessels designed to maximize carrying capacity, not speed. They increased sail capacity and improved ships' hulls. They extended the average life of Nova Scotia and New Brunswick vessels from a mere 9 years in the 1820s to 15 years by the end of the century. These shipbuilders also constructed their vessels cheaply. An iron steamer in Britain cost four or five times as much in the 1860s as did a wooden vessel from the Maritimes. The popularity of steamers, however, grew rapidly because of their speed and reliability, leaving only a tiny market for wooden ships by the end of the century.

BANKING

The financial needs of the merchants involved in the timber industry and shipbuilding led to the rise of banks. In Britain, commercial banks developed in the eighteenth century, and in the 1790s scores of them opened in the United States. The Halifax Banking Company, the first bank in Nova Scotia, began trading in money in 1825. A group of merchants founded the Bank of Nova Scotia in 1832, and by 1840 it had branches throughout Nova Scotia. New Brunswick's first bank, the Bank of New Brunswick, was chartered in Saint John in 1820; the second, the Commercial Bank, in 1834. Prince Edward Island's first bank opened in the mid-1850s. The banks dealt in foreign-exchange transactions, made loans, and circulated bank notes, on the understanding that the paper notes could always be redeemed, on demand, in real coinage. Depending on the risk the bankers were prepared to take, the banks could generally keep two or three times as many notes in circulation as they had gold or silver coins to redeem them. (The issuing of notes in place of coins allowed the banks to double or triple the amount of interest they collected.)

SAINT JOHN AND HALIFAX

Strong rivalries existed between the two major regional centres in the Maritimes: Saint John and Halifax. Initially Saint John held the advantage, since it was the largest city, controlled the timber trade of the Saint John River valley, had an important shipbuilding industry, and was the natural market for the farmers and fishers on both sides of the Bay of Fundy. Nearly half of the industrial output of New Brunswick was produced in and around Saint John. By the mid-nineteenth century, Saint John had emerged as the Maritimes' major industrial centre, with foundry, clothing, and foot-ware industries. Together they surpassed shipbuilding in value by the 1860s. But the great merchants of Saint John delayed investing in manufacturing iron and steel. Such financial conservatism held back the development of a viable industrial base in New Brunswick by two decades.

Halifax, the military headquarters for the region, had a large, secure, ice-free harbour, very close to major North Atlantic shipping lanes. It also benefited from the Caribbean trade and from its role as Nova Scotia's banking, judicial, and intellectual centre. In terms of industrial base, it developed a specialization in food-processing industries, such as sugar refining, brewing, and distilling. But it did not have a readily accessible hinterland. Also, unlike Montreal and Saint John, it lacked a major waterway comparable to the St. Lawrence or the Saint John River. Halifax did succeed in bringing Prince Edward Island, Cape Breton Island, and the Miramichi country of eastern New Brunswick into its commercial orbit, but it lost the important Bay of Fundy region to Saint John.

THE MARITIMES AND THE UNITED STATES

Issues of borders and trade dominated Maritime–American relations in the mid-nineteenth century. When Britain adopted free trade in the 1840s, many Maritimers looked to continental reciprocity — the free admission into British North America and the United States of each other's natural resources — as a viable alternative. New Brunswick saw reciprocity as the key to gaining entry for its timber into the American market of 23 million people. There could be no hope of reciprocity, however, until a border controversy between New Brunswick and Maine was settled. The Webster–Ashburton Treaty of 1842 resolved the controversy. It established the present-day New Brunswick–Maine boundary. The treaty left Maine a wedge of land projecting between New Brunswick and the Canadas, yet it kept intact the vital communication route between Quebec and Fredericton via Lake Témiscouata.

Reciprocity proposals met with a favourable response in Nova Scotia with its fish for export, in New Brunswick with its timber, and Prince Edward Island with its farm produce. The Americans, for their part, wanted access to the Maritime in-shore fisheries from which they had been excluded in 1818. The inclusion of the fisheries led the United States to sign a reciprocity agreement with the British North American colonies in 1854.

THE RECIPROCITY TREATY (1854–1866)

The treaty led to the desired increased trade with the United States. The Maritime colonies now bought one-quarter to one-half of their total imports from the Americans. In return, New Brunswick shipped to the United States increased amounts of lumber; Prince Edward Island shipped more foodstuffs; and Nova Scotia shipped a slightly greater amount of fish. Certainly, the twelve years of the reciprocity treaty proved prosperous, but not solely on account of the treaty. The high demand generated by the American Civil War (1861–65) led to high prices for the Maritimes' fish, timber, and foodstuffs. The carrying trade also benefited.

RAILWAYS

The leading Maritime cities sought to build railways inland to expand their economic hinterlands. Between 1853 and 1866, New Brunswick built 350 km of railways and Nova Scotia constructed 235 km. Maritime promoters envisaged one day linking the ice-free Maritime ports with the St. Lawrence valley and with the grain-producing American Midwest. Merchants in

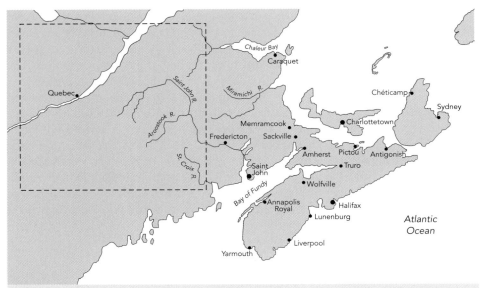

The Maritimes in the mid-nineteenth century. A detail of this map appears below.

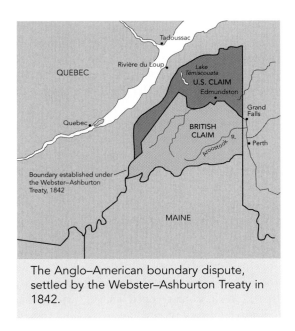

The Anglo–American boundary dispute, settled by the Webster–Ashburton Treaty in 1842.

Halifax and Saint John had visions of their respective cities serving as the focal point from which European commerce could be channelled into the continent and from which American and Canadian exports could be sent abroad.

Yet railways proved expensive both to build and to operate. A single kilometre of track could cost as much as a sizable sailing vessel. Moreover, operating costs were much higher by rail than by sea. To make money, the railway company owners needed both densely populated areas to provide local revenue and the shortest possible direct routes; neither Halifax nor even

Saint John had such hinterlands. The larger communities in the interior were too distant, in contrast with those neighbouring Boston, New York, or Montreal, and the land routes passed through long stretches of thinly populated territory.

THE POPULATION OF ATLANTIC BRITISH NORTH AMERICA

In the nineteenth century, thousands of Scottish and Irish immigrants crossed the North Atlantic to British North America to escape overcrowding, famine, and poverty. They joined those already-established residents: the Acadians, African Maritimers, First Nations people, and the descendants of the Planters and the white Loyalists, as well as recent English immigrants. The chart below reveals the changing ethnic composition of Maritime British North America.

 The number of permanent residents in Newfoundland doubled from about 20 000 in 1800, to about 40 000 in 1830. By the 1830s the Irish Catholic population numbered half the island's population. Most of the others were of English background. Mistrusting each other, the Irish and English communities separated themselves geographically.

THE FIRST NATIONS IN THE MARITIMES AND NEWFOUNDLAND

The Maritimers with the longest residency had the greatest difficulty in adjusting to changing conditions in the early and mid-nineteenth century. The British and the Maritime governments held that the Mi'kmaqs' and the Maliseets' title to the land had already been extinguished — first, by the fact that the French had occupied the area and, second, as a result of the Treaty of Utrecht in 1713, which the British claimed gave them sovereign title to Acadia. The New Brunswick government set aside reserves for the Mi'kmaqs and the Maliseets, but the lack of

NATIONAL ORIGINS: NOVA SCOTIA (1871), NEW BRUNSWICK (1871), AND PRINCE EDWARD ISLAND (1881)

	NORTH AMERICAN INDIAN NUMBER	%	ENGLISH AND WELSH NUMBER	%	SCOTS NUMBER	%	IRISH NUMBER	%	FRENCH NUMBER	%
Nova Scotia	1 666	0.4	113 520	29.2	130 741	33.7	62 851	16.4	32 833	8.5
New Brunswick	1 403	0.5	83 598	29.2	40 858	14.3	100 643	35.3	44 907	15.7
P.E.I.	281	0.3	21 568	19.8	48 933	44.8	25 415	23.3	10 751	9.9

	GERMAN NUMBER	%	DUTCH NUMBER	%	AFRICAN NUMBER	%	SWISS NUMBER	%	TOTAL POPULATION
Nova Scotia	31 942	8.2	2 868	0.7	6 212	1.6	1 775	0.5	387 800
New Brunswick	4 478	1.6	6 004	2.1	1 701	0.6	64	—	285 594
P.E.I.	1 076	1.0	292	0.3					108 891

Source: R. Cole Harris and John Warkentin, *Canada Before Confederation: A Study in Historical Geography* (Ottawa: Carleton University Press, 1991 [1974]), pp. 184–85. Data from Census of Canada.

proper legal descriptions and surveys of the reserve lands encouraged settlers to encroach into these areas. A similar situation developed in Nova Scotia. The first reserve was only established on Prince Edward Island in 1870. By the time of Confederation, the First Nations constituted roughly 0.5 percent of the total population of Nova Scotia, New Brunswick, and Prince Edward Island.

The Beothuks, Newfoundland's original inhabitants, did not survive European contact. In the seventeenth century they withdrew from the coastal areas where the European newcomers set up shore stations. They did not, as did the Mi'kmaqs in the Maritimes, trade and interact with the Europeans. Consequently, by staying in the interior to avoid the newcomers, they lost access to the valuable food supplies off the coast. They became greatly weakened by starvation and tuberculosis, which the Europeans had inadvertently introduced. By 1800, the Beothuks had almost totally disappeared.

The pressure on the Beothuks had grown in the eighteenth century. Several factors contributed to increased European settlement in the northeast and the interior: a salmon fishery developed near the river mouths of northeastern Newfoundland; settlers began to trap fur-bearing animals in the interior; and the spring seal hunt, which was best operated from the northeastern coast, grew rapidly. When the Beothuks encountered the Europeans on the northeastern coast, violence often erupted. The settlers harassed them and raided their camps. The Beothuks retaliated. According to contemporary reports and oral traditions, they killed about a

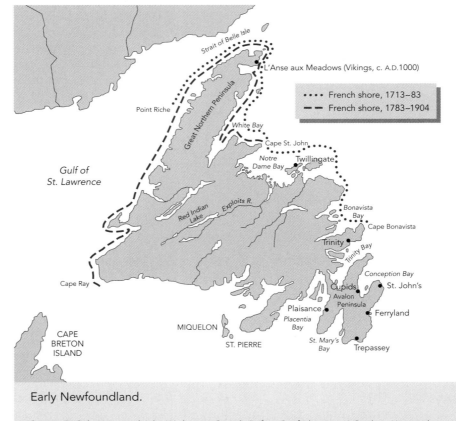

Early Newfoundland.

Source: R. Cole Harris and John Warkentin, *Canada Before Confederation: A Study in Historical Geography* (Ottawa: Carleton University Press, 1991 [1974]), pp. 184–85. Data from Census of Canada.

dozen settlers and wounded nearly as many more between 1750 and 1790. The settlers took their own revenge, killing and wounding Beothuks and destroying their wigwams. The Beothuks' lack of firearms weakened their ability to defend themselves.

Several naval officers and settlers in the late eighteenth and early nineteenth centuries worried about the Beothuks' fate, as it was already obvious that the First Nation was on the point of extinction. Demasduwit, a young woman, was taken captive in 1819 and lived for one year. Then, in 1823, three starving Beothuk women were captured. Both the mother and one of her two daughters died shortly afterward of tuberculosis. But the second daughter, Shawnadithit, called Nancy, a young woman between 16 and 20, survived for six years. She lived at first as a servant in the household of a justice of the peace, but spent the last year of her life in St. John's, informing William Cormack, a champion of the Beothuks, about her people's culture, history, and language. Shawnadithit died in 1829. Apart from two or three Beothuks who may have resided with the Newfoundland Mi'kmaqs, she was the last of the Beothuks.

POLITICAL CHANGES IN THE MID-NINETEENTH CENTURY

After the American Revolution, the British government imposed, as it did in the Canadas, rigid political structures, controlled from above. Reformers wanted the members of the Executive Council (or Cabinet) responsible to the majority party in the Assembly. If the Council lost a confidence vote in the Assembly, or lost support in a general election, its members must resign. Secondly, the governor must accept the recommendations of the Executive Council, dependent as it was, on majority support in the Assembly. This is what they meant by responsible government.

Joseph Howe led the Nova Scotia Reformers. In 1827, Howe purchased the *Novascotian*, a Halifax newspaper, which he remade into the most influential newspaper in the province. In the election of 1847, the Reformers fought on the issue of responsible government, and finally won a majority. On February 2, 1848, the Colonial Office agreed that henceforth the Executive Council must collectively resign if it lost the Assembly's confidence. Nova Scotia thus became the first British North American colony to obtain responsible government. New Brunswick, Prince Edward Island, and Newfoundland followed. All had responsible government by 1855.

WOMEN IN THE MARITIMES

The Maritimes, in the mid-nineteenth century, as was the case throughout North America, remained a male-dominated society. Men, for instance, owned almost all property and housing. At best, women had only limited rights under the law to protection and safety. In 1836 Prince Edward Island disenfranchised propertied women, as did New Brunswick in 1843 and Nova Scotia in 1851.

Although deprived of the vote, women could, and did, deliver petitions to their legislatures. They played a major role, for example, in petitioning for prohibition. On the positive side as well, after 1849 New Brunswick finally allowed women to attend the provincial Normal School. They numbered close to one-half of New Brunswick's teachers by the late 1850s. Yet, they were only paid the same wage as a domestic servant. And unlike men, who obtained higher wages and could teach the older students, women were still denied entrance to colleges.

In terms of women's rights, Nova Scotia in 1857 became the only British North American province prior to Confederation to allow legal divorce on the grounds of cruelty, such as wife battering. This was indeed an advance, but New Brunswick and Prince Edward Island took no immediate steps to imitate this legislation.

During the American Revolution Nova Scotia had remained in the British Empire. It became a place of refuge for the Loyalists after the British defeat. Yet, even with the Loyalist influx the colonies, Nova Scotia, Prince Edward Island, and the new colony of New Brunswick, remained relatively small in population, and weak economically. The War of 1812 proved a prosperous time for the British North Atlantic colonies. The economic upsurge after the war, led by ship-building, the timber industry, fishing, and agriculture, added to the region's development. By the mid-nineteenth century, the three Maritime colonies had become recognizable economic and political units. Eight of every nine people in the region had been born there.

But the inhabitants were far from homogeneous. Religious, ethnic, and provincial divisions remained, and some groups such as the Mi'kmaqs and the African Maritimers and, to a lesser extent, the Acadians, had been pushed to the margins of Maritime society. Women were politically disenfranchised and relegated largely to the domestic sphere. The colonies had become much more consolidated than half a century earlier, but even within their own provincial boundaries, regional loyalties remained strong. Many Maritimers were sceptical of the possibility of Maritime union when politicians first seriously discussed the idea in the early 1860s. Union with the Canadas seemed even more remote.

 As for Newfoundland in the 1860s it looked eastward toward Britain, not westward toward the mainland. Newfoundland's patterns of trade and settlement linked it to Europe, the West Indies, and the United States. The development of the western part of the island, which contained the land most suitable for agriculture, would have served as a bridge to Canada. Until 1904, however, the French held on to their treaty rights, first obtained in the Treaty of Utrecht in 1713, to dry fish on the western coastline. Newfoundland's geography and distinctive history placed it very much apart from the Canadas and even from the three Maritime colonies.

NOTES

1. George A. Rawlyk, "The American Revolution and Nova Scotia Reconsidered," *Dalhousie Review* 43 (1963–64): 379.
2. Paul H. Smith, "The American Loyalists: Notes on Their Organization and Numerical Strength," *William and Mary Quarterly*, 3rd series, 25 (1968): 269.
3. The estimates of the Loyalists' numbers appear in Wallace Brown and Hereward Senior, *Victorious in Defeat: The Loyalists in Canada* (Toronto: Methuen, 1984).

LINKING TO THE PAST

What Is a Loyalist?
http://www.uelac.org/whatis.html
Basic information about Loyalists as well as a summary of their immigration to the Maritime provinces and Quebec.

Black Loyalists
http://collections.ic.gc.ca/blackloyalists
An extensive, illustrated history of black Loyalists, from before the American Revolution to emigration to Sierra Leone. For information on one black settlement in Nova Scotia, Birchtown, visit http://museum.gov.ns.ca/arch/sites/birch.

From Slavery to Sierra Leone
http://collections.ic.gc.ca/port_royal/blkloyal.html
The site contains the story of a black Loyalist woman, from her escape from slavery and life in Nova Scotia to her decision to leave the continent.

History of Saint John, New Brunswick
http://www.city.saint-john.nb.ca/2.cfm?PageID=2-4-4

This site provides a look at the history of Canada's oldest incorporated city, from early exploration to the present.

The Maritime Shipyard
http://www.civilization.ca/hist/canp1/ca18eng.html

An overview is given of the nineteenth-century shipbuilding industry.

History of Law and Government in Newfoundland
http://www.heritage.nf.ca/law/default.html

This site provides an illustrated history of Newfoundland's government up to the time of Confederation. Go to http://www.heritage.nf.ca/law/admirals.html to read about the fishing admirals.

The Beothuks
http://www.delweb.com/nfmuseum/notes1.htm

From the Newfoundland Museum, an illustrated overview of what is known about these early inhabitants of Newfoundland.

1800s Newfoundland: A Pictorial
http://collections.ic.gc.ca/nfld

An extensive collection of photographs, most likely taken by Simeon H. Parsons (1844–1908), one of Newfoundland's earliest professional photographers.

BIBLIOGRAPHY

For a general overview of this period see Phillip A. Buckner and John G. Reid, eds., *The Atlantic Region to Confederation: A History* (Toronto: University of Toronto Press, 1994), pp. 156–260; Margaret R. Conrad and James K. Hiller, *Atlantic Canada. A Region in the Making* (Toronto: Oxford University Press, 2001); and W.S. MacNutt's *The Atlantic Provinces, 1712–1857* (Toronto: McClelland & Stewart, 1965), pp. 76–102. For bibliographical guides consult the essays in W. Brook Taylor, ed., *Canadian History: A Reader's Guide*, vol. 1, *Beginnings to Confederation* (Toronto: University of Toronto Press, 1994), by Barry Moody, "Acadia and Old Nova Scotia to 1784," pp. 76–111; Ian Ross Robertson, "The Maritime Colonies, 1784 to Confederation," pp. 237–79; and Olaf Uwe Janzen's essay, "Newfoundland and the International Fishery," in M. Brook Taylor, ed., *Canadian History: A Reader's Guide*, vol. 1, *Beginnings to Confederation* (Toronto: University of Toronto Press, 1994), pp. 280–324.

For articles on all aspects of British Atlantic Canada the three editions of Phillip A. Buckner and David Frank, eds., *Atlantic Canada Before Confederation*, vol. 1, *The Acadiensis Reader* (Fredericton: Acadiensis Press, 1985, 1988, 1998) are invaluable. Important portraits of Atlantic political, economic, and cultural leaders appear in the volumes of the *Dictionary of Canadian Biography* devoted to the nineteenth century. It is now available online: www.bibliographi.ca.

John Bartlet Brebner reviews Nova Scotia's response to the American Revolution in *The Neutral Yankees of Nova Scotia* (Toronto: McClelland & Stewart, 1969 [1937]). For an introduction to Henry Alline and his New Light movement see the booklet by D.G. Bell, *Henry Alline and Maritime Religion* (Ottawa: Canadian Historical Association, 1993). Valuable overviews of the Loyalists include Christopher Moore, *The Loyalists: Revolution, Exile, Settlement* (Toronto: Macmillan, 1984); and Wallace Brown and Hereward Senior, *Victorious in Defeat: The Loyalists in Canada* (Toronto: Methuen, 1984).

A review of Halifax's history by three professional historians is Judith Fingard, Janet Guildford, and David Sutherland, *Halifax: The First 250 Years* (Halifax: Formac Publishing, 1999). T.W. Acheson's *Saint John: The Making of a Colonial Urban Community* (Toronto: University of Toronto Press, 1985) studies New Brunswick's largest city. For the history of St. John's, consult Patrick O'Neill, *The Story of St. John's, Newfoundland* (Erin, Ontario: Boston Mills Press, 1975).

Graeme Wynn, a historical geographer, looks at early New Brunswick in *Timber Colony* (Toronto: University of Toronto Press, 1981). For background on Cape Breton Island see Stephen J. Hornsby's *Nineteenth Century Cape Breton: A Historical Geography* (Montreal/Kingston: McGill-Queen's University Press, 1992). J. M. Bumsted's *Land, Settlement, and Politics on Eighteenth-Century Prince Edward Island* (Montreal/Kingston: McGill-Queen's University Press, 1987) focuses on developments in Prince Edward Island. A lively popular history of the island is Douglas Baldwin's *Land of the Red Soil* (Charlottetown: Ragweed Press, 1990). Frederick W. Rowe's *A History of Newfoundland and Labrador* (Toronto: McGraw-Hill Ryerson, 1980) remains the most complete study of Newfoundland's history.

For background on the Native peoples in what is now Atlantic Canada consult, F.S. Upton, *Micmacs and Colonists: Indian–White Relations in the Maritimes, 1713–1867* (Vancouver: University of British Columbia Press, 1979); and Harold E.L. Prins, *The Mi'kmaq Resistance: Accommodation and Cultural Survival* (Fort Worth, TX: Harcourt Brace, 1996). In *We Were Not the Savages: A Micmac Perspective on the Collision of European and Aboriginal Civilizations* (Halifax: Nimbus, 1993), Daniel N. Paul provides a Mi'kmaq perspective on Native–Newcomer relations. On the Beothuk the most important study is Ingeborg Marshall, *A History and Ethnography of the Beothuk* (Montreal/Kingston: McGill-Queen's University Press, 1996).

Important maps of Atlantic British North America in the late eighteenth and nineteenth centuries appear in the first two volumes of the *Historical Atlas of Canada*, vol. 1, R. Cole Harris, ed., *From the Beginning to 1800* (Toronto: University of Toronto Press, 1987); and vol. 2, R. Louis Gentilcore, ed., *The Land Transformed, 1800–1891* (Toronto: University of Toronto Press, 1993).

THE NORTHWEST TO THE 1860s

TIME LINE

1690	Henry Kelsey, a Hudson's Bay Company employee, sets out on a journey into the interior of North America
1730s	Pierre La Vérendrye establishes French posts around Lakes Winnipeg and Winnipegosis
1761	French traders withdraw from the interior as a result of the French capitulation at Montreal
1780s	Formation of the North West Company
1812	The Selkirk colony is established on the Red River
1818	The 49th parallel becomes the boundary line between American and British claims from Lake Superior west to the Rocky Mountains
1821	Union of the Hudson's Bay Company and the North West Company
1849	Free trade is obtained in the Red River

The Blackfoot-speaking peoples occupied the rich buffalo ranges of present-day southern Alberta and northern Montana in the mid-eighteenth century. The horse, brought to Mexico by the Spanish, reached them about 1730, at about the same time that Cree middlemen brought them guns. Apart from possibly one or two "northern white men," as they later termed the English, the only Europeans that the Blackfoot speakers encountered on the northern plains in the 1740s and 1750s were French traders from Canada, whom they called "real white men."

After the fall of New France in 1760, hundreds of Europeans ventured into the interior from the north, the east, and the south. The best furs came from the Northwest, and independent fur traders from Montreal came to buy them. In the early 1780s, these Scottish and American fur traders formed the North West Company (whose agents came to be called Nor'Westers) to challenge the Hudson's Bay Company, already more than a century old. Thirty years of competition between the two companies ended with their merger in 1821. Even after the Métis broke the Hudson's Bay Company monopoly in the Red River in 1849, the company remained the leading commercial power in Rupert's Land.

THE FRENCH AND THE ENGLISH IN THE INTERIOR

The French came west in search of a short route to China. Well into the eighteenth century the French believed in the existence of a gulf that cut deeply into the continent from the Pacific, like Hudson Bay or the Gulf of Mexico. They hoped that somewhere between the 40th and 50th parallels of latitude a navigable strait joined the "Western Sea" to the Pacific Ocean. In 1730, Pierre Gaultier de Varennes et de La Vérendrye, commander of the fur-trading post on Kaministiquia (present-day Thunder Bay), offered to establish a post on Lake Winnipeg. He agreed to conduct explorations for the Western Sea from this base, at no expense to the Crown.

From Kaministiquia, La Vérendrye travelled westward in the 1730s, building fur-trading posts in the Lake of the Woods district and around Lakes Winnipeg and Winnipegosis. The French never found the Western Sea, but they did locate the key to the interior — the Saskatchewan River, whose twin branches flow through the central plains in a huge, wavering Y.

The English established trading posts in the late seventeenth century at the mouths of rivers emptying into Hudson Bay. From these forts they carried on a profitable trade with the Cree and Assiniboine, who, acting as middlemen, brought furs to them and came to dominate the exchange of furs. They charged the First Nations in the interior a considerable markup on the European goods they obtained from the English and, until 1713, from the French.

The Hudson's Bay Company sponsored only two inland expeditions southwest of York Factory, their major post on Hudson Bay. In 1690–91 they sent Henry Kelsey, a young employee, just out of his teens, known to the Hudson's Bay Company's committee in London as (to quote the original document) "a very active lad, delighting much in Indians' compa[ny], being never better pleased than when he is Travelling amongst

Indian Greeting White Man, a painting by the American illustrator Frederic Remington (1861–1909). "Real white men" is what the Blackfoot of Alberta call the French in the Blackfoot language, probably because traders from New France were the first Europeans to make contact with them.

Glenbow Collection, Calgary, Canada/60.2.20.

them,"[1] to explore the interior. He travelled from York Factory with a Cree band and reached the prairies, probably in present-day east-central Saskatchewan. But upon his return the company decided not to establish costly forts in the interior. As long as the Crees and the Assiniboines brought good furs to them, the English would stay on Hudson Bay.

Then a series of armed clashes occurred on Hudson Bay between the French and the English. By the Treaty of Utrecht in 1713, France recognized England's possession of the coastline of Hudson and James Bay. But the French continued to trade in the interior. So, more than half a century after Kelsey's journey, the English changed their minds. They now felt the effect of strong French competition. In 1754, they sent Anthony Henday inland to convince the First Nations to give up their trade at the French posts and to come to the bay. In the manuscript copies of his report, which is far more precise than Kelsey's, Henday identified the specific groups in the interior and provided notes on their way of life.[2]

THE IMPACT OF THE EUROPEANS ON THE FIRST NATIONS

The arrival of the Europeans greatly altered the First Nations' way of life through the introduction of guns, horses, and new trade patterns. It also led to the rise of a mixed people: the Métis.

The impact of firearms differed for the Woodland peoples such as the Woods Cree and the Woods Assiniboine; and those on the Plains, such as the Blackfoot. The Woodland peoples came to rely on guns much more than those on the Plains, who really only used them in warfare. For the Woodland First Nations, specialists in hunting furs, the gun generally proved more efficient than the bow and arrow as it eliminated long hours of trapping, waiting for the animal to weaken through loss of blood. Moreover, they had access to the service centres where gunsmiths could repair them; for instance, at York Factory on Hudson Bay, in what is now northeastern Manitoba. Hence, the Woodland groups, despite certain disadvantages — the awkward loading of powder and shot, barrels that were prone to explosion, and the firearms' easy breakage in cold weather — used them a great deal. This reliance on firearms tied them closely to the fur-trading posts.

Distant from service centres, the Plains peoples preferred to use in the buffalo hunt sinew-backed bows with metal-tipped arrows, which did not make a noise that prematurely stampeded a herd. Their experienced hunters could easily reload a bow on horseback. But in battle, the Plains peoples used firearms. Guns had obvious advantages. Bullets went a longer distance than arrows and had greater killing power. Rawhide shields and armour offered little protection against a musket ball. In addition, the gun's loud report gave its user a psychological advantage in battle.

In the early eighteenth century, the Chipewyans, armed with guns, moved further into the woodlands immediately north of the Woodland Crees. Directly supplied by the English at Churchill, the Chipewyans sold European goods to interior nations. Like the Woodland Crees farther south, the Chipewyans became the traders' middlemen. In addition, European guns gave them an advantage in their struggle with the Inuit to the north and the Crees.

Apparently, the Cree already lived along the North Saskatchewan River in the late eighteenth century, but their repeated intrusions ended their initially friendly relations with the Blackfoot or "Prairie People." Individual Cree bands travelled over the plains independently. No single chief co-ordinated the expansion.

The horse had a greater impact than the gun on the Native peoples of the prairies. The Blackfoot used horses for hunting buffalo. Horse-mounted warriors replaced those on foot in driving and luring the animals into buffalo pounds or over cliffs (buffalo jumps). Mounted hunters rushed straight into a herd, singled out an animal, rode beside it, and killed it at close range with two or three arrows from their bows. The horse caused a cultural revolution on the Great Plains. It became a symbol of wealth. Some rich individuals owned up to 100 horses. By giving away or even lending horses, individuals enhanced their prestige. Horses were borrowed for hunting and for war parties, with the borrower returning in payment a portion of the game killed or of the goods seized. The horse thus contributed to a class structure among the Native peoples of the prairies, based on the number of horses owned.

The introduction of the horse had other effects. It intensified warfare between First Nations. Combat on horseback with a bow and arrow, lance, war club, or knife — or a European rifle — led to increased casualties. The horse also enabled the Woodland Assiniboines and many of the Woodland Crees to hunt buffalo on the prairies, thus lessening their dependence on European guns and trade goods. In general, life became very mobile for the First Nations of the Great Plains, particularly for the equestrian Blackfoot-speaking communities.

THE FUR TRADE AFTER THE FALL OF NEW FRANCE

 After the fall of New France in 1760, the Hudson's Bay Company anticipated a trade monopoly in the Northwest. But the company soon faced new rivals: aggressive Scottish and American traders operating out of Montreal. In the early 1770s, these traders employed large numbers of French-speaking voyageurs and sent large shipments of goods to the West.

Their arrival on the prairies led to clashes with the First Nations population. In 1779, the Plains Cree attacked a trading post on the North Saskatchewan River, killing two traders. Other incidents occurred, including a battle at a post on the Assiniboine River in 1781, in which three traders and 30 First Nations people died. Only a smallpox epidemic in 1781–82 saved the traders from large-scale Native retaliation.

In the early 1780s, the Montreal traders combined their capital to form the North West Company, a decentralized fur-trading operation that soon expanded beyond the French fur trade in the West to include the Peace, Mackenzie, and Columbia River districts.

THE EMERGENCE OF THE NORTH WEST COMPANY

The North West Company employed experienced French-Canadian, Métis, and Iroquois canoeists. These hardy voyageurs would cross half a continent. As a rule, they were short (long legs were a definite disadvantage in a birchbark canoe), with great strength and endurance. On the journey, they slept only 5 to 6 hours a day. They paddled from 12 to 15, even 18, hours a day, if they had to. With their light paddles and rapid strokes, they made 40 to 60 strokes a minute. They regularly portaged loads of 80 kg, sometimes 120 kg, on their backs over rocky trails.

The North West Company underwent great expansion in the 1780s and 1790s. In 1778, fur trader Peter Pond reached the Athabasca and Peace River country (in present-day northern Alberta), rich with fur-bearing animals. In 1789, Alexander Mackenzie journeyed down the Mackenzie River and, in 1793, reached the Pacific Ocean. The company then opened up posts in the Mackenzie Basin and, later, along the Columbia River.

Despite its opponent's great territorial expanse, the Hudson's Bay Company had the advantage of a shorter, hence less expensive, transportation route — Hudson Bay was considerably closer than Montreal to the inland posts. The smaller company could take trade goods to the Athabasca country at about one-half the cost. The Hudson's Bay Company's York boats, although slower and much heavier than a canoe, could carry greater amounts of trade goods in, and more fur bundles out, than could the Nor'Westers' canoes.

A Historical Portrait

George Nelson

If asked to name the most celebrated fur traders of the late eighteenth and early nineteenth centuries, most historians would immediately mention Samuel Hearne, David Thompson, Alexander Mackenzie, Simon Fraser, Peter Fidler, or Peter Pond. A host of names would follow, but most likely it would be a long while before the name of the lowly, underpaid North West Company clerk George Nelson would surface. He produced no great maps or surveys, made no great voyages of exploration, rose to no great administrative heights. He achieved no fame in his lifetime at all, in contrast to his younger brothers, Wolfred Nelson, a Patriote in the Lower Canadian Rebellion of 1837 — and later mayor of Montreal; and Robert Nelson, the Patriotes' leader in 1838 and later a very successful surgeon in the United States.

But for the attention of fur-trade historians Jennifer Brown, Robert Brightman, and Sylvia Van Kirk, George Nelson might still be unknown to students of the Canadian fur trade. His chief distinction, as Brown and Brightman point out in their edited work, *"The Orders of the Dreamed": George Nelson on Cree and Northern Ojibwa Religion and Myth, 1823*[1] comes from his sensitive recording, in a memoir written nearly two centuries ago, of western Cree and Ojibwa beliefs. He listened to the people and carefully recorded their stories. Sylvia Van Kirk describes his memoir as "one of the finest early ethnographic documents of its kind."[2]

George Nelson (1786–1859) was the son of Loyalists from New York who fled to Quebec to escape the American Revolution. As the son of an English Protestant schoolmaster, George received a good education.

From the age of 16, when he entered the fur trade, he lived among First Nations people. From 1802 to 1823 Nelson served as a clerk in present-day Wisconsin, northwestern Ontario, Manitoba, and Saskatchewan. He married Mary Ann, an Ojibwa woman, who was a valuable helpmate in his work. Upon his retirement from the fur trade they settled with their four daughters at Sorel, just east of Montreal.

During his years in the Northwest, Nelson wrote constantly. Many of his fur-trade journals and his reminiscences (written 10 to 40 years after the events they describe) have survived and are valuable for an understanding of the Native peoples of the Northwest. But his memoir of 1823, written in his last year in the fur trade, while Nelson was stationed at Lac la Ronge in northeastern Saskatchewan, is the greatest ethnological treasure because it offers insight into the religion and myth of the Cree and Ojibwa.

In the text, Nelson provided "detail of their private life," including an account of the shaking tent ceremony used by religious leaders to provide a glimpse into the future. Nelson also discussed the importance of dreams to the Native peoples. Attention is given to the mythical being the Windigo: "Suffice it to say that they are of uncommon size — Goliath is an unborn infant to them: and to add to their dread, they are represented as possessing much of the Power of Magicians. Their head reaching to the tops of the highest Poplars (about 70, or 80, feet)."[3]

Nelson's life in Lower Canada after his retirement was not happy. His wife died in 1831. Only one of their children survived into adulthood. Nelson became estranged from his brothers, Wolfred and Robert, on account of their participation in the Rebellions of 1837–38. He regarded their activities as treason. As a farmer he had little success. Probably his greatest joy after his wife's death came from writing his reminiscences of his days in "Indian country." He died in 1859 at the age of 73.

[1] Jennifer S.H. Brown and Robert Brightman *"The Orders of the Dreamed": George Nelson on Cree and Northern Ojibwa Religion and Myth, 1823* (Winnipeg: University of Manitoba Press, 1988).
[2] Sylvia Van Kirk, in collaboration with Jennifer S.H. Brown, "George Nelson," *Dictionary of Canadian Biography*, vol. 8: *1851–1860* (Toronto: University of Toronto Press, 1985), p. 653.
[3] Nelson, *"The Orders of the Dreamed,"* p. 86.

RIVALRY BETWEEN THE NORTH WEST COMPANY AND THE HUDSON'S BAY COMPANY

Competition from the North West Company forced the Hudson's Bay Company to go farther inland to obtain the best furs. The expansion of the two companies led to the elimination of the Cree and Assiniboine middlemen, as both the Nor'Westers and the Hudson's Bay Company

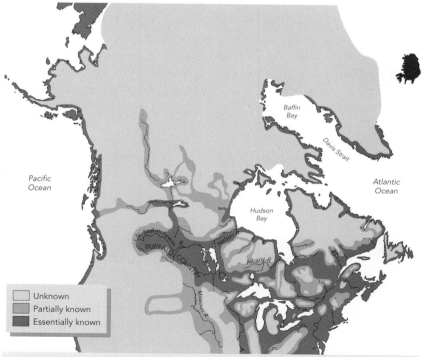

Non-Natives' knowledge of northern North America in 1795.

Source: Adapted from Richard I. Ruggles, *A Country So Interesting: The Hudson's Bay Company and Two Centuries of Mapping, 1670-1870* (Montreal/Kingston: McGill-Queen's University Press, 1991), p. 73.

established direct contact with the interior hunting bands. The Woodland Assiniboine and the Woodland Cree bands moved out onto the prairie and became provisioners, supplying the two trading companies with pemmican (dried buffalo meat mixed with buffalo fat and berries). Pemmican was easy to transport, kept well, and provided a nutritious, balanced diet. The demands for pemmican were enormous: a voyageur consumed nearly a kilogram a day — the equivalent of approximately three kilograms of fresh meat.

Where Historians Disagree
The First Nations' Role in the Fur Trade

For years, many fur-trade historians argued that the First Nations were passive agents in a trade dominated by more dynamic European traders. In *The Fur Trade and the Northwest to 1857*, for instance, E.E. Rich wrote that "within a decade of their becoming acquainted with European goods, tribe after tribe became utterly dependent on regular European supplies. The bow and arrow went out of use, and the Indian starved if he did not own a serviceable gun, powder, and shot; and in his tribal wars he was even more dependent on European arms."[1]

In the 1970s and early 1980s, Arthur J. Ray, Robin Fisher, Daniel Francis, Toby Morantz, and Paul C. Thistle challenged this interpretation. They underlined the independence of the Native peoples and their power in the trade. Historian Olive Dickason summarized the new approach in a review of Paul C. Thistle's *Indian–European Trade Relations in the Lower Saskatchewan River Region to 1840*: "Common to all of these works is the theme that Amerindians were as aware as Europeans in matters of self-interest, and during the early days of the fur trade at least, were able to manipulate matters to their own advantage. As long as they held the monopoly in fur production, they were also able to dictate the terms by which they were willing to trade. It was only when the exploitative nature of the fur trade began to affect the availability of resources, coupled with the widening technological gap that was a consequence of the Industrial Revolution, that Europeans were able to gain the upper hand."[2]

This led to a recognition of the First Nations' role in the fur trade as partners and initiators, as well as consumers. They became involved by their own choice. As historian Robin Fisher notes, concerning the early West Coast maritime fur trade, "The Indians of the northwest coast exercised a great deal of control over the trading relationship and, as a consequence, remained in control of their culture during this early contact period."[3] He added: "Even in these early years, the Indians were not passive objects of exploitation. Rather, they vigorously grew accustomed to the presence of the Europeans; they also became shrewder in trading with them."[4]

The absence of Native peoples' narratives remains the great weakness of research into the fur trade. Daniel Francis questions whether this has led historians to overemphasize the importance of the trading exchanges. In his *Battle for the West: Fur Traders and the Birth of Western Canada*, he observed that "the two groups met briefly at the posts to exchange goods, each receiving from the other things it could not produce for itself. Then they parted, the Indians returning to a world the trader never entered or understood, a world with its own patterns of trade, its own religion and social relations, its own wars and alliances.... [For] the most part traders were peripheral to the real concerns of the Indian people."[5]

Native-written studies have partially compensated for the absence of earlier First Nations accounts, including George Blondin's *When the World Was New: Stories of the Sahtú Dene* and Edward Ahenakew's *Voices of the Plains Cree.*[6]

[1] E.E. Rich, *The Fur Trade and the Northwest to 1857* (Toronto: McClelland & Stewart, 1967), pp. 102–103.
[2] Olive Dickason, "Review of Indian–European Trade Relations in the Lower Saskatchewan River Region to 1840 by Paul C. Thistle," *Western Canadian Publications Project Newsletter*, 21 (May 1987): 2.
[3] Robin Fisher, *Contact and Conflict: Indian–European Relations in British Columbia, 1774–1890* (Vancouver: University of British Columbia Press, 1977), p. 1.
[4] Ibid., p. 4.
[5] Daniel Francis, *Battle for the West: Fur Traders and the Birth of Western Canada* (Edmonton: Hurtig, 1982), p. 62.
[6] George Blondin, *When the World Was New: Stories of the Sahtú Dene* (Yellowknife: Outcrop Books, 1990); and Edward Ahenakew, *Voices of the Plains Cree*, ed., Ruth M. Buck (Regina: Canadian Plains Research Center, 1995; originally published, 1973).

THE RISE OF THE MÉTIS

French fur traders were established in the upper Great Lakes by the 1690s. As they intermarried with Native women, a group of "mixed-bloods," or Métis, appeared. The number of mixed marriages grew steadily. After a generation or two, Métis settlements extended from the upper Great Lakes west to the Red River and south through the Great Plains to the Arkansas River. Their culture uniquely blended Native and European customs. They saw themselves as constituting a "new nation."

THE MÉTIS AT THE RED RIVER

In the early nineteenth century, encampments of the French and their mixed-blood descendants developed at the junction of the Red and the Assiniboine rivers (at present-day Winnipeg). The increasing number of intermarriages furthered the growth of the "new nation" of the Métis. Like the mixed-bloods on the upper Great Lakes, the Red River Métis built homes of squared logs covered with bark roofs. They made a special baking-powder biscuit called "bannock," still a staple food in Métis communities today. Although they farmed a little, growing peas and potatoes in small gardens behind their cabins, they lived essentially off the buffalo hunt in the early nineteenth century.

They also introduced European technology to prairie life. For example, they introduced the small wagons used by the French Canadians in Quebec. These "Red River carts," built entirely of wood and tied together with leather, were easy to repair and very efficient. But the carts' constant rubbing of wood against wood made a terrible noise (one observer described it as the sound of a thousand fingernails being drawn

One of the earliest photographs taken in the Canadian West: a portrait of Susan, a Swampy Cree mixed-blood woman. Photographer Humphrey Lloyd Hime, then 24-years-old, took this shot while accompanying the Hind expedition in 1858.

Toronto Reference Library/T14359.

across a thousand panes of glass at the same time). As well, the carts stirred up clouds of dust that could be seen several kilometres away. Still, the Red River carts aided the Métis during the buffalo hunt. An ox-drawn cart could carry a load of 400 kg more than 30 km in a day. Several carts could be tied together in a caravan, enabling one driver to handle five oxen and carts. Soon the Red River cart trails rivalled the rivers as transportation routes.

ABORIGINAL WOMEN IN THE FUR TRADE

By the late eighteenth and early nineteenth centuries, many North West Company and Hudson's Bay Company employees had Native wives. Besides providing companionship and emotional support, Native wives offered voyageurs economic benefits too: the daughter of a leading hunter or chief brought to her new husband the trade of his new father-in-law, as well as his immediate relations. Native wives also taught the traders the customs and languages of the First Nations. As well, Native women acted as guides and interpreters for their husbands. Moreover, they made pemmican, gathered berries, fished, dressed skins, and made moccasins and snowshoes, all essential skills for the fur traders' survival.

By the early 1800s, interracial marriage between Europeans and the First Nations had become so common that about 1000 First Nations women and Métis children lived at North West Company posts. The company encouraged its labourers to marry the mixed-blood daughters of the older employees rather than First Nations women, in an effort to reduce the number of dependants at its posts, and thereby the demands for assistance. Many young Métis women had the ideal background for life as wives at a fur-trading post: they knew both the skills of their Native ancestors and the domestic duties required at the post — cleaning, planting, and harvesting.

THE RED RIVER COLONY

In 1811, Lord Douglas, the Fifth Earl of Selkirk, and a leading shareholder in the Hudson's Bay Company, persuaded the company to establish a European agricultural colony at the forks of the Red and Assiniboine rivers. The colony would provide a home to retire in for Hudson's Bay Company employees and their Native wives and families. It would also become an agricultural centre to supply provisions for the company's workforce in the interior. As well, the colony could serve as a refuge for evicted Scottish tenant farmers.

The following year, Selkirk recruited the majority of his settlers from Kildonan, Sutherlandshire, in Scotland, where the evictions of the tenant farmers to make sheep runs had been particularly brutal. After his family acquired a controlling interest in the Hudson's Bay Company, Selkirk obtained from the company an enormous land grant of 300 000 km^2 in the Red River valley — five times the size of Scotland — that he named Assiniboia. The location was contentious because it lay across the North West Company's vital pemmican supply line in the heart of the Red River valley, thus threatening to curtail its supply of pemmican. But the North West Company failed to prevent the founding of the colony.

THE ESTABLISHMENT OF THE SELKIRK COLONY

The advance party of 18 of Selkirk's settlers reached the Red River from Hudson Bay in late August 1812, and another 120 joined them in late October. Miles Macdonell, Selkirk's choice as governor, established the settlers near the junction of the Red and the Assiniboine rivers (now downtown Winnipeg).

The idealistic and impractical Lord Selkirk sent them off without ploughs, with only hoes and spades to use for cultivation. As well, the colony's lifeline of communication stretched back more than 1000 km to a tiny fort on Hudson Bay, visited once a year by ships from Britain. Only the assistance of the local Métis and North West Company traders enabled the Selkirk settlers to survive those first two years.

Then Macdonell unwittingly antagonized the Métis. He issued a "pemmican proclamation" in January 1814 that placed an embargo on the export of pemmican from the Red River settlement. This action hurt the North West Company because it depended on Red River pemmican to feed its voyageurs in the interior. The proclamation confirmed the Nor'Westers' suspicions that the Hudson's Bay Company had planted the Red River colony to ruin them.

In 1816 the rivalry intensified between the two companies. The Nor'Westers selected young Cuthbert Grant, the son of a Scottish Nor'Wester and a Cree mother, then in his early twenties, and three French-speaking Métis to head a movement of French-speaking Métis to drive out the Selkirk colonists.

SEVEN OAKS AND ITS AFTERMATH

On June 19, 1816, on a field called Seven Oaks, Grant and a party of some 60 or 70 Métis confronted Governor Robert Semple and some 25 settlers and Hudson's Bay Company employees. Fighting broke out, and Semple and 20 of his men lost their lives. Only one of Grant's men was killed.

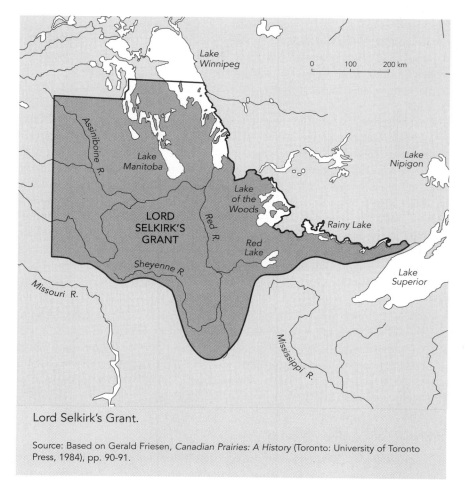

Lord Selkirk's Grant.

Source: Based on Gerald Friesen, *Canadian Prairies: A History* (Toronto: University of Toronto Press, 1984), pp. 90-91.

The victory strengthened Métis unity by reinforcing an identity that had already existed among the French-speaking Métis in the Red River valley. Within hours, Pierre Falcon, the Prairie Métis bard, told the story of the conflict in the "Chanson de la Grenouillère," or "Song of Frog Plain." That song became the French-speaking Métis' national anthem. Their collective memory of the victory gave the French-speaking Métis in the Red River a cohesion and a common identity that the English-speaking mixed-bloods (called the Country-born) around the Hudson's Bay Company posts to the north lacked.

The violence at Red River prompted the British government to seek a forced solution to the rivalry. It pressured the two financially exhausted companies to unite. In 1821, the Hudson's Bay and North West companies merged. The consolidated company, the Hudson's Bay Company, ended the North West Company's trade route via Montreal and shipped its furs through Hudson Bay. After 1821, only 5 percent of the furs exported from British North America passed through Montreal.

RED RIVER SOCIETY IN THE MID-NINETEENTH CENTURY

The Red River Scottish colonists and mixed-blood farmers faced many environmental challenges throughout the early nineteenth century: grasshoppers, early frosts, and floods. Whenever the Red River overflowed its banks, the water spread quickly over huge areas because of the flatness of the valley. Only by the 1840s did the settlement of some 6000 inhabitants achieve a level of stability and prosperity.

The Métis resided south and west of the forks of the two rivers. They numbered almost half the total population. To the north, down the Red River toward Lake Winnipeg, lived the Country-born who comprised about a third of the settlement. Their neighbours, the original Selkirk settlers, numbered about a tenth of the Red River population, and the First Nations another tenth.

The "Country-born," came from the northern Hudson's Bay Company posts. Many of their European ancestors came from the Orkney Islands, northwest of Scotland, a stopping point for the HBC vessels en route to Hudson Bay. Before 1800, the Hudson's Bay Company recruited more than 80 percent of its personnel there. Most of them were under 21 years of age. They worked as contract labourers for three or four years before returning home. Some, however, remained much longer; a few stayed for more than 20 years. These individuals fathered large families. Many used their savings to provide for their "country wives" and Native children before leaving to retire in the Orkneys or in Scotland. With the establishment of Selkirk's permanent settlement, many retired employees of the company now stayed in the Red River colony with their Native families. Their children were introduced to farming. Many also joined the Anglican Church, first established in the West by John West in 1820. A few obtained positions in the Hudson's Bay Company.

Although racial bonds and the common use of the Cree or Ojibwa languages united the Country-born and the French-speaking Métis, religion and their place of residence in the Red River colony divided them. Canadian historian John Foster wrote of the Country-born that a number "moved comfortably among the Métis. Others were more at home with the Indians.... Still others served a leadership role among the Kildonan Scots. Equal diversity could be found in terms of occupation and wealth."[3]

THE FRENCH-SPEAKING MÉTIS

The French-speaking Métis created a cohesive community, unified, in particular, by their Roman Catholic faith. The arrival of the first French-speaking priests in the Red River settlement in

Métis Encampment on a Buffalo Hunt, a painting by Paul Kane. The Upper Canadian painter is one of the best known early artists of the West.

Courtesy of the Royal Ontario Museum, Toronto/912.1.25 © ROM.

1818, followed by the first Oblate missionaries and the first sisters, the Grey Nuns, in the 1840s, strengthened the Métis' Christian faith as well as their knowledge of the language and culture of their French-Canadian ancestors.

The Métis also obtained a sense of community through participation in their expanding buffalo hunt. In the 1840s, they went on two annual hunts from the Red River — in June and in September or October. These expeditions included more than 1000 people. The Métis elected ten captains by vote at a general council, one of whom they named "chief of the hunt," or "governor." Each captain had ten "soldiers" under his command who helped the governor of the hunt maintain order. Rigid discipline prevented the premature stampede of the herds and was essential in the resistance to raids by the Sioux.

THE SAYER TRIAL, 1849

The Métis, the largest group in the Red River colony, came to resent the Hudson's Bay Company's tight control over the settlement. The test case of Métis power came during the trial of Pierre-Guillaume Sayer, a Métis trader arrested in 1849 on a charge of illegally trafficking in furs. The Hudson's Bay Company argued that Sayer violated its monopoly by selling goods to the colonists and trading with the First Nations. The judge, however, imposed no sentence. It would have been difficult to do so, because the Métis hunters constituted the most powerful military force in the colony. When Sayer emerged from the courthouse a free man, the Métis knew that they had broken the Hudson's Bay Company's monopoly. After the trial, the Hudson's Bay Company recognized French as an official language in the Red River colony.

The second test of Métis power came two years later. As the Métis moved farther to the southwest to hunt buffalo, they came into conflict

Pierre-Guillaume Sayer (left) and Louis Riel, Sr.

Provincial Archives of Manitoba/N1445.

with the Sioux. The Métis–Sioux wars intensified in the 1840s and came to a head in 1851, at the battle of Grand Coteau ("big hillock"), southeast of present-day Minot, North Dakota. The Métis victory at Grand Coteau over a numerically larger party of Sioux demonstrated their growing military supremacy in the Red River and surrounding areas.

THE END OF THE RED RIVER COLONY'S ISOLATION

By the 1840s, the Red River Métis had developed a largely self-sufficient economy based on the buffalo hunt, some small-scale farming, and seasonal labour for the Hudson's Bay Company. But it was in the 1850s that the colony's horizons grew enormously, mainly as a result of its more frequent contacts with St. Paul, Minnesota, to the south.

St. Paul gradually replaced York Factory on Hudson Bay as the Red River's major entrepôt. From 1851 to 1869, the number of Red River carts journeying to St. Paul, Minnesota, to sell furs and purchase supplies rose from 100 to 2500. Mail service to the Red River colony came through St. Paul after 1853, rather than by the slower and more cumbersome route through York Factory on Hudson Bay. A railway reached St. Paul in 1855, and within a year the Hudson's Bay Company itself used it to bring in supplies. The establishment of a regular steamboat connection with St. Paul and to the Red River colony in 1859 made the ties with Minnesota (with a population of nearly 200 000 by 1860) all the more binding. Fortunately for British North America the outbreak of the American Civil War in 1861–65, and the war between the Americans and the Sioux in 1862–64, prevented Minnesota's annexation of the Red River country in the 1860s.

Many Métis moved farther west in the early 1860s attracted by rising opportunities in the buffalo-hide trade. Those who spent the winter on the prairies to be nearer the herds became known as *hivernants* ("winterers"). The growing Métis involvement in the buffalo-robe trade led them to establish settlements at the forks of the Saskatchewan River, in the North Saskatchewan River valley, in the Cypress Hills area of present-day southwestern Saskatchewan, and at Lac Ste. Anne, about 80 km northwest of Fort Edmonton. Lac Ste. Anne became the largest Métis settlement in the Northwest outside of the Red River colony until St. Albert (about 15 km northwest of Edmonton) was founded in 1862. By the mid-1860s, the buffalo herds had migrated so far from present-day Manitoba that the Red River-based hunt had almost ended.

In 1871, approximately 2000–4000 mixed-bloods lived along the North Saskatchewan River between the Red River and the Rockies, and about 11 000 at the junction of the Red and the Assiniboine rivers. The Métis and Country-born population of 13 000–15 000 was approximately one-half of the estimated number of Plains First Nations in British North America. The mixed-bloods' increasingly frequent intrusions into the First Nations' hunting grounds in search of buffalo bred resentment.

THE PLAINS FIRST NATIONS IN THE MID-NINETEENTH CENTURY

While the Métis and Country-born population doubled in the Red River every 15–20 years, that of the Plains First Nations seriously declined in the mid-nineteenth century. In 1837–38, smallpox ravaged the Great Plains nations, just as it had a half-century earlier (in 1780–82). Such diseases tended to be carried along the trade routes — the drainage systems of the Missouri and Saskatchewan rivers. Non-Native crews usually carried the smallpox viruses. The boat brigades' tight schedules often caused crews to be dispatched while the men were still infectious. They moved into the interior and infected the First Nations who had gathered in their large summer camps. They, in turn, carried the disease farther inland.

Red River carts by the North Saskatchewan River, 1871.

National Archives of Canada/PA-138573.

Thanks to the efforts of the Hudson's Bay Company traders many of the Cree around the company's posts were saved. The discovery of a smallpox vaccine in Europe around 1800 checked the spread of the epidemic. The Hudson's Bay Company began an extensive vaccination program among the western Canadian Native peoples. The vaccinated population constituted an effective barrier, and the highly contagious disease spread no farther north than the Hudson's Bay Company posts on the northern fringes of the prairies. Saved from smallpox, the Cree became the most numerous First Nations group on the Canadian prairies. After the epidemic ran its course, the Crees could more readily move farther onto the prairies because the strength of the Blackfoot-speaking nations had been so reduced. But, smallpox continued to take its toll. In the epidemic of 1870 more than 3500 First Nations, Métis, and Country-born on the Canadian Plains died.

Other infectious killer diseases also ravaged the Native peoples. In 1864–65, more than 1000 Blackfoot-speaking people died of an outbreak of scarlet fever. A measles epidemic hit the Cree. Influenza and whooping cough also spread through their communities. A new disease — tuberculosis — arrived in the 1860s, brought by refugee Sioux from the United States and by Red River people moving west (both groups had already been exposed to the deadly bacterium).

THE ARRIVAL OF THE WHISKY TRADERS

In the mid-1860s, the Blackfoot experienced another assault: that of the American whisky traders. In the 1850s and the early 1860s, the Blackfoot had traded with both the Hudson's Bay Company and the American Fur Company. At Fort Edmonton and Rocky Mountain House they exchanged pemmican and horses, as well as the few beaver furs they trapped, for British trade goods. At Fort Benton, in Montana, they traded bulky buffalo hides and robes (which were difficult for the Hudson's Bay Company to transport profitably in their York boats) for American goods. The hides made excellent coats and robes. They could also be tanned into tough and durable leather suitable for making industrial machinery belts. The American Fur Company bought all that it could, shipping the furs down the Missouri by steamer to St. Louis.

The stability of the Missouri River fur trade suddenly ended, however, in 1864 with the collapse of the American Fur Company. Then, just after the end of the American Civil War in 1865, the discovery of gold brought a flood of prospectors and merchants to the mountains of Montana. With them came a flourishing whisky trade. After U.S. marshals began to enforce laws against the trade, many of the traders moved north to present-day southern Alberta and Saskatchewan to make their fortunes. Their arrival led to great social disruption among groups that had little acquaintance with alcohol and no social controls in place to deal with its consequences.

THE NORTHWEST ON THE EVE OF CANADIAN SETTLEMENT

Until the late 1850s, the fur traders and the early visitors to the Northwest had all reported that the treeless prairies, which stretched as far as the eye could see, were unsuitable for farming. This perception changed in the late 1850s, and by the 1860s, Canadians had come to covet the Northwest. The lack of good agricultural land in the United Canadas made the western lands more inviting. In the early 1860s, both the Canadian and the British expeditions to the Northwest published their findings. Of the two, the British-sponsored expedition led by John

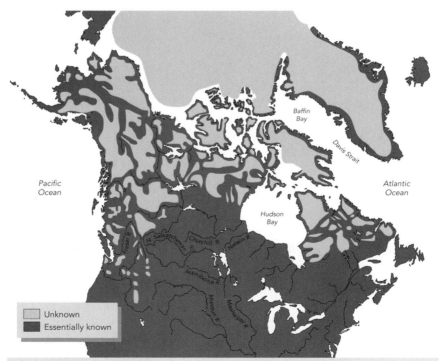

Non-Natives' knowledge of northern North America in 1870.

Source: Adapted from Richard I. Ruggles, *A Country So Interesting: The Hudson's Bay Company and Two Centuries of Mapping, 1670–1870* (Montreal/Kingston: McGill-Queen's University Press, 1991), p. 119.

Palliser is the best known. Dispatched in 1857, it was commissioned to report on the possibilities for agricultural settlement. In the same year, the Canadians sent out an expedition with Henry Youle Hind, a professor of geology and chemistry at Trinity University in Toronto, as scientific observer. Both expeditions reported on the magnificent possibilities for European agriculture, particularly in the Red River area and in the "fertile belt" of the North Saskatchewan River valley. These findings provided the incentive for the westward expansion of the eastern British North American colonies.

The First Nations remained the dominant group on the Plains until the late nineteenth century. By the 1860s, however, their political power had been reduced by severe population losses through epidemics, the rapidly diminishing buffalo herds, and the rise of a new mixed-blood population who now intruded into their hunting grounds. And, in the Red River area at least, small numbers of Canadians began to arrive.

NORTH OF THE PRAIRIES

The majority of the North's indigenous peoples, the First Nations and the Inuit, enjoyed uncontested political control of their homelands until the late nineteenth century and, in many more isolated areas, into the twentieth. Arctic explorers, fur traders, and Christian missionaries were the first non-Native newcomers to come north. A very small number of Christian missionaries, Roman Catholic and Anglican, arrived around 1850, or about half a century after the fur traders. Until the late nineteenth century, however, the number of church workers in the North remained quite small.

A decade or so after Alexander Mackenzie's voyage, in 1789, down the river that now bears his name, the North West Company established its first posts in the Mackenzie River valley. After the merger of the North West and Hudson's Bay Companies in 1821, the revitalized Hudson's Bay Company extended its operations throughout the Mackenzie River valley. By the 1840s, the company was expanding over the Mackenzie Mountains into the Yukon River valley.

As in the south European epidemics, inadvertently brought north by the fur traders, devastated Native communities. Anthropologist Shepard Krech III has written that the Gwitch'in (Kutchin) in the northern Yukon and adjacent area, for example, had an estimated population of about 5400 people in the early nineteenth century. By the 1860s, this number had been reduced to an estimated 850 to 900.[4]

In the early nineteenth century, British naval parties resumed the search for the Northwest Passage — not for economic reasons but for the international prestige of locating it. Sir John Franklin became one of the most famous explorers of all time. Sent off, in 1844, with the latest technological assistance, with ships heated by pipes fired from steam boilers, and with a three-year supply of canned food, the expedition seemed guaranteed of success. Yet Franklin, on this, his third Arctic expedition, refused to adapt to indigenous technology. He took no dogs, sleds, pemmican, or Inuit clothing. Within two years, the entire expedition of 129 men perished, as their ships became locked in pack ice near King William Island in the central Arctic. Even their great source of food, the canned provisions, turned out to be a liability, as the seams, soldered with lead, leaked toxic lead into the food.

Over 30 expeditions searched for Franklin and his missing party between 1847 and 1859: first, unsuccessfully, for survivors; and second, after evidence surfaced of their deaths, for explanations of the expedition's failure. The intensive search resulted in a large part of the Canadian Arctic Archipelago being charted and the northern limits of the North American continent established. Their sailing in and out of Arctic bays and inlets, and their wintering over on Arctic ice, led the English to claim sovereignty over the Inuit's homeland.

The fur trade attracted first the French to the Northwest, and later the British. Two rival companies in the British period — the Hudson's Bay Company (founded in 1670) and the North West Company (established in the 1780s) — vied for monopoly over the fur trade in the region. In 1821, the British government forced a merger of the two companies under the Hudson's Bay Company name. Settlement grew in the area, first at the junction of the Red and Assiniboine rivers, and later, in the 1860s, farther west, nearer the diminishing buffalo grounds. The intermarriage of fur traders and First Nations had led to the creation of two new peoples, the Métis and the Country-born. By the end of the 1860s, these two mixed-blood groups numbered from 13 000 to 15 000 in the Northwest, roughly half of the Plains First Nations population, estimated to be 25 000. It was the Métis, with their sense of constituting "a new nation," who would confront the Canadians when they tried to take control of the region in the late 1860s.

NOTES

1. The HBC Committee in London, quoted in K.G. Davies, "Henry Kelsey," *Dictionary of Canadian Biography*, vol. 2: *1700–1740* (Toronto: University of Toronto Press, 1969): 308.
2. Barbara Belyea presents all four surviving versions of Anthony Henday's report on his 1754–1755 journey in, *A Year Inland* (Waterloo, Ont.: Wilfrid Laurier University Press, 2000).
3. John Foster, "The Country-Born in the Red River Settlement (c. 1820–1870)," Ph.D. thesis, University of Alberta, 1973, p. 264.
4. Shepard Krech III, "On the Aboriginal Population of the Kutchin," in *Interpreting Canada's North. Selected Readings*, ed. Kenneth S. Coates and William R. Morrison (Toronto: Copp Clark Pitman, 1989): 66.

LINKING TO THE PAST

The Canadian West
http://www.archives.ca/05/0529/052901_e.html

This site provides a lavishly illustrated and cross-referenced history of the West. The section "Anticipation: Expectations for the New Land" covers some of the material discussed in this chapter.

Fur Trade and Mission History
http://collections.ic.gc.ca/abpolitics/alberta/fur_trade/index.html

This site provides an historical overview of the exploration, fur trade, and religious missions in the West, with a focus on present-day Alberta.

An Overview of the Métis
http://www.geocities.com/SoHo/Atrium/4832/metis.html

An overview of Métis history and culture is given.

Transfer of Power
http://www.canadiana.org/hbc/hist/hist8_e.html

This site reviews the merger of the Hudson's Bay Company and the North West Company. Navigate this extensive Website, which explores the history of the fur trade and HBC, for historical information, biographies of explorers, maps, stories, and more.

Bibliography

Gerald Friesen's *The Canadian Prairies: A History* (Toronto: University of Toronto Press, 1984) provides an excellent overview of the entire period; as does Sarah Carter, *Aboriginal People and Colonizers of Western Canada to 1900* (Toronto: University of Toronto Press, 1999). Two beautifully illustrated books are William R. Morrison, *True North: The Yukon and Northwest Territories* (Toronto: Oxford University Press, 1998); and John Herd Thompson, *Forging the Prairie West* (Toronto: Oxford University Press, 1998), both in Oxford's new "Illustrated History of Canada" series. For the Mackenzie River basin see Kerry Abel's *Drum Songs: Glimpses of Dene History* (Montreal/Kingston: McGill-Queen's University Press, 1993). R. Douglas Francis reviews changing perceptions of the Northwest in, *Images of the West* (Saskatoon: Western Producer Prairie Books, 1989). Kerry Abel provides a complete bibliographic guide to the historical literature in "The Northwest and the North," in M. Brook Taylor, ed., *Canadian History: A Reader's Guide*, vol. 1, *Beginnings to Confederation* (Toronto: University of Toronto Press, 1994), pp. 325–55.

For information on the First Nations in the eighteenth and nineteenth centuries consult Arthur Ray, *Indians in the Fur Trade* (Toronto: University of Toronto Press, 1974). John Ewers's *The Blackfeet* (Norman: University of Oklahoma Press, 1958), and his *The Horse in Blackfoot Indian Culture* (Washington, DC: Smithsonian Institution Press, 1955) are essential. On cultural change on the northern Plains, an essential work is Theodore Binnema's *Common and Contested Ground. A Human and Environmental History of the Northwestern Plains* (Norman: University of Oklahoma Press, 2001). For background on the impact of disease, see the early section of Maureen K. Lux, *Medicine that Walks: Disease, Medicine, and Canadian Plains Native People, 1880–1940* (Toronto: University of Toronto Press, 2001). Hugh Dempsey's recent study, *Firewater. The Impact of the Whiskey Trade on the Blackfoot Nation* (Calgary: Fifth House, 2002) reviews the topic of substance abuse.

E.E. Rich provides an overview of the fur trade in western Canada in *The Fur Trade and the North West to 1857* (Toronto: McClelland & Stewart, 1967). Another survey is that by Dan Francis, *Battle for the West: Fur Traders and the Birth of Western Canada* (Edmonton: Hurtig, 1982). For short sketches of the most important European fur traders see the essays on Kelsey, La Vérendrye, Henday, Hearne, Thompson, and others in the 14 volumes of the *Dictionary of Canadian Biography* (Toronto: University of Toronto Press, 1966–1998). (These sketches are now available online: www.biographi.ca.) The story of Native women and the fur trade is told by Jennifer S.H. Brown in *Strangers in Blood: Fur Trade Company Families in Indian Country* (Vancouver: University of British Columbia Press, 1980); and by Sylvia Van Kirk in *"Many Tender Ties": Women in Fur Trade Society in Western Canada* (Winnipeg: Watson & Dwyer, 1980).

The Métis are the subject of many studies. One popular work is D. Bruce Sealey and Antoine S. Lussier, *The Métis: Canada's Forgotten People* (Winnipeg: Manitoba Métis Federation Press, 1975). George Woodcock translated Marcel Giraud's classic *Le Métis Canadien* (Paris: Institut d'ethnologie, Université de Paris, 1945) into English, under the title *The Métis in the Canadian West*, 2 vols. (Edmonton: University of Alberta Press, 1986). Jacqueline Peterson and Jennifer S.H. Brown have edited *The New People: Being and Becoming Métis in North America* (Winnipeg: University of Manitoba Press, 1985).

Valuable maps of the Northwest appear in R. Cole Harris, ed., *Historical Atlas of Canada*, vol. 1, *From the Beginning to 1800* (Toronto: University of Toronto Press, 1987); R. Louis Gentilcore, ed., *The Historical Atlas of Canada*, vol. 2, *The Land Transformed, 1800–1891* (Toronto: University of Toronto Press, 1993); and Richard I. Ruggles, *A Country So Interesting: The Hudson's Bay Company and Two Centuries of Mapping, 1670–1870* (Montreal/Kingston: McGill-Queen's University Press, 1991).

CHAPTER 10

THE PACIFIC COAST TO THE 1860s

TIME LINE

1774 – The Spanish expedition led by Juan Pérez encounters the Haida off the Queen Charlotte Islands

1793 – Fur trader Alexander Mackenzie becomes the first European to cross the continent via Lake Athabaska to the Pacific Ocean

1827 – Fort Langley is built by the Hudson's Bay Company near the mouth of the Fraser River

1843 – The Hudson's Bay Company builds Fort Victoria on Vancouver Island

1846 – Under the Oregon Treaty, the 49th parallel becomes the international boundary between British and American claims from the Rocky Mountains to the Pacific

1849 – The colony of Vancouver Island is established by the Hudson's Bay Company at the request of the British Crown

1858 – The Fraser River gold rush leads to the establishment of the mainland colony of British Columbia, separate from the colony of Vancouver Island

1866 – The two colonies of British Columbia and Vancouver Island are united

The First Nations population of present-day British Columbia lived along the major salmon rivers, at scattered village sites along the ocean, and inland along the river systems. Europeans only made first contact with the First Nations of what is now coastal British Columbia in the 1770s, nearly three centuries after large-scale European contact with the First Nations of northeastern North America.

Initially, Spain, Russia, Britain, and the United States competed for control. Eventually, however, only Britain and the United States contested the sector between Russian Alaska and Spanish California. In 1818, they agreed to joint occupancy of the area. Twenty-eight years later, in 1846, the two countries consented to extend the international border along the 49th parallel from the prairies to the Pacific, and to include Vancouver Island in Britain's jurisdiction.

Immigrants first settled at the southern tip of Vancouver Island in the 1840s and then at the mouth of the Fraser River during the gold rush of 1858. In the 1860s, the newcomers claimed ownership of the entire coast and interior of British Columbia, even though well into the nineteenth century, the First Nations outnumbered them.

THE FIRST NATIONS OF THE NORTHWEST COAST

The First Nations have lived on the Pacific coast for thousands of years. One of the oldest archaeological sites on the North Pacific coast is the Fraser River canyon, which dates back at least 8500 years. The Native peoples probably arrived in successive waves, for nineteen distinct languages are represented on the British Columbia coast today. Hemmed in by towering mountains, the narrow coastline was heavily populated. It is estimated that nearly half of the total First Nations population of Canada lived in British Columbia at the moment of European contact. For these maritime people, salmon became the main food resource. They used red cedar for the construction of their plank houses, canoes, containers, and carved masks, as well as their most famous creations — totem poles.

NOTIONS OF PROPERTY

In several respects, the Northwest Coast peoples had a notion of property similar to that of Europeans. A large group of kinspeople, or a lineage — a group of people who shared a common ancestor in the real or mythological past — formed the primary unit of their societies. One or several kin groups might occupy the same winter village, and these villages in turn constituted independent units within the larger nation. Local kin groups claimed ownership of the fishing stations, berry patches, cedar groves, and stretches of beach. When they left their permanent winter villages for the salmon fisheries, they went to their own recognized stretches of the rivers. When the Europeans came, the chiefs or leaders of the kin groups made them pay for the wood and even the fresh water they used.

FIRST NATION IMPRESSIONS OF THE EUROPEANS

The Squamish of the Capilano reserve at Vancouver tell about the first time their ancestors encountered the newcomers, a century and a half earlier. As Chief Mathias told the story, the warriors hesitated going on board the floating island with cobwebs hanging from the sticks growing on it, until, with great misgivings, the bravest climbed the rope ladder onto the deck. The pale-faced captain, who looked like a corpse, advanced with outstretched hand. Never having heard of the handshake, the chief thought they were being challenged to a Native finger-wrestling match. He therefore waved away the man with whom the captain was trying to shake hands and called for the Squamish strongman to accept the challenge. Seeing he was

The beautiful sea-going canoes of the Northwest Coast were usually made of a single felled cedar, which was hollowed and shaped to meet specified requirements.

National Archives of Canada/C-30193.

Captain George Vancouver visited Chief Cheslakee's village on the Nimpkish River in July 1792. Each of the several dozen Kwakwaka'wakw (Kwagiulth or Kwakiutl) villages was socially and politically autonomous. This illustration is reproduced from Vancouver's *Voyage of Discovery*.

Glenbow Archives, Calgary, Canada/NA-528-1.

misunderstood, the captain shrugged and approached the chief with outstretched hand. The chief then said to the strongman, "He doesn't want you. He thinks you are not strong enough." With that, the chief refused to consider the captain's "challenge." The strangers' gifts also greatly puzzled Mathias's ancestors. It appeared to them that they had received snow in a sack (flour) and buttons (coins).[1]

EUROPEAN EXPLORATION OF THE NORTHWEST COAST

Although Spain was the first European power to reach the Pacific Ocean, it took the Spanish two and a half centuries to advance northward from Mexico. Crippled by economic depressions, epidemics, and defeats on European battlefields, Spain lost its pioneering spirit. Rival European empires had seized Spanish islands in the West Indies, but luckily for Spain, its European rivals seldom ventured to the Pacific, until Russians arrived in the eighteenth century.

RUSSIAN ACTIVITY IN THE NORTH PACIFIC

Vitus Bering, a Danish navigator in the Russian service, made the first documented Russian voyage to present-day Alaska. In 1728, he sailed along the eastern coast of Siberia until he found the strait that now bears his name. Then, in 1741, he explored an area in present-day southeastern Alaska. His voyage established Russia's claim to the Alaskan Panhandle and led to Russian economic expansion in the Pacific.

Rumours of the Russian activity prompted Spain to advance northward to protect Mexico. They established settlements in California at San Diego, Monterey, and San Francisco and sponsored expeditions to investigate Russian advances along the Northwest Coast and to assert Spanish sovereignty north of Mexico. Juan Pérez sailed in late January 1774 to Alaska, but bad weather forced him to turn back just north of the Queen Charlotte Islands. Pérez met 150 Haidas off the Queen Charlottes — the first recorded meeting between Europeans and British Columbian First Nations. The meeting was friendly, and the Spaniards traded small shipboard objects for Native artifacts.

THE ARRIVAL OF THE BRITISH

Instead of the Russians, the British became the Spaniards' greatest rival on the Pacific Northwest Coast. Captain James Cook, already renowned for his discoveries in Australasia and Antarctica, and who had been present at the French surrender of Louisbourg in 1758 and had helped to guide the English armada to Quebec, visited the Northwest Coast on his third expedition to the Pacific in the spring of 1778. Cook's two vessels, *Discovery* and *Resolution*, arrived at Nootka Sound, which had been sighted by Pérez four years earlier. Here, Cook spent a month refitting his ships. Since no other European power knew of the Spaniard's previous visit, Cook (who was killed in January 1779 by Natives in Hawaii) was credited with "discovering" Nootka, and the British claim to the Northwest Coast received international recognition.

The publication, in 1784, of the official account of Cook's third voyage proved a turning point. Captain James King, who had taken command shortly after the death of Cook, recounted in *A Voyage to the Pacific Ocean* (1784) how sea-otter pelts obtained in trade on the Northwest Coast had brought as much as $120 each at Canton, China. Other mariners saw their opportunity. British and American ships entered the North Pacific sea otter trade.

To strengthen their claim to the Northwest Coast, the Spanish in 1789 briefly established a colony at Nootka Sound for six years. Spain argued that it had the exclusive right to trade and to control the coast, while Britain claimed that navigation was open to any nation. But, in 1795,

Spain agreed to share the northern ports because it badly needed British assistance in its war against France. Thus ended Spain's attempts to exert a Spanish presence north of California.

IMPERIAL RIVALRY ON THE NORTHWEST COAST

The withdrawal of Spain in the mid-1790s left the Northwest Coast open to three contenders: Russia, Britain, and the newly independent United States. North of the present-day Alaskan boundary, the Russians now encountered intense British and American competition for sea-otter pelts. But the Russian traders laboured under several major handicaps. In contrast to both the Americans and the English, they possessed fewer and poorer trade goods and inferior trading vessels. The Russian advance slowed down in the Alaska Panhandle, where they faced strong competition from British and American traders and from Tlingit mid-

New tools and pigments became available to the Native peoples after contact with the fur traders. Carving became more elaborate and colourful. This photo, taken by C.F. Newcombe in 1901, shows the Kwakwaka'wakw village of Blunden Harbour.

Royal British Columbia Museum/PN 258.

dlemen, who traded European goods to the interior First Nations in what is now Yukon and northwestern British Columbia.

Britain strengthened its claim with the dispatch of a three-year expedition under George Vancouver, a naval officer who had served with Cook's expedition in 1778. From 1792 to 1794, Vancouver methodically and painstakingly charted the intricate coastline from Oregon to Alaska.

The outbreak of war between Britain and France in 1793, which lasted until 1815, curtailed British voyages to the Northwest Coast. As Britain withdrew men from its merchant ships for service in the Royal Navy, American entrepreneurs captured Britain's trade in the North Pacific. After the mid-1790s, American traders dominated the coastal trade until the mid-1820s, by which time the sea otter was virtually extinct due to over-hunting.

THE FIRST NATIONS AND THE MARITIME FUR TRADERS

The Northwest Coast First Nations welcomed the European fur traders with their iron trading goods. They wanted the metal to construct tools. The Spanish discovered that the First Nations coveted iron so much that they even removed the metal strapping from the sides of Spanish ships. Not even the rudder chains were safe. They paid careful attention to the quality of goods they purchased and refused iron that contained flaws or was too brittle. They also bought muskets. In addition to purchasing iron goods, the Native peoples bought cloth, clothing, and blankets. They also developed an appreciation of rum and another new trade good, molasses.

The coastal First Nations initially exercised considerable control over the early European fur trade, preventing the Europeans from coming into contact with the inland groups. Often the Native traders were middlemen who added a 200–300 percent markup to the furs and goods they traded. Women traders participated actively in the transactions with the newcomers.

Although the linguistic diversity of the Pacific coast exceeded that of Europe, a single trade language called "Chinook" came into use along the West Coast in the 1830s. In its vocabulary of about 300 key words are borrowings from First Nations languages, as well as English and French: "skookum" means powerful or fast, "chuck" — water; "cheechako" — newcomer; "Kinchotsh" (King George Man) — Englishman. It was spoken as well in the inland districts, and the middlemen knew that language. The entry around 1810 of European traders into the interior, however, took away much of the First Nations middlemen's trade. For nearly 40 years, the maritime fur trade prospered, but by 1825 the sea-otter population neared extinction.

The fur trade enriched the coastal peoples' culture. The tools they made from their new supplies of iron allowed them to produce better and more refined headdresses, costumes, and masks for feasts and ceremonies. As well, new dyes and pigments became available through the traders. Although the First Nations carvers favoured the traditional colours, weavers supplemented the original pigments — red and yellow ochres, black and blue-green copper oxide — with the whole spectrum of European trade colours. Wood carving expanded. During these years the totem poles, which displayed individual families' genealogies, underwent much elaboration and reached greater heights.

Although the Northwest Coast peoples enjoyed a higher standard of living after European contact, they also died in large numbers. The absence of accurate statistics makes it difficult to provide even rough estimates of the casualties, but European infectious diseases such as measles, mumps, and, especially, smallpox took their toll, as they did elsewhere in the Americas.

Securing the Inland Fur Trade

After European navigators reached the Northwest Coast by sea, European fur traders arrived by land. Anxious to find a short supply line to the Pacific Ocean, the North West Company searched for a route westward from Lake Athabasca to the Pacific. The Nor'Wester Alexander Mackenzie, the first European to canoe the northern river that now bears his name and to reach the Arctic Ocean, completed the first crossing of North America (north of Mexico) in 1793 by travelling down what is now called the Fraser River, then over to the Bella Coola River, and down to the Pacific. On a seaside rock he simply wrote, "From Canada. By Land." The arduous route proved useless for transporting furs, but the journey made the 24-year-old Mackenzie's reputation as a fearless and daring trader-explorer.

Two other Nor'Westers worked to find a commercial route to the Pacific. In 1808, Simon Fraser, who had first opened up fur-trading posts in the interior of what is now British Columbia, travelled with a small party down the treacherous river named after him. He succeeded, but concluded that the route was unnavigable.

Finally, in 1811, David Thompson, a partner of the North West Company, followed the Columbia River, and thereby connected the North West Company trade route from east of the Rockies to the Pacific Coast. A sea expedition sent by John Jacob Astor's Pacific Fur Company had arrived in late March 1811, just months before Thompson. On the basis of having founded Fort Astoria, the Americans claimed the Oregon country.

The Joint Occupation of the Oregon Territory

As a temporary compromise, Britain and the United States agreed in 1818 to occupy the Columbia country jointly and to decide its fate later. The agreement left commerce open to both British and American traders between latitudes 42° and 54°40' (from the northern boundary of California to the southern limits of Alaska).

With the merger of the North West Company and the Hudson's Bay Company in 1821, the new Hudson's Bay Company under the management of Sir George Simpson began to exploit the rich fur resources of the Northwest Coast. Having obtained from the British Crown a 21-year lease to the exclusive trade of the "Indian Territory" (the lands between the Rocky Mountains and the Pacific), Simpson located a Pacific depot at Fort Vancouver, in an area of good farmland 150 km up the Columbia River. Other forts followed. The three most important were Fort Langley, near the mouth of the Fraser River, built in 1827; Fort Simpson, on the boundary of the Russian territory to the north, in 1831; and Fort Victoria, strategically located on the southern tip of Vancouver Island, in 1843. The Hudson's Bay Company's energetic commercial activities established a strong British presence on the Pacific coast.

American interest in the Columbia country increased in the early 1840s. Americans began arriving in the 1830s, and by 1843 they numbered about 1000. In the next three years, another 5000 settlers arrived in the Columbia River valley. But thanks to the Hudson's Bay Company's network of posts, inland trails, and shipping routes, Britain dominated north of the Columbia River. Nevertheless, American president James Polk, who won the presidential election in December 1844 with the electoral slogan "54° 40' or fight," demanded all of "Oregon," between latitudes 42° and 54°40', up to the Russian border.

In his inaugural address in March, President Polk reaffirmed his position that the United States' title to Oregon was "clear and unquestionable." Great popular support existed for his stand. In the summer of 1845, the expansionist newspaper, *The United States Magazine and Democratic Review*, introduced in an editorial the phrase, "manifest destiny." The paper argued that foreign governments were attempting to check "the fulfillment of our manifest destiny to overspread the continent allotted by Providence for the free development of our yearly multiplying millions." Within months, the phrase became common usage throughout the United States.

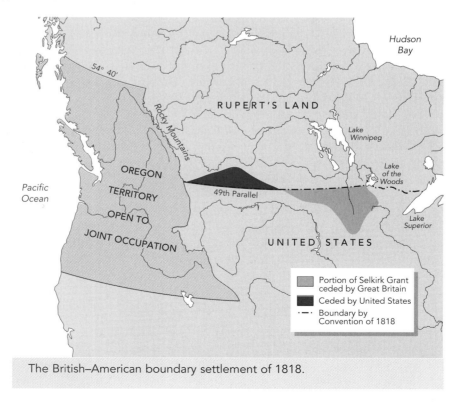

The British–American boundary settlement of 1818.

Fortunately for Britain's claim, the Americans began a war with Mexico in 1846 over Texas (and later New Mexico and California), and Polk did not want to fight with both Mexico and Britain at the same time. To avoid conflict, Britain retracted its claim to all the land south of the Columbia River. The Anglo–American treaty signed in June 1846 extended the 49th parallel (which had become the international border across the prairies in 1818) from the Rocky Mountains to the Pacific Ocean, and left all of Vancouver Island in British hands.

Anxious to counter the threat of American squatter settlement in its Pacific territory, the British government asked the Hudson's Bay Company to colonize, as well as to manage, Vancouver Island for ten years. A royal grant of 1849 stipulated that the company had to develop the island, make lands available to settlers at reasonable prices, and safeguard Aboriginal rights. By the end of 1849, Fort Victoria served as the company's western headquarters, its shipping depot, and its provisioning centre, as well as the capital of the colony of Vancouver Island. In 1852, the Colonial Office extended the jurisdiction of the governor of Vancouver Island to include the Queen Charlotte Islands.

At the time of the first census in 1855, less than 1000 non-Native inhabitants lived in the Pacific colony of Vancouver Island. The discovery of coal at Nanaimo on the east coast of the island had led to the founding of a small permanent European settlement there. But until the Fraser River gold rush in 1858, the colony continued primarily as a fur-trading region, with its centre at Fort Victoria.

The fur traders consisted of immigrants from places as diverse as the Orkney Islands and Hawaii, along with French Canadians, Iroquois, and mixed-bloods. Many of the non-Natives were married to First Nations, Country-born, or Métis women. The existence of virtually free land in Oregon and Washington attracted settlers there; on Vancouver Island, land had to be purchased. On Vancouver Island and the mainland, the Aboriginal peoples outnumbered the Europeans by roughly fifty to one.

JAMES DOUGLAS

James Douglas became governor of the colony of Vancouver Island in 1851. A "Scotch West Indian," Douglas was born in British Guiana (now Guyana), the son of "a free coloured woman" and a Scottish merchant. Sent to Scotland for his schooling at age twelve, James later left school at the age of sixteen and joined the North West Company as an apprentice. After the union of the two rival companies, he entered northern "Oregon," or New Caledonia, as the company called it. There, in 1828, he married Amelia Connolly, the daughter of William Connolly, a fur trader from Lower Canada, and his Cree wife. In 1830, the company transferred James to Fort Vancouver, and nine years later he became a chief factor. With his promotion to Fort Victoria in 1849, he became the senior company officer west of the Rocky Mountains.

JAMES DOUGLAS'S ABORIGINAL POLICY

Douglas refused to intervene in quarrels among the First Nations, but he did use his power, including Royal Navy gunboats, to settle disputes between them and Europeans. Shortly before he became governor, Douglas wrote that, in all his dealings with First Nations, he had

James Douglas played such an important role in the early history of British Columbia that he is called "the father of British Columbia." He and his wife, Amelia Connolly Douglas, had multi-ethnic backgrounds — Douglas was of Scottish and African origin, and his wife of Irish, French-Canadian, and First Nations descent.

The British Columbia Archives/HP 2656.

"invariably acted on the principle that it is inexpedient and unjust to hold tribes responsible for the acts of individuals." The governor meted out stern discipline to individuals he perceived as warranting such treatment, but not to their communities. Unlike many of the early settlers on the island, Douglas tried to understand First Nations society. Above all, he did not want the open warfare that had broken out between the American settlers and the Native peoples in the Washington Territory to spill over the border.

To avoid conflict between the First Nations and the settlers, Douglas purchased land from the First Nations before new settlement occurred. Between 1850 and 1854, he made fourteen treaties with groups living in areas that Europeans wanted to settle. In all, he purchased roughly 1000 km^2 of land, or about 3 percent of the total area of Vancouver Island. Douglas allowed the communities to select the land they wanted for their reserves and instructed the surveyors to meet the First Nations peoples' wishes.

In hindsight, Douglas was not overly generous with the amount of land allotted to reserves on Vancouver Island and later on the mainland. Just before he retired as governor of the mainland colony of British Columbia in 1864, he told the legislature, "The areas thus partially defined and set apart, in no case exceed the proportion of ten acres [4 ha] for each family concerned."

Some of the settlers complained that although Douglas handled First Nations well, he did not handle the colonists properly. They protested that he had not carried out his obligation to settle the island, that he ruled autocratically, and that he relied too heavily on the company's officials for advice. Most of all, they objected to his setting the price of land at £1 for one acre (0.4 ha) when land in the neighbouring American Pacific Northwest went for one-quarter the

At the first elections to the Vancouver Island Assembly in 1856, some 40 voters elected 7 members to North America's smallest legislature. Painting by Charles W. Simpson for a book celebrating the Diamond Jubilee of Confederation in 1927.

National Archives of Canada/C-013947.

price. The rising business class in Victoria objected to his "family-Company compact," composed of former Hudson's Bay Company officials and members of his own family.

When settlement on Vancouver Island grew in the late 1850s, Douglas made determined efforts to purchase the First Nations' land and to set aside reserves in the areas into which settlers were moving. But lack of funds made the process more difficult. In 1858, the governor left the Hudson's Bay Company and no longer had access to the company's storehouses. Moreover, the Aboriginal communities wanted larger payments for their land, as they now realized its true value to the newcomers. The Vancouver Island House of Assembly, established in 1856, asked Britain to lend it money for First Nations land payments. The Colonial Office refused and replied that the funds should be raised locally. As the colonial legislature considered itself unable to buy out Native title on Vancouver Island, it gave the First Nations no compensation for their lands after 1859. Without negotiating treaties, the Europeans settled along the Pacific coast. Their settlements were interspersed among small, autonomous Aboriginal villages. The government of Vancouver Island (and later British Columbia) set aside Native reserves without extinguishing the First Nations' title to the land. (Only a century and a half later, in the 1990s, would the treaty process resume on Vancouver Island and on the coastal mainland.)

DOUGLAS AND THE CREATION OF THE COLONY OF BRITISH COLUMBIA

When word of a big gold strike on the Fraser River reached California in the spring of 1858, the rush began. The California gold rush of 1849 had lost its momentum, and gold seekers headed north. A tent town arose at Victoria. Many new businesses or branches of American firms, financed by San Francisco capital, were established. One witness counted 225 new commercial buildings in Victoria in 1858.

Once in Victoria, the miners faced the challenge of reaching the gold fields in the interior. They needed boats to cross the Strait of Georgia to the mouth of the Fraser. Lacking the necessary boat-building skills, many launched their own hastily made vessels. Not surprisingly, some swamped, and their owners drowned. Once the would-be prospectors reached the mouth of the Fraser, they faced an additional 250 km journey up the river to the first big strike, just south of Yale, an old trading post. In the last two weeks of May 1858, 10 000 men travelled up the Fraser by canoe, sailboat, and raft. Another 15 000 arrived by the end of the year.

The arrival of thousands of Americans threatened British sovereignty and raised the danger of a war between prospectors and the First Nations. As the senior British official in the area, Douglas claimed the mainland and its minerals for the Crown. He drew up mining regulations, licensed miners, and hired constables. The Colonial Office praised Douglas, even though, strictly speaking, he lacked legal authority on the mainland. The British government remedied the legal shortcoming, and immediately established the colony of British Columbia on the mainland, separate from that of Vancouver Island.

James Douglas served as British Columbia's first governor while still continuing as governor of Vancouver Island (which in 1859 came under the direct control of the Colonial Office, after the royal grant to the Hudson's Bay Company ended). New Westminister located near the mouth of the Fraser River became the colony's new capital. Since no assembly was granted on the mainland — the British government did not wish to extend the electoral system to transients who had flocked into the Fraser River gold fields from California and Oregon — James Douglas retained great powers, including the power to legislate by proclamation. Together with Matthew Baillie Begbie, British Columbia's first chief justice, Douglas established a uniform judicial system for the colony. Judge Begbie's circuit court tours established a frontier version of British law in the scattered mining camps.

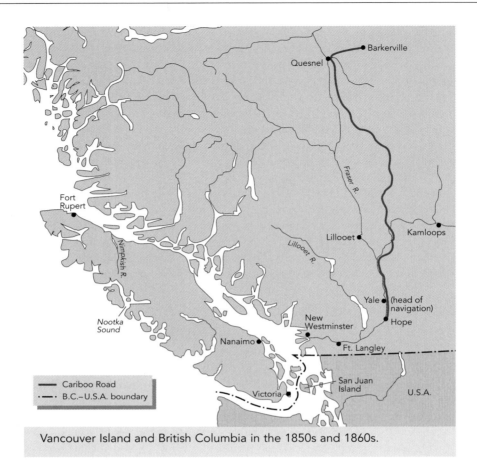

Vancouver Island and British Columbia in the 1850s and 1860s.

In 1860, British Columbia's gold rush frontier expanded. About 4000 gold miners (the majority from California and Oregon; the rest from eastern Canada, Britain, Europe, and even China) advanced eastward into potentially rich new gold fields, into the Thompson, Lillooet, and then the southern Cariboo regions. By 1861, with big strikes at Richfield, at Barkerville, and at Lightning on Williams Creek, the Cariboo region became the major mining field. To exploit the gold resources road links were necessary to the coast. Roads were also needed to guarantee British commercial and military control of the interior. Using public funds, Douglas built the 650 km Cariboo Road, completed in 1863, which connected the gold towns of Yale and Barkerville.

THE FIRST NATIONS AND THE IMPACT OF THE GOLD RUSHES

Apart from doing some backpacking and some work at the diggings, the First Nations obtained little economic benefit from the gold rushes. The miners had no intention of sharing British Columbia's rich lands and resources with the original inhabitants. Although James Douglas allowed the First Nations to choose the locations of their reserves, he made no treaties with them on the mainland. They received no compensation for the expropriation of their lands. Moreover, the miners intruded on their village sites, fishing stations, and cultivated areas. The increased number of non-Natives also resulted in the outbreak of disease, such as the smallpox epidemic of 1862 that claimed the lives of many First Nations living both along the coast and in the interior.

Where Historians Disagree

James Douglas's Contribution to British Columbia

In the historiography of British Columbia, James Douglas is a figure comparable to Champlain in Quebec and to Simcoe in Ontario. Few historians have been more laudatory of his contribution to British Columbia than historian Margaret Ormsby. In a biographical sketch of Douglas written in 1972, she states: "A man of iron nerve and physical prowess, great force of character, keen intelligence, and unusual resourcefulness, Douglas had had a notable career in the fur trade. As colonial governor his career was even more distinguished. Against overwhelming odds, with indifferent backing from the British government, the aid of a few Royal Navy ships, and a small force of Royal Engineers, he was able to establish British rule on the Pacific Coast and lay the foundation for Canada's extension of the Pacific seaboard. Single-handed in the midst of a gold-rush he had forged policies for land, mining, and water rights which were just and endurable."[1]

Recently, reassessments of Douglas have appeared, and his contribution, while still acknowledged as significant, is being judged more critically. In her study *The West beyond the West: A History of British Columbia*, Jean Barman introduced several criticisms of Douglas's administration. She noted his "overbearing style of governing" and the fact that he readily extended his authority beyond his legitimate power. Moreover, "he alienated newcomers from Ontario and the Maritimes through his haughty demeanour and preference for Britons over Canadians."[2] His feverish road-building program, she added, left the main-

land colony of British Columbia burdened by debt.

Douglas's Aboriginal policies have also been questioned. Political scientist Paul Tennant argued that the governor was far less generous to the First Nations than was formerly believed.[3] Earlier commentators such as Robert Cail,[4] Robin Fisher,[5] and Wilson Duff [6] have regarded the governor's Native policies favourably. Anthropologist Wilson Duff, for instance, wrote in *The Indian History of British Columbia*: "As colonization progressed, his main concerns, in addition to maintaining law and order, were to purchase the Indian ownership rights to the land and to set aside adequate reserves for their use."[7] Tennant himself admits that "at a time when aboriginal peoples elsewhere were routinely being forced from their lands and often actively exterminated, Douglas displayed a spirit of tolerance, compassion, and humane understanding."[8] Nonetheless, with the exception of fourteen small treaties signed between 1850 and 1854 on Vancouver Island, Douglas made no further attempts to negotiate the transfer of land title with the First Nations peoples. Moreover, the man who had complete control of the mainland from 1858 to 1864 made no treaties there at all. He, in fact, no longer supported the principle of Aboriginal land title. Instead, he spent large sums of money, principally on roads, to take miners in and out of the interior.

Tennant does acknowledge, however, that at least inadvertently, James Douglas made an enormous contribution to the survival of Aboriginal British Columbia. The governor's decision to set aside reserves for First Nations communities at locations of their own choosing helped to protect these groups from cultural extinction. As Tennant writes, "The surviving members of traditional communities could thus remain resident on preferred sites within their ancestral homelands and so could retain a sense of communal unity and an active connection with historic places and communal memories. Confined to their small reserves, they could nurture a deepening sense of injustice as they witnessed the takeover of their surrounding traditional lands without regard to aboriginal title. Douglas's approach thus facilitated the retention of the communal and tribal group identities that he assumed would vanish."[9]

Recently, after over a century of resistance, British Columbia has begun discussing land claims with Aboriginal groups. This has created much interest in James Douglas's early treaties on Vancouver Island, and, as well, in the reasons for his failure to complete further treaties on the Island and on the mainland of British Columbia. Historical assessment of Douglas's First Nations policies will lead, no doubt, to further discussion of his role in British Columbian history.

[1] Margaret Ormsby, "Sir James Douglas," *Dictionary of Canadian Biography*, vol. 10, *1871–1880* (Toronto: University of Toronto Press, 1972), p. 248.

[2] Jean Barman, *The West Beyond the West: A History of British Columbia* (Toronto: University of Toronto Press, 1991), pp. 80, 97.

[3] Paul Tennant, *Aboriginal Peoples and Politics: The Indian Land Question in British Columbia, 1849–1989* (Vancouver: University of British Columbia Press, 1990), p. 29.

[4] Robert Cail, *Land, Man and the Law: The Disposal of Crown Lands in British Columbia, 1871–1913* (Vancouver: University of British Columbia Press, 1974).

[5] Robin Fisher, *Contact and Conflict: Indian–European Relations in British Columbia, 1774–1890*, 2nd ed. (Vancouver: University of British Columbia Press, 1992 [1977]).

[6] Wilson Duff, *The Indian History of British Columbia*, vol. 1, *The Impact of the White Man* (Victoria: Royal British Columbia Museum, 1992 [1965]), p. 61.

[7] Ibid., p. 61.

[8] Tennant, *Aboriginal Peoples and Politics*, p. 29.

[9] Ibid., p. 38.

JAMES DOUGLAS'S ACCOMPLISHMENTS

Douglas remained in office as governor of both British Columbia and Vancouver Island until 1864. The settlers long complained about his autocratic ways and his "despotism," but in their haste to condemn him, they overlooked his accomplishments. On the mainland, he had confronted the Americans and firmly established British institutions. By building the Cariboo Road, he solved the problem of inland communication.

The governor's First Nations policy constituted another achievement. Thanks largely to Douglas, Vancouver Island and British Columbia were spared the fierce wars between First Nations and settlers that raged in the United States. The real test came in the Fraser River valley and the Cariboo country during the gold-rush days in the late 1850s and early 1860s. Apart from an attack in 1864 by Chilcotins on a road-building crew who had entered their territory uninvited, no major acts of First Nations armed resistance occurred.

BRITISH COLUMBIA IN THE MID-1860S

British Columbia experienced a post–gold-rush slump in the mid-1860s. Gold production fell, and people left the colony. Still, the region was rich in many natural resources. British Columbia's stands of Douglas fir produced ten times more wood per hectare than New Brunswick's Miramichi or the Canadas' Ottawa valley.[2] But high transportation costs in the 1860s ruled out large-scale exploitation. Beginnings had been made in lumber and fishing as export industries, but coal mining at centres on Vancouver Island, like Nanaimo, remained the most important industry. Some farming had begun, with specialization in wheat in the upper Fraser region, and with dairy and market gardening under way on the island. High American tariffs also reduced both British Columbia's and Vancouver Island's trade with the United States, although Vancouver Island did sell some coal to San Francisco.

In the late 1860s, about 12 000 non-Natives lived in British Columbia and on Vancouver Island, the majority around Victoria and its immediate surrounding area. Between 1000 and 2000 non-Natives resided in the lower Fraser valley. The remainder lived along the routes to the gold fields or at fur-trading posts. Since most Americans had left, at least three-quarters were British or Canadians and, of these, males predominated. In contrast the population of the First Nations, the overwhelming majority in both British Columbia and Vancouver Island, was about 25 000. A small community of African-American settlers from San Francisco, and a few settlers from the Caribbean, resided in Victoria and on the lower mainland. More than 1000 Chinese from California, mostly men, remained to work finds in the Cariboo. As late as 1871 there were only 53 Chinese women in the entire province. Most of the Chinese men came originally from poor rural backgrounds in southeastern China and could not bring over their families. (Other reasons for the small number of females include prejudices in Chinese society against emigration, and the hostile reception often given to Asians in British Columbia.)

CHRISTIAN MISSIONARIES AND THE PACIFIC COAST PEOPLES

Missionaries sought to convert the First Nations to Christianity in the 1850s. William Duncan began his work at Fort Simpson in 1857 and continued it at neighbouring Metlakatla, where he built a model mission. Other Anglican missionaries followed. Methodists from Canada West also came; Thomas Crosby worked on Vancouver Island and along the northern coastline. In the late 1850s, the Oblate Fathers established Roman Catholic missions along the south coast, in the Okanagan, and in the Fraser valley.

The missionaries tried to convert the First Nations into good European Christians. In their zeal, the missionaries at their Christian mission villages even banned totem poles. In 1900, the annual report of the federal Department of Indian Affairs noted that roughly 80 percent of British Columbia's First Nations were reported to be Christians.

It is difficult to judge the extent to which the First Nations adjusted to the new economic conditions. Independently of both mission and government direction, some First Nations tended potato gardens in the 1850s, and in the decades to follow, they started mixed farming. As early as the mid-1850s, independent Native loggers delivered logs to sawmills. Many of the Hudson's Bay Company supply ships and several private trading schooners employed First Nations as crew throughout the nineteenth century. First Nations-owned schooners began to appear in the 1870s, some of which they themselves had constructed. From the 1870s on, the First Nations entered the commercial fishing and canning industry. Thus, despite difficult circumstances, a number of them adjusted to the new conditions.

Community Portrait

The Black Community of Victoria

Canadians have long congratulated themselves on the improved state of race relations in Canada, and earlier in British North America, in contrast with that in the United States. While it is true that the British Empire abolished slavery in 1833, approximately one-third of a century before the United States, did African British North Americans achieve equality and full participation in their society? The existence of a vibrant, thriving community of people of African descent in Victoria, Vancouver Island, in the late 1850s and 1860s allows for comparisons to be made.

In the 1850s, African Americans faced increasing persecution and denial of civil rights in California. Several members of the African-American community in San Francisco sent a letter of enquiry to the government of the colony of British Columbia. Back came a favourable reply, they would be welcomed. It is interesting to note that James Douglas, the governor of Vancouver Island, had some African ancestry from his West-Indian mother.

The response that African Americans would be welcomed prompted the emigration of approximately 400 people of African background from California to Victoria in 1858 and 1859. Since California was not a slave state, those moving to Vancouver Island were already free. A number came with business experience, and with the advantage of knowing a trade. A few, such

When American forces threatened Vancouver Island in 1860 (during the dispute between Britain and the United States over the ownership of the strategic San Juan Island, near Fort Victoria), the black community formed a volunteer militia regiment to protect the colony. In 1872, international arbitration settled the boundary dispute in favour of the Americans, and San Juan Island became part of the United States.

Charles Gentile/National Archives of Canada/C-22626.

as Mifflin Gibbs, brought capital with them. Without a doubt one of the central figures in the migration was Gibbs, a free-born African American, originally from Philadelphia, the son of a Wesleyan Methodist minister. As a young man in his mid-twenties he had moved to San Francisco and, within a year, became a partner in a clothing business. But the discrimination against blacks rankled him. He became one of the first to emigrate northward. Once in the colony, he joined the Victoria Pioneer Rifle Corps, an all-black volunteer militia, known familiarly as the African Rifles, formed to protect the colony against possible American aggression.

In Victoria the newcomers pushed for integration. They sought what was denied to them in the United States: equal access to institutions, services, and the political process. Gibbs himself became a naturalized British subject, which allowed him to register as a voter. Elected to the Victoria city council in 1866, he served two terms — one as the chair of the important finance committee.

Unfortunately, full equality was not achieved. It soon became apparent that the African-American immigrants still suffered prejudice in their new home. Some churches established segregated sections. Some saloons and other public facilities refused service to them. Theatres made them sit for performances in the balcony seats. These divisions were backed up by physical intimi-dation. Even the loyal Pioneer Rifle Corps suffered humiliation, as they were barred from parades and public ceremonies. Legal equality prevailed, and some African Americans achieved acceptance, but the colour line remained.

By the late 1860s, a number of African Americans left the colony and returned to the United States. Gibbs himself departed in 1869, and settled in Little Rock, Arkansas. The Civil War had ended, and opportunities surfaced for many in the country of their birth, but the persistence of the colour bar in British North America had also contributed to the exodus. In their new home on Vancouver Island, African Americans had contended with much of the same bigotry that they had tried to escape in pre–Civil War California.

Further Reading

Sherry Edmunds-Flett, "Mifflin Wistar Gibbs," *Dictionary of Canadian Biography*, vol. 14: *1911–1920* (Toronto:University of Toronto Press, 1998): 398–399.

Crawford Kilian, *Go Do Some Great Thing. The Black Pioneers of British Columbia* (Vancouver: Douglas and McIntyre, 1978).

James W. St. G. Walker, *Racial Discrimination in Canada: The Black Experience*, Canadian Historical Association Booklet No. 41 (Ottawa: The Canadian Historical Association, 1985).

THE UNION OF THE TWO COLONIES

Major economic problems faced the two settler colonies of British Columbia and Vancouver Island in the mid-1860s. With the end of the gold rush, the economy was depressed and the two governments almost bankrupt. Anxious to save money in administrative costs, Britain promoted union of the two colonies. In 1866, the colonies joined together and New Westminster became the capital. (A vigorous lobby, however, later convinced the governor to move the capital to Victoria in 1868.) Despite the political consolidation of the two colonies, the depression continued. In 1867, a new issue arose: the American purchase of Alaska. This put in doubt the independence of British Columbia.

In 1867, the new united colony of British Columbia, only one year old, was the youngest of Britain's North American colonies. With the exception of a handful of fur traders, none of the approximately 8000 British Columbians of European descent in the colony had lived more than 25 years on Britain's Pacific coast. Thanks to the Hudson's Bay Company, Britain had retained this huge territory against Russian, and particularly against American, advances. But what would be the province's fate?

As the Canadas, New Brunswick, and Nova Scotia completed the final arrangements for their union, British Columbia's settler population debated its future. Apart from the old fur trade employees, few non-Natives had lived in either of the two colonies for more than fifteen years or so at best. At no point did the settlers consult the resident First Nations population, who, in the mid-1860s, outnumbered them by two to one. They proceeded as if the original inhabitants did not exist. British Columbia had three options: Britain, the United States, or Canada. Emotionally, most favoured the province's continuation as a British colony. Those seeking to increase British Columbia's trade with its most important trading partner, however, endorsed annexation to the United States. Many British Columbians who had been born in the Canadas and the Maritimes favoured union with Canada, as did those who saw Confederation as the best means of protecting British institutions on the Northwest Coast and of developing British Columbia's resources.

NOTES

1. Chief Mathias Capilano presents a Squamish version of the Europeans' arrival in "Strangers Appear on English Bay," in *Romance of Vancouver*, vol. 2, compiled by the Native Sons of British Columbia (n.p., 1926), pp. 5–6. A similar version, "How the Squamish Remember George Vancouver," was presented by Chief Philip Joe at the Vancouver Conference on Exploration and Discovery in April 1992; see Robin Fisher and Hugh Johnston, eds., *From Maps to Metaphors: The Pacific World of George Vancouver* (Vancouver: University of British Columbia Press, 1993), pp. 3–5.
2. Donald MacKay, *The Lumberjacks* (Toronto: McGraw-Hill Ryerson, 1978), p. 160.

LINKING TO THE PAST

Northwest Coast Native Culture
http://www.civilization.ca/aborig/grand/grandeng.html

The on-line version of this exhibition housed in the Canadian Museum of Civilization's Grand Hall features descriptions and photographs of artifacts related to Northwest Coast First Nations cultures. Check out the links at the bottom for additional artifacts and historical information.

Totem Poles: An Exploration
http://users.imag.net/~sry.jkramer/nativetotems

This site explains the meaning of totem poles and answers some of the most commonly asked questions about them.

Hudson's Bay Company at Fort Victoria
http://collections.ic.gc.ca/fortvictoria

This site provides an on-line exhibition on the inhabitants of and the daily life in Fort Victoria, with a virtual tour of the fort.

British Columbia Archives
http://www.bcarchives.gov.bc.ca/index.htm
The archives' extensive on-line collection includes images (photographs, paintings, drawings, and prints), government and private documents and records, and cartographic documents and maps of British Columbia from its beginnings to the present.

BIBLIOGRAPHY

Two excellent overviews of the history of the two Pacific colonies are Jean Barman's *The West beyond the West: A History of British Columbia* (Toronto: University of Toronto Press, 1991; revised edition, 1996) and Hugh J.M. Johnston, ed., *The Pacific Province: A History of British Columbia* (Vancouver: Douglas & McIntyre, 1996). A wealth of information on British Columbia can be found in Daniel Francis, ed., *Encyclopedia of British Columbia* (Madeira Park: Harbour Publishing, 2000). Tina Loo provides a very useful bibliographical guide in her essay "The Pacific Coast," in M. Brook Taylor, ed., *Canadian History: A Reader's Guide*, vol. 1, *Beginnings to Confederation* (Toronto: University of Toronto Press, 1994), pp. 356–93.

Reviews of British Columbia's Aboriginal past appear in Wilson Duff, *The Indian History of British Columbia*, vol. 1, *The Impact of the White Man* (Victoria: Royal British Columbia Museum, 1997 [1965]); Robin Fisher, *Contact and Conflict: Indian–European Relations in British Columbia, 1774–1890*, 2nd ed. (Vancouver: University of British Columbia Press, 1992 [1977]); and two volumes by historical geographer Cole Harris, *The Resettlement of British Columbia. Essays on Colonialism and Geographical Change* (Vancouver: University of British Columbia Press, 1997); and *Making Native Space. Colonialism, Resistance, and Reserves in British Columbia* (Vancouver: University of British Columbia Press, 2002). Paul Tennant's *Aboriginal Peoples and Politics: The Indian Land Question in British Columbia, 1849–1989* (Vancouver: University of British Columbia Press, 1990) is very useful. On the impact on the First Nations of European infectious disease, see: Robert Boyd, *The Coming of the Spirit of Pestilence: Introduced Infectious Diseases and Population Decline among Northwest Coast Indians, 1774–1874* (Vancouver: University of British Columbia Press, 1999).

For a survey of European and American activities in the North Pacific see John Kendrick's *Men with Wooden Feet: The Spanish Exploration of the Pacific Northwest* (Toronto: NC Press, 1985); and James R. Gibson's *Otter Skins, Boston Ships and China Goods: The Maritime Fur Trade of the Northwest Coast, 1785–1841* (Montreal/Kingston: McGill-Queen's University Press, 1992). Barry Gough reviews British contact in *The Northwest Coast: British Navigation, Trade, and Discoveries to 1812* (Vancouver: University of British Columbia Press, 1992); and in *Gunboat Frontier: British Maritime Authority and Northwest Coast Indians, 1846–90* (Vancouver: University of British Columbia Press, 1984). *The Dictionary of Canadian Biography*, vol. 4, *1771–1800* (Toronto: University of Toronto Press, 1979) contains sketches of James Cook by Glyndwr Williams, pp. 162–67, and of George Vancouver by W. Kaye Lamb, pp. 743–48.

On nineteenth century political developments Clarence G. Karr has written an interesting article on Douglas, "James Douglas: The Gold Governor in the Context of His Times," in E. Blanche Norcross, ed., *The Company on the Coast* (Nanaimo: Nanaimo Historical Society, 1983): 56–78. W. Peter Ward and Robert A.J. McDonald, eds., *British Columbia: Historical Readings* (Vancouver: Douglas & McIntrye, 1981) includes James E. Hendrickson's "The Constitutional Development of Colonial Vancouver Island and British Columbia," pp. 245–74. Tina Loo's *Making Law, Order, and Authority in British Columbia, 1821–1871* (Toronto: University of Toronto Press, 1994) is the first comprehensive legal history of British Columbia in the colonial period. In the field of gender and race history, Adele Perry has written *On the Edge of Empire. Gender, Race, and the Making of British Columbia, 1849–1871* (Toronto: University of Toronto Press, 2001).

For important maps consult the first two volumes of the *Historical Atlas of Canada*: vol. 1, R. Cole Harris, ed., *From the Beginning to 1800* (Toronto: University of Toronto Press, 1987); and vol. 2, R. Louis Gentilcore, ed., *The Land Transformed, 1800–1891* (Toronto: University of Toronto Press, 1993).

PART FOUR

BUILDING THE NEW DOMINION, 1867–1914

The mid- to late-nineteenth century saw the formation of European nation states, including Germany in 1866 and Italy in 1871; national consolidation — as occurred in the United States after the Civil War; and imperial expansion, as in the case of Britain, France, Germany, and the United States. Canada witnessed all three developments in a phenomenally short period of time: the three British North American colonies of Nova Scotia, New Brunswick, and the United Canadas came together in 1867 to create the new nation state of Canada; within ten years, the country had expanded to include all of the existing British North American colonies with the exception of Newfoundland. The new nation had also undertaken expansion to the Pacific and the Arctic Oceans. In the 1870s, Canada made seven treaties with the First Nations in Western Canada. The country also became involved in two conflicts with the Aboriginal peoples, first in 1869–70 in the Red River, and then in 1885 in the North-West Territories.

Creating the physical boundaries of a new nation state proved easier than fostering a sense of nationalism. Since the traditional components of cultural nationalism — a common language, a common cultural tradition, or a common religion — were absent, national enthusiasts looked to geography and especially to an economic policy of railway building, protective tariffs, and large-scale immigration to promote a feeling of nationalism.

This national policy, as well as the decision of the Fathers of Confederation to create a federal union with political power divided between Ottawa and provincial governments, necessitated the working out of Dominion–Provincial relations. This proved acrimonious. Also to be resolved were relations between French-speaking and English-speaking Canadians. A century of bitterness and suspicion preceded Confederation, yet a *modus vivendi* had existed in the union itself. Tension and compromise prevailed from 1867 to 1914. Finally, the new country needed to work out relations with Britain and the United States. Most Canadians favoured continued affiliation with the British empire; Dominion status did not mean independence. Equally,

Canadians sought trade with the United States, while clearly rejecting any form of political union with their southern neighbour.

For most Canadians, Confederation left their daily lives unaltered. They continued to identify more with their colonial (now provincial) and local area than with the country as a whole, and they pursued their livelihood as they had prior to Confederation. The year 1867 and the event of Confederation were not momentous. Still, the very act of union of the three British North American colonies put into place a new structure and a new dynamic for economic, political, and social change.

CONFEDERATION

Proposals for the union of the British North American colonies had been considered well before the 1860s, but they never became reality. By the 1860s, however, threats of an American takeover as a result of the Civil War, pressure from Britain for unification of the British North American colonies, internal problems in the colonies, such as heavy public debt from extensive railway building and, in the case of the Canadas, political deadlock (and the desire to acquire the Northwest), led politicians from both the Canadas and the Maritime colonies to consider union. These immediate circumstances, more than a spirit of nationalism, prepared the way for Confederation.

THE IMPACT OF THE AMERICAN CIVIL WAR

THE *ALABAMA* AND THE *TRENT* AFFAIRS

Fear of an American takeover during the Civil War contributed to British North American unification. Although Britain was officially neutral during the American Civil War, many Britons backed the Confederacy because of their dependence on southern cotton for the textile industry. The international rules of neutrality prevented the legal construction of Confederate warships in British shipyards, but the South secretly had the C.S.S. *Alabama,* a swift and powerful cruiser, built in a shipyard near Liverpool. During its 22-month rampage on three oceans, the *Alabama* burned or captured 64 Northern merchant vessels and a Union warship before it was sunk in June 1864. The North held Britain responsible for the destruction by the *Alabama* and other British-built Confederate vessels, since, Northern leaders argued, Britain knew the uses to which the South put these ships. As compensation, one Northern proposal included the takeover of all of British North America.

Adding to Anglo–American antagonism was the *Trent* affair. In November 1861, an American warship stopped the British steamer *Trent* and forcibly removed two Confederate envoys on their way to England to secure assistance for the Southern cause. Tempers flared on both sides, with Britain threatening retaliation if the North did not free these Confederate agents, seized in neutral waters, and the North denouncing Britain for aiding the Southern cause. In the end, President Abraham Lincoln released the prisoners on Christmas Day, 1861, to avoid war with Britain.

THE ST. ALBAN'S RAIDS

Meanwhile, by 1864, the Southern Confederacy planned attacks on the North via Canada. The largest of these attacks occurred at St. Alban's, Vermont, on October 19, 1864, during which 26 Confederate sympathizers terrorized the town, robbed three banks of $200 000, set several fires, wounded two men and killed another, and then fled to Canada. The government of the Canadas arrested them, but a Montreal magistrate released them on a legal technicality. This act of leniency infuriated Northerners. The Canadian government condemned the judge's decision. As well, the Canadian Assembly passed legislation to deport aliens involved in acts against a friendly foreign state. Nevertheless, Canada still remained suspect in American eyes.

The ensuing tension led Britain to send 14 000 soldiers to British North America to protect her colonies. Many of the troops had to reach their destination by sled since no rail link existed into the interior of British North America. Britain therefore saw a union of the British North American colonies as a means both to get the colonies to assume responsibility for their own defense, and to achieve a railway link to the Atlantic, by providing a larger financial base for railway construction.

NEGOTIATING CONFEDERATION

THE GREAT COALITION

In this tense atmosphere, the politicians in the United Canadas addressed the problem of political deadlock in their Assembly. Neither the Conservatives nor the Reformers could form a stable government. Between 1861 and 1864, for example, the Canadas experienced two elections and three changes of administration. On June 14, 1864, the most recent administration, the Macdonald–Taché coalition, went down to defeat. Governor General Monck urged John A. Macdonald, leader of the coalition, to negotiate with George Brown, leader of the Reform party, with the possibility of forming a larger coalition. Despite Brown and Macdonald's hostilities towards each other, the two men agreed. On June 30, a jubilant Assembly heard Brown announce that he and two other Reformers would enter a coalition cabinet to work for federation. Thus was born the "Great Coalition of 1864."

Brown made three demands in return for his support: a federation of all the British North American colonies; representation by population, or "rep by pop," as it became popularly known; and the incorporation of Rupert's Land into Confederation. Brown's interest in the Northwest lay in its benefits for the development of Canada West. On January 22, 1863, for example, the Toronto newspaper editor outlined his imperial vision:

> If Canada acquires this territory it will rise in a few years from a position of a small and weak province to be the greatest colony any country has ever possessed, able to take its place among the empires of the earth. The wealth of 400 000 square miles of territory will flow through our waters and be gathered by our merchants, manufacturers and agriculturists. Our sons will occupy the chief places of this vast territory, we will form its institutions, supply its rulers, teach its schools, fill its stores, run its mills, navigate its streams.

THE CHARLOTTETOWN CONFERENCE

In the early 1860s, the Maritime colonies of Nova Scotia, New Brunswick, and Prince Edward Island considered union among themselves. Despite reservations, the premiers of the three colonies agreed to meet. But before a date or place had been decided, the government of the Canadas asked permission to attend such a meeting so as to present a proposal for a wider British North American federal union. The Maritimers agreed. The meeting was set for September 1, 1864, in Charlottetown.

At the Charlottetown conference, the Canadian delegation presented an impressive *tour de force*. John A. Macdonald and George-Étienne Cartier set out the general terms of the Canadian proposal, particularly those aspects dealing with the division of powers between the central and provincial governments. Alexander Galt, the minister of finance in the Canadas, dealt with economic issues, while George Brown handled constitutional concerns. The main features of their proposal included: continued loyalty to the British Crown through membership in the British empire; a strong central government within a federal union in which the provinces retained control over their own local affairs; and representation in a lower house based on population and an upper house based on regional representation. Thomas D'Arcy McGee, the gifted poet-politician, spoke eloquently in terms of the need for a common British North American vision. Within seven days, the delegates agreed to meet again on October 10 at Quebec City to explore in greater detail the nature of a British North American federation.

The banquet and ball, the final night of the Charlottetown Conference, at Province House. The assembly chamber — now decorated with evergreens, flowers, and flags — became the ballroom. Under brilliant gaslight, delegates and their partners danced to the music of two Charlottetown bands from the gallery. At the front and centre of the re-creation by artist Dusan Kadlec appear John A. Macdonald and George-Étienne Cartier.

The Ball at the Legislature, 1864, by Dusan Kadlec. © Parks Canada.

THE QUEBEC CONFERENCE

At Quebec, the Canadian delegates presented the broad general principles set out at Charlottetown in the form of Seventy-Two Resolutions. Within a two-week period, these Resolutions were debated and slightly altered to become the British North American (BNA) Act, the political framework for a union of the British North American colonies.

At the conference Macdonald clearly favoured a legislative union, or a strong central government, believing that the Civil War in the United States was the result of overly powerful state governments. The Maritime delegates feared a loss of their identity in a legislative union and favoured instead a federal union with powerful local governments. George-Étienne Cartier also favoured a federal union, with a local government in Quebec strong enough to protect French Canadians' language, civil law, and customs.

The delegates reached a compromise. They granted powers to the provincial governments, but gave the central government residuary powers (powers not specifically assigned to the provinces). As well, they gave the central government the power "to make laws for the peace, order and good government of Canada." The federal government also gained the right to disallow provincial laws if they went against the national interest.

Community Portrait

The Charlottetown Conference as a Political Community

On September 1, 1864, political leaders from the Atlantic colonies and from the United Canadas met in Charlottetown to discuss the possibility of a British North American union. They came together as strangers to one another. So the success of the conference depended on the ability to create a sense of community—for the representatives to come to know and trust each other, and to believe that they had something in common. In this respect social events became as important as the political meetings. The wives of the politicians, especially the wives of the Island hosts who organized the social gatherings, made a very important contribution by helping to create this sense of community. As well, the presence of women reminded the politicians that their decisions affected all members of the community, including women and children. As a result, historians have now come to identify these women as the "Mothers of Confederation."

The politicians who met at Charlottetown came with quite different agendas, interests, and hopes. The resulting mistrust, divisiveness, and differences had to be overcome in order to find points of common interests, to cultivate a feeling of community. Luncheons, dinners, banquets, and balls became common occurrences designed to foster the feeling among the politicians that they belonged to a community. In a letter to his wife Anne Nelson, daughter of publisher William Nelson,* George Brown from Upper Canada noted the change that came over the delegates as they wined and dined: "Cartier and I made eloquent speeches, and whether as the result of our eloquence or of the goodness of our champagne, the ice became completely broken, the tongues of the delegates wagged merrily, [and] the banns of matrimony between all the provinces of British North America were formally proclaimed."

Brown failed to note in his letter the important role that the women played in forging this sense of political community. But at the final banquet, the delegates made the last toast to Mrs. Dundas, wife of the Lieutenant-governor of Prince Edward Island, and the other ladies present as acknowledgement of their important role in making the Charlottetown Conference a success. The Conference had shaped a political community of the leaders who would go on to forge the new nation of Canada.

Further Reading

Moira Dann, *Mothers of Confederation*. CBC Transcript (Toronto: Canadian Broadcasting Corporation, 1989).

Gail Cuthbert Brandt, "National Unity and the Politics of Political History," Presidential Address, *Journal of the Canadian Historical Association* (1992): 3–11.

Christopher Moore, *1867: How the Fathers Made a Deal* (Toronto: McClelland & Stewart, 1997).

J.M.S. Careless, "George Brown and the Mother of Confederation, 1864," Canadian Historical Association *Annual Report*, (1960): 57–73.

* Nelson, the publisher of your textbook, is a corporate descendant of William Nelson's publishing firm.

The delegates to the Charlottetown Conference, September 1864.

George P. Roberts/National Archives of Canada/C-733.

From left to right:

1. Charles Drinkwater, private secretary to John A. Macdonald
2. Hewitt Bernard, secretary to John A. Macdonald
3. Alexander T. Galt, Canada
4. Charles Tupper, Nova Scotia
5. Edward B. Chandler, New Brunswick
6. Hector-Louis Langevin, Canada
7. Edward Palmer, Prince Edward Island
8. John Hamilton Gray, New Brunswick
9. Robert Dickey, Nova Scotia
10. George-Étienne Cartier, Canada
11. Thomas D'Arcy McGee, Canada
12. William A. Henry, Nova Scotia
13. John A. Macdonald, Canada
14. William H. Steeves, New Brunswick
15. John Hamilton Gray, Prince Edward Island
16. John M. Johnson, New Brunswick
17. Samuel L. Tilley, New Brunswick
18. Adams G. Archibald, Nova Scotia
19. Andrew A. Macdonald, Prince Edward Island
20. William Campbell, Canada
21. William MacDougall, Canada
22. George Coles, Prince Edward Island
23. William H. Pope, Prince Edward Island
24. Jonathan McCully, Nova Scotia
25. George Brown, Canada

The delegates agreed on a federal lower house based on representation by population and an upper house based on regional representation, but disagreed on the number of representatives from each region in the upper house — the Senate. The smaller Maritime Provinces saw the Senate as a means of strengthening their regional representation to offset their numerical weakness in the lower house. In the end, the delegates agreed that the Maritimes would have 24 seats, the same number given to each of Ontario and Quebec.

The delegates also agreed, after much debate, that the new federal government would assume the public debts — up to a specified maximum amount — of each province that joined. In addition, the federal government would finance the Intercolonial Railway, linking the Maritimes to the Canadas.

To cover these costs, the federal government was given unlimited taxing powers, including the collection of both direct taxes and indirect taxes, such as customs and excise duties, one of the main sources of revenue at the time. In contrast, the provinces could levy only direct taxes.

To compensate the provinces for the cost of education, roads, and other local obligations, it was agreed that the federal government pay annual subsidies to the provinces based on 80 cents per head of their population.

THE DEBATE ON THE CONFEDERATION PROPOSALS IN THE CANADAS

After the Quebec Conference, the delegates returned to their respective provinces to secure approval for the resolutions. The Fathers of Confederation had considered submitting the draft constitution for popular approval but later decided to follow the British procedure of ratification by the politicians only. As a result, the Confederation agreement did not at the time (or since) form the basis of a political community with a clear sense of itself and its political rights and constitutional freedoms.

Absent entirely from the constitutional process were the First Nations. To the Fathers of Confederation, the First Nations were wards of the state, upon which sovereignty could be imposed, not people with rights of their own or members of the political community. As political scientist Peter Russell notes, "Aboriginal peoples were treated as subjects, not citizens, of the new dominion."[1]

In the Legislature of the United Canadas, considerable debate ensued. George Brown and his Reformers had some concerns about specific proposals but accepted the agreement reached at Quebec since it was based on "rep by pop." In general, Upper Canadian politicians favoured Confederation, realizing that they had the most to gain from the union.

In Canada East (Quebec), members of the Parti rouge, under the leadership of Antoine-Aimé Dorion, had serious reservations. Dorion argued: "It is not at all a confederation that is proposed to us, but quite simply a Legislative Union disguised under the name of a confederation. How could one accept as a federation a scheme ... that provided for disallowance of local legislation?" Furthermore, he pointed out that in the new House of Commons the English-Canadian representation from Canada West and the Maritimes would greatly outnumber the French-Canadian representation. As well, he denounced the Fathers of Confederation for refusing to put the issue to the people.

George-Étienne Cartier countered Dorion's criticisms. He emphasized that in the new federal union, French Canadians would control their own provincial government and legislature, have their own local administration, and retain the Civil Code. Furthermore, the French language would be official in the province of Quebec as well as in the federal administration, and the rights of religious minorities for separate schools would be recognized in all the provinces. On the question of English-Canadian dominance, Cartier pointed out that the "new nationality" would be a "political nationality" only, not a "cultural nationality," and therefore did not require French Canadians to suppress their cultural differences for the sake of some common pan-Canadian nationalism. He also reminded his French-Canadian compatriots of the importance of the British connection to offset the threat of American annexation and the loss of identity that would ensue.

Cartier also presented Confederation to French Canadians as their best hope for cultural survival in a world of limited possibilities. The existing union, crippled by deadlock, could not go on; for French Canadians, union with the United States would be the worst possible fate. The independence of Lower Canada was not feasible. Only a larger federation of British North American colonies offered French Canadians possibilities beyond their own provincial boundaries at the same time as it protected their affairs within their own province.

Cartier turned to the clergy for support for Confederation, despite his personal concerns about mixing politics and religion. Bishop Ignace Bourget of Montreal, the most powerful French-Canadian bishop, feared for the future of the church in the new political union with other English-speaking colonies with large Protestant populations. He kept silent about his misgivings, however, since the other Quebec bishops were more favourably disposed, at least in principle. They realized that the alternative to Confederation was support of their arch-enemies, the *rouges*, who were strongly anti-clerical.

In the final vote on Confederation in the Legislature of the United Canadas, 91 were in favour and 33 opposed. In the breakdown of votes in the two sections, 54 of the 62 members from Canada West favoured the proposal, as did 37 of the 62 members from Canada East. Of the 48 French-Canadian members present, 27 voted for and 21 against. Overall, Confederation won overwhelmingly, but among French Canadians the victory was narrow, indicating serious reservations on their part.

OPPOSITION TO CONFEDERATION IN ATLANTIC CANADA

In New Brunswick, Samuel Leonard Tilley, who had been premier since 1857 and who had represented the province at both the Charlottetown and Quebec conferences, argued the advantages of Confederation for New Brunswickers: Saint John would be a year-round, ice-free port for the export of Canadian goods, and a lucrative market would exist in central Canada for Maritime coal and manufactured goods. The promised Intercolonial Railway would make such trade possible.

IN NEW BRUNSWICK

But there existed strong opposition to Confederation in the Maritimes. In New Brunswick, A.J. Smith, the opposition leader, headed the anti-Confederate forces. He argued that no guarantee existed that the Intercolonial Railway would be constructed and, if it were built, where it would run and thus which area of the province, the north shore or the southern Saint John River valley, would benefit from it. He also pointed out that New Brunswick's economic trade pattern, especially since the Reciprocity Treaty of 1854, had been north–south rather than east–west. Commercial interests in the province had no economic ties with the Canadas. Furthermore, union with Canada could lead to a flooding of the New Brunswick market by Canadian imports, and a high tariff structure. In addition, New Brunswickers would be forced to assume a portion of the heavy Canadian debt from canal and railway building. Finally, Smith argued that Confederation would diminish New Brunswick's political power by giving the province representation of only 15 members of Parliament in a House of Commons with 194 members. The Roman Catholic clergy also opposed Confederation, believing that a Canada dominated by Protestant "extremists" in Upper Canada could threaten Roman Catholic schools and the church itself throughout the proposed union.

These arguments were debated in the election campaign of early 1865, an election fought chiefly on the issue of Confederation. New Brunswickers responded clearly and decisively — the Tilley pro-Confederation government lost heavily.

IN NOVA SCOTIA

In Nova Scotia, Charles Tupper, the pro-Confederation premier, faced a serious challenge from Joseph Howe, "Father of Responsible Government." Although he was no longer a member of the Assembly, Howe was still the most powerful political figure in Nova Scotia. He argued that in Confederation Nova Scotia would lose its identity and cease to be an important colony in the great British Empire. Furthermore, Howe pointed out that the province looked eastward to the Atlantic Ocean and Britain, rather than westward to the continent and the Canadas. As he vividly expressed it: "Take a Nova Scotian to Ottawa, away above tide-water, freeze him up for five months, where he cannot view the Atlantic, smell salt water, or see the sail of a ship, and the man will pine and die." He favoured continuing colonial ties to Britain. In the winter of 1866–67, Howe went to England to present his case for Nova Scotia staying out of Confederation.

IN PRINCE EDWARD ISLAND

In Prince Edward Island, support for Confederation went from modest to none. At the Charlottetown and Quebec conferences, the island's representatives had driven a hard bargain, pressing for better terms on representation in the Senate and in the House of Commons, and for better economic terms. But when they returned home, their enthusiasm and interest waned when they realized that the islanders themselves opposed Confederation for a number of reasons. One was the problem of absentee landlordism. For over a century, absentee British landlords had controlled the island, much to the resentment of the local population. In 1860, a British commission appointed to investigate the question issued a report favourable to the islanders, only to have it rejected by the proprietors and the Colonial Office. Thus, when the Colonial Office pressured Prince Edward Islanders to adopt Confederation, they resisted. Also, many islanders saw Confederation as simply replacing one set of distant landlords in Britain with another in Ottawa. In addition, islanders believed that Confederation would give them very little. Union would mean higher taxes to support the enormous costs of the Intercolonial Railway, and higher tariffs to create inter-provincial trade — neither of which would greatly benefit Prince Edward Island. They also disliked the proposed form of representation in the Senate and House of Commons, which would deny them a major voice in distant Ottawa.

IN NEWFOUNDLAND

Newfoundland failed to support Confederation out of apathy, not opposition. The Island had not participated in the Charlottetown Conference, although it did send two representatives to the Quebec Conference, both of whom endorsed Confederation. They returned to a colony that was initially mildly interested as a result of Newfoundland's declining fishing industry, agriculture, and the timber trade. But if Newfoundlanders initially hoped that joining Confederation might solve their economic ills, they soon believed that Canada was simply too far away to be of benefit to them. R.J. Pinsent, a member of the Legislative Council, summed up the prevailing opinion as follows: "There is little community of interest between Newfoundland and the Canadas. This is not a Continental Colony." Essentially, the island continued to look eastward to Britain rather than westward to Canada.

EXTERNAL PRESSURES

By the end of 1865, public support for British North American Confederation had waned, except in Canada West. All four of the Atlantic colonies opposed it, while Canada East had serious reservations. Two external developments, however, altered the situation: British intervention and the American threat.

BRITISH SUPPORT FOR CONFEDERATION

By the mid-1860s Britain wanted to rid itself of the expense of defending British North America, and to ease tension in its relations with the United States. Thus, when in the autumn of 1865 a pro-Confederation delegation from the Canadas arrived in London, it was warmly welcomed; a counter-delegation from Nova Scotia under Joseph Howe was not. Instead, the British government replaced the anti-Confederation governor of Nova Scotia with one more supportive. The Colonial Office also ordered New Brunswick Governor Arthur Gordon to intervene in his province's politics to ensure the success of Confederation. Finally, Britain guaranteed the loan interest for the proposed Intercolonial Railway on the assumption that the Maritimes would join Confederation.

THE AMERICAN CONTRIBUTION TO CONFEDERATION

While Britain applied direct pressure, the United States did so indirectly. When the Civil War ended in 1865, Northern extremists advocated using the Northern army to annex the British North American colonies. Also, influential politicians in the American Midwest advocated taking possession of the British Northwest, as part of the United States' manifest destiny. Other American politicians, including Hamilton Fish, the secretary of state in Ulysses S. Grant's administration, urged possession of all the British territory in North America.

Amidst such annexationist appeals, the American government announced that the Reciprocity Treaty of 1854 would terminate in 1866. American annexationists reasoned that the treaty's abrogation would cause such economic hardships for the British colonies as to force them to join the United States. Ironically, the announced abrogation of reciprocity had the opposite effect: it encouraged the colonies to consider an alternative commercial union among themselves.

Fenian raids also furthered the cause of Confederation. Fenians were fanatical republican Irishmen in the United States committed to fighting for the independence of Ireland. One scheme they devised was to capture the British North American colonies and use them as ransom to liberate Ireland from British rule. Their marching song explicitly set out their goals:

> We are the Fenian Brotherhood,
> skilled in the art of war,
> And we're going to fight for Ireland,
> the land that we adore.
> Many battles we have won, along with
> the boys in blue,
> And we'll go and capture Canada for
> we've nothing else to do.

The Fenians expected the support of Irish Catholics in the British colonies, but few supported them. Some prominent Irish individuals, such as Thomas D'Arcy McGee, spoke out strongly against them.

The Fenians posed little threat until the end of the American Civil War when thousands of Irish-American soldiers, trained, receptive to mobilizing in defence of their native country, and now idle, became available. Furthermore, the Fenians had the support of the American government that sympathized with their anti-British sentiments. Many American politicians also feared that if they failed to support the Fenians, then they would alienate the large number of American Irish Catholic voters.

The Fenian threat tended to be more psychological than physical. The actual military skirmishes were few and restricted to border areas. The two most important took place in New Brunswick and in the Niagara Peninsula. In New Brunswick in April 1866, a small band of Fenians crossed into New Brunswick, where they stole the flag from a customs house before the local militia and British regulars forced them back across the border. Although the raid was

In May 1866, the Fenians invaded the Niagara peninsula. Their banners bore the initials "I.R.A." (Irish Republican Army).

National Archives of Canada/C-18737.

insignificant in military terms, it helped to turn the tide in favour of Confederation in the New Brunswick election that was taking place at the time. Then in May, 1500 Fenians crossed the Niagara River into Canada West. At Ridgeway on June 2, the Fenians defeated the Canadian militia, but then withdrew, never to return, although they continued to pose a threat to Canada until 1870.

TURNING THE TIDE IN NEW BRUNSWICK

Finding it difficult to rule with a minority government, the Smith government resigned in April 1866. In the ensuing election campaign, Samuel Leonard Tilley resurrected his earlier arguments for Confederation and added new ones. He pointed out to the people of New Brunswick that in Confederation they could expect lower taxes, the Intercolonial Railway, a fair share in the running of the nation, and a market for their raw materials and manufactured goods — in other words, material progress and modernization.

During the campaign, both parties benefited from external funds. The anti-Confederates received money from Nova Scotia and possibly, it has been asserted, the United States, while the pro-Confederates obtained financial support from the government of the Canadas. "Give us funds," a desperate Tilley cabled John A. Macdonald. "It will require some $40 000 or $50 000 to do the work in all our counties." Macdonald agreed. He did not want Confederation to go down to defeat in New Brunswick simply for lack of money. Direct British intervention and threatened Fenian raids also assisted Tilley's cause. After his resounding electoral victory, Tilley had the New Brunswick legislature quickly endorse Confederation.

FINAL NEGOTIATIONS

In the autumn and winter of 1866, delegates from Nova Scotia, New Brunswick, and the United Canadas met in London to prepare the passage of the British North America Act through the British Parliament. Although the Maritime delegates pressed for modifications of those aspects of the Seventy-Two Resolutions that provided for a strong central government, in the end the Resolutions were accepted with only a few minor, but significant, changes. Subsidies to the provinces would be increased beyond the agreed 80 cents a head by a fixed grant from the federal government. The contentious issue of separate schools was settled by applying the Quebec clause on education, which safeguarded the Protestant separate schools in Quebec, to all other provinces in the union, or to new provinces that had separate schools "by law" at the time they joined Confederation. Furthermore, provisions were included for religious minorities to appeal to the federal government if a provincial government threatened their school systems, as they existed before Confederation.

 While the delegates were meeting in London to finalize the terms of Confederation, Joseph Howe continued his opposition to Nova Scotia joining Confederation. He urged British officials to reject union. But the British government refused to retract its support. When the British North America Act was signed on March 29, 1867, Howe returned to Nova Scotia cured "of a good deal of loyal enthusiasm" and embittered against the Canadians. He was not alone. Many Nova Scotians saw Confederation as the end not the beginning of a vibrant Nova Scotia. Elsewhere, Confederation was accepted, although not with enthusiasm, except in Ontario.

NAMING THE NEW NATION

John A. Macdonald wanted to call "the new nation" the "Kingdom of Canada," but the British government objected because it feared that the term would further offend the Americans, implying as it did a more autonomous country. Leonard Tilley had chanced upon an alternative title, as well as an appropriate motto, for the new country — *A Mari Usque Ad Mare* (From Sea to Sea) — while reading Psalm 72:

> He shall have dominion also from sea to sea,
> and from the river unto the ends of the earth.

On July 1, 1867, the Dominion of Canada was born. It consisted of the four provinces of Nova Scotia, New Brunswick, Quebec and Ontario.

POLITICS

The Conservative Party won the first federal election in November, 1867. John A. Macdonald became Canada's first prime minister. A man with warm personal charm and a sense of humour, he preferred practical politics to philosophical debate. A masterful politician, he remained in the prime minister's office, with the exception of a five-year Liberal interlude in the mid-1870s, from 1867 until his death in 1891. Thus the late nineteenth century is often referred to politically as the Macdonald era.

To win support in Quebec, Macdonald relied on George-Étienne Cartier, particularly as he himself did not speak French. Macdonald once referred to Cartier as "my second self," and indeed he was. From 1867 until his death in 1873, Cartier came second only to Macdonald in the Conservative party.

ESTABLISHING POLITICAL CONVENTIONS

Macdonald and Cartier began a political convention that has often been effectively used in Canadian politics: the co-operation within the governing party of an English-speaking prime minister and a politically powerful French-speaking lieutenant, or vice versa. Such an alliance has ensured the French-Canadian minority an influential voice in federal politics.

Macdonald also established a second political convention. For his first cabinet, he chose individuals from various regions and interest groups — Maritimers, Quebeckers, and Ontarians; Protestants and Roman Catholics; Irish, Scottish, English, and French Canadians; business-people, farmers, fishers, and, occasionally, even working people. The Conservatives also created the first federal bureaucracy. This meant jobs, or rather rewards, for the party faithful. Most of the approximately 500 civil-service positions went to former bureaucrats from the United Canadas, with only a few token positions going to Maritimers.

THE NATURE OF CONFEDERATION

Unity in diversity became the goal of the Fathers of Confederation. They sought to establish domestic peace between English- and French-speaking Canadians, and between Protestants and Roman Catholics, through the creation of a political rather than a cultural nationality. As Cartier noted during the Confederation debates in the United Canadas in 1865: "Now, when we were united together, if union were attained, we would form a political nationality with which neither the national origin, nor the religion of any individual, would interfere."

Despite their laudable intentions, Canada's founders built disunity into the political structure. The new Canadian system, by combining aspects of the American federal and the British parliamentary forms of government, resembled a carriage pulled by two horses moving in different directions.

DEBATING DOMINION–PROVINCIAL RELATIONS

For more than a century, historians, political scientists, and legal experts have debated the Fathers of Confederation's true intentions. Those who believe they sought to build a strong central government point out that the BNA Act delegated only precise and very circumscribed powers to the provincial governments. In contrast, the federal government gained the important economic and taxation powers, including the right to grant subsidies to the individual provinces. Ottawa also received the right to make laws for the "peace, order and good government of Canada" in relation to all matters not exclusively assigned to the provincial legislatures. Centralists also contend that the phrase "peace, order and good government of Canada" and the phrase "regulation of trade and commerce" incorporated all powers not exclusively given to the provinces; hence the residuum of powers lay with the federal government. Furthermore, they point out that the lieutenant governors of the provinces, appointees of the Dominion government, could reserve and disallow provincial legislation.

In contrast, provincial-rights advocates argue that since the colonies established the union, Confederation constituted a compact made among them: a provincial compact. Furthermore, they point to the general phrase "property and civil rights in the province" in section 92 of the BNA Act, which deals with the constitutional rights of the provinces, as proof of the provinces' broad powers. They also note that the provinces received a structure of government parallel to that of the federal government, implying that the provinces' association with the Crown was similar, not subordinate, to the Dominion's. Finally, they direct attention to legal tradition: in the late nineteenth and early twentieth centuries, the Judicial Committee of the Privy Council, the highest court of appeal in the British Empire, consistently interpreted the BNA Act in favour of the provinces.

CANADIAN–BRITISH–AMERICAN RELATIONS

Nationhood did not mean independence. By law and by desire, Canada in 1867 remained a British colony, with the British Parliament controlling Canada's external affairs. In 1867, Canadians, particularly English-speaking Canadians, considered the imperial connection as the best means for Canada to fulfill its destiny. The alternatives were possible annexation by the United States, or existence as an insignificant and isolated nation on the northern half of the North American continent, both of which Canadians considered undesirable choices.

THE ECONOMY

More than 80 percent of the Canadian labour force in 1867 worked in the primary industries — farming, fishing, and lumbering — to produce the staple products of trade: wheat, fish, and timber. The Maritimes were the centre of the shipbuilding industry. In 1865 alone, for example, the region built more than 600 vessels. The ports of Saint John, Halifax, and Yarmouth were the major shipbuilding centres in the Maritimes, along with Quebec and Montreal in the Canadas. But as steel ships replaced wooden ones, and as steam replaced sails as the source of energy, the era of wood, wind, and sails would soon decline. Some Maritimers equated the decline of their "golden age" with Confederation, and they resented union.

The vast majority of Canadians in 1867 lived on farms. Agriculture was important in Nova Scotia, especially in the Annapolis valley, while in New Brunswick, farmers made up more than half the labour force. In southern Quebec, dairy farming predominated. Some Quebec farmers, with the encouragement of the Roman Catholic Church and the Quebec government, colonized further north in the Saguenay–Lake St. Jean region, in the Laurentians, or in Témiscamingue in the upper Ottawa valley. These "colonist farmers" had to clear the land of forests before breaking ground. Even then, farming in these northern reaches was marginal because of poor soil, short frost-free periods, and long distances from market centres. As the joke went, northern farmers raised two crops: one stone, the other snow.

Wheat farming served as "the engine of economic growth"[2] in Ontario, according to the economic historian John McCallum. At the time of Confederation the best agricultural land lay in the province, where 60 percent of the working population farmed. Coarse grain or flour made up half of all exports at mid-century. By the time of Confederation, the peak of wheat production had been reached, with most of the good farmland occupied and some of the older districts becoming exhausted. Fortunately for Ontarians, just as they faced an agricultural crisis, the Canadian government acquired the vast prairie land to the west, which served as an outlet for aspiring young Ontario farmers.

URBANIZATION

In 1867, only one in five Canadians lived in urban centres, communities with a population over 1000. Canada had only three large cities: Montreal with 105 000 people; Quebec City with 60 000; and Toronto with 50 000. Six other cities had populations greater than 10 000: Saint John and Halifax in the Maritimes, and Hamilton, Ottawa, Kingston, and London in Ontario. A host of smaller towns in the range of 1000–5000 dotted the Canadian landscape. The larger metropolitan centres serviced a hinterland region that went beyond the adjacent rural area,

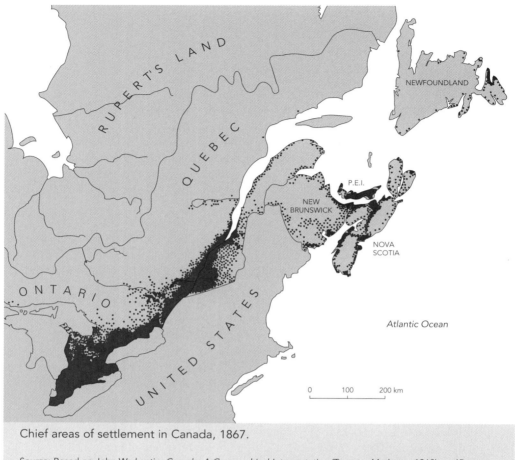

Chief areas of settlement in Canada, 1867.

Source: Based on John Warkentin, *Canada: A Geographical Interpretation* (Toronto: Methuen, 1968), p. 45.

thanks to their extensive rail connections. Montreal's hinterland, for example, included the rural areas of southwestern Quebec as well as eastern Ontario.

The Maritime cities of Saint John and Halifax grew slowly, compared with cities in central Canada. Many of the manufacturers in these two port cities faced hard times because they lacked a large local market and faced competition from wealthier entrepreneurs in central Canada. In 1867, industrialists in the Maritimes looked forward to the completion of the Intercolonial Railway, which would, they hoped, make Ontario and Quebec economic hinterlands of Halifax and Saint John.

Canadian cities in 1867 were, with the exception of Montreal, pre-industrial. This meant that rich and poor lived in close proximity, with social distinctions marked by the size of one's house, its location on the street, or by the location of a particular street in a district. In Montreal, however, there already existed predominantly working-class districts in the city core and along the St. Lawrence River and Lachine Canal. Well-to-do families were leaving the inner city to live in the spacious, clean, and airy suburban districts of the west end, with its numerous parks and good public services. Thus, in the case of Montreal, the modern industrial segregated city had made an appearance in 1867. By 1914, such segregated cities would be commonplace throughout the country.

POPULATION

In 1867, the total population of the new Dominion of Canada was 3.5 million. The First Nations numbered approximately 30 000, or roughly 1 percent. The three largest groups were: the Ojibwa (Anishinabeg), in Ontario; the Iroquois, in Ontario and Quebec; and the Mi'kmaq (Micmac), in Nova Scotia and New Brunswick.

Those of French descent made up roughly a third of the total population. More than 85 percent resided in Quebec and had roots in North America extending back two centuries. The Acadians in New Brunswick and Nova Scotia numbered nearly 10 percent of the French-speaking population. Only 3 percent of Canada's francophones lived in Ontario, mainly in the area adjacent to Quebec.

People of British descent accounted for 60 percent of Canada's population in 1867. Some were descendants of Loyalists who had settled on British territory after the American Revolution. Most, however, were British immigrants and their descendants who had arrived in British North America between 1815 and 1860, some 1.3 million in total. In 1867, the Irish made up 25 percent of the total Canadian population, the Scots 16 percent, the English 15 percent, and the Welsh 5 percent.

English-speaking and French-speaking Canadians lived in two separate worlds in 1867. P.-J.-O. Chauveau, the first premier of Quebec after Confederation, compared Canada to the famous staircase of the Château de Chambord in France, built to allow two persons to ascend it without meeting, and even without seeing each other except at intervals. "English and French, we climb by a double flight of stairs toward the destinies reserved for us on this continent, without knowing each other, without meeting each other, except on the landing of politics."

The remaining 8 percent of the Dominion's population consisted of non-British and non-French immigrants and their descendants from Europe and the United States. The majority was from German-speaking states and was welcomed because of the close links between the British monarchy and German principalities. There were, as well, about 65 000 African Canadians. While some were of American Loyalist descent, many had arrived in the mid-1800s, either as freed African Americans, now facing increased discrimination in racially torn America, or as fugitive slaves on the eve of the American Civil War via the Underground Railroad, a loose network of African Americans (sometimes ex-slaves) and white abolitionists who aided slaves. Although slavery had not existed in British North America since the early nineteenth century, racial prejudice existed. Blacks faced discrimination in land grants, schooling, employment, and voting rights.

Ontario and Quebec had nearly four-fifths of the new Dominion's population, with more than 1.5 million in Ontario and about one million in Quebec. The other fifth of Canada's population resided in the Maritime provinces: roughly 400 000 in Nova Scotia and 300 000 in New Brunswick.

SOCIAL LIFE

In 1867, most Canadians lived and worked on their own farms, as close to neighbours, kin, and their own ethnic group as possible. In Quebec, only thirteen years earlier, the seigneurial system had been abolished, which meant individual farmers had acquired title to their lands. Limited financial means made consumer goods a luxury. The village elite generally consisted of the curé, the doctor, the notary, and the local merchants. In Quebec City and Montreal, French Canadians lived amidst a substantial English-speaking population.

Next door in Ontario, most of the population consisted of recent British immigrants or children of immigrants. The majority were freehold farmers who had acquired their land within the

A Historical Portrait

☞ Josiah Henson

Josiah Henson was born into slavery on a Maryland plantation in 1789. His earliest recollection at the age of three or four was the day he saw his father return from a terrible beating. As Henson later recalled, "His right ear had been cut off close to his head and he had received a hundred lashes on his back." His "crime"? He struck a white man, the farm overseer, for brutally assaulting Josiah's mother.

Soon afterwards, the Hensons' master split the family up. He sold Josiah's father to a plantation in Alabama and auctioned off Josiah's mother, brothers, sisters, and Josiah himself to separate owners. Fortunately, Josiah was later reunited with his mother.

As slaves, Josiah and his mother lived in appalling conditions, eating corn meal and salted herring. "Our lodging," he recalled, "was in log huts, of a single small room, with no other floor than the trodden earth, in which ten or a dozen persons — men, women, and children — might sleep." By his twenties, the conscientious, hard-working man had so gained his master's respect that he appointed him farm superintendent. When it became clear, however, that his owner had no intention of granting him his freedom, Henson, who had married fifteen or so years earlier and now had a family, escaped with his wife and four children to Canada.

The Hensons spent six difficult weeks following the Underground Railway to Upper Canada. On October 28, 1830, they crossed the Niagara River. Immediately, Henson fell on his knees and gave thanks. In their new home, the Hensons founded an African

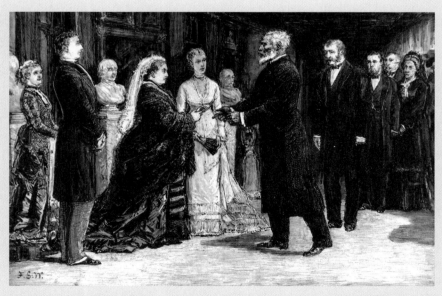

Queen Victoria receives Josiah Henson at Windsor Castle, March 5, 1877.
The American Museum in Britain, Claverton Manor, Bath, England.

community named Dawn, near present-day Dresden, Ontario. With the financial assistance of a group of Boston Unitarians, they began the British American Institute for Fugitive Slaves, a school to educate ex-slaves and to teach them a trade.

In the late 1840s, Henson dictated his life story. It was published in Boston as *The Life of Josiah Henson Formerly a Slave Now an Inhabitant of Canada* in 1849. Three years later Harriet Beecher Stowe's novel, *Uncle Tom's Cabin*, appeared. It proved a sensation, the most popular anti-slavery book published before the outbreak of the American Civil War. The fact that many

people identified Josiah Henson as the prototype for the fictional "Uncle Tom" made him famous. Stowe, however, never categorically stated this; people just inferred that it was true. As a result of his fame, Henson made several lecture tours of Britain to raise money for the Dawn settlement.

When the American Civil War ended, many African Americans in Upper Canada returned to the United States, and the community of Dawn died out. In his late eighties, Henson made his final visit to Britain to meet Queen Victoria at Windsor Castle. He died in Dresden in 1883.

last generation. In general, Ontario farmers were better off economically than their Quebec counterparts. They owned larger farms that were newly cultivated and subsequently more productive. People lived farther apart, however, and were divided by their different Christian denominational ties.

In the 1860s, Ontarians were on the move. A study of several townships along Lake Ontario near Port Hope revealed that within a five-year span more than half the people were recent occupants or had moved from one place to another within the region. David Gagan's study of Peel County at mid-century confirms this, as does Michael Katz's study of mid-century Hamilton.[3] An increasing number were leaving the country for the cities and towns. Physical mobility, however, did not necessarily mean social mobility, even though the incentive for moving was often to better one's life.

In the Maritimes, people lived predominantly in rural areas or in small towns. Given the sparse populations, poor roads, and a topography that encouraged settlement along the coast, communities were often isolated. In 1867, no major railways yet existed to link communities. In addition, the region's diversified economy of fishing, lumbering, mining, and farming segregated people according to interests and livelihood. As a result, Maritimers in 1867 identified with their particular locale and lacked a provincial and regional consciousness.

WOMEN

Women made up almost half of the population in 1867, yet they lacked basic rights: the right to vote; the right to higher education or professional training; and legal rights. They were not defined as individuals but by their role in the "domestic sphere," as wives and mothers at the service of husbands and children.

Women relinquished their personal property and any wages earned upon marriage. Under British common law, in effect everywhere except Quebec, husband and wife were legally one. A wife could not sign a contract, be sued in her own name, take her husband to court, or initiate divorce proceedings. Despite such restrictions, over 95 percent of women married. They also bore large families, 7.8 children on average by mid-century. By the end of the century, that number would decline to an average of only four children.

Marriage was more a communal than private affair. Courting occurred in supervised settings, and marriage was a public event. But the few surviving women's diaries of this period speak little of love and romance in marriage, and instead emphasize economic security.

In the days before modern conveniences, women's duties lay in the arduous work of keeping a good home. Their daily tasks would consist of cleaning house, cooking, sewing, weaving, and making butter, the rhythm being broken only by church services on Sundays. The change of seasons varied the pattern only slightly, and added garden and field work at harvest time.

A satirical cartoon in *L'Opinion Publique*, an illustrated journal of the day, reveals what many working-class women's sentiments must have been. The gruff-looking husband sits at the table heaped with food, while his wife, on her knees, scrubs the floor. In the background one sees laundry hanging. She comments to him: "You complain about your 10 hours of labour; I have just worked for 14 hours, and my day is not finished yet."

Children were the forgotten group in society, without any legal rights. Those from poorer families usually had to leave school early to help support their families. Most working-class children had little hope of rising above their parents' level and social status.

LE TRAVAIL.

u te plains, mon pauvre mari, de tes dix heures d'ouvrage ; voici quatorze heures que je travaille, moi, et je n'ai pas encore fini ma journée."

"Work," a drawing that appeared in the journal *L'Opinion Publique*, November 2, 1871. In the late nineteenth century, gender inequality was as common as class inequality.

National Archives of Canada/C-108134.

TRADE UNIONS

The federal government only legally recognized unions in 1872. In the 1860s, the unions that did exist represented skilled workers in a particular locale or a special trade, such as typesetting, shoemaking, and moulding. The first unions for non-skilled workers appeared in shops that introduced modern technology, a development that was beginning to undermine jobs. Increasingly, employers saw workers as employees rather than as apprentices. They brought workers under one roof and paid them according to the quantity, rather than quality, of their work.

Some workers responded to these changed conditions in the workplace by rioting. By 1867, however, strikes and parades were replacing riots as more acceptable forms of protest, and as a means to demand better wages and working conditions. On June 10, 1867, for example, 10 000 workers paraded in the streets of Montreal as a show of worker solidarity and as an appeal for improved wages and working conditions.

RELIGION AND EDUCATION

RELIGIOUS DENOMINATIONS

In 1867, almost all Canadians belonged to one of the major denominations. The Roman Catholic Church, the largest in Canada, claimed as members 40 percent of the country's population (in Quebec, 85 percent). In Quebec the Roman Catholic Church controlled the Catholic education system, supplying both its teachers and its curriculum.

Most of the teachers came from the female religious orders. The female orders also administered the hospitals and cared for the sick, the abandoned, and the poor. These female religious communities gave many of their members the opportunity to obtain an excellent education, to occupy responsible administrative positions, and to serve as teachers, nurses, and social-assistance workers. They also provided a strong sense of community.

In Protestant Canada, Anglicans slightly outnumbered Presbyterians, who outnumbered Methodists. These Protestant religious groups favoured voluntarism, the legal separation of church and state. They believed that religious instruction should be provided by the church only, in Sunday schools. The Roman Catholic Church, in contrast, maintained that the school system should provide religious, as well as regular, instruction. It therefore opposed the abolition of denominational schools.

SCHOOLING

Schooling had little priority in Canada in the 1860s, although most provinces moved to a form of taxation on property holders to finance state-operated schools. Children fortunate enough to receive formal education might have their classes in the corners of warehouses, blacksmith shops, stores, tanneries, or private homes. Their schooling rarely went beyond the basic "3 Rs" — "reading, 'riting, and 'rithmetic." Very often teachers had little more education than their students. The most important requisite to teach was simply a willingness to work for low pay and to enforce discipline.

In Ontario, the middle and upper classes paid fees for their children to attend grammar schools (renamed "high schools" in 1871 by the superintendent of education, Egerton Ryerson) and collegiate institutes. In high school, the students learned English, commercial subjects, and natural science, especially agriculture; and in collegiate institutes they also studied the classics in preparation for university. In Quebec, the Roman Catholic Church operated classical colleges, which trained the province's future lawyers, doctors, and priests. Most of the seventeen universities in existence in 1867 were affiliated with a religious denomination, but four exceptions already existed: the University of Toronto, McGill in Montreal, Dalhousie College in Halifax, and the University of New Brunswick in Fredericton. Universities served an elite of only 1500 students in total, mostly sons of the well-to-do (women were not admitted) or a few aspiring members of the upper middle class. Within the university curriculum, the faculties of arts and theology dominated, as teaching and the clergy were the favoured career options after graduation. The arts course was traditional, with an emphasis on classical languages, mathematics, and philosophy. Natural science was assuming greater importance. Engineering courses had not yet been introduced, but law and medicine were taught at some of the larger universities.

Community Portrait

◄ The Community of the Sisters of the Congregation of Notre Dame in the Late Nineteenth Century

Founded in 1653 by Marguerite Bourgeoys as a teaching order to provide schooling for the young women of New France, the Congregation of Notre Dame became, by the late nineteenth and early twentieth centuries, the largest and most prestigious religious community of women teachers in Quebec. By 1920, it had over 1600 members and over 150 Roman Catholic schools throughout Quebec, Nova Scotia, New Brunswick, and Ontario.

The Congregation of Notre Dame, like other women's religious orders, provided women with a community in which they could find meaningful work which, in the case of the Congregation, meant teaching. Many women who entered the Congregation of Notre Dame convents did so on the advice of family members who, in many cases, had preceded them. Thus a strong bond existed between members of the Congregation and their families. Even the terms "sisters" and "mothers" to identify members of women's religious communities, and, in the case of the Congregation of

Notre Dame, the epithet of "Les Filles de Marguerite Bourgeoys" (Daughters of Marguerite Bourgeoys) reinforced the familial link. Members of the order prayed to Marguerite Bourgeoys, their founder. Within the community, the Golden Rule applied: sisters were expected to be charitable and compassionate to fellow members. The young and healthy, for example, took care of the sick and elderly nuns. At the same time, the community also allowed for a relaxation of the order's rules and regulations to foster camaraderie. At the mother house of the Congregation, for example, sisters were permitted on special occasions to "let loose" by engaging in such communal fun as playing harmless pranks, wearing costumes, or performing imitations of their superiors.

As the Congregation grew, it also became more affluent. Its members enjoyed improved diets of fresh fruits, vegetables, butter, and pastries. The sisters had lighter manual workloads, and thus more time for leisure activities together and for communal prayers. But prosperity also caused strains in the Congregation's communal life. In the 1880s, les *soeurs converses*, or domestic servants, were brought into the community to do the manual work previously done by the sisters themselves. Thus a two-tiered social order emerged, evident in the separation of recreation, clothing habits, and assigned work of the two groups. Furthermore, the Congregation's growth resulted in a more bureaucratic structure that mitigated against its earlier sense of a community of equals. Now a General Superior ruled and administered affairs at the centre, while local and provincial superiors in the Congregation's six "provinces," each corresponding to the regional district of the schools owned by the community, carried out the rulings of the central council and regulated the everyday activities of the sisters. A constitution dictated the rights and responsibilities of each office and outlined the procedure for the appointment of superiors. Nominally, sisters who had been with the community for at least ten years could cast a vote for their leaders, but in reality each chapter selected delegates who made the final decision. And within the community, nuns from upper- and middle-class households wielded greater power than those nuns from working-class or farming backgrounds.

Still, the community of the Congregation of Notre Dame provided its members with a communal and supportive setting in which women lived a religious life while also acquiring a profession and the skills to play a meaningful role in society. In 1908, the Congregation supported the establishment of the first French-language women's college in Quebec; the École d'enseignment supérieur (renamed the Collège Marguerite Bourgeoys in 1926). In this way, the Congregation of Notre Dame assisted

The teachers of Mont Ste-Marie Convent School, 1889, Centre d'archives, Congregation of Notre Dame, Montreal.
Congrégation de Notre Dame, 2330 ouest, rue Sherbrooke, PQ, H3E 1G8, (514) 931-5891.

French-Canadian females to obtain an education equal to their male counterparts. Today, the Congregation of Notre Dame has a world-wide community of approximately 1700 sisters in Canada, the United States, Japan, Central and South America, and Africa.

Further Readings

Marta Danylewycz, *Taking the Veil: An Alternative to Marriage, Motherhood and Spinsterhood in Quebec, 1840–1920* (Toronto: McClelland and Stewart, 1987).

Danielle Juteau and Nicole Laurin, *Un métier et une vocation: Le travail des religieuses au Québec de 1901 à 1971* (Montreal: Presses de l'Université de Montréal, 1997).

Nadia Famy-Eid and Micheline Dumont, *Les couventines: l'éducation des filles au Québec dans les congrégations religieuses enseignantes, 1840–1960* (Montreal: Boréal, 1986).

Website address: www.cnd-m.com

This was the Canada of 1867 as the country embarked on its new experiment in nation building. It was a rural, predominantly farming, society. Social distinctions divided the rural population, and great physical distances isolated communities. In the few towns and cities, social distinctions existed, but segregation by social districts was only beginning. The Canadian economy remained largely pre-industrial, but manufacturing had started in a few large urban centres. Exports included mainly wheat, timber, and fish. Politically, the new nation was about to experiment with a new two-party system and with a new Constitution that left much to be resolved. The new Dominion also lacked a sense of nationalism. As Prime Minister John A. Macdonald put it: Confederation, "now in the gristle," needed to "harden into bone."

NOTES

1. Peter H. Russell, *Constitutional Odyssey: Can Canadians Become a Sovereign People?* 2nd ed. (Toronto: University of Toronto Press, 1993), p. 32.
2. John McCallum, *Unequal Beginnings: Agriculture and Economic Development in Quebec and Ontario until 1870* (Toronto: University of Toronto Press, 1980), p. 5.
3. David Gagan, *Hopeful Travellers: Families, Land, and Social Change in Mid-Victorian Peel County, Canada West* (Toronto: University of Toronto Press, 1981); and Michael Katz, *The People of Hamilton, Canada West: Family and Class in a Mid-Nineteenth Century City* (Cambridge, MA: Harvard University Press, 1975).

LINKING TO THE PAST

Canadian Confederation
http://www.nlc-bnc.ca/2/18/index-e.html

This site from the National Library of Canada offers extensive information on Confederation, the events that led up to it, and the people behind it. The site includes biographies of John A. Macdonald, George-Étienne Cartier, George Brown, Charles Tupper, and Alexander Tilloch Galt. For information on the influence of the American Civil War, go to http://www.nlc-bnc.ca/2/18/h18-2003-e.html. Also check out the full text of the Seventy-Two Resolutions, the British North America Act, and related historical documents at http://www.nlc-bnc.ca/2/18/h18-2600-e.html.

The Charlottetown Conference, 1864
http://collections.ic.gc.ca/charlottetown/

An extensive site that presents background material; a day-by-day summary of the conference, including description of the social events that took place; and a collection of newspaper clippings, paintings, and photographs.

The Fenian Raids of Upper and Lower Canada
http://www.doyle.com.au/fenian_raids.htm

A history of the Fenians and their raids, including the Battle of Ridgeway.

The BNA Act
http://www.canadahistory.com/sections/documents/documents.htm

The full text of the 1867 British North America Act, which marked the beginnings of Canada as a nation.

Congregation of Notre Dame of Montreal
http://www.newadvent.org/cathen/11127a.htm

A brief look at the history of the Congregation and of Marguerite Bourgeoys, its founding member.

BIBLIOGRAPHY

The three best general texts on Confederation, all written in the 1960s, are Donald Creighton, *The Road to Confederation: The Emergence of Canada, 1863–1867* (Toronto: Macmillan, 1964); W.L. Morton, *The Critical Years: The Union of British North America, 1857–1873* (Toronto: McClelland & Stewart, 1964); and P.B. Waite, *The Life and Times of Confederation, 1864–1867: Politics, Newspapers, and the Union of British North America* (Toronto: University of Toronto Press, 1962). The Canadian Historical Association has published a number of pamphlets on aspects of Confederation by leading scholars in their fields: J.M. Beck, *Joseph Howe: Anti-Confederate* (Ottawa, 1966); J.-C. Bonenfant, *The French Canadians and the Birth of Confederation* (Ottawa, 1966); P.G. Cornell, *The Great Coalition* (Ottawa, 1966); W.L. Morton, *The West and Confederation, 1857–1871* (Ottawa, 1962); P.B. Waite, *The Charlottetown Conference* (Ottawa, 1963); and W.M. Whitelaw, *The Quebec Conference* (Ottawa, 1966). Christopher Moore takes a more recent look at the topic in *1867: How the Fathers Made a Deal* (Toronto: McClelland & Stewart, 1997). A good primary source is P.B. Waite, ed., *The Confederation Debates in the Province of Canada, 1865* (Toronto: McClelland & Stewart, 1963).

On the Maritime provinces and Confederation in 1867 see Phillip A. Buckner, "The 1860s: An End and a Beginning," in Phillip A. Buckner and John G. Reid, eds., *The Atlantic Region to Confederation: A History* (Toronto: University of Toronto Press, 1994), pp. 360–86.

On the American influence on Confederation consult Robin Winks, *Canada and the United States: The Civil War Years* (Montreal: Harvest House, 1971 [1960], and Greg Marquis, *In Armageddon's Shadow: The Civil War and Canada's Maritime Provinces* (Montreal/Kingston: McGill-Queen's University Press, 1998). Studies of Britain's influence include C.P. Stacey, *Canada and the British Army, 1841–1871*, rev. ed. (Toronto: University of Toronto Press, 1963 [1936]) and Ged Martin, *Britain and the Origins of Canadian Federation, 1837–67* (Vancouver: University of British Columbia Press, 1995).

Portraits of Canada's first prime minister are available in Donald G. Creighton, *John A. Macdonald: The Old Chieftain* (Toronto: Macmillan, 1955); and P.B. Waite, *Macdonald: His Life and World* (Toronto: McGraw-Hill Ryerson, 1975). For studies of George-Étienne Cartier see Brian Young, *George-Étienne Cartier: Montreal Bourgeois* (Montreal/Kingston: McGill-Queen's University Press, 1981). Gordon T. Stewart discusses the formation of political parties in *The Origins of Canadian Politics: A Comparative Approach* (Vancouver: University of British Columbia Press, 1986).

For a review of the Canadian economy at the time of Confederation consult Michael Bliss, *Northern Enterprise: Five Centuries of Canadian Business* (Toronto: McClelland & Stewart, 1987); Kenneth Norrie and Douglas Owram, *A History of the Canadian Economy*, 3rd ed. (Toronto: Nelson, 2002), and in the case of Quebec, P.-A. Linteau, R. Durocher, and J.-C. Robert, *Quebec: A History, 1867–1929* (Toronto: James Lorimer, 1983).

For a study of social life in Montreal, see Bettina Bradbury, *Working Families: Age, Gender, and Daily Survival in Industrializing Montreal* (Toronto: McClelland & Stewart, 1993). Sandra Gwyn provides a glimpse of governing society in Ottawa from 1867 to 1914 in *The Private Capital: Ambition and Love in the Age of Macdonald and Laurier* (Toronto: McClelland & Stewart, 1984). For the story of the Native peoples see E.S. Rogers and Donald B. Smith, eds., *Aboriginal Ontario* (Toronto: Dundurn Press, 1994). The best overview of African Canadians remains Robin Winks, *The Blacks in Canada: A History*, 2nd ed. (Montreal/Kingston: McGill-Queen's University Press, 1997).

On women at the time of Confederation, see the relevant sections of Alison Prentice et al., *Canadian Women: A History*, 2nd ed. (Toronto: Harcourt Brace, 1996). For Quebec, see Marta Danylewycz, *Taking the Veil: An Alternative to Marriage, Motherhood, and Spinsterhood in Quebec, 1840–1920* (Toronto: McClelland & Stewart, 1987); for the Maritimes see Janet Guildford and Suzanne Morton, *Separate Spheres: Women's Worlds in the 19th-Century Maritimes* (Fredericton: Acadiensis Press, 1994).

Craig Heron's *The Canadian Labour Movement: A Short History*, 2nd ed. (Toronto: Lorimer, 1996) surveys Canadian labour history. See, as well, Bryan D. Palmer, *Working-Class Experience: Rethinking the History of Canadian Labour, 1800–1991* (Toronto: McClelland & Stewart, 1992).

For further discussion of religion see John S. Moir, "Religion," in *The Canadians: 1867–1967* (cited earlier), pp. 586–605; and John W. Grant, *A Profusion of Spires: Religion in Nineteenth-Century Ontario* (Toronto: University of Toronto Press, 1988). On education consult Susan E. Houston and Alison Prentice, *Schooling and Scholars in Nineteenth-Century Ontario* (Toronto: University of Toronto Press, 1988); Bruce Curtis, *Building the Educational State: Canada West, 1836–1871* (London: Althouse Press, 1988); and J. Donald Wilson, Robert M. Stamp, and Louis-Philippe Audet, eds., *Canadian Education: A History* (Toronto: Prentice-Hall, 1970).

CONSOLIDATION OF CONFEDERATION

In his first administration, John A. Macdonald worked to keep the fragile creation called Canada together and to round it out by purchasing Rupert's Land from the Hudson's Bay Company in 1869. From 1870 to 1872, he brought in Manitoba and British Columbia as provinces and prepared for Prince Edward Island's entry in 1873. Newfoundland, wanting better terms, refused to join. In 1880, Canada also acquired the Arctic region from Britain. As well, Macdonald had to persuade Nova Scotia, a reluctant partner in Confederation, to remain in Canada. Other challenges included American threats to the North-West Territories and even, on occasion, talk of annexing all of Canada, a result of some Americans' belief in their "manifest destiny" to control the entire North American continent.

THE NOVA SCOTIA REPEAL MOVEMENT

Nova Scotia had opposed union with the Canadas from the beginning. When Nova Scotians had a chance to vote on Confederation, in September 1867, they elected anti-confederates to 18 of the 19 federal seats. Only Charles Tupper won his seat for the confederates, and then by less than a hundred votes. In a provincial election the same year, Nova Scotians elected 36 anti-confederates and only 2 pro-confederates. In the first meeting of the provincial legislature, the anti-confederates presented repeal resolutions to end the "bondage" of Confederation.

 The Anti-Confederation League, later patriotically renamed the Nova Scotia Party, was formed in 1866 and led by Joseph Howe. Once again, he headed a committee to London in early 1868 to obtain the Colonial Office's sanction for Nova Scotia's release from Confederation. But the colonial secretary refused to meet Howe. While Howe wanted continued colonial ties with the British, other anti-confederates, particularly the business interests in the province, favoured annexation to the United States.

John A. Macdonald saw Canada's opportunity. He knew Howe opposed union with the United States. In return for joining his government, the prime minister promised Howe a cabinet position, control over provincial patronage, and better financial terms for Nova Scotia — an increased debt allowance and a 25 percent increase in the federal subsidy to the province. Although his opponents accused him of betraying Nova Scotia, Howe ran for federal office in a by-election. Assisted by a very generous campaign donation, supplied jointly by the federal Conservative government and central Canadian business interests, Howe won and subsequently joined the federal cabinet.

Howe's "conversion" to Canadian federalism weakened the repeal movement. Only the annexationists remained. In June 1869, the Anti-Confederation League formally changed its name to the Annexation League. The timing could not have been worse for them: their manifesto, advocating closer relations with the United States, coincided with a brief period of prosperity in the province, which undermined their economic grievances. Furthermore, the United States did not appear particularly interested at this time in annexing Nova Scotia.

The final offer of better terms for Nova Scotia won over the moderate anti-confederates. In order to weaken opposition to Confederation, Tupper, Howe, and New Brunswick's Charles Tilley successfully pressured Macdonald to give utmost priority to the construction of the Intercolonial Railway. The 800-km publicly funded railway line was completed in 1876 and ran from Rivière-du-Loup in Quebec, along New Brunswick's north shore, to link up with existing lines to Halifax and Saint John.

THE CANADIAN ACQUISITION OF RUPERT'S LAND

Macdonald's Conservative government also faced serious trouble in the Northwest. American senators and congressmen, particularly from the mid-west, talked openly of annexing the region. In 1864, the United States Congress granted a charter for the construction of the Northern Pacific Railway from St. Paul, Minnesota, to Seattle, Washington. It was to be built close to the international border with the intention of capturing more of the trade of the British territory through the building of spur lines.

In 1868, the Canadian government began negotiations in London with the British government and representatives of the Hudson's Bay Company (HBC) to acquire Rupert's Land, roughly defined as all territory whose rivers flowed into Hudson Bay. The agreement reached in 1869–70 constituted one of the largest real-estate deals in history. For an area ten times the size of what was then Canada, the Dominion government agreed to pay the HBC a cash sum of £300 000 (approximately $1.5 million at the time) and to allow the company to retain one-twentieth (roughly 2.8 million ha) of the land of the "fertile belt" (the area along the North Saskatchewan River), as well as the land immediately surrounding its trading posts. The company agreed to transfer the land to the British government, which then turned the territory over to Canada. Historian Chester Martin maintained that the land deal "transformed the original Dominion from a federation of equal provinces ... into a veritable empire in its own right."[1]

ADMINISTRATING THE NORTHWEST

While the negotiations were underway, the Canadian Parliament passed the Act for the Temporary Government of Rupert's Land and the North-West Territory. It provided for a colonial system of government with an appointed governor and council only. Representative and responsible government, and provincehood, would await a larger population. The Canadian government made immediate plans to build a road from the Lake of the Woods to Fort Garry in the Red River colony and dispatched a survey crew to the Red River for an eventual railway to link the Northwest to the rest of Canada. As well, it appointed William McDougall from Ontario as the first lieutenant governor. McDougall set off by way of St. Paul, Minnesota, to take up his administrative duties in the Red River colony. But he never reached his destination. A group of

Métis in the Red River colony, led by Louis Riel, a 25-year-old Métis from a well-established Red River family who had been educated in Montreal, forbade McDougall and his entourage to enter Rupert's Land. The Métis also drove out the survey crew.

The mixed-blood population in the Red River area consisted of three groups. About half were French Métis, offspring of the intermarriage of French fur traders and First Nations women. About another third were the "country born," descendants of Scottish and First Nations parents. The remaining group was the descendants of Selkirk's original Scottish settlers and newly arrived immigrants from the Canadas, who together numbered only about 1000 people, less than 10 percent of the total Red River colony's population in 1869.

THE MÉTIS RESISTANCE OF 1869–1870

The French Métis resented not being consulted over the sale of their homeland. They also disliked the aggressive action and haughty attitude of the small group of Canadian expansionists in the Red River colony working to bring the region into Confederation. In their local newspaper, *The Nor'Wester*, these Canadians ridiculed the Métis and proclaimed Canada's right to take control of the Northwest as part of the country's "manifest destiny." The Métis reacted by occupying Upper Fort Garry, the seat of government, on November 2, and establishing their own provisional government, thus gaining effective control of the Red River colony.

Prime Minister Macdonald opened negotiations with the Métis. Acting quickly, he dismissed William McDougall and asked the influential Bishop Alexandre Taché of the Red River colony to return from Rome, where he had been attending the Vatican Council, to assist in reaching a settlement. The prime minister also appointed Donald A. Smith of the Hudson's Bay Company to negotiate with the Métis on behalf of the Canadian government.

Riel's provisional government drew up a bill of rights in November 1869, outlining its grievances and demands. That bill became the basis for negotiations. At two public meetings in the Red River colony held in mid-January, Smith promised the Red River colony a better deal, to be decided by a committee of Métis and the Canadian government.

CLASH BETWEEN THE MÉTIS AND THE CANADA PARTY

Meanwhile, the Canadian expansionist party in the Red River colony took action into its own hands. Its members met at the general store owned by John Schultz, a sometime medical doctor and merchant and the leader of the Canada party. Schultz's store became the Canada party's headquarters for its attacks on Riel's provisional government. The Métis raided the store and imprisoned the Canadians. The Métis agreed to release those prisoners who promised either to leave the colony or to obey the provisional government. A few, like Schultz, refused to comply. He managed to escape from his Métis prison by using a knife, hidden in a pudding by his wife, to cut the ropes on the windows and to lower himself out. He then gathered together supporters for an ill-fated attack on Upper Fort Garry. The Métis captured members of the raiding party, including Thomas Scott, a virulent 28-year-old Protestant Irishman and member of the Orange Lodge.

Louis Riel (seated directly in the centre) with his council, 1870. Riel and his council's resistance to Canada's attempted seizure of the Red River led to the Manitoba Act of 1870, which brought Manitoba into Confederation as the first new province.

National Archives of Canada/PA12854; Manitoba Museum of Man and Nature/3661.

Thomas Scott, executed March 4, 1870.

Glenbow Archives/NA 576-1.

Scott proved a difficult prisoner. He insulted and provoked his Métis guards. Riel decided to hold a Métis court to try Scott for contempt of the Métis provisional government. The court voted to execute the trouble-maker. Riel agreed, in order, he claimed, "to make Canada respect us." (Some historians have since argued that Riel complied with the court order so as to maintain his control of the Métis.) On March 4, 1870, a firing squad executed Scott.

Scott's execution turned the Métis resistance from a distant western struggle into a national crisis. Protestant Ontario now had its martyr. When a group of Scott's Red River associates arrived in Toronto to enlist support for their cause, a huge crowd assembled to hear their version of the uprising in the West:

> It would be a gross injustice to the loyal inhabitants of Red River, humiliating to our national honour, and contrary to all British traditions for our Government to receive, negotiate or meet with the emissaries of those who have robbed, imprisoned and mur-dered loyal Canadians, whose only fault was zeal for British institutions, whose only crime was devotion to the old flag.

French Canadians, on the other hand, viewed Riel as the protector of the French-speaking Métis against an aggressive group of Canadianists from Ontario, backed by the Orange Order.

John A. Macdonald proposed a compromise. To appease the Métis and the French Canadians of Quebec, his government passed the Manitoba Act in May 1870, based on the negotiations between the Red River's three-person del-egation and the Canadian government. The Red River colony could enter Confederation as a province. To satisfy Ontarians, the prime minister agreed to send an armed force to the Red River colony immediately to secure the Northwest.

THE MANITOBA ACT

The Manitoba Act created the new province of Manitoba that geographically included only the 35 000 km^2 around the Red River settlement and Portage la Prairie to the west. The rest of the area became the North-West Territories. Manitoba received its own legislative assembly, four fed-eral members of Parliament, and two senators. But, unlike the other provinces in Confederation, Ottawa denied Manitoba control over its own public lands and natural resources. The same was true for the North-West Territories. The land and resources of the entire North West remained under the federal government's control, to be used "for the purposes of the Dominion."

The Manitoba Act addressed the issue of linguistic and educational rights of the French-speaking population. In 1867 the Fathers of Confederation had made no provision in the BNA Act for constitutional rights for French-speaking Canadians in new provinces joining Confederation. Thus, Manitoba became the test case. Should French be recognized as an official language? Should separate schools be permitted in provinces with a sizable Roman Catholic population at the time of union with Canada? The Manitoba Act recognized both French and English as official languages. It also established a confessional school system on the Quebec and Ontario models, with separate Protestant and Catholic divisions that would receive government funding.

THE WOLSELEY EXPEDITION

After Manitoba's entry into Confederation, tension continued in the region. In the spring of 1870, Macdonald sent out the promised military force under Lieutenant Colonel Garnet Wolseley. As the troops approached, Riel got word of their arrival and fled. Upon finding Fort Garry abandoned, Wolseley reported in his diary: "Personally, I was glad that Riel did not come out and surrender, as he at one time said he would, for I could not then have hanged him as I might have done had I taken him prisoner when in arms against his sovereign." Riel had left, convinced that he had achieved a great victory for his Métis people. He had won them provincial status, as well as land and cultural rights. Among those land rights was the agreement in the Manitoba Act to set aside a reserve of 600 000 ha for the Métis and their children.

Riel's victory proved transitory, however. Migrants from the rest of Canada, particularly Ontario, quickly moved into Manitoba and took over land once occupied by the Métis. One group of Ontarians seized Métis land on the Rivière aux Ilets de Bois and, in a symbolic gesture of defiance, renamed the river "the Boyne," after William of Orange's decisive victory over the Roman Catholics in Ireland on July 12, 1690. Ontarians soon dominated the political, economic, and social life of the new province. They worked to eliminate the land and cultural rights of the Métis population by introducing amendments to the Manitoba Act that made it difficult for the Métis to prove that they owned the land. Discouraged, many Métis left the province and went farther west into either the North-West Territories or to the Dakotas and Montana to live.

RELATIONS WITH THE FIRST NATIONS

TREATIES

In keeping with British tradition, the federal government negotiated treaties with the First Nations in the North West. Between 1871 and 1877, the government negotiated Treaties Number One to Seven, affecting the Native peoples in the area from northern Ontario to the Rockies.

According to the government's interpretation of the treaties, the First Nations agreed to "cede, release, surrender, and yield up to the Government ... all their rights, titles, and privileges whatsoever" to the lands in question forever in return for certain reserve lands, amenities, and the right to fish and hunt on Crown lands. In the case of Treaty Six with the Cree of present-day Central Saskatchewan and Alberta, the federal government also promised assistance in the event of "any pestilence" or "general famine," along with a "medicine chest" to be kept by every Indian agent.

THE INDIAN ACT

In 1876, the federal government passed the Indian Act, amended in 1880, to oversee Native affairs through its newly created Department of Indian Affairs and its Indian agents. It legally viewed the First Nations peoples as minors or special wards of the Crown, without citizenship privileges, such as the right to vote or to own private property. Government officials saw the reserves as training grounds for entrance into the larger society. As John A. Macdonald, the first Minister of the Department of Indian Affairs, pointed out: "The great aim of our legislature has been to do away with the tribal system and assimilate the Indian people in all aspects with the inhabitants of the Dominion, as speedily as they are fit for the change."

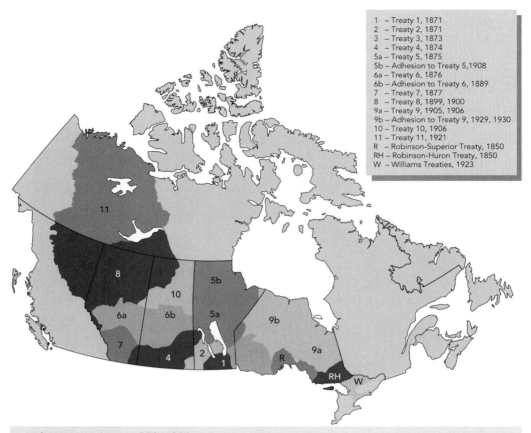

1 – Treaty 1, 1871
2 – Treaty 2, 1871
3 – Treaty 3, 1873
4 – Treaty 4, 1874
5a – Treaty 5, 1875
5b – Adhesion to Treaty 5, 1908
6a – Treaty 6, 1876
6b – Adhesion to Treaty 6, 1889
7 – Treaty 7, 1877
8 – Treaty 8, 1899, 1900
9a – Treaty 9, 1905, 1906
9b – Adhesion to Treaty 9, 1929, 1930
10 – Treaty 10, 1906
11 – Treaty 11, 1921
R – Robinson-Superior Treaty, 1850
RH – Robinson-Huron Treaty, 1850
W – Williams Treaties, 1923

Indian treaty areas, 1850–1930.

Source: Adapted from Energy, Mines and Resources Canada, *Canada/Indian Treaties* in *The National Atlas of Canada*, 5th ed., Ottawa: Geographical Services Division, 1991.

Map by Phillippe Garvie and Nooredin Azimi, 1996.

REPRESSIVE MEASURES

One way the federal government attempted to assimilate the Native people was by outlawing cultural practices. Particularly offensive from the government's perspective was the potlatch, the giving away of gifts in ceremonies, because it reinforced traditional Native beliefs and practices. The government used various tactics, including making it an offence "to encourage or participate in the potlatch." It instructed Indian agents to collect evidence to use in court cases, played off Christian Native converts who opposed the potlatch against traditionalists, and used extortion to pry ceremonial regalia from West Coast Native people. In spite of these efforts to end it, the potlatch survived and, in some areas, continued to flourish.

Schools became another of the government's assimilation schemes. Ottawa gave Christian missionaries control of the reserves and residential schools. Among residential schools were industrial schools that taught skills in agriculture and trades for boys and household skills for girls between the ages of 14 and 18. The first three were established in western Canada in 1883–84: at Qu'Appelle, Dunbow (just east of High River), and Battleford. By the turn of the century, 20 such schools operated in the West.

Where Historians Disagree

Interpreting Treaties One to Seven in Western Canada

Over the past thirty years the Supreme Court of Canada has upheld the argument that Aboriginal rights exist under Canadian law. Aboriginal rights include those outlined in treaties, possibly the best known of which are the numbered Treaties 1 to 7, signed between 1871 and 1877 in what is now Northwestern Ontario and the Prairie Provinces. According to Canadian judicial interpretation—before the Constitution of 1982—Aboriginal treaties could be amended or altered by federal statute, without the approval of the First Nations who were parties to them. The Constitutional Act of 1982 now entrenches treaty rights. How have historians interpreted the numbered treaties of the 1870s?

Duncan Campbell Scott, deputy superintendent of Indian affairs from 1913 to 1932, wrote the first history of federal Indian administration in 1914. The federal civil servant stressed the honourable and just nature of Indian policy: "As may be surmised from the record of past Indian administration, the government was always anxious to fulfil the obligations which were laid upon it by these treaties. In every point, and adhering closely to the letter of the compact, the government has discharged to the present every promise which was made to the Indians."[1] No subtleties of interpretation here, the treaties were fair and honourably respected by Ottawa.

George F.C. Stanley became the first university-trained historian to study the western treaties. In *The Birth of Western Canada* (1936) Stanley presents a far more sophisticated and rigorous analysis of the treaties than Scott, yet he reached a similar conclusion: "On the whole, Canada has followed the tradition of the Imperial Government in its relations with native tribes, and has endeavoured to deal fairly with her aboriginal wards."[2] For the next thirty-five years or so, historians essentially accepted the "honourable and just" interpretation of the treaties — or ignored the agreements altogether; in fact no real historical debate about the western treaties emerged until the 1970s.

Much of the new criticism came from First Nations people frustrated that their side of the story had not received attention. In 1969, Harold Cardinal, a young Cree politician and author, published *The Unjust Society*, a fiery indictment of Canadian Indian policy: "The truth of the matter is that Canadian Indians simply got swindled. Our forefathers got taken by slick-talking, forktongued cheats."[3] First Nation oral traditions of the treaties also appeared, such as the interviews in the timely book edited by Richard Price, *The Spirit of the Alberta Indian Treaties*.[4] More recently the Treaty Seven Elders and Tribal Council have made available First Nation accounts of Treaty Seven in what is now southern Alberta, in *The True Spirit and Original Intent of Treaty 7*.[5]

Other historians have joined in the debate.[6] Basically, they argue that the First Nations were active agents in the treaty process. The First Nations recognized that it was in their interest to secure the best terms possible in the treaty, that schools and a helping hand to adjust to farming would assist them. Problems arose, however, when the federal government did not fulfill the First Nations' oral understandings of the treaties.

In 1983, George F.G. Stanley re-entered the debate. He still dismissed the thought that there were deliberate attempts to deceive the First Nations during the treaty negotiations. Instead he saw the problems as arising from the misunderstandings of treaty terms. "The probability that promises were made to the Indians, which they remember and the Whites have forgotten, seems strong."[7] In short, a historical question that seemed in the early twentieth century to be well understood is now strongly debated. New readings of the old documentary evidence and the availability of Aboriginal oral testimony, as well as a new postcolonial context for discussion, have contributed to this debate.

[1] Duncan Campbell Scott, "Indian Affairs, 1867–1912," in Adam Shortt and Arthur G. Doughty, eds., *Canada and Its Provinces* (Toronto: Glasgow, Brook and Co., 1914), p. 600.

[2] George F.G. Stanley, *The Birth of Western Canada* (London: Longmans, Green, 1936; Toronto: University of Toronto Press, 1960), p. 214.

[3] Harold Cardinal, *The Unjust Society* (Edmonton: Hurtig, 1969), p. 39.

[4] Richard Price, ed., *The Spirit of the Alberta Indian Treaties* (Montreal: Institute for Research on Public Policy, 1979; 3rd ed., Edmonton: University of Alberta Press, 1999).

[5] Treaty Seven Elders and Tribal Council, *The True Spirit and Original Intent of Treaty 7* (Montreal/Kingston: McGill-Queen's University Press, 1996).

[6] To list several of them: John Leonard Taylor, in his essays, "Canada's Northwest Indian Policy in the 1870s: Traditional Premises and Necessary Interventions"; and "Two Views of Treaties Six and Seven," in Price, ed., *Spirit*, pp. 3–46. John L. Tobias, "Canada's Subjugation of the Plains Cree, 1879–1885," *Canadian Historical Review*, 64, 4 (1983): 519–48. David Hall, "'A Serene Atmosphere'? Treaty I Revisited," *Canadian Journal of Native Studies*, 4, 2 (1984): 321–58. Jean Friesen, "Grant Me Wherewith to Make My Living," in Kerry Abel and Jean Friesen, eds., *Aboriginal Resource Use in Canada: Historical and Legal Aspects* (Winnipeg: University of Manitoba Press, 1991), pp. 141–56.

[7] George F.G. Stanley, "As Long as the Sun Shines and Water Flows: An Historical Comment," in Ian A.L. Getty and Antoine S. Lussier, eds., *As Long as the Sun Shines and Water Flows* (Vancouver: University of British Columbia Press, 1983), p. 16.

The schools were intended to teach the Native children in English or, in many parts of southern Quebec, in French, to become Christians, to denounce their own cultural traditions, and to assimilate into "white" society, especially to become farmers. In the case of the latter objective, First Nations farms consisted of a small parcel of land, not always of good quality, and a few rudimentary implements — what historian Sarah Carter has described as "two acres and a cow."[2]

BRITISH COLUMBIA ENTERS CONFEDERATION

 With the Northwest secured, the Canadian government began negotiating with the colony of British Columbia to join Confederation. The colony had three options as to their future destiny: remain a separate British colony, join the United States, or unite with Canada.

Economically, British Columbia was tied closely to the United States. Many of the colony's business firms were branches of American establishments. Much of its trade of raw materials was to the south. In addition, the colony communicated with the outside world via the United States. American vessels, for example, provided the only regular steamship service. Mail required both local and American stamps on letters abroad since it went via San Francisco.

Before and after: Propaganda photos used to promote the benefits of Native residential schools. From Thompson Ferrier, *Indian Education in the North West* (Toronto: Department of Missionary Literature of the Methodist Church, 1906), pp. 4–5.

National Archives of Canada/C-104585 and C-104586.

When railways made transcontinental travel feasible, it was an American line, the Union Pacific, completed in 1869, that provided British Columbia with connections to the Atlantic seaboard.

British loyalties, however, remained firm. The Royal Navy provided protection. The colonial government followed British parliamentary tradition. The colony also had a predominance of British politicians, from the governor to the majority of representatives in the legislative council. By contrast the Americans, although large in numbers, had relatively few supporters in government.

The weakest link was with Canada. Few Canadians resided in the colony. Nor did any overland route exist to link this West Coast colony to the rest of British North America. Nevertheless, the small Canadian community that did reside in the colony constituted an influential and vocal minority: Amor de Cosmos ("Lover of the Universe," alias William Smith), originally from Nova Scotia, would become premier in 1872, while John Robson, from Ontario, headed the Confederation movement in the colonial assembly. Prime Minister Macdonald corresponded with these pro-Confederation politicians. As well, Macdonald had the British government appoint Anthony Musgrave, previously the governor of Newfoundland and a known supporter of Canadian Confederation, as the new governor of British Columbia when Governor Seymour, who had opposed union, died in 1869.

Britain valued British Columbia as an important link in its "all red route to the Orient" — an imperial trading network tying Britain to India and China through British territory. By convincing British Columbia to join Confederation, Britain could achieve both objectives. William Gladstone, Britain's prime minister, argued at the time that Victoria, as "the San Francisco of British North America," could achieve greater commercial and political power as part of Canada than as "the capital of the isolated colony of British Columbia."

British Columbia's settler population was very small in the 1870s. This photo, taken outside the legislative buildings in Victoria, shows the entire British Columbia civil service in 1878.

British Columbia Archives/HP-17826.

THE CANADIAN GOVERNMENT NEGOTIATES

Soon after taking office, Governor Musgrave appointed a three-member British Columbia delegation to open up negotiations with the Canadian government. The committee drew up its list of demands. British Columbia would consider joining Confederation if the Canadian government agreed to assume the colony's one million dollar debt, grant responsible government to the province, undertake a public-works program, and complete a road to link British Columbia with the rest of the country.

The British Columbia delegation found a receptive audience in Ottawa. A committee of the Canadian government, headed by George-Étienne Cartier, agreed to all the demands. Ottawa would assume the provincial debt, and request that Britain implement responsible government. It would also undertake a public works program that would include the underwriting of a loan to build a dry dock and to maintain a naval station at Esquimalt. Most importantly, the Canadian government promised to build not just a road but a railroad, to be begun within two years of British Columbia's entry into Confederation and completed within ten years — a most ambitious promise.

On July 20, 1871, British Columbia joined Confederation. Canada now stretched from the Atlantic Ocean to the Pacific Ocean. In the same year, Britain and the United States confirmed the borders between Canada and the United States in the Treaty of Washington, thus ending the threat of an American annexation of Canadian territory.

The agreement with British Columbia left one important issue unresolved, that of Aboriginal lands. At the time of British Columbia's entry into Confederation, land treaties had been concluded for only a tiny portion of Vancouver Island. In 1873, the federal government requested British Columbia to acknowledge Aboriginal land title and to increase the allotment of reserve land for a family of five from 10 to 80 acres (4 to 32 ha). The British Columbia government objected, claiming that the Native peoples already had enough land.

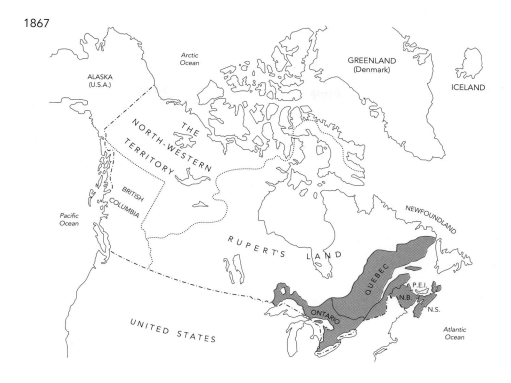

1867

1870

Canada's territorial evolution from a nation of four provinces (1867), to five (1870), to seven (1873), and to nine (1905).

1873

1905

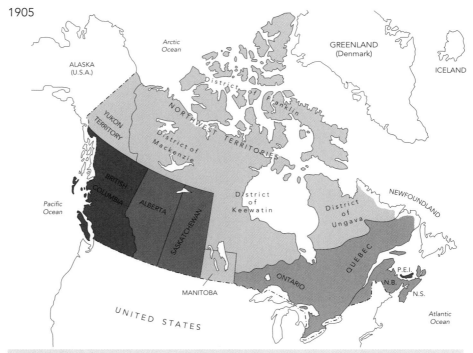

Source: These maps are based on information taken from National Topographic System map sheet number MCR 2306. © 1969, Her Majesty the Queen in Right of Canada with permission of Energy, Mines and Resources Canada.

AN UNWILLING NEWFOUNDLAND AND A RELUCTANT PRINCE EDWARD ISLAND

OPPOSITION TO CONFEDERATION IN NEWFOUNDLAND

 Only the British colonies of Newfoundland and Prince Edward Island remained as potential new provinces. Newfoundland trade had been with Britain and the West Indies, not with the other British North American colonies. Thus the Newfoundland merchants opposed Confederation. So too did Newfoundland's Roman Catholics because they feared that a wider union would offset their favourable position in the colony. They had their own government-funded schools, which many believed a union with "Protestant Ontario" might threaten. Also, Irish Catholics saw Confederation as comparable to the reviled union of Ireland and England.

Union with Canada became the chief campaign issue in the election of 1869. Charles Fox Bennett, a St. John's merchant, headed the anti-Confederation faction. He pointed out that Confederation would result in the imposition of Canadian taxes on boats and fishing gear, and in exploitive competition from the mainland. He reminded Newfoundlanders of Nova Scotia's opposition to Confederation, while injecting his own strong dose of local Newfoundland nationalism. As one contemporary folk song ran:

> Would you barter the rights that your fathers have won?
> No! Let them descend from father to son,
> For a few thousand dollars Canadian gold,
> Don't let it be said that our birthright was sold.
> Newfoundland's face turns to Britain
> Her back to the Gulf.
> Come near at your peril
> Canadian wolf!

Pro-Confederationists appeared on the defensive. They could only present union with Canada as an uncertain alternative to the current depressed economy of Newfoundland rather than as a bold positive move. Furthermore, an improved sealing and fishing season in 1869 worked against their cause. In the end, Newfoundlanders rejected Confederation, with nineteen seats in the colonial assembly going to anti-confederates and only eight to confederates. That defeat effectively ended the Confederation debate in Newfoundland for the next 25 years.

OPPOSITION TO CONFEDERATION IN PRINCE EDWARD ISLAND

Initially, Prince Edward Island opposed Confederation more strongly than did Newfoundland. If anything, islanders favoured economic union with the United States, seeing it as a possible return to the prosperity that the island had enjoyed during the period of the Reciprocity Treaty (1854–66). In 1868, American congressman Benjamin Butler visited Charlottetown to negotiate a reciprocal trade agreement.

Fear of American annexation of Prince Edward Island led Prime Minister Macdonald to reopen negotiations. Late in 1869, he extended another invitation to the islanders to join Confederation. He agreed to more generous financial terms than in 1864; guaranteed communication and transportation links with the mainland; and promised islanders assistance in buying off the remaining British absentee landlords who still owned large tracts. At the same time, the Canadian prime minister convinced Britain to block a reciprocal trade agreement between Prince Edward Island and the United States. Still the islanders resisted.

By the early 1870s, however, financial problems on Prince Edward Island made Confederation more appealing. A coalition government headed by J.C. Pope had embarked in 1871 on an ambitious railway-building scheme that threatened to push the island into bankruptcy. In 1872, work on the railway ceased for lack of funds. The Union Bank of Prince Edward Island, which held large numbers of the railway debentures, feared a financial collapse and appealed to Britain for assistance. London financiers replied that the island would be in a better negotiating position if it joined Canada.

This time Charlottetown approached Ottawa. In early 1873, the Canadian government renewed its earlier offer: to assume the island's debt; to pay the annual interest on an $800 000 imperial loan; to provide a special subsidy of $45 000 to buy out the absentee landowners and thus bring all land under provincial control; and to take over the railway guarantee. As well, it promised to establish and maintain an efficient all-year steamer service between the island and the mainland.

In the election of April 1873, the choice became Confederation or the imposition of increased taxes to pay off the debt. In the end, provincial debt and railways were the real "Fathers of Confederation" in Prince Edward Island. On July 1, 1873, Prince Edward Island joined the Dominion of Canada as its seventh province.

CANADIAN ACQUISITION OF THE ARCTIC ARCHIPELAGO

With the exception of Newfoundland and the Arctic archipelago, Macdonald had now completed the consolidation of British North America. Initially, Canada had no interest in the Arctic archipelago, seeing it only as a frozen wasteland. But in July 1880, the British government transferred title of its Arctic "possessions" to Canada. They did so without bothering to consult the First Nations peoples in the region, believing such consultation was not necessary.

Three oceans, one country — in just thirteen years, Canada had become Britain's largest colony. In the first decade after Confederation, the Dominion of Canada acquired three new provinces and an enormous geographical area. Fear of American encroachment was a factor in its rapid expansion, but internal economic pressures such as the need for more land for agricultural development, the necessity of east–west trade, and a growing railway-building program also contributed. By 1880, Canada had become a transcontinental nation. Now the challenge was to work out new Dominion–provincial relations, reconcile regional differences, and create a Dominion-wide economic policy.

NOTES

1. Chester Martin, *Dominion Lands Policy* (Toronto: McClelland & Stewart, 1973), p. 9.
2. Sarah Carter, "Two Acres and a Cow: 'Peasant' Farming for the Indians of the Northwest, 1889–97," *Canadian Historical Review* 70(1) (March 1989): 27.

LINKING TO THE PAST

Joseph Howe's Objections to Confederation
http://wwlia.org/cahi1867.htm
Joseph Howe's reply to the Speech from the Throne during the first session of Parliament.

The Rupert's Land Act, 1869

http://www.miredespa.com/wmaton/Other/Legal/Constitutions/Canada/English/rpl_1868.html

The full text of the Rupert's Land Act of 1869, which expanded Canada to include parts of the Northwest formerly controlled by the Hudson's Bay Company.

Louis Riel

http://library.usask.ca/northwest/background/riel.htm

A detailed biography of Louis Riel, who led the 1869 Métis resistance to the sale of Rupert's Land.

The Manitoba Act, 1870

http://www.solon.org/Constitutions/Canada/English/ma_1870.html

The full text of the Manitoba Act of 1870. A compromise between the Canadian government and the Métis on Rupert's Land, this Act brought Manitoba into Confederation as the first new province.

Treaties

http://www.ainc-inac.gc.ca/pr/trts/index e.html

This site from Indian and Northern Affairs Canada provides the full text to a number of treaties, including Treaties One to Seven, which covered the period 1871 to 1877 and dealt with the division of the Northwest.

British Columbia Terms of Union

http://www.miredespa.com/wmaton/Other/Legal/Constitutions/Canada/English/bctu.html

The original document detailing the terms of union under which British Columbia was admitted into Confederation.

Proposed Terms of Union, 1869

http://www.geocities.com/Yosemite/Rapids/3330/constitution/1869prop.htm

A document showing the proposed terms of union between Canada and Newfoundland in 1869. The agreement was defeated, however, and Newfoundland did not raise the issue for another 25 years.

Bibliography

Students interested in the Atlantic region's resistance to Confederation should consult Ged Martin, *Britain and the Origins of Canadian Confederation, 1837–67* (London: Macmillan, 1995); and his edited collection, *The Causes of Canadian Confederation* (Fredericton: Acadiensis, 1990). For Nova Scotia also see George Rawlyk, ed., *The Atlantic Provinces and the Problems of Confederation* (St. John's: Breakwater, 1979); and J. Murray Beck's booklet *Joseph Howe: Anti-Confederate* (Ottawa: Canadian Historical Association, 1965). On Newfoundland's resistance to Confederation see James Hiller, "Confederation Defeated: The Newfoundland Election of 1869," in *Newfoundland in the Nineteenth and Twentieth Centuries: Essays in Interpretation* (Toronto: University of Toronto Press, 1980), pp. 67–94; and the relevant section in Frederick W. Rowe, *A History of Newfoundland and Labrador* (Toronto: McGraw-Hill Ryerson, 1980). Francis Bolger reviews Prince Edward Island's decision to join Canada in *Prince Edward Island and Confederation* (Charlottetown: St. Dunstan's University Press, 1964). Popular studies include Donald Weale and Harry Baglole, *The Island and Confederation: The End of an Era* (Charlottetown: Williams & Crue, 1973).

Alvin C. Gluek, *Minnesota and the Manifest Destiny of the Canadian Northwest: A Study in Canadian–American Relations* (Toronto: University of Toronto Press, 1965), examines American annexationist sentiments toward the Canadian Northwest. On the Riel resistance, see W.L. Morton's introduction to *Alexander Begg's Red River Journal* (Toronto: Champlain Society, 1956); see also George F.G. Stanley, *The Birth of Western Canada* (London: Longmans, Green, 1936; rep. Toronto: University of Toronto Press, 1960), and J.M. Bumsted, *The Red River Rebellion* (Winnipeg: Watson & Dwyer, 1996). On Manitoba's entry into Confederation see W.L. Morton, *Manitoba: A History* (Toronto: University of Toronto Press, 1957). Sarah Carter's *Aboriginal People and Colonizers of Western Canada to 1800* (Toronto: University of Toronto Press, 1999) is a useful summary of developments in the Red River and on the prairies.

Useful surveys of First Nations relations with Canada that cover this period are J.R. Miller, *Skyscrapers Hide the Heavens: A History of Indian–White Relations in Canada*, 3rd ed. (Toronto: University of Toronto Press, 2000); Olive P. Dickason, *Canada's First Nations: A History of Founding Peoples from Earliest Times* (Don Mills, ON: Oxford, 2002); A.J. Ray, *I Have Lived Here Since the World Began* (Toronto: Key Porter, 1996); and his *The Canadian Fur Trade in the Industrial Age* (Toronto: University of Toronto Press, 1990). See as well J.R. Miller, *Canada and the Aboriginal Peoples 1867–1927.* CHA Historical Booklet No. 57 (Ottawa, 1997).

On the last numbered treaties on the Plains, see Richard Price, ed., *The Spirit of the Alberta Indian Treaties*, 3rd ed. (Edmonton: The University of Alberta Press, 1999). In *Indian Treaty-Making Policy in the United States and Canada, 1867–1877* (Toronto: University of Toronto Press, 2001), Jill St. Germain reviews American and Canadian experiences.

The Canadian government's Indian policy is reviewed by Brian Titley in the early chapters of his *A Narrow Vision: Duncan Campbell Scott and the Administration of Indian Affairs in Canada* (Vancouver: University of British Columbia Press, 1987). The government's farming policy for the Native peoples is outlined in Sarah Carter, *Lost Harvests: Prairie Indian Reserve Farmers and Government Policy* (Montreal/Kingston: McGill-Queen's University Press, 1990). Two historical studies of Indian residential schools are: J.R. Miller, *Shingwauk's Vision: A History of Native Residential Schools* (Toronto: University of Toronto Press, 1996); and John S. Milloy, *A National Crime: The Canadian Government and the Residential School System 1879–1986* (Winnipeg: The University of Manitoba Press, 1999).

On British Columbia and Confederation see Margaret Ormsby, *British Columbia: A History* (Toronto: Macmillan, 1958); Jean Barman, *The West Beyond the West: A History of British Columbia, rev. ed.* (Toronto: University of Toronto Press, 1996) and Hugh J.M. Johnston, ed., *The Pacific Province: A History of British Columbia* (Vancouver: Douglas & McIntyre, 1996).

For maps and charts see L.R. Gentilcore et al., eds., *Historical Atlas of Canada*, vol. 2, *The Land Transformed, 1800–1891* (Toronto: University of Toronto Press, 1993).

A "NATIONAL POLICY"?

TIME LINE

In 1874, Edward Blake, the premier of Ontario and future leader of the federal Liberal party, identified the issue: "The future of Canada depends very much upon the cultivation of a national spirit." In the late nineteenth century no agreement even existed on the definition of a Canadian, let alone the nature of a Canadian identity. When French-speakers referred to "les Canadiens," they spoke of themselves alone; they called English-speakers *les Anglais*. British Canadians, in turn, considered themselves the only Canadians and termed those speaking French, "French Canadians." The Native peoples did not use the term "Canadians" to describe themselves, because they had their own designations for their own nations, such as Dene, Anishinabeg (Ojibwa), or Innu (Montagnais), names which meant "people" or "human beings" in their languages.

Could common economic goals and interests unite Canadians? John A. Macdonald's Conservative government believed so. In 1879, his party proposed a Dominion-wide economic policy of nation building based on a "National Policy" or national tariff to protect Canada's infant industries. Once in place, the Conservatives believed, the tariff would provide the capital to pay the expenses of building the transcontinental railway. The railway, in turn, would link an industrialized East with the soon-to-be-developed agricultural West. The growth of central Canadian industry, the settlement of the West, and the building of the transcontinental railway would create a nation. After 1896, the Liberals under Wilfrid Laurier adopted their own version of the Conservatives' national policy.

Emerging English-Canadian and French-Canadian Expressions of Nationalism

In the spring of 1868, five young English-speaking Canadian nationalists met in Ottawa to launch the Canada First Movement. Concerned about the lack of myths, symbols, and national spirit surrounding Confederation, they sought to identify and promote a nationalism for the new Dominion of Canada. They believed that Canada's greatness lay in its northern climate and rugged landscape, which combined to create a superior Anglo-Saxon race. They saw English-speaking Canadians as the "Northmen of the New World."

French Canadians and the Native peoples rejected the Canada First Movement's vision of the new Dominion. In reality, "Canada First" meant "English Canada First." The members showed their true colours through their support of Dr. John Schultz's group of Canadian expansionists in the Northwest.

While Canada First sought a British and Protestant Canada, many French Canadians envisioned a French-speaking, Roman Catholic nation. In the late nineteenth century, Quebec became more French and Catholic than it had been since before the Conquest. The provincial government cultivated closer ties with France under Napoleon III, especially after the French helped to protect the papal lands in central Italy against Giuseppe Garibaldi's army that was fighting for the unification of Italy. Five hundred volunteer soldiers, the *Zouaves*, or "mercenaries of the Lord," left Quebec between 1868 and 1870 to serve in the papal army.

Ignace Bourget, the influential bishop of Montreal, and his disciple, Louis-François Laflèche, later named bishop of Trois-Rivières, led the ultramontane movement within the Roman Catholic church. Ultramontanes believed in the subordination of the state to the church. In their view, the pope constituted the supreme authority over religious and civil matters. Bourget reminded his followers in a circular in 1876: "Let us each say in his heart, 'I hear my *curé*, my *curé* hears the bishop, and the bishop hears the Pope, and the Pope hears our Lord Jesus Christ.'" Laflèche set down the basic principles of its nationalism in 1866:

> A nation is constituted by unity of speech, unity of faith, uniformity of morals, customs, and institutions. The French Canadians possess all these, and constitute a true

nation. Each nation has received from Providence a mission to fulfill. The mission of the French Canadian people is to constitute a centre of Catholicism in the New World.

The ultramontanes began a political movement in 1871. They issued a *Programme catholique*, which proclaimed the church's right to advise Roman Catholics on how to vote. Catholics were expected to vote for the *bleus* (Conservatives), blessed with the colour of heaven, and not for the *rouges* (Liberals), damned by the colour of the fires of hell.

Thus, by 1870, extreme and conflicting nationalisms had surfaced in both English- and French-speaking Canada. These movements reflected an attempt on the part of extremists in both linguistic groups to define a nation in cultural, rather than strictly political, terms.

LIBERAL RULE: 1873–1878

The Conservatives won the federal election of 1872, but just one year later a political scandal broke. It was revealed that Macdonald and Cartier had accepted more than $300 000 in campaign funds from Sir Hugh Allan, president of the Merchants' Bank and owner of the prestigious Allan Steamship Lines, whose newly created Canada Pacific Company was a major contender for the government charter to build the transcontinental railway promised to British Columbia. The major financial backing for Allan's group came from the United States. An American railway tycoon, angry at his exclusion from the consortium, supplied the Liberal opposition with the incriminating evidence of a financial kickback to the Conservatives from Allan and his American backers.

The Liberals accused the Conservatives of immorality and corruption. Macdonald denied involvement: "These hands are clean," he assured the House of Commons. But fearing a want-of-confidence vote, he announced his cabinet's resignation on November 5, 1873. The governor general asked the Liberals to form a government, which they did without an election being held. Two months later, in January 1874, the new prime minister, Alexander Mackenzie, dissolved Parliament and called an election, which the Liberals won.

Alexander Mackenzie, a stonemason, had replaced George Brown as leader of the Liberal Party in 1868. Mackenzie inherited numerous political problems. For one thing, the Liberal party had little internal unity. It was a free-wheeling coalition of factions — *rouges*, Clear Grits, and Liberal Reformers — who had come together less out of a sense of common philosophy or a unified party platform than out of a common dislike for the Conservatives and their program. The party also consisted of a number of "prima donnas" who challenged Mackenzie's leadership. George Brown, as the founding leader of the party, loomed large in the background; Richard Cartwright, a Conservative defector who left after Macdonald denied him the post of minister of finance, wanted a senior post; Antoine-Aimé Dorion led the party's *rouge* faction and sought the role of Mackenzie's Quebec lieutenant. Finally, Mackenzie faced the enigmatic Edward Blake, former premier of Ontario (1871–72) and a brilliant parliamentary debater, who appeared indecisive about whether or not to stay in the party, yet seemed to aspire to lead it.

Another political problem lay in the fact that the Liberals took office just as Canada entered an economic depression. As trade declined, the federal debt increased sharply. Mackenzie responded by slowing down the railway-building scheme the government had inherited from the Conservatives, thus alienating advocates of the railway and especially British Columbia, which threatened to leave Confederation if the railway was not built as promised.

The Liberals did excel in bringing in a number of constitutional and political reforms. In 1875, they established the Supreme Court of Canada as a national appeal court. While final appeal still rested with the Judicial Committee of the Privy Council in Britain and continued to do so with regards to civil matters until 1949, the Supreme Court became the first Canadian

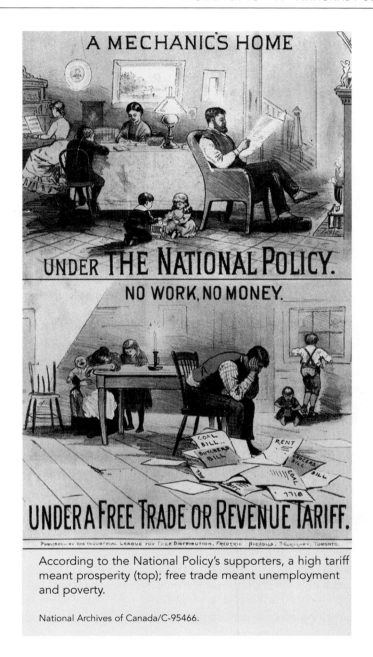

According to the National Policy's supporters, a high tariff meant prosperity (top); free trade meant unemployment and poverty.

National Archives of Canada/C-95466.

court to review Canadian laws. The Liberals also restricted the powers of the governor general, Britain's representative in Canada, by withdrawing his right to disallow legislation without consulting the Canadian Parliament.

Among political reforms, the Liberals introduced the secret ballot and the practice of holding federal elections on the same day in each constituency across the country. They also closed the taverns on election day to reduce the possibility of buying votes for drinks. Controverted elections were transferred out of the hands of parliamentarians and into the courts. Mackenzie and his cabinet extended the federal franchise effectively to all non-Native males, whether they held property or not. The Liberals also ended the system of dual representation that allowed an individual to hold a federal and a provincial seat simultaneously.

THE NATIONAL POLICY OF JOHN A. MACDONALD

The Mackenzie administration lacked an economic agenda. It had wanted a reciprocity treaty with the United States similar to the one signed in 1854, and had in 1874 successfully drafted such a treaty. But the highly protectionist American Senate defeated the bill, leaving the Liberals without a viable commercial policy.

The Conservatives promoted an alternative economic agenda in a protective system of higher tariffs. Macdonald pointed out how import duties in Britain and the United States had enabled these countries to advance industrially and claimed that the same could happen in Canada. Macdonald maintained that the creation of an east–west economy by means of a transcontinental railway provided the answer to the depression of the 1870s. Western Canadian farmers could help their Ontario counterparts to feed the growing number of industrial workers in central Canada, who in turn could supply the farmers throughout Canada with agricultural equipment and other manufactured goods. In 1878 the Conservative party returned to power with a majority government on the basis of its National Policy.

This policy of nation building — the "national policy," as Macdonald called it — rested on three essentials: the National (capital N) Policy, or high protective tariff; the completion of a transcontinental railway; and the settlement of the West through immigration. It is debatable to what extent the Conservatives envisioned an integrated national policy at the time. Nevertheless, in 1879, the Conservatives raised the tariff on textiles, iron and steel products, coal, and petroleum products by 10 to 30 percent, thus achieving their first objective of a high protective tariff.

Advocates of the National Policy argued that a protective tariff would shift trade from a north–south to an east–west axis. It would provide Canadians with their own national market, thus reducing their dependency on the United States. Furthermore, manufacturers — both Canadian and foreigners building plants in Canada — would ensure more jobs for Canadian workers, technicians, and managers.

In contrast, the Liberals argued that the tariff would erect a fiscal barrier around the country. Furthermore, they maintained that, while the tariff or National Policy was "National" in name, it was regional in interest. It served the needs of central Canadians alone, and more specifically, the needs of the manufacturers and industrialists of the urban centres of Ontario and Quebec who could live off the bounty of the government. Furthermore, it would put the burden of national unity on the hinterland regions, which would become the suppliers of raw materials for the prosperous metropolitan centres of central Canada. In social terms, a corresponding inequality would develop, since workers, farmers, and fishers would have to pay a higher price for consumer goods, whether imported (as a result of the higher tariff) or produced in Canada (as a result of higher production costs).

Despite Liberal opposition to the implementation of the National Policy in 1879, when the Liberal party under Wilfrid Laurier came to power in 1896, it adopted its own version of the National Policy. As the United States still refused to discuss free trade, the Liberals had little choice. In 1897, W.S. Fielding, the Liberal finance minister, introduced a tariff that maintained high duties on imported goods, such as textiles and iron and steel products coming from the United States, and goods from other countries that restricted the entry of Canadian goods. At the same time, the new policy lowered tariffs to any country admitting Canadian goods at a rate equal to the minimum Canadian tariff. As Britain already adhered to such a policy, it became known as the "British tariff."

TRANSCONTINENTAL RAILWAYS

BUILDING THE CANADIAN PACIFIC RAILWAY

Even before the formulation of the national policy, a transcontinental railway was considered an indispensable part of nation building. Settlers wishing to go from Toronto to Manitoba via British territory in the 1870s, for example, had to travel via the United States or else by steamboat and wagon. Furthermore, British Columbia's entry into Confederation depended on the "trail of iron" as the only means to link this isolated colony to central Canada. Finally, a transcontinental railway, it was felt, would permit Canada to compete with the United States as a great North American nation.

Where Historians Disagree
The National Policy

The national policy of high tariffs, railway building, and development of the West, first established by the Conservative government in the late nineteenth century, generated considerable debate at the time and much debate since among historians and economists. Historian Donald Creighton spoke for many in the central Canadian nationalist tradition in arguing that the national policy, especially the protective tariff of 1879, was an essential component of Canada's growth as an independent nation. Creighton writes: "In international affairs, the tariff asserted the principle of independence as against both Britain and the United States. In domestic matters, it expressed the hope for a new varied and self sufficient national life."[1] Craig Brown notes the success of the national policy in instilling a feeling of nationalism in Canada when traditional national symbols, such as a common language, a common cultural tradition, or a common religion, were absent.[2]

Historian Ben Forster has noted how other factors — besides or possibly instead of, nationalism — were important in shaping Canada's national policy. He points to a wide range of political and economic factors and interests — including business, industry, agriculture, and government — as all having made a contribution from 1825 to 1879 in shaping the policy.[3]

Economist John Dales has questioned the success of the national policy as a policy of nation building. Dales argues that the national policy was from the beginning a "dismal failure."[4] Railway building became an expensive undertaking for the Canadian taxpayer through heavy government subsidies to the Canadian Pacific Railway Company, established in 1880 to build the transcontinental line. Second, immigration and the settlement of the West did not occur until well after the national policy was in place and then for reasons independent of the national policy itself. Third, the high tariff placed region against region. It also created an artificial climate for industrial growth that ironically made Canada more, not less, dependent on the United States through a branch-plant economy. Dales also questioned to what extent international economic trends dictated Canadian economic policy.

Historian Michael Bliss agrees that the protective tariff fostered the "Americanization of the Canadian economy," but points out that that was exactly what it was intended to do. "By 1911," he writes, the "concern … was not to limit what had already been called an American 'invasion' of Canada, but rather to sustain and encourage the branch-plant phenomena."[5]

Some historians in western Canada and the Maritimes have presented the negative impact of the National Policy of tariff protection, especially on their regions. David Bercuson writes: "The ill effects [of the National Policy] abound: high prices for the manufactured products of Central Canada (added to by shipping costs) and the loss to East and West of significant commercial intercourse with New England and the northwestern areas of the United States."[6] It resulted in the growth of industry in central Canada at the expense of the hinterlands.

Economist Kenneth Norrie has countered this viewpoint in reference to western Canada.[7] He argues that the lack of industrial development in the West had nothing to do with the National Policy and everything to do with the West's location — away from the heart of North American development — and its lack of a sufficient population base to make industrialization viable.

The debate on the National Policy received renewed vigour during the national debate over both the Canada–United States and the North American free-trade agreements in the late 1980s and early 1990s. Central to any discussion of the future of Canada, the National Policy will long be a subject of debate.

[1] Donald Creighton, *Dominion of the North* (Toronto: Macmillan, 1957), p. 346.

[2] Craig Brown, "The Nationalism of the National Policy," in R. Douglas Francis and Donald B. Smith, eds., *Readings in Canadian History: Post-Confederation*, 6th ed., (Toronto: Nelson Thomson Learning, 2002), pp. 3–8.

[3] Ben Forster, *A Conjunction of Interests: Business, Politics, and Tariffs, 1825–1879* (Toronto: University of Toronto Press, 1986).

[4] John Dales, "Canada's National Policies," in Francis and Smith, eds., *Readings in Canadian History: Post-Confederation* (cited above), pp. 8–17.

[5] Michael Bliss, "Canadianizing American Business: The Roots of the Branch Plant," in I. Lumsden, ed., *Close the 49th Parallel etc.: The Americanization of Canada* (Toronto: University of Toronto Press, 1970), p. 29.

[6] David Bercuson, ed., *Canada and the Burden of Unity* (Toronto: Macmillan, 1977), pp. 3–4.

[7] Kenneth Norrie, "The National Policy and Prairie Economic Discrimination, 1870–1930," in Donald Akenson, ed., *Canadian Papers in Rural History*, vol. 1 (Gananoque, ON: Langdale, 1978).

Macdonald's Conservative government favoured a private company to undertake the project. Two companies competed for the contract: the Interoceanic Company, headed by Senator David Macpherson of Toronto and backed by British financiers; and the Canada Pacific Company, a Montreal consortium under Sir Hugh Allan, with American financial backing. Macdonald favoured a merger of the two companies, but neither Macpherson nor Allan would agree. In the end, the government awarded the contract to the Canada Pacific Company in return for generous financial contributions on Allan's part to the Conservative campaign fund in the election of 1872. The resulting "Pacific Scandal" forced the Macdonald Conservative government to resign and ended the short-lived Canada Pacific Company.

Mackenzie's Liberal government continued the railway, but only on those sections where settlement warranted construction and only as public money became available, relying on waterways and even American lines to fill the gaps. To move slowly, however, meant reneging on the Conservatives' promise of completing the railway to British Columbia in ten years. An annoyed Edgar Dewdney, an MP for British Columbia, insisted on "The Terms, the Whole Terms and Nothing but the Terms."

When the Conservatives returned to office in 1878, the building of a transcontinental railroad became the second component of the national policy. A new private company emerged: the Canadian Pacific Railway Company (CPR), made up of a group associated with the Bank of Montreal, headed by George Stephen, R.B. Angus, and Donald Smith. The syndicate agreed to build the railway across northern Ontario from Callander (near North Bay) to Port Arthur and from Winnipeg to Kamloops by May 1, 1891. In return, the government offered $25 million in financing and 25 million acres (10 million ha) of land consisting of alternate sections not already sold in a belt nearly 40 km wide on both sides of the track across the Prairies. Land not "fit for settlement" could be exchanged for better land elsewhere. The company also obtained free of charge the 1200 km of track already completed or under construction, which had an estimated worth of $31 million. The government promised exemption of construction materials from duty. As well, CPR property and its capital stock would be free from taxation. Its grant of 10 million ha of land remained tax exempt for 20 years or until sold. Finally, the government agreed to a monopoly clause: no competing line could be built south of the main CPR line until 1900.

In Parliament, Liberals and even some Conservative backbenchers questioned the need for such generous terms. The two-month debate that followed proved one of the longest and most acrimonious in the history of Parliament. Yet Macdonald held his party together, and the Conservatives voted down the 25 amendments proposed by the Liberal opposition.

Very early on the new CPR Company altered the route of the railway from that proposed by Sandford Fleming's survey team in the early 1870s along the North Saskatchewan River and through the Yellowhead Pass to a southerly prairie route through Pile O' Bones Creek (Regina), Swift Current, Fort Calgary, and the Kicking Horse Pass. A number of reasons account for this sudden shift. First, the company feared that the American Northern Pacific Railway would siphon off the trade of the southern prairies, bringing the region within the American sphere of influence. Second, Elliott Galt, the son of Alexander Galt, a Father of Confederation, had discovered coal deposits near Lethbridge that could be exploited as a source of fuel for the locomotives on the southern route. Third, John Macoun, a botanist and recent leader of a scientific expedition in the West, reported that the southern prairies were not the desert that John Palliser had earlier described. Most important, the company hoped through the sudden switch to bypass speculators, who had bought up land along the proposed northern route. When speculators attempted to do the same along the southern route — guessing where divisional points and stations might be — the company arbitrarily changed its plans and placed stations and divisional points on property it owned.

Once the government agreed to the route, construction began. In 1881 the syndicate hired William Cornelius Van Horne, an experienced American engineer, as general manager to oversee construction. Van Horne drove his men without mercy. He boasted that his construction gang, which at one time had 5000 workers and 1700 teams of horses, could lay 800 km of prairie track in a year. Already by August of 1883, the line had reached Calgary.

Still ahead lay the difficult mountain terrain. Surveyors had already chosen the Kicking Horse Pass through the Bow River valley, despite its steep incline, as the best route through the Rocky Mountains. Only late in the summer of 1882, however, did Major A.B. Rogers, an experienced railway surveyor, locate a pass that allowed the CPR to cross the more westerly Selkirk Mountains. Difficulties abounded: laying track along the sides of mountains, blasting tunnels through rock, bridging swift mountain rivers. The construction of the British Columbia section, particularly that built by Andrew Onderdonk from Port Moody on the coast nearly 400 km into the interior, cost enormous amounts of time and money and took the lives of hundreds of the estimated 15 000 Chinese workers who had been hired as cheap labour to do the difficult and

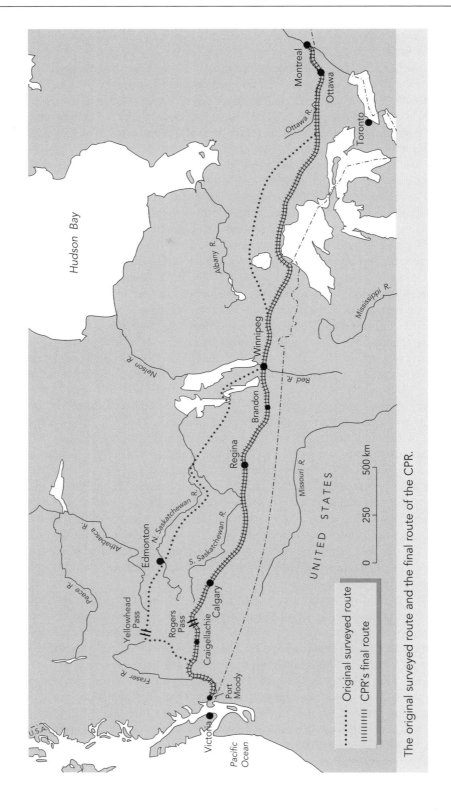

The original surveyed route and the final route of the CPR.

dangerous tasks of tunnelling and handling explosives. Chinese Canadians had a saying that "for every foot of railway through the Fraser Canyon, a Chinese worker died." Onderdonk himself estimated that three Chinese died for every kilometre of track that was laid.

Construction costs rose. For one thing Van Horne insisted on the best materials to ensure long-term use. Also Macdonald insisted on building along the north shore of Lake Superior instead of relying on the inefficient waterway system or on competing American lines. This meant blasting through hundreds of kilometres of Precambrian rock. In addition, the company had to buy up eastern lines to connect the Pacific railway with Toronto and Montreal. When the CPR's construction boss was asked about the prospect of not having sufficient funds to complete the project, he replied: "If we haven't got enough, we'll get more, that's all about it." The money did come — from investors, from the sale of stock, and from bank loans. When these sources proved inadequate, the company turned to the only remaining source, the government.

In the summer of 1883, the syndicate asked the government for an additional $22.5 million, the equivalent of a year's revenue for the federal government. Macdonald was about to turn them down when J.H. Pope, his secretary, reminded him: "The day the Canadian Pacific bursts, the Conservative party bursts the day after." Macdonald convinced his party to agree to another loan, but only after the CPR agreed to mortgage the entire main line, all the rolling stock, and everything else connected with the railway. The money kept construction going through 1884, but by the end of that year, the company once again plunged toward bankruptcy.

On the evening of March 26, 1885, George Stephen met with Macdonald to appeal for more government money. The prime minister turned him down. Stephen returned home convinced the railway would, after all, go under. Then, in the morning, came the extraordinary news: the Métis had rebelled under Louis Riel, defeating the North-West Mounted Police in a battle near Duck Lake in the North-West Territories. Macdonald's luck had saved him once again. The uprising justified the railway. That day in Parliament, the government voted to send troops out on the railway to fight Riel and the Métis. It also introduced a bill to finance the remaining mountain section of the railway.

On November 7, 1885, Donald Smith drove in the last spike at Craigellachie, a proud moment for all who had been involved in the project. The American-born Van Horne remarked that "to have built that road would have made a Canadian out of the German Emperor." But the cost of such national pride was high. In the end, the Pacific railway cost the Canadian government 10.4 million ha of the best prairie land, an estimated $63.5 million in public funds, and government loans of $35 million. Yet as a private company it did very well, and by 1905 it would have capital of $228 million. Was the project worth the costs to the government? People then and since have debated that question.

TWO NEW TRANSCONTINENTAL RAILWAYS

During the economic boom of the Laurier era (1896–1911), Canada added two new transcontinental railways. The first was the Canadian Northern Railway, begun by Donald Mann and William Mackenzie, two Ontario-born entrepreneurs, who had bought up defunct lines in the West to have substantial holdings by 1901. They applied to the federal government for financial assistance to build from Port Arthur (now Thunder Bay) to Montreal. The Grand Trunk Railway, an eastern-based company, wanted to build a line westward to profit from prairie grain traffic. The logical solution would have been for the two companies to co-operate, but both feared that the other would dominate in any joint venture. At the same time, Laurier believed the country could support three transcontinental railways.

The Liberals backed the Grand Trunk but insisted that in the east the new rail line go through northern Ontario and Quebec to its terminus at Moncton, New Brunswick. The federal

The driving of the last spike, November 7, 1885, 9:30 a.m., at Craigellachie, British Columbia. The important CPR financial backer Donald A. Smith (later Lord Strathcona) holds the heavy spike hammer. Behind Smith stands white-bearded Sandford Fleming, former engineer-in-chief; to the left is the burly figure of W.C. Van Horne, CPR general manager.

Glenbow Archives, Calgary, Canada/NA-218-3.

government even offered to underwrite the costs of the 2880-km-long eastern section. This section, known as the National Transcontinental, would be leased to the Grand Trunk for 50 years at a modest annual rate of 3 percent on construction costs. The first seven years of operation would be rent free. A new company, the Grand Trunk Pacific, a subsidiary of the Grand Trunk, would build the western section from Winnipeg to the Pacific. The federal government agreed to guarantee 75 percent of the bond money for its construction.

Meanwhile, Mann and Mackenzie went ahead with their transcontinental line, convinced that Ottawa would, if they encountered difficulties, assist. As a result, in many areas of the West, these competing lines ran parallel to each other and sometimes within sight of one another.

In the meantime, the two companies added 18 000 km of prairie railway — six times more line than the CPR had when completed in 1885. It gave Canada the dubious distinction of having by 1914 more kilometres of rail line per capita than any other country in the world. The new lines also opened up lucrative mining areas in northern Ontario and Quebec, and provided employment for thousands during the construction and operational phases.

NEW INVENTIONS

 Other technological inventions in the nineteenth century helped unite the country. In 1884, the first electric telegraph line was built in the United States. Soon other countries, such as Canada, realized the benefits of this new rapid means of communication for business and for pleasure.

Then in 1876, Scottish-born Alexander Graham Bell, at the time a Canadian resident, invented the telephone in a successful call between Brantford and Paris, Ontario. Before long, every business and household coveted a telephone. In the late nineteenth century, the energetic Sandford Fleming, dubbed "the Father of Canadian Communications," turned his attention to build first a transatlantic and then a transpacific underwater cable to link Canada to Britain and to the other British possessions in the Pacific. Then in 1901, Guglielmo Marconi picked up the first wireless signal sent across the Atlantic Ocean by erecting an antenna on Signal Hill in St. John's, Newfoundland. Marconi's Wireless Telegraph Company of Canada, created in 1902, operated a transatlantic radio link between Glace Bay, Nova Scotia, and London, England.

Such rapid means of communication and trade heightened the inadequacy of recording time by astronomical calculations in each locality. It proved difficult, for example, to create a train schedule in which the time varied from place to place. So railway companies demanded a standardized approach. It was Fleming once again who devised a solution by "inventing" standard time, dividing the world into twenty-four time zones and persuading governments throughout the world to standardize time within their own time zones so as to ensure conformity and uniformity.

THE DOMINION'S STRATEGY FOR THE NORTHWEST

Development of the West constituted the third component of Macdonald's national policy. Without a populated West, no justification existed for a transcontinental railway. Without a railway, east–west trade could not occur. And without internal trade, the National Policy of tariff protection was meaningless.

In preparation for settlement, the Canadian government surveyed the land into townships of 36 square miles (92 km^2) and consisting of 36 sections. Each section, one square mile (2.6 km^2) in size, contained 640 acres (259 ha). Sections were subdivided into more manageable quarter-sections of 160 acres (65 ha).

Not all land was available for settlement. The HBC received "one twentieth of the land of the fertile belt" as part of the sale of Rupert's Land to the Canadian government in 1869. In Manitoba, the Canadian government appropriated, as part of the Manitoba Act of 1870, 1.5 million acres (600 000 ha), or one-seventh of the new province, for the benefit of the Métis. The CPR received 25 million acres (10 million ha), and other railway companies also received land as part of their contracts until the practice ended in 1894. Additional land was set aside for schools. The remaining land belonged to the federal government to sell or to turn over to private land companies to sell. This latter scheme proved disastrous. Most of the 26 colonization companies in existence in 1883 were owned by friends of Macdonald's government and held up to 3 million acres (1.2 million ha) of land, most of which remained idle either as a result of failed immigration or speculation on the part of the companies that land prices would rise.

To encourage settlement, the government passed the Dominion Lands Act in 1872. It provided a quarter-section free to each head of family or 21-year-old male if he did the following: paid a $10 registration fee, resided on the land for three years, cultivated 30 acres (12 ha), and built a permanent dwelling.

Women's property rights in the West were seriously curtailed. Married women did not qualify for free land under the Dominion Lands Act, and only a few widowed women succeeded in receiving the 160-acre land grant. In 1886, the North-West Territories government abolished a woman's right to the dower — a one-third interest in her husband's property upon widowhood. Western Canadian women protested the dower legislation for over thirty years before it was rescinded in 1917.

NWMP Commissioner James Macleod, standing second from right, with his men at Fort Walsh in the Cypress Hills, in what is now southwestern Saskatchewan, in the late 1870s. Macleod treated the Native peoples with dignity and respect. The Blackfoot called him "Stamixotokan," or "Bull's Head," and welcomed his promise of a new order.

Glenbow Archives, Calgary, Canada/NA-52-1.

To ensure peaceful settlement, the federal government established territorial courts and created its own police force in 1873, the North-West Mounted Police (NWMP). They established important posts throughout the West: Fort Walsh in the Cypress Hills, Fort Macleod on the Old Man River, and Fort Calgary at the junction of the Bow and Elbow rivers. The NWMP administered Canadian law to the Native peoples, curtailed the whisky traders, and assisted the early settlers. Their success lay in what they represented: their red tunics and white helmets symbolized British over American law and tradition, a collective as opposed to an individual authority. As the American writer Wallace Stegner pointed out, "One of the most visible aspects of the international border [in the West] was that it was a colour line: blue below, red above, blue for treachery and unkept promises, red for protection and straight tongue."[1]

IMMIGRATION AND THE SETTLEMENT OF WESTERN CANADA

Up until the turn of the century, only a limited number of immigrants entered the Northwest from outside Canada. They consisted of 7000 Mennonites from southern Russia who were being persecuted under a policy of Russification by the Tsarist government that demanded universal conscription, a policy that went against the pacifist nature of Mennonites.

Also, 2000 Icelanders left their homeland, with its limited supply of fertile land and declining fishing industry, to settle on the shores of Lake Winnipeg. Selected groups of Jewish immigrants came in the 1880s. Sir Alexander Galt, Canada's high commissioner in London, joined the archbishop of Canterbury and several titled English gentlemen in aiding victims of

Russia's pogroms (massacres of Jews) and offered the Canadian prairies as a refuge. The Canadian government encouraged the new settlers to farm, but many chose instead to become small shopowners, merchants, or labourers in urban centres, particularly Winnipeg.

The Mormons were the largest single American group to arrive in western Canada before 1896. Charles Ora Card, a religious leader, entrepreneur, and colonizer from Utah, led them northward in 1887 to establish farms at Lee's Creek (later renamed Cardston in his honour), Sterling, and Magrath in present-day southern Alberta, where they hoped to avoid the discrimination they had experienced in the United States due to their practice of polygamy, or multiple marriages. The Canadian government encouraged them to settle in the Palliser Triangle area since they had practised dryland farming in Utah.

Most new settlers in the West prior to 1896 were migrants from Ontario, English-speaking Quebec (French-speaking Quebeckers did not move out West in great numbers), and the Maritimes. Being the first to arrive, they became the established commercial and political elite, ensuring that the region became integrated with the rest of the country.

Between 1896 and 1914, more than one million people immigrated to western Canada, thus ensuring the success of the third component of the "national policy" — settlement of the West. What had changed after 1896 to account for this tremendous influx of immigrants? Both "push" and "pull" factors played a role. The push factors varied as widely as did the migrants themselves but included such elements as limited agricultural land, a desire to escape from the drudgery of working in factories and living in urban slum areas, religious persecution, and simply adventure and the prospect of a better life.

The pull factors were equally varied and related to world conditions in general and the Canadian West's attractions in particular. The rapid growth of international trade after 1896 meant jobs. Prosperity also increased demand for raw materials, especially for food for the growing urban population. Farmers in the West could benefit from a ready market and a high price for Canadian wheat. Increased prosperity also meant declining interest rates and lower freight rates, which in turn resulted in higher profits for exports of Canada's bulky natural resources. Most important of all, Canada benefited from the closing of the American frontier after 1890. After the best land — especially well-watered land — in the American West ceased to be available, the Canadian prairies became the "last best West."

Improved farming conditions also made the Canadian West attractive. Better strains of wheat, such as Marquis, that matured earlier than Red Fife, could thus be grown in northern areas of Alberta and Saskatchewan without risk of frost damage. The price of wheat quadrupled between 1901 and 1921. Better machinery such as the chilled-steel plough (introduced from the United States), improved harrows and seed drills, and tractors and threshers also aided western farmers. A steam-thresher could process more in a day than a farmer could by physical labour for an entire season.

Credit also goes to Clifford Sifton, an energetic Manitoba politician with a business background, and Laurier's minister of the interior. He pressured the HBC and the CPR to sell their reserved lands at reasonable rates to prospective settlers. He discontinued the practice of using land grants as incentives to railway promoters. He also simplified the procedure for obtaining a homestead and encouraged settlers to buy up an adjacent section, if available, by allowing them the right to pre-empt such land by making an interim claim on it and to purchase it at a reduced rate from the government later on.

As well, his department produced numerous pamphlets —such as *The Wondrous West*; *Canada: Land of Opportunity*; *Prosperity Follows Settlement*; and *The Last Best West* — which contained glorified descriptions of conditions in the Canadian West. In 1896 alone, his department printed 65 000 pamphlets; four years later, the figure reached one million. Millions of brochures were sent out to prospective immigrants in the United States and Europe, in over a dozen languages. As well, he advertised in thousands of newspapers, arranged for lecture tours and promotional trips for potential settlers (particularly Americans), and offered bonuses to steamship agents based on the number of immigrants they brought to Canada.

IMMIGRANT GROUPS

British immigrants came mostly on their own and at their own expense. There were exceptions. The Barr colonists, a group of Londoners who came together under the aegis of Reverend Isaac Barr at the turn of the century, settled in the Lloydminster area on the border between Saskatchewan and Alberta. Also, some 80 000 "Home Children" came to Canada between 1867 and 1924 to work as agricultural and domestic servants. Despite some known incidences of gross neglect and child abuse, the government supported the movement and deemed it successful. Most British immigrants adjusted relatively easily to Canadian life. They did not have to learn a new language or radically different customs, and many were relatively well off. Those who lacked farming experience, however, had a more difficult time adjusting. But not all British received a warm welcome; some employment ads read, "No English Need Apply." Canadians resented the haughty attitude of upper-class Englishmen in particular, many of whom refused to fit into Canadian society.

American immigrants were high on Sifton's list of desirable settlers. Although not British, the majority of them were of Anglo-Saxon extraction. As they already spoke English, they mixed easily with their Canadian neighbours and participated fully in their new communities. As well, many were experienced farmers. Many ex-Canadians returned. About a third of those coming from the United States were newcomers from Europe, such as Germans and Scandinavians who had initially settled in the American West.

In an age of racial-superiority theories, African Americans were not welcomed. While Canadian agents told white Americans that the climate of the Northwest was mild and healthy, they informed black Americans of the region's rigorous and severe climate. When a group of well-to-do African Americans from Oklahoma crossed into Canada in 1910, local newspapers, especially the Edmonton *Journal* (Edmonton was reported to be their destination), warned of an "invasion of Negroes." In the end, the effort to restrict black immigrants succeeded. Between 1901 and 1911, fewer than 1500 African Americans came to Canada, compared with hundreds of thousands of other Americans.

A Historical Portrait ☙

☞ Robert, a Barnardo Boy

Robert* was a "Home Child," one of some 80 000 British boys and girls sent to Canada between 1868 and 1925 to work as agricultural and domestic servants. He belonged to the Barnardo Homes, the largest of the child-care organizations in England, begun by Dr. Thomas Barnardo in 1870 in London's East End, to assist waifs, strays, orphans, and street urchins by providing them with a "home." The original Barnardo Home had a sign out in front that read: "No destitute child ever refused admission." While in operation, the Barnardo Homes took in over 30 000 destitute children.

Robert was one of them. He was admitted into the home on November 23,

1921, at the age of 9, along with an older brother, Alfred, and a younger brother, Harold. Another brother, Sidney, was old enough to be on his own. Their mother, Emily, had died from pregnancy complications in 1920, and their father, Edward, a brewer's labourer, died a year later from pneumonia. A maiden aunt, Annie, took them in for a brief time, but when she was unable to care for them any longer, they were admitted to the home. They were given the familiar Barnardo uniform of a tunic, a pair of red-striped trousers, and a hat like that of a Salvation Army officer.

From the beginning, Dr. Barnardo had arranged to send "his" children overseas to "the colonies," where he believed they had a better chance at a new life than in the slums of London. Robert had a choice of going to either Canada or Australia, and chose Canada. He and his brother Harold left England on the *SS Melita* on September 18, 1924, with the customary "Barnardo trunk" that contained all of their earthly possessions; Alfred stayed in England with Sidney. It was the last time the four brothers would see each other.

Upon arrival in Canada Robert and Harold were sent to the Barnardo's Canadian Office and Distributing Home for Boys in Toronto. From here, they were sent north to Bracebridge to a bush farm in Muskoka, where a widow requested two boys as farm workers. Like so many Home Children, the boys did not have a good initial experience in Canada. She saw them as indentured labourers. They ate separately from the family and slept in an unheated section of the house. They were underfed, and Robert recalled drinking the cow's milk from the bucket before taking it into the house. They attended school but missed many days when needed around the farm. Robert wrote to the officials in Toronto to complain about the harsh conditions, and an inspector came

out, but only after informing the lady of his impending visit. Robert recalled that day as the only time he ate with the family and had a scrumptious meal. When the official left, conditions became even more intolerable.

It was customary for employers of Home Children to pay them a wage when they reached the age of 15. When Robert became 15, the lady let the boys go. They were then sent down to the Niagara Peninsula, where a large number of Barnardo boys were located, to assist on the fruit and vegetable farms. Robert's new "home" was a wonderful contrast to his first; the farm owner, Sidney Wright, had been a Barnardo boy himself. Robert got to be part of the family, enjoying the privileges of regular family members. Unfortunately, he was let go when, during the depression, the family could no longer afford him. He moved to another farm in the area, where once again he was treated as "just a Barnardo boy." He stuck it out until he married a local girl whose parents owned a farm, at which time he took over the family farm. The couple had three children and lived in the community for the remainder of their lives.

*Robert is Robert Francis, the father of one of the textbook authors.

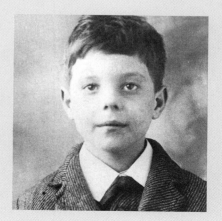

Robert Francis, as a young boy.
Doug Francis' personal photo collection.

The Canadian government had little success in attracting large numbers of western Europeans. The French government openly discouraged Canadian immigration agents because it feared a future war with Germany, whose population was almost double that of France. The Scandinavian countries also restricted emigration, fearing the negative result of such migration, especially of skilled workers, on their own economies. Germany prohibited immigration agents within its borders and fined steamship lines for carrying emigrants.

To get around these emigration restrictions, Clifford Sifton allowed W.T.R. Preston, Canada's immigration inspector in London, to set up a clandestine organization, the North Atlantic Trading Company, in 1899 to work with European shipping agents to bring western Europeans to Canada. Each agent received a $5 bonus for every healthy man, woman, or child over twelve who was a bona fide farmer, farm worker, domestic servant, or accompanying family member. This illegal scheme ended in 1905 after public outcry against undue profiteering, but not before the company had succeeded in bringing in fifty thousand emigrants from Western Europe.

Sifton encouraged immigrants from Eastern Europe. Ukrainians were particularly targeted because they were considered hardworking and experienced farmers. By World War I, 170 000 Ukrainians had come to Canada from the Austro-Hungarian empire. The first group of 4000 Ukrainians — or Galicians, as the immigration agents called them because they came from the province of Galicia — settled at Star and Josefberg, 65 km east of Edmonton.

Some 7000 Doukhobors (meaning "spirit wrestlers") came from Russia in the late 1890s because of persecution for their pacifist and anti-tsarist beliefs. Leo Tolstoy, the noted Russian novelist, and Peter Kropotkin, a leading Russian anarchist, admired their simple, communal lifestyle and assisted them to emigrate from Russia. James Mavor, a professor of political

Doukhobor women pulling a plough. During their first spring in Canada the Doukhobors had a limited number of beasts of burden. With most of their men away working on railway construction to earn money for the community the women hitched themselves to the plough.

Saskatchewan Archives Board #SPA R-B 1964(1).

economy at the University of Toronto and a friend of Kropotkin's, helped settle them in Canada. They founded three colonies, two near Yorkton, Saskatchewan, and another near Saskatoon.

All was peaceful until a radical Doukhobor wing calling itself the Sons of Freedom marched toward Winnipeg in search of Christ and a new earthly paradise, and in expectation of the arrival of their leader, Peter Veregin, recently released from captivity in Russia. The group walked naked through the Doukhobor villages in a quest for a state of purity akin to that of Adam and Eve before the Fall. Public outcry provided an excuse for Frank Oliver, Clifford Sifton's successor as minister of the interior (1905–11), to confiscate half of their Saskatchewan land. In protest, 5000 Doukhobors trekked to the Kootenay district near Grand Forks, British Columbia, where Peter Veregin had purchased private land.

Although he tolerated eastern European immigrants as potentially good farmers, Sifton disdained southern Europeans. He believed them to be migratory labourers who would only settle in the urban centres.

 Asian immigration occurred mainly on the West Coast. To restrict Asian immigration, the federal government imposed a head tax on Chinese immigrants — $50 in 1885, $100 in 1900 and as high as $500 by 1903. The government would have done the same with Japanese immigrants, but Japan was a military ally of Britain and a major trading partner of Britain and Canada. Instead, the Canadian and Japanese governments mutually agreed to restrict Japanese immigrants to Canada to 400 a year.

A few immigrants came from India. As British subjects, they had a special claim for entry into another country within the British Empire. But West Coast citizens opposed their entry. In

The tax certificate for Lau Shong (or Shing), 1912, for $500, the amount required to bring in Chinese immigrants.

National Archives of Canada/C-96443.

May 1914, the ship the *Komagata Maru* brought nearly 400 Punjabis, mostly Sikhs, to Vancouver. But for two months, port authorities refused them entry. In the end, the Punjabis were forced back to India, amid cries of "White Canada forever" and the refrain of "Rule Britannia."

NATIVIST ATTITUDES

An ethnic hierarchy of preferred immigrants developed among English Canadians. Not surprisingly, the British and Americans, for the most part "Anglo-Saxon" Protestants, stood at the top of the list. Next came the northern and western Europeans, particularly Scandinavians, Germans, and Dutch, considered by many English Canadians to have the best qualities of "Anglo-Saxons" and thus welcomed. After the "chosen races" came the central and eastern Europeans, seen as industrious people and good farmers. Less tolerated in this group were Ukrainians and Doukhobors because of their exclusiveness and "strange" customs. Lowest in the hierarchy of European immigrants came Jews and southern Europeans, both considered difficult to assimilate and regarded as poor farmers. Ranked well below Europeans came those of African background and Asians (Japanese, Chinese, and South Asians) — all believed to be unassimilable. They were denied the franchise, barred from the professions, and subjected to discrimination in housing and in access to public places.

The First Nations people also faced discrimination. Both the Liberal and the Conservative administrations put intense pressure on First Nation communities to surrender reserve land. A number of illegal losses of reserve lands occurred, particularly in the last years of Laurier's administration. Frank Oliver, as Laurier's minister of Indian affairs and minister of the interior, passed a law in 1908 that allowed the government to remove Native people from reserves near towns of more than 8000 residents. Then, in 1911, he amended the Indian Act to allow companies and municipalities to expropriate reserve land for roads, railroads, or other public purposes.

Underlying these racist attitudes was the belief that "foreign" immigrants could only become Canadians by abandoning their own customs and language so as to assimilate. Few English Canadians at this time thought in terms of a culturally pluralistic society. Their only concern was how best to integrate the various ethnic groups into a unified Canada. They looked to the churches and especially the schools to inculcate British-Canadian customs and one language.

By 1914, the era of nation building was complete with a national economic policy: the National Policy, or high tariff; the completion of the transcontinental Canadian Pacific Railway; and settlement of the West through large-scale immigration. But certain groups, classes, and regions of the country felt alienated or neglected. Their discontent contributed to a new era of protest and a resurgence of regionalism.

NOTE

1.   Wallace Stegner, *Wolf Willow: A History, a Story, and a Memory of the Lost Plains Frontier* (New York: Viking, 1966), p. 101.

LINKING TO THE PAST

Alexander Mackenzie
http://www.nlc-bnc.ca/primeministers/h4-3050-e.html

Facts about and a brief biography of Alexander Mackenzie, the second prime minister (and the first Liberal prime minister) to hold office.

Canada, by Train
http://www.nlc-bnc.ca/trains/index-e.html

An exhaustive multimedia site tracing the history of railways (and railway advertising) and the contribution of railways to the growth of Canada. Immigration, urban growth, and technology and communications are among the topics explored.

Connexions: An Exhibit on Communications
http://www.sciencetech.technomuses.ca/english/collection/conn1.cfm

An exhibit from the Canada Science and Technology Museum tracing the development and popularization of the telegraph, telephone, radio, and television.

The Chinese Immigration Act, 1885
http://www.asian.ca/law/cia1885.htm

Selections from the 1885 Chinese Immigration Act, which restricted Asian immigration to Canada.

Becoming Canadian: Pioneer Sikhs in Their Own Words
http://collections.ic.gc.ca/sikh/

An illustrated history of Sikh immigrants based on personal recollections.

BIBLIOGRAPHY

The nationalism of the Canada First movement is discussed in the chapter "The First Fine Careless Rapture," in F.H. Underhill, *The Image of Confederation* (Toronto: Canadian Broadcasting Corporation, 1964); and in David Gagan, "The Relevance of 'Canada First,'" *Journal of Canadian Studies* 5 (November 1970): 36–44. On the rising French-Canadian nationalism of the 1870s see Arthur Silver, *The French-Canadian Idea of Confederation, 1864–1900*, 2nd ed. (Toronto: University of Toronto Press, 1997); and Mason Wade, "Growing Pains: 1867–96," in his *The French Canadians: 1760–1945* (London: Macmillan, 1955), pp. 331–92.

Dale Thomson's *Alexander Mackenzie: Clear Grit* (Toronto: Macmillan, 1960) gives a good portrait of Canada's second prime minister. The ideas underlying Canadian liberalism in the 1870s are examined by F.H. Underhill in "The Political Ideas of the Upper Canadian Reformers, 1867–1878," in his *In Search of Canadian Liberalism* (Toronto: Macmillan, 1960), pp. 68–84; and by W.R. Graham in "Liberal Nationalism in the 1870's," *Canadian Historical Association Report* (1946): 101–19. On the politics of the Laurier era see R.C. Brown and R. Cook, *Canada, 1896–1921: A Nation Transformed* (Toronto: McClelland & Stewart, 1974). On the national policy see the endnotes to "Where Historians Disagree: The National Policy" in this chapter.

Pierre Berton's two-volume popular study, *The National Dream: The Great Railway, 1871–1881* (Toronto: McClelland & Stewart, 1970) and *The Last Spike: The Great Railway, 1881–1885* (Toronto: McClelland & Stewart, 1974), describes the building of the Canadian Pacific Railway. For a less nationalistic view of the railway see A.A. den Otter, "Nationalism and the Pacific Scandal," *Canadian Historical Review* 69 (3) (September 1986): 315-39. On the Chinese contribution to the building of the CPR, see Paul Yee, *Building the Railway: The Chinese and the CPR* (Toronto: Umbrella Press, 1999).

On railway building during the Laurier era consult T.D. Regehr, *The Canadian Northern Railway: Pioneer Road of the Northern Prairies, 1895–1918* (Toronto: Macmillan, 1976); and G.R. Stevens, *Canadian National Railways*, 2 vols. (Toronto: Clarke Irwin, 1960). In *The Canadian Pacific Railway and the Development of Western Canada* (Montreal/Kingston: McGill-Queen's University Press, 1989), John A. Eagle examines the CPR's contributions to western Canadian economic growth between 1896 and 1914. Suzanne Zeller's *Inventing Canada: Early Victorian Science and the Idea of a Transcontinental Nation* (Toronto: University of Toronto Press, 1987) and her *Land of Promise, Promised Land: The Culture of Victorian Science in Canada* (Ottawa: Canadian Historical Association, 1996), examine the role of scientists in shaping the idea of a transcontinental nation.

On the development of the Canadian West in the 1870s and 1880s see Gerald Friesen, *The Canadian Prairies: A History* (Toronto: University of Toronto Press, 1984). Also useful for primary sources is L.G. Thomas, ed., *The Prairie West to 1905: A Canadian Source Book* (Toronto: Oxford University Press, 1975). For an account of homesteading see the essays in David C. Jones and Ian Macpherson, eds., *Building Beyond the Homestead: Rural History on the Prairies* (Calgary: University of Calgary Press, 1985). A detailed study of settlement in one prairie town is Paul Voisey, *Vulcan: The Making of a Prairie Community* (Toronto: University of Toronto Press, 1988). On the North-West Mounted Police, see R.C. Macleod, *The North-West Mounted Police and Law Enforcement, 1873–1905* (Toronto: University of Toronto Press, 1976), and William Baker, *The Mounted Police and Prairie Society, 1873–1919* (Regina: Canadian Plains Research Center, 1998).

Overviews of immigration to western Canada are available in R.C. Brown and R. Cook's chapter "Opening Up the Land of Opportunity," in *Canada, 1896–1921: A Nation Transformed* (Toronto: McClelland & Stewart, 1974); Pierre Berton's *The Promised Land: Settling the West, 1896–1914* (Toronto: McClelland & Stewart, 1984); and Gerald Friesen's *The Canadian Prairies: A History* (Toronto: University of Toronto Press, 1984). See as well, Paul Robert Magocsi, ed., *Encyclopedia of Canada's Peoples* (Toronto: University of Toronto Press for the Multicultural Society of Ontario, 1999).

On immigration to western Canada in the pre-1896 era see Norman Macdonald, *Canada: Immigration and Colonization, 1841–1903* (Toronto: Macmillan, 1966); and the relevant articles in Franca Iacovetta et al., *A Nation of Immigrants: Women, Workers, and Communities in Canadian History, 1840s–1960s* (Toronto: University of Toronto Press, 1998). Clifford Sifton's role in promoting immigration to the West is examined in D.J. Hall, "Clifford Sifton: Immigration and Settlement Policy, 1896–1905," in Howard Palmer, ed., *The Settlement of the West* (Calgary: University of Calgary Press, 1977), pp. 60–85, and in D.J. Hall's two-volume biography, *Clifford Sifton*, vol. 1, *The Young Napoleon, 1861–1900* (Vancouver: University of British Columbia Press, 1981), and vol. 2, *The Lonely Eminence, 1901–1929* (Vancouver: University of British Columbia Press, 1985).

The immigration of British home children is the subject of Joy Parr's *Labouring Children: British Immigrant Apprentices to Canada, 1869–1924* (Montreal/Kingston: McGill-Queen's University Press, 1980); and Kenneth Bagnell's *The Little Immigrants: The Orphans Who Came to Canada*, rev. ed. (Toronto: Dundurn Press, 2002). On American farmers' immigration to western Canada see Carl Bicha, *The American Farmer and the Canadian West, 1896–1914* (Lawrence, KS: Coronado Press, 1968); and Harold Troper, *Only Farmers Need Apply* (Toronto: Griffin House, 1972). European immigration is discussed in Donald Avery, *"Dangerous Foreigners": European Immigrant Workers and Labour Radicalism in Canada, 1896–1932* (Toronto: McClelland & Stewart, 1979). George Woodcock and Ivan Avakumovic's *The Doukhobors* (Toronto: McClelland & Stewart, rep. 1977) deals with this important group. The story of Jewish immigration to Canada is told in Irving Abella, *A Coat of Many Colours: Two Centuries of Jewish Life in Canada* (Toronto: Lester & Orpen Dennys, 1990); and Gerald Tulchinsky, *Taking Root: The Origins of the Canadian Jewish Community* (Toronto: Stoddart, 1992).

Black immigration to western Canada is covered in Robin Winks, *The Blacks in Canada: A History*, 2nd ed. (Montreal/Kingston: McGill-Queen's University Press, 1997). On Asian immigration to British Columbia in the pre-World War I era see Jin Tan and Patricia E. Roy, *The Chinese in Canada* (Ottawa: Canadian Historical Association, 1985); Peter Ward, *White Canada Forever: Popular Attitudes and Public Policy toward Orientals in British Columbia*, 3rd ed. (Montreal/Kingston: McGill-Queen's University Press, 2002); Patricia Roy, *A White Man's Province: British Columbia Politicians and Chinese and Japanese Immigrants, 1885–1914* (Vancouver: University of British Columbia Press, 1989); and Hugh Johnston, *The Voyage of the Komagata Maru: The Sikh Challenge to Canada's Colour Bar* (Delhi: Oxford University Press, 1979). On nativist attitudes see Howard Palmer, *Patterns of Prejudice: A History of Nativism in Alberta* (Toronto: McClelland & Stewart, 1982).

CONFLICTING VISIONS: 1867–1914

"We have come to a period in the history of this country when premature dissolution seems to be at hand." So wrote Wilfrid Laurier, the official leader of the opposition, in the early 1890s. Canada appeared to be a failure. Bickering between Ottawa and the Dominion's seven provinces had become endemic. A provincial-rights movement flourished in Ontario; secessionist sentiments resurfaced in Nova Scotia; and regional protest arose in the Northwest. In Quebec, French-Canadian nationalist feeling strengthened in reaction to the execution of Louis Riel, and in the course of the debate concerning the Jesuits' Estates Act, and denominational schools in Manitoba. As well, a deep economic depression resulted in one million people leaving for the United States in the 1880s. As a result of these problems, Canadians doubted the ability of the country to survive as a fully independent country. But they disagreed whether Canada's future should lie in closer relations with the United States, in a federated union with Britain, or in formulating its own foreign policy as an autonomous nation within the British Empire. No one seemed to know the solution to Canada's problems; some, like Laurier, questioned whether or not a solution existed.

THE PROVINCIAL-RIGHTS MOVEMENT IN ONTARIO

Oliver Mowat, Liberal premier of Ontario from 1872 to 1896, can rightfully be considered the "father of provincial rights." He endorsed the concept known as the provincial-compact theory — a belief that Confederation constituted a compact entered into by the provinces of their own volition, and one that could be altered only with their consent. As premier of Ontario, Mowat continued the policy of Edward Blake, his predecessor, of making the province dominant within the federation. One opportunity to do so arose over the question of the boundary line between Ontario and Manitoba.

THE ONTARIO BOUNDARY DISPUTE

The origins of the Ontario–Manitoba boundary dispute dated back to pre-Confederation days. The British had never established a precise boundary line between Rupert's Land and the colony of Upper Canada (Ontario). Mowat argued that Ontario's western boundary should run due north from the source of the Mississippi River, which was slightly west of Lake of the Woods at a place called Rat Portage (present-day Kenora). In contrast, Macdonald and the federal Conservatives wanted to draw the boundary between Ontario and Manitoba near Port Arthur on Lake Superior.

The issue remained unresolved when in 1881 Macdonald unilaterally awarded the disputed territory — from Lake of the Woods eastward to Thunder Bay — to Manitoba. Since the federal government owned Manitoba's natural resources, it was in a position to control the land and the mineral rights. Nonetheless, Ontario continued to dispute the awarded area granted to Manitoba.

After two years of legal chaos, both governments agreed to submit the issue to the Judicial Committee of the Privy Council in London, the supreme legal authority in the British Empire. In 1884 the Judicial Committee fixed the western limits of Ontario at the northwest angle of Lake of the Woods (the present boundary). But not until 1889 did the federal government confirm Ontario's boundaries and the province's right to the natural resources within the disputed territory.

POWERS OF THE LIEUTENANT GOVERNOR AND FEDERAL DISALLOWANCE

Mowat also won a series of victories in other disputes with the federal government, notably over the powers of the lieutenant governor, and the federal power of disallowance (the right granted to the federal government in the BNA Act to disallow any provincial law considered to conflict with federal law). Mowat argued that the lieutenant governor had the same position in the province as the governor general in the federal government, thus making the provinces co-ordinate sovereignties on a par with the federal government on constitutional matters. The Judicial Committee of the Privy Council upheld Mowat's position. Next Mowat argued that the provinces had certain legal powers before Confederation that they retained after 1867, thus making their jurisdiction independent of that of the federal government rather than subordinate to it. Once again, he won his case. Thus, by 1896 and the end of Conservative rule, Mowat had succeeded in strengthening provincial powers and Ontario's rights, at the expense of the federal government.

PROTEST IN ATLANTIC CANADA

Mowat had allies in Atlantic Canada in his fight with the federal government. The anti-confederate sentiments of the mid-1860s re-emerged in the 1880s as Maritimers protested their perceived inferior position in the new Dominion.

The Maritimes faced difficult economic times in the 1880s. The Conservatives' high protective tariff of 1879 contributed to regional dissatisfaction. Fish and lobster exports had dropped a staggering 75 percent in the early 1880s when the Americans raised their import duty on Maritime fish in response to the high Canadian tariff. Shipbuilding declined, as iron steamers replaced wooden sailing ships. Yarmouth, for example, once a thriving centre of Nova Scotia's shipbuilding industry, built only six vessels in 1880, four in 1884, and none in 1887. Many Nova Scotians left in search of jobs elsewhere.

SECESSION THREATS IN NOVA SCOTIA

From 1878 to 1884, Nova Scotia's Conservative government asked Ottawa for financial assistance. But Macdonald's top priority remained the CPR and the development of the West. The unwillingness of Ottawa to help contributed to the Liberals' provincial victory in 1884 under their leader W.S. Fielding on a wave of anti-confederate sentiment. Fielding also attempted to extract larger subsidies from Ottawa. When he too failed, he introduced a secessionist resolution in the Nova Scotia legislature in 1886. The premier appealed to the other Maritime provinces to secede as well but they declined. Fielding even found little sustained support in his own province. Once again, the secessionist movement in Nova Scotia died out.

DISCONTENT IN THE NORTHWEST

Macdonald faced more serious problems in the Northwest. The First Nations, particularly the Crees in the Treaty Number Six area, felt betrayed by the federal government's failure to keep its treaty promises of providing food rations in time of scarcity. The Native peoples also resented the government's refusal to allow them to choose their own reserve lands, as promised in the treaty.

The Western Métis were also angry with Ottawa. After the Red River resistance of 1869–70, many of the Manitoba Métis moved to the South Saskatchewan River Valley. Once again, their livelihoods appeared threatened as settlers moved in. They appealed to the federal government to recognize their land claims. But by the end of 1884, Ottawa had still not responded to their petitions.

Many of the settlers in the northern region were also discontented. The CPR's decision to reroute the railway through the southern region left them hundreds of kilometres away from a rail link to eastern markets. As well, the more politically active settlers demanded an elected assembly for the North-West Territories and representation in the federal Parliament in Ottawa.

In 1884, the Métis, with the support of the "country-born" (English-speaking mixed-bloods) in the Prince Albert area, welcomed back Louis Riel to lead their protest. They believed that Riel could obtain for the Northwest what he had for Manitoba fifteen years earlier. But the Riel who returned in 1884 was not the Riel of 1869. During the intervening years, he had been hospitalized in two mental asylums in Quebec and had spent years in exile in the United States. He became convinced that God had chosen him to be the "prophet of the New World," responsible for creating a reformed Roman Catholic state on the prairies. He saw his invited return to western Canada as part of God's plan.

THE NORTH-WEST REBELLION OF 1885

Initially, Riel and his followers avoided violent action. They petitioned Ottawa on December 16, 1884, to ask for more liberal treatment for the Native peoples, a land grant for the mixed-bloods, responsible government for the North-West Territories, western representation in Ottawa, a reduction of the tariff, and the construction of a railway to Hudson Bay as an alternative to the CPR. The federal government acknowledged receipt of the petition and promised to appoint a commission to investigate problems in the Northwest. But apart from making a list of mixed-bloods, it took no further action.

In mid-March, Riel established a provisional government with himself as president for the purpose of once again taking up arms against the federal government as he had done in 1869. But the situation was different in 1885. A federal police force now existed in the North-West Territories; thousands of settlers had located there; and a newly completed railway linked the region to central Canada.

Where Historians Disagree

The Causes of the North-West Rebellion of 1885

Earlier generations of English-speaking Canadian historians blamed the North-West Rebellion of 1885 on one man: Louis Riel. The rebel leader, a madman, incited violence. In 1905, R.G. MacBeth wrote that "rebellion was rampant with a madman at its head."[1] In contrast, French-Canadian historians saw Riel as a misguided leader acting out of concern for his Métis people. Both groups of historians saw Riel and the rebellion largely in terms of the continuing controversy of English Canadians versus French Canadians, Protestants versus Catholics.

Canadian historiography took a new turn in the 1930s. Influenced in part by the "frontier" school of thought, already well established in American historiography, several Canadian historians saw the Métis as frontier hunters and nomads who opposed the advancing frontier of a different cultural group. Historian George F.G. Stanley saw the rebellion of 1885 as a clash between "primitive and civilized peoples."[2] French ethnologist Marcel Giraud also subscribed to this cultural-conflict thesis, while American popular writer Joseph Kinsey

Howard depicted Riel as the symbolic leader of all North American Aboriginal peoples struggling to free themselves from white domination.[3]

Historian W.L. Morton denied that the Métis were "primitive": they were an advanced society, whose interests and values simply differed from those of other Canadians. Moreover, by 1885, the Métis formed part of a larger western Canadian society that felt aggrieved by the indifference of Ottawa to western concerns. The rebellion of 1885 was therefore more than a Métis uprising incited by one man; it was a resistance by the people of the Northwest as a whole, and in this respect the first of a series of western protest movements against central Canada in general, and the federal government in particular, for their failure to address western complaints.

Thomas Flanagan questions whether the Métis had to rebel to force the Conservative government to act. He argues that "the Métis grievances were at least partly of their own making; that the government was on the verge of resolving them when the Rebellion broke out; that Riel's resort to arms could not be explained by the failure of constitutional agitation." Flanagan does not exonerate Ottawa, but claims that the government's mistakes were "in judgment, not part of a calculated campaign to destroy the Métis or deprive them of their rights."[4] Flanagan argues that Riel acted as much out of self-interest or, at least, private motives, as for his Métis followers.

Historian D.N. Sprague has challenged Flanagan's assertion that the government was playing fair. He argues that Métis grievances over land claims in Manitoba during and after the resistance of 1869–70 continued to poison Métis–Ottawa relations in Saskatchewan, where so many Métis had fled when the situation in Manitoba became intolerable. Sprague implies that the federal government deliberately provoked Riel into forming a second provisional government so as to accuse him of treason.

Recently, the debate has shifted away from Riel to the Métis themselves. Why did they follow Riel? The shift in perspective has led to the study of Métis society in an effort to explain what conditions prevailed within the community that would have caused its members to follow Riel into rebellion. Diane Payment has examined Métis society in the South Saskatchewan River valley.[5] Noting that not all Métis supported Riel, historian David Lee examines the reasons why some Métis did and others did not support their leader.[6]

In *Homeland to Hinterland*, Gerhard Ens argues that the economy and society of the Red River Métis underwent dramatic change between 1840 and 1890 from being pre-capitalist and "subsistence" to a dynamic capitalist market economy, based on the buffalo-robe trade, in the North-West Territories. The result was out-migration from the Red River Colony well before 1870. Ens maintains that migration after 1870 was part of this earlier trend as economic opportunities for the Métis in Manitoba continued to decline, along with the added economic difficulties the Métis experienced as a result of the "intolerant actions and behaviour of the incoming Protestant settlers from Ontario,"[7] rather than as a result of any action by the Canadian government. Furthermore, he argues that the Métis who supported Riel in the uprising of 1869–70 came from those Métis who believed Manitoba could still be their economic "homeland." Those who did not, simply moved further West in search of better economic opportunities, only to re-enact, unfortunately, the same scenario 15 years later. By this time, however, the West as a whole had become an economic "hinterland" to central Canada.

[1] R.G. MacBeth, *The Making of the Canadian West* (Toronto: W. Biggs, 1905), p. 144.
[2] George F.G. Stanley, *The Birth of Western Canada* (London: Longmans, Green, 1936), p. vii.
[3] Joseph Kinsey Howard, *Strange Empire: The Story of Louis Riel* (Toronto: James Lewis & Samuel, 1952).
[4] Thomas Flanagan, *Riel and the Rebellion: 1885 Reconsidered* (Saskatoon: Western Producer Prairie Books, 1983), pp. 146, 147.
[5] Diane Payment, *The Free People—Otipemisiwak": Batoche, Saskatchewan, 1870–1930* (Ottawa: National Historic Parks and Sites Canada, 1990).
[6] David Lee, "The Métis Militant Rebels of 1885," in R. Douglas Francis and Donald B. Smith, eds., *Readings in Canadian History: Post-Confederation*, 6th ed. (Toronto: Nelson Thomson Learning, 2002): 45–62.
[7] Gerhard Ens, *Homeland to Hinterland: The Changing Worlds of the Red River Métis in the Nineteenth Century* (Toronto: University of Toronto Press, 1996), p. 170.

The Military Campaign

Meanwhile, the Métis took action into their own hands. On March 26, 1885, the Métis militant leader Gabriel Dumont and his followers successfully routed a group of about 100 settler-volunteers and the North-West Mounted Police at Duck Lake, near Batoche. Subsequently, a band of Crees surrounded Battleford, while militant Cree warriors killed nine people near Frog Lake, northwest of Battleford.

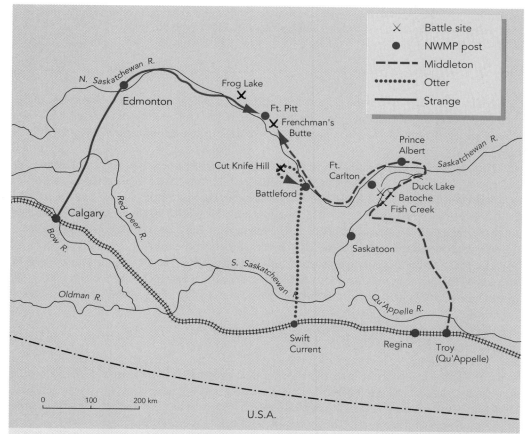

Military operations in the North-West Rebellion, 1885. This map shows the routes of the three military columns: to Batoche, under Major General Middleton; to Battleford, under Lieutenant Colonel Otter; and to the Ft. Pitt area, under Major General Strange.

Big Bear (front row, second from the left) and Poundmaker (front row, far right), shown at their trials, 1885. Father André (back row, second from the right) spent the night before Riel's execution in prayer with him, and walked with him to the scaffold.

Glenbow Archives, Calgary, Canada/NA-3205-11.

Within a month, the federal government dispatched 3000 troops to the Northwest under the command of Major General Frederick Middleton, to join the 2000 volunteers and Mounties already in the region. Middleton organized the troops in three columns: at Qu'Appelle, Swift Current, and Calgary.

The Métis ambushed Middleton at Fish Creek, south of Batoche, on April 24. Lieutenant Colonel William Otter successfully relieved Battleford, but on May 2, Cree chief Poundmaker defeated Otter's force at Cut Knife Hill. Major General Thomas Bland Strange led the Alberta Field Force from Calgary, by way of Edmonton and the North Saskatchewan River, against another Cree chief, Big Bear, and his band at Frenchman's Butte in late May. As at Fish Creek, the encounter was a draw, with both sides retreating at the same time.

The main battle took place at Batoche, Riel's headquarters, beginning on May 9. Within three days, Middleton's superior troops forced the Métis to retreat. Riel surrendered on May 15, while Dumont and others fled to the United States. Poundmaker and Big Bear surrendered soon afterwards.

RIEL'S TRIAL

In the trials that followed, the Canadian government prosecuted more than 125 Native people and hanged eight of them publicly. This mass hanging was intended to send a message to the First Nation community against further opposition. Big Bear and Poundmaker each received prison sentences of three years. They were released before their terms ended, because of poor health; both died within a year of their release.

A jury of six men, all of British background, tried Louis Riel for treason in a Regina court-room. Riel pleaded not guilty. Two psychiatrists examined Riel during the trial. Both concluded that Riel was sane, that he could distinguish right from wrong.

Louis Riel's address to the jury during his trial at Regina, July 1885.

Glenbow Archives, Calgary, Canada/NA-1081-3.

Riel's speech in English to the jury eloquently explained his reasons for involvement in the rebellion:

> No one can say that the Northwest was not suffering last year ... but what I have done, and risked, and to which I have exposed myself, rested certainly on the conviction I had to do, was called upon to do something for my country.... I know that through the grace of God I am the founder of Manitoba.... Even if I was going to be sentenced by you, gentlemen of the jury, I have the satisfaction if I die — that if I die I will not be reputed by all men as insane, as a lunatic.... Gentlemen of the jury, my reputation, my liberty, my life are at your discretion.

The jury deliberated for an hour before reaching its verdict: Riel was guilty of treason.

Prime Minister John A. Macdonald twice postponed the execution. Then on November 16, 1885, Riel mounted the gibbet at Regina. The trap door was sprung. A Métis, a French-Canadian, and later a western-Canadian martyr was born.

While Riel's execution gained Macdonald support in Ontario, it cost him support in Quebec. In hindsight, it is evident that Riel's execution contributed to the demise of the Conservatives in Quebec in the 1890s and to the rise of the Liberals.

SIGNIFICANCE OF THE NORTH-WEST REBELLION

The North-West Rebellion of 1885 marked a transition on the Prairies; henceforth the settler society would dominate. Many events symbolized the transition: the execution of Riel and the imprisonment of Big Bear and Poundmaker; the use of the newly completed CPR to transport troops west to suppress the insurgents; and the establishment of an elected territorial assembly a year later, in 1886, in which no Métis were present. Possibly the most poignant, however, was

Immediately after Riel's execution on November 16, 1885, French Canadians rose in protest against the federal government. In Montreal, demonstrators burned Sir John A. Macdonald in effigy at the base of the statue of Queen Victoria in Victoria Square.

From *Frank Leslie's Illustrated Newspaper*, November 28, 1885. Saskatchewan Archives Board/R-D1776.

the animus generated over the capture of two Ontario women — Theresa Delaney and Theresa Gowanlock — by a group of Cree during the rebellion. In accounts of the capture, confinement, and ultimate release of these two women, they came to embody the virtues of the "civilizers" from the East and, by contrast, the "barbaric" nature of the indigenous Native population, especially Native women. The liberation of these captives at the hands of the supposedly cruel, treacherous "savages" marked the triumph of the forces of "good" over "evil" and provided a rationale for the "necessary" suppression of the minority by the dominant society.

RISING FRENCH-CANADIAN NATIONALISM

The Riel controversy intensified the nationalist sentiment of some French-Canadian leaders. Honoré Mercier, leader of the Quebec wing of the Liberal party after 1883, expressed this nationalist position at a rally in Montreal: "Riel, our brother, is dead, victim of fanaticism and treason — of the fanaticism of Sir John and some of his friends, of the treason of three of our people who sold their brother to keep their portfolios." He appealed to his fellow Quebeckers to form a Parti national, an exclusive French-Canadian party. His new party won the provincial election of 1886.

THE FIRST INTERPROVINCIAL CONFERENCE

Mercier then called an interprovincial conference to challenge the federal government's hegemony. The provincial premiers summed up the provincial-rights position. They argued that Confederation was a contract among the British North American colonies that had agreed to establish a new country. Therefore, the provinces should control the federal government. Among their demands were appeals for larger federal subsidies, abolition of the federal power of disallowance, and Senate reform to strengthen provincial power.

In 1887, Wilfrid Laurier became the federal Liberal leader. He proposed a French-Canadian nationalism that was an alternative to Mercier's, one that included French Canadians across the country. It was a nationalism based on compromise between French Canadians and English Canadians.

CULTURAL AND RELIGIOUS FEUDS

Unfortunately, Laurier's appeal for unity between English and French Canadians and Protestants and Roman Catholics went unheeded in the ethnically and religiously intolerant atmosphere of the late nineteenth century. Two issues — the Jesuits' Estates Act and the Manitoba Schools Question — revealed just how bitter ethnic relations and religious differences had become.

A photo of the first interprovincial conference, called by Honoré Mercier in 1887, to challenge the authority of the federal government. The Quebec premier appears seated second from the left. Ontario's Oliver Mowat, the "Father of Provincial Rights," is seated in the centre. W.S. Fielding, who tried during his premiership to take Nova Scotia out of Confederation, is beside Mowat on the right.

National Archives of Canada/C-11583.

THE JESUITS' ESTATES CONTROVERSY

The dispute over the Jesuits' Estates began in 1888 when the Jesuits appealed to the provincial government of Quebec to have their property, which had been confiscated after the conquest, returned or else that they receive financial compensation for their losses. Premier Mercier appealed to the pope to act as arbiter. Based on the pope's recommendation, Mercier implemented the Jesuits' Estates Act.

D'Alton McCarthy, an anti-Catholic and a Conservative MP from Ontario, insisted that the pope had no right to meddle in Canadian affairs. He moved a resolution in the House of Commons to have the federal government disallow the Jesuits' Estates Act. He considered the Act to be the latest in a series of attempts by the Jesuits and French-speaking Roman Catholics to rule Canada. McCarthy failed to get sufficient support in the Conservative Party to disallow the Act, but succeeded, through his actions, in diminishing the support for the Party in Quebec.

THE MANITOBA SCHOOLS QUESTION

Ethnic and religious tensions next focussed on the school question in Manitoba. By 1890, the English-speaking Protestant population in Manitoba had increased tenfold, greatly outnumbering the French-speaking population that had essentially remained static. This imbalance did not appear to cause problems in Manitoba until D'Alton McCarthy delivered an emotional speech at Portage la Prairie in August of 1889 against denominational schools in Manitoba as undermining the future greatness of Canada. A few months earlier, he had helped form an Equal Rights Association, which claimed in its platform to stand for "equal rights of all religious denominations before the law, special privileges for none." He objected that the French-Canadian and Métis Roman Catholics in the West, should not, as a minority, have "special privileges." On the same platform as McCarthy sat Joseph Martin, attorney general for the Manitoba government. He pledged his government's support in abolishing the dual school system, as well as French as an official language, in Manitoba.

In 1890, the Manitoba government passed a Schools Act that established a provincial department of education and a system of non-sectarian public schools that alone would receive the provincial grant for education. Denominational schools could still exist, but without government funding. Those contributing to such schools must do so in addition to their public-school taxes. The same session of the legislature abolished French as an official language, contrary to section 23 of the Manitoba Act of 1870.

MANITOBA CATHOLICS FIGHT SCHOOL LEGISLATION

Discontented Roman Catholics had three options: appeal to the federal government to use its right of disallowance of provincial legislation; take the issue to the courts to have the legislation declared *ultra vires*, or unconstitutional; or appeal to Ottawa to intervene on behalf of the minority through remedial legislation as set out in section 93 of the BNA Act. Eventually, they pursued all three possibilities.

Macdonald resisted using the federal government's right of disallowance, fearing that the Manitoba electorate's disapproval of such an action would strengthen the provincial government's power. He favoured court action and agreed that the federal government pay the legal costs of the appellant. The case, known as *Barrett v. the City of Winnipeg*, went through the provincial court, which upheld the Manitoba government's position, to the Supreme Court of Canada, which upheld the right of the Roman Catholic minority to have state-supported separate schools. Then, the Judicial Committee of the Privy Council in London reversed this decision in favour of the Manitoba government's position.

One final option remained. The Manitoba Roman Catholics appealed to the federal government for remedial action. The Conservatives introduced the remedial legislation bill in Parliament in January 1896. It provided for a nine-member board to run the separate-school system, to be supported by the Roman Catholics' own tax monies; the schools in this system would share a portion of the provincial educational grant; and, to ensure proper standards, the separate schools would be inspected regularly and funds would be withheld if they were judged inefficient. Clearly, remedial legislation favoured the Roman Catholic position. But Parliament dissolved on April 23, with the bill still not passed into law. Four days later, Mackenzie Bowell resigned as Conservative leader under pressure from the Orange wing of his party, angered over his handling of the schools question.

THE ELECTION OF 1896

The Conservatives entered the federal election of 1896 with a new leader, Charles Tupper — the party's fifth leader in five years. The Manitoba Schools Question proved only one of several contentious issues in the election, although an important one. In Quebec, the Conservatives stressed during the election campaign that they had introduced remedial legislation on behalf of the Manitoba Roman Catholics. In English-speaking Canada, Conservative candidates emphasized that the bill was not, and might never become, law.

The Liberals were in an enviable position. As the opposition, they could denounce the Tories without offering concrete alternative policies. On the controversial schools question, Laurier simply promised that his Liberal government, if elected, would end the dispute through compromise with the Manitoba Liberal government in a way that would respect provincial rights.

The Liberals narrowly won the election of 1896. Outside Quebec, they tied the Conservatives in the number of seats. But in Quebec they obtained two-thirds of the province's share.

THE LAURIER–GREENWAY CONTROVERSY

 Laurier and Manitoba's Premier Greenway struck a compromise: religious instruction would be allowed in the public schools for half an hour at the end of each day. Roman Catholic teachers could be employed in urban schools with 40 Roman Catholic pupils or in rural districts with 25. On the language question it was agreed that, when ten of the pupils in any school system spoke the French language or any language other than English as their native language, the teaching of such pupils would be conducted in English and French or the other language "upon the bilingual system."

The French-Canadian Roman Catholic minority in Manitoba would have obtained more under the Conservatives' remedial legislation. Laurier's compromise allowed religious instruction but led to the abolition of the state-supported separate-school system. French would be retained only when sufficient population warranted it; hence, it lost the status of equality with English that it had had under the Manitoba Act of 1870. Moreover, it became a language like any other in Manitoba, all of which were unofficial except English. (In 1916, at the height of World War I, even the bilingual clause of the Laurier–Greenway compromise was abolished, making English the only language of instruction in the province's schools.) The Roman Catholic hierarchy in Canada accused Laurier of capitulating to the English-Canadian Protestants but in the end was persuaded to accept "the compromise" as the best that could be hoped for, given the Roman Catholics' minority position.

THE SCHOOLS QUESTION IN ALBERTA AND SASKATCHEWAN

The schools question in the West arose again in 1905, with the creation of the two new provinces of Saskatchewan and Alberta. The original ordinances of the North-West Territories Act of 1875, as amended in 1877, had provided for both Protestant and Roman Catholic schools to receive public funding. As well, both French and English could be used as languages of instruction. In the early 1890s, however, the territorial government made English the official language of instruction in the Roman Catholic school system, restricting French to the primary grades only for French-speaking children. Then, in 1901, the territorial government restricted religious instruction to the last half hour of the school day, as was the case in Manitoba.

When the time came to draw up the autonomy bills to bring Saskatchewan and Alberta into existence, Charles Fitzpatrick, the federal minister of justice and a Quebec Roman Catholic, and Henri Bourassa drafted the educational clause to restore the original system of 1877. The clause permitted the free establishment of Roman Catholic and Protestant schools as well as the use of French in the school system. The powerful Clifford Sifton, who had once been a cabinet minister under Manitoba premier Greenway, opposed the educational clause, claiming it went against the wishes of the government of the North-West Territories. He resigned from the cabinet in protest.

Laurier intervened and allowed Sifton to redraft the educational clause, although he did not invite him back into the cabinet. Sifton's revised clause restricted the rights of the French-Canadian Roman Catholic minorities to the limited concessions granted in the ordinance of 1901. Laurier accepted the "honourable compromise," as he described the Sifton amendment. But Bourassa denounced it as a sell-out. It infringed on the rights of French Canadians as set out in the original North-West Territories Act. In the end, however, the Sifton amendment became law.

At the same time that the country was facing conflicting visions internally, it was also having to deal with conflicting visions as to its destiny in relation to Great Britain and the United States.

CONTINENTALISM

The Liberals favoured stronger continental ties in the 1880s and 1890s. Closer links could take many forms. Some Liberals wanted a restricted reciprocity agreement, which would apply to natural products only. Others favoured unrestricted reciprocity, or free trade, in some manufactured goods as well as in natural resources. Still others proposed commercial union — an integrated economic union with a free interchange of all products, a sharing of internal revenue taxes, and a common tariff policy against other countries. At the extreme end of this spectrum came political union. Goldwin Smith, an outspoken critic, advocated political union with the United States in his book, *Canada and the Canadian Question* (1891).

THE TRADE QUESTION AND THE 1891 ELECTION

Laurier, as Liberal leader, favoured commercial union in principle but he believed it was too extreme a position for a party platform, so he committed the party to unrestricted reciprocity instead in the election of 1891. Macdonald claimed that unrestricted reciprocity threatened Canada's independence because it would ultimately lead to political union with the United States. He maintained that protectionism was the means to prevent American assimilation and to uphold the British connection. He declared his loyalty to Britain in his popular campaign slogan, "A British subject I was born, and a British subject I will die," and proceeded to drape himself in the British flag.

The Conservatives won the election of 1891, but only by a narrow majority of 27 seats. They lost seats to the Liberals in close votes in the rural areas, which tended to support free trade, but won most of the urban vote in Ontario and Quebec, where protectionism was strong. The election of 1891 ended unrestricted reciprocity as a Liberal policy and the party moved toward its own version of a national policy, including a high tariff. Two decades would pass before the Liberals would champion "continentalism" once again in the election of 1911.

IMPERIALISM

Many English-speaking Canadians favoured stronger British ties through imperial federation. After 1875, British leaders came to appreciate the importance of colonies in maintaining Britain's military and economic supremacy in the world. In particular, overseas colonies proved important for British hegemony as Germany and Italy became major European powers and as the United States threatened to supplant Britain as the leading English-speaking country in the world. Furthermore, rivalry between imperial countries meant competition for colonial markets and for world trade, thus giving an economic emphasis to the new imperialism. The cry from imperialists that "trade follows the flag" led British manufacturers and many in the working class to support imperialism in the late nineteenth century.

THE GRIT TOBOGGAN SLIDE, AND WHERE IT LEADS TO!

GRIT POLICY

UNRESTRICTED RECIPROCITY

ANNEXATION

But the Canadian People will come to the Aid of their Patriotic Premier on the 5th of March, and Rescue their Country from the impending Danger.

The cartoon shows Liberal leader Wilfrid Laurier, and Richard Cartwright, his Liberal financial critic, on a toboggan slipping down the slope of "Unrestricted Reciprocity" with the symbolic Miss Canada between them. With the knife of Reciprocity, Cartwright is cutting the rope that prevents the toboggan from falling into "Annexation." Macdonald, straining to hold the toboggan back, calls for help to save Canada in the forthcoming federal election, March 5, 1891.

By Bengough, National Archives of Canada, March 5, 1891.

RACE THEORY AND IMPERIALISM

The new imperialism, however, represented for many of its followers much more than trade, tariffs, and guns. It was an intellectual and spiritual force. Imperialists distorted Charles Darwin's theory of evolution in the animal kingdom by applying it to society, in a concept known as Social Darwinism. Race theorists argued that some groups or races were born "superior" — were better fit to survive — than others, and that, in Britain and in colonies settled by whites, the Anglo-Saxon "race" constituted the elite. Imperialists argued that their "race's" superior position made it imperative for "Anglo-Saxons" to spread their "virtues" — their British values and Christian beliefs, the two being considered synonymous — to the less fortunate "infidels" of Asia, Africa, and the Pacific. They believed they must take up this "white man's burden," as the British author Rudyard Kipling expressed it.

Women played an important role in the imperialist movement. Organizations such as the Imperial Order Daughters of the Empire (IODE), founded by Margaret Polson Murray, became strong advocates of imperial sentiment. Its motto—"One Flag, One Throne, One Country"—

summarized its aspirations. By World War I, it would become one of the largest English-Canadian women's voluntary associations.

British women, however, were much more than advocates of imperialism; they were also symbols, or icons, of imperialism, as representatives of the moral, religious, and spiritual components of its ideology. They were the bearers of the finest British civilization and thus the true "empire builders." Their children were the offspring of the dominant race, and thus the means to ensure its survival. English-Canadian imperial literature extolled the virtues of the fairer sex of the empire builders, by contrasting the noble attributes of British women with the degenerate qualities of "coloured women" in the subservient colonial society. As well, protecting this "fairer sex" became a pretext for suppressing and controlling the indigenous population.

IMPERIALISM AND CANADIAN NATIONALISM

English-Canadian imperialists believed that Canada could offer the British Empire much, economically, militarily, and spiritually. In turn, the empire could advance Canada's national interests. English-Canadian imperialists envisioned imperial federation as a means to free Canada from economic depression, ethnic tension, provincialism, and threatened American annexation, thus enabling it to reach greater heights — "a sense of power" — in the world. In this sense, as historian Carl Berger has written, "imperialism was one form of Canadian nationalism."[1]

Imperialism drew its greatest support in Canada from a small English-speaking social and political elite, mainly Protestant ministers, lawyers, teachers, and politicians. In 1887 they formed a Canadian branch of the Imperial Federation League, an organization begun in Britain three years earlier. Descendants of United Empire Loyalists joined in large numbers, seeing imperialism as the fulfilment of their long-time dream of a "United Empire," which gave the League its greatest support in Ontario and the Maritimes.

Where Historians Disagree
The Nature of Imperialism

Historians have debated the nature and impact of imperialism in Canada's past. Inspired by William Lyon Mackenzie King's efforts to achieve Canadian independence, liberal nationalist historians of the interwar years viewed imperialism as an obstacle in the way of Canada's evolution from colony to nation. In his study of Wilfrid Laurier, Oscar Skelton, later undersecretary of state for external affairs (1925–41), argued that imperialism hindered the growth of Canadian independence. It also caused disunity, as French Canadians could not identify with the imperial vision.[1]

Liberal nationalist historian Frank H. Underhill equated imperialism with colonialism in his writings in the 1930s. The British connection embroiled Canadians in imperial wars of no direct interest to them. On one occasion, Underhill wrote: "We must ... make it clear to the world, and especially to Great Britain, that the poppies blooming in Flanders fields have no further interest for us." And when British imperialists ask for assistance "the simplest answer is to thumb our noses at them."[2]

In the post–World War II era, Donald G. Creighton and other conservative-nationalist historians looked to the imperial connection as the counterforce to the menacing pull of continentalism, and thus Canada's means of maintaining independence in North America. Creighton depicted John A. Macdonald as the great Canadian statesman who had understood the importance of British imperialism in safeguarding Canada against American continentalism. "The diplomatic and military support of Great Britain," Creighton wrote, "could alone offset the political preponderance of the United States; and Macdonald proposed therefore to bring in the old world to redress the balance of the new."[3] Historian Norman Penlington has argued that English-Canadian imperialists in general had seen the empire as Canada's means to strengthen its position vis-à-vis the United States.[4]

Historian Carl Berger shifted the focus of the debate. He showed that imperialism was more an intellectual than a political, economic, or military phenomenon, that it was primarily a concept in the mind of those who endorsed it. In reality, Berger argued, imperialism was "one variety of Canadian nationalism."[5] Canadian imperialists believed that Canada could achieve a "sense of power" and thus fulfill its destiny as a great nation through the imperial connection.

Berger's argument that imperialism was an indigenous phenomenon promoted largely by an elite of English-Canadian thinkers has been challenged by historian Robert Page. In a review of Berger's book, Page wrote that "external events and a very strong international climate of opinion,"[6] including such phenomena as the popular enthusiasm surrounding Queen Victoria's Diamond Jubilee and the patriotism that came forth during the Boer War, also contributed. Furthermore, Page questions Berger's strictly nationalist and intellectual perspective on imperialism, arguing that a study of the attitudes toward imperialism among businesspeople, for example, would undoubtedly yield a different, more economic, perspective.

[1] O.D. Skelton, *The Life and Letters of Sir Wilfrid Laurier* (Toronto: Oxford University Press, 1921).

[2] Quoted in R. Douglas Francis, *Frank H. Underhill: Intellectual Provocateur* (Toronto: University of Toronto Press, 1986), p. 106.

[3] Donald Creighton, "Macdonald and the Anglo-Canadian Alliance" in *Towards the Discovery of Canada: Selected Essays* (Toronto: Macmillan, 1972), p. 223.

[4] Norman Penlington, *Canada and Imperialism, 1896–1899* (Toronto: University of Toronto Press, 1965).

[5] Carl Berger, *The Sense of Power: Studies in the Ideas of Canadian Imperialism, 1867–1914* (Toronto: University of Toronto Press, 1970), p. 9.

[6] Robert Page, "Carl Berger and the Intellectual Origins of Canadian Imperial Thought, 1867–1914," *Journal of Canadian Studies*, 5 (August 1970), p. 40.

British imperialism peaked in the 1890s. Joseph Chamberlain, appointed Colonial Secretary in 1895, personified the imperial spirit and spearheaded the movement. Two years later, Queen Victoria celebrated her Diamond Jubilee — 60 years as the ruling monarch — in a spectacular celebration to show the world the splendour and the might of the British Empire. Special commemorative stamps were issued, among them a Canadian stamp showing a map of the world splashed with red for all the British possessions. The inscription read: "We hold a vaster empire than has been." A year after Queen Victoria's Diamond Jubilee, several Canadian provinces established Empire Day on May 23 — the day before Queen Victoria's birthday.

THE SOUTH AFRICAN WAR

The supreme moment for English-Canadian imperialists came with the outbreak of the South African War in 1899. Britain appealed to the Dominions to assist in fighting the Boers, descendants of European settlers, mainly Protestants from the Netherlands, in South Africa. The English-language newspapers, especially those in Montreal and Toronto, demanded immediate Canadian participation. Lord Minto, the governor general, and Major General Edward Hutton, commander of the Canadian militia, worked out plans for a Canadian contingent, without informing Prime Minister Laurier. A cable from Joseph Chamberlain, the British colonial secretary, thanked Canada for its "offer to serve in South Africa." His thanks were premature, however, since the Canadian government had not yet made an official statement of support.

Meanwhile, anti-imperialistic sentiments towards the South African war arose in Quebec. If French Canadians sympathized with anyone in the struggle, it was with the Boers, whom they regarded as a kindred oppressed minority. Henri Bourassa, a young politician and brilliant orator like his grandfather, the legendary Louis-Joseph Papineau, leader of the Rebellion of 1837 in Lower Canada, opposed Canadian involvement in this distant imperialist war. Bourassa equated imperialism with militarism and commercialism, and thus condemned the British Empire "not because it is British, but because it is Imperial. All empires are hateful. They stand in the way of human liberty, and true progress, intellectual and moral. They serve nothing but brutal instincts and material objects." Bourassa also argued that the sending of Canadian troops to South Africa would establish a "dangerous precedent" for future imperial wars to which Britain would expect Canada to contribute.

For two days, Laurier's cabinet met to find a solution. On October 13, 1899, Laurier devised a compromise. He proposed that the Canadian government equip and transport a volunteer force of 1000 men for service on the British side. Once in South Africa, however, the troops would become the British government's responsibility and would fight as British soldiers. Laurier reminded imperialists and French Canadians alike that this decision to send troops should not be "construed as a precedent for future action." (Eventually Canada sent 7300 men to South Africa, of whom 245 died overseas, more than half from disease.) While Laurier's compromise did not satisfy the extremists on both sides, it did succeed in keeping the Liberal Party and the country together. But Bourassa resigned from the party in protest and ran instead as an independent.

GROWING FRENCH-CANADIAN NATIONALISM

Imperialist sentiments in English-speaking Canada contributed to a parallel French-Canadian nationalism in Quebec. In 1903, a group of young French-Canadian nationalists, inspired by Henri Bourassa, founded the Ligue nationaliste and their own newspaper, *Le Nationaliste*, a year later. The organization had a three-point program: Canadian autonomy within the British Empire; provincial autonomy within a federal state; and the rational development of Canada's resources. Other French-Canadian nationalists founded the Association catholique de la jeunesse canadienne-française (ACJC), or "Catholic Association of French-Canadian Youth," in 1904. This group, under the leadership of Lionel Groulx, a Catholic priest and teacher, recruited new members from the classical colleges. They saw the Roman Catholic church as playing an important role in shaping Quebec nationalism.

Jules-Paul Tardivel, a Franco-American born in Kentucky, who came to Quebec in 1868 to study French and then took up the causes of ultramontanism and French-Canadian nationalism, took a more extreme position. In his newspaper, *La Vérité*, and in his futuristic novel, *Pour la Patrie* (1895), Tardivel proposed Quebec's separation from Canada to create a Roman Catholic state on the banks of the St. Lawrence River. In an exchange published in 1904, Tardivel and

The members of the Prince Edward Island Transvaal contingent before their departure for South Africa. In total, some 7300 Canadian volunteers fought in the South African War (1899–1902).

The Patent and Copyright Office Collection/National Archives of Canada/C-7983.

Bourassa outlined their differing conceptions of French Canada at this time. Tardivel distinguished between his exclusive French-Canadian form of nationalism and Bourassa's broader Canadian nationalism. Tardivel wrote: "Our own nationalism is French-Canadian nationalism.... For us our fatherland is — we do not say precisely the Province of Quebec — but French Canada; the nation we wish to see founded at the hour marked by Divine Providence is the French-Canadian nation." Bourassa replied:

> For us the fatherland is all Canada, that is, a federation of distinct races and autonomous provinces. The nation that we wish to see develop is the Canadian nation, composed of French Canadians and English Canadians, that is of two elements separated by language and religion, and by the legal dispositions necessary to the preservation of their respective traditions, but united in a feeling of brotherhood, in a common attachment to the common fatherland.

In this interchange lay the essence of two currents of twentieth-century French-Canadian nationalism: one leading to separatism, the other to a bilingual and bicultural nation.

RELATIONS WITH THE UNITED STATES

THE ALASKA BOUNDARY DISPUTE

At the turn of the century a new dispute arose between Canada and the United States, this time over the boundary between Alaska and the Yukon Territory. The news that gold had been discovered in the Yukon in 1897 suddenly made the boundary question of utmost importance. The Americans sought a continuous border along the Pacific coast, thus denying Canada's claim to several fiords with access to the Yukon.

The Canadians and the Americans, along with the British, agreed to settle the issue through a six-member tribunal, three from each side, to review the disputed border. Britain appointed a British judge and two Canadian lawyers for its side. In the end, Lord Alverstone, the lone British member of the tribunal, sided with the Americans who claimed that the boundary line should be around the heads of the inlets, giving the United States territorial control of them. Many Canadians at the time, including the prime minister, considered Alverstone's decision to side with the Americans to be "one of those concessions which have made British diplomacy odious to Canadian people." Such action increased the will of Canadian leaders to gain greater control of their own foreign policy.

RENEWED PROSPECTS OF RECIPROCITY

After the contentious Alaska boundary dispute, Canadian–American relations actually improved. On January 26, 1911, the Liberals made a surprise announcement in Parliament that a reciprocal trade agreement had been reached with the Americans that allowed Canadian natural products free entry into American markets in exchange for letting American manufactured goods into Canada at a lower tariff rate. The agreement only required ratification by the Americans and Canadian governments. The American Congress passed the legislation in July 1911. It remained only for the Canadian Parliament to give its approval.

Very quickly, opposition to the reciprocity agreement arose in central Canada. A group of eighteen prominent Toronto manufacturers, industrialists, and financiers petitioned the government against the agreement. The group went on to become the core of a newly created Canadian National League. The league published a pamphlet, *The Road to Washington*, in which it warned that the reciprocity treaty was the first step towards American annexation of Canada.

Inopportune statements by imprudent American politicians aided the league's campaign. Champ Clark, speaker-designate of the House of Representatives, said of the agreement: "I am for it, because I hope to see the day when the American flag will float over every square foot of the British North American possessions clear to the North Pole." President Taft himself noted: "Canada stands at the parting of the ways." By this he meant that Canada had to choose between remaining an isolated protectionist country or trading with the Americans. But anti-American proponents in Canada interpreted the statement to mean that Canada had to choose between Britain and the United States. Emotional arguments about loyalty and nationalism replaced economic ones.

THE NAVAL CRISIS

The controversy over reciprocity coincided with the contentious naval question. In 1908, the British press warned of Germany's growing naval strength that threatened Britain's control of the high seas. The British Conservative opposition demanded that the British government immediately build eight super-battleships, or dreadnoughts. Many English Canadians insisted that Canada contribute to the cause. Canadian Conservatives wanted an emergency direct cash contribution to Britain in the present crisis, while the ruling Liberals favoured the immediate establishment of a Canadian navy under Canadian command, to be used by Britain in the event of war if the Canadian Parliament approved. In January 1910, Laurier introduced the Naval Service Bill. It proposed that Canada construct five cruisers and six destroyers and establish a naval college to train Canadian officers. The Canadian government could, "in case of war," place the force under imperial command with the Canadian Parliament's approval.

Opposition to the Naval Service Bill arose at both extremes. English-Canadian imperialists denounced this "tin-pot navy," as they described it, as a disgrace to Canada's role in the empire. French-Canadian nationalists, led by Henri Bourassa, opposed the proposed navy because it could be used to fight imperial wars of no interest to Canada. Bourassa was in favour of a navy for home defence but not one that would involve Canada in the "whirlpool of militarism." He questioned whether Canada needed a navy at all, since the only threat to the country could come from the United States, with whom Canadians had enjoyed a century of peace.

During the 1911 federal election campaign, Laurier faced vigorous attacks from both imperialists in Ontario, who branded him a continentalist on the reciprocity issue, and French-Canadian nationalists, who called him an imperialist on the naval issue. "I am neither," an exasperated Laurier protested during an election rally in St. Jean, Quebec. "I am a *Canadian*." His policy, he claimed, was one of "true Canadianism, of moderation, or conciliation." Nevertheless, the Liberals lost the election due to the combined opposition of Ontario imperialists and Quebec nationalists.

Robert L. Borden became the new prime minister. One of his government's first decisions concerned the naval issue. Despite strong Quebec opposition, the Conservative government introduced the Naval Aid Bill that provided a direct cash contribution of $35 million to Britain to build three dreadnoughts. The Liberals attacked the Naval Aid Bill as a sham and as an inadequate alternative to Laurier's naval program. They used their strong majority in the Senate to defeat the bill. Thus, on the eve of World War I, Canada had neither made a contribution to the British navy nor built up a navy of its own.

The period from 1880 to 1914 saw a resurgence of regionalism internally, and debate over the future of Canada externally. Provincial-rightists successfully challenged the power of the central government on a number of constitutional issues, thus making Canada in practice a federal state with a more even division of power between the federal and provincial governments. Regional protests arose in the Maritimes with the attempt by Nova Scotia once again to secede from Confederation, and in the West over the North-West Rebellion of 1885. As well, English- and French-speaking Canadians feuded over Riel's execution, over the Jesuits' Estates Act in Quebec, and over linguistic and religious rights in schools, first in Manitoba and then in Saskatchewan and Alberta.

Canadians also debated the nation's destiny in the world. Most English Canadians favoured some form of association with either Britain, in an imperial federation, or with the United States, in a continental association, to Canadian independence. French-Canadian leaders preferred either an autonomous Canadian nation within the British Empire, or greater autonomy for Quebec within Canada. Few Canadians thought in terms of Canadian independence; most felt that the country was not yet strong enough, or sufficiently united, to be independent.

NOTE

1. Carl Berger, *The Sense of Power: Studies in the Ideas of Canadian Imperialism, 1867–1914* (Toronto: University of Toronto Press, 1970), p. 259.

LINKING TO THE PAST

The Ontario Boundary Act, 1889
http://www.miredespa.com/wmaton/Other/Legal/Constitutions/Canada/English/coba_1889.html

The full text of the 1889 Ontario Boundary Act, which settled the dispute between Ontario and Manitoba and fixed the western limits of Ontario.

The North-West Rebellion of 1885
http://www.schoolnet.ca/collections/E/

Scroll down to "History" under the subject listing, and then choose "Northwest Rebellion of 1885," which features a wide range of information about the rebellion. By following the table of contents link to "The 1885 Resistance," you will also find a detailed chronology of events, including biographies of key participants.

Quebeckers, the Roman Catholic Church, and the Manitoba Schools Question
http://www2.marianopolis.edu/quebechistory/chronos/manitoba.htm

A descriptive chronology of the developments related to this controversy.

The Laurier–Greenway Compromise
http://www.ola.bc.ca/online/cf/documents/1896ManitobaSchool.html#top

The Laurier–Greenway Compromise, also known as the Manitoba School Act of 1896, attempted to resolve the issue of religion and language in education.

The Program of the Ligue Nationaliste
http://www2.marianopolis.edu/quebechistory/docs/nligue/eng.htm

The 1903 document outlining the goals of Quebec's Ligue nationaliste.

BIBLIOGRAPHY

For an overview of Dominion–provincial relations in the late nineteenth century see P.B. Waite, *Canada, 1874–1896: Arduous Destiny* (Toronto: McClelland & Stewart, 1971). The provincial-rights movement in Ontario is discussed in Christopher Armstrong, *The Politics of Federalism: Ontario's Relations with the Federal Government, 1867–1942* (Toronto: University of Toronto Press, 1981); and Paul Romney, *Getting It Wrong: How Canadians Forgot Their Past and Imperilled Confederation* (Toronto: University of Toronto Press, 1999). On political protest in Atlantic Canada in the 1880s see Judith Fingard, "The 1880s: Paradoxes of Progress," in E.R. Forbes and D.A. Muise, eds., *The Atlantic Provinces in Confederation* (Toronto: University of Toronto Press, 1993); T.W. Acheson, "The Maritimes and 'Empire Canada,'" in D.J. Bercuson, ed., *Canada and the Burden of Unity* (Toronto: Macmillan, 1977), pp. 87–114; and George Rawlyk, ed., *The Atlantic Provinces and the Problem of Confederation* (St. John's: Breakwater Books, 1979).

The most authoritative account of the North-West Rebellion is Bob Beal and Rob Macleod, *Prairie Fire: The 1885 North-West Rebellion* (Edmonton: Hurtig, 1984). For the Native perspective on the 1885 Rebellion see Blair Stonechild and Bill Waiser, *Loyal Till Death: Indians and the North-West Rebellion* (Calgary: Fifth House, 1997). For a historical perspective on the Delaney–Gowanlock captivity see Sarah Carter, *Capturing Women: The Manipulation of Cultural Imagery in Canada's Prairie West* (Montreal/Kingston: McGill-Queen's University Press, 1997). On Louis Riel see the readings cited for Chapter 12 of this book, as well as the titles listed in "Where Historians Disagree" in this chapter. A historiographical article is J.R. Miller, "From Riel to the Métis," *Canadian Historical Review* 69(1) (March 1988): 1–20.

Quebec's views on federal–provincial relations are analyzed in R. Cook, *Provincial Autonomy: Minority Rights and the Compact Theory, 1867–1921* (Ottawa: Queen's Printer, 1969); and Arthur Silver, *The French-Canadian Idea of Confederation, 1864–1900* (Toronto: University of Toronto Press, 1982). J.R. Miller's *Equal Rights: The Jesuits' Estates Act Controversy* (Montreal: McGill-Queen's University Press, 1979) deals with that subject in depth. On the Manitoba schools question and its impact on the election of 1896 consult Paul Crunican, *Priests and Politicians: Manitoba Schools and the Election of 1896* (Toronto: University of Toronto Press, 1974). Lovell Clark has compiled a collection of sources in *The Manitoba School Question: Majority Rule or Minority Rights* (Toronto: Copp Clark, 1968). Treatment of the schools question in Alberta and Saskatchewan can be found in Manoly R. Lupul, *The Roman Catholic Church and the North-West School Question: A Study in Church–State Relations in Western Canada* (Toronto: University of Toronto Press, 1974). The politics of the 1890s are discussed in John T. Saywell's introduction to *The Canadian Journal of Lady Aberdeen, 1893–1898* (Toronto: Champlain Society, 1960), P.B. Waite, *The Man from Halifax: Sir John Thompson, Prime Minister* (Toronto: University of Toronto Press, 1985); and H. Blair Neatby, *Laurier and a Liberal Quebec: A Study in Political Management* (Toronto: McClelland & Stewart, 1973).

The most comprehensive survey of Canada's relations with Britain and the United States remains C.P. Stacey, *Canada and the Age of Conflict: A History of Canadian External Relations*, vol. 1, *1867–1921* (Toronto: Macmillan, 1977). Canadian–American relations in the late nineteenth century are dealt with in John Herd Thompson and Stephen J. Randall, *Canada and the United States: Ambivalent Allies*, 3rd ed. (Montreal/Kingston: McGill-Queen's University Press, 2002); J.L. Granatstein and Norman Hillmer, *For Better or For Worse: Canada and the United States to the 1990s* (Toronto: Copp Clark Pitman, 1991); and C.C. Tansill, *Canadian–American Relations, 1875–1911* (Toronto: The Ryerson Press, 1943).

Norman Penlington's *The Alaska Boundary Dispute: A Critical Appraisal* (Toronto: McGraw-Hill Ryerson, 1972); and John Munro's *The Alaska Boundary Dispute* (Toronto: Copp Clark, 1970) cover this issue.

Carl Berger's *The Sense of Power: Studies in the Ideas of Canadian Imperialism, 1867–1914* (Toronto: University of Toronto Press, 1970), analyzes the beliefs of English-Canadian imperialists. Carman Miller, *Painting the Map Red: Canada and the South African War 1899–1902* (Montreal/Kingston: Canadian War Museum, McGill-Queen's University Press, 1992) discuss Canadian imperialism in the context of the South African War.

French-Canadian views on imperialism and nationalism during this era can be found in M. Wade, *The French Canadians, 1760–1945* (Toronto: Macmillan, 1955), pp. 447–535; and in Susan Mann, *The Dream of Nation: A Social and Intellectual History of Quebec*, 2nd ed. (Montreal/Kingston: McGill-Queen's University Press, 2002), pp. 167–83. Joseph Levitt's pamphlet, *Henri Bourassa, Catholic Critic* (Toronto: Canadian Historical Association, 1976), summarize the ideas of this French-Canadian thinker.

The issue of reciprocity in the 1911 election is analyzed in L.E. Ellis, *Reciprocity, 1911: A Study in Canadian–American Relations* (Toronto: The Ryerson Press, 1939).

URBAN AND INDUSTRIAL CANADA

TIME LINE

1869 – The beginning of the T. Eaton Company

1872 – Trade Union Act passed

1873 – Beginning of an economic recession

1883 – Founding of the Trades and Labor Congress of Canada (TLC)

1889 – Royal Commission on the Relations of Labour and Capital issues report

1894 – Labour Day established as a national holiday

1908 – Henry Ford introduces the Model T

1917 – Order of Sleeping Car Porters, the first African-Canadian railway union in North America, formed

By the turn of the century, a number of factors — worldwide prosperity, the success of the national policy, better world prices for raw materials, a decline in freight rates, and a new attitude toward business — combined to enable Canada to undergo its industrial revolution. Not all regions experienced uniform and sustained economic growth. The Maritimes languished, and the West developed as a great agricultural area, while central Canada became the heartland of industrial growth. Nor did all classes benefit equally. The upper- and middle-classes benefited at the expense of the poorer class. But overall, Canada entered an age of general prosperity through industrialization and resource extraction.

Canada's Economic Expansion

By the turn of the century, the national policy finally worked as intended. Growth in the primary industries increased the demand for secondary industry. The CPR and the two new transcontinental railways — the Canadian Northern and Grand Trunk Pacific/National Transcontinental — brought hundreds of thousands of immigrants westward and took away to market the West's natural resources. Equally, a growing rural population in the West required eastern manufactured goods, from agricultural implements to common household items. Stimulated by additional foreign investment, industry and manufacturing expanded to meet the increased demand for consumer goods. This meant jobs for workers. Service industries, as well as governments (national, provincial, and municipal), also became major employers. Indeed, by 1921 as many people worked in service industries as in the primary sector.

Canada became an attractive country for investment. The federal government provided financial assistance to private companies. The governments of Quebec and especially Ontario offered bonuses, subsidies, and guarantees to industrialists to locate new plants within their borders. Banks provided another source of internal revenue. The three largest — the Bank of Montreal, the Royal Bank (also with its headquarters in Montreal), and the Toronto-based Bank of Commerce — centralized their operations, invested in new industries, and provided capital for entrepreneurs. Foreign investment increased as well. British financiers invested chiefly in the form of indirect portfolio investments (loans in the form of bonds). In contrast, American investors preferred ownership to indirect investment through the establishment of branch plants.

	Canada's Population (in Thousands), 1861–1921				
Year	Natural Increase*	Immigration	Emigration	Net Migration	Population
1861					3230
1861–71	610	260	410	−150	3689
1871–81	690	350	404	−54	4325
1881–91	654	680	826	−146	4833
1891–01	668	250	380	−130	5371
1901–11	1025	1550	740	810	7207
1911–21	1270	1400	1089	311	8788

* Natural increase is the number of births minus the number of deaths.

Source: From *Canada: Our Century, Our Story: Ontario Edition*, Student text by Fielding/Evans. © 2001. Reprinted with permission of Nelson, a division of Thomson Learning: www.thomsonrights.com. Fax 800-730-2215.

Large corporations emerged. In 1902, a handful of consolidated companies existed; by 1912, there were nearly 60. The most noteworthy included: Dominion Canner Limited, which in 1910 amalgamated 34 smaller canning factories; Canada Cement, a consolidation of eleven cement companies in 1909; and Stelco (the Steel Company of Canada), formed in 1910 out of several small Ontario and Quebec iron and steel mills.

ROLE OF GOVERNMENT IN THE ECONOMY

Ottawa did nothing to regulate the monopolies, apart from passing the Combines Investigation Act of 1910. The Act allowed government to investigate monopoly price-fixing, but during its nine-year life span, the investigation board dealt with only one case. As well, corporations took advantage of the division of powers between the federal, provincial, and municipal governments over regulations to play one government off against the other.

Limited state involvement in the economy did occur, however. In the case of Ontario Hydro, when it seemed likely that a small, privileged business group alone might harness the tremendous energy power of Niagara Falls, business interests rallied behind Adam Beck, a manufacturer of cigar boxes and the Conservative member for London in the Ontario legislature, to urge the Ontario government to create a Crown corporation of the hydro-electric power industry. Under Beck, the Hydro-Electric Power Commission of Ontario became the largest publicly owned power authority in the world.

A NEW ATTITUDE TOWARD BUSINESS

The new economy necessitated a new managerial class and a skilled industrial labour force. In many ways, schools became training grounds for the workplace. In factory-like institutions, teachers taught young people the values of punctuality, obedience, thrift, and self-discipline — values essential for an industrial society. As well, girls could now study domestic science, and boys either manual training or how to prepare for business.

In Canada's "gilded age," Canadians honoured business successes. In a poll taken in 1908 by the *Canadian Courier*, a major newspaper, nine out of ten of those named "Canada's Top Ten Biggest Men" were captains of industry or railway magnates. The philosophy of Social Darwinism prevailed: survival belonged to the fittest, the successful believed. Their wealth proved their virtue. Many young English-speaking Canadians accepted the theory of the popular American writer Horatio Alger that anyone could rise from rags to riches through hard work, thrift, and self-discipline.

English-speaking Canadians had numerous role models for success: Herbert Holt, the billion-dollar recluse who founded the Montreal Light, Heat and Power Company in 1902 and became president of the Royal Bank; Henry Pellatt, active in the formation of Canadian General Electric and owner of Toronto's Casa Loma, one of the most palatial residences in North America; Joseph W. Flavelle, president of the William Davies Meat Packaging Plant in Toronto and chair of the Bank of Commerce and the National Trust Company; Francis H. Clergue, founder of the Algoma Steel Company of Sault Ste. Marie, Ontario; Patrick Burns, owner of the Burns Meat Packing Company of Calgary; and Max Aitken (later Lord Beaverbrook), a millionaire by the age of 30, who used his Royal Securities Corporation as an investment bank to fund his many mergers.

Few Canadian merchants eclipsed the success of Timothy Eaton, who opened his Toronto dry-goods store at the corner of Yonge and Queen Street in 1869. He introduced two new revolutionary practices to Canadian merchandising. First, he accepted cash only. Second, he promised "money refunded if goods not satisfactory." Eaton also knew the value of advertising and took out full-page ads in the Toronto newspapers. By 1882, his business had grown to such an extent that he transformed his operation into a department store that had three floors, 35 departments, electric lights (the first in a Canadian store), the first elevator, and the first store restaurant-café. By the time of his death in 1907 at age 72, Timothy Eaton employed over 9000 people. His "empire" extended across the country and the world.

Canadian entrepreneurs and other corporate leaders relied on a new, skilled managerial class to run the complex, day-to-day operations of their expanded business: increased production data, costs, personnel, and internal communications. These managers were often trained in "scientific management," a term coined by the American Frederick W. Taylor. "Scientific managers" used workers to complete simple and routine jobs at a proficient speed for a minimum wage. Success was judged only in terms of efficiency. Beneath this managerial class and closely supervised by it came the clerical workers who carried out the daily routine office jobs. Increasingly, women performed the mechanized and highly specialized jobs, but under the supervision of male managerial clerks.

Community Portrait

The T. Eaton Company: A Community Store

Timothy Eaton's ability to create Canada's most successful department store by the early twentieth century was due to a variety of factors, but clearly one of the most important was his ability to create a sense of community among his employees. They proudly identified themselves as "Eatonians," an identity that not only linked them to Timothy Eaton and his family but also to a community of fellow workers who had one thing in common: they were employees — or what Eaton preferred to call "associates" — of the T. Eaton Company.

"The Governor," as he became known, cultivated a close personal relationship with his staff, his "loyal subjects," that engendered respect, co-operation, and enthusiasm on their part. Stories became legendary of his kindness and generosity to loyal workers who experienced financial difficulties. Employees absent from work for extended periods of time due to illness continued to receive their pay, often along with

an order of coal to keep them warm if the illness occurred in the winter months.

When his Toronto store at the corner of Queen and Yonge became too large for him to supervise his staff by himself, and when other stores opened across the country, Eaton hired managers. He handpicked and trained them himself to ensure that they had the qualities to cultivate a sense of community among employees. "The Governor" personally held meetings in his store at which employees could air grievances and suggest ways to improve good relations (and thus increase sales). To cultivate the sense of community, Eaton provided his "associates" with additional benefits such as a 10 percent discount on merchandise, low-interest rate loans to those wishing to buy a home, a welfare department, a pension and life-insurance plan, and deposit accounts with generous interest rates.

Timothy Eaton cultivated the same strong sense of community among his customers, many of whom also considered themselves "Eatonians." As one store brochure stated: "The Eaton Spirit is the combined faith and enthusiastic loyalty we have for the store and for our fellow employees." With the beginning of the Eaton's catalogue in 1884, the "wider community" of Eatonians stretched across the country. During World War I, the catalogue even cultivated a sense of community among Canadian soldiers on the front. Among soldiers, the catalogue became known as "The Wish Book" since soldiers ordered items that they wished to own, such as a wristwatch—and that Eaton's often provided at no cost—or dreamed of having when they returned home.

When Eaton died on January 31, 1907, several thousand of his employees followed the funeral entourage from Timothy Eaton Methodist Church to the Mount Pleasant Cemetery. In 1919, on the occasion of the fiftieth anniversary of the founding of the T. Eaton store, company employees presented a life-size bronze statue of Timothy Eaton for the main store as a gift to the Eaton family. A copy of the statue was also given to the main Western Canadian store in Winnipeg. From that day on, passers-by would rub the toe of the left shoe to the point of making it shiny, hoping that Eaton's good fortune might rub off on them. The T. Eaton Company remained in operation until 1999 when it filed for bankruptcy. A number of reasons account for its demise, but clearly one was the failure of the company to continue to engender the sense of community loyalty that its founder had so successfully cultivated.

Photo of a woman touching the boot of the statue of Timothy Eaton in the Winnipeg downtown Eaton's store. People rubbed the boot for good luck.

Winnipeg Free Press, October 23, 2002, p. A5.

Further Readings:

Joy L. Santink, *Timothy Eaton and the Rise of His Department* Store (Toronto: University of Toronto Press, 1990).

Rod McQueen, *The Eatons: The Rise and Fall of Canada's Royal Family*, rev. ed. (Toronto: Stoddart, 1999).

Patricia Phenix, *Eatonians: The Story of the Family Behind the Family* (Toronto: McClelland and Stewart, 2002).

ECONOMIC DEVELOPMENT IN THE EAST AND WEST

In the Maritimes, the resource-based economy lost some of its momentum. The West Indies sugar trade fell dramatically in the 1870s, resulting in a decline in trade between Nova Scotia and the West Indies. In the same decade, Britain's demand for Maritime lumber and wooden ships fell, seriously weakening Nova Scotia's and New Brunswick's economies. An industrial economy did emerge, based largely on the Cape Breton coal fields. In fact, at one point in the early 1880s, thanks in large part to the Intercolonial Railway, the National Policy of tariff protection, and a vigorous iron and steel industry, Nova Scotia's industrial growth on a per capita basis actually outstripped that of Ontario and Quebec.

In the long run, however, the Maritimes' industrial expansion faltered. Some historians have pointed out that the region lacked resources as extensive or diverse as, for example, Ontario's. As well, distance from the large markets of central Canada and the small regional population in Atlantic Canada combined to create a significant obstacle to expansion for factories in the region. Furthermore, Maritime investors, like their Canadian counterparts elsewhere, saw western and central Canadian development as potentially more lucrative. As a result, Maritime cities grew at a slower rate than those elsewhere across the country. Many of them also became dependants of Montreal and, to a lesser extent, of Toronto.

GROWTH IN THE WEST

British Columbia's economy shifted from its Pacific orientation (southward to California) toward central Canada, thanks to the completion of the CPR. The provincial economy remained still predominantly resource-based: mining, forestry, fisheries, and agriculture. Mining speculation ran at a fever pitch by the turn of the century. Extraction of lode gold and silver began in the Slocan and Boundary districts in the 1890s, but copper, lead, and zinc superceded precious metals after 1900. Coal mining, especially in and around Nanaimo on Vancouver Island, also contributed to the province's economy. Forestry outdistanced mining in terms of both wealth and employment. Logging increased by an astonishing 400 percent between 1900 and 1910. Fisheries, especially the salmon fisheries, expanded and consolidated in a highly competitive business. British Columbia Packers Association emerged as the most powerful salmon packing company after 1902, and the small port of Stevetson became known as "the sockeye capital of the world."

Agriculture was slow to get established in British Columbia, but by World War I it ranked second to forestry in terms of output. Fruit farming was the most commercially viable, especially after the introduction of refrigerated rail cars at the turn of the century, since much of the fruit was exported. Manufacturing grew in the late nineteenth century, contributing 5 percent of the country's output by 1890. Still, the province's distance from the centre of the industrial development in central Canada, combined with the high freight rates and the small regional market, prevented the province from becoming a substantial and ongoing secondary-manufacturing base. Rather, British Columbia, like the Maritimes, became another hinterland region to central Canada.

The two urban centres of Victoria and Vancouver vied for dominance in West Coast trade. Vancouver won out by 1914 because of the excellent dock and terminal facilities on Burrard Inlet and its role as the western terminus of the CPR. The completion of the Panama Canal in 1914 enabled Vancouver to surpass Winnipeg as Canada's major western city, by enabling prairie farmers to ship their wheat to European markets via the Pacific.

On the Prairies, wheat was king. Hardier strains of wheat and the world demand for wheat after 1896 opened up areas on the northern fringe and in the arid Palliser Triangle to production, thus increasing substantially both the wheat lands and yields. In terms of yields, that amounted to a record 208 million bushels in 1911. Such growth justified and necessitated new rail lines, especially to service the new areas of settlement. But the Prairies faced the same problem that British Columbia and the Maritimes faced: too small a regional market to foster substantial secondary manufacturing. Thus, as intended by the National Policy, the Prairies became subservient to central Canada in terms of economic growth and dominance.

Urbanization occurred at a rapid rate on the Prairies. In 1870, no urban centres existed in the region; by 1911, there were seventeen incorporated cities and 150 incorporated towns. Five dominant cities emerged by servicing surrounding agricultural hinterlands: Winnipeg, Saskatoon, Regina, Edmonton, and Calgary.

Winnipeg's location as the "gateway to the West" with rail links to the East made the entire prairie west its hinterland. Thanks to this strategic location, it became the third-largest manufacturing city in pre–World War I Canada. Nicknamed the "Hub City," it stood at the junction of three transcontinental railways. The city employed thousands in its rail yards, the largest in the world by 1904, with as many as 1800 freight cars passing through in a single day. But Toronto and Montreal dominated even Winnipeg. Ultimately, all western rail lines led to central Canada.

INDUSTRIALIZATION IN CENTRAL CANADA

At the turn of the century, industrialization occurred largely in Ontario and Quebec. Ontario's growth initially was based on small-scale consumer goods industries in a series of towns and cities throughout southern Ontario that depended chiefly on coal as a source of energy and on iron production. In both cases, Ontario benefited from the province's proximity to the Pennsylvania coal fields and the Minnesota iron ranges, although Ontario created its own iron and steel companies as well. Also, a network of rail lines crisscrossed Ontario, linking the numerous towns and cities to the rural countryside and to other urban centres. These centres produced such goods as engines, farm implements, stoves, furniture, and canned goods. Hamilton, predominantly a steel-producing town, also became the home of large rail-car shops. But most of Ontario's largest head offices, financial institutions, factories, and warehouses were located in Toronto.

In Quebec, much of the new industry was small-scale and labour-intensive: shoes, textiles, lumber, and foodstuffs (flour, sugar, dairy products). These industries were also concentrated mainly in two cities: Montreal and Quebec City. Montreal had the advantage over Quebec City, the latter becoming more isolated from the major canals and rail networks without a bridge over the St. Lawrence. Montreal also had the majority of financial institutions to provide capital for businesses in the city.

Beginning in 1911, a second industrial revolution occurred when hydro-electric power replaced steam as the main source of industrial energy. Now pulp and paper, and later minerals, became the new resource products. Initially, the pulp produced by Canadian-based companies went for processing in the United States. But at the turn of the century, the Quebec government, at the urging of Quebec nationalists, placed an embargo on exports of pulp from Crown lands. Subsequently, Quebec pulp mills began producing their own newsprint for export. By 1914, Quebec had become a leading industrial province. More than two-thirds of its population worked in non-agricultural activities, and roughly one-half of its population lived in urban centres.

THE UNIQUENESS OF QUEBEC'S INDUSTRIAL DEVELOPMENT

For French Canadians, however, Quebec's industrialization had a unique and disturbing aspect: they had almost no control over it. In 1910, of Canada's entrepreneurs, only one out of 40 was French speaking. French Canadians were the labourers, not the owners of industry.

An immigrant woman and her children waiting on a curb in front of the CPR Station in Winnipeg, around 1909. Almost everyone who came west came through this station, built in 1904. In 1992 the Aboriginal Centre of Winnipeg Inc. bought the building. The refurbished Aboriginal Centre is now a modern office space.

The United Church Archives, Toronto/93.049P/3111N.

French-Canadian theorists began to question why. Was this imbalance due to French Canadians' limited pool of capital? Perhaps in part, but French-speaking Canadians in the Dominion faced a larger obstacle: the language of business was English. Education might also have been a factor. The Roman Catholic church tended to emphasize a humanistic education, particularly at the classical college level, over science and commerce. The Quebec government tried to correct this imbalance by offering financial support for the establishment of technical schools. In 1907 it created the École des Hautes Études Commerciales (HEC), a university-level business school. Yet, many graduates still faced the need to work in English, at least at the managerial level.

"NEW ONTARIO"

Industrialization advanced fastest and farthest in southern Ontario, especially in the period from 1890 to 1914. One decisive factor was the wealth of timber and minerals in northern Ontario. Suddenly this area — "New Ontario" — ceased to be perceived as an unproductive wasteland of rocks, lakes, and muskeg, and was seen instead in terms of its resource potential. By 1914, the mineral-resource base of northern Ontario had become accessible through rail transport to major urban centres outside the region.

Where Historians Disagree
Industrial Growth in Quebec

Two questions relating to the industrialization of Quebec have led to much discussion. First, why did Quebec lag behind neighbouring Ontario in its industrialization, or did it? Second, why were French Canadians excluded from the control of industry in their province when industrialization finally occurred?

In the early 1950s, Quebec economists Albert Faucher and Maurice Lamontagne argued that Canadian industrialization occurred in two stages, or two "industrial revolutions" — one from 1866 to 1911, the other after 1911. In the first, industrial growth depended chiefly on the ability to produce iron and steel, resources that Quebec had in short supply and that were unavailable nearby. Ontario, by contrast, benefited from its proximity to the Pennsylvania coal fields and the Minnesota iron ranges while also creating its own iron and steel centres. In the second stage, growth depended on the availability of hydro-electric power, which by 1911 had become the new source of industrial energy. Here Quebec was well blessed, but by this time Ontario had already developed an industrial infrastructure, and Quebec could not catch up.[1]

Other economic historians have questioned Faucher and Lamontagne's identification of the "industrial takeoff" period in Quebec. John Dales contends that hydro-electricity experienced its greatest growth — 310 percent — in the first decade of the twentieth century.[2] André Raynauld argues that in some decades, such as the period 1910–20, Ontario accelerated faster than Quebec, but that over the extended period 1870–1957, the two provincial economies grew at almost parallel rates, each one taking its turn as the leader in industrial growth. Thus, overall, Quebec did not lag behind.[3]

Historians H.V. Nelles and C. Armstrong agree. They argue that by 1920, both Ontario and Quebec produced the same quantity of hydro-electric power. But the two provinces differed in the nature of control of this key energy source. In Ontario it was publicly owned through Ontario Hydro, thus making it available to a larger industrial base, whereas in Quebec two very large privately owned companies controlled profits and alone benefited.[4]

Economic historian John Isbister looks to the differing agricultural economies of the two provinces for his explanation. Quebec produced insufficient surplus food to serve its urban centres. Agriculture was in the province "a subsistence sector, economically isolated, not integrated into the wider market system," unlike in Ontario. Cultural explanations, according to Isbister, explain the difference: Quebec had "a different attitude toward the farming life. The Quebec habitant was a peasant, poor and self-sufficient, not a man of business."[5] Only in the twentieth century would this attitude change, and by then Ontario farmers had surged ahead.

More recently, Quebec historians Paul-André Linteau, René Durocher, and Jean-Claude Robert have questioned whether Quebec industrialized at a slower pace than Ontario even at the turn of the century. They argue that by dwelling on the resource-oriented industries, historians and economists have overlooked the sustained growth in manufacturing in Quebec at the turn of the century, which shows the period to be one of industrial takeoff.[6]

The second question — why French-speaking Quebeckers failed to become the leaders of industry in their own province —

has also proven to be contentious. Historians Maurice Séguin and Michel Brunet blame the Conquest of 1759–60 for the disadvantage. They contend that New France had a dynamic business class, but that its members were forced to return to France after the conquest because of poor business opportunities under the British conquerors. With the departure of the French bourgeoisie, British interests stepped in, causing French Canadians to lose their economic role from that point onward.[7]

Historian Fernand Ouellet has challenged this interpretation.[8] He denies the existence of a viable business class in New France. Rather the French-Canadians' non-progressive business mentality led to British commercial superiority. In any event, both sides agree that anglophone business interests already controlled the economy of Quebec in the nineteenth century, and continued to do so.

Current debate has revolved around the question of how this small Anglo minority was able to maintain its favoured position. Some historians blame the church-dominated educational system, with its emphasis on a classical education rather than on training in science and commerce, for the failure of French-speaking Canadians to succeed in business. But recent research does not entirely bear this out. Some science and commerce courses were in fact part of the school curriculum in Quebec.[9] Historians Craig Brown and Ramsay Cook argue that where the church and the schools erred was in putting nationalism ahead of practical economic considerations: "Education ... had a moral and patriotic function, to which practical training for economic life was secondary."[10] Historians Paul-André Linteau, René Durocher, and Jean-Claude Robert explain the gap in industrial leadership of French-Canadian businesspeople in terms of limited technological know-how. Unlike English-speaking immigrants in Quebec, whose contact with their place of origin provided them with important business links and an international perspective, French Canadians lacked an "information network."[11] Their contacts and know-how never extended beyond the confines of Quebec.

[1] Albert Faucher and Maurice Lamontagne, "History of Industrial Development," in Marcel Rioux and Yves Martin, eds., *French-Canadian Society: Volume 1* (Toronto: McClelland and Stewart, 1964), pp. 257–270.

[2] John Dales, *Hydroelectricity and Industrial Development in Quebec, 1898–1940* (Cambridge, MA: Harvard University Press, 1957).

[3] André Raynauld, *Croissance et structure économique de la Province de Québec* (Quebec: Ministère de l'industrie et du commerce, 1961).

[4] H.V. Nelles and C. Armstrong, "Contrasting Development of the Hydro-Electric Industry in the Montreal and Toronto Regions, 1900–1930," in Douglas McCalla, ed., *The Development of Canadian Capitalism: Essays in Business History* (Toronto: Copp Clark Pitman, 1990), pp. 167–190.

[5] John Isbister, "Agriculture, Balanced Growth, and Social Change in Central Canada Since 1850: An Interpretation," in Douglas McCalla, ed., *Perspectives on Canadian Economic History* (Toronto: Copp Clark Pitman, 1987), p. 67.

[6] Paul-André Linteau, René Durocher, and Jean-Claude Robert, *Quebec: A History 1867–1929* (Toronto: James Lorimer, 1983).

[7] Maurice Séguin, "The Conquest and French-Canadian Economic Life," translated from "La Conquête et la vie économique des Canadiens," *Action nationale*, 28 (1947): 308–26, in Dale Miquelon, ed., *Society and Conquest: The Debate on the Bourgeoisie and Social Change in French Canada, 1700–1850* (Toronto: Copp Clark Publishing, 1977), pp. 67–80; and Michel Brunet, "The British Conquest and the Decline of the French-Canadian Bourgeoisie," translated from "La Conquête anglaise et la déchéance de la bourgeoisie canadienne," in *La Présence anglaise et les Canadiens* (Montreal: Beauchemin, 1958), pp. 49–109; also in Miquelon, *Society and Conquest*, pp. 143–61.

[8] See the conclusion of Fernand Ouellet's *Histoire économique et sociale du Québec 1760–1850* (Montreal: Fides, 1966), pp. 539–596. This work is available in translation, *Economic and Social History of Quebec 1760–1850* (Toronto: Gage, 1980), pp. 547–609.

[9] W.J. Ryan, *The Clergy and Economic Growth in Quebec, 1896–1914* (Quebec: Presses de l'Université Laval, 1966).

[10] R.C. Brown and R. Cook, *Canada, 1896–1921: A Nation Transformed* (Toronto: McClelland and Stewart, 1974), p. 132.

[11] Linteau, Durocher, and Robert, *Quebec: A History, 1867–1929*, p. 404.

Northern mining required sophisticated and expensive equipment and large consolidated companies. In 1902, the Canadian Copper Company at Sudbury amalgamated with several smaller American companies to form the International Nickel Company of Canada (Inco). In the Porcupine district, three large companies — Hollinger (Canadian-owned), Dome (American-owned), and McIntyre (Canadian-owned after 1915) — soon controlled 90 percent of the gold production. In Sault Ste. Marie, F.H. Clergue, an American-born entrepreneur, built an industrial empire, the Consolidated Lake Superior Company, by using largely American capital.

A host of mining towns arose at the turn of the century. Some, such as Golden City, Elk Lake, and South Porcupine, were little more than camps made up of shacks and log cabins; others became company towns, built and owned by the town's only employer. Only a few, such as Sudbury and Timmins, became main service or distribution centres for the entire region. Over time, all of these northern Ontario mining communities depended on the capricious rise and fall of world metal prices. In time they also came under the dominance of Toronto, the provincial capital, their main supply base, the focus of their rail transport, and the source of money for many of the mining and forestry companies.

THE IMPACT OF INDUSTRIALIZATION

IMPACT ON RURAL SOCIETY

 The introduction of labour-saving machines — hay mowers, reapers, threshers, and tractors — enabled a farmer to bring more land under cultivation, and by 1900, to produce a bushel of wheat in one-hundredth of the time required only 30 years earlier. But a farmer now required greater revenue from the farm to pay for the expensive equipment he used. Large-scale farms became common. Dairy and fruit farming also became agribusiness.

The nature of work changed too. It became more routine and specialized. Farmers also began to take over what had previously been considered women's work. Large-scale dairy farms produced the milk to supply cheese factories that, by 1901, produced 40 percent of Canadian cheese. As was the case with cheese, the production of butter and the canning of fruit, traditionally women's work, now occurred in factories instead of on farms. Mechanization also reduced the number of older children needed to work the farm. This encouraged some youth to seek jobs or at least to work seasonally in the cities. Better-paying jobs and better working conditions also lured the younger generation from the land. Rural depopulation became a concern.

IMPACT ON NATIVE PEOPLE

On the West Coast, salmon processing came under the control of the British Columbia Packers Association after 1902. The company replaced Aboriginal people with Japanese as fishers, boat builders, and processors, since the latter would work for lower wages, could be relied on for year-round fishing, and were less prone to strike. Asians also replaced Native people in the canneries, although both groups were subordinate to Euro-Canadians as managers. The introduction of modern assembly line and processing equipment eliminated jobs in general in fish-processing plants.

Native peoples were also adversely affected by commercialization in the northern fur trade. The influx of non-Native hunters and trappers led to increased competition, and a rapid decline in furs. The federal and provincial governments introduced conservation methods and laws to provide protection for wildlife, but they failed to appreciate the Aboriginal peoples' commercial, ceremonial, and subsistence needs and treaty rights in those areas under treaty.

URBANIZATION

Industrial growth required factories, large banks, commercial institutions, and transportation services in large urban centres. During the period from 1890 to 1920, Montreal and Toronto, the two largest and most advanced industrial cities, almost tripled their population, each surpassing the half-million mark. But the most rapid urban growth in this time period occurred in the West. Winnipeg's population increased sevenfold; Vancouver's, twelvefold (growing at a rate of 1000 new residents per month in the peak year of 1910); and Calgary's, sixteenfold. From 1901 to 1911, the Canadian urban population increased 63 percent. In 1901, Canada had 58 urban centres with a population greater than 5000; by 1911, that number had grown to 90.

Canadian urban centres grew to prominence by becoming heartlands that controlled their surrounding hinterlands, providing the rural inhabitants with manufactured goods and services. Only two Canadian cities had heartlands that extended across the country: Montreal and Toronto.

LIFE IN THE INDUSTRIAL CITY

As a result of industrialization, cities became more socially stratified, with working-class districts physically separated from middle- and upper-class areas. The introduction of the electric streetcar and the automobile enabled the middle and upper classes to leave the inner city for suburban districts away from downtown congestion and pollution. The city centres became ghettoized and undesirable places to live. The Commission of Conservation, established by the federal government in 1909, noted in its *Annual Report* in 1914: "Industrial smoke disfigures buildings, impairs the health of the population, renders the city filthy, destroys any beauty with which it may naturally be endowed and tends, therefore, to make it a squalid and undesirable place of residence, and this at a time when economic influences are forcing into cities an ever increasing proportion of our population."

In Montreal and Toronto, most working-class people rented rooms in either boarding or tenement houses — old wooden cottages or two-storey buildings with little or no yard area. Rent could be as high as $10 or $12 a month for basement rooms, roughly 25 percent of an unskilled worker's wages. Few families had the luxury of owning their own houses, since house prices remained well beyond the means of the ordinary worker. In Montreal, an average working-class family of five typically lived in a one-or-two-room flat: damp, unventilated, inadequately lighted, and poorly heated. Overcrowding remained a constant problem. In Toronto, some families lived in hastily constructed shacks, in backyard tents, or even on the street. In summer, a stench rose from the cesspools and outdoor privies.

Wife beating and the sexual abuse of children were common among all classes. Very often such violence in working-class districts was associated with drinking, unemployment, and destitution. Wives had little legal recourse because male-dominated courts rarely challenged the husband's proprietary right over his wife's person and her sexuality. If anything, judges questioned the woman's character. Because of high legal costs, divorce also remained out of the question for most abused women. Children, particularly those of the working class, enjoyed fewer rights and privileges than did women at the turn of the century. They had to assume family responsibilities at an early age, and to grow up and mature quickly.

Education was at a premium. In Montreal, a maximum grade three education was common for working-class children. They had to enter the work force as soon as possible (age 11 or 12 being the norm) to supplement the family income. The census of 1871 reveals that 25 percent of boys and 10 percent of girls between the ages of 11 and 15 held jobs outside the home; these statistics did not include boys hired to do odd jobs or girls working as domestics. Ontario and

Untreated waste from Toronto, and virtually every other municipality in the Great Lakes area, in both Canada and the United States, polluted the region's water systems.

City of Toronto Archives Fonds 1244, Item 1122A.

Quebec passed Factory Acts prohibiting the hiring of boys under 12 and girls under 14, but they had little impact due to poor enforcement and the difficulty of taking recalcitrant factory owners to court. Those children unfortunate enough to end up in court were more likely to be penalized than protected, and sent to harsh probationary institutions.

Recent research enables us to make some generalizations about those children most likely to work outside the home and those who stayed home. Young daughters were less likely than young sons to be employed outside the home, since girls, by the age of 15 or 16, made only half to two-thirds of the wages paid to boys of the same age for doing a similar job. Also patriarchal attitudes militated against daughters working in factories. As well, girls up to the age of 16 were required at home to help run the household and tend to younger family members. Still, poorer working-class families had to send their daughters out to work because of economic necessity.

Industrialization created harsh working conditions. In times of demand the average labourer spent at least ten to twelve hours a day, six days a week, at work. Factories were poorly ventilated, noisy, and dirty. Factory foremen ran the factory ruthlessly to ensure maximum efficiency. They often fined workers for tardiness or for talking to fellow workers on the job. Industrial accidents and deaths occurred frequently.

Job security did not exist. Victims of industrial accidents had no workers' compensation. Layoffs, especially during the slower winter months, occurred regularly. Even in good times, unemployment was common, a byproduct of the capitalist system. Before the federal government introduced unemployment insurance in 1940, layoffs meant months of subsistence without wages.

The cost of living in urban centres rose continually and outpaced urban wages. The federal Department of Labour issued "typical weekly expenditure" budgets listing those items necessary for a family of five to enjoy a minimum standard of living. Although it allowed for only 0.6 kg of fresh meat per week per person, less than a litre of milk a day for a family of five, and no fresh vegetables or fruit, this minimum was more than the average working-class family could afford. In 1901, the estimated cost of living was $13.38 a week. But, at best, the average male worker could, without layoffs, make $425 a year in 1901, or an average of $8.25 a week. Thus many working-class families needed at least two incomes to survive.

HEALTH

Frequent illness complicated the normal daily problems of living and working. Montreal in particular remained a most unhealthy city in which to live, especially for children. At the turn of the century, approximately one out of every four infants died before the age of one. This was due to impure water, unpasteurized milk, and the limited use of vaccines for smallpox, diphtheria, and tuberculosis.

Society denounced attempts to limit family size. Limitation of family size, especially among those of British stock, was considered "race suicide." Section 179 of the Criminal Code of Canada, prepared in 1892, made it a criminal offence and liable to two years' imprisonment for anyone who attempted "to sell, advertise, publish an advertisement of or have for sale or disposal any medicine, drug or article intended or represented as a means of preventing conception or causing abortion." Despite such threats, many married women sought birth-control information.

WORKING IN THE NEW INDUSTRIAL ECONOMY

WOMEN IN THE WORKPLACE

At the turn of the century, women made up about one-seventh of the paid work force. Usually they worked outside the home only between the ages of 14, the youngest age permissible for girls to work after 1885, and 24, the normal marrying age. The routine of housework — rearing children, cleaning, cooking, washing, mending, and shopping — meant full and exhausting days in an era before labour-saving devices. Marriage, motherhood, and domesticity remained intertwined in the minds of most women, no matter to which class they belonged. The home was considered women's "proper sphere." Men dominated the "public sphere." Nevertheless, many women supplemented the family income by taking in boarders, doing part-time sewing, or doing laundry.

The most economically pressed mothers had no choice but to work outside the home in female-related jobs, such as in textile factories, as waitresses, or as domestics. Women without familial support had to find work. In these cases, they had to rely on friends, neighbours, relatives, or on working-class associations to assist with children. Sometimes immigrant women could count on the support of ethnic groups to provide mutual aid and, occasionally, employment agencies. Increasingly, however, there arose a segment of working women who were single, non-immigrant girls, popularly known as "working girls," who performed non-domestic waged work outside the home. Being single, young, independent and alone, they became the concern of moral reformers who saw them as a threat to the ideal Canadian society as made up of morally upright, married, and motherly women.

Middle-class women depended on domestic help at the turn of the century. Families were larger then, homes harder to keep clean, and food preparation much more time-consuming. Domestics tended to be young girls from rural areas or immigrant women. Indeed, the demand for domestic servants was so great that they were considered "preferred" immigrants. In 1891, 40 percent of all women working outside the home were employed as domestics.

This store at the turn of the century shows the diversity of items available to those who had money to purchase them, including Jello, which had just come on the market in 1897.

Provincial Archives of New Brunswick/P18-163.

Amherst, Nova Scotia Telephone Exchange, around 1909. Telephone operators belonged to the elite of female clerical workers. (Cumberland County Historical Society.)

Cumberland County Museum, 184-78-2.

Women preferred factory work to domestic service because of higher wages and shorter hours. Still, in 1900, most women in factories worked up to 60 hours a week. Textile and shoe factories hired women because they could pay them lower wages (approximately half of what men earned) and because they were better workers for the type of work to be done.

Even more preferable for women were office jobs away from the noise and pressure of the factory. By the turn of the century, women were employed in most of the clerical jobs. Conventional wisdom held that women's "natural" feminine characteristics — sympathy, adaptability, courtesy, and even nimble fingers — made them particularly suitable for clerical work. Women also worked as department-store clerks or telephone operators, two of the most "feminized" occupations at the turn of the century.

After domestic, factory, and office work, teaching was the most important female occupation. Teaching was considered an acceptable occupation for women, and one that allowed for the possibility of some upward social mobility, although it provided little financial security. Women received low salaries and had little chance of advancing to become department heads or principals.

A small number of women worked as nurses. Many gravitated towards the Victorian Order of Nurses (VON), formed in 1897, as a model public-health nursing service. Only a handful of women entered Canadian medical schools. For one thing, few hospitals would provide them with hospital privileges after graduation. Unable to attract enough patients, a number of Canada's early female doctors became medical missionaries overseas instead. In all the professions that women entered in small numbers at the turn of the century, they experienced lower pay than men, lack of control over their work, and pressure to quit once they married.

CHARITABLE AND SOCIAL INSTITUTIONS FOR THE WORKING CLASS

At the turn of the century, churches and private philanthropic organizations administered limited charitable help. Since generally society held that, with the exception of the handicapped and the aged, individuals alone remained responsible for their plight, charities provided only temporary relief as a stop-gap measure – usually a meal of soup, bread, and tea, and a bath and a bed. Skilled workers looked to fraternal organizations – lodges such as the Orange Lodge, the Masons, the Oddfellows, and the Independent Order of Foresters – for financial and emotional support. Some sporting clubs gave their male members a sense of importance and self-worth and a feeling of camaraderie. Females were forbidden to belong to these fraternal or sporting clubs, but in some instances, such as the Oddfellows, women could belong to a parallel organization, such as the Rebekahs. Some associations had mutual-aid plans to care for sick members and to assist widows and orphans in the event of a member's death. They also gave workers a means to express publicly and collectively their discontent with industrial capitalism by supporting parades through the streets of towns and cities to show both solidarity and defiance.

UNIONS

Between 1850 and 1890, labour unions took root in Canada. At first, most unions were local, dispersed across the country, and specialized. Initially, the government refused to grant them legal recognition or to accept workers' right to collective bargaining. But in 1872, Macdonald's Conservative government enacted the Trade Union Act, which recognized the right of unions to exist and to organize without fear of prosecution as illegal associations, so long as they registered with the government. However, at the same time, the Criminal Law Amendment Act imposed severe penalties, including a prison sentence, for most forms of picketing and union pressure.

Knights of Labor procession, King Street, Hamilton, 1885. Parades were an expression of workers' solidarity and a means to achieve public recognition.

W. Farmer/National Archives of Canada/PA-103086.

In the late nineteenth century, only a minority of Canadian workers belonged to unions, and those who did affiliated with a variety of groups, among which three stand out: the Knights of Labor, the Provincial Workmen's Association, and the American Federation of Labor.

The Knights of Labor, an American organization founded in 1869, enjoyed its greatest success among workers in Ontario and Quebec, although it had branches across the country. The Knights developed a working-class consciousness through the organization of workers by industry rather than by craft. The organization favoured arbitration over strikes, an eight-hour day, an end to child labour, the passage of health and safety legislation, and equal pay for equal work. The Knights took in semi-skilled and unskilled workers as well as women and blacks, although not Asians.

Most unions refused to support women, arguing that by improving women's wages they encouraged women to remain at work, where they took jobs away from men. In some industries, women formed their own unions. In the garment industry, for example, a number of women joined locals of the International Ladies' Garment Workers Union. Their success in this particular industry might have come partially from the support of male trade unionists who needed their female counterparts to mount effective strikes. Still, unionized women workers remained more the exception than the rule.

Most unions also refused to support visible minorities such as blacks and Asians, seeing them as cheap labour that would undermine unionization. Since these minorities ended up working only part-time or seasonal jobs, it was difficult for them to form their own unions. One exception was the occupation of railroad employees. In 1917, porters formed the Order of Sleeping Car Porters—the first African-Canadian railway union in North America. Although the

Canadian Brotherhood of Railway Employees initially refused to accept the union, it did so in 1919, making it the first craft union to lift racial restrictions on memberships.

The Provincial Workmen's Association, founded in 1879 by the coal miners of Springfield, Nova Scotia, became the Maritime equivalent of the Knights of Labor, and Canada's first industrial union. In 1909, however, the Scottish immigrant James Bryson McLachlan helped introduce to Cape Breton a more militant union, a branch of the American-based United Mine Workers of America. Ten years later, the miners at last gained the eight-hour day and made important gains in their standard of living.

 In Newfoundland, William Ford Coaker, a local fisher, founded the Fishermen's Protective Union (FPU) in 1908 to protect fishers from the vagaries of curing weather, fish migration, and volatile markets. Its motto was "To each his own," believing fishers did not enjoy the benefits of their own labour nor the right to a decent living. Coaker advocated a "national plan" that consisted of free and compulsory education, a night-school system, non-denominational education in small outposts, outpost hospitals, and universal old-age pensions. The FPU turned to politics to attempt to achieve its objectives, and won eight seats in the Newfoundland Legislature in the 1913 election. But even here, it faced an uphill battle.

The Trades and Labor Congress of Canada (TLC), the central labour organization founded in 1883, established strong ties with the American Federation of Labor (AFL), a strictly craft-union organization. The conservative leadership of the AFL believed that the primary purpose of unions should be simply to improve the material benefits of its workers — better wages and hours and safer working conditions — rather than to radically reform the capitalist system.

Unskilled workers looked increasingly to politics or radical unions to achieve their objectives. Some worked to create an independent socialist party, while others supported radical unions, such as the Industrial Workers of the World (IWW), founded in 1905. The "Wobblies," as they became known, attempted to organize all workers, regardless of their trade, skill, or sex, into one large union for the purpose of calling a general strike to bring down the capitalist system. The IWW had little impact in eastern Canada but greater success in western Canada.

In the West, conditions remained poor for western workers. Wages were exceptionally low, inflation high, employment sporadic, especially in the primary industries, and working conditions, especially in the mines and railway camps, atrocious.

In Quebec, the Roman Catholic church formed church-affiliated unions as an alternative to what it considered to be socialist and anti-clerical international unions that undermined the church's position among the working class. The largest was the Confédération des Travailleurs Catholiques du Canada (CTCC), an exclusively Roman Catholic organization founded in 1921, with a priest, as chaplain, effectively in charge of each local.

LIMITATIONS OF UNIONS IN THE PREWAR ERA

In general, unions had limited success prior to World War I. As late as 1911, less than one-tenth of the national work force belonged to unions. Most unskilled workers and virtually all women remained non-unionized. Unions were also divided, and their leaders suspicious of one another. Furthermore, unions had few rights. Employers could still fire union workers at will or demand that workers sign contracts in which they promised not to join a union. As well, employers brought in immigrant labourers on the condition that they work as strike breakers or for extremely low wages. Nevertheless, unions did organize strikes — 1000 disputes were recorded between 1900 and 1911. Many of them erupted into physical violence, with the government calling out the militia to end them. This happened on more than 30 occasions before 1914. Most strikes ended without workers gaining any significant concessions.

Governments clearly favoured business interests over workers. The federal Conservative government did, however, establish the Royal Commission on the Relations of Labour and Capital, which in its Report in 1889 documented the negative impact of industrialization in Canada. Few reforms resulted from the Report. In 1894, the Conservatives established Labour Day, the first Monday of September, as a national holiday for working people. The Laurier Liberal government created the Department of Labour in 1900 to prevent and settle strikes as well as to enforce a fair wage policy.

Skilled workers tried to gain influence through politics. They set out their own agenda, such as the sixteen-point program of the Trades and Labor Congress passed at its meeting in 1898, in which they demanded free compulsory education, an eight-hour day, a minimum wage, tax reform, public ownership of railways and telegraphs, extension of the franchise, abolition of the Senate, prohibition of prison and contract labour, legislative elimination of child labour, and opposition to Chinese immigration — the Chinese being perceived as a threat to labour's employment opportunities and wages. Then they tried to pressure the two traditional parties to adopt some or all of their recommendations. When this approach failed, they fielded their own labour candidates in federal, provincial, and municipal elections. While a few were elected, most labour politicians had limited success and impact, particularly at the federal and provincial levels. Overall, workers had a weak political voice in the pre–World War I era.

From 1880 to 1914, Canada underwent its industrial revolution as a result of the success of the national policy, large-scale financial investment from within the country and abroad, and a new, more positive attitude towards business. Manufacturing and large-scale industrial production, and accompanying urban growth, meant increased prosperity and an overall higher standard of living. But not all regions of the country, nor all social classes, benefited equally from the economic expansion. The social costs of rapid change were high especially for the urban poor. In times of need, they looked to charitable and social institutions, and ultimately to unions, for assistance. By the early twentieth century the injustices had become so noticeable that they gained public attention, especially among a rising group of middle-class social reformers.

LINKING TO THE PAST

The Substance of Development, 1871–1928
http://www.upei.ca/~rneill/canechist/topic_18.html

A detailed account of Canada's economic development during the period 1871–1928.

British Columbia's Resource Development
http://www.bcarchives.gov.bc/exhibits/timemach/galler09/frames/index.htm

A detailed look at the economic development of British Columbia and its dependence on natural resources. Through description and photographs, this site examines the historical growth of industries such as forestry, mining, and fishing in the province.

A Village in the Lower Ottawa Valley
http://collections.ic.gc.ca/cumberland/index.htm

The Cumberland Heritage Village Museum is a re-creation of a village of the Lower Ottawa Valley during the 1900s. Explore the virtual village to discover how industrialization, mechanization, and the Great Depression affected the people of the Cumberland area.

The Peopling of Canada, 1891–1921
http://www.ucalgary.ca/applied_history/tutor/canada 1891

This site features information on Canadian population and society at the turn of the century, including immigration and migration patterns, settlement of the West, and descriptions of urban rural life.

North of the Colour Line
http://www.historycooperative.org/journals/llt/47/02mathie.html

An article that tells the story of black workers on Canadian railways and their struggle for job security and unionization.

1880s Newfoundland
http://collections.ic.gc.ca/nfld

Photographs of Newfoundland, including scenes from the streets of St. John's, pictures of fishing communities, and rural images.

BIBLIOGRAPHY

Michael Bliss's *Northern Enterprise: Five Centuries of Canadian Business* (Toronto: McClelland & Stewart, 1987) provides a comprehensive history of Canadian business. On economic developments consult Kenneth Norrie and Douglas Owram, *A History of the Canadian Economy*, 3rd ed. (Toronto: Nelson, 2002). Also of importance is Christopher Armstrong and H.V. Nelles, *Monopoly's Moment: The Organization and Regulation of Canadian Utilities, 1830–1930* (Philadelphia: Temple University Press, 1986). On Quebec consult also Paul-André Linteau, René Durocher, and Jean-Claude Robert, *Quebec: A History, 1867–1929* (Toronto: James Lorimer, 1983). Michael Bliss deals with Canadian business's attitudes in *A Living Profit: Studies in the Social History of Canadian Businessmen, 1883–1914* (Toronto: McClelland & Stewart, 1974).

On industrialization in the Maritimes see T.W. Acheson, D. Frank, and J. Frost, *Industrialization and the Underdevelopment in the Maritimes, 1880 to 1930* (Toronto: Garamond Press, 1985); and Kris Inwood, *Farm, Factory and Fortune: New Studies in the Economic History of the Maritime Provinces* (Fredericton: Acadiensis Press, 1993). For Newfoundland, see David Alexander, "Economic Growth in the Atlantic Region, 1880–1940," in E. Seager, L. Fisher, and S. Pierson, comp., *Atlantic Canada and Confederation: Essays in Canadian Political Economy* (Toronto: University of Toronto Press, 1983), pp. 51–78. For studies in English of industrialization in Quebec, consult the endnotes for "Where Historians Disagree: Industrial Growth in Quebec" in this chapter. For Ontario's resource development see H.V. Nelles, *The Politics of Development: Forests, Mines and Hydro-Electric Power in Ontario, 1849–1941* (Toronto: Macmillan, 1970). For a general debate on industrialism in Ontario consult Ian Drummond, Louis P. Cain, and Majorie Cohen, "CHR Dialogue: Ontario's Industrial Revolution," *Canadian Historical Review* 69 (3) (September 1988): 283–314. On British Columbia see Allen Saeger, "The Resource Economy, 1871–1921," in Hugh J.M. Johnston, ed., *The Pacific Province: A History of British Columbia* (Vancouver: Douglas & McIntyre, 1996), pp. 205–52; and Martin Robin, *The Rush for Spoils: The Company Province, 1871–1913* (Toronto: McClelland & Stewart, 1972).

For the impact of industrialization and urbanization and resource developments on the Native peoples in Ontario consult Edward S. Rogers and Donald B. Smith, eds., *Aboriginal Ontario* (Toronto: Dundurn Press, 1994); and for British Columbia, Rolf Knight, *Indians at Work: An Informal History of Native Labour in British Columbia, 1848–1930* (Vancouver: New Star Books, 1996).

On urban trends in Canada, see J.M.S. Careless's booklet *The Rise of Cities in Canada before 1914* (Ottawa: Canadian Historical Association, 1978). For urbanization in the Maritimes see J.M.S. Careless, "Aspects of Metropolitanism in Atlantic Canada," in M. Wade, ed., *Regionalism in the Canadian Community, 1867–1967* (Toronto: University of Toronto Press, 1969), pp. 117–29. On British Columbia see Robert A.J. McDonald, *Making Vancouver: Class, Status, and Social Boundaries, 1863–1913* (Vancouver: University of

British Columbia Press, 1996). On the Prairies consult Paul Voisey, "The Urbanization of the Canadian Prairies, 1871–1916," *Histoire Sociale/Social History* 8 (1975): 77–101; and A.F.J. Artibise, ed., *Town and City: Aspects of Western Canadian Urban Development* (Regina: Canadian Plains Research Center, University of Regina, 1981).

On the dynamics between rural life and urban and industrial growth are: Daniel Samson, ed., *Contested Countryside: Rural Workers and Modern Society in Atlantic Canada, 1800–1950* (Fredericton: Acadiensis Press, 1994); R. W. Sandwell, ed., *Beyond the City Limits: Rural History in British Columbia* (Vancouver: UBC Press, 1999); and Kenneth Michael Sylvester, *The Limits of Rural Capitalism: Family, Culture and Markets in Montcalm, Manitoba, 1870–1940* (Toronto: University of Toronto Press, 2001).

For the impact of industrialization and commercialization on the First Nations see Arthur Ray, *I Have Lived Here Since the World Began* (Toronto: Key Porter, 1996).

Working-class life in the major industrial city of Montreal at the turn of the century is discussed in T.J. Copp, *The Anatomy of Poverty: The Condition of the Working Class in Montreal, 1897–1929* (Toronto: McClelland & Stewart, 1974). For family life in Montreal see Bettina Bradbury, *Working Families: Age, Gender and Daily Survival in Industrializing Montreal* (Toronto: McClelland & Stewart, 1993). For Toronto see Gregory Kealey, *Toronto Workers Respond to Industrial Capitalism, 1867–1892* (Toronto: University of Toronto Press, 1980); and Michael Piva, *The Conditions of the Working Class in Toronto, 1900–1921* (Ottawa: University of Ottawa Press, 1979).

On women workers see the relevant sections in Alison Prentice et al., *Canadian Women: A History*, 2nd ed. (Toronto: Harcourt Brace, 1996). For Ontario see Marjorie Griffin Cohen, *Women's Work: Markets and Economic Development in Nineteenth-Century Ontario* (Toronto: University of Toronto Press, 1988); and for the Maritimes see Janet Guildford and Suzanne Morton, *Separate Spheres: Women's Worlds in the 19th-Century Maritimes* (Fredericton: Acadiensis Press, 1994).

On changing notions of sexuality consult Angus McLaren and Arlene Tigar McLaren, *The Bedroom and the State: The Changing Practices and Politics of Contraception and Abortion in Canada, 1880–1980* (Toronto: McClelland & Stewart, 1986).

The labour movement is discussed in Craig Heron, *The Canadian Labour Movement: A Short History*, rev. ed. (Toronto: James Lorimer, 1996); and Bryan Palmer, *Working-Class Experience: Rethinking the History of Canadian Labour, 1800–1991* (Toronto: McClelland & Stewart, 1992).

SOCIAL REFORM AND CULTURE: 1890–1914

TIME LINE

1874 –	Founding of the Woman's Christian Temperance Union (WCTU)
1877 –	Toronto Women's Literary Club becomes Canada's first women's suffrage organization
1880 –	Calixa Lavallée composes "O Canada"
	Beginning of the Canadian Academy of the Arts
	Ned Hanlan wins the world rowing championship
1885 –	Banff National Park established
1886 –	Founding of the Amateur Hockey Association of Canada, the first national hockey association
1887 –	First North American bird sanctuary established at Last Mountain Lake, Northwest Territories
1893 –	Lord Stanley donates Stanley Cup
1894 –	Fred Victor Mission founded in Toronto
	Founding of the Toronto Mendelssohn Choir
1909 –	Governor General Earl Grey donates Grey Cup

Various social reform movements — the social gospel movement, educational reformers, urban reformers, conservationists, women's reform and suffrage, and prohibition — arose to correct injustices brought about by large-scale industrialization and rapid urbanization at the turn of the century. Each offered its own solution. Together, these reformers transformed Canadian society on the eve of World War I. Canadian high culture —art, music, literature, and theatre — and an emerging popular culture, along with sports — reflective of rising middle-class and working-class cultures — also underwent a transformation at the turn of the century as a result of large-scale urbanization and industrialization. By 1914, Canada was a more culturally sophisticated and socially conscious society than it had been in 1867.

SOCIAL GOSPEL AND CATHOLIC SOCIAL ACTION

THE PROTESTANT SOCIAL GOSPEL MOVEMENT IN ENGLISH CANADA

The social gospel movement, part of a larger religious revival movement in Britain and the United States, aimed at applying Christianity to solving society's ills so as to create a perfect "Kingdom of God on Earth." The movement developed partially in response to a challenge to religious beliefs from the Darwinian concept of evolution. In *The Origin of Species* (1859) and *The Descent of Man* (1871), Charles Darwin, an English naturalist, advanced his theory that humans had evolved, over millions of years, from earlier forms of life in the animal kingdom. Darwin's arguments challenged the orthodox Christian belief that God created humans in his own likeness and as special beings during the six days of creation.

At the same time that science challenged contemporary Christian theology, a new philosophy of "higher criticism" presented the Bible as a document written by humans, and therefore not the divine and absolute word of God. The Bible may contain moral and religious, but not historical and scientific, truths. In response, a number of church leaders directed their attention away from theological questions to social issues. The new emerging industrialized Canada had a host of social problems that needed to be addressed.

Social gospellers regarded people as inherently good. If individuals erred, they did so, not because of any basic weakness or maliciousness of character, but because of their environment. Social gospellers believed in environmental determinism. If they could improve social conditions, then people's character would change for the good, which would result in an ideal Christian society.

Social gospellers wanted the church to concern itself with social problems: prostitution, alcoholism, and intolerable living and working conditions, rather than with such "personal sins" as drunkenness, sex, and slovenliness. Social gospellers strove to create in this world a humane society based on the Christian principles of love, charity, humanity, brotherhood, and democracy.

While united in their aspiration to improve the quality of life, social gospellers were divided on the means to achieve it. As many ways to regenerate and reform society existed as there were regenerators and reformers. But social gospellers can be classified into four broad categories: advocates of direct social assistance; social purity activists who focused on eradicating "evils" associated with sex; those who looked to education and a change of attitude as the means to social change; and those who saw state intervention as the best means to bring the "Kingdom of God on Earth."

What one might call the "direct social assistance group" of social reformers worked to give immediate aid to society's destitute through the establishment of missions and settlement houses. In 1890, the Reverend D.J. Macdonnell founded St. Andrews Institute in Toronto to bring the Presbyterian church closer to the working people. Four years later, with financial assistance from the wealthy Massey family of Toronto, a group of Methodists founded the Fred Victor

A Salvation Army meeting in Calgary, late August 1887. Meetings featured testimony, prayer, music, and song. The Salvation Army, begun by General William Booth in England, came to Canada in 1882.

National Archives of Canada/C-14426.

Mission in Toronto. In Newfoundland, Dr. Wilfred Grenfell established his Grenfell Mission in 1893 to help improve the appalling social conditions he found in northern Newfoundland outposts and along the Labrador coast. His efforts led to the establishment of a Newfoundland public health movement that addressed in particular the serious tuberculosis epidemic in the British colony.

Sara Libby Carson started the first settlement house in 1902 and helped found the Toronto and McGill University settlements. By 1920, at least thirteen settlement houses existed in Canada, offering the basic necessities of food and shelter and, often, a night school and a library. Many provided medical care. Others included gymnasiums, clubrooms, savings banks, and nurseries.

The Salvation Army, started by William Booth in England, also established centres in Canada at the turn of the century to help the poor. They modelled themselves after the regular army. Their members wore military-style uniforms and insignia. The ministers were called "officers," and the converts were "soldiers." At their peak, their "field force" enlisted nearly 150 000 in Canada to fight sin and poverty. Among them were a number of women — "Hallelujah lasses" — who preached on street corners and worked in shelters and homes to alleviate the misery of their "sisters."

A second group, social purity activists, concerned themselves with issues of sexual vice, such as prostitution (often referred to as "the social evil"), homosexuality, venereal disease, "feeblemindedness" (which they believed resulted from masturbation), and abortion. They sought to eliminate these "evils" by regulating and legislating sexual relations as a means to ensure racial purity and social control.

Sexual control took many forms. Churches hired "morality experts" to address, or had ministers preach on, moral concerns such as extramarital sex, masturbation, homosexuality, prostitution, and abortion. The Methodist and Presbyterian churches established social reform agencies under the umbrella of the Moral and Social Reform Council of Canada, established in 1907, which later changed its name to the Social Service Council of Canada. The Methodist church also recommended and distributed sex manuals, especially the popular eight-volume "Self and Sex" series. The Woman's Christian Temperance Union (WCTU) hired purity reformers such as William Lund Clark, Arthur Beall, and Beatrice Brigden to tour schools to warn young people against self-abuse and sexual promiscuity.

Increasingly, however, regulation of sex came under the control of the state. Cities hired social workers, experts on prisons, and psychiatrists to present the latest "scientific" theories, to educate the public on proper moral standards, and to work with the "sexual deviants" in the jails and mental institutions. Some social theorists, known as eugenicists, argued for selective breeding by preventing people deemed to have undesirable mental and physical traits from reproducing. All too often the "unfit" and "inferior" were also foreigners, thus adding an ethnic component to the eugenics movement.

The courts assisted the state in regulating morality. In 1892, the Criminal Code itemized offences to "protect" young girls and women by imposing stiff penalties of up to 14 years on brothel operators and those who enticed women into prostitution. It also legislated against "gross indecency," which referred to homosexual acts. Punishment was set at a minimum of five years, with provisions for whipping. In Toronto, both juvenile and women's courts were established to deal with issues of promiscuity and "vagrancy."

A third group of social gospellers worked to change people's attitudes. They believed that attitudes of greed, competition, and materialism caused society's problems. Through education, people could learn of the greater benefits of living in a society governed by Christian principles of love, charity, brotherhood, and democracy. In 1918, William Lyon Mackenzie King, about to become the leader of the federal Liberal party, published *Industry and Humanity* in which he argued that social salvation would come to a society that practised the ethical laws of Christianity. Education, he believed, would teach those ethical laws and inculcate proper moral values.

A final group of social reformers believed in state intervention. They argued that the concept of laissez-faire — the belief that governments should not upset the natural laws of the marketplace — had been used by the wealthy in society to exploit the poor. They advocated, instead, state intervention to provide essential social services and welfare assistance for the unemployed and the disabled, and to regulate industry and nationalize key industries to ensure that they served the public good.

For a few social gospellers, such as J.S. Woodsworth — then a Methodist minister, later the founder of the Co-operative Commonwealth Federation (CCF) — innovative reforms and state-regulated social services could only come about through a fundamental restructuring of society. Woodsworth believed that the "ideal Kingdom of Jesus" was a socialist paradise where everyone worked for the well-being of the whole rather than for its individual parts. True social reform meant replacing the profit motive of capitalism with Christian charity through socialism.

THE ROMAN CATHOLIC SOCIAL ACTION MOVEMENT IN QUEBEC

The origins of social reform in Quebec lay in the Roman Catholic church's emphasis on personal humanity and on its principles of social justice and Christian charity. Catholic social reformers in Quebec looked to the family and the church, rather than to the state, as the best institutions to deal with social problems.

The Roman Catholic church initiated and supported various social-reform movements in Quebec. In 1911, for example, the Jesuits founded the Montreal-based École Sociale Populaire (ESP) to develop a social doctrine for the church. The ESP published pamphlets, organized study groups and retreats, and worked to sensitize the clergy to the social needs of their parishioners.

Many priests supported the *caisses populaires*, the credit unions founded in 1900 by Alphonse Desjardins, as their way of improving Quebec society. Desjardins established his savings and lending co-operatives to assist French-Canadian enterprises to get started in the hopes of improving the living standards of the working class and of bringing economic liberation to the Quebec people. By the time of Desjardins's death in 1920, more than 200 *caisses populaires* existed, mainly in Quebec but also among French-speaking Canadians in Ontario, Manitoba, and Saskatchewan, as well as among Franco-Americans in the New England states.

French-Canadian priests also promoted Catholic unions for Quebec workers. Church leaders feared that workers in secular unions, especially American-controlled ones, would become too materialistic and too socialistic in their outlook.

The church also lent its moral support to the Ligue nationaliste, a middle-class group of reformers, founded in 1903. They formulated a French-Canadian and largely Catholic response to problems arising out of Quebec's urbanization and industrialization on the assumption that French Canadians needed to retain their identity in an increasingly secularized society. They believed in the family as the fundamental social unit of society and in Christian values as the bulwark of society. The state, they argued, should curtail the excessive monopolization of big business by preventing private control of utilities. Ultimately, they favoured a society based on Christian values of co-operation and a concern for the public good.

EDUCATIONAL REFORMERS

By the turn of the century, a new generation of educational reformers, strongly influenced by Friedrich Froebel, a European philosopher, advocated a child-oriented education that treated children as children, not miniature adults, by providing them with love and by protecting them from the harsh realities of adult life.

To some educational reformers, kindergartens provided the answer. James L. Hughes, a Toronto school inspector, and his future wife, Ada Marean, established the first Canadian public-school kindergarten in 1883. Four years later, Ontario formally incorporated kindergartens into the public-school system. The Free Kindergarten Association in Winnipeg advocated the same for Manitoba, arguing that "the proper education of children during the first seven years of their lives" did "much to reduce poverty and crime in any community."

In Montreal and Quebec City, nuns ran *salles d'asile* or day-care centres for children of working parents. Between 1898 and 1902, more than 10 000 children attended. In addition to these centres, which offered care on a daily basis, orphanages, provincial asylums, and homes for the poor also provided care for children of destitute families.

Other educational reformers pursued temperance education to warn children of the evils of alcohol, while still others asked for social programs in public health and in physical and mental hygiene. All educational reformers appreciated the importance of extended and free schooling. They succeeded by 1905 in getting all provinces except Quebec to legislate free schooling and compulsory attendance for youngsters up to the age of 12.

Two exceptional educational reformers were John Kelso and Alfred Fitzpatrick. Kelso, a young police reporter for the Toronto *World*, was concerned about the street urchins who could not be reached through the regular educational system. He quit journalism and began the Humane Society. When its members seemed only marginally interested in the plight of children, he began yet another organization, the Children's Aid Society. In 1899, Rev. Alfred Fitzpatrick, a Presbyterian minister from Nova Scotia, created the Reading Camp Association, later called Frontier College, to bring education to immigrant workers in the lumber shanties and railway bunkhouses across northern Canada.

THE URBAN REFORM MOVEMENT

Urban reformers formed an important part of social reform at the turn of the century. Inspired by the "City Beautiful" movement in the United States and Europe, they believed that reform must include a humane and beautiful urban environment — the physical structure of the city, its aesthetic nature, and the quality of its municipal government.

A host of professionals — engineers, architects, surveyors, medical people, and urban planners — offered advice on how to create the perfect city. Architects emphasized the need for stately buildings, while urban planners stressed parks, treed boulevards, and adequate housing. Medical professionals argued for clean water and air, and campaigned for pasteurized milk as a means to decrease the high rate of infant mortality in Canadian cities, especially Montreal and Toronto.

WILDERNESS AND WILDLIFE CONSERVATION

The idea of conservation emerged slowly in Canada. In 1885, the federal government took the first step in the creation of Canada's national parks by reserving more than 26 km^2 of land around the mineral springs near the railway station of Banff. Two years later, it extended the area to 675 km^2 and officially turned the reserve into a national park, Rocky Mountains Park (renamed Banff in 1930).

In 1887, the first bird sanctuary in North America opened at Last Mountain Lake, in present-day Saskatchewan. In 1893, the Ontario government established Algonquin Park, south of North Bay, as the province's first wilderness area. Other provinces followed Ontario's example in establishing their own provincial parks.

By the early twentieth century, the overexploitation of the country's wildlife was becoming obvious. Major improvements in firearm technology, combined with the rapidly increasing commercial value of certain types of wildlife, led to the extermination of certain species. The Plains bison herds disappeared on the Canadian side of the border as early as 1879. By 1900, the great prairie herds of pronghorn antelope declined to a tiny fraction of their original number. Hunted thoroughly, the passenger pigeon had vanished from Nova Scotia by 1857, from Manitoba by 1898, and from Ontario by 1902. (The last surviving member of this once abundant species died in an Ohio zoo in 1912.) By 1900, trumpeter swans had disappeared from eastern Canada, as had wild turkeys before them.

Slowly, a conservation mentality developed, cultivated by back-to-nature movements, such as the Alpine Club and Field-Naturalists' Clubs. Woodcraft Clubs, and the Boy Scout and Girl Guides movements, promoted the importance of a wilderness experience for good health, spiritual rejuvenation, and refuge from hectic city life. Schools in British Columbia, Nova Scotia, Ontario, and Alberta initiated nature study classes in the first decade of the twentieth century through the initiative of naturalists' societies, farm organizations, and experimental farms. Novelist Ernest Seton wrote realistic animal stories, such as *Wild Animals I Have Known* (1898), that were popular with Canadian youth.

The federal government responded slowly to the need for conservation. It established the Commission of Conservation (1909–21), which helped to secure the passage in 1917 of the Canada–United States Migratory Birds Convention Treaty, an agreement that was supposed to ensure international protection for migratory bird populations throughout their ranges. In 1919, the Canadian government also convened the first national wildlife conference to discuss with the provinces how best to conserve the country's wildlife.

Later, in the 1930s, the popularity of Grey Owl assisted the conservation movement. Born Archie Belaney, he took on the identity of an Ojibwa upon coming to Canada from England in 1907. He learned the Native view of the world, based on a belief that all animals, fowls, fish, trees and stones were endowed with immortal spirits and possessed supernatural powers. Humans were a part of this animated world, not its master. Through his books, films, and lectures, he presented this Native perspective, and promoted the protection of Canada's wilderness and wildlife.

WOMEN AND SOCIAL REFORM

By the 1890s, a "new woman" had appeared, demanding an active role in reforming society. Local, provincial, and national women's organizations such as the Woman's Christian Temperance Union, the National Council of Women, the Young Women's Christian Association (YWCA), and the Dominion Women's Enfranchisement Association were a few of the organizations that assisted women in reaching out to society. By 1912 an estimated one out of every eight adult women — the majority of them middle-aged, middle-class, English-speaking Protestants — belonged to a women's group, thus making these organizations influential agents of social change.

Two women cyclists, Flo and Jessie McLennan, Owen Sound, Ontario. Bicycles liberated women from restrictive clothing — and from chaperones.

Glenbow Archives, Calgary, Canada/NA-2685-61.

Most women accepted the prevailing "scientific" stereotyping of them as womanly and motherly whose primary task was to maintain the home. But a few women came to believe that their maternal instincts should be used to reform society. "Rocking the cradle for the world" was how Nellie McClung, an influential reformer, saw women's new role. These reform-minded women argued that men had controlled society for ages without making any appreciable improvements; now it was women's turn. As McClung explained it:

> Women must be made to feel their responsibilities. All this protective love, their instinctive mother love, must be organized in some way, and made effective. There is enough of it in the world to do away with all the evils which war upon childhood: undernourishment, slum conditions, child labour, drunkenness. Women could abolish all these if they wanted to.

Adelaide (Hunter) Hoodless helped to further the women's cause in another way. Her fourth child died in 1889, at the age of 18 months, from the unpasteurized milk that farmers delivered in open cans, which exposed it to bacterial contamination. Seeing an urgent need to teach women nutrition and proper health measures, she offered domestic science or home economics classes through the YWCA. Later she assisted in having the subject introduced in the schools and, eventually, at the Ontario Agricultural College in Guelph and at McGill University in Montreal. In 1897, she started the first Women's Institute near Stoney Creek, south of Hamilton, Ontario. The new organization helped women to increase their knowledge of farm and household management. She also helped found the Victorian Order of Nurses to offer nursing and housekeeping services to impoverished invalids.

THE WOMEN'S SUFFRAGE MOVEMENT

Women reformers saw the right to vote as the means by which women could obtain the power to reform society. The women's suffrage movement began in Ontario with leaders such as Dr. Emily (Jennings) Stowe. But further momentum came from the Prairie provinces. In the newer settler society of the West, women had found a greater degree of equality. In establishing a homestead and building a farm, women worked alongside their husbands. Early on, they won the support of western farm organizations that also struggled for national recognition and were, therefore, better able to empathize with women's efforts for equality. The prairie farmers' newspaper, the *Grain Growers' Guide*, founded in 1908, added a women's column to its paper in 1911, while the Grain Growers' Association of Manitoba, Saskatchewan, and Alberta endorsed women's suffrage as early as 1912.

The West had several outspoken women actively involved in the struggle for female suffrage, such as Henrietta Edwards, Emily Murphy, Louise McKinney, Nellie McClung, and Irene Parlby. Perhaps Nellie McClung, with her gift for oratory, her energy, and her delightful sense of humour, best epitomized the suffrage movement. Her spirited leadership rallied many others to the cause of women's suffrage.

Nellie (Mooney) McClung was born in Ontario in 1873 but educated in Manitoba, where her family began homesteading in 1880. After attending Winnipeg Normal School and teaching for several years, she married Wes McClung, a pharmacist and later an insurance company

Where Historians Disagree
Women and Reform

Although a relatively new field of historical study, Canadian gender history has already raised a healthy historical debate. One contentious issue has been the primary motive behind the women's reform movement. The first historians to write on the subject in the 1960s and early 1970s argued that women reformers sought only the right to vote — women's suffrage — believing that political equality would bring about an era of societal reform. This narrow focus on the ballot box seemed to explain why the movement for reform died out so rapidly in the 1920s, once women's suffrage had been achieved.

Some historians see women's reform as part of a greater "progressive reform" movement that went well beyond a concern for the enfranchisement of women. In his introduction to a reprint of Catharine L. Cleverdon's classic study, *The Woman Suffrage Movement in Canada*, Ramsay Cook linked women's reform to the larger social gospel movement. "The suffragists were a part of a more general, middle-class reform movement that was concerned to remove a wide range of injustices and evils that afflicted the country."[1]

Other historians question this idealized image of women reformers as being motivated purely by religious zeal. Historian Veronica Strong-Boag argues that power, fame, and influence motivated them, at least those associated with the influential National Council of Women of Canada. She notes that "the female relatives of Canada's powerful men, energized by a changing external environment and by their own recent access to higher education and the professions, had few formal ways of expressing their complementary desires for national leadership and influence."[2] In short, these middle-class women reformers worried more about their own position of power in society than about the disadvantaged.

Carol Bacchi applied the feminist theories of the 1980s to the leaders of the suffrage movement in the 1910s, and found the suffragists wanting.[3] She argued that suffrage leaders were middle-class reformers more than they were feminists, and as such were more conservative than radical in outlook. They succeeded in getting the vote for women, according to Bacchi, only because men in positions of power at the time realized that giving women the right to vote would not upset the status quo. In a review of Bacchi's book,[4] which was based essentially on a study only of women leaders in Montreal, Toronto, and the Prairies, historian Ernest Forbes, relying on his own work on Halifax women reformers, challenged her conclusions. In Halifax, at least, according to Forbes, suffrage leaders were feminists before they were reformers, and used their position to encourage women to get out of the home, and even provided them with opportunities to do so. In this respect, they were "revolutionary" in aspiration. Furthermore, he argued that although Halifax suffragists were from the middle class, they addressed working-class issues. Thus Forbes appealed for more "local studies" to help draw a definitive conclusion about suffragists on a national level.

Historian Margot Iris Dudley took up Forbes's challenge and examined the women's suffrage movement in Newfoundland.[5] She discovered a group of women reformers who crossed class lines and even religious divisions between Catholics and Protestants, and who allied themselves with the International Alliance of Women, based in London,

England. Her study brought into question the assumption that the women's suffrage movement in Canada was middle-class, Protestant, and narrowly national.

More recently, some women historians have concentrated on the 1920s to see whether the women's reform movement died out after political emancipation as previously believed. Historians Linda Kealey and Joan Sangster have studied a group of "radical women" in the 1920s to show that, for these women, left-wing politics became the means to achieve real change, something that was not possible in the more conservative social reform movement.[6] Nevertheless, these women had to adopt male tactics and abandon the "private sphere" in order to succeed in the traditionally male-dominated "public sphere."

Veronica Strong-Boag has re-entered the debate to argue that the real struggle for reform did not take place in politics — in the public sphere — but rather in a highly politicized private sphere. "Theirs was the feminism of the workplace, day-to-day life. It was not for the most part an organized movement as the campaign for enfranchisement had been, but it flowed from a similar awareness of women's oppression and a desire to end it."[7] Strong-Boag's study underlines the need to rethink the categories of political/apolitical, public/private, and male/female.

Linda Kealey appeals for a broader definition of "public" and "political" in dealing with women reformers to include "the home, the neighbourhood, and the community, as well as ... the union, the party, or the workplace."[8] She argues that some socialist women reformers were concerned with women workers as wage earners or working-class wives and mothers, while others advocated a radical transformation of the industrial capitalist system. In either case, they succeeded in bringing working-class women's issues into the public domain, despite opposition from men and even middle-class female reformers.

Janice Newton shows how Canadian women reformers within the socialist movement rejected the middle-class obsession of the suffragists to get the vote and instead worked for equality of working-class women through such organizations as the Canadian Socialists League, the Socialist Party of Canada, and the Social Democratic Party.[9]

It is ironic that just as Canadian women obtained a political voice, First Nations women were denied one. Under their traditional system of governance, for example, the women of the Six Nations (Iroquois) Confederacy chose the Confederacy's chiefs, but under the Indian Act of 1880, they did not even have a vote in community decisions. This topic deserves to be studied.

[1] Ramsay Cook, "Introduction" to Catharine L. Cleverdon, *The Woman Suffrage Movement in Canada* (1950). Reprint. (Toronto: University of Toronto Press, 1974), p. xvii.

[2] Veronica Strong-Boag, *The Parliament of Women: The National Council of Women of Canada, 1893–1929* (Ottawa: Canadian Museum of Civilization, 1976), p. 410.

[3] Carol Bacchi, *Liberation Deferred? The Ideas of the English Canadian Suffragists, 1877–1918* (Toronto: University of Toronto Press, 1983).

[4] Ernest Forbes, "The Ideas of Carol Bacchi and the Suffragists of Halifax," *Atlantis*, 10, 2 (Spring 1985): 119–26.

[5] Margot Iris Dudley, "The Radius of Her Influence for Good: The Rise and Triumph of the Women's Suffrage Movement in Newfoundland, 1909–1925," in Linda Kealey, ed., *Pursuing Equality: Historical Perspectives on Women in Newfoundland and Labrador* (St. John's: Institute of Social and Economic Research, Memorial University, 1993).

[6] Linda Kealey and Joan Sangster, *Beyond the Vote: Canadian Women and Politics* (Toronto: University of Toronto Press, 1989).

[7] Veronica Strong-Boag, "Pulling in Double Harness or Hauling a Double Load: Women, Work and Feminism on the Canadian Prairies," *Journal of Canadian Studies*, 21 (Fall 1986): 34.

[8] Linda Kealey, *Enlisting Women for the Cause: Women, Labour, and the Left in Canada, 1890–1920* (Toronto: University of Toronto Press, 1988), p. 10.

[9] Janice Newton, *The Feminist Challenge to the Canadian Left, 1900–1918* (Montreal/Kingston: McGill-Queen's University Press, 1995).

Presentation of a petition by the Winnipeg Political Equality League for the Enfranchisement of Women, December 23, 1915. Mrs. Amelia Burritt, then 93 years old, gave the document to the provincial government. In 1916, Manitoba became Canada's first province to grant women the franchise.

Provincial Archives of Manitoba/Events 173/3 (N9905).

manager, in 1896. Her fiancé promised her before marriage that he would not stand in the way of her writing career, a promise he kept. Between 1897 and 1911, she had four sons and a daughter, but still found time to write — first poems, sketches, and editorials for Sunday school publications, and later adult stories in leading North American magazines.

Early on, her interest in reform led her to write her best-selling novel, *Sowing Seeds in Danny*. In 1912, she joined the Winnipeg Political Equality League, whose president was Lillian Beynon Thomas, another reformer. Nellie wrote her witty but powerful social commentary on suffrage, *In Times Like These*, for the 1916 election in Manitoba, in which suffrage was the major issue. The suffragists made their first breakthrough in that election when the Liberals came to power. The new government introduced a suffrage bill, making Manitoba the first province in Canada to grant women the right to vote.

WOMEN REFORMERS IN QUEBEC

Women involved in social reform in Quebec had a more difficult battle than their sisters in English-speaking Canada, since the image of women as mothers and guardians of the home was more entrenched in the French-Canadian ethos than it was in English Canada. Nevertheless, several French-Canadian women spoke out for the feminist cause, often through membership in the local council of the National Council of Women of Canada, founded by Marie Lacoste Gérin-Lajoie, Caroline Béique, and Josephine Dandurand in 1907, or through the Fédération nationale Saint-Jean-Baptiste. The Fédération fought for such causes as the pasteurizing of milk to reduce infant mortality, better working conditions for women, and the elimination of alcoholism and prostitution. It also contributed to better women teachers' pensions, improved working conditions for women in factories and stores, increased home-economics courses, and established pure milk depots.

Marie Lacoste Gérin-Lajoie led the fight for women's suffrage in Quebec. With an English-speaking colleague, she created the Provincial Franchise Committee in 1921 to put pressure on Quebec politicians to grant women the franchise. When her efforts failed, Marie Lacoste Gérin-Lajoie resigned her post as head of the francophone section of the Provincial Franchise Committee, although she continued to promote women's rights. Women in Quebec finally obtained the provincial franchise in 1940, a generation later than women in other provinces.

THE PROHIBITION MOVEMENT

Throughout Canada, many women reformers worked for prohibition. Prohibitionists argued that the only way to eradicate drinking was to prohibit it through government legislation. But the division of jurisdiction over alcohol between the federal and provincial governments complicated the question. The federal government had the power to restrict the manufacture of, and interprovincial trade in, alcoholic beverages, but provincial governments controlled retail sales. Thus, prohibitionists had to apply pressure on both levels of government.

They achieved an initial victory in 1878 with the passage of the Scott Act, which allowed the residents of each municipality or county to decide by a simple majority vote whether their constituency would be "wet" or "dry." Prohibitionists, however, demanded that governments outlaw the liquor trade completely. The federal Conservative government delayed acting on the issue until the mid-1890s, when it established the Royal Commission on the Liquor Traffic. During the election campaign of 1896, Laurier and the Liberals promised a plebiscite on the question of prohibition if they gained office. When they won, the prohibitionists held them to their promise.

The results of Canada's first plebiscite were split. Every province except Quebec voted on the dry side. But voter turnout throughout Canada had been low — only 44 percent. Furthermore, of those who did vote, only a small majority of about 13 000 had favoured prohibition. Laurier used these "indecisive" results to avoid enacting legislation that he feared would divide the nation. The Liberals' refusal to follow through on their promise angered the prohibitionists and gave them even greater resolve to banish alcohol.

Protestant churches provided many of the leaders of the prohibition movement. For them, the struggle became part of a religious battle. They urged drinkers to sign "the pledge" card, where they promised, "by the help of God, to abstain from the use of all intoxicating drinks as a beverage."

The Woman's Christian Temperance Union (WCTU), formed in Ontario in 1874, and quickly becoming a national organization with some 16 000 members by 1914, identified alcoholism as the greatest single cause of domestic violence and divorce. They linked prohibition with women's suffrage. If women had the right to vote, they argued, alcohol abuse would end. As Mrs. Jacob Spence, first superintendent of the Ontario WCTU's Franchise Department, noted: "The liquor sellers are not afraid of our conventions but they are afraid of our ballots." For many prohibitionists, drunkenness became associated with "foreigners." Controlling alcohol offered a means of regulating immigrants and of ensuring their conformity in a heterogeneous society.

Despite their efforts, however, prohibitionists remained in the minority before World War I. On the eve of the Great War, only Prince Edward Island had implemented provincial prohibition, while on the national level the federal government had resisted pressure to restrict the production, and interprovincial distribution, of "demon rum" and all liquor in general.

Canadian High Culture

The Promotion of Canadian Culture

Canada's viceroys played an important role in promoting English-Canadian and French-Canadian culture. They hosted important cultural activities across the country, and they bought and displayed Canadian art. The Marquis of Lorne, Canada's fourth governor general, brought the Royal Canadian Academy of the Arts and the National Gallery of Canada, its successor, into existence in the brief interlude of prosperity in the early 1880s. Governor General Earl Grey sponsored the Earl Grey Musical and Dramatic Trophy Competition, a national competition designed to elevate the quality of Canadian talent. A fervent imperialist, he also sponsored lecture tours to promote the British empire both within Canada and abroad. To promote the study of Canadian and British history, Grey founded the Historical Landmark Association of Canada in 1907.

By the turn of the century, the growing business community also provided financial support for the arts. The CPR hired artists in the 1880s to create works of art for their hotels, châteaus, railcars, and offices and to design their promotional posters. The wealthy Massey family of Toronto established a company band — the Massey Concert Band — a glee club, an employees' orchestra, and even a literary magazine, *Massey's Illustrated*, published between 1882 and 1895. As well, the Massey family purchased a number of church organs for Methodist churches in Toronto. In 1894, Hart Massey built the magnificent Massey Hall, with a seating capacity of 4000, and underwrote the costs of the Toronto Symphony Orchestra and the Toronto Mendelssohn Choir.

Canadian Art

In 1867, the Society of Canadian Artists formed. It set an ambitious goal: to foster a pan-Canadian artistic tradition so as to make Canadian artists known both within Canada and abroad. The Ontario Society of Artists followed in 1872. They promised to do everything in their power to promote Canadian art, including holding annual exhibitions of their works and working toward the building of a permanent public art gallery in Toronto. Out of these two societies came the beginnings of the Canadian Academy of the Arts, founded in 1880 with the help of Governor General Lord Lorne. A year later, Queen Victoria officially prefixed "Royal" to its title. Women countered with their own organization, the Women's Art Association, founded in 1890.

When *Picturesque Canada*, the most ambitious publishing project of the day, was launched, O'Brien was the chief Canadian contributor, with almost one-quarter of the over 500 illustrations in the two volumes. George Munro Grant, principal of Queen's University and a Canadian enthusiast, edited the text. He underscored the importance of the volumes for the growth of a pan-Canadian nationalism. "I believe that a work that would represent its characteristic scenery and the history and life of its people, would not only make us better known to ourselves and to strangers, but would also stimulate national sentiment and contribute to the rightful development of the nation."

Lucius R. O'Brien, *Sunrise on the Saguenay*, 1880. This painting, first exhibited at the opening of the Royal Canadian Academy of the Arts in 1880, won O'Brien much praise and recognition. O'Brien became the first president of the Canadian Academy of the Arts in 1880, a position he held for ten years.

National Gallery of Canada, Ottawa. Royal Canadian Academy of Arts diploma work, deposited by the artist, Toronto, 1880.

Another opportunity for Canadian artists to achieve international fame and recognition came with the holding of a Colonial and Indian Exhibition in London in 1886 — the year preceding Queen Victoria's Golden Jubilee. The Canadian display included works by such established painters as Adolph Vogt, William Raphael, John A. Fraser, and O'Brien. But it was the paintings by a younger, Paris-trained group — Homer Watson, William Brymner, Paul Peel, Robert Harris, and Percy Woodstock — that caught the English critics' attention.

One of the finest Quebec artists of the late nineteenth century was Napoleon Bourassa, who was influenced by Ingres, the French neoclassicist, and by historic painting. His student, Louis-Philippe Hébert, achieved great renown in sculpture, with commemorative statues across Canada, including those of both Macdonald and Cartier on Parliament Hill in Ottawa. Another talented French-Canadian artist of the period, Ozias Leduc, lived in seclusion, unknown to most of his contemporaries except for a handful of devoted artistic friends. His still-life paintings of simple Quebec subjects show a heightened sensitivity and an appreciation of beauty in the ordinary. Most of his income derived from church decoration. He completed some 150 large paintings for 27 cathedrals, churches, and chapels.

At the turn of the century, painting in English-speaking Canada came of age. Maurice Cullen of Quebec became a leading Canadian practitioner of Impressionism, and James Wilson Morrice, also from Quebec, a leading modernist. Ironically, both men achieved fame in Europe before acquiring it in Canada. But A.Y. Jackson, a young Montreal revolutionary artist of the time and a future member of the Group of Seven, recalled of Cullen: "To us he was a hero."

MUSIC

Music was widespread in both English-speaking and French-speaking Canada at the turn of the century. Sacred music flourished because the churches played a large role in the musical life of the communities. Almost all cities in Canada had singing groups; for example, Halifax had the Orpheus Club, and Saint John, the Saint John Oratorio Society. Bands and orchestras were equally popular. Most brass bands formed around the militia camps but also included a number in Indian residential schools as a means to impose discipline and order.

A few noted composers emerged. Calixa Lavallée, considered in his day to be Canada's greatest musician, composed "O Canada." Also well known in Quebec for his religious compositions was Guillaume Couture, organist and conductor of the

Calixa Lavallée, the composer of "O Canada." Ironically, Canada's national anthem since 1980 was originally composed in 1880 for St. Jean Baptiste Day, now recognized as Quebec's national holiday.

Heritage Canada 5 (2) (May 1979): 13.

Montreal Philharmonic Society. In English Canada, Alexander Muir, a Toronto school principal, was famous for writing "The Maple Leaf Forever." William Reed's *Grand Choeur in D Major* was considered one of the finest organ works ever written by a Canadian, while Clarence Lucas was known for being a prolific composer of orchestral music.

The nineteenth century is often referred to as the "age of the virtuoso" — a time when gifted soloists astounded the public with superb performances. Canada became home to four world-class soloists. One was Frantz Jehin-Prume, a violinist from Belgium who came to live in Montreal. Another violinist, Luigi von Kunits, from Vienna, had a similarly successful career in Toronto. In the 1910s and 1920s, Calgary-born Kathleen Parlow, an internationally renowned violinist, toured Europe, Russia, North America, and Asia. But the most famous of all was Emma Albani. Born Marie Lajeunesse in Chambly, near Montreal, in 1847, she adopted the stage name Emma Albani while on a European tour in the early 1870s. The French-Canadian diva sang at the best opera houses in Europe. She made various visits from her home in England to Canada — in 1883, 1889, and a grand tour from Halifax to Victoria in 1896–97.

CANADIAN LITERATURE

Canadian poetry in English became established in the 1880s. The "Confederation Poets" — the name literary critics have given to the four poets Charles G.D. Roberts, Bliss Carman, Archibald Lampman, and Duncan Campbell Scott — sought the essence of Canada in nature: the world of rocks, streams, and woods, and the lifestyle of the farmer and lumberjack. These poets depicted nature in the highly romantic terms of the British Romantic poets, such as Wordsworth, Keats, and Shelley, who inspired them. Isabella Valancy Crawford also drew inspiration from the Canadian landscape. She depicted nature as possessing a soul that was very much in tune with the human soul.

The most famous female poet in the late nineteenth century was Pauline Johnson — or Tekahionwake, her Mohawk name. Born the daughter of a Mohawk chief and his English wife,

Pauline Johnson (1861–1913).

National Archives of Canada/C-85125.

Émile Nelligan (1879–1941), the legendary Quebec poet and member of the École littéraire de Montréal. The intense young man already was confined to a mental asylum at the time this photo was taken in 1904.

National Archives of Canada/C-88566.

Johnson celebrated her Iroquois heritage while at the same time expressing a Canadian, and an imperial, vision. In her poem, "Canadian Born," for example, she wrote:

> The Dutch may have their Holland, the Spaniard have his Spain,
> The Yankee to the south of us must south of us remain;
> For not a man dare lift a hand against the men who brag
> That they were born in Canada beneath the British flag.

Quebec's poetry came into its own with the founding of the École littéraire de Montréal in 1895. Its poetry broke free of the patriotic-romantic verse that then dominated. Its most famous member was Émile Nelligan. This poet of genius produced some 170 poems when he was between the ages of 17 and 20. Perhaps his best known is "Le Vaisseau d'or" (Ship of Gold). Nelligan found his inspiration for poetry less in romantic nature, historical subjects, or patriotic fervour, and more in what Wordsworth called "the still, sad music of humanity," the poetry of the spirit. Exhausted and ill, Nelligan lost his grip on reason in 1899, at the age of 21, and spent the last 41 years of his life in mental institutions.

English-Canadian novelists and short-story writers emerged in the late nineteenth century. Ernest Thompson Seton and Charles G.D. Roberts pioneered the writing of realistic animal stories. Seton also published *Two Little Savages*, his classic of children's literature based on his boyhood experiences of "playing Indian" in Ontario.

Many of the best Canadian novels had regional settings. Norman Duncan's *The Way of the Sea* (1903) and Theodore Goodridge Roberts' *The Harbour Master* (1913) were set in Newfoundland. Lucy Maud Montgomery's first novel, *Anne of Green Gables* (1908), captured the spirit of her native province of Prince Edward Island through her beloved orphan character, Anne Shirley. Stephen Leacock acquired international recognition as one of Canada's great humorists with his *Sunshine Sketches of a Little Town* (1912), an affectionate satire of small-town (Orillia) Ontario life, and *Arcadian Adventures of the Idle Rich* (1914), a parody of city life, earning him a reputation as the "Mark Twain of the British Empire." Gilbert Parker's *The Seats of the Mighty* (1898), a historical novel about New France, became an international bestseller.

Popular French-Canadian novels of the Quebec rural countryside appeared, one of the most popular being Ernest Choquette's *Claude Paysan* (1899). But Charles Chiniquy outdistanced all of his Quebec contemporaries in terms of the number of editions and translations of his works. His *The Priest, the Woman and the Confessional* (1875); *Fifty Years in the Church of Rome* (1885); and *Forty Years in the Church of Christ* (1899) were popular among Protestant extremists throughout the world because of their vitriolic attacks on the Roman Catholic church.

In the West, authors such as Ralph Connor (Charles Gordon), Robert Stead, Nellie McClung, and Janey Canuck (Emily Murphy), wrote of the settlement experience of the Canadian prairies with highly utopian depictions of the West. Ralph Connor's novels sold in the millions and had a larger audience outside the country than within it. All of his western novels capitalized on the romance, adventure, and physical beauty of the early West. In British Columbia, Martin Allen Grainger's *Woodsmen of the West* (1908) captured life in the logging industry on the West Coast. Robert Service's verse, published in his *Songs of a Sourdough* (1907), *The Spell of the Yukon* (1907), and *Ballads of a Cheechako* (1909), established his reputation as a writer of humorous ballads, such as Sam McGee and Dan McGraw.

CANADIAN THEATRE

English-Canadian theatre grew slowly in the period from 1867 to 1914 because of an anti-theatre attitude. One reason was the association of theatre with "immorality and debauchery" in the mind of church leaders. The stage was regarded "as the gate of Hell." No doubt contributing to this perception were the controversial performances of the flamboyant French actress Sarah Bernhardt. Despite the Roman Catholic church's condemnation of her "heretical" theatre productions, she performed to a full house in Montreal. She was equally popular in English-speaking Canada during her several visits to Canada.

Another reason for the unpopularity of theatre was its "foreign" nature. American touring companies provided nearly all the English-language entertainment. They made no attempt to use local talent and in fact discouraged the growth of indigenous talent by getting Canadians accustomed to looking beyond Canada's borders for theatrical talent.

Some patrons of the arts became concerned about the "Americanization of English-Canadian theatre." But instead of supporting Canadian actors, they brought in British touring groups. For a while, in the period 1910–1914, a battle existed between these two external groups for the domination of Canadian theatre. With the outbreak of war, however, the British "theatrical invasion" of Canada ended. The Great War also curtailed American productions in Canada. Only in the interwar years would a respectable Canadian theatre develop, in competition with the new moving-picture industry.

POPULAR CULTURE

Canada's first permanent movie house, the Edison Electric Theatre, opened on Cordova Street in Vancouver in 1902. It was followed by Winnipeg's Unique and Dreamland in 1903, Montreal's Nationale and Palais Royale (an impressive 1000-seat cinema) in 1904, and St. John's York in 1906. Each charged its customers a nickel, from whence derived the name "nickelodeon." One of the great American stars of the era was Gladys Mary Smith — or, to use her stage name, Mary Pickford — who was born in Toronto in 1893 but moved with her family to New York at the age of five.

SPORTS

Sports came into its own as a popular form of culture in the years 1867 to 1914. Sports clubs provided social meeting places for Canada's political, economic, and commercial elites. Women were active in these clubs, although in a clearly defined and subservient role, while racial minorities were barred entirely. Instead, these minority groups created their own teams and clubs. In Nova Scotia, African Canadians in the community of Africville, formed their own baseball and hockey teams, while on the West Coast, Japanese formed a baseball team, called the Asahi.

Organized team sports, such as football, baseball, lacrosse, and ice hockey, grew as well in popularity as people in urban centres had more time for sports. Better transportation facilities

The University of Toronto and McGill University football teams in action during an intercampus match, 1909. Later that fall, the U of T team defeated Toronto Parkdale to win the first Grey Cup.

Canadian Football Hall of Fame and Museum.

and communication links also enabled intercity competition. The standardization of rules in sports, in turn, led to the creation of local, provincial, and national associations.

Although football made its debut in Canada in the late nineteenth century, it only became a recognized national sport when Governor General Earl Grey donated the cup that bears his name in 1909. At first the sport remained largely the preserve of an anglophone Canadian elite associated with universities of central Canada. Only in the first decade of the twentieth century did football spread to the smaller towns of Ontario and the Prairies. Baseball, the most Americanized sport in Canada, became the most Canadian sport in terms of those who either played or watched the game, since it required minimal facilities to play.

Many Canadians considered lacrosse Canada's national sport. The National Lacrosse Association's slogan, "*Our* Country and *Our* Game," certainly claimed that status. Lacrosse was also closely associated with the game of baggataway, which was played by several First Nations. On the very day of Canada's creation — July 1st, 1867 — the native team of Kahnawake took the Dominion lacrosse title — at the time, the equivalent of world championship — by defeating the Montreal Lacrosse Club 3 to 2. The game changed from being amateur to professional in the 1880s. This change could be seen in the shift from exhibition games that were arranged occasionally to systematized leagues that met and competed on a regular basis for spectators. The game also became a "national" sport, with teams located in urban centres across the country, although the sport lacked a national association until 1912.

Ice hockey had already become *the* Canadian sport by World War I. The first regulated game dates back to 1875 in Montreal, when two nine-man teams from the Montreal Football Club, looking for some winter training, confronted each other. Many of the early teams began in

Canada's mining, lumbering, and farming towns, resulting in tough games and ferocious inter-community rivalry. The sport caught on quickly. By 1880, the number of players per side had been reduced from nine to seven, and a standardized set of rules was also in place. Montreal hosted the "world championship" in 1883, in which the McGill University team was victorious.

In 1909, the National Hockey Association, the forerunner of today's National Hockey League, launched its inaugural season with seven teams: three from Montreal, one of which was the Canadiens, the new French-Canadian team, with other teams from Ottawa, Renfrew, Haileybury, and Cobalt. They employed professional players. By 1912, the three small-town teams had folded, victims of rising costs. The league now consisted of two teams from Montreal, two new ones from Toronto, and a team from both Ottawa and Quebec City. Also by 1912, the first artificial-ice rinks appeared, making playing conditions more stable and also allowing ice hockey to become a West Coast sport. A Pacific Coast Hockey Association formed, which, in 1917, affiliated with the National Hockey Association to create the National Hockey League (NHL).

In four major sports in Canada at the turn of the century — football, baseball, lacrosse, and ice hockey — professionalization had taken over by World War I. From this point onward, money and victory overrode gentlemanly conduct and pleasure as the objectives of sports. Sports had become a business.

Toronto's first sport hero, Edward "Ned" Hanlan, "the Boy in Blue," contributed to the professionalization of sports. Known for his long, smooth strokes and sharp clean "catch," he gained fame as the best sculler in Ontario in a series of races between 1873 and 1876. He dominated the professional rowing world from 1877 to 1884, winning the Canadian Championship on Toronto Bay in 1877, the Championship of America on the Allegheny River in 1878, the Championship of England on the Tyne River in 1879 (beating the English champions by an astonishing eleven lengths), and ultimately the Championship of the World against Australia's E.A. Trickett in 1880.

MIDDLE-CLASS CULTURE

At the turn of the century, the middle class had more time and money for leisure. In the cities, leisure centres arose such as roller-skating rinks, dance halls, amusement parks, theatres, and fairs. The most popular in the Victorian era became Toronto's Industrial Exhibition, the forerunner of the Canadian National Exhibition. Founded in 1879, it entertained a broad segment of the populace of Toronto and its surrounding towns in the last few weeks of summer. Industrial fairs expressed the perspective of the dominant or hegemonic groups in society, usually the industrial and mercantile members of the rising middle class.

WORKING-CLASS CULTURE

A working-class culture fully emerged in both English-speaking and French-speaking Canada in the late nineteenth century through a proliferation of associations, societies, clubs, and lodges. They provided a meeting place where male workers (female workers could not belong) of common background and interest could meet and enjoy each other's company. Taverns served the same purpose in larger urban centres. "Joe Beef's Canteen," established in Montreal in the 1860s by Charles McKiernan, an Irish Protestant ex-soldier, became one such place. It offered its working-class clientele food, drink, and accommodation — a blanket and access to a tub, a barber, "medical" advice, and "cures" — all for ten cents.

By the 1880s, larger working-class associations such as the Knights of Labor assumed the role that Joe Beef's Canteen and other similar establishments, such as Dan Black's Tavern in

Hamilton, had played. Through the American-based organization's ritualistic procedure of secret pledges, obedience, and committed charity, working men and women formed a common bond and a sense of pride. Festivals, dinners, picnics, and workers' balls provided social gatherings to "cement the bonds of unity."

NATIVE CULTURE

Although many English and French Canadians in the late nineteenth century had a sentimental regard for the Native peoples, it did not extend to a belief that First Nations had a right to keep their ancestral cultures and religions. Canadians, like the rest of the western world, believed that the First Nations were inferior and therefore had to be assimilated into the "superior" Western European culture. This negative perspective justified suppressing any aspect of Native culture that might get in the way of achieving assimilation.

Yet, with a peculiar twist of irony, as Canadians believed that the First Nations were about to disappear, they became more fascinated with this "quaint" and disappearing "race." They wanted to include First Nations ceremonies and customs in their country fairs and stampedes. The government opposed such trends since it went against their policy of assimilation.

By the turn of the century, the cultural traditions of other ethnic groups also emerged, as immigrants came in large numbers and brought their customs, ceremonies, and special festivities with them. The fact that many of these customs were frowned upon by the host society did not prevent newly arrived ethnic groups from enjoying their own customs within their own communities.

On the eve of World War I, social-reform movements had accomplished much, but they still fell short of their ultimate goal of social regeneration. The War would spur many of these reforms forward, particularly women's suffrage and prohibition. In terms of culture, both English and French Canada had brought forth a small number of internationally renowned musicians, visual artists, actors, writers, and sports figures, but greater strides would be made in the interwar years.

LINKING TO THE PAST

J.S. Woodsworth
http://timelinks.merlin.mb.ca/referenc/db0031.htm
A brief biography of J.S. Woodsworth, a prominent Canadian social reformer of the early twentieth century.

Votes for Women
http://www.niagara.com/~merrwill/vote.html#anchor1855139
A brief description of the main legislative acts relevant to women's suffrage in Canada. This site also provides the dates on which women gained the right to vote and to stand for office in each province. Biographies of key women in Canadian history, such as Emily Jennings Stowe, Adelaide Hoodless, and Nellie McClung, are available at http://niagara.com/~merrwill.

Nellie McClung
http://www.nlc-bnc.ca/2/12/h12-304-e.html
A detailed biography of Nellie McClung, teacher and suffragist in the Canadian West.

The National Anthem of Canada
http://www.pch.gc.ca/progs/cpsc-ccsp/sc-cs/anthem_e.cfm
The history of "O Canada," including brief biographies of the musicians and writers who helped create it.

English-Canadian Literature
http://www.canadiana.org/eco/english/collection_eng_lit.html
This collection, part of Early Canadiana Online, contains images of early editions of over 800 works of drama, poetry and fiction, biography, and exploration accounts written before 1900. Use the "Search the Collections" button to enter search criteria or to browse.

BIBLIOGRAPHY

Chapters 15 and 16 in R.C. Brown and R. Cook, *Canada, 1896–1921: A Nation Transformed* (Toronto: McClelland & Stewart, 1974) provide an overview of the social-reform movements. Paul-André Linteau, René Durocher, and Jean-Claude Robert, *Quebec: A History, 1867–1929* (Toronto: James Lorimer, 1983) deals with social reform in Quebec.

The social gospel is examined in Richard Allen's, *The Social Passion: Religion and Social Reform in Canada, 1914–28* (Toronto: University of Toronto Press, 1971), and Ramsay Cook, *The Regenerators: Social Criticism in Late Victorian English Canada* (Toronto: University of Toronto Press, 1985). On religion and moral reform consult Mariana Valverde, *The Age of Light, Soap, and Water: Moral Reform in English Canada, 1885–1925* (Toronto: McClelland & Stewart, 1991).

Educational reform in the context of social reform is the subject of Neil Sutherland's *Children in English-Canadian Society* (Toronto: University of Toronto Press, 1976). On higher education see Paul Axelrod and John Reid, eds., *Youth, University and Canadian Society: Essays in the Social History of Higher Education* (Montreal/Kingston: McGill-Queen's University Press, 1989). Paul Rutherford's "Tomorrow's Metropolis: The Urban Reform Movement in Canada, 1880–1920," *Canadian Historical Association Report* (1971): 203–24 deals with urban reform. Janet Foster discusses the early conservation movement in *Working for Wildlife: The Beginning of Preservation in Canada* (Toronto: University of Toronto Press, 1978).

For women and social reform see Chapter 7, "The 'Woman Movement,'" in Alison Prentice et al., *Canadian Women: A History*, 2nd ed. (Toronto: Harcourt Brace, 1996); and the endnotes of "Where Historians Disagree: Women and Reform" in this chapter. On the Woman's Christian Temperance Union see Sharon Anne Cooke, *"Through Sunshine and Shadow": The Woman's Christian Temperance Union, Evangelicalism, and Reform in Ontario 1874–1930* (Montreal/Kingston: McGill-Queen's University Press, 1995).

A synthesis of the arts in Canada has yet to be written. For an overview consult Maria Tippett's *Making Culture: English-Canadian Institutions and the Arts Before the Massey Commission* (Toronto: University of Toronto Press, 1990). Music is discussed in Helmut Kallmann, *A History of Music in Canada, 1534–1914* (Toronto: University of Toronto Press, 1960). On the history of painting consult J. Russell Harper, *Painting in Canada: A History*, 2nd ed. (Toronto: University of Toronto Press, 1966); and Dennis Reid, *A Concise History of Canadian Painting*, 2nd ed. (Toronto: Oxford University Press, 1988). For Quebec see, as well, Guy Viau, *Modern Painting in French Canada* (Quebec: Department of Cultural Affairs, 1967). For architecture consult Harold Kalman, *A Concise History of Canadian Architecture* (Toronto: Oxford University Press, 2000).

Literary history is well documented in Carl F. Klinck, ed., *Literary History of Canada*, 2nd ed. (Toronto: University of Toronto Press, 1976). For Quebec see Guy Sylvestre, *Literature in French Canada* (Quebec: Department of Cultural Affairs, 1967). On Pauline Johnson, see Veronica Strong-Boag and Carol Gerson, *Paddling Her Own Canoe: The Times and Texts of E. Pauline Johnson* (Toronto: University of Toronto Press, 2000). The life of Charles Chiniquy is told by Marcel Trudel in *Chiniquy* (Trois-Rivières: Editions du Bien Public, 1955).

For the history of Canadian theatre in English-speaking Canada see Murray D. Edwards, *A Stage in Our Past: English-Language Theatre in Eastern Canada from the 1790s to 1914* (Toronto: University of Toronto Press, 1968). For Western Canada, consult E. Ross Stuart, *The History of Prairie Theatre: The Development of Theatre in Alberta, Manitoba and Saskatchewan 1833–1982* (Toronto: Simon and Pierre, 1984). For Quebec see Jean Hamelin, *The Theatre in French Canada* (Quebec: Department of Cultural Affairs, 1967).

For sports in Canada see Alan Metcalfe, *Canada Learns to Play: The Emergence of Organized Sports, 1807–1914* (Toronto: McClelland & Stewart, 1987); and Colin Howell, *Blood, Sweat, and Cheers: Sport in the Making of Modern Canada* (Toronto: University of Toronto Press, 2001).

For a discussion of an emerging middle-class culture in English-speaking Canada see Lynne Marks, *Revivals and Roller Rinks: Religion, Leisure, and Identity in Late Nineteenth Century Small-Town Ontario* (Toronto: University of Toronto Press, 1996); and Keith Walden, *Becoming Modern in Toronto: The Industrial Exhibition and the Shaping of a Late Victorian Culture* (Toronto: University of Toronto Press, 1997).

On working-class culture the best source is Bryan Palmer, *Working-Class Experience: The Rise and Reconstitution of Canadian Labour 1880–1991*, 2nd ed. (Toronto: Butterworths, 1993). An insightful article on taverns and working-class culture is Peter de Lottinville, "Joe Beef of Montreal: Working-Class Culture and the Tavern, 1869–1889," reprinted in R. Douglas Francis and Donald B. Smith, eds., *Readings in Canadian History: Post-Confederation*, 6th ed. (Toronto: Nelson Thomson Learning, 2002), pp. 195–216.

PART FIVE

THE IMPACT OF TWO WORLD WARS AND THE GREAT DEPRESSION, 1914–1945

Like two bookends on a shelf, two world wars enclose the years 1914–1945. The international events of war, economic growth in the 1920s, and depression in the 1930s affected Canada in profound ways. In this 31-year period, Canada became part of the global community.

The country felt the impact of the wars in significant ways. In human terms, Canada sent over 600 000 men out of a population of only 8 million to fight in World War I, and nearly 1 million out of 11.5 million in World War II. Canadian soldiers, sailors, and pilots distinguished themselves in battle, thus contributing greatly to the Allied cause, and advanced Canada's national recognition abroad. But at great cost. Over 60 000 — one-tenth of the total number of Canada's soldiers — died in World War I; some 40 000 died in World War II. An even greater number returned home maimed in body and in mind.

World War I transformed the country in other ways. Energy was directed principally toward the production of war-related materials. Since insufficient numbers of men were available to work in the factories and munitions plants, more women were called upon to work outside the home. This did not, however, result in gender equality in the workplace, although it did contribute to women getting the franchise. Women continued to face wage discrimination and were the first to be let go when the economy lagged. War also had a political impact. The state intervened in the lives of Canadian citizens to a greater extent than ever before, regulating and restricting what people could buy; dictating wages and working conditions; introducing new forms of revenue, such as the income tax and the sale of victory bonds; and reallocating resources to maximize war production. Government also took responsibility for the enlistment, equipping, and training of troops. In 1917, the Borden government created a Union party made up of Conservatives and a number of English-Canadian Liberals as a united war effort. It implemented military conscription. Conscription divided English-speaking and French-speaking Canadians to an unprecedented degree and left a legacy of bitterness that endured long after the war was over.

In the 1920s, economic prosperity eventually returned. A new economy of pulp and paper, mineral production, and the manufacturing of consumer goods replaced the old wheat economy. But the age-old regional, cultural, ethnic, gender, and class divisions remained. Politically, the two traditional parties survived the war, but a new third party, the Progressive party, challenged them. A new political tradition of federal multi-party rule began. Internationally, Canada took control over its foreign relations and achieved independent status.

The Great Depression of the 1930s affected the country profoundly. It occurred at the same time as severe climatic conditions in the Canadian West, making this one of the hardest-hit regions of the country. New political parties, and new radical left- and right-wing movements, emerged, desperate to find a solution to the economic crisis.

World War II might have ended the depression, but it plunged the country into something even more horrific. Although the King government was reluctant to get involved in the war on a major scale, it had no alternative as Hitler's army swept through western Europe. Once again, women were called upon to work outside the home for the war effort. This time they experienced greater gender equality than they did during World War I, but not without a struggle. The war raised the issue of Dominion–provincial relations and of Canada's relationship to Britain and the United States. The King government appointed the Royal Commission on Dominion–Provincial Relations in an attempt to find a solution to the tension between the two levels of government. Internationally, the signing of the Ogdensburg Agreement with the United States in August 1940 saw Canada agree to join in Canadian–American defence of North America. This proved to be the turning point from an era of British alliance to American protection.

The Canada that emerged from World War II in 1945 proved as different from the Canada that entered World War I as pre-1914 Canada was from the Canada of 1867. While changes had occurred in all areas, perhaps the most significant was the development of an increasingly interventionist state. Internationally the closer military and economic ties with the United States had a profound impact on Canada's foreign policy.

THE GREAT WAR: THE ROAD TO NATIONHOOD

TIME LINE

1914 –	World War I begins
	Canadian Parliament passes War Measures Act
	First Division of the Canadian Expeditionary Force leaves for England
1915 –	John McCrae writes "In Flanders Fields"
1916 –	Battle of Beaumont-Hamel
	Women in the four western provinces are the first to get the right to vote provincially
1917 –	Battle of Vimy Ridge
	Military Service Act (the conscription bill) becomes law
	Election of Union government under Robert Borden
	Halifax explosion
1918 –	Armistice signed ending World War I
	Women over 21 (except female status Indians and female Asians) get the right to vote
	Outbreak of Spanish flu epidemic
1919 –	Winnipeg General Strike
	Canada joins the League of Nations
	Death of Sir Wilfrid Laurier

World War I marked a turning point in Canadian development. Between 1914 and 1918, Canada sent 625 000 men and several thousand women to war — an enormous contribution for a nation of only 8 million people. One in ten of those who fought on the battlefields of Europe died; an even greater number were wounded in deadly trench warfare. The numbers were even higher proportionately for Newfoundlanders; an estimated one out of four died. During the war, the government intervened in the affairs of the state to an unprecedented degree, establishing such institutions as the Canadian National Railways, the Canadian Wheat Board, and a federal income tax. The war also initially united, and then divided, Canadians. Conscription set English-speaking against French-speaking Canadians. Workers and capitalists also quarrelled bitterly over who contributed the most to the war effort. Social reformers, particularly women suffragists and prohibitionists, used this "war to end wars" to advance their causes. By the war's end, Canadian leaders sought to gain full control over the Dominion's military and foreign affairs.

CANADA JOINS THE WAR EFFORT

The murder of Archduke Ferdinand, heir to the Austro–Hungarian throne, by a young Serbian nationalist in June 1914 began a chain of events that led to World War I. Austria attacked Serbia, an ally of Russia. Germany backed Austria, while France came to the defence of Russia. Britain, an ally of France had promised to defend Belgium's neutrality. When Germany invaded Belgium, Britain declared war (August 4, 1914). As a member of the British Empire, Canada was automatically at war.

Initially, Canadians united behind the war effort. Throughout the country, loyal demonstrations occurred, involving impromptu parades, flag waving, and, in the streets of Montreal, the singing of "La Marseillaise" and "Rule Britannia." Even the anti-imperialist Henri Bourassa initially supported Canadian participation, seeing the survival of France and Britain as vital to Canada. Most English-speaking Canadians viewed the war in black-and-white terms: good versus evil; democracy versus tyranny; the Anglo-Saxons versus the "Huns." Many believed that the Allies would achieve a quick victory — by Christmas.

Parliament unanimously passed the War Measures Act in 1914, which gave the cabinet the right to suspend the civil liberties of anyone suspected of collaborating with the enemy and to regulate any area of society deemed essential for the conduct of the war. Under the act, Ottawa required all those classified as "enemy aliens" — people who held citizenship in enemy countries, mostly German and Austro-Hungarian immigrants — to carry identity cards and to report once a month to the local police or to the Royal North-West Mounted Police. Ottawa also established 24 internment camps, from Halifax to Nanaimo, and interned those who were considered dangerous, as well as anyone who refused to register. During the war years, the Canadian government imprisoned about 8000 individuals.

THE CANADIAN EXPEDITIONARY FORCE

Canada's permanent army in July 1914 numbered only 3000, with an additional 60 000 in the militia. Its navy consisted of only two antiquated British cruisers, the *Niobe* and the *Rainbow*, and Canada did not have enough sailors even to serve these two. Cadet training had been implemented in schools and some universities in most provinces. Sam Hughes, who had been a "volunteer" since the age of 12, and had fought in the South African War, served as the minister of militia. He had also worked in his own determined way to build up the volunteer sector of the Canadian militia between 1911 and 1913. It would be the volunteer nature of the Canadian

Internment camp at Castle Mountain, Banff National Park, Alberta, 1915.

Glenbow Archives/NA-1870-6.

Corps and the absence of class divisions that would prove to be the great strengths of the Canadian army in the Great War.

At first, tens of thousands of young men answered the call for volunteers. Within two months, 30 000 Canadian volunteers were trained at Valcartier, a military camp 25 km north-west of Quebec City. Pleased by the enlistment results and anticipating a short war, Prime Minister Borden promised that he would not implement conscription.

The First Division of the Canadian Expeditionary Force of some 36 000 sailed for England on October 3, 1914, the largest convoy ever to cross the Atlantic until that time. More than 60 percent of the troops, known as "Hughes's Boys" after Sam Hughes, were recent British immi-grants, mostly unmarried, frequently unemployed, and emotionally close to Britain. Native-born Canadians of British stock made up 25 percent of the soldiers. The remainder included French Canadians, non-British immigrants, and Native Canadians. Among the Force were 101 volun-teer nurses. After training on Salisbury Plains in southern England, the First Canadian Division joined the British Army under the command of Lieutenant General E.A.H. Alderson for action in Flanders, in northwestern Belgium and adjacent France.

A "WHITE MAN'S WAR"

From the beginning, the war was considered a "white man's war." As in other allied armies, the Canadian army discouraged visible minorities from enlisting. When fifty African Canadians from Sydney, Nova Scotia, attempted to enlist, the recruiting officers told them: "This is not for you fellows, this is a white man's war." They then pressed for a totally African-Canadian bat-talion. Major-General Willoughby Gwatkin, Canada's chief of the General Staff, agreed if offi-cered by "white men." Daniel Sutherland, a contractor from Nova Scotia experienced in railway construction, commanded the No. 2 Construction Battalion (Coloured), the only African-Canadian battalion in Canadian military history. Nearly 600 of them went overseas to southern France, but on a separate transport ship so as to avoid "offending the susceptibility of other troops." They joined the Canadian Forestry Corps where they played an important role in the lumber camps. The battalion engendered pride in the African-Canadian community both at the time and since.

Japanese Canadians also faced discrimination in their effort to enlist. When Canadian military authorities denied them the right to join regular units, the Canadian–Japanese Association of Vancouver raised an exclusively Japanese unit. The 227 enlistees drilled at their own expense but under British veteran and militia captain R.S. Colquhoun. Eventually 185 of them served overseas in different battalions.

First Nations men faced similar obstacles to enlisting. The Canadian Militia Council forbade the enlistment of status Indians on the belief that "Germans might refuse to extend to them the privileges of civilized warfare." Still, they persisted. Sam Hughes permitted them to establish their own units so long as they were under the watchful eye of "white" officers who could cultivate their "natural" talents as fighters and marksmen. The 114th became an all-First Nations unit, but was broken up upon arrival in England, its members dispersed to various battalions, where many ended up doing mainly labour duty.

By 1917, the Canadian authorities, now desperate for all possible human power, lifted restrictions on the enlistment of visible minorities. By the end of the war, a significant number had enlisted: some 3500 First Nations (registered Indians under the Indian Act), probably several thousand Métis, over 1000 African Canadians, and several hundred Japanese Canadians. Unfortunately, they gained little in return for their service. At war's end, they were still denied respect and equality.

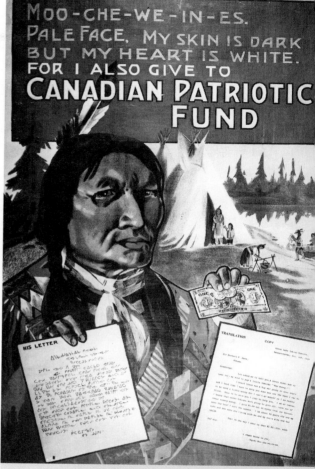

"My Skin Is Dark But My Heart Is White," Canadian Patriotic Fund Poster. It is ironic that the Canadian Patriotic Fund was using a First Nations to solicit war fund donations when First Nations men were facing obstacles to enlisting.

Toronto Reference Library.

The Nature of the Great War

From the outset the Great War was a war of attrition, one designed to kill as many of the enemy as possible. The fundamental concept of war remained Napoleonic. Like the French emperor a century earlier, the belligerent parties tried to destroy the main enemy army. They made no attempt to hit a tactical point, and in fact *blitzkreig* tactics — short, quick military attacks — would only develop in the last months of the war.

As early as October 1914, deadlock developed on the Western Front. The two opposing sides faced each other across a narrow "No Man's Land," in deep trenches stretching from

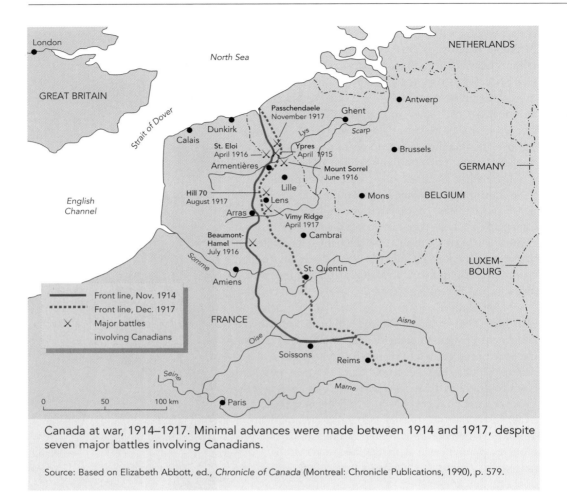

Canada at war, 1914–1917. Minimal advances were made between 1914 and 1917, despite seven major battles involving Canadians.

Source: Based on Elizabeth Abbott, ed., *Chronicle of Canada* (Montreal: Chronicle Publications, 1990), p. 579.

Switzerland to the North Sea. Four years of trench warfare began for an area no bigger than southern Ontario. From the beginning, the Canadian troops were singled out for their skill at trench raiding. It was the Princess Patricia's Canadian Light Infantry who first used the tactic of surprise attacks on enemy trenches at night in the first battle of St. Eloi in February 1915, and their success greatly boosted the morale of the Canadian Corps.

On the Western Front, all soldiers faced the same intolerable conditions: mud, vermin, rotten food, and the stench of rotting flesh. The soldiers spent hours digging trenches, tunnels, dugouts, and underground shelters, only to have them washed away by the rain and mud or abandoned in haste. Then there was the noise. As Canadian military historian John Swettenham has written: "It has been likened to an infernal orchestra made up of ear-splitting crashes from heavy artillery, the deeper roar of mined charges, the flailing crack of field pieces, the higher-pitched note of rifles, the ghastly staccato rattle of machine-guns, the shriek and wail of shells, and the insect zip and whine of bullets, but no words can ever describe it adequately."[1]

Amid these horrors came something worse — chemical warfare. The Germans first used chlorine gas, a greenish substance that caused coughing, choking, and burning eyes and skin, on April 22, 1915, at the Battle of Ypres. One Canadian officer described it vividly: "A great wall of green gas about 15 or 20 feet high was on top of us. Captain McLaren gave an order to get handkerchiefs, soak them and tie them around our mouths and noses." A British soldier later recalled what he saw when he and his contingent arrived to relieve the Canadians: "We stopped at a ditch at a first-aid clearing station. There were about 200 to 300 men lying in that ditch. Some were clawing their throats. Their brass buttons were green. Their bodies were swelled. Some of them were still alive. Some were still writhing on the ground, their tongues hanging out." Half of the men in surgeon John McCrae's brigade were killed or wounded. While waiting on the rear step of an ambulance for the wounded to arrive, he wrote "In Flanders Fields," the most popular poem of the Great War. The poem made the poppy flower the enduring symbol of those who died.

At Ypres, the Canadians made their reputation by preventing a German breakthrough in the Allied lines to drive to the English Channel. But nearly 2000 Canadians lay dead, with another 3410 wounded and 775 taken prisoner – out of a total divisional fighting strength of 10 000. After Ypres, historian Daniel Dancocks explains, "there was no more bravado about an early victory over the Hun, no more fears of missing out on 'the fun.'"[2]

In 1915 and 1916, three more Canadian divisions joined the 1st Canadian Division in France. Lieutenant General Sir Julian Byng, a British regular officer, replaced Alderson as commander of the Canadian Corps. There was also a change of equipment. The Canadian-built Ross rifle, insisted upon by Sam Hughes, jammed in trench warfare. In the spring of 1916, the Canadian cabinet overruled Hughes and officially replaced the Ross rifle with the better-built British Lee-Enfield.

The Ross rifle fiasco highlighted the incompetence of Sam Hughes as minister of militia and defence. Accused of corruption, of failure to attend to his departmental duties, and of incompetence in handling the administration of the war, Hughes had his responsibilities reduced by Prime Minister Borden. Then, in November 1916, Borden sacked Sam Hughes, chiefly for openly criticizing the prime minister.

THE INTERVENTIONIST STATE

The war led Ottawa to intervene in Canada's economic, social, and military affairs to an unprecedented degree. Through the newly created Board of Grain Supervisors (after 1919 the Canadian Wheat Board), the government regulated all aspects of the production and distribution of wheat. Hectarage in wheat doubled, and the price per bushel increased by more than 50 percent. The government also regulated the production, distribution, sale, and consumption of coal, wood, and gas fuels. As well, the government nationalized two new transcontinental railways, the Canadian Northern and the Grand Trunk Pacific. Between 1917 and 1920, the Canadian government incorporated these railways into the publicly owned Canadian National Railways (CNR).

The federal government also got involved in selling "Victory Bonds" to finance the war. They proved to be immensely popular — more than one million Canadians purchased the bonds by war's end, thus generating close to $2 million in revenue. The government also introduced another important financial innovation: direct taxation. First it imposed a business-profits tax; then, in 1917, it imposed its first federal income tax. Ottawa promised that the new tax would only remain for the duration of the war. While these new sources of revenue helped, costs continued to outdistance revenue, thus forcing the government to borrow vast sums at home and abroad, at high interest rates. The national debt increased fivefold, from $463 million in 1913 to $2.46 billion by 1918.

WOMEN AND THE WAR

Women made major contributions to the war effort. Twenty-five hundred women served as nursing sisters in the Canadian Army Medical Corps, working overseas at station hospitals, on hospital ships, and on ambulance trains. Forty-three died in the service of Canada. Margaret

Macdonald, director of the army nursing sisters, received the Royal Red Cross and the Florence Nightingale Medal for her effort, while Matron Ethel Ridley was invested into the Order of the British Empire for her efforts as principal matron in France.

Women also contributed through their work for voluntary organizations, including the Imperial Order Daughters of the Empire (IODE), Red Cross clubs, the Great Veterans' Association, the Next-of-Kin Association, the YWCA, and the Women's Patriotic Leagues. They rolled bandages and knitted socks, mitts, sweaters, and scarves for the troops; raised money to send cigarettes and candy overseas; and marshalled support for the cause, not least by persuading wives and mothers to allow their men to enlist. They headed the Canadian Patriotic Fund, established in 1914, to assist families of soldiers overseas. They lobbied for mothers' pensions, day nurseries, and health inspection. By 1918, the government established federal agencies, such as the Women's Bureau and the Food Board, to assist them in the war effort. Some women also encouraged their children to help by growing "victory gardens" to increase the amount of food available for overseas.

Unmarried women entered the work force in large numbers, as did some married women, to ease the wartime labour shortage. On farms, in factories, and in offices, women filled positions previously occupied by men. In summertime, the YWCA recruited hundreds of female volunteers in the cities and towns to help on farms. The Women's Canadian Club organized a Women's Emergency Corps to recruit women for the munitions-production industries.

In wartime industries, however, gender discrimination remained: lower wages for women, lack of union support, and inadequate day-care facilities. Nevertheless, a number of women used their new bargaining position to raise social issues such as women's suffrage, child labour, and conditions in jails and asylums.

FIGHTING ON THE BATTLEFIELDS OF EUROPE

 On June 1, 1916, Canadian soldiers contributed to the Battle of Sorrel in the Ypres Salient, a small triangular area around the town of Ypres. The Germans began an intense artillery barrage that enabled them to break through the Allied lines to capture Mount Sorrel. Arthur Currie led the First Division troops that began the counterattack. By June 13th, the Canadian Corps had recaptured all that had been lost to the Germans, a great victory but at the loss of 8000 men in just 12 days of fighting.

A month later, Canadian and Newfoundland soldiers joined British and French soldiers in the massive but ill conceived Battle of the Somme against heavily fortified German positions. On July 1, the first day of the Big Push or Grand Assault at Beaumont-Hamel, the Newfoundland Regiment suffered 720 casualties — three-quarters of the unit. It was the greatest single disaster in Newfoundland's history, and the heaviest loss by any army on any single day in the history of the Great War. Britain recognized Newfoundland's efforts by awarding its regiment the title "Royal." At the end of the war, the people of Newfoundland purchased the land at Beaumont-Hamel, and erected a statute of a lone bull caribou, the regiment's emblem. For Newfoundlanders, the battle, commemorated annually on July 1, came to represent what Vimy Ridge did for Canadians.

Canadian soldiers made their major contribution to the Battle of the Somme in the assault on the Regina Trench, a shallow ditch on the outskirts of the town of Courcelette. The Royal 22nd Regiment, the famous "Vandoos," led the attack. Their commanding officer, Lieutenant-Colonel Thomas Tremblay, wrote: "If hell is as bad as what I have seen at Courcelette, I would not wish my worst enemies to go there." After a week of fierce fighting and heavy casualties, the Canadians captured the Regina Trench and the town of Courcelette. This battle was one of the last — and few victories — in the infamous Battle of the Somme in which, during the three-month period, the Canadian Corps lost close to 2500 men.

Canada's finest hour came in the Battle of Vimy Ridge. On Easter Monday, April 9, 1917, some 70 000 Canadian soldiers, under the command of Julian Byng, along with British units, made a major attack against the German-held Vimy Ridge. Earlier in the war, both the British and French armies, with heavy losses, had failed to dislodge the Germans. This time, the Canadians took it. David Lloyd George, the British prime minister, recalled in his memoirs: "The Canadians played a part of such distinction ... that thenceforth they were marked out as storm troops; for the remainder of the war they were brought along to head the assault in one great battle after another." The cost for such praise and national honour was devastating: 3598 killed and 7004 wounded.

CANADA'S ENLISTMENT/CASUALTY RATE, 1917

Month	Enlistments	Casualties
January	9 194	4 396
February	6 809	1 250
March	6 640	6 161
April	5 530	13 477
May	6 407	13 457
June	6 348	7 931
July	3 882	7 906
August	3 177	13 232
September	3 588	10 990
October	4 884	5 929
November	4 019	30 741
December	3 921	7 476
Total	64 339	122 946

Source: From *Canada: Our Century, Our Story: Ontario Edition*, Student text by Fielding/Evans. © 2001. Reprinted with permission of Nelson, a division of Thomson Learning: www.thomsonrights.com. Fax 800-730-2215.

Canadians and Newfoundlanders also served with distinction in the air and on the sea. Canada did not have an air force of its own, but some 2500 Canadian flyers, trained in Canada by the Royal Flying Corps after 1917, joined the Royal Air Force (RAF). A number became high scoring "aces," such as British Columbia's Raymond Collishaw, Manitoba's "Billy" Barker, Ontario's Ray Brown (credited with shooting down the notorious Baron von Richthofen — the "Red Baron" — in April 1918), and the legendary Billy Bishop, who was credited with shooting down 72 German fighters, earning him a Victoria Cross. But casualties were high. As the British never issued parachutes in World War I, there were no parachute escapes for Canadians from burning or disabled aircraft. The airplanes, too, were very flimsy; more pilots died in crash landings than in the air. Canadians wanting to serve at sea joined the Royal Canadian Navy, under the command of the British Royal Navy. Some 8800 Canadians and 200 Newfoundlanders joined. Among their duties was the patrolling of Canadian and Newfoundland waters against German U-boats (submarines).

"INVITE US TO YOUR COUNCILS"

As the war progressed, Canadian politicians demanded a greater voice in Britain's war policy. At the outset of the war, the British government treated Canada and the other dominions as colonial subordinates, neglecting to consult with them about war strategy or even to keep them informed of developments.

When David Lloyd George became prime minister in December 1916, he implemented changes. He invited the dominion prime ministers to London to meet as an Imperial War Cabinet, a group consisting of the British War Cabinet and dominion representation. There, in March 1917, for the first time, Borden learned about the Allied position, discussed strategy, and, most important, became involved in the decision-making process.

Borden also gradually replaced British senior officers with Canadian commanders. Then in June of 1917, Arthur Currie, the commander of the First Canadian Infantry Division, was appointed commander of the entire Canadian Corps.

RECRUITMENT

With continuous high casualties in Europe, Ottawa stepped up its recruitment drive. In his New Year's Day address of 1916, Borden announced his "sacred promise" that Canada would send a total of 500 000 to the war front, double the current numbers. In the first half of the year, it appeared that the government could honour its commitment. By June 1916, the total number of wartime recruitments numbered over 300 000. Then recruitment dropped off dramatically. In summer, farmers needed young men to help on the farms. Munitions factories were in need of more workers. The government responded by establishing the National Service Board, which had a mandate to "determine whether the services of any man of military age are more valuable to the state in his present occupation than in military duties and either to permit or forbid his enlistment." The government assigned registration cards to every male of military age. It concluded that 475 000 potential recruits existed.

Borden next established the Canadian Defence Force in the spring of 1917. This force was designed to get men who opposed fighting overseas to sign up for home defence. They would replace those already in uniform who were willing to serve on the war front. This last desperate attempt to get more troops without conscription failed. In the first month of operation, fewer than 200 signed up for home defence.

NATIONAL DISUNITY

As voluntary enlistment dried up, complaints arose about those groups who appeared reluctant to give their full support to the war effort. Once again, this exposed the geological fault line that divided French and English Canadians. Several reasons can be given for the coolness of French Canadians to the war effort. To them, the war was alien and remote. They had few or no emotional ties to Britain or even to France. Few of the officers at the Royal Military College in Kingston, the training school for military officers, were French-speaking, since English remained the sole language of instruction. In Quebec, an English-speaking elite with little sympathy for, and even less contact with, French Canadians headed the recruitment effort. As well, Sam Hughes, the minister of militia and defence, did little to encourage French-Canadian enlistment. He placed French Canadians in English-speaking units and seldom appointed or promoted French Canadians to the rank of officer. Initially, apart from the one French-language battalion, the "Vandoos" (the Royal 22nd Regiment of Quebec), English ruled as the language of the army.

THE ONTARIO SCHOOLS QUESTION

The question of language rights for French Canadians outside Quebec also poisoned relations between French-speaking and English-speaking Canadians during the war years. This time the controversy centred on Ontario. By 1910, French Canadians made up nearly 10 percent of Ontario's population. These Franco-Ontarians appealed to the Ontario government to protect their bilingual schools (or "English–French schools," as they were called) and to promote French-language interests.

These English–French schools came under attack from both the Orange Order and Irish Catholics. The Orange Lodge believed that the use of the French language in schools undermined the unity of Canada and of the British empire. Irish Catholics feared that language concessions to French Catholics would give French Canadians control of the separate-school system. The Irish Catholics favoured Roman Catholic — but not bilingual — schools.

James Whitney, the Ontario premier, appointed a commission to investigate. The commissioners pointed out the inadequate training of many teachers in the English–French schools but stopped short of making any recommendations to solve the problem. In 1912, the Whitney government implemented Instruction 17, or "Regulation 17," which made English the official language of instruction and restricted French to the first two years of elementary school. A year later, Whitney amended Regulation 17 to permit French as a subject of study for one hour a day.

French-speaking Canadians in Ontario and Quebec reacted. At the Guigues school in Ottawa, an "army" of French-speaking mothers, brandishing long hatpins, stood ready to prevent any entry by authorities to remove the bilingual teachers. In Quebec, Henri Bourassa denounced the Ontario government as more Prussian than the Prussians: French Canadians need not go to Europe to fight the enemy; it resided next door. Bourassa carried his message into Ontario. Everywhere he went in Ontario, he met hostility from English-speaking Canadians.

The Ontario schools controversy dragged on for years, during which time Franco-Ontarians were deprived of schooling in their own language. Not until 1927 did the Ontario government find a solution: each school designated for bilingual education would be considered on its merits by a departmental committee.

ETHNIC TENSIONS

The wartime hysteria poisoned relations with various ethnic groups. Whereas prior to the war, Germans were considered ideal immigrants, now they were vilified as "blood-crazed madmen." The Canadian propaganda machine, through newspaper editorials, books, advertisements, movies, songs, and church sermons, ensured that this image of the enemy prevailed. It also presented the counter image of the Allies, and especially the Canadian soldiers, as brave and noble warriors. Such propaganda played out in various ways. In Berlin, Ontario, the city government held a plebiscite on whether or not to change the name of this city. Although over two-thirds of the city's population was of German descent, it was decided, by a narrow vote, to rename the city "Kitchener," after the British military hero who drowned at sea on June 5, 1916.

THE CONSCRIPTION CRISIS

In the spring of 1917, Prime Minister Borden visited Canadian soldiers in British hospitals and at the front while attending a meeting of the Imperial War Cabinet in London. The desperate situation and the British pressure on Canada to increase its commitment of men convinced him to break his promise, made at the outset of the war, not to introduce conscription for overseas military service.

Slander!

That man is a slanderer who says that

The Farmers of Ontario

will vote with

**Bourassa, Pro-Germans,
Suppressors of Free Speech and Slackers**

Never!

They Will Support Union Government

Citizens' Union Committee

An ad placed in *The Farmer's Advocate*, December 13, 1917, by the "Citizens' Union Committee." The federal election of December 1917 was one of the most divisive in Canadian history as a result of the implementation of the Military Service Act, or conscription bill, that past summer.

Courtesy University Archives, Killam Memorial Library, Dalhousie University.

He favoured a coalition government of Conservatives and Liberals as the best means to introduce compulsory service, so he approached Wilfrid Laurier, leader of the Liberal Party, about the possibility. While Laurier agreed with the need for a coalition government for the war's duration, he opposed a union government that would introduce conscription, which neither he nor his Quebec followers favoured. "I oppose this bill," he warned when the Conservatives introduced the Military Service Act in Parliament, "because it has in it the seeds of discord and disunion, because it is an obstacle and bar to that union of heart and soul without which it is impossible to hope that this Confederation will attain the aims and ends that were had in view when Confederation was effected."

OPPOSITION TO CONSCRIPTION

The Military Service Act, the official title of the conscription bill, became law in July 1917. Throughout that summer, anti-conscriptionist riots broke out in Montreal. More riots followed in the spring of 1918, after the actual implementation of conscription in January 1918.

Others, besides French Canadians, opposed conscription. Farmers resented their sons' forced departure from the farm, where they contributed to the war effort through food production. Workers saw military conscription as the first step toward compulsory industrial service, forcing them to remain at one job for the war's duration. Both groups demanded the "conscription of wealth" — heavier taxes on the rich and the nationalization of banks and industries — to ensure that financiers and businesspeople made their sacrifice for the war effort.

Some pacifist groups, such as the Quakers and the Mennonites, opposed wars as inherently evil and immoral. Others, not having a religious affiliation, opposed war as a wasteful and destructive means of settling world problems. The Canadian Women's Peace Party, forerunner of the Women's International League for Peace and Freedom, advocated a non-violent struggle at home rather than war abroad as a means to reform society in order to root out the inherent causes of violence and war.

UNION GOVERNMENT AND THE ELECTION OF 1917

Despite Laurier's refusal to join Borden in a coalition government, Borden did convince a number of Liberal members of Parliament and provincial Liberal leaders to join his Union government. Then he dissolved Parliament and called an election.

Before dissolving Parliament, the Unionists implemented two bills to strengthen their chances at the polls. The Military Voters Act enfranchised all members of the armed forces, no matter how long or short a time they had lived in Canada. The governing party could use the soldiers' vote in whatever constituency it wished, where a constituency was not indicated. The Wartime Elections Act gave the vote to Canadian women who were mothers, wives, sisters, or daughters of servicemen (this did not apply to female relatives of status Indian servicemen), but denied the vote to conscientious objectors and to naturalized Canadians from enemy countries who had settled in Canada after 1902.

Both the Unionists and the Liberals fought the election largely along cultural lines. A Unionist election poster claimed that a vote for Laurier was a vote for Bourassa, the Kaiser, and the Germans. A group of Union supporters issued a map of Canada with Quebec in black, the "foul blot" on the country. On the Sunday before the election, an estimated three-quarters of the Protestant ministers across Canada responded to a Unionist circular, appealing for support of the Union party in their sermons.

In Quebec, political leaders painted conscriptionists as a greater danger to the country than the Germans. Bourassa and the *nationalistes* argued that Canada had done enough for the war. "Every Canadian who wishes to combat conscription with an effective logic," he declared, "must have the courage to say and to repeat everywhere: No Conscription! No Enrolment!"

The outcome of the election proved predictable. The Union party won two-thirds of the constituencies outside of Quebec but only three seats, all in English-speaking ridings, in the province. Ninety percent of the soldiers' vote went to the Union government. The federal government was now literally an English-Canadian government. The Liberals won 62 of the 65 seats in Quebec but only 20 seats in the rest of the country.

FINAL YEAR OF THE WAR

Meanwhile, the situation in Europe deteriorated. In October 1917, revolution broke out in Russia, and by November, Lenin led the Bolsheviks to power. They immediately made peace with Germany. Now the Germans could concentrate on the Western Front. The Germans' unrestricted submarine warfare in the North Atlantic brought the United States into the war against Germany in April 1917, but American troops would not be mobilized in force in Europe until the summer of 1918. In October and November, the Allies suffered hundreds of thousands of casualties in the last phase of Field-Marshal Haig's Flanders offensive, including 16 000 Canadian deaths in the battle of Passchendaele, an attempt to take an insignificant ridge in a sea of mud.

Finally, in the spring of 1918, came the all-out German counteroffensive. Once again the Allies faced defeat. Only with the Germans' "black day" at Amiens on August 8, 1918, the beginning of the final "Hundred Days" campaign, did the Allies turn the tide. The Canadian Corps under Currie's command played a key role in the final assault. With victories at Drocourt-Quéant, Cambrai, and Valenciennes, the Canadians pushed on to the city of Mons. As the site of Britain's first defeat at the hands of the Germans in 1914, the recapture of Mons on the night of November 10th held symbolic importance. The next morning at 11 a.m., the Germans surrendered and signed the Armistice. The "Great War" was over.

Few Canadian conscripts ever fought on the battlefield in the Great War. While the implementation of conscription put 100 000 more men into the army by the war's end, only one-quarter of them reached the front before the armistice. Overall, some 600 000 Canadians fought in the Great War; 60 000 of them died.

SUCCESS OF THE CANADIAN CORPS

The Canadian Corps proved itself in the Great War. In assessing its success, historians have pointed to its volunteer nature, the absence of class distinctions and of preconceived rules of conduct of military operations (both of which hindered the established European armies), the fact that the Corps stayed together during the war, the rural and small-town roots of many of the soldiers who were used to a rugged lifestyle, and finally the fact that Canadian soldiers had something to prove: a pride in being Canadian.

THE WAR AND SOCIAL REFORM

The war greatly advanced the cause of social reform. During the war, English-Canadian reformers argued that just as the troops fought for a noble cause on the battlefront, so should those at home — against materialism, alcoholism, and corruption. Social gospellers saw the war as the final struggle for bringing God's kingdom to earth.

THE SUCCESS OF WOMEN'S SUFFRAGE AND PROHIBITION

Women's suffrage and prohibition both gained support during the war. Women reformers argued that men's aggressive nature, often aggravated by alcohol, had caused the worldwide cataclysm. If women had the right to vote and an opportunity to rule, wars would cease. They also pointed out the inconsistency of fighting for democracy abroad while denying women the democratic right to vote at home.

In 1916, the four western provinces granted women the right to vote in provincial elections. Ontario followed in 1917, Nova Scotia in 1918, New Brunswick in 1919, Prince Edward Island in 1922, and Quebec in 1940.

Federally, the franchise came in three stages: the Military Voters Act of 1917 awarded the vote to women serving in the armed forces or as nurses in the war; the Wartime Elections Act extended voting privileges to women, aged 21 years and over, whose fathers, husbands, or sons served overseas; and finally, in 1918, all women, recognized as British citizens in Canada, over the age of 21, gained the right to vote federally. Still excluded from the franchise were status Indians, Asians, and conscientious objectors, including Mennonites and Hutterites.

For What? by Frederick Varley, one of the four war artists who later joined the Group of Seven. Varley's bleak painting of a burial party at work behind the front lines makes a horrible statement on the futility of war.

F.H. Varley, *For What?* Accession number: 19710261-0770, Catalogue number: 8911, Beaverbrook Collection of War Art © Canadian War Museum (CWM).

The war also helped the cause of prohibition, at least temporarily. Prohibitionists equated their struggle with that of the men at the front. As well, prohibitionists criticized human and material resources being wasted to make liquor at this time of critical shortage. The prohibitionists' first victory came in 1915, when the Saskatchewan Liberal government closed all bars, saloons, and liquor stores. Immediately, this move brought liquor under the control of provincially operated outlets. Alberta went further by endorsing outright provincial prohibition later the same year. Manitoba followed in early 1916. By the end of 1917, every provincial government except Quebec had implemented prohibition legislation. In 1918, the newly elected federal Union government imposed prohibition on Quebec. Within a week of his electoral victory in December 1917, Prime Minister Borden moved to prohibit the manufacture, importation, and transportation of any beverage containing more than 2.5 percent alcohol.

FRENCH-CANADIAN REFORMERS IN THE WAR YEARS

French-Canadian clerics and laypeople pressed for social, not political, reform during the war period. In 1917, Father Joseph-Papin Archambault, of the Jesuit-inspired École sociale populaire, issued a tract, *La question sociale et nos devoirs de catholiques*, in which he appealed to Roman Catholics to reach out to the working class. In 1920, he began the Semaines sociales, an annual weeklong meeting of clerics and laypeople to discuss social questions.

In Bourassa's view, French-Canadian regeneration had to remain linked to Canadian Roman Catholic reform in general. At the turn of the century, most French-Canadian nationalists, including Bourassa, looked to all of Canada as their homeland. After the conscription crisis of 1917, however, perspectives changed. A small group of nationalists, led by Abbé Lionel Groulx, advanced the idea of an independent, Roman Catholic, and rural French-Canadian nation in the St. Lawrence valley. As historian Mason Wade wrote of Groulx in the early 1920s: "For him the French Canadians possessed most of the essential attributes of a nation, and their attainment of political independence would be a normal part of their coming of age as a people."[3]

ENGLISH-CANADIAN REFORMERS AND THE WAR

English-Canadian reformers regarded the Allied victory as the beginning of regeneration for a "New Canada." Some wrote books associating war with reform. In *The New Christianity* (1920), Salem Bland, a leading figure in the social gospel movement and a professor at Wesley College in Winnipeg, presented his vision of a socialist Canada operating on the Christian principles of love, equality, brotherhood, and democracy through a new labour church. Stephen Leacock, the political economist-cum-humorist, had doubts about the utopian nature of socialism. In his *Unsolved Riddle of Social Justice* (1920), he favoured instead legislation designed to make the workplace more appealing. In *Wake Up Canada* (1919), C.W. Paterson saw educational reform as the answer to society's ills. Two agrarian reformers, W.G. Good in *Production and Taxation in Canada* (1919) and William Irvine in *The Farmers in Politics* (1920), proposed rural values as the ideal of the future. William Lyon Mackenzie King welcomed the new urban–industrial society in *Industry and Humanity* (1918), provided that "regenerated men" directed it on Christian principles of co-operation and brotherhood.

POSTWAR PROBLEMS

In 1919, the Canadian government faced insurrection among its soldiers stationed in demobilized camps in Britain and Europe. In early 1918, it had created the Department of Soldiers' Civil Re-establishment in anticipation of this problem. But even its personnel were unprepared for the difficulties involved in arranging for 300 000 troops to return and be integrated back into society.

The problem of treating disabled soldiers paled in comparison with an even greater domestic crisis in the immediate postwar era: the Spanish influenza epidemic, brought back home almost certainly by returning soldiers. The first major outbreak occurred in September 1918 in Quebec. In some cities, people were ordered to wear gauze masks in public; in others, theatres and schools were closed, public meetings were banned, and church services were cancelled in an effort to check the deadly disease. Labrador was devastated by the influenza, with a third of the Inuit dying between November 1918 and January 1919. In the fall of 1919, the federal government established the Department of Health to deal with the epidemic. Eventually an estimated 50 000 Canadians died from this "silent enemy" — almost as many as had died in the Great War itself.

THE WINNIPEG GENERAL STRIKE

Widespread labour unrest followed the armistice. Strikes broke out from Halifax to Vancouver as workers tried to make up for the restraints applied in wartime and to protect themselves in an inflationary economy. At the annual meeting of the Trades and Labor Congress in Quebec City in

"Bloody Saturday," June 21, 1919, a violent confrontation that occurred between peaceful marchers and the Mounties and special police during the Winnipeg General Strike. Note the burning streetcar.

David Miller Collection/National Archives of Canda/C-33392.

1918, the western delegates broke rank with the conservative eastern members who controlled the meeting. A month later, the Western Labour Conference called for a single industrial union, the One Big Union (OBU), at its meeting in Calgary. But before its organizers could hold the founding convention, new developments broke out in Winnipeg. On May 1, 1919, metalworkers' and builders' unions struck for better wages and improved working conditions. Other Winnipeg union workers, including police officers, fire fighters, and telephone and telegraph operators, joined them on May 15, swelling the numbers of strikers to some 3000, thus enabling them virtually to close down the city. To provide essential services and to regulate the strike, the organizers created a central strike committee. Business and government officials saw this committee, with its power to dictate what went on in the city, as the beginnings of a "Bolshevik uprising." They countered by creating the Citizens' Committee of 1000, an anti-strike organization.

Fearing that the strike would spread to other centres, the federal government intervened. Arthur Meighen, the minister of justice and minister of the interior, and Gideon Robertson, acting minister of labour, arrived in Winnipeg to assess the situation. They came already convinced that the strike was a conspiracy.

On the night of June 16, Meighen ordered the Royal North-West Mounted Police to arrest ten of the Winnipeg strike leaders, along with labour newspaper editors, including J.S. Woodsworth, and some returned soldiers. In protest, the strikers organized a silent parade on Saturday, June 21. Violence erupted, and the mayor of Winnipeg called in the Mounties to disperse the crowd. The confrontation saw one man killed and another wounded and many others injured. "Bloody Saturday," as it became known, ended with the dispersal of the workers and the establishment of military control of the city. On June 26, the strike committee called off the strike, without the workers having gained any of their objectives.

Where Historians Disagree

The Winnipeg General Strike

Canadian labour and working-class historians agree on the importance of the Winnipeg General Strike of 1919, but on little else. Initially, the historiography reflected the opposing ideological perspectives of the two sides at the time: the strike opponents seeing it as a revolution aimed at creating a Soviet-style regime in Canada; its supporters seeing it as a legitimate tool by which workers could obtain collective bargaining to secure better wages and working conditions.

Historian D.C. Masters wrote the first scholarly study of the strike. He emphasized the British background of the strike leaders so as to reinforce the legitimacy of the strike within the British democratic tradition and denied any connection between the strike and the One Big Union (OBU) (often seen as an attempt to create a working-class solidarity as a prelude to a Bolshevik-style revolution). He also challenged those who saw the strike as a spontaneous uprising, claiming "it came at the end of a series of controversies which had raged in a crescendo since at least 1917." Thus, he concluded that "there was no seditious conspiracy and that the strike was what it purported to be, an effort to secure the principle of collective bargaining."[1]

In contrast, sociologist S.D. Clark emphasized the importance of the One Big

Union in his introduction to D.C. Masters' study, which was part of a series under Clark's general editorship. Clark saw the OBU, along with the Progressive party among western farmers, as "expressions of protest against eastern dominance ... in the tradition of American frontier radicalism."[2] In this respect, Clark concluded, "the movement was revolutionary" — ironically, a direct contradiction to the conclusion that Masters, whose book Clark was introducing, had drawn!

Historian David Bercuson provided a comprehensive study of the general strike in *Confrontation at Winnipeg*. He traced the roots of the strike back to labour unrest in the city in 1906, if not to the turn of the century. The massive influx of immigrants came at a time of major social and industrial changes that turned Winnipeg into a city sharply divided along class lines. Bercuson denied that the strikers were revolutionaries; instead they were striking for legitimate working-class concerns. But, he argued, the fact that they failed to achieve their objectives set back "the cause of labour for at least another generation."[3] Fellow labour historian Irving Abella concurred. "Labour's trauma started at Winnipeg in 1919," he wrote. "With the suppression of the Winnipeg General Strike ... the rapid demise of organized labour in Canada began."[4]

Historian Norman Penner disagreed with this negative assessment of the strike's aftermath. "[F]or more than a year," he wrote, "the Winnipeg General Strike and the trials of its leaders kept the labour movement in a constant state of agitation and turmoil which succeeded in translating the economic struggle into a political victory.... Hence the Winnipeg General Strike must be seen as part of the cumulative impact of labour on Canadian life, a constant force which accounts for labour's strength and status in Canada today."[5]

Bercuson introduced a new issue into the debate in an article that examined the strike in the context of the larger issue of western labour radicalism.[6] He argued that western workers were more radical than elsewhere in the country because of unique western frontier conditions, including immigrants who came with utopian dreams of a better lifestyle, only to find themselves up against ruthless and repressive industrialists who thwarted their hopes. Failed expectations, Bercuson argued, were a sure cause for radicalism. He concluded that the Canadian western industrial frontier bred class consciousness and radical working-class attitudes rather than equality and harmony.

Labour historian Greg Kealey vehemently disagreed with Bercuson's theory that the West was more radical than the rest of the country. Also, Kealey questioned Bercuson's implication that the Winnipeg General Strike could only have occurred in Winnipeg, the most urban of societies. Kealey pointed out that that year was punctuated by strikes and labour unrest throughout the country; in fact, labour unrest in Canada in 1919 was really part of an international working-class solidarity. He went on to argue as well that the strike was part of "larger structural changes in capitalist organization on both a national and international scale."[7] Seen from this wider perspective, the strike was not a failure, but only a momentary defeat before labour emerged even stronger in the move toward industrial unionism in the 1940s.

Bercuson dismissed Kealey's argument in a historiographical chapter that appeared in a revised edition of *Confrontation at Winnipeg*. He claimed that evidence of numerous strikes and/or revolts across the country did not constitute proof of working-class revolt. Few of these strikes were "politically motivated and those that were — the

Vancouver general strike, for example — were dismal failures." Nor had Kealey proven that the strikers were consciously trying to overthrow capitalism. Kealey's essay, he claimed, was "little more than pamphleteering. He is rallying the revolutionary troops; he is certainly not advancing scholarship." Then Bercuson criticized Marxist history in general as reading back into the past the present dreams of workers. In the case of the Winnipeg General Strike, there was no evidence of any connection whatever between the strike and the rise of industrial unionism in the 1940s, and "only the most slender thread connecting the strike to the rise of the CCF."[8] As for the significance of the Winnipeg General Strike in Canadian history, it lay in "its unique occurrence that took place for particular reasons and which had specific consequences" and not for some "hidden inner meaning" found only in the minds of historians.

Bryan Palmer entered the debate to argue that the significance of the strike lay in the fact that it reflected both "the continuity of class struggle and the changes that had taken place as a consequence of the twentieth-century conditions of monopoly capital, state intervention, and labour market segmentation."[9] Craig Heron agreed with those labour historians who saw the strike as only one of a series of strikes between 1917 and 1925 in industrial centres across the country, where "workers formed their own organizations, marched off the job in record numbers, engaged in defiant acts of solidarity, and made bold new demands."[10] He urged labour historians to study the ethnic and gender component of workers' revolts.

The debate on what happened in Winnipeg in 1919 and its consequences continues. Clearly, though, the strike remains the best-known example of a general strike in Canadian history.

[1] D.C. Masters, *The Winnipeg General Strike* (Toronto: University of Toronto Press, 1950), pp. 127, 134.

[2] S.D. Clark, "Introduction" to Masters, *The Winnipeg General Strike*, p. viii.

[3] David Bercuson, *Confrontation at Winnipeg* (Montreal/Kingston: McGill-Queen's University Press, 1974), p. 176.

[4] Irving Abella, "Introduction" to *On Strike: Six Key Labour Struggles in Canada, 1919–1949*, ed. by Irving Abella (Toronto: James Lewis & Samuel Publishers, 1974), p. xii.

[5] Norman Penner, *Winnipeg 1919: The Strikers' Own History of the Winnipeg General Strike*, 2nd ed. (Toronto: James Lorimer, 1975), pp. xxiii, vii–viii.

[6] D. J. Bercuson, "Labour Radicalism and the Western Industrial Frontier: 1897–1919," *Canadian Historical Review*, LVIII, 2 (June 1977): 154–75.

[7] Gregory Kealey, "1919: The Canadian Labour Revolt," *Labour/Le Travail*, 13 (Spring 1984): 15.

[8] Bercuson, *Confrontation at Winnipeg*, rev. ed. (Montreal/Kingston: McGill-Queen's University Press, 1990), pp. 202, 205.

[9] Bryan Palmer, *Working-Class Experience: Rethinking the History of Canadian Labour, 1880–1991* (Toronto: McClelland & Stewart, 1993), p. 180.

[10] Craig Heron, "Introduction" to *The Workers' Revolt in Canada, 1917–1925*, ed. by Craig Heron (Toronto: University of Toronto Press, 1998), p. 4.

ADVANCES TO NATIONHOOD

Prime Minister Robert Borden was determined to ensure that Canada benefited from its major contribution to the war through enhanced national status. First he pressed for dominion representation in the British empire delegation at the Paris Peace Conference, which met in 1919 to settle the war. In the end, he won representation for Canada as a power in its own right at the Paris Peace Conference, in addition to its collective representation as a member of the British empire delegation.

Borden also insisted on Canada's right to membership in the League of Nations' General Assembly as well as eligibility for membership in the governing council of the new international body. Once in the League of Nations, however, Canada wanted to limit its commitment. It opposed Article 10 of the league's charter, which bound members to come to the aid of other league members in times of attack. Borden feared that this agreement would commit Canadians to involvement in world disputes that were of no interest to them. (In the end, Article 10 remained in place.) Clearly, by the end of the war and in the immediate postwar period, Canada had taken the first few important steps along the road from colony to nation. The sense of nationalism that these events reflected was one of the enduring legacies of the Great War for Canadians. As Jonathan Vance has shown in *Death So Noble*, the pride in Canada's soldiers infused the memories, stories, and myths of the Great War.

The wartime rhetoric that the war would lead to a better Canada, a glorious nation of peace and prosperity, rang hollow in 1919. The war had strained English- and French-Canadian relations to an unprecedented extent. Equally, the war had taxed the nation's capacity in both industrial production and human resources. While Canada had made important strides on the road to nationhood, it had done so at great expense. The total of all Canadian casualties — killed, missing, prisoners of war, or wounded — reached a quarter of a million people.

Canada had also lost its optimism. Fifteen years earlier, Prime Minister Wilfrid Laurier had predicted that the twentieth century would be Canada's, just as the nineteenth century had been that of the United States. In 1919, Laurier died. His vision had perished before he did, another casualty of the killing fields of Europe.

NOTES

1. John Swettenham, *To Seize the Victory: The Canadian Corps in World War I* (Toronto: Ryerson Press, 1965), p. 106.
2. Daniel Dancocks, *Welcome to Flanders Fields: The First Canadian Battle of the Great War, Ypres, 1915* (Toronto: McClelland & Stewart, 1988), p. 249.
3. Mason Wade, *The French Canadians, 1760–1967*, 2 vols. (Toronto: Macmillan, 1968), p. 872.

LINKING TO THE PAST

The Great War and the African-Canadian Soldier
http://www.qesn.meq.gouv.qc.ca/mpages/unit5/u5toc.htm

Documents and images that relate the story of African-Canadian soldiers' participation in World War I.

Canadians in World War I
http://www.civilization.ca/cwm/chrono/1914first_ww_e.html

The Canadian War Museum offers an on-line tour of World War I that includes photographs and descriptions of the weapons used in trench warfare.

Canada and World War 1
http://www.archives.ca/05/0518_e.html

Biographies, first-person accounts, and stories of ordinary and famous Canadians who served in the war.

Citizens' Committee of 1000
http://timelinks.merlin.mb.ca/refernc/db0121.htm
A short description of the Citizens' Committee of 1000, which played a prominent role in Winnipeg's General Strike of 1919, with links to additional information about the strike.

BIBLIOGRAPHY

For overviews of Canada during World War I see Desmond Morton and J.L. Granatstein, *Marching to Armageddon: Canada and the Great War, 1914–1919* (Toronto: Lester & Orpen Dennys, 1989); Daniel Dancocks, *Spearhead to Victory: Canada and the Great War* (Edmonton: Hurtig, 1987); and Bill Freeman and Richard Nielson, *Far From Home: Canadians in the First World War* (Toronto: McGraw-Hill Ryerson, 1999). On Robert Borden see R.C. Brown, *Robert Laird Borden: A Biography*, 2 vols. (Toronto: Macmillan, 1975, 1980); and John English, *Borden: His Life and World* (Toronto: McGraw-Hill Ryerson, 1977). For a study of party and politics during the Borden era consult John English, *The Decline of Politics: The Conservatives and the Party System, 1901–1920* (Toronto: University of Toronto Press, 1977).

John Swettenham, *To Seize the Victory* (Toronto: Ryerson Press, 1965) and Robert James Steel, *The Men Who Marched Away: Canada's Infantry in the First World War, 1914–1918* (St. Catharines: Vanwell, 1989) describe Canadian involvement at the front, as does Sandra Gwyn's *Tapestry of War: Politics and Passion: Canada's Coming of Age in the Great War* (Toronto: HarperCollins, 1992). G.W.L. Nicholson, *The Fighting Newfoundlander: A History of the Royal Newfoundland Regiment* (Ottawa: Government of Newfoundland, 1964) recounts Newfoundland's contribution to the Allied army. On Canada's first military commander consult A.M.J. Hyatt, *General Sir Arthur Currie: A Military Biography* (Toronto: University of Toronto Press, 1987). On the Canadian air force see S.F. Wise, *Canadian Airmen and the First World War* (Toronto: University of Toronto Press, 1980); and for the navy, Michael L. Hadley and Roger Sarty, *Tin-Pots and Pirate Ships: Canadian Naval Forces and German Sea Raiders 1880–1918* (Montreal/Kingston: McGill-Queen's University Press, 1991).

James W. St. G. Walker looks at race relations in the Canadian army in "Race and Recruitment in World War I: Enlistment of Visible Minorities in the Canadian Expeditionary Force," *Canadian Historical Review* 70(1) (March 1989): 1–26. On Native soldiers see Fred Gaffen, *Forgotten Soldiers* (Penticton, BC: Theytus Books, 1985); and James Dempsey's *Warriors of the King: Prairie Indians in World War I* (Regina: Canadian Plains Research Center, 1999). On Ukrainian internments, see Frances Swyripa and John Herd Thompson, eds., *Loyalties in Conflict: Ukrainians in Canada During the Great War* (Edmonton: Canadian Institute of Ukrainian Studies, 1983). For information about the nearly 4000 Canadians held in German prison camps in World War I see Desmond Morton, *Silent Battle: Canadian Prisoners of War in Germany, 1914–1919* (Toronto: Lester, 1992). The role of propaganda on the war effort is examined in Jeffrey A. Keshen, *Propaganda and Censorship During Canada's Great War* (Edmonton: University of Alberta Press, 1996).

The question of government intervention in the state during the war is discussed in R. Cuff, "Organizing for War: Canada and the United States During World War I," *Canadian Historical Association Report* (1969): 141–56. For women's contributions to the war effort, see the relevant sections of Alison Prentice et al., *Canadian Women: A History*, 2nd ed. (Toronto: Harcourt Brace, 1996). The Halifax explosion is well documented in Alan D. Ruffman and Colin D. Howell, eds., *Ground Zero: A Reassessment of the 1917 Explosion in Halifax Harbour* (Halifax: Nimbus, 1994).

The conscription crisis is covered in J.L. Granatstein and J.M. Hitsman, *Broken Promises: A History of Conscription in Canada* (Toronto: Copp Clark Pitman, 1985 [1977]). The Canadian peace movement is studied in Thomas Socknat, *Witness against War: Pacifism in Canada, 1900–1945* (Toronto: University of Toronto Press, 1987). Often forgotten are the veterans; consult D. Morton and G. Wright, *Winning the Second Battle: Canadian Veterans and the Return to Civilian Life, 1915–1930* (Toronto: University of Toronto Press, 1987). Jonathan F. Vance looks at the construction of a myth of the Great War in *Death So Noble: Memory, Meaning and the First World War* (Vancouver: UBC Press, 1997).

For the Ontario schools questions, see Chad Gaffield, *Language, Schooling, and Cultural Conflict: The Origins of the French-Language Controversy in Ontario* (Montreal/Kingston: McGill-Queen's University Press, 1987). For the impact of World War I on social reform, consult John Herd Thompson, *The Harvests of War: The Prairie West, 1914–1919* (Toronto: McClelland & Stewart, 1978). On the flu epidemic of 1918 see Eileen Pettigrew, *The Silent Enemy* (Saskatoon: Western Producer Prairie Books, 1983). On the Winnipeg General Strike see the references listed at the end of "Where Historians Disagree: The Winnipeg General Strike" in this chapter.

TIME LINE

1921 – Liberals come to power under William Lyon Mackenzie King

Agnes Macphail becomes the first woman elected in a federal election

1929 – The Persons Case recognizes women in Canada as "persons" for legal purposes

The New York stock market crashes

1930 – Conservatives come to power under R.B. Bennett

1931 – Statute of Westminster recognizes Canadian independence from Britain

1934 – Birth of the Dionne quintuplets, the world's first surviving quintuplets

1935 – Liberals return to power under Mackenzie King

On-to-Ottawa Trek by unemployed workers; riots break out in Regina

1937 – Establishment of the Royal Commission on Dominion–Provincial Relations

The 1920s were a decade of adjustment to new postwar conditions. In politics, both major federal political parties chose new leaders, and regional protest movements surfaced in the Maritimes and in the West. In foreign affairs, Canada continued to move toward autonomy. Economically, Canadians looked increasingly to the United States rather than to Britain for both financial needs and foreign trade. Socially, reform declined, but disadvantaged groups such as women and workers continued their fight for recognition and rights.

The Great Depression dominated the 1930s. The stock market crash in New York in October 1929 signalled the crisis, and began the downward spiral. Prices for commodities fell, international trade declined as nations erected higher tariff walls, and unemployment rose substantially as industries cut back production. Thousands of Canadians faced, for the first time, the degradation of going on public relief. Farm organizations, trade unions, and co-operatives attempted to protect the interests of their members, but with limited success. Increasingly, people looked to government for answers. Although the Conservatives and the Liberals were voted into office during the Great Depression, in 1930 and in 1935 respectively, many Canadians looked to new third parties, and some even turned to extreme right- and left-wing organizations for solutions. Popular entertainment became a means of escape from the depressed conditions of everyday life.

NEW POSTWAR POLITICAL LEADERS

As the 1920s began, William Lyon Mackenzie King succeeded Laurier as Liberal leader, while Arthur Meighen succeeded Robert Borden. These two leaders had completely opposite approaches to politics. King sought compromise. To him, right answers did not exist in politics, only answers that seemed better because they offended fewer people. As a result he often spoke in ambiguities and in generalities. Meighen, by contrast, stated his position clearly and unequivocally. He upheld principles over compromise and believed that Canadians should be made to see the truth as he saw it. To him, every problem had a solution, and he clearly articulated solutions often without regard for the possible political repercussions.

REGIONAL PROTEST

THE MARITIME RIGHTS MOVEMENT

Regional protest movements arose in both eastern and western Canada. In the Maritimes, the Maritime Rights movement fought for a greater Maritime voice in national politics. By the 1920s, the number of seats from the Maritimes in the House of Commons had fallen by one-quarter (to 31) and even more in proportion to other areas of the country where the population was expanding, as a result of depopulation, as thousands left the region in search of work. Economically, manufacturing companies in the region re-established themselves in the larger markets of central Canada. A decline in demand for Cape Breton coal and steel hurt that regional industry. Shipbuilding also went into decline as Britain, the United States, and Canada all competed for international sales.

The Maritimes also suffered from tariff reductions throughout the 1920s. A rise in freight rates, of 200 percent or more, on the Intercolonial Railway also hurt the region's economy. As well, when the Canadian government nationalized the Intercolonial Railway as part of the Canadian National Railways (CNR), it moved the Intercolonial's head office from Moncton to Montreal, and thus ceased to promote regional interests.

A.P. Paterson, a grocer from Saint John, New Brunswick, led a group of influential business and professional people in the region to launch the Maritime Rights movement. The group

Arch Dales' cartoon in the *Grain Growers' Guide* in 1915 conveys western farmers' views of Canada's political and economic reality.

Glenbow Archives, Calgary, Canada/NA 3055-24.

demanded increased federal subsidies for the Maritime provinces, more national and international trade through the ports of Halifax and Saint John, and improved tariff protection to strengthen the region's steel and coal industries.

In the federal election of 1921, the movement pressed Maritime Liberal candidates to swear "to advocate and stand by Maritime rights first, last and all the time." The Liberals won all but six of the Maritime constituencies. But the Maritime members of Parliament could not keep their promises since Mackenzie King's Liberal minority government depended too much on Prairie support to be able to cater to Maritime needs, and especially to raise the tariff.

Disillusioned, Maritime voters switched to the Conservatives in the 1925 federal election, giving the party all but three of the 31 seats. Unfortunately for Maritimers, the Liberals returned to power in 1926. King established a royal commission to investigate the group's complaints. But before reporting, the Maritime Rights movement had disbanded.

THE PROGRESSIVE MOVEMENT

In the West, farmers had been demanding for some time reduced freight rates, an end to the monopoly of eastern-owned grain-elevator companies, an increase in the CPR's boxcar allotment for grain trade, a railway to Hudson Bay to rival the CPR, and most of all, a reduction in the tariff. With the election of a "non-partisan" Union government in 1917, farmers hoped that it would remove the tariff. When it failed to do so, Thomas Crerar, the minister of agriculture from Manitoba in the Union government, resigned from the cabinet in 1919. Nine other western Unionist MPs followed. They formed the nucleus of a new National Progressive party.

The party won an amazing 65 seats in the federal election of 1921. They won 39 of the 56 seats in the West, and gained a significant 24 in Ontario. But the party had no seats in Quebec and just one in the Maritimes. The party was also weakened by an internal split between a

Manitoba-based wing under Crerar and an Alberta-based wing under Henry Wise Wood, an American populist farmer who came to Alberta in 1905 and became president of the United Farmers of Alberta (UFA) in 1916. Crerar wanted the Progressives to act as a pressure group to force the minority Liberal government to implement policies favourable to farmers. Wood saw political parties as inherently evil, and favoured replacing them with "group government" made up of all occupational groups in society.

Unable to resolve their differences, the party proved to be politically ineffective. They declined the role of official opposition. Then, in 1922, Crerar resigned as leader. His successor, Robert Forke, had no better luck at uniting the party. The party lost political strength throughout the 1920s, and was, by the election of 1930, a spent force.

THE KING–BYNG AFFAIR

The Liberals lost heavily in the election of 1925, going from 116 to 99 seats. The Conservatives won 116 seats. Nevertheless, King decided to stay in office, believing he could win enough support from the Progressives to win any non-confidence votes. But in 1926, a custom department scandal broke out with evidence of some civil servants accepting bribes to allow liquor smuggling into the United States, where prohibition remained in force. On this issue, the Progressives threatened to vote against the government. King asked the governor general, Lord Byng, to dissolve Parliament and call an election before a loss-of-confidence vote could be taken in the House. Lord Byng refused King's request. King promptly resigned as prime minister and announced to a surprised House of Commons that the country was without a government.

The governor general asked Meighen to form a government, and he agreed. The new Conservative government lasted only three days. Now, the governor general had no choice but to dissolve Parliament and call a new election. During the election campaign, King accused Byng of acting unconstitutionally, thus enabling him to sidestep the custom scandal. King won his first majority government.

Where Historians Disagree

 ## Causes of Regional Protest Movements in Eastern and Western Canada in the 1920s

Historians have debated the reasons for the rise of differing protest movements on the Prairies and in the Maritimes immediately after World War I. Initially, they explained such protests as indigenous to the regions. As a frontier community inhabited by irascible farmers, the prairie West naturally protested against everything from the weather to railways, grain merchants, and the federal government. Political scientist Walter Young, for example, wrote: "It was thoroughly consistent with the frontier tradition of self-sufficiency and independence that they [the people of the West] should form their own political machines to influence or wrest power from the old and insensitive engines of government in the east."[1] By contrast, commentators viewed Maritimers as innately conservative, fighting changes that threatened to undermine their way of life. In short, earlier analysts regarded the West as a region that looked to the future and favoured change, while the Maritimes looked to the past and wanted to maintain the status quo.

This perspective gave way to a view of regions as dynamic entities, changing to fit the larger Canadian context. In the case of the Maritimes and the West, both regions served as hinterlands for the metropolitan centres of central Canada. Such a relationship disadvantaged both regions, thus leading to protest. In the "Bias of Prairie Politics,"[2] historian W.L. Morton describes how an initial bias of inequality when the West joined Confederation set off a series of protests that came to include the Progressive movement. Maritimers also identified their decline with Confederation and the beginning of their regional protest. Historian George Rawlyk argues that this feeling of persecution in Confederation created a "paranoid style," in which Maritimers "felt that the hostile and almost conspiratorial world of 'Upper Canada' was directed specifically against their beloved Nova Scotia."[3] Such feelings of regional protest tended to erupt in times of economic crises, as happened in the 1920s.

Recent studies of the prairie West and the Maritimes in the interwar years have linked political protest with a wider social reform tradition. Historian Richard Allen links the leadership, ideology, and aspirations of the Progressive movement to the social gospel movement,[4] while Maritime historian Ernest Forbes has tied the Maritime Rights movement to a "progressive ideology of the period, which increased the pressure upon the small governments for expensive reforms while at the same time suggesting the possibility of limitless achievement through a strategy of unity, organization and agitation."[5] This broadening of perspective offers a fuller understanding of the complexity and dynamics of regional protest.

[1] Walter Young, *Democracy and Discontent: Progressivism, Socialism and Social Credit in the Canadian West*, 2nd ed. (Toronto: McGraw-Hill Ryerson, 1978), p. 111.

[2] W.L. Morton, "Bias of Prairie Politics," (1955) reprinted in A.B. McKillop, ed., *Contexts of Canada's Past: Selected Essays of W.L. Morton* (Toronto: Macmillan in association with the Institute of Canadian Studies, Carleton University, 1980), pp. 149–160.

[3] George Rawlyk, "Nova Scotia Regional Protest, 1867–1967," *Queen's Quarterly*, 85 (Spring 1968): 107.

[4] Richard Allen, "The Social Gospel as the Religion of the Agrarian Revolt," in Carl Berger and Ramsay Cook, eds., *The West and the Nation: Essays in Honour of W.L. Morton* (Toronto: McClelland and Stewart, 1976), pp. 174–186.

[5] Ernest Forbes, *The Maritime Rights Movement, 1919–1927: A Study in Canadian Regionalism* (Montreal/Kingston: McGill-Queen's University Press, 1979), p. 38.

FROM COLONY TO NATION

In the interwar years, King's Liberal government made significant advances towards Canadian autonomy. In 1922, King refused to automatically come to Britain's defence when British troops were threatened by Turkish nationalists while maintaining the neutrality of the Dardanelle straits that linked the Black Sea to the Mediterranean Sea. When pressured by British leaders, King replied that only the Canadian Parliament could decide Canadian participation. By the time Parliament met, the crisis had passed. A year later, the Canadian government signed the Halibut Treaty, a Canadian–American agreement relating to fishing rights on the Pacific coast, without acquiring British parliamentary approval, the first time that Britain had been bypassed in signing international agreements affecting Canada.

The next step towards Canadian autonomy came with the signing of the Balfour Declaration at the Imperial Conference of 1926. It recognized the dominions as "autonomous communities within the British empire, equal in status, in no way subordinate to one another in any respect of their domestic or external affairs, though united by a common allegiance to the Crown, and freely associated as members of the British Commonwealth of Nations."

The final step to securing full Canadian autonomy occurred in 1931 with the signing of the Statute of Westminster. This act prohibited the British Parliament from declaring any law passed by the Canadian Parliament as being *ultra vires*, or unconstitutional, except for laws amending the British North America Act. Canada insisted on continued British approval for these latter laws because of the failure of the federal and provincial governments to agree among themselves on an amending formula.

THE ECONOMICS OF ADJUSTMENT

In the 1920s, the Canadian economy shifted from the old staple economy of fish, timber, and wheat to a new resource economy of pulp and paper, mining, and the production of consumer goods. The new economy made Canada more dependent on the United States, as its major trading partner. In 1923, for the first time, Canadians exported more to the United States than to Britain. Pulp and paper became Canada's leading new export. At the beginning of the 1920s, paper mills in Canada produced 938 million tons of newsprint; by the end of the decade, this production increased more than threefold to 2981 million tons — enough to print 40 billion newspapers a year. Mining followed a similar pattern. After a sluggish period in the early 1920s, it revived as a result of an American demand for Canadian-based metals to produce such consumer goods as automobiles, radios, and electrical appliances. Whole new areas opened up across the country, but particularly in the Laurentian Shield area of northern Ontario and Quebec, with the discovery of new lodes of copper, zinc, lead, and precious metals. Hydroelectric production quadrupled in the mid-1920s, providing power for the pulp and paper industry and for the refineries.

A REVOLUTION IN TRANSPORTATION AND COMMUNICATION

Growth in the primary sector multiplied markets in the secondary sector. The most spectacular secondary growth occurred in the automotive industry. Next to the United States, Canada became in the 1920s "the most motorized country on the globe."

Initially, Canada produced its own cars. At one time as many as 70 small companies manufactured, assembled, or sold automobiles in Canada. But Canadian companies failed to keep pace with their automated American counterparts, and eventually sold out to the American giants. By the end of the decade, the American "big three" manufactured three-quarters of the cars purchased in Canada.

The car revolutionized the Canadian landscape. Roads were built everywhere, and in the cities, paved streets became commonplace. Tire companies and factories emerged to produce tires and spare parts, service stations sprang up, and tourism prospered. The car made it easier to get to vacation areas.

Aviation also expanded greatly in the 1920s. Veteran World War I flying aces assisted in opening up the North by flying geologists and prospectors into remote areas of the Canadian Shield and providing service to isolated northern settlements. In 1924, Laurentide Air Services began Canada's first regular air-mail service, into the Quebec gold fields at Rouyn–Noranda. Other companies followed, and for several years the Canadian government permitted each company to print and issue its own postage stamps.

Important communications inventions became popular in the 1920s. The telephone became a standard household item. Radios, the great communications invention of the 1920s, helped to end isolation and loneliness. The first scheduled broadcast in North America took place in Montreal in May 1920, when station XWA (later CFCF) relayed a musical program to a Royal Society of Canada meeting in Ottawa.

DISILLUSIONMENT AND THE DECLINE OF REFORM

Idealism and reform declined by the mid-1920s. In part, this was due to the success of each of the reform movements achieving their goals. By 1921, workers had a higher standard of living and had achieved better recognition from employers. Women had the franchise federally and in most provinces. Prohibitionists had succeeded in eliminating legalized drinking. Educational reformers' achievements included better schools, children staying in school longer, and better-qualified teachers. Yet, in a sense, all these groups had failed in their ultimate objective: a new, regenerated, harmonious, and utopian Canada.

In some instances, a reaction to reform set in. Prohibitionists, for example, saw the provincial temperance acts removed one by one. By the end of the decade, government-regulated outlets sold liquor in every province except Prince Edward Island

Social gospellers within the mainstream churches retreated during the prosperous 1920s, as churchgoers became more concerned with personal prosperity and individual salvation than with social regeneration. Church reformers within the Methodist, Presbyterian, and Congregationalist churches did succeed in 1925 in creating the United Church of Canada. They hoped that this new church would rejuvenate the reformers' zeal and challenge the secularization of Canadian society. But when the new church challenged society, it appeared to some as too radical and reform-minded. Many members left and joined fundamentalist churches that upheld more traditional values and beliefs, or they became members of conservative sects and cults.

In Quebec, the Roman Catholic community reacted to the growing secularization of society. Abbé Lionel Groulx, the editor of *L'Action française,* saw the onslaught of urban and industrial society as an anathema to everything French Canadians believed in: the land, the church, the family, and the French-Canadian nation. In his journal, he launched an all-out attack — *l'action française* — on those forces that he believed were contributing to the anglicization and Americanization of Quebec.

WOMEN IN THE 1920S

Women made only modest gains in the 1920s. The women's suffrage movement had obtained the vote, but the electorate returned few women to either federal or provincial governments. Agnes Macphail was the only woman elected in the federal election of 1921 making her Canada's first woman member of Parliament. Provincially, women did better at entering politics, although the results were a far cry from their expectations. As late as 1940, only nine women sat in provincial legislatures, all of them in the four western provinces.

 Women still faced discrimination. For example, not until 1929 in the famous "Persons Case" were women considered "persons" and thus eligible for membership in all Canadian legislative bodies. Five Alberta women reformers — Emily Murphy, Irene Parlby, Nellie McClung, Henrietta Edwards, and Louise McKinney, fought the court case up to the highest court of appeal, the Judicial Committee of the Privy Council in England.

Few women had the opportunity for a secondary education; in 1929, only a quarter of the national secondary-school student body was women. Of the few who entered the professions, most became teachers or nurses, while only a handful became physicians, lawyers, or professors, and a very tiny number, engineers.

Women who worked outside the home in industry or business — 20 percent of the labour force in 1929 — held traditional female jobs as secretaries, sales clerks in department stores, and domestics. Others worked on assembly lines in textile or tobacco factories, canneries, or fish plants. In these jobs, women earned considerably less than men doing the same job. Economic equality, like political equality, remained an elusive goal for women.

Unions did little to organize working women, even in the female-dominated industries. Seldom did they support women on strike. Agreements with employers commonly included lower female wage scales. In some cases, male-dominated unions demanded equal pay for women and men — not to combat discrimination against women but rather to ensure that employers would have no financial reason to replace male employees with females.

Although many farms were becoming more mechanized in the 1920s, the farmhouses remained basic. Prairie farm wives were also expected to help outside the house at critical times of the year, while they continued caring for the children, cooking, cleaning, laundering, and sewing. Rural reform leaders advocated household-science courses, co-operation, and the use of more household appliances as ways of alleviating the burden.

Urban middle-class women enjoyed a higher standard of living than their rural counterparts. Many benefited from modern labour-saving devices such as refrigerators, electric stoves, and vacuum cleaners, and from such luxuries as electricity and running water. Ironically, however, these "conveniences" increased the amount of time women spent in the home.

THE NATIVE PEOPLES

The experience of the Native peoples in the 1920s varied across Canada. In the northern forested areas, the First Nations and Métis suffered greatly when boom prices for furs led to an influx of non-Native trappers. As well, intensive trapping resulted in a serious depletion in the numbers of beaver. Some First Nations and Métis people worked as tourist guides, in commercial fishing, as miners, railway workers, and loggers. In the south, farming on the reserves declined as heavy expenditures became necessary for the new farm machinery. Among the Iroquois, high-steel rigging, although dangerous work, was popular and lucrative. On the Pacific coast, Native people could obtain jobs in logging and commercial fishing. A number of independent First Nations operators owned and operated gas-powered gillnetters, trollers, and seine boats.

LABOUR IN THE 1920S

Labour unions faced difficult times in the 1920s, as wage cuts, industrial consolidation, improved technology, and managerial efficiency all weakened the labour movement. Workers retaliated by staging strikes. Most strikes failed to improve wages or working conditions, and many ended in physical violence. Union membership plummeted by more than one-third by mid-decade, reaching a low of 260 000 members.

Unions were also divided. The conservative Trades and Labor Congress (TLC) continued to favour craft unions and to advocate advancement only through conciliation and government intervention. In 1927, a new militant All-Canadian Congress of Labour (ACCL) union was established. It favoured industry-wide unions and strike action. In Quebec, some workers and farmers joined Roman Catholic unions, guided by priests and sanctioned by the church. These unions attempted to isolate their members from the more secular and often socialistic "foreign" — American or English-Canadian — unions. Throughout the 1920s, unions in Quebec never succeeded, however, in attracting much more than one-quarter of the total Quebec union membership.

CULTURAL DEVELOPMENTS

ART

Cultural life flourished in the 1920s. In English-speaking Canada, the Group of Seven dominated contemporary art. Their first exhibition was held in May 1920. The exhibition catalogue claimed that art must reflect "the spirit of a nation's growth." The Group of Seven believed that "spirit" could best be found in the land — in the trees, rocks, and lakes of the Ontario northland. They depicted the land in brilliant mosaics of bright colours. For the Group of Seven, the Ontario northland symbolized the nation in the same way that the West did in the American tradition — a mythical land that became a metaphor for the Canadian people. As well, the "North" represented a counterforce to the "South," especially the United States, where urbanization, industrialism, and materialism threatened to undermine the Canadian spirit.

Community Portrait

The Arts and Letters Club as a Cultural Community

Founded in 1908, Toronto's Arts and Letters Club brought together writers, architects, musicians, artists, and dramatists, with a minority membership of non-professionals "with artistic tastes and inclinations" to promote an appreciation of the arts. The membership, restricted to men, expanded rapidly in the 1910s to comprise a significant number of the Toronto arts community; it also included several wealthy Toronto entrepreneurs, friends of the arts. These entrepreneurs greatly assisted an emerging group of artists, who in 1920 became the "Group of Seven." Art historian Peter Mellen notes that "the friendly atmosphere of the club" provided the members of the Group of Seven "with an opportunity to meet Toronto's wealthy elite, who were to become their first patrons." These entrepreneurs found in the Club a haven from the purely commercial nature of modern Toronto. In the words of Augustus Bridle, a founding member, the Club's president in 1913–1914, and author of *The Story of the Club*, the Club provided for all its members "absolute escape from all that otherwise made Toronto."

The members consciously created a sense of community through the Club's location, its décor, and the members' activities. Members believed that poverty would help to draw them together as a community. Hence, despite the wealth of a number of Club members, they chose very modest locations for their headquarters. Their first locale was a garret next door to the Brown Betty restaurant, which was opposite—not in—the opulent King Edward Hotel. It consisted of one room and a cubbyhole in which to make coffee. Evicted ten months later, Club members moved to the old Assize Court room behind No. 1 Police Station, "the most impressive, inaccessible room in Toronto." Bridle boasted: "just before the inaugural dinner day we had neither gas in the kitchen nor electricity in the hall." Yet, the event was a great hit as members rallied in support.

In the 1920s, the Club leased St. George's Hall at 14 Elm Street, where it remains today. According to Bridle, each move heightened the mythical belief in the spirit of community that had prevailed in the previous locale, and made Club members

Members of the Group of Seven at 1920 luncheon at the Arts and Letters Club. From left to right: A.Y. Jackson, Fred Varley, and Lawren Harris; Barker Fairley, a strong supporter of the Group but not a member; Frank Johnston, Arthur Lismer, and J.E.H. MacDonald. Absent was Frank Carmichael.

Photo by Arthur Gross, The Arts and Letters Club, Toronto.

determined to create a similar ambience in the new locale. So the first thing Club members did in their St. George location was to build a "collegiate-gothic fireplace." Then they commissioned Club member artist George Reid to paint a mural panel of the Club's Viking crest on the adjacent wall to the fireplace. The crest had been the work of artist J.E.H. MacDonald, who joined the Club in 1911. It consisted of a "Viking ship with the sails full spread before the rising sun to remind us of the open sea and the great adventure."

Club members performed rituals along medieval lines, drawing examples in particular from "the brotherhood of medieval monks," according to Bridle, believing that in medieval times a sense of community and camaraderie existed that was lacking in modern times. Members also purchased a farm to which they could retreat from the stresses of modern life. Camping and canoeing, and other Club activities, contributed to a life of simplicity and friendship, they believed. As well, Club members got involved in social reform activities in Toronto to enhance the sense of community in the

city at large. Of particular importance to members, especially for University of Toronto political economist James Mavor, was the Guild of Civic Art.

Nearly a century after its founding, the Club continues to have a sense of community, but with one notable change: women can now be members. In 1986, the Club finally purchased its current location, St. George's Hall at 14 Elm Street.

Further Readings

Augustus Bridle, *The Story of the Club* (Toronto: The Arts & Letters Club, 1945).

Peter Mellen, *The Group of Seven* (Toronto: McClelland and Stewart, 1970).

Charles C.H. Hill, *The Group of Seven: Art for a Nation* (Toronto: McClelland and Stewart, 1995).

Karen Leslie Knutson, "Absolute Escape from all that Otherwise Made Toronto: Antimodernism at the Arts and Letters Club, 1908–1920," MA Thesis, Queen's University, 1995.

Website address: http://home.interlog .com/~artslets/history.html

Frederick Philip Grove in the early 1920s, rafting on Lake Winnipeg with his daughter, May. He was actually Felix Paul Greve, a German translator and writer who faked his own suicide in 1909 by appearing to throw himself off a boat. Having successfully escaped his creditors, three years later he surfaced as Frederick Philip Grove in Manitoba. In his lifetime no one in Canada knew his real identity. The true story was only revealed 25 years after his death, when D.O. Spettigue published his biography of Grove, *FPG: The European Years* (1973).

University of Manitoba Archives and Special Collections, The Libraries/PC 2, No. 10.

In British Columbia, Emily Carr had begun in 1908 to visit First Nations communities and to paint scenes of their villages, buildings, and totem poles. In 1932, at age 57, Carr launched into the most productive period of her artistic career. At the start, she emphasized nature themes and was beginning to focus on First Nations subjects in her paintings.

On the Prairies, Lionel LeMoine FitzGerald, of Winnipeg, and Illingworth Kerr, from Lumsden, Saskatchewan, captured the region's uniqueness on canvas. In the Maritimes, a group of local artists arranged for their own exhibition and issued their own magazine, *Maritime Art*, which by 1940 had become Canada's first full-fledged art magazine. This Maritime group assisted Jack Humphrey and Miller Brittain, both born and raised in Saint John, New Brunswick, where they spent most of their lives, in becoming internationally recognized Maritime artists.

LITERATURE

A new literary culture emerged in the 1920s. In English-speaking Canada, two new journals captured and epitomized the cultural renaissance: the *Canadian Forum* and the *Canadian Historical Review*. The Canadian Authors' Association (CAA), founded in 1921 for the purpose of using literature "to articulate a national identity and to foster a sense of community within the country," aided young English-Canadian writers in publishing their works.

In poetry, E.J. (Ned) Pratt of Newfoundland used familiar Canadian historical events as the subjects for his poems and elevated them to mythical proportions. Some of his most famous were *Brébeuf and His Brethern*, about the heroic seventeenth-century French Canadian martyr, and *Towards the Last Spike,* about the building of the Canadian Pacific Railway.

At McGill University, a group of young, rebellious poets known as the "Montreal group" — F.R. Scott, A.J.M. Smith, A.M. Klein, and Leo Kennedy — endorsed the modernist movement. They wrote in free verse, discarded the norms of punctuation, and chose their subject material in the modern city. They began two small literary journals, the *McGill Fortnightly Review* (1925–27) and the *Canadian Mercury* (1928–29), as vehicles for their works.

In French-speaking Quebec, a group of young poets challenged the establishment in the pages of *Le Nigog*, the first arts magazine in Quebec, and founded by architect Fernand Préfontaine, writer Robert de Roquebrune, and musician Léo-Paul Morin. Ironically, although this group and the "Montreal group" resided in the same city, they worked in isolation from one another.

While most novels continued to be romantic and escapist, three stood out for their realism: Frederick Philip Grove's *Settlers of the Marsh* (1925), in which Grove explored the inner psychic tension of a Norwegian settler on the Prairies; Martha Ostenso's *Wild Geese* (1925), about the tyrannical patriarch Caleb Gare, who aims to dominate both his land and his family and in the process destroys himself; and R.J.C. Stead's *Grain* (1926), which describes the tensions that farm boy Gander Stake faces in having to choose between life on the farm and in the city.

MUSIC

The radio and the phonograph brought music directly into Canadian homes in the 1920s. Radio was used to celebrate the Diamond Jubilee of Confederation in 1927. Beginning in 1929, the Toronto Symphony Orchestra was heard throughout the country performing 25 concerts over the radio, the last of which was devoted entirely to music by Canadian composers.

POPULAR CULTURE

English-speaking Canadian popular culture became more Americanized in the 1920s. Canadians who had never set eyes on the *Canadian Forum* or even the mass-circulation *Maclean's* knew about such popular American magazines as *Ladies' Home Journal*, *McCall's*, and *Saturday Evening Post*. Canadian newspapers also adopted an "American" style: glossy, plenty of advertising, sensational headlines and stories, comic strips, substantial sports sections, and a heavy reliance on American wire services for international coverage.

Canada's first radio program was transmitted in 1920. By the end of the decade, some 60 Canadian stations existed across the country, consisting mainly of news, lectures, or recorded music. But most of them carried American material. As a result, in 1928, the Canadian government established the Aird Commission to review public broadcasting. The Aird Report recommended that broadcasting become a public monopoly, without competitors and with limited commercial content. The Canadian Radio League, founded by English-Canadian nationalists Alan Plaunt, Graham Spry, and Brooke Claxton, concurred. Out of their efforts came the Canadian Broadcasting Corporation (CBC) in the 1930s.

Movies contributed to the Americanization of Canadian culture in the 1920s. Initially, it did not appear that this would be the case; between 1919 and 1923, Canada had a thriving domestic feature film industry that used Canadian settings, casts, and crews. But thereafter, what Canadian companies existed succumbed to the American "Big Five" studios — Paramount, MGM, Warner Brothers, Fox, and RKO.

SPORTS

The professionalization and Americanization of Canadian sports continued in the 1920s. At the beginning of the 1920s, professional hockey was solely Canadian. Then the National Hockey League expanded into the lucrative urban market of the United States. By 1930, only two of the NHL teams were Canadian: the Toronto Maple Leafs and the Montreal Canadiens, although almost all the players were Canadians.

In other sports, a number of Canadian amateurs won international recognition. Track and field athletes Percy Williams and Ethel Catherwood won gold medals at the 1928 Olympics. George Young made a name for Canada in swimming by winning the 32-km race from the California mainland to Catalina Island. In the Maritimes, Captain Angus Walters sailed the *Bluenose* to three successive wins in the International Fisherman's Trophy — in 1921, 1922, and 1923. The famous Edmonton Grads women's basketball team, formed from students and graduates of an Edmonton high school, set a world record by winning 502 games and losing only 20 during its entire career from 1915 to 1940.

THE ADVENT OF THE GREAT DEPRESSION

 On October 29, 1929 — "Black Tuesday" — stock markets around the world crashed. The Great Depression that followed lasted a decade and affected the entire western world. The depression hit Canada severely because the national economy had expanded so rapidly and so extensively

Dust storm near Lethbridge, Alberta — a familiar sight in Prairie Canada during the "Dirty Thirties."

Glenbow Archives, Calgary, Canada/NA-1831-1.

in the first three decades of the twentieth century. In essence, having risen so high, it had further to fall. Within Canada, the Prairie West and British Columbia probably suffered most because of the dependence of these regions on primary industries, especially wheat production, and their over-expansion in the previous decades. As well, the Prairie West suffered from a climatic disaster: ten years of exceptional and persistent drought, extreme summer and winter temperatures, unusual weather patterns, and grasshopper infestations. The topsoil turned to dust and blew away. British Columbia had to contend with high numbers of transients; Vancouver became known as "the Mecca for the unemployed."

From 1928 to 1932 wheat prices fell from $1.29 to 34 cents a bushel for No. 1 Hard, the best wheat on the market. Prices for lesser grades were considerably lower. Also, farmers themselves paid for the cost of shipping the grain to the Lakehead, eroding profit even further. Some western farmers found it cost less to burn their crops than to harvest them. The wheat pools went bankrupt.

Similar dramatic conditions prevailed in other primary resource sectors. Mines closed down for lack of business and thousands of investors lost everything. The pulp and paper industry had overexpanded in the 1920s. When the depression hit, the newsprint market collapsed, and, along with it, the pulp and paper industry.

Money markets followed. Banks and other financial institutions had generously approved loans in the 1920s. When the depression hit, they recalled loans and demanded mortgage payments. But the average Canadian investors could not retrieve their money or cover their debts. Many people abandoned their homes and farms, leaving banks with property that no one could afford, and hence had little monetary value.

Companies and factories cut back on wages and on employees. By 1933, over 20 percent of the entire Canadian labour force remained unemployed. In some regions of the country, the figures rose as high as 35 percent and even 50 percent.

THE R.B. BENNETT GOVERNMENT'S RESPONSE TO THE DEPRESSION

The Conservatives under R. B. Bennett won the election of 1930 on the promise that they would solve the problems of the depression. Bennett introduced a high-tariff policy on manufactured goods as one solution to the depression. Unfortunately, the high tariff hurt Canadian trade especially with the United States, which retaliated with their own high tariff.

Bennett also introduced the Unemployment Relief Act, which provided $20 million of assistance to the poor. But Bennett soon discovered that much more was needed. Between 1930 and 1938, Ottawa would provide nearly $350 million in relief for the jobless and for destitute farmers, while municipal and provincial governments added another $650 million.

RELIEF

For the first time, thousands of Canadians faced the personal degradation of going on relief — the "pogey," as it was called. In a society built on a philosophy of self-help, relief was an admission that one could no longer fend for oneself. Many people lost their sense of self-worth.

Those on relief faced the further humiliation of having to acknowledge their failure publicly. They lined up in a church basement or fire hall waiting for relief. When their turn came, they had to proclaim their destitution, by swearing that they did not own a car, a radio, or a telephone and that they were in arrears in rent payments, and had received notice of discontinuation of electricity and water service, as well as impending eviction. Then the authorities gave them food vouchers to purchase the minimum necessities at local stores — a further reminder of their impoverished condition.

To give those on relief the illusion of working for their relief payments, governments created make-shift jobs known as "boon-doggling." The town of New Toronto, Ontario, for example, required relief workers to haul large stones to vacant lots, where they were smashed and used for road construction. Winnipeg men on relief sawed wood, pulled weeds along city boulevards, and swept the city streets. Rumours abounded of some municipalities that had "relief men" dig holes one day and fill them in the next, simply to keep them occupied.

To avoid drifters coming into town for assistance, most municipalities had lengthy residence requirements to qualify for relief. This hurt immigrants in particular. The Immigrant Act allowed for the deportation of immigrants on relief. Between 1930 and 1935, Ottawa returned an unprecedented 30 000 immigrants to Europe.

RELIEF CAMPS AND THE ON-TO-OTTAWA TREK

By 1932, more than 1.5 million Canadians (15 percent of the nation's population) depended on relief. The country seemed ripe for rebellion. Of particular concern were unemployed single men, many of whom "rode the rods" across Canada in search of work, begged for food and clothing, camped in shantytowns on the outskirts of cities, and lined up at soup kitchens and hostels for food and shelter. To deal with these transient unemployed single men, the Bennett government established relief camps across the country. During the four-year period that they existed, an estimated 20 000 single, homeless male "volunteers" lived in intolerable conditions and worked long hours at menial jobs designed simply to keep them busy for a meagre 20 cents a day.

In the spring of 1935, men in British Columbia work camps jumped the trains en route to Ottawa to protest conditions. They picked up other camp men and unemployed workers along the way. By the time they reached Regina they were over 2000 strong. The federal government ordered the RCMP to break up the march. The ensuing confrontation, on Dominion Day, 1935, left one plainclothes policeman dead and numerous strikers and police officers injured. The police arrested 120 of the trekkers and convicted eight of them. Only strike leader Arthur Evans and a few others were permitted to continue to Ottawa, where Bennett denounced them as "red" agitators and dissidents.

Canada's millionaire prime minister came to represent the callous indifference of the rich to the suffering of the unemployed and destitute. In fairness to Bennett, beneath his cold exterior existed a warm generosity. Thousands of Canadians wrote personal letters to him expressing their hardships and appealing for help. Very often he sent them money from his own pocket.

A demonstration of strikers at Market Square on the eve of the Regina Riot on Dominion Day, 1935. During the riot, one plain-clothes policeman was killed and numerous strikers and police officers were injured.

Dick and Ada Bird Collection/Saskatchewan Archives Board/R-A27560-1.

BENNETT'S NEW DEAL

Bennett also enacted a number of measures that, over time, strengthened Canada's economy. He established the Bank of Canada, to "promote the economic and financial welfare of the Dominion." His government passed the Natural Products and Marketing Act, which set up a federal marketing board with authority over all "natural products of agriculture and of the forest, sea, lake or river." The Conservatives also introduced the Canada Grain Board Act, which gave Ottawa control of the marketing of coarse grains, including wheat. In 1934, Bennett also appointed the Royal Commission on Price Spreads to investigate the buying practices of major department stores and the labour conditions in certain industries. Out of that commission came legislation to institute unemployment insurance and to regulate wages and working hours. Unfortunately both bills were struck down by the Judicial Committee of the Privy Council as unconstitutional.

Despite these measures, Bennett's Conservatives were defeated in the election of 1935, and the Liberals under Mackenzie King returned to power. But in the popular vote, more than 25 percent of Canadians voted for one of the new parties that entered the election.

THIRD PARTIES

THE CCF

Two of those new parties began on the Prairies. The Co-operative Commonwealth Federation (CCF) drew together dissident groups of farmers, labourers, socialists, academics, and disenchanted Liberals. At the party's first convention in Calgary in August of 1932, it chose Labour

MP J.S. Woodsworth, a prominent social gospeller and one of those arrested for supporting the Winnipeg General Strike of 1919, as their leader.

From the beginning, the CCF distanced itself from the two mainline parties by having a clear socialist program, the "Regina Manifesto," to deal with the Great Depression. The CCF favoured government control of the economy through the nationalization of the means of production, distribution, and exchange. It also worked for a more equitable distribution of wealth, the creation of a welfare state, and the pursuit of international peace through the League of Nations.

The CCF entered the federal election in 1935 in high hopes of becoming a major party. But the party won only seven seats, all from the West. Nevertheless, the party did acquire the reputation of being "the conscience of the House of Commons."

SOCIAL CREDIT

In Alberta, the Social Credit party began in 1935. It blamed the depression on the financial institutions that hoarded money, thus preventing consumers from buying the abundant goods that the capitalist system produced. The party's solution was for the government to inject money into the economy by giving each adult a monthly "national dividend" of $25.00. To people without sufficient money to buy even the necessities of life, the theory proved appealing.

Social credit found a popular leader in the charismatic William "Bible Bill" Aberhart. He used his popularity as a lay preacher on the radio to attract financial contributions from his listeners to build his Prophetic Bible Institute in Calgary, which he later used to distribute Social Credit material once he "converted" to Social Credit in the summer of 1932. But only on the eve of the 1935 provincial election did he form his Social Credit party. The party swept Alberta, winning 56 of the 63 seats.

The federal CCF caucus meets with its secretary J.S. Woodsworth, who is standing in the centre. On the extreme left sits Tommy Douglas, later Premier of Saskatchewan, and the first federal leader when the CCF changed its name to the New Democratic Party.

National Archives of Canada PA 167544.

An anti-Semitic poster at Sainte-Agathe, a resort area in the Laurentians north of Montreal, 1939.

National Archives of Canada/PA-107943. Reprinted with permission of *The Gazette*, Montreal.

UNION NATIONALE

In Quebec, a new Union Nationale party, under the leadership of Maurice Duplessis, the Conservative leader, emerged and won power by allying with a dissident left-wing group within the Liberal party called Action libérale nationale, headed by Paul Gouin. After the election, the right-wing Duplessis purged his government of the Gouin faction.

Duplessis attacked a number of dissident groups in the province, including socialists, communists, and trade unionists. In 1937 he introduced the "Padlock Law," which made it illegal for any group to use a house or hall "to propagate communism or bolshevism" or to publish or distribute literature "tending to propagate communism." Duplessis used the law to lock premises suspected of being used for communist activities, to ban publications, and, on a couple of occasions, to arrest dissidents.

COMMUNISTS AND FASCISTS

Extreme left- and right-wing political movements, such as the Communist Party and fascist groups, grew during the interwar years. The Communist Party of Canada, founded in 1921 in Guelph, Ontario, thrived in the economic-crisis conditions of the depression, especially among immigrants threatened with deportation. The federal government attempted to repress the party by invoking section 98 of the Criminal Code, which made it illegal to advocate "governmental, industrial or economic change within Canada by the use of force, violence or physical injury to persons or property, or by threats of such injury." Nevertheless, on the eve of World War II, the Party had 16 000 members. But when the Soviet Union signed a non-aggression pact with Adolf Hitler that summer, many members quit the party in protest. In June 1940, the Canadian government declared the Communist Party illegal.

Fascists proved less numerous than communists. The Deutscher Bund Canada, founded in 1934 and led by German Canadians, never had more than 2000 members, while the Canadian Nationalist Party, founded by right-wing militants, and the allied Swastika clubs, added a few thousand more. In Quebec, Adrien Arcand's National Social Christian party, modelled on the Nazi party, claimed to represent the last stand of Roman Catholicism against communists and other "atheist" groups. While Arcand remained a marginal and eccentric character, anti-Semitism found support among nationalist movements in the province, such as the Jeune-Canada and the Ligue d'Action nationale. Not surprisingly, thousands of persecuted Jews fleeing Nazi Germany found Canada's doors firmly closed. A leading member of the immigration department summarized the department's viewpoint toward Jewish immigrants, with the comment: "none is too many."

LABOUR IN THE GREAT DEPRESSION

Workers became more militant in the desperate conditions of the Great Depression. "Red" trade unions grew, and some affiliated with the Communist Party of Canada. For example, the Workers' Unity League (WUL) was born out of a directive from Moscow that communist-led unions should separate from "reformist" unions, and prepare for the coming world revolution. At its peak in 1932, the WUL had an estimated 40 000 members. It claimed leadership of most of the strikes across the country in the early 1930s.

In 1935 a new union, the American-based Congress of Industrial Organizations (CIO), emerged in Canada to "organize the unorganized." The Canadian CIO's greatest success occurred in 1937, when the CIO-inspired United Auto Workers led the strike at the General Motors factory in Oshawa, Ontario. The CIO also organized Montreal's female garment workers, as well as coal miners in Nova Scotia. But elsewhere in the country, the CIO made little headway in the 1930s.

WOMEN IN THE 1930S

Initially, the depression benefited women who wanted to work because they could be hired at half a man's wages. Soon, however, a backlash occurred. Women were accused of taking jobs away from unemployed men who had wives and families to support. Women also faced difficulties getting relief even if they were eligible for it. Authorities reasoned that single unemployed women posed no threat to society, as did single unemployed men. Furthermore, they assumed that these women would be cared for by their families. As well, authorities feared that relief to women would contribute to the breakdown of the family.

Birth control was seldom an option women could consider, although by 1937 birth-control clinics existed in Toronto, Hamilton, and Windsor. Also available was A.H. Tyrer's popular book, *Sex, Marriage and Birth Control* (1936). The popular belief of the day was expressed by Dr. Helen McMurchy, director of the Dominion Division of Child Welfare, who described birth control among those of British background as "race suicide." French-Canadian nationalists used the same argument in Quebec. Still, a few doctors provided birth-control information and devices, but they did so at the risk of losing their medical licence. For some women, self-induced miscarriages seemed to be the only alternative to unwanted children or children they simply could not afford.

MACKENZIE KING'S GOVERNMENT'S RESPONSE TO THE DEPRESSION

Once back in power after the federal election of 1935, Mackenzie King's Liberals continued some of the Conservatives' policies to cope with the depression and added some of their own. The Liberals, for instance, supported the Bank of Canada and made its governor responsible to Parliament for monetary policy. But the Liberals abolished the Conservatives' high tariff policy by negotiating low tariff agreements with both Britain and the United States.

PRAIRIE FARM REHABILITATION PROGRAM

The Liberals continued the Conservatives' policy of aid to the drought-stricken farmers of western Canada and extended it further by implementing the Prairie Farm Rehabilitation Act (PFRA). The Act provided money to the experimental farms in the dry-belt area of the Palliser Triangle to apply the latest scientific knowledge to attempt to get the soil to regain its productivity. Two innovations followed: first, the Noble plough, invented by Charles Noble of Nobleford, Alberta, which cut the roots of weeds without turning over the topsoil to expose it to sun and wind; second, "trash farming" — instead of ploughing and harrowing their fields to make them look neat and clean, farmers were encouraged to leave the dead plants and grain stubble on the field to prevent wind erosion. The PFRA's program also provided money to build dugouts for spring runoff water for cattle, helped reseed vacant and pasture land, and, in the case of destitute farm families in the Palliser Triangle area, assisted relocation to better farming areas to the north.

CBC AND TCA

The Liberals created two innovative national institutions and introduced two important social-security measures in the 1930s. In 1936, they reorganized the Canadian Radio Broadcasting Commission into the Canadian Broadcasting Corporation (CBC). The CBC's mandate was to regulate private broadcasting and to develop its own network across the country with Canadian content in both official languages. In 1937, the Liberals also established Trans-Canada Air Lines (TCA), the forerunner of Air Canada, as a Crown corporation. Two other federal initiatives proved successful: the Municipal Improvements Assistance Act, which authorized $30 million in federal loans at 2 percent interest for special municipal public-works projects, and the National Housing Act (NHA), which made federally backed mortgages easier to obtain.

The King government also established the National Employment Commission to re-examine and restructure the administration of direct relief. The commission made two important recommendations: first that the federal government takes over unemployment payments because this was too big and expensive an undertaking for municipal or provincial governments; and second that the government adopts a policy of deficit financing to provide additional relief and stimulate economic growth.

ROYAL COMMISSION ON DOMINION–PROVINCIAL RELATIONS

Before moving on either issue, King created the Royal Commission on Dominion–Provincial Relations to explore all aspects of relations between these two levels of government in light of the current economic crisis. The Commission recommended a stronger federal-government economic presence. But its report did not appear until 1940. In the meantime, Parliament imposed the War Measures Act, which gave the government licence to impose many aspects of the report's centralist agenda without consulting the provinces, at least for the duration of the war.

RELIGION

The trend in the 1930s was to move away from radical religion, with its emphasis on social reform, to a more conservative faith, with its emphasis on personal salvation and the importance of tradition. Nevertheless, a few radical groups gained some support during the depression. The Fellowship for a Christian Social Order, founded by members of the United Church, argued for an overthrow of the capitalist system and replacing it with socialism as their answer to the economic crisis. The Student Christian Movement (SCM) provided study groups on most Canadian university campuses in the 1930s to discuss social issues and advocate social change.

Conservative and fundamentalist groups flourished in the decade. Disciples of the British Oxford Movement toured Canada, delivering a message of "revelation, not revolution" to overflow audiences. In Quebec, many in the Roman Catholic Church supported a back-to-the-land movement as the best means to combat both unemployment and "moral decrepitude."

Still others, particularly in the Maritimes, looked to co-operatives as the answer. Moses Coady, director of the extension department at St. Francis Xavier University in Antigonish, Nova Scotia, and Jimmy Tompkins, a fellow priest, worked to improve the lives of poor farmers, miners, fishers, and their families through co-operatives. The co-operatives might be credit unions, or perhaps co-operatives for selling fish or farm produce.

CULTURE IN THE 1930s

During the 1930s, entertainment often became a means of escape from the realities of the depression. Owners of radio sets in English-speaking Canada listened to the American comedy show *Amos 'n Andy*, the most popular program of the decade, and *Hockey Night in Canada*, with Foster Hewitt. Recording artists such as Willie Eckstein, Percy Faith, Guy Lombardo and his Royal Canadians, and Don Messer got their start on Canadian radio. French Canadians enjoyed the successful serials written specifically for radio, such as "Le Curé de Village" and "La Pension Velder."

Mass magazines, both Canadian and American, featured stories of wealth and glamour, while films from Hollywood portrayed romance and fantasy. The birth of the Dionne quintuplets near Callander, Ontario, in May 1934, attracted worldwide attention and brought over 3 million people to see a glimpse of them at a special hospital set up to care for them under the auspices of the Ontario government — a government that quickly appreciated the profit to be made from this "tourist attraction." Even this real-life event was a form of escape for the many that came.

SPORTS

Sports became another form of popular entertainment and a distraction during the depression. In winter, hockey dominated. Hockey stars became household names among sports-minded families: the Toronto Maple Leafs' famous "Kid Line" of Charlie Conacher, Joe Primeau, and Busher Jackson; the legendary Eddie Shore of the Boston Bruins, known for his speed and scoring flair; Francis "King" Clancy of the Toronto Maple Leafs, who once played every position on the ice in a single game; and Howie Morenz of the Montreal Canadiens, with his speed and flashy stick handling, who was easily the greatest hockey superstar of the 1930s. In summer, baseball continued to be Canada's most popular sport. Every community had a local team, and the larger towns and cities enjoyed franchises in minor professional leagues.

ART

In 1933, the Canadian Group of Painters (CGP) formed as a loose-knit association that provided moral support for artists who were affiliated with it. Art education became one of their goals. French-Canadian painters in the 1930s showed a fascination with the land. Marc-Aurèle Fortin, for example, painted scenes of the village of Sainte-Rose and along the north shore of Montreal Island. Religious subjects appeared in the early paintings of Jean-Paul Lemieux. He chose colourful Fête-Dieu processions in Quebec streets and other religious events as subjects for his paintings. They too, like Fortin's, were noted for their quiet nostalgia and gentle lyricism.

LITERATURE

In literature, Morley Callaghan's three novels — *Such Is My Beloved* (1934), *They Shall Inherit the Earth* (1935), and *More Joy in Heaven* (1937) — stood out as good examples of realistic novels, a reaction to the sentimental and romantic literature of an earlier generation. Irene Baird's *Waste Heritage* (1939) dealt with labour unrest and unemployment in Vancouver during the depression. The most outstanding French-Canadian novel in the 1930s was Ringuet's (Philippe Panneton's) *Trente Arpents*, translated into English as *Thirty Acres*, a realistic novel that follows the fall of its central character, Euchariste Moisan, from initial prosperity on his farm to a broken man in a New England factory town.

THEATRE

During the 1930s in Quebec, several of the best-known French-Canadian playwrights, such as Gratien Gélinas, made a living by writing scripts for radio productions, especially for the

Canadian Broadcasting Corporation (CBC). Although the Roman Catholic Church opposed public theatre for entertainment purposes, the clergy did support amateur theatre for educational purposes. In English Canada, professional theatre languished to be replaced by amateur theatre groups. Governor General Lord Bessborough assisted amateur theatre by founding in 1932 the Dominion Drama Festival, an annual competition. The best provincial productions went on to national finals, held each year in a different major city.

Working-class political theatre was popular during the depression, especially the agitprop troupe (agitprop is a combination of the words "agitation" and "propaganda") theatre used by communist sympathizers to advance class struggle. The Workers' Experimental Theatre became the first agitprop troupe in Canada. It held its first performance on May 6, 1932, at the Ukrainian Labour Temple, followed in the summer of 1933 by three tours through southern Ontario. But its greatest success occurred in December 1933 when the group staged *Eight Men Speak*, a mock trial drama of the arrest two years earlier in 1931 and attempted assassination at the Kingston Penitentiary of Tim Buck, leader of the Communist Party, to an audience of 1500 at the Standard Theatre in Toronto. Many of the actors themselves risked arrest (and in some cases deportation) for taking part in the play, while theatre owners were threatened with having their licences revoked should they permit the play to be staged in their theatre.

The depression affected all aspects of Canadian society. Out of desperation, people turned to the government for financial assistance. Governments, in turn, reluctantly accepted new economic and social responsibilities. New political parties appeared, each one offering its own solution to the depression. Women and labourers made only marginal gains. Many turned to religion for guidance. Popular culture flourished as people sought an escape from the harsh reality around them.

LINKING TO THE PAST

Winged Messenger: Airmail in the Heroic Era, 1918–1939
http://www.civilization.ca/cpm/courrier/wm00eng.html
This virtual exhibition from the Canadian Museum of Civilization offers information on early developments in the airplane industry and on the delivery of airmail.

Biographies of the First Women to Be Elected or Appointed to Political Positions in Canada: The Famous 5
http://collections.ic.gc.ca/famous5
A site about the lives and achievements of Emily Murphy, Henrietta Muir Edwards, Louise McKinney, Irene Parlby, and Nellie McClung, who won the "Persons Case," achieving the recognition of women as persons under the BNA Act.

The Group of Seven and Their Contemporaries
http://www.mcmichael.com/group.htm
This site from the McMichael Canadian Art Collection includes biographies of, and reproductions of works by, the members of the Group of Seven and their associates, as well as a brief history of the group.

The Great Depression
http://www.canadianencyclopedia.com/index.cfm?PgNum=TCE&TCE_Version=A&ArticleId=A0003425&MenuClosed=0
An article tracing the economic, political, and social aspects of the depression years. Follow the links on this page to learn more.

The Bank of Canada Act
http://laws.justice.gc.ca/en/B-2
The full text of the Bank of Canada Act, which established the Bank of Canada in 1935.

75 Years of Struggle: History of the Communist Party of Canada
http://www.communist-party.ca/archive/index.html
All illustrated history of the Communist Party of Canada, from its formation in 1921 to the present.

BIBLIOGRAPHY

For an overview of the interwar years, consult John Herd Thompson with Allen Seager, *Canada, 1922–1939: Decades of Discord* (Toronto: McClelland & Stewart, 1985). On the 1930s see Michiel Horn's booklet *The Great Depression of the 1930s in Canada* (Ottawa: Canadian Historical Association, 1984).

On politics in the interwar years, see H.B. Neatby, *The Lonely Heights*, vol. 2, *1924–1932*; and *The Prism of Unity*, vol. 3, *1932–1939* (Toronto: University of Toronto Press, 1970; 1976) for Mackenzie King. Roger Graham's *Arthur Meighen* (Ottawa: Canadian Historical Association, 1965) deals with King's political rival in the 1920s, and Richard Wilbur's booklet, *The Bennett Administration* (Ottawa: Canadian Historical Association, 1969) deals with King's rival in the1930s. H. Blair Neatby provides an overview of politics in the 1930s in *The Politics of Chaos: Canada in the Thirties* (Toronto: Macmillan, 1972).

Maritime protest in the 1920s is discussed in E.R. Forbes, *The Maritime Rights Movement, 1919–27: A Study in Canadian Regionalism* (Montreal/Kingston: McGill-Queen's University Press, 1979). On the Progressive movement see W.L. Morton, *The Progressive Party in Canada* (Toronto: University of Toronto Press, 1950). On the CCF in the 1930s, see Walter Young, *The Anatomy of a Party: The National CCF* (Toronto: University of Toronto Press, 1969). On Social Credit see David R. Elliott and Iris Miller, *Bible Bill: A Biography of William Aberhart* (Edmonton: Reidmore Books, 1987); and Alvin Finkel, *The Social Credit Phenomenon in Alberta* (Toronto: University of Toronto Press, 1989). On the Union Nationale in Quebec, see Richard Jones's booklet, *Duplessis and the Union Nationale Administration* (Ottawa: Canadian Historical Association, 1983); and H.F. Quinn, *The Union Nationale*, rev. ed. (Toronto: University of Toronto Press, 1979). For the Communist Party see Norman Penner, *Canadian Communism: The Stalin Years and Beyond* (Toronto: Methuen Publications, 1988). Extreme right-wing movements are examined in Martin Robin, *Shades of Right: Nativist and Fascist Politics in Canada, 1920 to 1940* (Toronto: University of Toronto Press, 1991). Irving Abella and Harold Troper, *None Is Too Many: Canada and the Jews of Europe, 1933–1948*, 3rd ed. (Toronto: Lester, 1991), is a poignant account of Canada's treatment of Jewish refugees.

On the economics of the interwar years, see Michael Bliss, *Northern Enterprise: Five Centuries of Canadian Business* (Toronto: McClelland & Stewart, 1987); and Kenneth Norrie and Douglas Owram, *A History of the Canadian Economy*, 2nd ed. (Toronto: Harcourt Brace, 1996).

How Canada dealt with jobless or "radical" immigrants is discussed in Barbara Roberts, *Whence They Came: Deportation from Canada, 1900–1935* (Ottawa: University of Ottawa Press, 1988). James Struthers has studied the relief question in *No Fault of Their Own: Unemployment and the Canadian Welfare State, 1914–1941* (Toronto: University of Toronto Press, 1983). On the On-to-Ottawa trek, see Bill Waiser, *All Hell Can't Stop Us. The On-to-Ottawa Trek and the Regina Riot* (Calgary: Fifth House, 2003).

On women in the interwar years consult the relevant chapters in Alison Prentice et al., *Canadian Women: A History*, 2nd ed. (Toronto: Harcourt Brace, 1996); and Veronica Strong-Boag, *The New Day Recalled: Lives of Girls and Women in English Canada, 1919–1939* (Toronto: Copp Clark Pitman, 1988). The equivalent study for Quebec women is Andrée Lévesque, *Making and Breaking the Rules: Women in Quebec, 1919–1939* (Toronto: McClelland & Stewart, 1994).

Birth control is the subject of Angus McLaren and Arlene Tigar McLaren, *The Bedroom and the State: The Changing Practices and Politics of Contraception and Abortion in Canada, 1890–1980* (Toronto: McClelland & Stewart, 1986). On the Dionne quintuplets see the special issue of the *Journal of Canadian Studies* 29 (4) (Winter 1995).

Labour in the interwar years is discussed in Bryan D. Palmer, *Working-Class Experience: Rethinking the History of Canadian Labour, 1800–1991* (Toronto: McClelland & Stewart, 1992); and Irving M. Abella, *Nationalism, Communism and Canadian Labour: The CIO, the Communist Party and the Canadian Congress of*

Labour, 1935–1956 (Toronto: University of Toronto Press, 1973). On labour in Quebec in the 1930s, see Evelyn Dumas, *The Bitter Thirties in Quebec* (Montreal: Black Rose Books, 1975).

Canadian culture is dealt with in "The Conundrum of Culture," in *Canada, 1922–1939* (as cited earlier), pp. 158–92. On cultural nationalism see Mary Vipond, *The Mass Media in Canada* (Toronto: James Lorimer, 1992). On the Group of Seven consult Peter Mellen, *The Group of Seven* (Toronto: McClelland & Stewart, 1970) and Charles C. Hill, *The Group of Seven: Art for a Nation* (Ottawa: National Gallery of Canada, 1995). On working-class theatre see Richard Wright and Robin Endres, eds., *Eight Men Speak and Other Plays from the Canadian Workers' Theatre* (Toronto: New Hogtown Press, 1976); and Toby Gordon Ryan, *Stage Left: Canadian Theatre in the Thirties* (Toronto: CTR Publications, 1981). University education in the 1930s is the subject of Paul Axelrod's *Making a Middle Class: Student Life in English Canada During the Thirties* (Montreal/Kingston: McGill-Queen's University Press, 1990). Radio is discussed in Mary Vipond, *Listening In: The First Decade of Canadian Broadcasting, 1922–1932* (Montreal/Kingston: McGill-Queen's University Press, 1992). For Canadian sport, see Colin Howell, *Blood, Sweat, and Cheers: Sport in the Making of Modern Canada* (Toronto: University of Toronto Press, 2001).

Important reviews of Native history in the interwar years include Arthur Ray, *The Canadian Fur Trade in the Industrial Age* (Toronto: University of Toronto Press, 1990); and John Leonard Taylor, *Canadian Indian Policy during the Inter-War years, 1918–1939* (Ottawa: Indian and Northern Affairs Canada, 1984).

CANADA IN WORLD WAR II

TIME LINE

1939 –	World War II begins
1940 –	Unemployment Insurance scheme begun by federal government
	Canada and the United States sign the Ogdensburg Agreement
1941 –	Canadian Women's Army Corps established
1942 –	Plebiscite on conscription held in April
	Canadian troops participate in raid on Dieppe
1943 –	Canadian troops join Allied forces in the invasion of Italy
1944 –	The Family Allowance Act comes into effect
	Canadian troops participate in the invasion of Normandy
	Conscription decreed
1945 –	World War II ends
	Canada joins the United Nations Organization

On September 1, 1939, the German army invaded Poland. Two days later, Britain and France declared war on Germany. Canada's own declaration of war followed on September 9. Surely few people imagined at this moment that the world would have to endure fully six years of untold destruction and violent death.

The war and its immediate aftermath forced Canadians to reflect upon their international responsibilities. To what degree and in what manner should they participate in the war effort? And how should Canada contribute to maintaining the peace that finally returned in 1945? These questions often provoked bitter controversy.

The development of a huge war industry brought a rapid end to the depression that had gripped Canada during the 1930s. In response to citizens' demands, the federal government also began to set up social programs to alleviate economic hardship. The role of women changed, as women left the home to work in industry, partly to replace men who had joined the armed forces. Union membership climbed rapidly, as unemployment fell to low levels. In federal–provincial relations, the war effort brought Ottawa to centralize power at the expense of the provinces. In international affairs, Canada shifted its focus from Britain to the United States as its major ally and trading partner. Indeed, the war transformed Canada in many ways.

NEUTRALITY AND APPEASEMENT IN THE 1930S

In the 1930s, Canada used its newly won autonomy in foreign affairs to avoid military entanglements overseas. When, for example, Italian dictator Benito Mussolini invaded the independent African kingdom of Abyssinia (Ethiopia) in 1935, Prime Minister Mackenzie King made it clear that Canada should not become involved. He disavowed the Canadian representative at the League of Nations who had spoken in favour of imposing severe sanctions upon Italy. Britain and France saved Canada from further embarrassment when, in exchange for peace, they offered Mussolini the territory he had already overrun.

Adolf Hitler, who became chancellor of Germany in 1933, posed the greatest threat to world peace. Systematically, he set out to increase Germany's power. First, he reoccupied the hitherto demilitarized zone of the Rhineland in 1936, in violation of the Treaty of Versailles. Then, in 1938, he annexed Austria. Next, he seized the western part of Czechoslovakia, a conquest that Britain and France accepted, in the hope of avoiding war. Then, in March 1939, the German leader annexed what remained of Czechoslovakia. Throughout all these acts of aggression, Canada supported Britain and France's policy of appeasement, of making concession after concession.

Many supporters of appeasement in Canada saw Hitler and Mussolini as bulwarks against the spread of communism, as defenders of order in an era of chaotic revolution. Yet other explanations exist for Canada's support of appeasement. King and his foremost advisers favoured it out of fear that British policies might undermine Canadian autonomy and again draw the country into imperial conflicts. With his sure political instincts King also knew that another war, just like World War I, risked dividing Canadians in a bitter internal conflict that could destroy national unity as well as his government and the Liberal party.

Furthermore, isolationist sentiment ran deep in Canada, as it did in the United States, which had never even joined the League of Nations. Historian Frank Underhill said it more bluntly than most: "All these European troubles are not worth the bones of a Toronto grenadier."

In any case, many Canadians wondered, what impact could Canada have upon events? In 1938–39, the country's total budget for the armed forces was a trifling $35 million. The navy had fewer than a dozen fighting ships, and the air force, only 50 modern military aircraft. The professional army had just 4000 troops; the navy, 3000; and the air force, only 1000. Twenty years of neglect had gravely weakened Canada's defences. Clearly, the nation could not even defend its own coasts, let alone dispatch fully equipped and trained forces to Europe.

CANADA AND THE WAR AGAINST THE AXIS

When Britain declared war on Germany, Canada's support was not in doubt. Theoretically, Canada could have remained neutral, as the United States did until the Japanese attack on Pearl Harbor in December 1941. But Canada's strong emotional ties with the mother country made this option impossible.

Thanks to the "phoney war," as those months of relative quiet in the early months of the conflict were called, the Canadian government was able to postpone making wrenching decisions concerning the nature of Canada's participation. Nevertheless, during this period one vitally important part of Canada's contribution to the war got under way: the British Commonwealth Air Training Plan (BCATP), which was conducted in, and heavily funded by, Canada.

Negotiations with Britain to establish the terms of Canada's involvement proved arduous, even rancorous. As historian Desmond Morton observes, "King's attachment to England did not always extend to Englishmen."[1] The final plan gave control of the schools to the Royal Canadian Air Force (RCAF), which the federal government had organized immediately after World War I. By the end of the war, the BCATP had trained 130 000 aviators, nearly half the Commonwealth's air crews. The project also gave a tremendous boost to the aeronautics industry and, thanks to the more than $2 billion spent, to the Canadian economy in general.

THE WAR EFFORT, 1940–1942

The Nazis' invasion of western Europe in the spring of 1940 transformed the war. The rapid German advance led to the near capture of the entire British Expeditionary Force at Dunkirk. After France fell in June, Britain and its dominions stood alone against Germany. Overnight,

Trainee pilots at No. 5 Elementary Flying Training School, Kenyon Field, Lethbridge, August 1940.

Glenbow Archives, *Calgary Herald*, NA-2864-3445.

Canada became Britain's chief ally. Until the German invasion of the Soviet Union in June 1941, it remained so. During these dark months, Britain's surrender seemed highly possible.

To assist Britain and combat the Nazis, Canada built up a much larger army, constructed dozens of warships and hundreds of aircraft, and converted the entire economy to war production. In response to Britain's wartime financial needs, Canada lent, and then gave, huge sums of money through mutual-aid agreements, with no strings attached, although most of the money was spent in Canada on war materials destined for Britain.

Combat action for Canadian troops came first in the Pacific theatre. In hindsight, the federal government had foolishly agreed to reinforce British troops in Hong Kong. The colony fell to the Japanese on Christmas Day, 1941. More than 550 Canadians perished either in the attack or afterwards in the harsh conditions of Japanese slave labour camps. Later, Canada played a relatively minor role in the war in the Pacific. Plans to increase Canada's air and sea participation in summer 1945 were cancelled after the Americans dropped atomic bombs on two Japanese cities.

Canadians in Europe experienced their baptism of fire in August 1942, in the ill-conceived major Allied raid on the French coast at Dieppe. In a few terrible hours, more than 60 percent of the 5000 Canadian participants were killed or captured. For long months after that tragedy, Canadian troops continued garrison duty in Britain. They were not completely inactive: indeed, thousands of marriages between Canadian servicemen and British women took place. One Montreal journalist commented that the Canadian army was "the first formation in the history of war" in which the birth rate exceeded the death rate!

A Historical Portrait 🖎

🖝 Sir Frederick Banting and Pilot Joseph Mackey

Sir Frederick Banting is well known as the discoverer, with Charles Best, of insulin, used in the treatment of diabetes. Joseph Mackey was an American pilot, one of several hundred pilots and crew who worked for Ferry Command, an enterprise set up by the British and responsible for flying more than 9000 planes across the Atlantic for delivery in Great Britain.

The first flights began in February 1941. Banting, wanting to go to England, sought space on an aircraft as a passenger. He was assigned to the Lockheed Hudson piloted by Mackey. After bad weather finally cleared, five planes, including Mackey's, took off from Gander airport in Newfoundland. Shortly after takeoff, the left engine of Mackey's plane failed. The pilot turned back. Then the right engine lost power and the plane crashed. Mackey was injured, but not seriously. The other two crew members were killed. Banting suffered a concussion and internal bleeding. He died a few hours later despite Mackey's efforts to save his life. Three days later, Mackey was spotted by a plane and rescued. He later sold his story to a Toronto newspaper and then donated the proceeds to the children of his deceased radio officer.

More than 500 airmen lost their lives while working for Ferry Command, often in crashes of large Liberator bombers used to bring the crews home. About 50 passengers were killed, too. Banting was the first.

This story is told in Carl A. Christie, *Ocean Bridge: The History of RAF Ferry Command* (Toronto: University of Toronto Press, 1995), pp. 62–72.

Canadian–American Wartime Relations

War inevitably drew Canada closer to the United States. In August 1940, King and the American president, Franklin D. Roosevelt, signed the Ogdensburg Agreement, which created the Permanent Joint Board on Defence (PJBD), responsible for discussing military questions of mutual interest. As early as 1938, the two countries had begun to exchange military information. In the summer of 1940, King himself pushed for talks on common defence planning. Most Canadians approved of the continental defence tie, as they believed Canada could not rely on its own (then virtually non-existent) defences or on Britain's. Thus, when Roosevelt proposed the PJBD, King was delighted, although he apparently had some doubts about making the board permanent.

Historians differ in their interpretations of this *rapprochement*. Donald Creighton, always alert to the imperial designs of Canada's southern neighbour, saw the Ogdensburg Agreement as a major step toward the Liberals' surrender of Canadian autonomy."[2] In contrast, J.L. Granatstein and Norman Hillmer have argued that King "wanted to protect Canada and to help Great Britain as much as possible, and he understood and accepted that this obliged him to seek even closer relations with Roosevelt's America."[3] Indeed, during the early months of war, Canada seems to have enjoyed some influence in the United States, notably through King's use of quiet diplomacy with the president.

The Hyde Park Declaration

King and Roosevelt signed a second agreement, the Hyde Park Declaration, in April 1941. It proved an even more important milestone in Canadian–American relations than the Ogdensburg Agreement.

Canada's wartime economic relations with both Britain and the United States led to this understanding. Since 1939 Britain had ordered ever-increasing amounts of war supplies from Canada and the United States, but it lacked the dollars to pay for them. Meanwhile Canada had accumulated huge deficits in its American trade, largely because of its enormous purchases of equipment destined for Britain. When in 1941 the United States passed the Lend-Lease Act, which exempted Britain from making cash payments on its orders for war materials, Canada worried that it would now lose British business.

King nevertheless managed to get a reasonably satisfactory agreement with the Americans: the United States promised to increase its defence purchases in Canada substantially, enabling Canada to make its own purchases of war equipment in the United States. Britain could continue buying Canadian goods and Canada could even get relief, through Lend-Lease, for its American purchases of war supplies to be sent via Canada to Britain. The agreement ended Canada's dollar shortage by 1942. Some scholars see the Hyde Park Declaration as another blow to Canadian independence. In view of Canada's precarious situation, however, the country probably could not have obtained better financial terms.

After Hyde Park, Canada's influence with the United States waned. The American entry into the war in December 1941 substantially changed American perspectives. Relinquishing its isolationism, the United States became more concerned with global rather than hemispheric issues. Canada lost its special status and became a junior partner in the Anglo-American-Russian alliance to defeat the Axis powers from 1942 to 1945. Even at the two wartime conferences held in Quebec City that brought together the British and the American war leaders, Winston Churchill and Franklin D. Roosevelt, Canada acted merely as host. King's presence was largely confined to the official photos.

The Wartime Economy

On the eve of war, 20 percent of Canadian workers lacked jobs. Barely a year later, full employment was within sight. The wartime emergency led to large-scale federal economic intervention. Soon Canada produced 4000 airplanes a year, as well as ships, tanks, and huge quantities of shells and guns. Investment in industry doubled between 1939 and 1943. War materials had priority over civilian goods, whose production was severely curtailed.

Just as during World War I, the burgeoning economy generated inflationary pressures. Prices spiralled upwards. In response, Ottawa implemented drastic wage and price controls. The government also resorted to so-called voluntary measures. It exhorted homemakers to put their savings into Victory Bonds and urged merchants to offer customers their change in war savings stamps. The government used the revenue from the bonds and stamps to purchase arms and build bombs. And that — as one patriotic poster proclaimed — was how homemaker "Mrs. Morin bombarded Berlin"! Women also established branches of the Consumers Service that, among other activities, denounced merchants who violated the law. Such measures succeeded in curtailing inflation.

Fitting the guns on a 28-ton tank at Montreal Locomotive Works, Montreal, around 1942.

Photograph Collection and Library Services Canada/ Science and Technology Museum, Image CN 001876.

Rationing

The relative scarcity of various consumer goods led to rationing. The government issued books of coupons and recruited thousands of female volunteers to distribute them to shoppers. Sugar became the first product to be rationed. Later, Ottawa added tea, coffee, butter, meat, and gasoline to the list. Occasionally, shortages provoked an outcry. When brewers could not supply enough beer, Ontario workers threatened to boycott the sale of Victory Bonds. "No beer, no bonds!" was their warning.

The lack of automobiles and of the gasoline to make them run explains, together with full employment, an enormous increase in the use of urban public transport. During the war, buses and trams were often severely overcrowded. Mothers shopping for food had to compete with commuters for space. The media urged shoppers to avoid travelling at peak hours. Women frequently faced sexual harassment as men complained about "feminine intrusion into their cultural privacy and social space," particularly "their" smoking section at the rear of the bus.[4]

Business leaders improved their public image, tarnished during the depression years, by helping the federal government organize the country's war production. Proud to be called "Howe's boys," many went to work, often for a symbolic annual salary of one dollar, for the powerful C.D. Howe, minister of munitions and supply, the department in charge of all war procurement. Howe set up numerous Crown corporations and adopted the techniques of private enterprise. He also avoided the accusations of graft and profiteering that had so plagued Robert Borden's government during World War I.

WOMEN AND THE WAR EFFORT

According to traditional Canadian beliefs and practices, married women belonged in the home. Yet many women, particularly unmarried women, had worked outside the home long before the war, generally in low-paying occupations such as teaching, office work, retail sales, factory labour in textile and clothing mills, and as domestics. Now, in response to the general labour shortage created by the war, many more women entered the civilian work force. Department of Labour advertisements urged women to "roll up [their] sleeves for victory"; the men overseas needed support and women had to "back them up — to bring them back."

Women often did what was traditionally men's work. When a plywood factory opened in Port Alberni on Vancouver Island in 1942 to supply plywood for ammunition boxes, 80 percent of the workers hired were women. Many of these affectionately nicknamed "plywood girls" had brothers who were in the armed forces.

To attract women to factories from small towns and rural areas, employers offered women relatively attractive wages, particularly in war industries; indeed, women's wages increased faster

Women war workers return home after shift change, Edmonton, 1943.

National Archives of Canada/PA-116122.

than men's wages during the war years, although they remained substantially lower. Ottawa, for its part, temporarily amended the income tax laws to make it possible for husbands to continue to enjoy a full married exemption while their wives earned wages. Then, in mid-war, when a chronic lack of "manpower" made it essential to recruit mothers, the provinces of Ontario and Quebec set up a modest number of government-funded nurseries. Most women, however, had to leave their children in the care of relatives and friends.

Patriotic appeals drew thousands of women into volunteer work. They recuperated and recycled such items as paper, metal, fat, bones, rags, rubber, and glass. They also collected clothes for free distribution and prepared parcels to be sent overseas. Together with their unpaid labour in the home, women's voluntary efforts constituted, in the words of historian Ruth Roach Pierson, "far and away the largest contribution made by Canadian women to the war effort."[5]

WOMEN IN THE ARMED SERVICES

For the first time, women served in the armed services. By the end of the war, 50 000 women had enrolled, but these "Jill Canucks" were not "pistol-packing Mommas" and they did not hurl grenades.[6] The armed services assigned them positions considered proper to their sex and always paid them less than males. They remained subordinate to men of the same rank, and they commanded only other women. Such auxiliary women's units as the Canadian Women's Army Corps, created in 1941, supplied female support staff to release men for combat training and other duties.

Efforts to achieve fairness and equality did not permeate all aspects of life in the services. Male dominance of the military meant a double standard on sexual morality; literature on venereal disease, for example, warned servicemen to beware of "diseased, predatory females," but women received no similar advice regarding "loose men." Pregnancy was cause for an immediate discharge on medical grounds.

THE WAR AND NATIONAL UNITY

The Canadian government worked to keep support high for the war effort. The National Film Board (NFB), founded in 1939, produced "progressive film propaganda" designed to enhance Canadians' faith in their country. In the same year, Ottawa set up the Bureau of Public Information to promote patriotism and "Canadianism" among all ethnic groups in English-speaking Canada. The bureau published hundreds of pamphlets, arranged for news stories, magazine articles, and radio broadcasts, and subsidized "loyal" segments of the foreign-language press.

WARTIME TREATMENT OF MINORITY ETHNIC GROUPS

The federal government also took measures to combat widespread anti-immigrant attitudes during the war. Ironically, while attempting to unite Canadians, the government meted out harsh treatment to members of ethnic groups whose homelands were at war with Canada, believing that they constituted a danger to the state. Under the War Measures Act, the federal government interned hundreds of German Canadians, although the RCMP found no evidence of domestic subversion. Upon Italy's entry into the war, the RCMP began to fingerprint and photograph thousands of Italian Canadians, and arrested some 700. Businessman James Franceschini was one of those interned; he saw his businesses placed in the hands of the Custodian of Alien Property and the equipment sold off at fire-sale prices to his Montreal

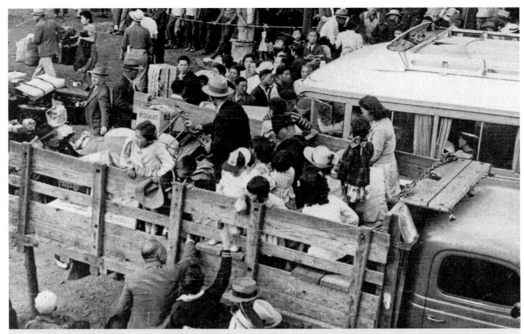

Japanese Canadians being "relocated" to camps in the interior of British Columbia. More than 20 000 Japanese and Japanese Canadians were relocated and their property confiscated during the war.

Tak Toyota/National Archives of Canada/C-46350.

competitors. A few members of the clergy and university professors questioned the arrests. Most Canadians appeared, by their silence, to acquiesce.

More than any other group, Japanese Canadians felt the brunt of Canadians' animosity. After the Japanese surprise raid on Pearl Harbor in December 1941, which brought fears of an invasion of the Pacific coast, the federal government evacuated the more than 20 000 Japanese and Japanese Canadians living in coastal British Columbia. Most evacuees were transported to camps in the interior of the province, but several hundred males deemed "dangerous" were placed under armed guard at a camp in the Lake Superior bush country. Those interned saw their property confiscated and auctioned off. After the war, Ottawa resettled the Japanese Canadians across Canada and even attempted to deport thousands — many of whom were Canadian citizens — to Japan.

Most historians view wartime government policy toward the Japanese in Canada as the result of longstanding racial hostility toward this group. "The threat of Japanese subversion was created by the union of traditional racial attitudes and perceptions shaped by the fears and anxieties conjured up by war," historian Peter Ward contends.[7] A hostile public easily convinced federal politicians to act. Historians Patricia Roy and others, however, have argued that Ottawa carried out the evacuation of the Japanese "as much for their own protection, and, by implication, the protection of Canadians in Japanese hands."[8] Forty years later, the federal government apologized to Japanese Canadians for their wartime treatment and offered financial compensation.

FRENCH CANADA AND THE WAR

French Canada posed a special challenge. Although French Canadians generally accepted participation, as in World War I they remained adamantly opposed to compulsory military service for overseas operations. The stringent Defence of Canada Regulations, which provided for the censorship of anti-war sentiment in the media, attempted to curb opposition to government war policy in Quebec. The CBC also acted as a "propaganda vehicle" in favour of the war effort.

Several reasons help to explain French Canada's lack of enthusiasm for the war. During the 1930s many French-Canadian intellectuals showed sympathy for the fascist leaders of southern Europe whom they viewed as stalwart opponents of communism. Traditionalists predicted that the war would cause the break-up of families because it brought women into the factories. For their part, the defenders of provincial autonomy attacked Ottawa's wartime intrusion into the provincial government's jurisdiction. Furthermore, nationalists denounced the danger of linguistic assimilation by a Canadian army in which the French language was often proscribed.

Most French Canadians, however, simply did not feel immediately concerned by a war in Europe. Having been estranged from France politically, culturally, and demographically for nearly two centuries, they had few ties with that country. They certainly felt no strong loyalty to England. Most, however, agreed to Canada's involvement on the condition that enlistment be voluntary.

PLEBISCITE OF 1942

As the war dragged on and military leaders demanded reinforcements, many English-speaking Canadians called for conscription. They interpreted King's refusal to consider conscription as putting political advantage, especially his solid support in Quebec, ahead of the war effort. King certainly moved cautiously. In mid-1940, his government decreed compulsory military training but for home service only. When recruiting for overseas service lagged in 1941, the government decided to retain the home-defence conscripts for the duration of the war, in the hope that many would volunteer to serve overseas. When few signed up, and pressure mounted for King to send more troops, King decided to ask Canadians, by plebiscite, to release his government from its anti-conscriptionist commitments. In Quebec, nationalists accused the prime minister of betraying his sacred promises, and urged French Canadians to vote "non." The results of the vote, held in April 1942, revealed the deep division between Quebec and the rest of Canada. While 72 percent of Quebecers answered "no," 80 percent of the electorate of the other provinces responded "yes."

Still Mackenzie King delayed. When asked if the time had come to implement conscription, he replied evasively: "Conscription if necessary, but not necessarily conscription." Remembering the disastrous consequences of the conscription crisis of 1917 for national unity and for both major political parties, King hoped that conscription would never be necessary. Until late 1944, Canada continued to rely on voluntary enlistments, although some of the volunteers were home-defence conscripts, "convinced" by moral pressure and even physical abuse to "go active."

CANADA INTENSIFIES ITS WAR EFFORT

On the Atlantic ocean, the Royal Canadian Navy (RCN), which enlisted a total of 100 000 men and 6500 women during the war, took on the responsibility of defending the convoys that transported troops and supplies to Britain. The job was dangerous. Moreover, living conditions on the escorting corvettes were often dreadful, as seawater penetrated continually during bad weather. "The smell just got worse and worse," one sailor remembered. "The ship was a floating pigpen of stink. You couldn't get away from it..."

In the first years of the war, Allied naval losses were staggering; shipyards were unable to build replacements fast enough. Initially, the Canadian navy had few successes in the

Members of the Fusiliers Mont-Royal Regiment in Falaise, France, just after the Normandy invasion.

National Archives of Canada/PA-115568.

anti-submarine war. But once properly trained and equipped, it played a significant role in the Battle of the Atlantic by sinking, or helping to sink, many German U-boats.

On land, Canadian troops saw sustained combat from July 1943. In the mistaken hope that casualties would be light, King pressured the British to allow Canadian forces to join in the Allied invasion of Sicily. Nearly 100 000 Canadian troops took part in the lengthy Italian campaign that followed. Some 6000 Canadian soldiers lost their lives, and another 20 000 were wounded. The fierce battle to capture the strategic town of Ortona alone cost the Canadians 700 dead: they fought from doorway to doorway, from rooftop to rooftop, sometimes even moving from house to house without going outside, through a technique of breaking through the walls between houses known as "mouse-holing." Although they faced Germans who often were better armed, the Canadians relentlessly pushed north, breaching the imposing German fortifications of the Gothic Line in September 1944.

Canadians also played a significant role in the Normandy invasion of June 6, 1944. Assisted by the RCN, Canadian troops took an entire German-held beach. The Canadian division suffered greater casualties than the British formations, but it also advanced further inland than any other Allied division on D-Day. Over the next few weeks, the Canadian army's progress across Normandy was slowed by several costly failures. In possibly the Canadians' worst reversal, a complete battalion, the Canadian Black Watch, was virtually annihilated on July 25 in an unsuccessful attempt to take Verrières Ridge, south of Caen.

Allied bombing errors resulted in substantial Canadian casualties. Moreover, at least 150 Canadian deaths were in reality cold-blooded murders by German soldiers, well behind the lines. In one notorious incident, a group of Canadian prisoners was marched to the Abbaye d'Ardennes, where they were shot in the garden after interrogation. The German commander held responsible later served some time in prison before being released to a hero's welcome in Germany.

The Canadians also organized the bloody sieges of Boulogne, Calais, and Le Havre. Then, in autumn 1944, in dreadful conditions of cold and mud, Canadian troops played a major role in the fight to secure the approaches to the Belgian port city of Antwerp. One effort involved an attempt to dislodge the Germans on Walcheren Island, at the mouth of the Scheldt delta. The approach by land was over a long rock-and-earth causeway that became a veritable hell for Canadian attackers raked by intense enemy bombardment. After heavy losses, the Canadians managed to establish a bridgehead on the island; then the British modified their strategy and decided to attack elsewhere.

CONSCRIPTION AND THE END OF THE WAR

By late 1944, after several months of fighting in France and in the face of an important German counteroffensive, Canadian officers overseas were demanding reinforcements, particularly the well-trained home-defence conscripts. The Conservatives, in opposition, urged the government to decree conscription. Within the cabinet, Colonel J.L. Ralston, the minister of national defence, also pushed for compulsory military service. King, still not ready, replaced Ralston with General McNaughton, who failed to recruit the necessary volunteers. On November 22, just as several of his English-speaking cabinet ministers prepared to resign, King yielded. Canada would again have conscription.

Few Canadian conscripts ever served overseas, however, and conscription ultimately had no effect on winning the war. In spite of the criticism from both supporters and opponents of conscription, and perhaps because the criticism came from both ends of the spectrum, King was able to portray himself as a moderate. He and his Liberal party managed to survive the crisis. To their credit, they had limited the ethnic bitterness that occurred in the conscription crisis in 1917.

Where Historians Disagree
Canadian Participation in the Land War in Northwestern Europe

Throughout the early 1990s, the media extensively marked the fiftieth anniversary of the events of World War II. Canadian historians also showed new interest in that conflict and, in particular, in the role Canadians played in combat in northwestern Europe.

The tragedy at Dieppe in August 1942 has been the subject of several studies. In *Unauthorized Action: Mountbatten and the Dieppe Raid*, Brian Loring Villa assigns

British Chief of Combined Operations Lord Louis Mountbatten responsibility for having ordered the raid. Villa quotes Canadian newspaper magnate Lord Beaverbrook who bitterly accused Mountbatten of having the blood of "thousands of my countrymen on your hands."[1] But Villa also notes that General A.G.L. McNaughton, commander of Canadian forces in Britain, had delivered numerous bellicose statements. When, at last, an opportunity to use Canadian troops presented itself, McNaughton could scarcely decline the offer. Even the cautious Prime Minister King had to take into account the rising criticism of Canadians who wanted to see their country's troops take a more active part in the struggle.

For J.L. Granatstein, General H.D.G. Crerar, who commanded the 1st Canadian Corps, shares responsibility. Crerar, he says, "had come to England convinced that the army had to see action soon, both for its own morale and for domestic Canadian consumption."[2] After Dieppe, Crerar's approach was to rationalize the raid by speaking of lessons learned, an approach that Granatstein says "may even be right." Peter Henshaw also believes that the Canadian commanders were primarily responsible for the Dieppe fiasco: "Their struggle for autonomy, and for a leading Canadian role in raids, interacted with British interservice rivalries in a way that was decisive for the progress of the planned raid."[3]

Denis and Sheilagh Whitaker, the former a captain at Dieppe, blame British Prime Minister Winston Churchill, who needed to prove to Soviet dictator Joseph Stalin that it was impossible in 1942 to open a second front against the Germans. They argue that Churchill's strategy "was successful, no matter how high the costs."[4] Moreover, the Allies gained essential experience at Dieppe in preparation for D-Day. The lessons learned, they say, "saved countless lives as a result of their far-reaching influence on the success of future operations."[5] W.A.B. Douglas and Brereton Greenhous agree. Because of Dieppe, the Allies realized that "objectives must be more realistic, tactics more sophisticated, and training more rigorous. Communications must be more comprehensive, equipment more appropriate, and, most of all, fire support by sea and air must be overwhelming."[6]

Canadians participated actively in the lengthy campaign in northwestern Europe that followed the invasion of Normandy. Casualties were high. Indeed, in John A. English's view, "the lives of many soldiers were unnecessarily cast away." Who should be blamed? English responds, "those who left them exposed in open wheatfields to be harvested like so many sheaves.... The responsibility must rest with the high command."[7] English argues that senior officers had little idea of how to direct a modern army in field operations, while many officers at the divisional and brigade levels were of doubtful professional competence.

The Valour and the Horror, a television series on Canada's role in World War II broadcast by the CBC and Radio-Canada in January 1992, provoked bitter controversy. War veterans and several historians accused the writer-producers, Brian and Terence McKenna, of distorting history and of unduly maligning military commanders. A Senate subcommittee held hearings on the series — a gesture that the media attacked as a threat to freedom of expression.

In a review commissioned by the CBC, historians S.F Wise and David J. Bercuson both found the series to be "bad history."[8] Wise, for example, refuted the film's portrayal of poor Canadian generalship. Bercuson, while affirming a general belief that "the Canadian Army as a whole did not acquit itself well in the Normandy fighting," decried the "failure" to put events in Normandy into a broader context.[9] In a report partly based on the reviews done by Wise and Bercuson, the CBC ombudsman concluded that the series failed to "measure up to the CBC's demanding policies and standards."[10] The McKennas responded that the ombudsman's choice of historical advisers was "prejudicial" to them and that his judgments were "almost entirely unsubstantiated in fact."[11]

Clearly the controversies that have developed concerning Canada's participation in the war illustrate the problems of interpreting history and defining the "truth."

[1] Brian Loring Villa, *Unauthorized Action: Mountbatten and the Dieppe Raid*, 2nd ed. (Toronto: Oxford University Press, 1994), p. 18.

[2] J.L. Granatstein, *The Generals: The Canadian Army's Senior Commanders in the Second World War* (Toronto: Stoddart, 1993), p. 102.

[3] Peter Henshaw, "The Dieppe Raid: A Product of Misplaced Canadian Nationalism?" *Canadian Historical Review* 77 (1996): 252.

[4] Denis and Sheilagh Whitaker, *Dieppe: Tragedy to Triumph* (Toronto: McGraw-Hill Ryerson, 1992), p. 290.

[5] Ibid., p. 304.

[6] W.A.B. Douglas and Brereton Greenhous, *Out of the Shadows: Canada in the Second World War*, rev. ed. (Toronto: Dundurn Press, 1995), p. 128.

[7] John A. English, *The Canadian Army and the Normandy Campaign: A Study of Failure in High Command* (New York: Praeger, 1991), p. 256.

[8] S.F Wise and David J. Bercuson, *The Valour and the Horror Revisited* (Montreal/Kingston: McGill-Queen's University Press, 1994), p. 10.

[9] Ibid., p. 51.

[10] Ibid., p. 72.

[11] Ibid., p. 88.

AN EVALUATION OF CANADIAN PARTICIPATION

During the last months of the war, in early 1945, Canadian troops participated in the liberation of the Netherlands and in the final offensive against Germany. By the war's end, 250 000 troops had served in the Canadian army in northwestern Europe; more than 11 000 of them died. In addition, from 1942, Canadian aviators conducted thousands of perilous night-bombing missions that destroyed most of Germany's large cities; Canadians eventually made up about a quarter of Bomber Command's crews. More than 17 000 of the nearly quarter-million Canadians who served in the RCAF lost their lives. All told, more than 1 million Canadians out of a total population of 11.5 million saw military service in Canada and overseas during World War II. About 42 000 were killed, and nearly 55 000 were wounded; many of these would never recover.

Over 3000 status Indians enlisted, mostly in the army; indeed, until 1943, Navy regulations required that enlistees be "British born subjects, of a white race." Some 200 died in service. These figures do not include the Metis, Inuit, or non-status Indians, for whom no information is available.

The war caused innumerable personal tragedies, as thousands of Canadians lost a loved one. Sometimes the sad announcement came brutally. One Canadian girl wrote to her soldier boyfriend in France, and after a few

Private Huron Eldon Brant, member of the Tyendinaga Mohawk community, receiving the Military Medal for bravery at Grammichele, Sicily, 1943, from General Bernard Montgomery. One year later he was shot and killed during an attack near Rimini.

Captain Frank Royal/National Archives of Canada/PA-130065.

weeks the letter came back stamped "Killed in action." The soldiers' return, in some cases after five years of absence, provoked poignant emotions: time brought change, and lengthy absences had often altered perceptions of relationships. The divorce rate rose substantially.

Was Canada's role essential to the Allied victory over the Axis powers? Canada's military strength certainly paled in comparison with the resources that its huge southern neighbour was able to mobilize. Yet, for a small country, Canada's contribution was enormous. In the war in Italy and in northwestern Europe, Canadian forces made a decisive contribution. It is safe to say that, without their aid, the war, and the terrible suffering that it wrought, would have dragged on even longer.

ORGANIZED LABOUR DURING THE WAR

Organized labour made significant gains in the war years. Thanks to the war, the labour surplus of the 1930s became a shortage in the early 1940s. As employment rose, so, too, did union membership, particularly in the new industrial unions, which combined all workers in a particular industry in a single union. Between 1940 and 1945, union membership doubled to more than 700 000.

Although the war brought jobs and, in general, higher wages, grievances remained. Employers fiercely resisted union attempts to impose collective bargaining. The federal government intervened constantly to prevent strikes that could hurt war production. It applied wage controls that labour denounced as inequitable. Moreover, as historian Laurel Sefton MacDowell has shown, it sought particularly "to conciliate business, its wartime ally in developing the war economy."[9] For example, business representatives sat on government policy boards; labour did not.

INDUSTRIAL CONFLICTS

Workers' growing resentment contributed to a wave of industrial conflicts that peaked in 1943. That year, one union member in three went out on strike. The government responded to the unrest with new rules which recognized the right of workers in industries under federal jurisdiction to join unions and to bargain collectively. It established certification procedures, set out penalties for unfair labour practices by which employers commonly interfered with workers' attempts to set up unions, and established a labour-relations board to administer the law. After the war most provinces adopted comparable rules.

A bitter strike at the Ford motor plant in Windsor, Ontario, in 1945 concerned labour security, among other issues. The union wanted an agreement specifying that all employees had to belong to the union and that the company had to deduct union dues from wage cheques — "union shop and checkoff" was the workers' demand. Ford adamantly refused. To ensure a tight picket line, militant strikers set up a massive automobile blockade in the streets around the plant. Federal and provincial authorities as well as the Canadian Congress of Labour itself intervened, without success.

Finally, both sides agreed to accept binding arbitration. Justice Ivan Rand of the Supreme Court of Canada proposed what became known as the Rand Formula: since all employees benefited from union activities, all should pay union dues, to be collected by the company and remitted to the union. Workers need not join the union, however. Rand also recommended heavy penalties for unauthorized, or "wildcat," strikes. Although he admitted that a strike was not a "tea party," he strongly condemned the workers' motor blockade.

The late 1940s saw more dramatic confrontations between labour and management, often in provinces whose governments sided openly with employers. Still, unions felt more secure as the war years ended. The relative labour peace of the 1950s resulted, in part, from these wartime gains.

THE STATE'S NEW ROLE

Though the war eliminated unemployment and restored a degree of prosperity, it exacted heavy financial sacrifices from people. By 1943, as war fatigue set in and increasing Allied success pointed the way to final victory, Canadians reflected on the postwar society they wanted to build. In particular, many wanted governments to introduce measures that would help those in need and establish greater equality within society.

SOCIAL-WELFARE MEASURES

In 1940, after obtaining the consent of the provinces to amend the British North America Act, the federal government adopted an unemployment-insurance plan. Then, in 1943, the government's Committee on Reconstruction urged the immediate creation of a full welfare state, with a national health-insurance scheme, old-age pensions, and children's allowances. Fearful of the costs involved, Ottawa adopted a cautious and piecemeal approach. In 1944, it introduced a family-allowance program providing monthly payments to help Canadian mothers support their children. King, worried about the left-wing CCF's high ratings in the polls, hoped that the measure would boost support for the Liberals. Certain Conservatives denounced the project as a "baby bonus" designed to benefit Quebec with its alleged big families, while nationalists in Quebec condemned it as an infringement upon provincial autonomy. Business reacted favourably; it hoped that the allowances would diminish pressure to raise wages. Undoubtedly, King's cautious, reformist approach to social problems helped ensure the Liberals' re-election in 1945, as CCF support weakened.

Housing became a serious problem for increasing numbers of urban Canadians during the war years. As migrants flocked to cities to work in war-related industries, many families lived in garages, empty warehouses, shacks, chicken-coops, "and indeed, in anything that will hold a bed," as one report put it. As the war ended, Canada's rental-controls administrator estimated that at least 200 000 Canadian households were now living "doubled up" or even "tripled up." Ottawa ignored pleas for public intervention to provide low-rental housing; instead, it acted to reduce down payments and to guarantee mortgages in order to stimulate the building of new homes and enable families with moderate incomes to purchase property.

WOMEN IN POSTWAR CANADA

In the middle of the war, Ottawa established a special subcommittee to study the role of women in postwar Canada. The members, all women, assumed that many female workers would return to the home. For those who remained employed outside the home, the subcommittee's report recommended expanded employment opportunities, equal pay, better working conditions, and the granting of children's allowances.

These proposals stirred up substantial opposition. Government planners wanted women out of the work force to make room for returning soldiers and workers in shut-down war industries. Unions did not want to see women competing for scarce jobs with men. Polls showed that most Canadians — women as well as men — wanted women back in the home after the war. The war experience was the exception, not the rule. In this climate, as historian Gail Cuthbert Brandt wrote, the subcommittee's report was "pigeon-holed and forgotten."[10]

Things appeared to return to "normal" at the end of the war. Many of the barriers blocking women from the work force went back up again. Historian Susanne Klausen recounts that the "plywood girls" of the Port Alberni plywood factory now became "plywood bags," a derogatory term often used by other women who wished to express their disapproval of young female workers who were occupying jobs that, in their view, should rightfully be given to returning veterans.[11] The proportion of women working outside the home plummeted. Although women slowly began to return to the work force in the early 1950s, not until the 1960s would the proportion of female workers return to what it had been in 1944 — 27 percent.

FEDERAL–PROVINCIAL RELATIONS: TOWARD FEDERAL SUPREMACY

The depression had restricted the autonomy of the provinces, forcing them to rely increasingly on Ottawa for financial assistance. The war created conditions that furthered centralization, as the federal government now took the dominant role in organizing the Canadian economy.

THE ROWELL–SIROIS REPORT

The Rowell–Sirois Commission on Dominion–Provincial Relations, set up by the King government in 1937, made public its report in 1940. With the objective of stabilizing provincial finances and giving equal services to all Canadians, the commissioners recommended that Ottawa collect all income taxes and, in return, make unconditional grants to the provinces. Disadvantaged provinces should receive special subsidies to enable them to offer social and educational services equivalent to those of other Canadian provinces. The federal government should also assume all provincial debts.

Provincial autonomists condemned the report as a veritable centralizer's "Bible." They argued that its recommendations would place provincial treasuries at Ottawa's mercy and that the federal government would determine provincial activities by what it was willing to pay out. For their part, federal ministers and bureaucrats endorsed the recommendations strongly, particularly those relating to money. Ottawa wanted to ensure control over fiscal policy to pay for the war as well as to diminish inflationary pressures. It thus urged the provinces to "rent" their tax fields to the federal government, at least for the duration of the war, and it proposed to compensate the provinces more generously. All the provinces yielded, although some did so reluctantly.

After 1943, the economic planners in Ottawa set forth their designs for the immediate postwar era. The federal government, they urged, should act as the "balance wheel" of the economy. If it kept its hand firmly on taxation, it could combat cyclical tendencies, either deflationary busts or inflationary booms; it could maintain high and stable employment; and it could offer costly social-security measures to all citizens, thus supporting consumer buying power. For these civil servants, economic, political, and humanitarian objectives dictated that the federal government continue to take charge.

As the war ended, King sought to convince the provinces to continue to allow Ottawa to levy all income taxes in return for increased provincial grants, with no strings attached. The federal government also offered to pay part of the cost of a comprehensive health-insurance plan and of old-age pensions, and to expand the coverage of federal unemployment insurance. Ottawa eventually managed to reach agreement on the tax proposals with all but Ontario and Quebec. The federalism of the next decade thus remained highly centralized.

THE PROVINCES IN THE WAR YEARS

The war and the after-effects of the depression fostered the uneven development of regional economies and thus contributed to the growth of regionalism in Canada. The war had diversified Canada's manufacturing capacity, as well as further promoting its resource-based industries. Quebec, British Columbia, and especially Ontario made dramatic advances. In Quebec, industries such as chemical products and aluminum refining expanded rapidly. In Ontario, factory employment increased greatly. On the Pacific coast, the port of Vancouver prospered. Its shipyards and those of Victoria employed 30 000 workers at their peak. In spite of the war, tourism continued to contribute to Vancouver's development, and wartime promotion ensured that the sector would be poised for rapid postwar expansion.

THE NORTH

In 1942, the United States Army Corps of Engineers coordinated the construction teams that built, for defence purposes, a 2500-km highway from Dawson Creek in northeastern British Columbia to Fairbanks, Alaska. This rough American military road, built largely on Canadian soil, was then transformed into a permanent civilian highway. The attack on Pearl Harbor also led American defence planners to worry about the threat to energy supplies in the Northwest; oil tankers now appeared vulnerable to Japanese submarine attack. As a result, the Canadian Oil (Canol) project was begun to pipe oil from the Imperial Oil Company's field at Norman Wells, on the Mackenzie River.

CHANGES IN THE CENTRAL PROVINCES

In Quebec the war-time Liberal government of Adélard Godbout initiated important reforms. In 1940, women in Quebec finally obtained the right to vote, despite the vigorous objections of the church and conservative groups. The government also created Hydro-Québec, a publicly owned hydro-electric utility in the Montreal region. To boost educational levels, it made school attendance obligatory until age fourteen, a measure hitherto opposed by the Roman Catholic clergy. In the area of labour–management relations, it set out the rules intended to force companies to negotiate with their unionized employees.

In Ontario, the Conservatives regained power in 1943. They denounced the supposed threat posed by the socialists of the provincial CCF party, but they also energetically pursued reform policies, notably in health, education, and housing. Provincial planning became important in areas such as forest conservation, industrial development, and water use. By 1945, the CCF was in decline, the Conservatives easily won a majority, and Ontario settled into what would become more than 40 years of Conservative government.

THE MARITIMES AND NEWFOUNDLAND

The war brought fewer economic benefits to Canadians in the three Maritime provinces, although war spending did boost the regional economy. By 1943, some 75 000 men and women were building and repairing vessels in Maritime shipyards, even at night under floodlights. Halifax became Canada's major port for shipping munitions and other supplies to western Europe.

Yet, according to historian Ernest Forbes, the impact of Ottawa's war policies on the Maritimes was "largely negative. While the government did generate economic activity, it created relatively little new industry in the region."[12] According to Forbes, C.D. Howe believed it was more efficient to develop industry along the St. Lawrence and in the Great Lakes region, a conviction reinforced by his regional prejudices.

Economic weakness meant that governments lacked funds for investment in health and education. In 1945, Prince Edward Island had only half the number of doctors needed to meet national standards. New Brunswick had Canada's highest infant and maternal death rate, and Nova Scotia followed closely. Teachers in the region were often poorly qualified, and salaries were low. New Brunswick had Canada's highest illiteracy rate, affecting particularly the province's French-speaking Acadian population, who also suffered linguistic discrimination.

In Newfoundland, low fish prices and uncertain markets left the population of the outports in appalling poverty. Eventually, though, the war created a temporary boom in employment through the construction and maintenance of huge American defence projects. As the war came to a close, Britain came to an understanding with the Canadian government to encourage the island's eventual incorporation into Canada.

The West

The Prairie provinces, hard hit by the depression of the 1930s, recovered slowly. Farmers did increase their incomes, thanks to higher prices and to improved harvests. Yet most rural homes still had no indoor plumbing or electricity, and farm villages enjoyed few services.

The family of Private Louis Zarowny welcomes him home, at Mewata Stadium in Calgary, in July 1945. Wounded twice, Zarowny served with The Loyal Edmonton Regiment in Italy and Northwestern Europe.

Glenbow Archives, Calgary, Canada/Herald Collection/NA-2864-3448.

The war boosted crude-oil production in Alberta, at least until the Turner Valley field near Calgary went into decline after 1942. Coal mines prospered, too, and in Prairie cities the construction industry flourished. But the war did not create the diversified economy that many residents felt the region needed.

Politically, third parties on the Prairies grew stronger, although they tended to moderate their ideology. Social Credit leaders in Alberta denounced socialism and centralization, promised able, businesslike administration, and gently laid Social Credit doctrine to rest. The CCF scored its first victory in Saskatchewan in 1944. Its ambitious program promised public ownership of natural resources, security of land tenure for farmers, collective bargaining for workers, and a universal socialized health plan. Once in power, the CCF launched major reforms, but financial and other factors soon forced it to make pragmatic policy adjustments. In British Columbia, the old political order also changed, as Liberals and Conservatives formed a coalition to counter the CCF's growing popularity.

TOWARD A NEW INTERNATIONALISM

The war in Europe ended when Germany capitulated in May 1945. By September, Japan also surrendered. Peace brought with it new problems and, in particular, the difficult question of how to maintain it. In contrast to its position after World War I, Canada was ready to accept responsibility in world affairs. Canada thus participated in the founding conference of the United Nations at San Francisco in April 1945, where it worked to ensure that both the United States and the Soviet Union became members.

Canada also pushed for world economic and social co-operation. Canadian diplomat Lester Pearson chaired the founding meeting of the United Nations Food and Agriculture Organization in Quebec City. As a member of the United Nations Relief and Rehabilitation Administration, Canada became a major supplier of aid to war-torn countries. Canada also joined the International Monetary Fund, as well as the International Civil Aviation Organization, whose headquarters came to Montreal. Canada willingly recognized that its influence was less than that of the United States, but at the same time it attempted, with some success, to get recognition from the Great Powers for states like itself.

World War II changed Canada profoundly, in the country's relations with the world and at home as well. It effectively ended the isolation of the 1930s. Involvement in world affairs brought benefits but carried a price. Despite Canada's attempts to develop relationships with multilateral associations of states, it also developed closer ties to the United States. For supporters of the *rapprochement*, the closer links brought security and economic prosperity through trade and investment. For critics, the triumphant move toward nationhood in the interwar years appeared to have abruptly ended, with Canada being relegated once more to colonial status — this time, as a colony of the United States.

At home, the war created an economic boom that instilled hopes among Canadians for a better life. Trade-union organizations made notable gains, as governments enacted legislation establishing a new framework for the conduct of industrial relations. The entry of large numbers of women into the work force announced a substantial change in their role. New federal social programs meant that Canadians took a significant step in the direction of the welfare state. In federal–provincial relations, Ottawa reasserted a pre-eminence that endured for two decades. Voters in several provinces elected new governments that stayed in office for lengthy periods. In Ottawa, however, Canadians continued to support King, perhaps because he was, in historian Frank Underhill's words, the leader "who divides us least."[13]

NOTES

1. Desmond Morton, *Canada and War: A Military and Political History* (Toronto: Butterworths, 1981), p. 106.
2. Donald Creighton, *The Forked Road: Canada, 1939–1957* (Toronto: McClelland & Stewart, 1976), p. 43.
3. J.L. Granatstein and Norman Hillmer, *For Better or For Worse: Canada and the United States to the 1990s* (Mississauga, ON: Copp Clark Pitman, 1991), p. 144.
4. Donald F. Davis and Barbara Lorenzkowski, "A Platform for Gender Tensions: Women Working and Riding on Canadian Urban Public Transit in the 1940s," *Canadian Historical Review* 79 (1998): 442–43.
5. Ruth Roach Pierson, *"They're Still Women After All": The Second World War and Canadian Womanhood* (Toronto: McClelland & Stewart, 1986), p. 33.
6. Ruth Roach Pierson, "'Jill Canuck': CWAC of All Trades, But No 'Pistol Packing Momma,'" *Historical Papers/Communications historiques* (1978): 106–33.
7. W. Peter Ward, *White Canada Forever: Popular Attitudes and Public Policy Toward Orientals in British Columbia* (Montreal: McGill-Queen's University Press, 1978), p. 146.
8. Patricia Roy et al., *Mutual Hostages: Canadians and Japanese During the Second World War* (Toronto: University of Toronto Press, 1990), p. 215.
9. Laurel Sefton MacDowell, "The Formation of the Canadian Industrial Relations System During World War Two," *Labour/Le Travailleur* 3 (1978): 186.
10. Gail Cuthbert Brandt, "'Pigeon-Holed and Forgotten': The Work of the Subcommittee on the Post-War Problems of Women, 1943," *Histoire sociale/Social History* 15 (1983): 239–59.
11. Susanne Klausen, "The Plywood Girls: Women and Gender Ideology at the Port Alberni Plywood Plant, 1942–1991," *Labour/ Le Travail* 41 (1998): 199–235.
12. Ernest R. Forbes, *Challenging the Regional Stereotype: Essays on the 20th Century Maritimes* (Fredericton: Acadiensis Press, 1989), p. 195.
13. Frank Underhill, "The End of the King Era," *Canadian Forum* (September 1948); reprinted in F.H. Underhill, *In Search of Canadian Liberalism* (Toronto: Macmillan, 1960), p. 127.

LINKING TO THE PAST

C.D. Howe
http://www.schoolnet.ca/collections/wayfarers/cdhowe.htm

An illustrated biography of C.D. Howe.

Women in the War
http://www.valourandhorror.com/DB/ISSUE/Women/

An illustrated history of Canadian women's participation in World War II, both on the home front and in Europe.

The National Film Board of Canada
http://www.nfb.ca/e/history/index.html

A brief history of the National Film Board of Canada. Check out "1940s" for more information about the NFB's activities during that decade.

Years of Sorrow and Shame
http://www.japanesecanadianhistory.net/overview/part2.htm

A brief account of the treatment of Japanese Canadians during World War II.

The 1940 Unemployment Insurance Act
http://www.hrdc-drhc.gc.ca/insur/histui/ui_hist/chap04/chap4_e.html

A detailed explanation of the 1940 Unemployment Insurance Act.

RELATED READINGS

The following articles from R. Douglas Francis and Donald B. Smith, eds., *Readings in Canadian History: Post-Confederation*, 6th ed. (Toronto: Nelson Thomson Learning, 2002), deal with topics relevant to this chapter: James Eayrs, "'A Low Dishonest Decade': Aspects of Canadian External Policy, 1931–1939," pp. 347–61; J.L. Granatstein and Desmond Morton, "The War Changed Everything," pp. 323-28; and W. Peter Ward, "British Columbia and the Japanese Evacuation," pp. 328-43.

BIBLIOGRAPHY

Surveys of Canadian foreign policy from 1930 to 1945 include James Eayrs, *In Defence of Canada*, vol. 2, *Appeasement and Rearmament* (Toronto: University of Toronto Press, 1965); and C.P. Stacey, *Canada and the Age of Conflict: A History of Canadian External Policies*, vol. 2, *1921–1948: The Mackenzie King Era* (Toronto: University of Toronto Press, 1981). Both foreign and domestic policy issues are examined in J.L. Granatstein, *Canada's War: The Politics of the Mackenzie King Government, 1939–1945* (Toronto: University of Toronto Press, 1975, 1990); and in Desmond Morton, *Canada and War: A Military and Political History* (Toronto: Butterworths, 1981).

Among the numerous works discussing Canada's participation in the war see W.A.B. Douglas and Brereton Greenhous, *Out of the Shadows: Canada in the Second World War*, rev. ed. (Toronto: Dundurn Press, 1995); David J. Bercuson, *Maple Leaf Against the Axis: Canada's Second World War* (Toronto: Stoddart, 1995); and appropriate chapters in J. L. Granatstein, *Canada's Army: Waging War and Keeping the Peace* (Toronto, University of Toronto Press, 2002).

Canada's military leaders are studied in Bernd Horn and Stephen Harris, eds., *Warrior Chiefs: Perspectives on Senior Canadian Military Leaders* (Toronto: Dundurn Press, 2001). Other useful works include Terry Copp and Bill MacDraw, *Battle Exhaustion: Soldiers and Psychiatrists in the Canadian Army, 1939–1945* (Montreal/Kingston: McGill-Queen's University Press, 1990); Jonathan Vance, *Objects of Concern: Canadian Prisoners of War through the Twentieth Century* (Vancouver: University of British Columbia Press, 1994); and Peter Nearby and J. L. Granatstein, eds., *The Veterans Charter and Post-World War II Canada* (Montreal/Kingston: McGill-Queen's University Press, 1998).

For writings on naval and airforce history see Marc Milner, *Canada's Navy: The First Century* (Toronto: University of Toronto Press, 1999); the same author's *The U-Boat Hunters: The Royal Canadian Navy and the Offensive against Germany's Submarines* (Toronto: University of Toronto Press, 1994); Brereton Greenhous, Stephen J. Harris, William C. Johnston, and William G.P. Rawling, *The Crucible of War, 1939–1945: The Official History of the Royal Canadian Air Force*, vol. III (Toronto: University of Toronto Press, 1994); and Spencer Dunmore, *Wings for Victory: The Remarkable Story of the British Air Training Plan in Canada* (Toronto: McClelland & Stewart, 1994).

Government mobilization policies are looked at in J.L. Granatstein and J.M. Hitsman, *Broken Promises: A History of Conscription in Canada*, rev. ed. (Toronto: Copp Clark Pitman, 1985); and Michael D. Stevenson, *Canada's Greatest Wartime Muddle: National Selective Service and the Mobilization of Human Resources during World War II* (Montreal/Kingston: McGill-Queen's University Press, 2001). Larry Hannant, *The Infernal Machine: Investigating the Loyalty of Canada's Citizens* (Toronto: University of Toronto Press, 1995), deals with questions of internal security and civil liberties. On the wartime treatment of Japanese Canadians see Peter Ward, *White Canada Forever: Popular Attitudes and Public Policy toward Orientals in British Columbia*, 2nd ed. (Montreal/Kingston: McGill-Queen's University Press, 1990).

Nancy Christie studies social issues in *Engendering the State: Family, Work and Welfare in Canada* (Toronto: University of Toronto Press, 2000). See also Doug Owram, *The Government Generation: Canadian Intellectuals and the State, 1900–1945* (Toronto: University of Toronto Press, 1986). On women during World War II see Ruth Roach Pierson, *"They're Still Women After All": The Second World War and Canadian Womanhood* (Toronto: McClelland & Stewart, 1986); Carolyn Gossage, *Greatcoats and Glamour Boots: Canadian Women at War, 1939–1945*, rev. ed. (Toronto: Dundurn Press, 2001); and Alison Prentice et al., *Canadian Women: A History*, 2nd ed. (Toronto: Harcourt Brace, 1996), Chapter 12. Maria Tippett examines culture in wartime in *Making Culture: English-Canadian Institutions and the Arts before the Massey Commission* (Toronto: University of Toronto Press, 1990). Union activity is described in Desmond Morton with Terry Copp, *Working People: An Illustrated History of the Canadian Labour Movement*, 3rd ed. (Toronto: Summerhill Press, 1990).

PART SIX

MODERN CANADA, 1945–2003

Canada emerged in the last half of the twentieth century as an important industrial nation and a respected secondary world power. Such achievements brought both benefits and problems. Overall, Canadians have enjoyed one of the highest standards of living of any country in the world, although certain groups within Canadian society remain seriously disadvantaged and some regions of the country experience greater hardships and fewer advantages than others. How to ensure that all Canadians, regardless of ethnic origin, class, gender, or place of dwelling have equal opportunities continues to be one of the challenges facing Canadian leaders. Canadians have also had to learn to live in a global economy, where they have less control over their economic destiny than ever before.

Internationally, Canada emerged from World War II prepared to play a more active role on the world stage. Caught in the middle of the Cold War between the United States and the Soviet Union, the country chose to play the role of middle power, a role well-suited to the country's historic position as the mediator between Britain and the United States. To offset American dominance in the North American defence program, of which Canadians found themselves a part, Canadians have taken an active role in such international organizations as the United Nations, the British Commonwealth of Nations, and the North Atlantic Treaty Organization (NATO). Still, some foreign analysts have criticized Canada for becoming too closely allied to the United States, thus limiting the country's ability to help mediate international disputes.

Politically, one of the two traditional parties has shown incredible resilience at adapting to changes — the Liberal party, having ruled for three-quarters of the time since the end of World War II. Still, third parties have emerged in what has become at times a multi-party system, as a constant reminder that no party has enjoyed complete support from all regions and all groups within the country. Regional parties have been particularly strong in the West and in Quebec, challenging political leaders to find consensus.

As Canada has modernized, it has become more of a consumer society. Culturally, too, it has taken on the attributes of a mass culture, in which the emphasis is on a popular, mass audience. Both of these trends have moved the country, particularly English-speaking Canada, socially and culturally into the American orbit, making it difficult to maintain a distinctive Canadian identity. Yet, at the same time, regional and local cultural differences have continued to challenge these universal homogenizing trends, thus enabling Canada to offer an alternative North American lifestyle and a counter-culture to that of the United States.

CHAPTER 20

TOWARD A MORE AFFLUENT SOCIETY: 1945–1960

TIME LINE

1947 –	The Leduc oil field in Alberta begins operation
1949 –	Newfoundland enters Confederation
	Canada joins the North Atlantic Treaty Organization
1950 –	Outbreak of the Korean War
1952 –	Canada's first television station begins broadcasting in Montreal
1954 –	Construction begins on the St. Lawrence Seaway
1956 –	Founding of the Canadian Labour Congress
1957 –	Lester Pearson wins Nobel Peace Prize
	The Liberals defeated by John Diefenbaker's Conservatives in the federal election
1959 –	Newfoundland loggers' strike

After a decade of economic depression and six years of war, Canadians wanted to make up for lost time, forget a bleak past, and look toward the future. Workers sought stable jobs and better wages. Consumers wanted cars, household appliances, adequate housing, and more leisure. Yet modest family budgets, limited availability of goods, particularly in the immediate postwar years, and fears that prosperity would not continue, forced them to be patient and prudent. In addition, the insecurity of the recent past made Canadians look increasingly to governments to provide an array of health, educational, and social services as a safety net against misfortune. In regard to the world outside, they took pride in Canada's prestigious role in international organizations, and in the welcome their country extended to immigrants from war-torn and economically ravaged Europe.

Attitudes remained basically conservative. Traditional values and beliefs continued to govern the behaviour of a majority of Canadians. Although more women worked outside the home, long-held notions concerning the role of women in society loosened only gradually. By the late 1950s, however, attitudes were changing. Slower growth with rising unemployment disrupted the postwar boom. People tired of unimaginative politicians who boasted of past successes and talked in platitudinous generalities. They were now ready to welcome new leaders who would put forth new ideas and propose new solutions.

ECONOMIC NIRVANA IN CANADA?

Postwar Canada prospered. Construction boomed. Total industrial output rose by half in the 1950s, and productivity soared thanks to technological innovation. The lighting of the flame on Leduc no. 1 oil well in a farmer's field near Edmonton on a cold February day in 1947 signalled large-scale job creation and rapid population growth in Alberta. The discovery of large deposits of base metals in northern New Brunswick raised hopes for significant job creation in that province. In Ontario, demand for a wide array of goods stimulated industrial expansion. By 1951, 10 percent of the Canadian labour force had jobs related to motor vehicles, mostly in southern Ontario.

The average worker had reason to feel satisfied. Rapid economic growth meant that unemployment rates remained very low. Pay packets for factory workers doubled between 1945 and 1956. In spite of significant increases in the prices of food and consumer goods, workers saw their living standards improve. They also worked less, as the 40-hour week became the norm. In addition, federal transfer payments, like family allowances and old-age pensions, put more money into consumers' pockets.

THE AGE OF THE CONSUMER

The era of the consumer introduced a new lifestyle. In towns, people discarded their ice-boxes and equipped their kitchens with electric refrigerators. Coal merchants' sales tumbled as homeowners bought electric ranges and switched to cleaner and more efficient gas and oil heat. Families acquired a variety of new appliances intended to reduce the drudgery of housework. Sales of new automobiles mounted in the 1950s as Canadians bought sleek American Fords and Chevrolets, or slim British Morrises and Austins.

Subdivisions proliferated around major cities. In historian Doug Owram's words, "the rise and triumph of low-density residentially-oriented communities was the single most significant urban event of the postwar decades."[1] A million new homes were built between 1945 and 1960. Proud new homeowners hurried to vary the colour of the trim or to plant shrubs in order to distinguish their dwelling from the identical constructions on all sides. Roofs acquired an

Supermarkets became a symbol of postwar prosperity. Woodward's department store, Vancouver, was one of the first in Canada. It included in-store home economists and baby seats in the shopping carts.

Vancouver Public Library/25644.

important new use — as supports for forests of television antennas. Shopping centres sprang up, the first appearing in a Toronto suburb in 1946.

The Environment

More prosperous Canadians posed new threats to the environment as well as having an increased interest in protecting it. In search of new outdoor recreational opportunities, more mobile urban dwellers invaded provincial parks. Existing parks quickly became saturated. In response to this demand, Ontario, for example, embarked upon a major program of park expansion. By the late 1950s, however, conservationists worried that increased outdoor recreation threatened the survival of natural areas, and they called for the establishment of nature preserves.

Conservation practices had not yet influenced the methods of the forest industry. Harvesting aimed at maximum profits. Clearcutting, facilitated by the mechanization of the industry, was the primary method employed, because it permitted lower labour costs while hugely increasing logging volumes.

The Less Advantaged

Yet Canadians were often unhappy when they compared themselves, as they did obsessively, with better-off Americans. Canadians complained that refrigerators costing $400 at home could be had for only $275 in the United States. Journalist Blair Fraser remarked that, for Europeans still rebuilding their war-torn economies, second-place Canadians must have seemed like the impoverished tycoon who was down to his last million. Nevertheless, many people of talent, especially entertainers, researchers, and engineers, migrated south, while those who remained behind bemoaned the "brain drain."

A Historical Portrait 🖋

🖙 Betty, Ruby, and the Others

At the conclusion of World War II, most working women left the work force and became homemakers for their breadwinner husbands, and full-time mothers of the two, three, or often more children who quickly made their appearance. The gendered division of labour seemed normal and natural. The happiest women were supposedly those whose husbands were able to purchase a modest bungalow on a small lot in one of the new suburbs.

Do the life stories of these ordinary women confirm the myths of contentment in the home in suburbia? Betty's husband bought a bungalow in Cooksville, Ontario, a west Toronto suburb. Betty, who had a B.A. in music and had worked until her marriage, now settled in as a full-time homemaker. Some modern appliances supposedly made her work easier. In 1950, she already had an automatic washer. Historian Joy Parr shows that, in this regard, Betty, an American immigrant, was not typical of her Canadian neighbours, the majority of whom used labour-intensive wringer washers until the mid-1960s. Such washers cost much less, they consumed far less water, and they enabled users to assert more control over the washing process; the wringers, however, did pose some dangers to children's hands![1]

Betty's husband, John, commuted to work in downtown Toronto. He did not have a job, he had a "vocation." The distinction signified that John viewed his work as "socially important" and that he had to

devote virtually all his time to it. Betty was thus often home alone with the children because John was away on business. She was convinced that she was doing what was expected of her. "A woman's place is in the home," she repeated. John agreed. He was sure that women working outside the home were an important cause of divorce and of juvenile delinquency.

One day Betty decided to begin giving piano lessons at home. Perhaps she merely wanted some extra spending money of her own; perhaps she felt that her musical talents were being wasted; perhaps she was

Mrs. Hugh Hawkins of Ottawa doing the washing with a traditional labour-intensive wringer washer, 1947. Modern automatic washers were as yet rarely seen in Canadian homes.

National Archives of Canada/PA-115254.

simply bored and lonely. Earnings from the job were modest; indeed, John often belittled his wife's efforts. At the same time he did not hesitate, over Betty's protests, to delve into the piano money box when he needed some spare change.

Ruby was another Ontario homemaker in the 1950s. Her sister, Edna Staebler, has edited the letters that Ruby wrote to members of her family. Ruby worried about her appearance — she constantly complained about being overweight. She talked a lot about her children. She also got a job outside the home. In a touching letter to sister Kay, she expounded upon her decision.

> I'm so thrilled and so nervous I don't know what to do... You know I've been talking about getting a job for so long because (husband) Fred wasn't earning enough and I guess he got sick of hearing about it.... I'm to go to Musser's store on Monday afternoon and start selling gloves.

I'm so scared. I'll have to make change and fit people and be on my feet all those hours — and what will Fred say when he comes home tonite and I tell him?

> Gosh, why did I do it? I could be so comfortable here just watching TV and working on my rug and I wouldn't need many clothes.... If I work ... I'll always be in a rush with my housework and have to make dinner at noon. And I won't be home when the kids get here from school.... (But) it would be good training. And I could use the extra money for so many things we need around here....[2]

"Home dreams" did not fully meet the aspirations of all Canadian women after 1945, as historian Veronica Strong-Boag concludes.[3] Yet much work still needs to be done to reconstitute the life experiences of ordinary women in this period and to re-examine traditional interpretations.

[1] Joy Parr, *Domestic Goods: The Material, the Moral, and the Economic in the Postwar Years* (Toronto: University of Toronto Press, 1999), ch. 10.
[2] Edna Staebler, ed., *Haven't Any News: Ruby's Letters from the Fifties* (Waterloo, ON: Wilfrid Laurier Press, 1995), p. 58.
[3] Veronica Strong-Boag, "Home Dreams: Women and the Suburban Experiment in Canada, 1945–60," *Canadian Historical Review* 72 (1991): 504.

Many Canadians saw no boom at all. Few men and far fewer women held the university diplomas that guaranteed good jobs. Salaries were often low, especially for non-unionized workers, immigrants, and women. In rural Canada before 1950, only a minority of households even had electricity. The 1951 census revealed that half of Canadian families still did not own an electric refrigerator or a vacuum cleaner; 60 percent had no car; 40 percent had no telephone; and 25 percent did not have an electric washing machine. Indeed, one dwelling in three did not have hot and cold running water. Thousands of small farmers, incapable of earning a living, abandoned their land. Incomes of residents of the Atlantic provinces remained nearly 40 percent below the Canadian average. Thousands of Montrealers with incomes below the poverty line lived in the tenements of St. Henri, which were portrayed poignantly by Gabrielle Roy in her novel *Bonheur d'occasion* (*The Tin Flute* in English). Many First Nations people began to flee poverty and unemployment on the reserves, in search of better opportunities in urban centres. Disadvantaged provinces offered social services of inferior quality. Throughout Canada, the underprivileged, whether unemployed or sick, handicapped or elderly, could not count on the array of social welfare benefits that, in spite of recent cutbacks, still exist today.

Canada had many second-class citizens, too. French-speakers suffered a linguistic disadvantage, even within Quebec. Women did not enjoy the same employment opportunities as men. Discrimination also afflicted Canada's Aboriginal peoples as well as African Canadians, recent immigrants, and Jews. In 1948, Pierre Berton, a young reporter for *Maclean's*, set out to investigate anti-Semitism. When, for example, he attempted to reserve a room at summer resorts north of Toronto, he had much more success using the name "Marshall" than when he identified himself as "Rosenberg." To help combat such discrimination through education, the newly founded Canadian Council of Christians and Jews instituted Brotherhood Week, a major program, in 1948.

Society in this era emphasized family and reproductive heterosexuality, and psychologists warned that over-protective mothers and absent fathers risked provoking homosexual tendencies in their sons. Most homosexuals hid their sexual orientation except perhaps from a few persons close to them. Those who did not faced social stigma as "perverts" and "sex deviates," as well as job discrimination. Gay men were often viewed as potential child molesters and, in the climate of the Cold War, as security risks to be purged from government service. Yet gay and lesbian networks expanded in Canadian cities. Gay men met in bars, baths, parks, and theatres; indeed newspapers reported frequent arrests in such places. Lesbians socialized at bars that women could frequent and at house parties.

The inequalities suffered by many Canadians engendered increasing discontent. Not clearly articulated in the 1950s, dissatisfaction provoked far-reaching change beginning in the 1960s.

PROSPERITY AND TRADE

After demobilization, the federal government worked to convert the Canadian economy back to a free-enterprise system and to avoid a repetition of the severe recession that followed World War I. To achieve this objective, C.D. Howe, now in charge of the country's postwar reconstruction, sold war plants for a fraction of their cost, on condition that they reopen for business. He also wanted to liberalize international trade: only if markets abroad were open, he believed, could a country like Canada, with its economy largely based on exports, prosper. He also wanted the government to use tax policy to promote investment and create jobs.

Canada's trade did expand, albeit unevenly. From the late 1940s, the country had a persistently negative trade balance as imports rose faster than exports. Most Canadian-made manufactured products could not compete in international markets. Canadian production costs remained high because Canadian companies manufactured a wide variety of products in small quantities, and they often relied heavily on imported American components.

After World War II, Canada moved to establish closer economic ties with the United States. Indeed, by 1947, as imports from the United States increased sharply and British regulations made it impossible for Canada to convert into dollars the pounds it earned in trade with Britain, Canada experienced a severe shortage of American dollars. King succeeded in convincing the Americans to permit European countries receiving American aid through the Marshall Plan to use a portion of it to buy Canadian goods, thus resolving the dollar crisis. Ottawa also placed much hope in the General Agreement on Tariffs and Trade (GATT), a multilateral trade agreement, signed in Geneva in 1947, which aimed at stimulating world trade by reducing tariffs.

AN INVESTMENT BOOM

Continental economic integration proceeded apace. Foreign capital poured into Canada, particularly during the Korean War, 1950 to 1953. The Americans sought Canada's resources, as production of some important minerals declined in the United States. Moreover, to gain access to the Canadian market, protected by high tariffs, American multinational corporations established, especially in central Canada, numerous branch plants that manufactured consumer products and industrial goods.

Most provinces, in their quest for jobs, actively encouraged the entry of foreign capital by keeping taxes and labour costs down. Nevertheless, some observers worried about the "complacency" with which Canadians sold out the country's resources. In particular, the Royal Commission on Canada's Economic Prospects recommended in 1956 that Canada move to control foreign investment. Howe disagreed strongly: Canada needed American enterprise and capital to assure rapid growth.

For the moment, then, there would be no controls. Investment, both Canadian and foreign, financed several important development projects. Pipelines carried oil and gas from Alberta to markets in Ontario and the United States; a railway nearly 600 km long, running north from Sept-Îles, Quebec, opened up ore-rich Labrador; and the construction of the St. Lawrence Seaway and the TransCanada Highway began.

Then the boom ended. By 1958, slow growth raised unemployment to nearly 10 percent. Automation eliminated some jobs. When railways switched to diesel engines, for example, they needed fewer machinists, blacksmiths, and firemen. The high-valued Canadian dollar, which brought a premium when exchanged for an American dollar, hurt exports.

A GOVERNMENT OF EFFICIENT ADMINISTRATORS

In the postwar years, voters wanted politicians who would manage the country efficiently and achieve greater prosperity. They also called upon the state to protect them from the risks of unemployment, illness, and poverty. The Liberal government of businessmen and administrators largely fulfilled this need. It was a regime that reflected an era.

When William Lyon Mackenzie King finally retired in 1948, he had led the Liberal party for nearly 30 years and could boast of having been the longest-serving prime minister in the history of the British empire. Jurist Frank Scott, who objected indignantly to King's being given credit for everything but putting the oil under Alberta, attributed King's success to his blandness: "He will be remembered wherever men honour ingenuity, ambiguity, inactivity, and political longevity."

Yet many observers of Canadian politics admired King for his accomplishments, even though they disliked him personally and found him uninspiring. Like Macdonald and Laurier before him, he had held the country together effectively through difficult times. His government had also taken the first steps toward establishing a welfare state in Canada.

Louis St. Laurent (right) and Prime Minister Mackenzie King (centre), at the national Liberal convention of 1948 at which St. Laurent was chosen to succeed King as Liberal leader and prime minister. In the background is a portrait of former Liberal leader and prime minister Wilfrid Laurier.

William Lyon Mackenzie King Collection/ National Archives of Canada/CV-23278.

THE ST. LAURENT GOVERNMENT

Louis St. Laurent, chosen as King's successor in 1948, was a former corporation lawyer from Quebec City and the second French-speaking, though fluently bilingual, prime minister. Denounced in his home province during the war for his approval of military conscription, he was clearly no Quebec nationalist. On constitutional questions he opposed the provincial autonomists in Quebec and elsewhere. In foreign affairs, he appeared more internationalist than most Canadians.

The new prime minister followed his predecessor's "accommodative" approach, acting only after general agreement had been reached. Under his leadership, the Liberals continued to occupy the centre of the political spectrum and thus established the consensus so necessary to govern Canada. Prosperity facilitated their task.

NEWFOUNDLAND ENTERS CONFEDERATION

 In 1949, Newfoundland became Canada's tenth province. Confederation had been preceded by months of bitter struggle. Joey Smallwood, leader of the confederate forces, campaigned tirelessly to prove that Newfoundlanders "would be better off in pocket, in stomach, and in health" within Canada. Anti-confederationists denounced those who would "lure Newfoundland into the Canadian mousetrap."

The referendum held in June 1948 allowed Newfoundlanders to choose among three options: Confederation, favoured by both Britain and Canada; responsible government or dominion status; and the unpopular existing system, by which a commission of British-appointed officials governed Newfoundland. Responsible government won; Confederation placed second. Since no clear majority had emerged, a second referendum was held in July in an atmosphere of sectarian bitterness. Most Roman Catholics, fearing loss of their denominational schools, spoke against Confederation, while many Protestants favoured it. In addition, the urban commercial classes generally opposed Confederation, fearing the competition of the big Canadian mail-order companies. The confederates won narrowly this time, with a majority of 52 percent. Canadians and Newfoundlanders now set about negotiating the final terms of union.

Historian David Alexander argues that the decline of the fishing economy, which fell victim to tumbling prices and oversupply, "led Newfoundlanders reluctantly into Confederation."[2] Poverty was endemic. Canada's "safety net" of social programs looked inviting. In addition, Britain clearly desired to quit Newfoundland. For its part, Canada wanted Newfoundland, having discovered the island's strategic and economic importance during World War II. Canadians also worried that the United States might seek to strengthen its ties with the island.

Newfoundland's integration into Canada proceeded rapidly. Immediately upon confederation, family allowances and other federal social programs were ready to function. Income levels improved. Yet the federal government did little to favour the province's economic development, and the province simply "shifted its dependence from London to Ottawa."[3]

FEDERAL–PROVINCIAL TENSIONS

The Liberal government's preoccupation with maintaining a buoyant economy had serious implications for Canadian federalism. Ottawa sought to maintain and even strengthen the fiscal and legislative pre-eminence that it had acquired during the wartime emergency. But several provinces objected to the federal government's aggressive centralization. Nova Scotia premier Angus L. Macdonald complained that federal subsidies destroyed provincial independence and transformed the provinces into "mere annuitants of Ottawa." Ontario insisted on its right to formulate its own economic priorities and programs. In Quebec, the Duplessis government feuded continuously with Ottawa over federal tax and spending policies.

TOWARD A WELFARE STATE

Neither federal–provincial tensions nor the Liberals' moderate conservatism halted Canada's movement toward a welfare state. In 1951, after all the provinces had agreed to the requisite constitutional amendment, federal legislation authorized sending monthly old-age-security cheques to all Canadians over the age of 70 and to needy Canadians over 65. Family allowances, also a universal program covering all children, now took second place. For the government, the allowances, instituted in 1944, had served their purpose: workers' wages had increased, there had been no postwar depression, and the socialist CCF no longer posed a threat. The government thus chose not to increase allowances to compensate for higher living costs.

Ottawa also adopted other measures concerning health and welfare. In 1948, it enacted the National Health Program, which provided for federal grants to each province in the fields of hygiene and health. In 1956, after a national publicity campaign by the Canadian Welfare Council, Parliament adopted the Unemployment Assistance Act, a shared-cost program designed to assist employable persons on welfare. Provinces also spent significantly more on welfare as case numbers increased. Yet such aid failed to take into account increased housing and clothing costs. For historian James Struthers, in Ontario "the poor went hungry to pay the rent."[4]

Canadians who became seriously ill in the 1950s knew the prohibitive cost of health care. Increasingly, they called for a national health plan. Several provincial premiers, especially those from the western provinces most of which had already established hospital insurance, pressured Ottawa into acting. Finally, in 1957, Parliament adopted the Hospital Insurance and Diagnostic Services Act which provided federal financial assistance to provinces willing to set up a publicly administered hospital-insurance program with universal coverage.

THE GOLDEN AGE OF CANADIAN DIPLOMACY

After 1945, Canada had to adapt to a new world power structure. It could no longer rely on a permanently weakened Britain as a counterweight to American influence. To offset growing American power, Canada worked to build strong multilateral institutions. At the same time, it did not want world organizations to interfere in its relations with the United States, which it believed it could conduct better alone.

CANADA IN THE COLD WAR ERA

Disappointments were rife in these years, as the postwar era rapidly gave way to the Cold War. As relations between the United States and the Soviet Union soured, Canadian foreign-affairs officials feared that the often bellicose attitude of the United States would only make matters worse. However, events soon shook Canadians' faith in the West's capacity to reach some kind of reasonable entente with the Soviet Union. In late 1945 Igor Gouzenko, a cipher clerk at the Soviet embassy in Ottawa, defected. He revealed the existence of a Soviet espionage network in Canada that reached into several government agencies.

The intensification of the Cold War led Canada into ever-closer relations with the United States. Britain's own decline left Canada little choice. "London's impotence," historian Jack Granatstein argues, compelled Canadian governments to seek "shelter within Uncle Sam's all-encompassing embrace."[5]

As people lost hope that the United Nations could assure world peace through collective security, the Canadian government pushed for an Atlantic alliance for mutual self-defence. After arduous negotiations, the North Atlantic Treaty Organization (NATO) came into existence in April 1949. Canada had hoped that NATO would contribute to the economic and social development of the member nations, but rising East–West tensions, especially the outbreak of war in Korea in 1950, turned the organization into an almost exclusively military alliance. Canada's influence declined as its defence spending fell and its priorities became continental.

NEW INTEREST IN THE NORTH

The Cold War made the Canadian North an area of vital strategic interest to both Canada and the United States. Acting together, the two countries worked to provide a warning system in the event of a Soviet nuclear attack on Canadian and American cities. A chain of more than 40 Distant Early Warning (DEW) Line stations was built in the 1950s across the Arctic. The system remained in full operation for nearly a decade, until intercontinental ballistic missiles largely replaced the bomber threat. Defence relations between Canada and the United States became even closer in 1957 when the two countries signed the North American Air Defence Agreement (NORAD), which formally co-ordinated their air forces.

The DEW Line and other American proposals revived fears about Canada's sovereignty in the Arctic. Recognizing that one of the surest grounds for Canada's claim would be "effective occupation," the federal government in 1953 arranged for several Inuit families from northern Quebec and Baffin Island to relocate nearly 2000 km away, on Cornwallis and Ellesmere islands in the high Arctic. The migrants lost contact with their communities and, the government's promises aside, found themselves in a much more inhospitable environment than the one they had left behind.

THE COMMONWEALTH

In keeping with its desire to balance closer links to the United States with an increased international participation, Canada looked with hope to the evolving British Commonwealth of Nations. The Commonwealth was rapidly changing and becoming more diversified, with the addition of new members such as India, Pakistan, and Sri Lanka (then Ceylon). Canada helped move the Commonwealth in directions that made it an acceptable organization for these new states. It also supported and contributed to the Colombo Plan, which was set up at a meeting of Commonwealth foreign ministers in 1950 to promote economic development in Commonwealth countries in Asia.

PEACEKEEPING

Canada's early attempts at peacekeeping produced some positive results. In 1950, when communist North Korea invaded South Korea and the United Nations Security Council denounced this act of aggression, Canada contributed a brigade to fight alongside mostly American troops in the name of collective security. As the war moved toward a stalemate, Lester B. Pearson, Canada's minister of external affairs, helped to restrain the "overzealous" Americans from actions that risked bringing China and the Soviet Union into the war.

Then, in 1956, came what many considered to be Canada's greatest contribution internationally. In October, despite strong American opposition, Israel, together with Britain and France, invaded Egypt, in response to Egypt's nationalization of the Suez Canal. Wary of the dangerous split developing in the western alliance, Pearson proposed the creation of a multinational United Nations emergency peacekeeping force in the region. He then lobbied tirelessly to have the plan accepted by the General Assembly. For his efforts, he won the Nobel Peace Prize in 1957. According to biographer John English, Pearson's initiative "strengthened the United Nations, moderated the tensions between Washington and London, and helped to maintain both the Commonwealth and NATO."[6]

Canada's United Nations peacekeeping missions, from 1947 to the 1990s.

Source: Adapted from *The Integrated Atlas: History and Geography of Canada and the World* (Toronto: Harcourt Brace, 1996), p. 120. Reprinted by permission of Harcourt Canada Ltd.

YEARNING FOR POLITICAL CHANGE

The Progressive Conservatives' narrow victory at the polls in 1957 surprised most observers. Certainly the Liberals had boasted during the election campaign that voters would not "shoot Santa Claus." Yet not all Canadians were prosperous. Residents of the Prairies and the Maritimes complained of their regions' underdevelopment. Many senior citizens endorsed Conservative assertions that unindexed old-age pensions were scandalously insufficient. Other voters agreed with new Conservative leader John Diefenbaker's denunciations of the "dictatorial" tactics employed by the Liberals in 1956 as they pushed a bill through the House of Commons that arranged for an important loan to a private pipeline company. But most of all, many Canadians simply wanted a change from what appeared increasingly to be cold, insensitive, uncreative leadership by an aging Liberal gerontocracy.

THE "DIEFENBAKER PARTY"

John Diefenbaker surely played a significant role in the success of what became known as the "Diefenbaker party." Diefenbaker sought to change voters' traditionally negative image of the Tories. He wrested control of the party from the Toronto business elite and gave it to "outsiders," many of whom came from western Canada. His oratorical talents, which he used to proclaim Canadians' "appointment with destiny," far outshone anything the Liberals could muster.

The new government barely had time to adopt a few popular measures designed to assist the unemployed, Prairie farmers, and Maritimers before Diefenbaker, anxious to form a majority government, called a new election in March 1958. The prime minister then presented his "vision of opportunity" for Canada, a vision based on the development of resources and of the North. New Liberal leader Lester B. Pearson attempted to brush off what he termed the "oracular fervour and circus parades." The result was a Diefenbaker landslide, with the Progressive Conservatives winning what was proportionally the greatest majority in Canadian electoral history: 208 of the 265 seats in the House of Commons, including 50 seats from Quebec.

From the start, the Conservatives had difficulty governing. Ministers lacked experience and distrusted civil servants inherited from the Liberals; Diefenbaker, a unilingual Anglophone from Saskatchewan, knew little about Quebec and entrusted no senior cabinet portfolios to Quebeckers, and his vision of northern development did not capture the imagination of southern Canadians. The Conservative government's major problem, however, arose from the country's deteriorating economic situation. It responded to rising unemployment with subsidies and increased welfare benefits. Budgetary deficits grew and the business community complained of financial mismanagement.

A campaign poster. John Diefenbaker with his hero, Sir John A. Macdonald.

Diefenbaker Centre Poster Collection. Diefenbaker Centre, University of Saskatchewan.

Labour Relations in Prosperous Times

Postwar economic growth gave a powerful boost to the unions. In 1950, union membership passed the one million mark, or 30 percent of the work force. "Elite" unions in sectors such as heavy manufacturing enjoyed strong bargaining power and succeeded in negotiating high wages. They had frequent recourse to strikes, aimed at forcing employers to recognize union rights, improve working conditions, and increase salaries. In retaliation, companies frequently hired strikebreakers, and violent confrontations sometimes ensued. Provincial governments supported employers directly through anti-union legislation and the use of the police and the courts.

Industrial Unrest

Although most workers signed contracts without going on strike and although sickness resulted in far more loss of work time than did strike activity, certain sensational confrontations earned a place in the annals of Canadian working-class history. In one dramatic encounter in 1946, Steel Company of Canada (Stelco) management used airplanes and boats to avoid picket lines and to transport food and supplies to strikebreakers inside its plant at Hamilton, Ontario. In the same year, textile workers, many of them women, struck in Valleyfield, Quebec. Led by Madeleine Parent and Kent Rowley, the strikers obtained recognition for their union only after bloody skirmishes with police. Parent was then convicted of seditious conspiracy. In 1949, 5000 Quebec asbestos workers struck for five months to improve wages and working conditions. The Duplessis government defended the companies, decertified the union, and sent in special police squads. Some members of the clergy, including Archbishop Joseph Charbonneau of Montreal, defied the government and sided openly with the strikers, one of whose supporters was a young Montreal lawyer, Pierre Elliott Trudeau. Though the settlement gave workers no significant material gains, the strike itself took on great symbolic value: Quebec sociologist Jean-Charles Falardeau even viewed it as a "quasi-revolution."[7]

Conflict continued into the 1950s, as major strikes occurred among loggers, fishers, government employees, and longshoremen in British Columbia, building-trades workers in Halifax and Vancouver, gold miners in Ontario and Quebec, and automobile workers and employees of the International Nickel Company (Inco) in Ontario. In August 1950, 130 000 employees of Canada's two major railways left their jobs, but the government, declaring that "the country cannot afford a railway strike," ordered the workers back. Copper workers at Murdochville, Quebec, struck for seven months in 1957 in a violent but vain confrontation. In 1959, Newfoundland loggers, members of the International Woodworkers of America (IWA), went on strike. Violence broke out when the company recruited fishers to replace strikers. In an effort to break the IWA, Premier Joseph Smallwood set up a union and had the legislature outlaw the IWA in the province. The federal government refused to send the RCMP reinforcements that Smallwood demanded, but the strike nonetheless failed.

WORKERS VERSUS WORKERS

Workers not only fought management and governments, they also feuded with one another for political and personal reasons. On the left, communists and democratic socialists battled each other furiously. Both clashed with conservative unionists, who viewed all political links as dangerous for the labour movement.

Anti-communists in the Canadian Congress of Labour (CCL) insisted that, to fight the bosses, "we must get rid of the communists." The communist-led Canadian Seamen's Union (CSU) was crushed when the Canadian and American governments combined with the shippers and Trades and Labor Congress (TLC) officers to replace the CSU with a rival union. Some Canadian unionists thought that the battle against communists merely permitted American unions to reinforce their hold in Canada. According to labour historian Irving Abella, the communist purge did little to strengthen the union movement and, in hindsight, was probably "neither necessary nor wise."[8]

Greater labour unity came in 1956, when the TLC and the CCL formed the Canadian Labour Congress (CLC), with one million members. This union followed the merger in 1955 of the American labour congresses, the AFL and the CIO. The costly raids by TLC and CCL unions on each other, with no total gain in membership, then ended. Many of the CLC unions were affiliated with the AFL–CIO, and they remained subject to American influence. Indeed, most Canadian workers who were employed by American branch companies found nothing unusual in belonging to American-dominated unions.

Although unions made major gains in the postwar period, much work remained. Collective agreements generally left managers with complete authority over the work process on the shop floor. Vast numbers of workers, particularly in the service sector, remained outside unions. The increasing bureaucratization of the union movement, fostered by what labour historian Peter McInnis has termed the "excessively legalistic and rigid framework" that came to characterize industrial relations, tended to exclude the rank and file from decisions.[9] Labour legislation in several provinces was unsympathetic to unions. Automation made job security an increasingly serious issue. Worker safety also caused serious concern. When fire killed five Italian labourers laying a water main in the Hogg's Hollow district of Toronto, the coroner denounced management's "callous attitude" toward worker safety and noted that almost all the safety regulations had been violated.

THE STATUS OF WOMEN

After World War II, most women workers, especially married women, left the paid work force. Women who continued in paid employment outside the home still had to perform all the domestic and family chores. Cultural stereotypes reinforced the "traditional" role of women: school textbooks depicted men in interesting careers while portraying women as staying at home, cooking meals, and scolding children. Women's magazines such as *Chatelaine* and the *Canadian Home Journal* wrote about sewing, homemaking, gardening, and fashion.

WOMEN IN THE WORK FORCE

Slowly, however, female participation in the work force increased. Mothers began to rejoin the work force after their youngest children enrolled in school. Most women worked as secretaries, nurses, sales personnel, and clerks; only a handful were professionals.

Where Historians Disagree
Women and Unions in Postwar Canada

Most working women in 1960 were employed in non-unionized sectors of activity, such as clerical and domestic work. Women made up only about one-sixth of the unionized work force. Did these women see themselves simply as workers who, like the men, wanted to improve wages and working conditions? Or did they see themselves primarily as women with objectives that were different from, and at times contradictory to, those of men? And how did men react to the entry of women into "their" workplace?

Labour historians, preoccupied with labour's battles against employers, did not at first ask these questions. Bryan Palmer, for example, notes that women comprised one-quarter of the membership of the militant United Electrical, Radio and Machine Workers' Union (UE), but he does not view their struggle as other than a workers' struggle against the bosses.[1] Craig Heron, for his part, does state that industrial unions of these years had difficulty eliminating the segregation of women into low-wage job ghettos, but he then comments, revealingly, that "even if the male unionists' pride had allowed more equity, most men still assumed that women should be at home, supported by a male wage."[2]

In her study of working women in Peterborough, Ontario, Joan Sangster shows

how unions have been arenas of both gender conflict and class solidarity.[3] Looking at the UE, she notes that union leadership endorsed gender equality, partly in order to gain women workers' support for the UE's struggle against a rival union. The UE also tried to focus on grievances that could unite men and women, such as more equal pay rates, because men feared the substitution of female for male labour. While the union itself gave pre-eminence to class rather than to gender, separate organizations for women within unions eventually provided an innovative means for women to demand better working conditions and wages.

Julie Guard has also studied the experience of women within the UE. Like Sangster, she shows that the union was interested primarily in the class struggle, not in women's rights. It made slow progress in endorsing equal pay for women, in spite of women's attempts to prove that low pay for women put a brake on male wages. She too observes that few women participated in union leadership, a fact that men attributed to personal choice rather than to the "inherent gender bias of union structure and culture."[4]

Joy Parr has examined the effect of gender on strike action against a textile company in Paris, Ontario, in 1949. About one-half of the workers were women and, although women were less inclined to join the union than were men, female militancy on the picket line was considerable. Yet, whereas the union itself whipped up male strikers' militancy, female militancy was "forged and sustained in family and neighbourhood relationships" rather than through union organization.[5]

In her study of the United Auto Workers in Canada, Pam Sugiman argues that the traditional view of the UAW as a progressive union that gave vocal support to women's rights is only partly true; the UAW also showed persistent gender bias and allowed blatant inequalities to persist in the working environment. Male union officials were reluctant to view the special concerns of female dues-paying members as legitimate union issues. In the immediate postwar years, women did not generally challenge gender ideologies, separate seniority lists, and large pay differentials. Even in the 1950s, women still did not "openly contest their subordination as a sex" although they did develop "a stronger self-identification as wage earners and as unionists."[6] Thanks to improving economic conditions, women became bolder and made use of grievance procedures to try to improve working conditions.

Interest in the situation of women within postwar unions is relatively recent. Many other case studies will have to be carried out on different aspects of the question before it will be possible to reach general conclusions.

---

[1] Bryan Palmer, *Working Class Experience: Rethinking the History of Canadian Labour, 1800–1991*, 2nd ed. (Toronto: McClelland & Stewart, 1992), p. 287.

[2] Craig Heron, *The Canadian Labour Movement: A Short History*, 2nd ed. (Toronto: James Lorimer, 1996), p. 78.

[3] Joan Sangster, *Earning Respect: The Lives of Working Women in Small-Town Ontario, 1920–1960* (Toronto: University of Toronto Press, 1995), p. 167.

[4] Julie Guard, "Fair Play or Fair Pay? Gender Relations, Class Consciousness, and Union Solidarity in the Canadian UE," *Labour/Le Travail* 37 (1996): 176.

[5] Joy Parr, *The Gender of Breadwinners: Women, Men, and Change in Two Industrial Towns, 1880–1950* (Toronto: University of Toronto Press, 1990), p. 108.

[6] Pam Sugiman, *Labour's Dilemma: The Gender Politics of Auto Workers in Canada, 1937–1979* (Toronto: University of Toronto Press, 1994), p. 99.

For female workers, inequality abounded. Men generally received higher wages than women for performing the same tasks. Ontario adopted the Female Employees Fair Remuneration Act in 1951, but historian Shirley Tillotson's research shows that it had little tangible effect.[10] Nor did women have equal opportunity for promotions, even in female-dominated sectors such as teaching. Minimum wage rates, fixed by governments, were usually lower for women than for men.

Churches such as the United Church of Canada which accepted women as ministers nevertheless placed numerous obstacles in the paths of those seeking ordination. United Church moderator James Mutchmor gave Lois Wilson, a minister's wife, reasons for objecting to her ordination: who would "wear the pants" in the family? Who would have priority in the use of the car? Wilson succeeded in gaining ordination because prominent men supported her. She later became the United Church's first woman moderator.

Only a few women held positions of influence in business or politics in the 1950s. Between 1930 and 1960, the federal government named only seven women senators, while more than 250 men received the coveted lifetime appointment. Few women ran in elections. Only in 1957 did a prime minister, John Diefenbaker, appoint a woman to a federal cabinet post — Ellen Fairclough, from Hamilton, Ontario. Many observers saw this nomination as only a modest beginning. Charlotte Whitton, Ottawa's feisty mayor, clairvoyantly predicted that women were growing so impatient with "the man-made messes of a man-made world" that they would soon insist on a much larger voice in public affairs.

THE BABY BOOM

With good times, a higher proportion of young adults married. They also married earlier. As Mary Louise Adams explains, "Marriage was a legitimate avenue of sexual expression for those men and women who felt caught between the incitement to sex in the culture at large and the proscriptions against their own engagement in it. Early marriage was one way to bring changes in sexual behaviour into line with the established moral order."[11]

As North American women began, on an impressive scale, to have children, a veritable "baby boom" set in. By 1947, the birth rate in Canada had increased to nearly 29 per thousand, and the average family had three or four children. This relatively large contingent of youth has had enormous repercussions on Canadian society. The precise nature of the impact would alter with time, as the baby boomers went through childhood, adolescence, young adulthood, and middle age. The baby boom led to a rapid increase in Canada's population. Including immigration, the annual growth rate exceeded 3 percent, equivalent to that experienced by many developing countries today.

HIGHER EDUCATION

Few Canadians attended colleges or universities in the 1950s. In 1951, Canada's institutions of higher learning had only 60 000 students, barely 4 percent of the eligible age group. Only about one university student in four was a woman. Most female students enrolled in programs in education or the liberal arts; few entered the sciences or the professional schools. In Quebec, until 1960, the provincial government denied classical colleges for women the state funds that were made available to all-male colleges. In Toronto, the elite University of Toronto Schools (whose graduates almost all went on to university) admitted no women, even though it was largely state-supported.

In 1951, the Royal Commission on National Development in the Arts, Letters and Sciences, chaired by Vincent Massey, recommended direct federal financial support for universities. The Soviet launching of *Sputnik*, the first space satellite, in 1957, proved an unforeseen boon to Canadian universities. The fear of Soviet scientific superiority convinced many Canadians that governments should invest much more in higher education. Provincial authorities loosened the purse strings and the federal government instituted a system of grants. Several new universities came into being in the late 1950s.

Zoologist William Rowan lecturing at the University of Alberta, Edmonton, before 1957. Beginning in the 1960s, class sizes would expand to the bursting point with the arrival of the baby boomers at universities.

University of Alberta Archives/Acc. 82-29-37.

CULTURE: CANADIAN VERSUS AMERICAN

In the postwar era, Canadian nationalists increasingly felt the dangers of dependence upon American culture. Reduced funding for the Canadian Broadcasting Corporation (CBC) threatened to undermine public broadcasting. Private broadcasters, who wished to offer more American-produced commercial programming, resented the CBC's regulatory role. The federal government also reduced the National Film Board's budget after the war, and private filmmakers sought to obtain its work. Institutions such as the Public Archives of Canada and the National Museum of Canada suffered from lack of co-ordination, while the country still had no national library.

Cultural associations that enjoyed strong cabinet support brought the government to establish the Massey Commission. In 1951, the commission recommended the establishment of a national arts-funding body, one free of partisan and bureaucratic control. Finally, in 1957, the Liberals founded the Canada Council. It used its endowment to help a multitude of arts organizations, among them ballet companies, theatre troupes (including the Stratford Shakespearean Festival), and orchestras. The council also gave grants to writers and scholarships to graduate students.

POPULAR CULTURE

Prosperity enabled many Canadians to spend money on entertainment. They purchased new long-playing records, often of poor quality and relatively costly. They flocked to the movie theatres that proliferated, to watch mostly American-made films. Censorship in all provinces regulated the movies Canadians saw. The British Columbia Moving Pictures Act, for example, outlawed films "considered injurious to morals or against public welfare, or which may offer evil suggestions to the minds of children." Alberta's censors watched carefully for "any materialistic, undemocratic, un-Christian propaganda disguised as entertainment."

The real revolution in the entertainment industry, however, came in the early 1950s with television. At first, television sets were a status symbol because of their relatively high cost. By 1952, Canada's own television broadcasting began in Toronto and Montreal, then quickly expanded to other cities. The CBC and the French-language Radio Canada aired many news programs, and also presented numerous cultural programs, which attracted a small, but influential, audience.

Although the CBC presented Canadian variety shows such as *Showtime*, which featured dance, song, music, and comedy, it also imported popular American variety shows to boost its ratings and increase its commercial revenues. On Sunday evenings, millions of Canadians loyally watched the most famous and longest-lasting of these, *The Ed Sullivan Show*. Sullivan introduced Elvis Presley and his hip gyrations to Canadians in September 1956. He also boosted the fortunes of Canadian comedians Johnny Wayne and Frank Shuster. Both CBC and private television imported popular American comedies such as *I Love Lucy* and *The Jackie Gleason Show*, and presented contemporary American singers like Perry Como and Dinah Shore. Baby-boom children watched Roy Rogers, Lassie, Walt Disney programs, and the popular American puppet show, *Howdy Doody*.

French-language television had more local content. While it beamed a French-speaking *Hopalong Cassidy* and many other programs dubbed in French into Quebec living rooms and kitchens, it also carried original productions, such as a series adapted from novelist Roger Lemelin's *La famille Plouffe*. Children watched a captivating Quebec-made puppet show called Pépino. The CBC's very successful variety show, *Music Hall*, produced in Montreal, featured French stars such as Edith Piaf, Maurice Chevalier, and Charles Aznavour. By 1957, television

The Schiefners, a farm family living outside of Milestone, Saskatchewan, on a Saturday evening in 1956. "Hockey Night in Canada: Toronto versus Detroit," will be broadcast at 9 p.m.

National Archives of Canada/PA-111390.

production in Montreal, historian Susan Mann writes, was "third in the world to New York and Hollywood and second to none in French."[12]

The advent of television increased popular interest in sport. Armchair spectators marvelled at the exploits of the Edmonton Eskimos' football dynasty. Watching "La Soirée du hockey," or "Hockey Night in Canada," became a popular pastime on Saturday night. Fans avidly discussed the feats of Syl Apps, Maurice "The Rocket" Richard, and Gordie Howe, and celebrated the Stanley Cup triumphs of the Toronto Maple Leafs in the late 1940s and of the Montreal Canadiens in the late 1950s.

English-speaking Canadians enjoyed newspaper supplements like the *Star Weekly* and *Weekend*, while French Canadians read a variety of tabloid newspapers. By the end of the 1950s, however, American mass-circulation magazines, among them *Time*, *Reader's Digest*, and its French edition, *Sélection du Reader's Digest*, accounted for 75 percent of the Canadian general-interest magazine market.

LITERATURE

Canadian literature in both languages came into its own in the post–World War II era. In Montreal, Hugh MacLennan published his celebrated novel *Two Solitudes*, with its theme that Canada's two major linguistic communities needed to demonstrate more mutual tolerance. In *The Mountain and the Valley*, Maritimer Ernest Buckler examined the dilemma faced by a brilliant and ambitious Nova Scotia boy who found his creativity stifled by his deep attachment to rural life. W.O. Mitchell, in *Who Has Seen the Wind*, interpreted the struggles of a small-town

Saskatchewan boy at the time of the depression. Throughout the 1950s, Mitchell produced his highly successful "Jake and the Kid" stories for magazine and radio.

Mordecai Richler's *The Apprenticeship of Duddy Kravitz*, a portrait of a young Montreal Jewish entrepreneur, established the Montreal author as a successful novelist. Adele Wiseman's first novel, *The Sacrifice*, was strongly influenced by the experiences of her Russian-Jewish parents. Robertson Davies gained early recognition as an essayist and brilliant novelist. Poet Dorothy Livesay won Governor General's awards for *Day and Night*, in 1944, and *Poems for Peace*, in 1947, while the versatile and flamboyant Irving Layton produced numerous volumes of love poems and prose.

At the same time, an "aesthetic thaw" came slowly to Quebec. In *Refus global*, a manifesto written in 1948, Paul-Émile Borduas condemned Quebec's asphyxiating orthodoxy. The artist's cry for the right to total freedom of expression led to his departure from Quebec. Novelists cast aside traditional themes of religion and rurality. Some, such as Roger Lemelin in *Au pied de la pente douce*, used urban working-class settings. Others, such as Anne Hébert in *Le Torrent* and André Langevin in *Poussière sur la ville*, forcefully portrayed personal dramas. Yves Thériault won international fame with *Agaguk*, a novel about the Inuit. Professional theatre troupes proliferated, with some of their repertories supplied by Quebec playwrights. The play *Tit-Coq*, by Gratien Gélinas, as well as the film that followed, encountered spectacular success. Quebec culture seemed to have attained new vibrancy, despite the province's small market.

RELIGION

Religion "stands out as one of the great gulfs" separating the 1950s from today, writes historian Doug Owram.[13] The majority of Canadians still attended church or the synagogue regularly. Religion was present in most schools across the country, even in so-called public schools. Nevertheless, the influence of religion often appeared superficial. Possibly, religious practice was linked more to socialization than to faith. The *United Church Observer* frequently bemoaned the limited commitment of many adherents. Presumably church-going Quebeckers bought a million copies each weekend of sex-and-crime tabloids like *Allo Police*, which flourished in spite of — and possibly because of — the opposition of the Roman Catholic church.

The quiet Sundays of English-speaking Canada also came under attack. It was said that in Toronto one could harmlessly fire a cannon ball down Yonge Street on a Sunday, and the local press editorialized in favour of the maintenance of Toronto's "typically Canadian" Sunday. Then the citizens of "Toronto the Good" voted in favour of Sunday sports in a plebiscite and, in 1951, elected as their mayor a churchgoer who had pledged to make it possible to watch doubleheaders on Sundays at Maple Leaf Stadium. Across English-speaking Canada, provincial drinking restrictions that determined who could drink, where they could drink, and under what conditions, were increasingly challenged as attitudes changed. In British Columbia, for example, citizens voted in 1952 to authorize the sale of liquor and wine by the glass in respectable cocktail lounges. The beer parlours, often viewed as indecent working-class centres of excess, continued to exist, however, with separate sections for men, and for ladies and escorts.[14]

In the late 1940s and the 1950s, Canadian consumers had more money to spend and new products to spend it on. Workers in most regions of the country easily found jobs, and pay scales increased substantially. Governments went about the task of managing economic growth. For a time, Canada's postwar prosperity camouflaged the poverty and inequalities that remained the lot of many Canadians, in spite of the appearance of several new social programs. When, by the late 1950s, the postwar boom appeared to have run its course, new tensions emerged in society. Canadians now seemed to believe that it was time for a change.

NOTES

1. Doug Owram, "Canadian Domesticity in the Postwar Era," in Peter Neary and J. L. Granatstein, eds. *The Veterans Charter and Post-World War II Canada* (Montreal/Kingston: McGill-Queen's University Press, 1998), p. 213.

2. David G. Alexander, *Atlantic Canada and Confederation: Essays in Canadian Political Economy* (Toronto: University of Toronto Press, 1983), p. 32.

3. Raymond Blake, *Canadians at Last: Canada Integrates Newfoundland as a Province* (Toronto: University of Toronto Press, 1994), p. 6.

4. James Struthers, *The Limits of Affluence: Welfare in Ontario, 1920–1970* (Toronto: University of Toronto Press, 1994), p. 180.

5. J.L. Granatstein, *How Britain's Weakness Forced Canada into the Arms of the United States* (Toronto: University of Toronto Press, 1989), p. 3.

6. John English, *The Worldly Years: The Life of Lester Pearson*, vol. II, *1949–1972* (Toronto: Knopf Canada, 1992), p. 145.

7. J.-C. Falardeau, *Bulletin des Relations industrielles* 4 (1949), quoted in Fraser Isbester, "Asbestos 1949," in Irving Abella, ed., *On Strike: Six Key Labour Struggles in Canada, 1919–1949* (Toronto: James, Lewis & Samuel Publishers, 1974), p. 163.

8. Irving Abella, *Nationalism, Communism, and Canadian Labour: The CIO, the Communist Party, and the Canadian Congress of Labour, 1935–1956* (Toronto: University of Toronto Press, 1973), p. 221.

9. Peter S. McInnis, *Harnessing Labour Confrontation: Shaping the Postwar Settlement in Canada, 1943-1950* (Toronto: University of Toronto Press, 2002), p. 13.

10. Shirley Tillotson, "Human Rights Law as Prism: Women's Organizations, Unions, and Ontario's Female Employees Fair Remuneration Act, 1951," *Canadian Historical Review* 72 (1991): 532–57.

11. Mary Louise Adams, *The Trouble with Normal: Postwar Youth and the Making of Heterosexuality* (Toronto: University of Toronto Press, 1997), pp. 105–106.

12. Susan Mann, *The Dream of Nation: A Social and Intellectual History of Quebec* (Montreal/Kingston: McGill-Queen's University Press, 1982, 2002), p. 284.

13. Doug Owram, *Born at the Right Time: A History of the Baby-Boom Generation* (Toronto: University of Toronto Press, 1996), p. 103.

14. Robert A. Campbell, *Sit Down and Drink Your Beer: Regulating Vancouver's Beer Parlours, 1925–1954* (Toronto: University of Toronto Press, 2001).

LINKING TO THE PAST

Louis St. Laurent

http://www.nlc-bnc.ca/history/4/h4-3300-e.html

Facts about and a brief biography of Louis Stephen St. Laurent, with excerpts from his speeches.

The Newfoundland Act, 1949

http://www.geocities.com/Yosemite/Rapids/3330/constitution/1949ntu.htm

The full text of the Newfoundland Act of 1949, which made Newfoundland Canada's tenth province.

The Inuit Resettlement Project, 1953

http://www.carc.org/pubs/v19no1/2.htm

This essay, "A Case of Compounded Error: The Inuit Resettlement Project, 1953, and the Government Response, 1990," by Shelagh D. Grant (published by the Canadian Arctic Resources Committee) evaluates the government's 1953 decision to relocate seven Inuit families and the aftermath of this decision.

John Diefenbaker

http://www.primeministers.ca/diefenbaker/intro.php

Quick facts about and a biography of John Diefenbaker.

The Canada Council
http://laws.justice.gc.ca/en/C-2/index.html
The full text of the Canada Council for the Arts Act, from the Department of Justice. To find out more about what the Canada Council for the Arts does, visit http://www.canadacouncil.ca.

RELATED READINGS

Three essays in R. Douglas Francis and Donald B. Smith, eds., *Readings in Canadian History: Post-Confederation*, 6th ed. (Toronto: Nelson Thomson Learning, 2002), pertain to topics in this chapter: Hector Mackenzie, "The Cold War and the Limits of 'Internationalism' in Canada's Foreign Relations, 1945–1949," pp. 362–76; Veronica Strong-Boag, "Home Dreams: Women and the Suburban Experiment in Canada, 1945–60," pp. 380–403; and John Herd Thompson, "Canada's Quest for Cultural Sovereignty: Protection, Promotion, and Popular Culture," pp. 404–16.

BIBLIOGRAPHY

Useful general works on this period include Robert Bothwell, Ian Drummond, and John English, *Canada since 1945: Power, Politics, and Provincialism*, rev. ed. (Toronto: University of Toronto Press, 1989); Doug Owram, *Born at the Right Time: A History of the Baby-Boom Generation* (Toronto: University of Toronto Press, 1996); and Kenneth Norrie and Douglas Owram, *A History of the Canadian Economy*, 3rd ed. (Toronto: Nelson Thomson, 2002).

Joy Parr offers a critical study of consumerism in *Domestic Goods: The Material, the Moral, and the Economic in the Postwar Years* (Toronto: University of Toronto Press, 1999). Among works on social history see Alvin Finkel, *Our Lives: Canada after 1945* (Toronto: James Lorimer, 1997); James Struthers, *The Limits of Affluence: Welfare in Ontario, 1920–1970* (Toronto: University of Toronto Press, 1994); Jacqueline S. Ismael, ed., *The Canadian Welfare State: Evolution and Transition* (Edmonton: University of Alberta Press, 1987); Peter Neary and J. L. Granatstein, eds., *The Veterans Charter and Post–World War II Canada* (Montreal/Kingston: McGill-Queen's University Press, 1998); and John R. Miron, *Housing in Postwar Canada: Demographic Change, Household Formation, and Housing Demand* (Montreal/Kingston: McGill-Queen's University Press, 1988).

Aspects of environmental history are studied in George M. Warecki, *Protecting Ontario's Wilderness: A History of Changing Ideas and Preservation Politics, 1927–1973* (New York: Peter Lang, 2000); Alan MacEachern, *Natural Selections: National Parks in Atlantic Canada, 1935–1970* (Montreal/Kingston: McGill-Queen's University Press, 2001); and Richard A. Rajala, *Clearcutting the Pacific Rain Forest: Production, Science and Regulation* (Vancouver: UBC Press, 1998).

The numerous studies available on politicians and politics include Dale C. Thomson, *Louis St. Laurent, Canadian* (Toronto: Macmillan, 1967); Denis Smith, *Rogue Tory: The Life and Legend of John G. Diefenbaker* (Toronto: Macfarlane Walter & Ross, 1995); and Reginald Whitaker, *The Government Party: Organizing and Financing the Liberal Party of Canada, 1930–58* (Toronto: University of Toronto Press, 1977). On Newfoundland's entry into Confederation, see Peter Neary, *Newfoundland in the North Atlantic World, 1929–1949* (Montreal/Kingston: McGill-Queen's University Press, 1988); and Raymond B. Blake, *Canadians at Last: Canada Integrates Newfoundland as a Province* (Toronto: University of Toronto Press, 1994).

Canadian foreign policy in this period is examined in James Eayrs, *In Defence of Canada: Growing Up Allied* (Toronto: University of Toronto Press, 1980). See also John W. Holmes, *The Shaping of Peace: Canada and the Search for World Order, 1943–1957*, 2 vols. (Toronto: University of Toronto Press, 1979, 1982); David Bercuson, *Blood on the Hills: The Canadian Army in the Korean War* (Toronto: University of Toronto Press, 1999); and Joseph Levitt, *Pearson and Canada's Role in Nuclear Disarmament and Arms Control Negotiations, 1945–1957* (Montreal/Kingston: McGill-Queen's University Press, 1993). Postwar trade issues are discussed in Michael Hart, *A Trading Nation: Canadian Trade Policy from Colonialism to Globalization* (Vancouver: UBC Press, 2002).

For Canadian–American relations in the defence sector see Joseph T. Jockel, *No Boundaries Upstairs: Canada, the United States and the Origins of North American Air Defence, 1945–1958* (Vancouver: University of British Columbia Press, 1987). The history of Canada's atomic energy program is discussed in Brian Buckley, *Canada's Early Nuclear Policy: Fate, Chance, and Character* (Montreal/Kingston: McGill-Queen's University Press, 2000). Issues linked to internal security are examined in Reg Whitaker and Gary Marcuse, *Cold War Canada: The Making of a National Insecurity State, 1945–1957* (Toronto: University of Toronto Press, 1994).

Labour has been much studied for this period. Consult Bryan D. Palmer, *Working-Class Experience: Rethinking the History of Canadian Labour, 1800–1991*, 2nd ed. (Toronto: McClelland & Stewart, 1992); Peter S. McInnis, *Harnessing Labour Confrontation: Shaping the Postwar Settlement in Canada, 1943–1950* (Toronto: University of Toronto Press, 2002); and Charlotte Yates, *From Plant to Politics: The Autoworkers Union in Postwar Canada* (Philadelphia: Temple University Press, 1993). Two excellent general syntheses of women's history are Micheline Dumont et al., *Quebec Women: A History* (Toronto: Women's Press, 1987); and Alison Prentice et al., *Canadian Women: A History*, 2nd ed. (Toronto: Harcourt Brace, 1996).

Works on cultural history include Paul Litt, *The Muses, the Masses, and the Massey Commission* (Toronto: University of Toronto Press, 1992); and Paul Rutherford, *When Television Was Young: Primetime Canada 1952–1967* (Toronto: University of Toronto Press, 1990). On heterosexuality and homosexuality, see Mary Louise Adams, *The Trouble with Normal: Postwar Youth and the Making of Heterosexuality* (Toronto: University of Toronto Press, 1997); and Gary Kinsman, *The Regulation of Desire: Homo and Hetero Sexualities*, 2nd ed. (Montreal: Black Rose Books, 1996).

AN ERA OF CHANGE: THE 1960s

TIME LINE

1961	Launching of the New Democratic Party (NDP); Tommy Douglas chosen as leader
1962	Opening of the Trans-Canada Highway from St. John's to Victoria
1963	The Liberals, led by Lester B. Pearson, regain office
1965	The maple leaf flag replaces the Red Ensign
	The Auto Pact establishes free trade between Canada and the United States in the automobile industry
	Canada Pension Plan set up
1967	Canada celebrates its centennial
	Expo 67 (Canadian Universal and International Exhibition), held in Montreal, welcomes 50 million visitors
	The Royal Commission on the Status of Women is appointed
	The National Health Insurance Program (medicare) comes into being
1968	Pierre Elliott Trudeau becomes prime minister
1969	Parliament adopts the Official Languages Act

Canada experienced profound social, cultural and political upheavals in the 1960s. Young people, in particular, challenged authority. The universities became centres of protest as demonstrations erupted on campuses. Youth began to reject traditional social and cultural values, and sexual taboos weakened.

Other groups as well wanted to be heard. Women questioned the inequalities of their condition. So did gays and lesbians. Labour became more militant in its attacks on the business "establishment." French-speaking Canadians sought linguistic rights that would place them on an equal footing with English-speaking Canadians. An important minority in Quebec believed that only independence could ensure real equality. English-speaking Canadian nationalists denounced the powerful American presence in most aspects of Canadian life. A Native resurgence began in reaction to fears of assimilation and to federal proposals, formulated in a White Paper in 1969, to end special status. No longer was it acceptable for a small group of middle-aged and elderly men, primarily of British origin, to rule Canada. As a multitude of new interest groups entered the political forum, many observers concluded that diversity had now triumphed over unity within Canada.

The economic stability of the postwar years ended in the 1960s. As the decade opened, Canada faced the highest unemployment levels since the Great Depression. Although prosperity returned, rapidly rising prices became a problem in the late 1960s. Economic difficulties led to social problems. Canadians demanded that their governments at all levels intervene more actively to find solutions.

The political stability of the postwar years also disappeared in the 1960s; indeed, in Ottawa minority governments ruled for much of the decade. Several of the provinces also saw political change. Canadians sought new leaders, but tired of them rapidly when they failed to deliver what was expected of them.

REVOLT AND PROTEST

Canadian society in the 1960s became more secular. In Quebec, the influence of the Roman Catholic church waned as that institution largely abandoned to the state its historic role in education and in social institutions and as church attendance declined. Many clergy left the orders, and new recruitment fell rapidly.

Elsewhere in Canada, the major Protestant denominations also lost ground. (Many Protestants who felt that the traditional denominations had become too liberal joined conservative fundamentalist groups such as the Pentecostals, which grew prodigiously.) Sunday school attendance fell sharply. In a controversial book, author Pierre Berton attacked the churches for their lack of relevance, as they vainly attempted to combat the supporters of beer parlours, Sunday movies, and Sunday sports. Rev. James Mutchmor, the head of the United Church's board of evangelism and social service and later moderator of the church, outspokenly denounced the new trends. The "voice against vice" became the most-quoted cleric in Canada in the mid-1960s. Mutchmor's critics mocked: "Let's have much less of Mutchmor!"

Much of the revolt against established social and cultural patterns was superficial. High school boys put away their hair oil and deserted barbershops, while their mothers remonstrated with them in vain. "Flower children" dressed in fringes and beads and displayed psychedelic colours. Blue jeans became the uniform of a generation. College students and non-students began to sport moustaches, sideburns, and beards. Youth denounced age and experience and promised to stay young. A drug culture flourished, as did sexual experimentation.

 Young English-speaking Canadians empathized with the peace-and-love message of such American folk singers as Bob Dylan and Joan Baez. But Canadian folk singers, including Ian and Sylvia Tyson, Gordon Lightfoot, and Joni Mitchell, also achieved an international reputation.

The Tysons became popular in the United States at the start of the folk revival in the 1960s, paving the way for other Canadian performers at a time of limited recording opportunities in Canada. Orillia-born Lightfoot began his career in coffee houses and bars; as composer of such pieces as "Early Morning Rain" and "For Lovin' Me," he soon drew crowds to his performances at the Mariposa folk festival and elsewhere.

In French Canada, young people flocked to listen to the *chansonniers* who sang, accompanied only by their guitars or the piano, in the *boîtes à chansons* that sprang up across Quebec in the early 1960s. At first, the lyrics dwelt on apolitical themes such as love and nature. Later, as a powerful nationalist current surged through the province, new themes bearing on the historical experience of Quebec's people and their identity dominated singers' repertories. Gilles Vigneault became one of the most well-known singer-songwriters of the era — and his "Mon pays" became the anthem of nationalist youth. The *chansonniers* soon gave way to popular singers, among whom figured a strong feminine contingent, including Ginette Reno, Renée Claude, Pauline Julien, and Monique Leyrac. Robert Charlebois's audacious creativity, evident in his recording of "Lindberg" in 1968, made him one of the most popular male performers of the era.

Many young Canadians listened avidly to rock music during the 1960s. Enthusiastically they fell victim to Beatlemania, especially during the shaggy-haired foursome's tour of Canada in September 1964. On September 8, the *Toronto Star* headlined: "200 girls swoon in battle of the Beatles." Vancouver's Empire Stadium saw even greater hysteria, during a concert by the Fab Four, as 2000 fans rushed the stage and screams drowned out the singing. As the decade advanced, literally thousands of Canadian rock bands sprang up, usually modelled on British and American groups. Canadian singers received a substantial boost in 1970, when the Canadian Radio-Television and Telecommunications Commission (CRTC) established Canadian-content rules for broadcasters.

Protest against the war in Vietnam.

Toronto Star Syndicate.

CAMPUS UNREST

For historian Doug Owram, the 1960s constituted "the moment in history that forever defined the baby boom as a distinct generation."[1] The boomers' centres of activity were the university campuses (although the majority of boomers never went to university). Canadian students, like American and western youth in general, picketed against the war in Vietnam and for a wide range of reformist causes. Nationalist protest took root and flourished, often tended closely by university professors. Academics in the social sciences, particularly in Toronto, prepared research studies to show the extent to which Canada had become an American colony, and proposed measures for buying or taking it back. In Quebec's universities, equal fervour was applied to proving that Quebec was a Canadian colony and to devising plans for liberating it.

University protest had political repercussions. In Quebec, where most intellectuals were strong nationalists, it contributed to bringing the language question to the floor of the National Assembly and assisted the rise of the Parti Québécois. In Ottawa, it helped Pierre Trudeau, who appeared to challenge the establishment and who brought new ideas to the fore, to win the Liberal leadership and the federal election of 1968. In addition, by 1970, the nationalist outcry from many English-Canadian universities, particularly in Ontario, caused the Liberals to question the continentalism they had espoused in the 1950s.

Students abandoned classes and occupied administrative offices, demanding more active participation in the university community and the recognition of students' rights. At the University of Toronto, for example, students protested against recruiting on campus by a manufacturer of napalm used by the American military during the Vietnam War. Such protests were all the more visible, in part, because students were now far more numerous. University enrolments doubled during the 1950s, then tripled during the 1960s and 1970s. The parents of baby boomers, many of whom had never finished high school, preached the virtues of a university degree as the key to a bright future.

HIGHER EDUCATION

Provincial governments, convinced that higher education would bring enormous economic benefits to society, dramatically increased spending on universities and established a host of new institutions. One of these was Simon Fraser University, situated atop Burnaby Mountain, near Vancouver, which opened in 1965 with 2500 students. (The main building was well-known architect Arthur Erickson's first major commission. Some critics later blamed Erickson for student unrest because his design of the campus encouraged student interaction.) In Ontario, York University admitted its first 75 students in 1960; a year later the province gave York 500 acres in northwest Toronto for the building of a campus. Laurentian, Trent, Brock, and Lakehead universities were also set up. Quebec established the public Université du Québec in Montreal with several regional affiliates. The University of Alberta, Calgary branch, became the separate University of Calgary in 1966. New Brunswick's francophones obtained their own university at Moncton. Regional and community colleges began operations in several provinces. The federal government, which had been making grants directly to the universities since 1951, began in 1966 to make contributions to provincial governments for the financing of postsecondary education. In all, government spending on universities increased sevenfold during the 1960s.

The magnificent University of Lethbridge, main building, designed by famed architect Arthur Erickson. Construction was completed in 1971.

Communications Office, University of Lethbridge.

A Historical Portrait ☞

☞ The Student Radicals at Sir George Williams University

The late 1960s saw frequent protests against virtually all aspects of the established order. Students militated for a wide variety of causes, some of which regarded the universities themselves, while others were concerned with the wider society, such as the ban-the-bomb protests. Preferred methods were strikes, sit-ins, teach-ins and occupations of buildings.

Some militants were ready to take extreme measures in defence of causes that appeared increasingly imprecise. The events of February 11, 1969, at Sir George Williams University (today Concordia University) in Montreal appeared to mark a watershed.

"Police rout SGWU militants; $1 million computer centre wrecked." Thus read the *Montreal Star*'s headline that day. The damage figure was revised upward the next day to $2 million, or approximately $10 million in today's dollars.

In December 1968, some students had levelled charges of racism against a biology professor at the university. In early February 1969, they occupied the Faculty Club in the nine-storey Henry Hall Building in support of their cause. At first they succeeded in generating considerable sympathy. Over time, however, the militant group, thanks to new additions, became more radical, and moderates tended to distance themselves. One prominent militant proclaimed that he didn't really care about the charges of racism against the professor. "All we want to do is burn down the university. We want the police to come, we want violence."

Militants then broke into the cafeteria on the seventh floor and hurled chairs and tables down escalators, stairwells, and elevator shafts. As police moved against the crowd, occupants turned on the fire hoses against them, then retreated to the computer centre on the ninth floor. When police attempted to evict them from the centre, militants threw computers, punch cards, tapes, and furniture onto the street, and then set fire to the centre.

Police made 90 arrests; those arrested included 42 non-nationals, mainly from the Caribbean and from England. Thirty of those arrested were not students at Sir George Williams.

The events at Sir George Williams provoked a sharp backlash and a demand for a return to order. The *Montreal Star* denounced what it termed "an indefensible act by student anarchists." Acts of intimidation, disruption, and even violence were occurring at the same time on other campuses. But for historian Doug Owram, the SGWU episode, because of the degree of violence and destruction, "foreshadowed the end of the 1960s era."[1]

---

[1] Doug Owram, *Born at the Right Time: A History of the Baby-Boom Generation* (Toronto: University of Toronto Press, 1996), p. 286.

As a result of their rapid growth, universities faced serious shortages of trained staff. English-speaking universities recruited heavily on American campuses. Critics accused universities of ignoring Canadian university graduates in their hiring policies. Carleton University professors Robin Mathews and James Steele, after reviewing the statistics on university hiring policies, called for the Canadianization of faculties.

GOVERNMENT INTERVENTION

Although university teachers and students were among the loudest voices calling for change, Canadians in general endorsed increased state intervention, at all levels, as a necessary tool for reform. They pressured municipal governments to improve the quality of life in cities by controlling the heights of buildings, curtailing expressway expansion, promoting urban transit, fighting urban blight, and improving parks and libraries. They demanded that governments take measures to protect society's weaker elements, and that they act to protect consumers, promote the equality of women, and combat discrimination against minority groups. The cultural lobby requested financial aid to assist Canadian cultural development, while sport organizations urged Ottawa to fund amateur sport and to work to improve Canadian athletes' performances in international competitions.

The Canadian welfare state became entrenched during this period. Canadians acquired new rights for which all residents, through the state, now became collectively responsible. In 1966, for example, the federal government adopted the Canada Assistance Act, a coordination of largely existing provincial measures designed to aid persons who were unable to work or were ineligible for unemployment insurance. In 1971, it substantially widened coverage under the Unemployment Insurance Act, partly to benefit regions where little full-time year-round work existed.

 The most important programs launched in the 1960s concerned pensions and medical care. After 1967, low-income pensioners became eligible for a guaranteed income supplement to their old-age pensions. More importantly, in 1965, Ottawa established the Canada Pension Plan, a compulsory and completely portable contributory plan paid for by workers and employers. Quebec set up its own provincial plan, respecting the principles edicted by the federal government; money deposited in the fund was then reinvested.

Canadians increasingly called for the state to provide universal medical care. Saskatchewan set up a health insurance plan in 1962. Only in 1968 did Ottawa enact into law a national health scheme that provided for financial contributions to provincial medicare plans all of which had to be universal, comprehensive, portable and publicly administered. Social and health programs proved costly: health expenses alone nearly doubled to $6 billion between 1965 and 1970. Ottawa registered what would be its last budgetary surplus for nearly 30 years in 1969–70.

Governments also intervened modestly to supply disadvantaged Canadians with low-income housing. The 1960s saw the construction of large apartment buildings in central urban areas, often with little public space, a situation that gave rise to a variety of social problems. Toronto's Cabbagetown district, Vancouver's Strathcona area, Halifax's Uniacke Square, and Montreal's Jeanne Mance Park saw such developments.

Most Canadians dreamed of owning a house in the suburbs. Federal government programs made low-cost mortgages available, provincial governments built roads, and local authorities installed services. The Don Mills community of Toronto, built in 1952–62, served as the prototype of a planned corporate suburb. Around a core area containing a shopping centre and a high school at the intersection of two arterial roads, developers built small apartment buildings and townhouses. Beyond them were four low density neighbourhood units. Edmonton had its own planned suburb, Mill Woods. Developers made plans for a population of 100 000, which was to live in 23 neighbourhoods that were focused on a town-centre complex containing the necessary services. All large Canadian cities saw these suburbs mushroom in the 1960s.

THE CULTURAL REVOLUTION

Both English-language and French-language cultural expression underwent a renaissance in the 1960s. Universal education increased the potential market for cultural products, and higher disposable incomes and more leisure time made it possible for people to enjoy them. Federal and provincial grant agencies gave considerable assistance to a wide variety of cultural endeavours.

LITERATURE

The 1960s saw the rapid growth of a vibrant and diverse literature in both English and French, due in part to government support programs. By 1970, most universities in English-speaking Canada offered courses in Canadian literature in English, as did Quebec universities on French-Canadian literature. New literary periodicals were established to publish and critique Canadian writing. Several new publishing houses also appeared.

Many of the most popular writers of the decade were women. Margaret Laurence, who spent her early life in Neepawa, Manitoba, wrote *The Stone Angel* and *A Jest of God*, two novels set in the fictitious town of Manawaka, which bore a close resemblance to Neepawa. In some of her short stories set in Ontario's Huron County, Alice Munro examined the difficulties experienced by an adolescent girl in coming to terms with her family and with life in a small town. Margaret Atwood published her first novel, *The Edible Woman*, in 1969, on the theme of women's alienation in modern consumer society.

A sense of place and of identity was important for many novelists. Ernest Buckler situated his *Ox Bells and Fireflies* in Nova Scotia. Robert Kroetsch, who grew up in rural Alberta, published an "Out West" series of novels before moving mainly into poetry. Rudy Wiebe, a Mennonite from the prairies, set out to explore the tensions between pacifism and war in *Peace Shall Destroy Many*.

The revolution in poetry brought youth to the fore. Indeed, a volume on Canada's fifteen most outstanding poets in 1970 featured only three who were well known before 1960. Irving Layton, a Romanian Jew whose family settled in an impoverished immigrant district in Montreal, filled his poems with his early impressions and experiences. Gwendolyn MacEwen demonstrated her grasp of the poetic dimensions of history, while Al Purdy chronicled the geographical and historical complexities of Canada in such volumes as *The Cariboo Horses*, which he wrote after a trip to Baffin Island. Milton Acorn's populist poetry featured left-wing causes popular in this era. Leonard Cohen of Montreal achieved renown, both as a poet and as a singer and songwriter. Raymond Souster continued to influence the direction of Canadian poetry by editing the volumes of many poets. A number of Canadian poets, including Souster, gave public readings at the Bohemian Embassy, a Toronto coffee house established in 1960. (Bell Canada, not yet "in," listed this establishment in its yellow pages under the general heading "Embassies and consulates.")

Some Quebec authors found their inspiration in the turbulent nationalism of the Quiet Revolution. Poet Fernand Ouellette dwelt upon the alienation and oppression of the Québécois in *Le Soleil sous la mort*, while Jacques Ferron's short stories dealt with the problems of maintaining Quebec's cultural identity. Hubert Aquin wrote *Prochain épisode* while being held in a Montreal psychiatric clinic pending trial on a weapons charge; the novel's narrator, also confined to a psychiatric hospital, awaits trial on charges related to his underground activities as a revolutionary separatist.

Nationalism formed only part of the general theme of liberation being experienced in Quebec during these years. Many novelists examined the emancipation of the person in relation to society. *Une saison dans la vie d'Emmanuel*, which presented a sombre portrait of a Quebec family dominated by a tyrannical father, brought novelist Marie-Claire Blais a wide international audience. Feminist concerns permeated Françoise Loranger's *Encore cinq minutes*, while themes of war, sexual repression, and exploitation of the weak were central to Roch Carrier's highly acclaimed work *La guerre, yes sir!*

A deep concern for Aboriginal rights inspired much of the work of Quebec novelist Yves Thériault. In his *Ashini*, the hero, a Montagnais or Innu, commits suicide in the hope that his death will awaken his people from their apathy and bring them to claim their ancestral lands. Playwrights Marcel Dubé and Michel Tremblay made major contributions to French-language theatre; Tremblay's *Les belles-soeurs* violated traditional codes by being the first play to be written entirely in joual, or working-class slang.

FILM-MAKING

Canada's film industry in both languages underwent substantial development in the 1960s. Through its diverse activities, the National Film Board made Canadians more conscious of their history and culture. In English, producers worked mainly on documentaries. *Memorandum*, whose subject was Hitler's "final solution" to the "Jewish question," helped build an enviable reputation for producer Donald Brittain, who had previously directed *Fields of Sacrifice*, a memorial to Canadians killed in action during World War II. Canada's centennial year, 1967, saw other noteworthy productions, including *Labyrinth*, which used the Greek myth of Theseus, who entered a labyrinth to find and kill the Minotaur, to symbolize the universality of a person's journey throughout the world. The lavish film, seen by 1.3 million people at Expo 67 in Montreal, attracted much positive press reaction internationally.

French-language filmmakers experimented with subjects linked to French Canada's social ferment. Denys Arcand's *On est au coton* was a film about the textile industry and workers' fears of unemployment because of factory closures. Pierre Perrault's *L'Acadie! L'Acadie!* featured the struggle by Acadian students at the Université de Moncton for the recognition of language rights. Quebec film-makers also set about making what one magazine called "maple leaf porno." Denis Héroux produced *Valérie* in 1969, asserting the need to "undress the Quebec female." One-third of Quebec's population went to the movies in 1970 to see Claude Fournier's *Deux femmes en or*, a similar production.

POPULATION TRENDS

Demographically, the 1960s saw the baby boom of the late 1940s and 1950s turn into a "baby bust." In one decade, the rate of growth of Canada's population dropped by nearly half. The two-child family — the minimum to maintain the current size of the population — briefly became the norm in Canada. Then single-child or childless families became increasingly numerous.

Demographers and sociologists had difficulty explaining the demographic revolution, which other industrialized countries also experienced. Many observers emphasized the availability of better contraceptive methods, particularly the birth-control pill, which became available in Canada in 1966. Contraception and birth-control methods did indeed gain much more exposure and publicity. Only in 1969, however, did Parliament amend Canada's Criminal Code to permit the distribution of birth-control information and devices.

Obviously, Canadians wanted fewer children, and they wanted them later in life. A century earlier, large families had been a necessity — on farms, for example, children meant additional workers and, in general, the extended family cared for its elderly members. In Canada's modern social welfare state, the aged relied less on adult children for financial assistance. As well, the ever-increasing costs of raising and educating them made children appear as financial liabilities. Children could also be perceived as a brake on career development.

CHANGING FAMILY PATTERNS

A general revolution in family patterns began in the 1960s. Conservative-minded Canadians had long looked askance at the frequency of marriage breakdown in the United States, symbolized by the rapidly moving love-lives of glamorous Hollywood stars. After 1968, when Parliament modified Canadian laws, divorce became frequent in Canada, too.

Traditional sexual taboos gradually became more relaxed as society became more tolerant. Gay and lesbian themes began to feature in films and literary works, among them Jane Rule's first novel, *The Desert of the Heart*, and Quebec writer Michel Tremblay's plays. Same-sex relationships became more open after the government, promising to stay out of the nation's bedrooms, legalized homosexual practices between consenting adults in private in 1969. Many opposition parliamentarians denounced the changes on religious and moral grounds. In spite of their apparent victory, gays and lesbians worried that their concerns had now been reduced to narrow issues of criminal-law reform. A coalition of gay and lesbian liberation groups stated that, in spite of the reform, "we are still confronted with discrimination, police harassment, exploitation and pressures to conform which deny our sexuality."

Young people in general began to experiment with different types of living arrangements. For a time, communes were in fashion, although few lasted long. "Living together," or common-law marriage, hitherto frowned upon socially, gained popularity. Some women favoured living together because they opposed marriage in principle as a form of economic servitude — women working without pay — disguised by the myth of romantic love. In most cases, for both women and men, convenience was probably a compelling factor in favour of such unions.

WOMEN: THE LONG ROAD TOWARD EQUALITY

The desire for smaller families symbolized a more general wish by women for a change in their condition. A half century earlier, women had struggled to obtain the right to vote. Now, in an age of protest, women's groups began to demand that governments intervene to promote equality. Thus began the "second wave" of the women's movement.

Women disagreed strongly over the nature of the "ideal woman." Historian Valerie Korinek describes a contest created by *Chatelaine*, Canada's only mass-market women's magazine. The goal of the contest was to discover Canada's foremost homemaker, "Mrs. Chatelaine," a stay-at-home wife and mother who also did volunteer work and could serve as a role model for readers of the magazine. Some women, however, proposed other models. One suggested setting up a "Mrs. Slob contest," and named herself as winner. She admitted that she did not always serve nourishing meals, she liked fish and chips, she "entertained" only when her neighbours came in to gab, and she didn't find time to do much volunteer work. She offered her philosophy: "Be happy, don't worry. You do what you can with what you've got when you feel like it."[2]

As the 1960s began, many women felt ready to speak out about the affairs of the country. When journalist Lotta Dempsey lamented what appeared to be the increasing danger of nuclear war and wondered where the voice of women was, she hit a raw nerve: hundreds of women turned out for a public meeting at Massey Hall in Toronto. Thus was born the Voice of Women, whose membership grew to 10 000 in less than a year. Many of its participants later became activists in other women's associations.

Convinced that much more needed to be done, Laura Sabia, president of the Canadian Federation of University Women, promoted the establishment, in 1966, of a new group, the Committee for the Equality of Women in Canada. The coalition pressed Ottawa to create a royal commission on the status of women. Thérèse Casgrain and other members of the Fédération des femmes du Québec also attended in order to demonstrate that francophone women were making the same demands as their anglophone sisters. The federal government agreed to set up a commission, but only after the committee threatened to organize a huge march on Ottawa.

The Royal Commission on the Status of Women, chaired by professional broadcaster Florence Bird, held hearings across Canada and received nearly 500 briefs. Issued in September 1970, the "Bird Report," which one journalist called "a bomb, already primed and ticking," called for a societal change of attitude toward women. It proposed dozens of recommendations concerning women in the workplace, in political life, in education, and in family life.

WOMEN IN THE PAID WORK FORCE

Male-dominated legislatures did adopt some laws that improved the lot of women. They made divorce simpler and maternity benefits more generous, and they granted tax deductions for child-care expenses. Ontario adopted the Women's Equal Employment Opportunity Act in 1970. In spite of many loopholes, the law provided for legal unpaid maternity leave and banned the firing of women upon marriage. Business complained that maternity leaves would eventually lead to paid leaves, a kind of "reward for pregnancy."

Women's major demands for change — and, indeed, the changes themselves — occurred in the workplace. In 1961, only one married woman in five was in the labour force, often in part-time employment. Public attitudes still strongly disapproved of married mothers taking paid employment. By 1971, however, as increasing numbers of married women sought jobs outside the home, the proportion had risen to one in three. By 1981, it reached one in two. Women who worked outside the home needed to find some type of day care for their small children. It would be necessary to wait until the 1970s, however, before even modest state subsidies for provincial day-care centres became available.

Sex segregation in the workplace, resulting in "pink-collar ghettos," still remained the norm. Many women found jobs as salesclerks in the retail stores which proliferated. The expansion of health care and education also created traditional employment for women. In the late 1960s, the federal government became the largest employer of women in Canada: most female employees worked in office or administrative-support jobs, while men dominated in the higher-level, better-paying managerial positions.

Women disagreed over the means to effect necessary changes and, indeed, over the changes that they should seek. Some shared the liberal view that legislative reform would give women more equal opportunities. Other younger, more radical feminists believed that only a fundamental transformation of the economic and social structures that perpetuated the dominance of men would end female oppression. This group regarded the Bird Report as far too conservative. From the late 1960s, these women waged a militant campaign for women's liberation, often on university campuses, through newsworthy demonstrations and rallies, in innumerable organized discussions, and in newspapers.

ECONOMIC CHANGE

Canada in the 1960s entered a postindustrial era, in which services, such as those provided by governments, schools, hospitals, the communications industry, retail trade, and financial institutions, constituted the largest sector of employment. Manufacturing placed second.

Primary industries, including agriculture, came last — a complete reversal of the Canada of 1867.

Such sectors as transportation and communications developed spectacularly as a result of new technologies. Many workers faced painful adjustments in the wake of job losses. Employees in traditional "soft" industries such as footwear and textiles, hard hit by lost markets and cheap imports, suffered particularly. Shipbuilders laid off thousands of workers as the federal government reduced subsidies and Canadian shipyards remained internationally uncompetitive.

Declining prices for their products and fierce competition from abroad led Canada's important natural-resource industries to modernize in order to reduce costs. In addition, an increasingly vocal environmental movement now pointed to pulp and paper companies and smelters as major polluters of the nation's air and water. They urged governments to force such companies to bear some of the huge costs of cleaning up the production process.

Technological change and market forces led to new challenges in agriculture. Large farms, with the equipment necessary to work more land and boost yields, became the norm. Small farmers lacked the means to make the necessary adjustments, and many abandoned the land that their families had farmed for generations.

Some regions of Canada — southern Ontario, the West Coast, and Alberta — prospered in the climate of change during the 1960s. For others, including the Atlantic provinces, much of Quebec, and parts of the Prairies, change brought unemployment and poverty and provoked widespread discontent.

BUST AND RECOVERY

The great postwar economic boom ended in the late 1950s as Canada entered its most serious recession since the Great Depression of the 1930s. Jobless rates increased sharply, as industry encountered more difficulty in selling goods to foreign markets. Worldwide overproduction and declining prices hit farmers particularly hard. John Diefenbaker's Progressive Conservative government, first elected in 1957 and re-elected in 1958 with an overwhelming majority, tried to attack unemployment by means of higher tariffs, and also increased spending which caused rising budget deficits.

In 1962, the government devalued the Canadian dollar, pegging it at a relatively low (for that era) 92.5 cents (U.S.). This measure provoked both outright condemnation by importers and enthusiastic approval by exporters. The Liberals protested noisily that devaluation would mean higher prices for consumers. They printed thousands of so-called "Diefenbucks" — 92.5-cent dollars adorned with the prime minister's likeness — which they used effectively during the election campaign of June 1962. Diefenbaker lost his majority in Parliament that year. Then, in 1963, he lost power to the Liberals.

INFLATION

By 1963, recovery seemed well under way as unemployment dropped. By 1966, however, a new, worrisome trend became evident: prices were moving up more quickly. Angry shoppers boycotted supermarkets, accusing them of price gouging. Prime Minister Lester B. Pearson's Liberal government raised some taxes in an effort to dampen demand. The Conservative opposition boldly compared the Liberal minibudget to then fashionable miniskirts: "Taxes are getting higher and higher and covering less and less." Most Canadians strongly disagreed with the economists' explanation that inflation was caused by the fact that consumers had too much money to spend.

Canadians battled inflation in various ways. The members of strong unions in key sectors of the economy, such as transportation, sought, and often obtained, massive pay increases. These large wage increases added to inflationary pressures. In 1967, while inflation showed no signs of abating, the economy slowed down noticeably. Economists coined a new word — *stagflation* — to describe the phenomenon of inflation at a time of slow economic growth. First-year economics textbooks insisted that this combination could not occur — but it did, in Canada and throughout much of the world.

Not all economic news was bad. Canada's foreign-trade balance on goods improved in spite of a growing deficit on finished products. Early in the 1960s, the Diefenbaker government finally found markets — in the People's Republic of China, the Soviet Union, and eastern Europe — for Canada's surplus grain. These new sales improved many western farmers' incomes.

Environmental Concerns

Some Canadians came to realize that economic development was having deleterious effects upon the physical environment. In Ontario, environmentalists focussed their attention on water quality in heavily industrialized areas of the province. A Hamilton newspaper worried in 1962: "Sewage, detergents, sludges, chemicals, oil ... they all pour into the harbour." Detergent manufacturers vied with each other to create the longest-lasting suds for washing machines and dishwashers. These suds eventually piled up along the shores of lakes and rivers. Finally, in the face of public outcry, the industry regulated itself and developed more biodegradable detergents.

Later, in the 1960s, algae proliferated in southern Ontario's waters, depleting oxygen levels and killing multitudes of fish. The cause was phosphates, again from detergents. At the University of Toronto, anti-pollution campaigners founded Pollution Probe, staging such events as a mock funeral for Toronto's "dead" Don River. After 1970, governments agreed to take steps to cut phosphate use dramatically in an effort to improve water quality.

Economic Relations with the United States

Throughout the 1960s, Canada registered trade deficits with the United States. Although the Diefenbaker devaluation of the dollar in 1962 did stimulate exports, Canadian subsidiaries sent back dividends to the United States and Canadian visitors spent heavily there.

One measure in particular did increase exports to the United States. In 1965, the Liberal government signed the Automotive Products Agreement with the United States. The "Auto Pact" provided for free trade among the manufacturers, who could now rationalize production. Canadian plants began specializing in producing relatively few models. Most economists agree that the pact, accompanied by a lower Canadian dollar, strongly benefited the economy of southern Ontario, where most of Canada's automobile and automotive parts industry are concentrated.

Canadians passionately debated the issue of American ownership of Canadian industries in the 1960s. In 1966, Walter Gordon, the Liberal finance minister, set up a task force to study "the significance — both political and economic — of foreign investment." At this time, however, the Liberal government contained very few economic nationalists. Indeed, Canadians themselves had not reached a consensus on the issue.

Business and Labour

In the 1960s radicals in the universities, in the churches, and in the media joined economic nationalists and reformist political parties such as the Parti Québécois, with its initial pro-worker bias, and the New Democratic Party, the beneficiary of considerable union support, to criticize

Prime Minister Lester B. Pearson visits President John F. Kennedy, spring 1963.

National Archives of Canada/C-90482.

the large multinational corporations. They castigated business in general for its unquenchable thirst for profits and for its failure to display any social or environmental conscience. They flayed developers for destroying old urban neighbourhoods to build highrise luxury apartment buildings and office towers. Finally, in this age of rising inflation and of concern for consumers' rights, they denounced companies for "gouging" consumers by endlessly raising prices.

UNIONS

The major organized assault on business, however, came from unions. Canadian workers, particularly younger ones from the first cohorts of baby boomers, became increasingly restive during the 1960s. Many of these new workers had high expectations, which they hoped to realize quickly. As well, in the late 1960s, rising consumer prices made it imperative for workers to obtain generous wage settlements.

The union rank and file vigorously attacked authority. Militant workers frequently rebelled against their conservative leaders by launching wildcat strikes (illegal work stoppages), some of which paid handsome dividends. A lengthy wildcat strike by Inco workers at Sudbury, for example, brought miners the highest wages in North America. Another clash at the Stelco plant in Hamilton, with much violence and destruction of property, enabled steelworkers to obtain very substantial wage increases.

Many unionized workers were women. In contrast with the 1950s, when women often hesitated in their resistance to discriminatory practices in the workplace, they now began to wage "a more concerted and organized campaign for gender equality." Results came slowly. In 1968, women employees of General Motors with six years' seniority were being laid off while the company continued to hire new men. One woman vented her frustration with a poem in the newspaper of the local United Auto Workers to which she belonged:

> I read that whole darn paper and never make the grade;
> Do they just count the females when union dues are paid?
> We wait on recognition and it better show up soon,
> I feel more isolated than the men that walked the Moon.
> So all you fancy journalists, here's one thing to remember:
> I'm classed as just a female, but I'm still a union member.[3]

Workers, often women, in the rapidly growing public sector — teachers, hospital workers, civil servants, municipal employees, and others — also sought to improve salaries and working conditions. They successfully lobbied governments to place them on an equal footing with workers in the private sector, to recognize their right to form unions and, in many cases, to strike. Public sector unions soon became the largest in Canada and among the most militant. Lengthy work stoppages in the post office, for example, became notorious.

POLITICS IN THE AGE OF MASS MEDIA

Since Confederation, Canadian politics has focussed increasingly on personalities. Political scientists have attempted to explain this tendency by suggesting that the major political parties have come to differ less and less on questions of basic principle. Leadership has been either a significant asset or a grave liability for parties.

The advent of television increased this focus on the leader. Through the news and televised events such as election campaign debates, it has brought politicians into the homes of Canadians. At the same time, as political scientist Frederick J. Fletcher has pointed out, television has inhibited the thoughtful exposition of policies and promoted "simple and flashy promises and one-line put-downs of the opposition."[4] The media have stressed conflict and confrontation in their coverage, emphasizing sensational and exciting occurrences. Prime Minister Lester Pearson once complained that "when we do discuss policies seriously ... reporters do not even appear to listen, until we say something controversial or personal, charged with what they regard as news value." In spite of television's particular deficiencies, it began to play a major role in moulding the images — favourable and unfavourable — of politicians.

DIEFENBAKER: A PROPHET OUTCAST

Progressive Conservative leader John Diefenbaker, prime minister from 1957 to 1963, benefited in 1957 and again in the electoral triumph of 1958 from a remarkably positive image. By 1960, however, he had acquired a very negative one. In 1962, he barely managed to retain power with a minority government. In 1963, he returned to the opposition benches. It took only five short years to destroy the boundless confidence that Canadians had placed in "Dief the Chief."

This downfall, in part, arose from the Conservatives' weak basis of support, notably in Quebec, where the party's organization had long been deficient. Moreover, Diefenbaker understood little of Quebec's awakening in the early 1960s. Conservatives also quickly found that they could not easily reconcile the interests of urban and rural voters, or those of central Canadians and Canadians living in other provinces. The government also seemed disorganized and rife with dissension. Most to blame, in journalist Peter Newman's opinion, was Diefenbaker himself, a "renegade in power" who had conquered a generation and brought only disillusionment.[5]

To some extent, the controversial prime minister became a victim of circumstances. After 22 years in opposition, the Conservatives had no experience with the art of governing.

Moreover, the severe recession of 1960–61 undermined the government's popularity. Certainly Diefenbaker's critics, especially in the cities of central Canada, did not hesitate to charge him with economic mismanagement.

STRAINED CANADIAN–AMERICAN RELATIONS

Other critics deplored strained Canadian–American relations. Shortly after the 1957 election, Diefenbaker had, without benefit of cabinet scrutiny, committed Canada to the North American Air Defence Command (NORAD), the continental air-defence alliance headed by a U.S. Air Force general. Then, in 1962–63, in a reversal of his original position, he refused to accept the nuclear warheads that the Americans wanted installed in their anti-aircraft missiles on Canadian soil. Moreover, he intensely disliked President Kennedy, a feeling the American president reciprocated.

In these years of renascent Canadian nationalism, Canadians began to agonize over the kind of relationship they wanted with their southern neighbour. Diefenbaker's decisions reflected the will of part of the electorate, but they also provoked the disgruntlement of many other Canadians. In addition, as historians John Herd Thompson and Stephen Randall point out, Canadian and American priorities moved increasingly apart. While the United States was determined to confront the Soviet threat and was turning into a warfare state, Canada in the 1960s gave greater priority to advancing the welfare state.[6]

POLITICS IN DISARRAY

Politics in the early 1960s promoted cynicism among many voters. The country faced grave problems with, at the beginning of the decade, more Canadians out of work than at any time since the Great Depression. The increasing cost of living provoked costly demands from some unions. Relations with the provinces were strained, while growing discord also characterized ties with the United States. Yet neither Progressive Conservative leader John Diefenbaker nor Liberal leader Lester B. Pearson appeared to have a vision or long-term plan about what could be done.

Four times these two knights in tarnished armour faced each other on the electoral battlefield; in 1962, 1963, and again in 1965, neither won enough seats in the House of Commons to form a majority government. Each made numerous — and costly — promises in attempts to rally more voter support. Some of their techniques, borrowed from Madison Avenue, elicited mockery and disdain. The Liberals, for example, published colouring books portraying Diefenbaker riding backwards on a rocking horse. They also formed a short-lived "truth squad" to pursue the Conservatives relentlessly across the country to make sure they told the truth. Once elected, Canada's parliamentarians devoted themselves to discussing a seemingly endless succession of alleged scandals. In his memoirs, Pearson gave the title "Politics in Disrepute" to a chapter on the years 1964 and 1965.

Some voters showed their dissatisfaction with both the Conservatives and the Liberals by supporting third parties. In Quebec, Social Credit, a fringe group since the 1930s, surprised and even stupefied most observers when it won one-quarter of the province's seats. Leader Réal Caouette, an automobile salesman from Rouyn, in northern Quebec, appealed to Quebeckers' obvious desire for change. Promising a national dividend to all citizens to raise consumers' buying power, as well as help for the aged, the unemployed, and large families, Caouette carried his crusade through rural and small-town Quebec as well as to weekly television audiences.

Less spectacular was the reconstitution of the national CCF. In 1961, in an effort to broaden its support, the CCF co-operated with the Canadian Labour Congress and with various left-wing organizations to launch the New Democratic Party. The party's reformist program called for jobs,

John Diefenbaker looks on, as Lester Pearson attempts to uncoil the cord of a translation earpiece. After the 1960s, it became much more important for federal Anglophone politicians to be able to speak French.

John McNeill.

health insurance, free education, and a policy of "co-operative federalism" in federal–provincial relations. Yet electoral results during the 1960s at both the federal and provincial levels proved disappointing. In particular, even most union members failed to support the NDP, which in turn feared becoming too closely identified with unions.

The Pearson Years

While in office from 1963 until 1968, Lester B. Pearson attempted to find solutions to Canada's problems. He sought to conciliate the provinces and initiated a series of federal–provincial conferences on the Canadian Constitution. In answer to French Canadians' claims for linguistic equality, he set up the Royal Commission on Bilingualism and Biculturalism to study the issue and make recommendations. His government adopted numerous social measures, such as the Canada Pension Plan and universal medicare. Also, after weeks of debate, the Pearson government gave Canadians a national flag.

Pearson's Critics

Yet Pearson and his government had numerous critics. Most reproached him for his failure to give the country firm and sure leadership (in the direction they wished). Business considered his election promises irresponsibly costly and blamed him for surrendering too easily to the unions. Labour portrayed itself as the victim, not the cause, of inflation. Canadian nationalists accused him of doing little to counter the Americanization of Canada in the areas of culture and investment. And they decried Pearson's decision to reverse his earlier position and to authorize nuclear warheads for American missiles in the country.

Quebec nationalists thought that Pearson was resisting their province's legitimate demands, while strong centralists declared that his concessions to Quebec and the other provinces were balkanizing the country. Monarchists censured him for tolerating creeping republicanism, while French Canadians and new Canadians favoured a loosening of Canada's ties with the British crown. Unhappy residents of the Atlantic provinces thought he was doing little to alleviate regional disparities, and westerners judged him ill-attuned to their region's interests. In sum, Pearson endeared himself to virtually none of the regions or major interest groups.

Perhaps Pearson and his Liberal administration should not have been expected to build a consensus on the major questions of the day when Canadians themselves disagreed so strongly on the answers. The 1960s were a time of increasing polarization. In that climate, Pearson manoeuvred with some skill. The policy of "co-operative federalism," by which Ottawa showed greater sensitivity to provincial concerns, was perhaps the best that could be hoped for in an era of confrontation between Ottawa and the provinces, particularly Quebec. As for the economy and the growing problem of inflation, no obvious long-term solutions existed. Also, even though the Pearson government did have more than its share of scandals, the prime minister's own conduct remained above suspicion.

Finally, concerning American–Canadian economic and cultural relations, Canadians first had to debate options before they could make decisions. American participation in the Vietnam War certainly poisoned relations between the North American neighbours. Pearson provoked the ire of U.S. President Lyndon B. Johnson when, in a speech in Philadelphia in April 1965, the prime minister urged Americans to stop bombing North Vietnam. As the war escalated, so did Canadian criticism of American actions in Vietnam. The American government could only express regret for the lack of support from its northern ally.

TRUDEAUMANIA

 Many Canadians have viewed the Diefenbaker–Pearson years as the culminating point of a bygone and increasingly repugnant brand of politics. The public longed for a new style, a new type of leadership, an imaginative and refreshing approach to the complex issues of the day. In 1968, as the Liberals searched for a successor to Pearson, many believed that they had found all this in Pierre Elliott Trudeau. Trudeau, as justice minister, attracted much attention at the constitutional conference in early 1968, where he jousted with Premier Daniel Johnson of Quebec over the role of the federal government.

TRUDEAU'S BACKGROUND

Trudeau had been elected for the first time in 1965, when Pearson had convinced him to enter the House of Commons to help renew Quebec's presence in Ottawa. During the Duplessis years in Quebec, Trudeau had been a bitter critic of the Union Nationale regime and had helped establish a small-circulation magazine called *Cité libre* to give a voice to liberal-minded Quebeckers. He had also studied at Harvard and the London School of Economics, and travelled widely. Yet Quebec nationalists had no liking for this intellectual who incessantly stigmatized nationalism. Nor did business have confidence in a candidate who lacked experience in the corporate world.

Nevertheless, Trudeau's style and background intrigued delegates at the Ottawa leadership convention. His image was of a wealthy bachelor surrounded by beautiful women. He was athletic, drove a Mercedes-Benz sports car, and often dressed flamboyantly. As *The Globe and Mail* put it: "He is the man we all would like to be: charming, rich, talented, successful." This image was certainly at the base of the wave of "Trudeaumania" that broke out during the Liberal leadership race and reached its zenith during the June 1968 federal election, which the Liberals won easily.

The election of Pierre Elliott Trudeau as Liberal Party leader, spring 1968.

National Archives of Canada/PA 111214.

TRUDEAU'S PROGRAM

In marked contrast to Pearson and Diefenbaker, Trudeau made few specific promises designed to buy blocks of voters with their own money. Rather, he expressed a number of general priorities. He spoke of building a "just society" in which personal and political liberties were ensured by a charter of rights, a society in which minorities would be sheltered from the caprices of majorities, in which regions and social groups who had not participated fully in the country's material abundance would have greater opportunities. He wanted to discuss with Canadians their country's future. This emphasis on participatory democracy appealed to and attracted many electors.

Trudeau had much to say on the constitutional question as well. When he asked for a strong mandate to oppose the Quebec government's ambitions to play a role in international affairs, Toronto newspapers congratulated him for his "firmness." For advocates of a strong central government, here was someone who would stand up to the provinces, which they viewed as continually encroaching upon Ottawa's authority. Trudeau could also promise Quebec that he would promote bilingualism in Canada, notably in the federal civil service, and that he would give Quebec and French Canada a major role to play in federal politics. Trudeau's triumphant victory in the 1968 election suggested that he might succeed in building a new consensus among Canadians if he could overcome the Liberals' weakness in the West.

THE CANADIAN CENTENNIAL, 1967

The 1960s were a time of celebration as well as confrontation. In 1967, the year of the Canadian centennial, provinces and municipalities organized various festivities to mark the event. Typically subdued Canadians gave vent to few of the effusions of American-style patriotism, and many wondered whether the country was going to succeed in holding itself together.

Expo 67, Montreal 1967 — an exciting celebration of Canada's centennial year. Canada put forward its very best and invited the world. Some 50 million visitors attended.

Malak/National Archives of Canada/C-18536.

w w w

One centennial activity was not restrained: Expo 67, staged on an island in the St. Lawrence River at Montreal. The showpiece event brought together more than 60 nations to celebrate the theme "Man and His World." Fifty million visitors passed through the turnstiles, and governments, both federal and provincial, spared no expense, perhaps unfortunately for the taxpayer.

The Canada of 1970 differed greatly from the country that had timidly embarked on an era of change a decade earlier. Materially, most Canadians were now better off; they were also better educated and certainly more liberal in their views. As we shall see in the following chapters, such minority groups as Native Peoples, French-speaking Canadians and new Canadians of neither French nor British heritage sought to defend their interests more vigorously and found that society was at least somewhat more attentive to their claims.

Many Canadians, particularly older Canadians, found it difficult to accept the rapid pace of change. They criticized what they saw as a general decline in respect for authority and particularly the many excesses that accompanied social transformation. Others felt that the heightened individualism of the era was incompatible with the need to preserve the nation's unity. For the moment, however, these voices of caution had little impact. Indeed the 1970s would bring more change against a background of increasing economic difficulties and political disunity.

NOTES

1. Doug Owram, *Born at the Right Time: A History of the Baby-Boom Generation* (Toronto: University of Toronto Press, 1996), p. 159.

2. Valerie J. Korinek, "'Mrs. Chatelaine' vs. 'Mrs. Slob': Contestants, Correspondents and the Chatelaine Community in Action, 1961–1969," *Journal of the Canadian Historical Association/Revue de la Société historique du Canada* 7 (1996): 266.

3. Pamela Sugiman, *Labour's Dilemma: The Gender Politics of Auto Workers in Canada, 1937–1979* (Toronto: University of Toronto Press, 1994), p. 136.

4. Frederick J. Fletcher, "Playing the Game: The Mass Media and the 1979 Campaign," in Howard R. Penniman, ed., *Canada at the Polls, 1979 and 1980: A Study of the General Elections* (Washington, D.C.: American Enterprise Institute of Public Policy Research, 1980), p. 319.

5. Peter C. Newman, *Renegade in Power: The Diefenbaker Years*, rev. ed. (Toronto: McClelland & Stewart, 1989).

6. John Herd Thompson and Steven Randall, *Canada and the United States: Ambivalent Allies*, 3rd ed. (Montreal/Kingston: McGill-Queen's University Press, 2002), p. 243.

LINKING TO THE PAST

Canadian Music Encyclopedia
http://www.canoe.ca/JamMusicPopEncycloPages/
Biographies of 1200 Canadian music artists from the 1950s to the present, including Joni Mitchell, Gordon Lightfoot, and Ian and Sylvia.

The History of Canada's Public Pensions
http://www.civilization.ca/hist/pensions/cpp1sp_e.html
Click on "1952–1967" to read about the introduction of the Canada Pension Plan. For the full text of the Canada Pension Act, go to http://laws.justice.gc.ca/en/C-8/index.html.

The Cradle of Collective Bargaining
http://www.humanities.mcmaster.ca/~cradle/
This site presents a history of unionization in Hamilton, Ontario. Check out the slide show for an illustrated overview of the labour movement (including strikes at the Stelco plant between the 1940s and the 1970s) and read the essay "Women, Work, and Unions" to learn about women's working conditions.

Lester B. Pearson
http://www.primeministers.ca/pearson/intro.php
Quick facts about and a biography of Lester B. Pearson.

Trudeaumania
http://archives.cbc.ca/300c.asp?IDCat=69&IDDos=73&IDLan=1&IDMenu=69
Video and audio clips related to Trudeaumania, from CBC Archives.

Expo 67
http://www.archives.ca/05/0533_e.html
A multimedia account of a visit to Expo 67 in Montreal.

RELATED READINGS

The following article in R. Douglas Francis and Donald B. Smith, eds., *Readings in Canadian History: Post-Confederation*, 6th ed. (Toronto: Nelson Thomson Learning, 2002), relates to a topic in this chapter: Jennifer Read, "'Let Us Heed the Voice of Youth': Laundry Detergents, Phosphates, and the Emergence of the Environmental Movement in Ontario," pp. 416–35.

BIBLIOGRAPHY

Many works listed in the bibliography of Chapter 20 also contain material on the 1960s. Books on the evolution of Canada's welfare state include Allan Moscovitch and Jim Albert, eds., *The 'Benevolent' State: The Growth of Welfare in Canada* (Toronto: Garamond Press, 1987); Penny E. Bryden, *Planners and Politicians: The Liberal Party and Social Policy, 1957–1968* (Montreal/Kingston: McGill-Queen's University Press, 1997); and Rodney S. Haddow, *Poverty Reform in Canada, 1958–1978: State and Class Influences on Policy Making* (Montreal/Kingston: McGill-Queen's University Press, 1993). Among studies of housing are John R. Miron, ed., *House, Home, and Community: Progress in Housing Canadians, 1945–1986* (Montreal/Kingston: McGill-Queen's University Press, 1993); and John C. Bacher, *Keeping to the Marketplace: The Evolution of Canadian Housing Policy* (Montreal/Kingston: McGill-Queen's University Press, 1993).

On higher education, see Paul Axelrod and John G. Reid, eds., *Youth, University and Canadian Society: Essays in the Social History of Higher Education* (Montreal/Kingston: McGill-Queen's University Press, 1989). For further study of Canadian literature, W. H. New, ed., *Encyclopedia of Literature in Canada* (Toronto: University of Toronto Press, 2002) is indispensable. Books on cultural policy include Gary Evans, *In the National Interest: A Chronicle of the National Film Board of Canada from 1949 to 1989* (Toronto: University of Toronto Press, 1991); Michael Dorland, *So Close to the State/s: The Emergence of Canadian Feature Film Policy* (Toronto: University of Toronto Press, 1998); Andrew Stewart and William H.N. Hull, *Canadian Television Policy and the Board of Broadcast Governors, 1958–1968* (Edmonton: University of Alberta Press, 1994); Ted Magder, *Canada's Hollywood: The Canadian State and Feature Films* (Toronto: University of Toronto Press, 1993); and Mary Vipond, *The Mass Media in Canada* (Toronto: James Lorimer, 1989). Sport history is discussed in Colin Howell, *Blood, Sweat, and Cheers: Sport and the Making of Modern Canada* (Toronto: University of Toronto Press, 2001).

On the role of women in politics see Sydney Sharpe, *The Gilded Ghetto: Women and Political Power in Canada* (Toronto: HarperCollins, 1994); Sylvia Bashevkin, *Toeing the Lines: Women and Party Politics in English Canada*, 2nd ed. (Toronto: Oxford University Press, 1993); and Linda Kealey and Joan Sangster, eds., *Beyond the Vote: Canadian Women and Politics* (Toronto: University of Toronto Press, 1989). How the media responded to the feminist movement is discussed in Barbara Freeman, *The Satellite Sex: The Media and Women's Issues in English Canada, 1966–1971* (Waterloo, ON: Wilfrid Laurier University Press, 2001). Valerie Korinek shows how one popular women's magazine viewed women's issues in *Roughing It in the Suburbs: Reading Chatelaine Magazine in the Fifties and the Sixties* (Toronto: University of Toronto Press, 2000). On birth control consult Angus McLaren and Arlene Tigar McLaren, *The Bedroom and the State: The Changing Practices and Politics of Contraception and Abortion in Canada, 1880–1980* (Toronto: McClelland & Stewart, 1986). Legal aspects of homosexuality are discussed in Bruce MacDougall, *Queer Judgments: Homosexuality, Expression, and the Courts in Canada* (Toronto: University of Toronto Press, 2000). Secret activities of the RCMP on university campuses are discussed in Steve Hewitt, *Spying 101: The RCMP's Secret Activities at Canadian Universities, 1917–1997* (Toronto: University of Toronto Press, 2002).

Among syntheses of labour history containing material on the 1960s are Desmond Morton with Terry Copp, *Working People: An Illustrated History of the Canadian Labour Movement*, 3rd ed. (Toronto: Summerhill Press, 1990); and Craig Heron, *The Canadian Labour Movement: A Short History*, rev. ed. (Toronto: James Lorimer, 1996). Politics in the 1960s is examined in J.L. Granatstein, *Canada, 1957–1967: The Years of Uncertainty and Innovation* (Toronto: McClelland & Stewart, 1986). Studies of prime ministers include Garrett Wilson and Kevin Wilson, *Diefenbaker for the Defence* (Toronto: James Lorimer, 1988); John English, *The Worldly Years: The Life of Lester Pearson*, vol. 2: *1949–1972* (Toronto: Knopf Canada, 1992); Norman Hilmer, ed., *Pearson: The Unlikely Gladiator* (Montreal/Kingston: McGill-Queen's University Press, 1999); and Stephen Clarkson and Christina McCall Newman, *Trudeau and Our Times*, vol. 1, *The Magnificent Obsession* (Toronto: McClelland & Stewart, 1990).

On aspects of Canada's international relations see John English and Norman Hillmer, eds., *Making a Difference? Canada's Foreign Policy in a Changing World Order* (Toronto: Lester, 1992). Studies of Canadian–American relations include J.L. Granatstein and Norman Hillmer, *For Better or For Worse: Canada and the United States to the 1990s* (Toronto: Copp Clark Pitman, 1991); and John Herd Thompson and Steven Randall, *Canada and the United States: Ambivalent Allies*, 3rd ed. (Montreal/Kingston: McGill-Queen's University Press, 2002).

CHAPTER 22

ABORIGINAL CANADA: WORLD WAR II TO THE PRESENT

Since 1950 the Native peoples have become the fastest-growing group in Canada. The birth rate among the Inuit and status Indians — those registered under the federal Indian Act — is the highest in the country. What a contrast with the situation immediately after Confederation, when the Aboriginal population continued to decline due to tuberculosis and other communicable diseases introduced by Europeans. As late as 1932, Diamond Jenness, the distinguished Canadian anthropologist, affirmed: "Doubtless all the tribes will disappear. Some will endure only a few years longer; others, like the Eskimos, may last several centuries."[1]

The growing perception after World War II that the Native peoples were not "vanishing" led to the development of a more positive attitude in the dominant society. Equally important, particularly from the 1930s onward, a new group of politically conscious Aboriginal leaders, with a knowledge of the larger society and an ability to articulate their demands in English or French, made their voices heard. The Indian resistance to the federal government's assimilationist "White Paper" of 1969 led to its withdrawal. Land claims began in the mid-1970s for over half of Canada. Successful political lobbying in the 1970s contributed to the inclusion of the Aboriginal peoples — Indians, Inuit, and Métis — in Canada's new Constitution in 1982. Widespread recognition of the concept of Aboriginal rights, including Native self-government, followed in the late 1980s and early 1990s. In 1999 the federal government created Nunavut, a separate political jurisdiction in the eastern Arctic, which the Inuit controlled due to their numerical dominance.

THE YALE–TORONTO CONFERENCE ON THE NORTH AMERICAN INDIAN

The University of Toronto and Yale Conference on the North American Indian that met in Toronto in 1939 symbolized the transition from the old to the new Canada on Native issues. Organized by Tom McIlwraith, the first academic anthropologist employed at a Canadian university (the University of Toronto), the conference was designed "to reveal the conditions today of the white man's Indian wards, and in a scientific, objective and sympathetic spirit, plan with them for their future." Over 70 Canadian and American government officials, missionaries, and academics attended. More importantly, thirteen invited Native people participated. It was the first conference ever held to discuss First Nations welfare and the first scholarly meeting to include Native delegates.

For nearly two weeks, the conference delegates discussed North American Native cultures, reserve economics, health, and education. Perhaps the most revealing information about Canada's Native peoples came from federal government officials who pointed out that, beginning in the mid-1930s, Canada's status Indian population had reversed its previous decline and was increasing annually by 1 percent, thanks to both an increase in the birth rate and a decline in the death rate. On the last day of the conference, delegates passed resolutions urging greater attention to "the psychological, social, and economic maladjustments of the Indian populations of the United States and Canada." They established a committee to oversee the publication of the conference's papers and the dissemination of information on North America's Native peoples.

Then a dramatic event occurred. The Native delegates broke from the main group and met separately to pass their own resolutions. They objected to government officials, missionaries, and non-Native sympathizers speaking for them. "We hereby go on record as hoping that the need for an All Indian Conference on Indian Affairs will be felt by Indian tribes, the delegates to such a conference be limited to *bona fide* Indian leaders actually living among the Indian people of the reservations and reserves, and further, that such a conference remain free of political, anthropological, missionary, administrative, or other domination." This appeal went largely

The delegates to the Yale–Toronto Conference on the North American Indian, Toronto, September 1939. This was the first conference held in Canada to discuss Native welfare and the first scholarly conference to include First Nations delegates.

Pringle and Booth/Courtesy of Ken Kidd, a delegate at the conference.

unheard by a Canadian public totally preoccupied by the entry of Canada into World War II, but in retrospect the conference was a turning point.

THE NATIVE PEOPLES IN WARTIME

During the war, the status Indian population experienced increased oppression. Acting against verbal promises at several treaty negotiations in western Canada, the federal government initially tried to include status Indians among those eligible for overseas military conscription. Other arbitrary wartime measures included the seizure of reserve lands, the transfer of reserve populations, and the revision of band membership lists. When, for example, the federal government decided in 1942 that it needed a military training facility on Lake Huron, it invoked the War Measures Act to appropriate Ontario's Stoney Point Reserve to establish Camp Ipperwash.

Financial exigency during the war also contributed to First Nations resentment. To save money and promote self-sufficiency, the Indian Affairs Branch unilaterally proposed a centralization plan designed to remove status Mi'kmaq (Micmac) in Nova Scotia from nineteen small reserves to two large inland ones. The abandoned reserves were to be sold. Only mounting Native opposition led to the cancellation of the proposal. Then, in northern Alberta, an Indian Affairs Branch official created havoc when he revised the membership lists in the Lesser Slave Lake agency to eliminate 700 individuals who he claimed were not "true Indians." First Nations reacted by working to strengthen their already existing political organization, the Indian Association of Alberta.

Such actions undermined the Indian Affairs Branch's credibility among the First Nations, as did the fact that the branch's 65 members included only two Native persons in 1944. Indeed, the war years proved demoralizing for the First Nations. Many enlisted in armed services during the war, but were denied benefits given to the other veterans. Furthermore they continued to be "wards of the state" without the right to vote. Still the period contributed to fostering a greater political consciousness among Native peoples.

THE ABORIGINAL PEOPLES OF THE NORTH

In the interwar years, First Nations people in sparsely populated areas in the North escaped the full weight of the Indian Act. The federal government paid little attention to such groups as the Dene in the Mackenzie River valley and the Cree in the James Bay area. During the war, however, the isolation ended for the northern First Nations, Métis, and Inuit. Thousands of armed-service personnel and civilians established military airstrips and radio stations in the North. Small communities arose around these posts. Furthermore, in the late 1940s, with the collapse of the fur market and the failure to meet the migrating caribou herds, starving Inuit depended on the federal government for help. Ottawa responded by flying hungry families to fur trading posts, where food supplies existed. The federal government also brought in nurses and doctors to look after the Inuit refugees coming off the land, and it built hospitals and schools, as well as living quarters. As soon as these non-Native medical personnel, administrators, and teachers arrived, even on a semi-permanent basis, the federal government built permanent installations, such as power plants, water and sewer systems, and roads. The small non-Native bureaucracy that administered the social-assistance programs gained enormous control over the Inuit.

For those Inuit who had tuberculosis or other communicable diseases, the government provided medical assistance, such as X-rays and immunization. Those patients requiring immediate hospitalization were sent south by plane or boat. By the 1950s, hundreds had been hospitalized and the Department of Health and Welfare had succeeded in lowering substantially the high mortality rate among the Inuit.

Ottawa now saw its task as bringing the Mackenzie valley First Nations to a level comparable to that of the Inuit in the eastern Arctic. In the Mackenzie valley, the Native peoples had not experienced the same economic collapse as the Inuit had after World War II. Moreover, they already lived in semi-permanent camps around Hudson's Bay Company posts and Christian missions. Ottawa replaced the mission schools with public schools and provided the same medical services and administrative help as in the eastern Arctic. The government clashed, however, with local chiefs and elders who resented its intrusion into their communities. Up to this time the First Nations in the Mackenzie valley had run their own affairs.

A NEW POSTWAR ATTITUDE TOWARD THE NATIVE PEOPLES

After World War II, Canadians developed a more positive attitude toward Native peoples. Several reasons explain this change. First, social scientists discredited earlier pseudoscientific race theories that had held certain "races" to be inherently inferior to others. Second, many Canadians learned through the media of the impoverished living conditions of the northern First Nations and Inuit. Improvements in water and especially air transportation brought even the most remote regions of the Arctic into the southern Canadian consciousness. Third, the expansion of the natural-resource frontier took southern Canadians into Aboriginal territory (a situation that brought Aboriginal land claims throughout northern Canada to the public's attention). Fourth, the decolonization movement in Asia and Africa and later the civil-rights movement in the United States in the 1950s and early 1960s contributed to a new consciousness of injustices to minorities, including the Native peoples. Most importantly, Aboriginal leaders now made their demands known. A number of demobilized First Nations veterans, for example, demanded freedom from tutelage, and recognition of their civil rights. Modern technology enabled the new Native leadership to communicate easily in a new common language, English, and, in parts of southern Quebec, French.

After the war, the Indian Association of Alberta campaigned to have Parliament review the Indian Act. Some veterans' organizations and church groups assisted Native political leaders in pressuring Ottawa to relax the powerful controls it exercised over the reserves. For the first time, Parliament listened. Several provincial Indian organizations participated in the hearings of the Joint Committee of the House of Commons and the Senate on the Indian Act, held from 1946 to 1948. Out of these deliberations came a new revision of the Indian Act in 1951.

The new Indian Act allowed band councils more authority. Women also gained the vote in band council elections. It lifted bans on the potlatch and Sun Dance, an important religious ceremony. Compulsory enfranchisement, by which male First Nations people could relinquish Indian status in return for full citizenship privileges, was swept away. Yet, the new Indian Act's underlying goal remained the assimilation of the status Indian. It made it easier for individuals to give up their Indian status. It included new provisions to allow the placement of First Nations children in integrated provincial schools.

By the 1970s, Ottawa had phased out most of the residential schools and had integrated First Nations children into provincially controlled programs. But integrated schooling did not prove entirely successful. Its shortcomings led a number of bands in the early 1970s to call for community control of their schools. Blue Quills, near St. Paul, Alberta, became the first band-controlled school in 1970. Others followed, and in 1973 the federal government endorsed Native-controlled schools.

Gradually the federal government softened its stance on local band government. In 1960, for example, the Walpole Island band council in southwestern Ontario assumed responsibility for road improvements and other public works on the reserve. Later, the same band council gained control over the administration of its own local affairs. Many bands in Ontario began to administer their own welfare services. Other bands created their own police forces, as Walpole Island did in 1967.

During the 1950s and early 1960s, the dominant society showed a greater sensitivity to some Aboriginal issues. Gradually the provinces granted the provincial franchise to status Indians. In 1960, Ottawa extended the right to vote in federal elections to all status Indians (at that time approximately three out of four could not vote in federal elections), without requiring First Nations people to give up their Indian status. A federally appointed commission reported in the mid-1960s that Native people occupied the lowest economic rung on Canada's economic ladder. The Hawthorn commission held in conclusion that "in addition to the normal rights and duties of citizenship, Indians possess certain rights as charter members of the Canadian community." After the publication of the report, Prime Minister Lester Pearson committed his government to revising the Indian Act, after prior consultation with First Nations people.

The federal government, which now adopted a more supportive role, helped to build a pavilion for the First Nations at Montreal's Expo 67. The Native organizers of the pavilion used the building to tell the story of Aboriginal Canada. At the entrance, a message greeted visitors: "The Indian people's destiny will be determined by them and our country, Canada, will be better for it." Inside, visitors saw, in bold script, statements such as "Give us the right to manage our own affairs" and "Help us preserve the moral values, the meaningful way of life, the inheritance of our forefathers." These anti-assimilationist messages announced the First Nations' political agenda for the remainder of the century.

FROM THE "WHITE PAPER" OF 1969 TO THE CONSTITUTION OF 1982

In 1969 the recently elected Liberal government of Pierre Trudeau inadvertently contributed to the Native resurgence. The Hawthorn Report had recommended that First Nations people be

Jean Chrétien, Minister of Indian Affairs, meeting with a delegation from the Indian Association of Alberta and other First Nations groups in Ottawa, June 1970. Prime Minister Pierre Trudeau is seated beside Jean Chrétien. The First Nations representatives have just presented the "Red Paper," their response to the government's controversial "White Paper."

Duncan Cameron/National Archives of Canada/PA-170161.

treated as "citizens plus." Trudeau's predecessor, Lester Pearson, had promised that the Indian Act would be revised after prior consultation with Indian people. But, without any meaningful prior consultation, the Trudeau administration now promoted an end to the Indian Act, to the reserves, to the concept of "citizens plus." First Nations people would be brought immediately into the mainstream society. In the "White Paper" on Indian policy, Minister of Indian Affairs Jean Chrétien called for the end of the Department of Indian Affairs, the repeal of the Indian Act, the elimination of reserves, and the transfer to the provinces of many of the federal government's responsibilities for Indian affairs. Trudeau also announced his government's refusal to negotiate land settlements for the roughly one-half of the country that was not under treaty.

Without delay, young educated First Nations leaders joined ranks with Native elders to oppose the government's position paper. Although unsatisfied with the colonial relationship imposed by the Indian Act, the First Nations leaders realized that the legislation did at least recognize their special constitutional status. Without the act, they risked being absorbed into the mainstream of non-Native Canadian society. The fact that the federal government began to provide core funding for First Nations political organizations in 1970 helped strengthen them. By forming a united front First Nations organizations succeeded in convincing the Liberal government to withdraw the White Paper in March 1971. The provincial and territorial Native political associations representing status Indians in Canada and the National Indian Brotherhood, founded in 1968, then began to work to secure the constitutional entrenchment of Aboriginal and treaty rights.

Assisting the Native activists in their cause was the decision of the Supreme Court of Canada in the *Nisga'a* case of 1973. Although it went against the Nisga'a on a legal technicality, the Supreme Court did agree that the First Nations held Aboriginal title to their lands. Thus the federal government was pressured into accepting comprehensive claims in the areas of Canada where treaties had not been signed, and accepting specific claims elsewhere. More limited than comprehensive land claims, specific claims usually relate to demands for compensation or the restitution of land or money on the basis of the unfulfilled terms of an existing treaty, or formal legal agreement with the government. In 1974, Ottawa established an Office of Native Claims, a branch of the Department of Indian Affairs and Northern Development, to rule on Aboriginal claims.

The first comprehensive land claim signed immediately after the enactment of the new federal policy in 1974 was the James Bay and Northern Quebec Agreement in 1975. By this treaty, the Cree and Inuit surrendered their Aboriginal rights to a huge area of 1 million square kilometres of land. In return, they gained ownership, in and around their communities, of over 14 000 km^2, as well as exclusive hunting, fishing, and trapping rights over 150 000 km^2. Both they and the general public would obtain equal access to the rest of the land. The Cree and the Inuit were also awarded $225 million over a period of 25 years. In 2002, the Grand Council of the Cree and the Quebec government reached an understanding to extend the original agreement. In exchange for permitting further hydro-electric development on the Rupert and Eastmain Rivers, the Cree will obtain payments valued at $3.5 billion over a fifty-year period. They also received important commitments relating to employment, land, and co-management of the region's resources.

The early and mid-1970s were marked by greater Native activism. In the United States the rise of the Red Power movement led to a series of confrontations. Canada also saw heightened unrest. In late 1971 Alberta First Nations began a six month sit-in at the Department of Indian Affairs offices in Edmonton to protest the inferior conditions at reserve schools. Ojibwa (Anishinabeg) occupied Anicinibe Park in Kenora, northwestern Ontario, in the summer of 1974, in a land-claim dispute. A Native caravan from Vancouver reached Parliament Hill in September 1974 to protest poor housing and social services on reserves, as well as land-claim issues.

The emergence of constitutional issues after the election of the Parti Québécois in Quebec in 1976 provided Canada's Aboriginal peoples with an opportunity for constitutional advancement. Among the Native political organizations which entered the constitutional debate were the National Indian Brotherhood (which became the Assembly of First Nations in 1982), the first permanent national organization for Status Indians; the recently-formed Native Council of Canada (now the Congress of Aboriginal Peoples), which represented Métis and off-reserve and non-status Indians; and the Inuit Tapirisat of Canada, the Inuit political organization. A strong campaign by Aboriginal groups led to the inclusion of Section 35 (2) in the Constitution of 1982 which gave constitutional protection for the first time to the "existing Aboriginal and treaty rights of the Aboriginal peoples of Canada." The new Constitution also identified the Métis, with the Indians and Inuit, as an Aboriginal people.

FIRST NATIONS POLITICAL DEMANDS IN THE 1980S AND 1990S

The definition of Aboriginal rights and the issue of self-government became the major constitutional questions for Aboriginal people in the 1980s and early 1990s. Yet, at a series of four subsequent meetings held between 1983 and 1987, the prime minister, the provincial premiers, and Native representatives failed to reach agreement either on the meaning of the phrase "Aboriginal rights" or on a definition of Native self-government. These meetings did, however, give Aboriginal issues a very high public profile. In 1983, the House of Commons Committee on

A Canadian soldier and a Native come face to face in a tense standoff at Kanesatake (Oka), Quebec, summer 1990.

CP Picture Archive/Shaney Komulainen.

Indian Self-Government in 1983 had endorsed the concept of full Native control over matters such as education, child welfare, health care, and band membership. For the first time in a federal document, the term "First Nation" was used.

With the end of the constitutional conferences on Aboriginal rights in 1987, the battleground between Native groups and the federal government shifted back to the courts. Since the mid-1980s, Supreme Court rulings have provided an expanding interpretation of Aboriginal and treaty rights. In *Guerin* (1984) the court established the concept of a trust-like, or "fiduciary," relationship between the Crown and the Aboriginal peoples. The federal government had a trust-like duty to act in the best interests of the First Nations it represented. The following year the judges in *Simon* (1985) ruled that Indian treaties must be given a "fair, large and liberal interpretation." In 1990 in the *Sparrow* case, the Supreme Court drew on the Constitutional Act of 1982 to draw up rules to restrict to a minimum government's infringement of Aboriginal and treaty rights.

At the four special constitutional conferences on Aboriginal issues in the mid-1980s the question of an Aboriginal right to self-government had remained unresolved. The federal government argued that First Nations self-government would be a right delegated from the Crown. The First Nations contended that it was an inherent right that they possessed from their historical occupation of what was now Canada. It would take another decade of discussion before the federal government in 1995 accepted the inherent right of self-government as a matter of policy. It then began negotiations with a number of First Nations to implement Aboriginal self-government in conjunction with existing federal and provincial jurisdictions.

The growing influence of the Aboriginal peoples was demonstrated in the failure of the Meech Lake Accord in 1990. The federal government and the provinces agreed in 1987 to respond to Quebec's constitutional demands, and the province's opposition to the 1982

Constitution. But the Meech Lake Accord omitted to address Aboriginal concerns. Elijah Harper, an Aboriginal MLA in the Manitoba legislature, managed, on a technical point, to delay Manitoba's ratification of the accord until the deadline for its approval was reached. Manitoba's (and Newfoundland's) failure to ratify the accord ensured its demise.

The Charlottetown Accord, a comprehensive agreement, followed. Unlike Meech it promised to address the constitutional concerns of the Aboriginal peoples as well as those of Quebec. Aboriginal leaders joined the federal and provincial and territorial leaders in negotiations. The accord promised recognition of the inherent Aboriginal right of self-government within Canada. It recognized Aboriginal governments as one of Canada's three orders of government. It opened the Senate and the House of Commons to Aboriginal representation. But Canadians had grown weary of constitutional discussions. The Charlottetown Accord failed to win majority support in the referendum in 1992, even in First Nations communities.

During the 1990s Native protests provided much of the momentum for recognition of Aboriginal issues. The inability of the federal government to settle the complex, two-centuries-old land claim of the Mohawks at Kanesatake (Oka) contributed to the outbreak of violence in the summer of 1990. The Mohawks resisted attempts by the town of Oka, 50 km west of Montreal, to extend a golf course over disputed lands. Barricades led to a shoot-out in which a Quebec provincial police constable died, and then to a 78-day armed stand-off between the Mohawks and the federal and Quebec governments. The Oka Crisis provided the catalyst for Ottawa to create a commission to study the condition of Aboriginal peoples.

THE ROYAL COMMISSION ON ABORIGINAL PEOPLES

The federal government established the Royal Commission on Aboriginal Peoples in April 1991. Four of its seven commissioners were Aboriginal. Its mandate was "to examine the economic, social and cultural situation of the Aboriginal peoples of this country." In 1996, the commissioners tabled their five-volume final report in the House of Commons. Their 440 recommendations covered a wide range of Aboriginal issues, but essentially all focussed on four major concerns: the need for a new relationship in Canada between Aboriginal and non-Aboriginal peoples; Aboriginal self-determination through self-government; economic self-sufficiency; and healing for Aboriginal peoples and communities. The report and its accompanying research papers constitute the most in-depth analysis ever undertaken on Aboriginal people in Canada.

In January 1998, after waiting fourteen months, the federal government finally issued its response in a document entitled *Gathering Strength: Canada's Aboriginal Action Plan*. Although the statement committed the federal government to a new approach to Aboriginal policy in Canada, it replied directly to only a few of the commission's recommendations. In general terms, Ottawa accepted the treaty relationship as the basis for Canada's relationships with First Nations. Second, it promised a more stable, long-term fiscal relationship with Aboriginal groups. Third, in future, it would increase efforts to prepare First Nations for self-government. Fourth, increased access would be given to land and resources. The federal government also agreed to set aside $350 million to support community-based healing initiatives for First Nations people affected by the legacy of Indian residential schools.

Currently the federal government is engaged in talks with the churches in the hope of reaching an agreement over the liability for abuses. At present over 11 500 former students have filed civil lawsuits that name the Government of Canada, church organizations, and former school employees. Ottawa has budgeted $1.7 billion to settle the claims. Another controversial issue involves the federal government's "First Governance Act," which attempts a massive reform of the Indian Act, but many First Nations leaders oppose the initiative as a flawed document that fine-tunes colonialism rather than replacing it.

Where Historians Disagree
The Debate over Indian Residential Schools, 1879–1986

For nearly a century a church–state run system of residential schools worked to assimilate First Nations children into the dominant Euro-Canadian society. Each of the four Christian denominations responsible — the Anglicans, Presbyterians, Roman Catholics, and the United Church — have in recent years formally apologized for their role in this assimilationist program. On January 7, 1998, the federal government also apologized in its Statement of Reconciliation:

> This system separated many children from their families and communities and prevented them from speaking their own languages and from learning about their heritage and cultures. In the worst cases, it left legacies of personal pain and distress that continue to reverberate in Aboriginal communities to this day. Tragically, some children were the victims of physical and sexual abuse.

Church historian John Webster Grant was one of the first academics to identify the issue. Without any attempt to hide the reality he explained that many First Nations people fought the forced assimilation: "Resistance to enrollment was widespread, and school burnings were more common than mere accidents would explain."[1] Financial handicaps, poor teachers, unhealthy buildings, few amenities, all plagued the system. Yet, he argues, in the face of these difficulties, in an age when non-Native Canadians were as culture-bound as any people of their own time or ours, some schools performed well.

"Despite its shortcomings, the residential school evidently met a need."[2]

Historian Scott Trevithick shows that the participants in the debate over residential schools "do not fit conveniently into two distinct and opposing camps, but rather find themselves spread out at various places across the playing field."[3] Another early contributor to the discussion in the 1980s was historian Celia Haig-Brown. From her study, rich in oral testimony, of the Kamloops Indian Residential School in central British Columbia, one gains a fuller understanding of residential schools. Reflecting her interviewees' vivid and painful memories she emphasizes "the injustice of the system

Cree children attending an Anglican Church school, Lac La Ronge, Saskatchewan, March 1945.
National Archives of Canada, Photo by Bud Glunz, PA-124110.

which attempted to control and to transform them."[4] Yet she points out: "Even with the controls already described well in place, the students found time and space to express themselves and to produce a separate culture of their own within the school."[5]

By 1990 the subject of residential schools began to enter into the general public's consciousness. The statement by Phil Fontaine, then chief of the Assembly of Manitoba Chiefs, that he had suffered sexual abuse as a student at a Manitoba residential school, broke other former students' silence. A number came forward to reveal their own stories of physical, sexual, and emotional abuse. The hearings of the Royal Commission on Aboriginal Peoples also helped publicize the Indian residential school system's weaknesses. Then, in 1996, J.R. Miller published an important study in which he notes that, at the high point of the Indian residential school system, in the early twentieth century, probably about one-third of the eligible Inuit and status Indians of school age attended.[6] He concludes: "It seems clear that the schools performed inadequately in most respects, and in a few areas, wrought profoundly destructive effects on many of their students."[7] For his part, historian John S. Milloy, who wrote a report for the Commission on residential schools, strongly criticized the church–state partnership for its assault on the well-being of the First Nations. Both groups' original good intentions paved the way to a form of absolute hell. "In thought and in deed the establishment of this school system was an act of profound cruelty rooted in non-Aboriginal pride and intolerance and in the certitude and insularity of purported cultural superiority."[8]

Much of the challenge of this topic for academic historians resides in the lack of consensus in the oral evidence. As J.R. Miller wrote: "The existence of former students who hold positive memories of residential school and many others who recall it as a living hell seriously complicates a later age's ability to reach a firm, overall assessment of the problem of abuse in these institutions." He concludes: "In a pathetic sense, that emotional confrontation is also a form of abuse perpetuated indirectly by the residential school system."[9]

---

[1] John Webster Grant, *Moon of Wintertime: Missionaries and the Indians of Canada in Encounter Since 1534* (Toronto: University of Toronto Press, 1984), p. 179.
[2] Ibid., p. 183.
[3] Scott Trevithick, "Native Residential Schooling in Canada: A Review of Literature," *The Canadian Journal of Native Studies*, 18, 1 (1998): 53.
[4] Celia Haig-Brown, *Resistance and Renewal: Surviving the Indian Residential School* (Vancouver: Tillacum Library, 1988), p. 115.
[5] Ibid., p. 88.
[6] J.R. Miller, *Shingwauk's Vision: A History of Native Residential Schools* (Toronto: University of Toronto Press, 1996), p. 142.
[7] Ibid., p.418.
[8] John S. Milloy, *'A National Crime': The Canadian Government and the Residential School System, 1879 to 1986* (Winnipeg: The University of Manitoba Press, 1999), p. 302.
[9] Miller, *Shingwauk's Vision*, pp. 341–342.

ABORIGINAL RIGHTS

 The 1990s marked the beginning of a treaty process in British Columbia. From its entry into Confederation in 1871 the province had refused to acknowledge that the Aboriginal peoples had any treaty rights or ancestral claims over traditional lands. In 1990 British Columbia made a historic change of policy and agreed to enter into treaty negotiations with First Nations groups. Parliament ratified the Nisga'a Treaty in 1999, the first comprehensive claim to be settled south of the Yukon and Northwest Territories since the James Bay Agreement in 1975. The Nisga'a obtained control over 2000 square kilometres of their territory, as well as nearly $120 million in compensation for their lost lands. Currently, approximately 50 First Nations are involved in negotiations to make similar agreements. British Columbia's Aboriginal groups might obtain firm title to about 5 percent of the province's land mass, an amount of land that currently corresponds to the Aboriginal proportion of the province's total population.

In 1997 in the *Delgamuukw* case the Supreme Court enlarged and clarified the definition of Aboriginal title in Canada. The court recognized in this British Columbian case that Aboriginal title could extend over large areas of traditional lands. The landmark decision also accepted the validity of using Aboriginal oral history and testimony from elders in cases involving Aboriginal title.

Advances have been made elsewhere in the 1990s. In the early 1990s the federal government negotiated a $450 million settlement in Saskatchewan for treaty land entitlement. The settlement will compensate for illegal losses of reservation lands in the province. It will also allow for the granting of additional lands to those communities entitled to larger land areas in their historic treaties.

Another confirmation of the growing legal and political recognition of Aboriginal rights came in 1999 with the Supreme Court's *Marshall* decision, which concluded that the peace and friendship treaties made in 1760–61 between the Mi'kmaq and the British gave the Mi'kmaq a treaty right to a "moderate livelihood" in the Atlantic commercial fishery. Ottawa's continued attempt to try to regulate the Mi'kmaq fishery resulted in sporadic violence in the 2000 and 2001 fishing seasons, particularly at the Mi'kmaq community of Burnt Church, in New Brunswick's Miramichi Bay.

Contemporary Aboriginal issues abound. The claim of the Cree of Lubicon Lake in northern Alberta still remains unresolved. Geographical remoteness kept this community out of Treaty Eight signed in 1899. The Cree of Lubicon Lake have taken their case to the United Nations. But the community's distance from major southern urban centres has denied its claim the same attention as Oka received. The breakdown in negotiations in the 1990s came over the nature of the claim. The federal government will recognize the claim only as an unfulfilled treaty entitlement, a specific claim, based on Treaty Eight. In contrast, the Cree of Lubicon Lake argue that they have unextinguished Aboriginal title and consequently a comprehensive claim. They seek a modern-day treaty similar to that of the James Bay Cree or the Nisga'a in British Columbia.

Land-claims issues remain contentious. First Nations groups contend that the whole federal claims-resolution process is unfair. Ottawa sets the rules and controls the agenda. Under the existing system, Aboriginal communities lacking sufficient economic resources must obtain research and legal funds from the same government that will decide whether or not to accept their claim for negotiation.

The danger of violence over unresolved land-claims issues remains very real, as Oka showed in 1990. Five years after Oka, a land-claim dispute in Ontario over an Aboriginal burial site at Ipperwash Provincial Park led to an incident in which an Ojibwa protester was killed. Another confrontation occurred in British Columbia that same summer, at Gustafsen Lake, where First Nations individuals claimed the private ranchland they occupied was a sacred site. Attempts to negotiate peace with the militants failed. During a police operation that followed, shots were exchanged and arrests were made, but there were no casualties. Twenty-one militants received sentences.

ABORIGINAL CANADA IN THE 1980s AND 1990s

The findings of the Royal Commission on Aboriginal Peoples in the mid-1990s confirmed the continuing economic and social inequality of the Native peoples in Canada. For nearly one-half of the registered Indians living off the reserves, the quality of life remains substantially below that of the average non-Native Canadian.

Before World War II, nearly all First Nations people lived in rural areas. Then, large numbers migrated to cities in search of industrial jobs. Many experienced discrimination, from the refusal of accommodation to discrimination in hiring processes. Those who lacked academic and vocational credentials experienced the greatest difficulties. Although Native friendship centres did help individuals adjust to urban life, they could not alter economic conditions.

Great challenges remain. The life expectancy of a registered Indian remains about 6 years shorter than for the general Canadian population. Tuberculosis and other diseases continue to ravage many First Nations communities. Equally worrisome, as Marianne O. Nielsen points out, Canada's Aboriginal population is "seriously and tragically overrepresented among the inmates incarcerated in federal and provincial correctional institutions."[2]

Yet, on the positive side, a number of improvements have been made. The number of individuals identifying themselves as Aboriginal has increased. According to the 2001 census there were approximately 610 000 Indians, 290 000 Métis and non-status Indians, and 45 000 Inuit in Canada, or over 3 percent of Canada's total population, far more than in the 1996 census. Natural increase alone cannot explain such rapid growth. It appears that many more individuals now identify with their Aboriginal ancestry, indicating an increased pride in their heritage.

"IT'S ALL VERY WELL TO ACCUSE THE JUSTICE SYSTEM OF FAILING NATIVES.... BUT WHERE'S YOUR PROOF."

This cartoon captures the reality of the situation facing many Native people in the Canadian judicial system.

Malcom Mayes, *Edmonton Journal*, March 28, 1991, p. A22.

Education is another area in which significant improvement has occurred. In 1995 the federal government published data that showed that almost three-quarters of status Indian students reached Grade 12, compared to only one-fifth in 1970. Similarly the number of status Indians and Inuit in post-secondary education has jumped from 4500 in 1970 to 27 000 in 2001.

Since 1975, numerous Native authors, artists, and performers have emerged. Writers such as Maria Campbell, Thomson Highway, and Basil Johnston have achieved prominence. They join a growing number of Native artists, such as Robert Davidson, Norval Morrisseau, Daphne Odjig, Bill Reid, and Allen Sapp, who have used art to strengthen and affirm their Aboriginal identity. Several Inuit artists enjoy a world-wide reputation. The musical group Kashtin and Inuit singer Susan Aglukark gained notoriety in popular music. Tom Jackson achieved a prominent role in both music and acting. Architect Douglas Cardinal won numerous international awards for his work. He designed the Canadian Museum of Civilization in Hull, Quebec, and the National Museum of the American Indian in Washington, D.C. Advancement has occurred on other fronts as well. Over the past decade Aboriginal people have served in many important administrative posts, including the CBC board of directors (John Kim Bell), ombudsman of Ontario (Roberta Jamieson), the lieutenant-governor of Ontario (James Barteleman), and chancellor of Trent University (Mary Simon). Annually the National Aboriginal Achievement Awards have recognized the successes of Aboriginal people in Canada.

Economic progress has been made in a number of communities. The fact that some First Nations and Inuit people have gained ownership over huge chunks of territory, land where

Native elder Elmer Courchene performs a "cleansing ceremony" at Prime Minister Paul Martin's swearing-in, December 2003.

CP Picture Archive/Jonathan Hayward.

resource companies have huge investments, has helped. Oil and gas have provided supplementary income to some First Nations communities. A few others have obtained a measure of economic self-sufficiency from running casinos. Tourism and successful small businesses have also helped. An entrepreneurial class is emerging. But great challenges remain. Large numbers of status Indians have left their reserves to escape their depressed economic conditions. Many of the over 2350 reserves (and many rural communities of non-status Indians and Métis) are very small, scattered, and distant from large urban areas, and they lack the resources and the necessary infrastructure to sustain their increasing populations.

Since the mid-1980s the number of status Indians has increased substantially on account of the passage of Bill C-31 in 1985. It restored Indian status to all Native women who requested it, in particular to those women who had married non-Indians and subsequently lost their status under the Indian Act. It also gave status to their immediate descendants, increasing the number of registered Indians by 115 000 from 1985 to 2001. Reinstatement as a status Indian entitled the individual to receive free medical care, subsidies for housing and higher education, and exemption from all federal and provincial taxation on monies earned on any reserve. Those gaining membership in a specific Indian band (many bands now control their own individual membership) obtain a share of the band's assets, the right to reside on the band's reserve, all hunting and fishing rights, eligibility for federal loans and grants to establish reserve businesses, and free schooling on the reserve.

Women play a very prominent role in today's First Nations communities. Of the 625 communities represented by the Assembly of First Nations, over one hundred are led by female Aboriginal chiefs. Women are also very prominent in their communities as band councillors. In the non-political sector many women work as teachers and social workers in their communities.

THE MÉTIS, THE INUIT, AND THE FEDERAL GOVERNMENT

The Métis position differs from that of status Indians. The federal government has maintained that Canada's obligations to the Métis ended once it had dealt with the Métis land claim under the Manitoba Act and issued land allowances (or the money equivalent) to the Métis in the North-West Territories in 1885 and in 1899–1900. The federal government contends that the provinces have responsibility for the Métis. A high point of the Métis's political struggle for recognition came when they succeeded in achieving identification in the Constitution Act of 1982 as an Aboriginal people. One of the difficulties of describing the Métis, however, lies in the lack of an easy definition of Métis ethnicity. Both the Native Council of Canada and the Métis National Council, formed in 1983 to represent the five Métis provincial organizations west of Quebec, participated in the Charlottetown Accord discussions in 1992.

Of the three Native groups, the Inuit have the best chance of retaining control of their lands, because they constitute over three-quarters of the population in the eastern Arctic. Due to the remoteness of the area and, from a southerner's perspective, the severity of its climate, the Inuit will probably always be the majority on the treeless northern tundra. Nunavut (meaning "our land" in Inuktitut), created in 1999, is now Canada's third territory.

THE ABORIGINAL NORTH SINCE THE 1970s

The northern First Nations and Inuit have contributed greatly to the placing of Aboriginal issues on the public-policy agenda. Native political awareness arose in the Yukon in the late 1960s when Elijah Smith, the late chief of the Champagne Aishihik First Nations, urged his people to start looking for guarantees of their rights to their homeland. In the Yukon, and indeed throughout Canada, a new generation of bilingual Native leaders came forward to fight for

Aboriginal land claims and an end to the federal government's assimilationist policies. In 1973, the Yukon Native Brotherhood began formal talks with the federal government about unsurrendered Aboriginal rights in the Yukon.

Aboriginal demands for political control in the neighbouring Northwest Territories date back to Canada's centennial activities in 1967, when the federal government brought communities in the Mackenzie valley together to celebrate the event. In effect, these gatherings helped to bring about a new political awareness and Native pride. Discussions begun in 1968 resulted in the formation of the first territorial Aboriginal organization, the Indian Brotherhood of the Northwest Territories, later called the Dene Nation. In 1970, the Committee for the Original Peoples' Entitlement (COPE) was formed in Inuvik to protect the interests of the Inuit in the Mackenzie Delta — or the Inuvialuit, as the Inuit of the western Arctic refer to themselves. In 1971 an Inuit organizing committee formed the Inuit Tapirisat of Canada, a pan-Inuit organization with a mandate to address questions of northern development and to work to preserve Inuit culture. COPE became one of the regional associations affiliated with the Inuit Tapirisat of Canada. Later, the Inuit of the eastern and central Arctic established the Tungavik Federation of Nunavut to represent their specific regional concerns. Then, in 1973, the Métis formed their own association, the Métis Association of the Northwest Territories, which eventually joined with the Dene Nation to submit a joint land claim.

The Berger Inquiry, headed by Judge Thomas Berger in the mid-1970s, brought notoriety to First Nations and Inuit concerns. In 1972, the building of a Canadian pipeline to carry American oil and gas from the vast Prudhoe Bay field on the northeastern coast of Alaska south through the Mackenzie valley seemed a certainty — until a commission was set up to investigate its feasibility. Berger undertook a free-ranging and comprehensive environmental, social, and cultural impact study, holding community hearings in settlements potentially affected by the pipeline. His report called for the prior settlement of Native land claims and a ten-year delay on the development of the Mackenzie valley pipeline. The report eloquently conveyed the Native peoples' conviction that the North was their own distinct homeland, and not simply a resource frontier for southern Canada. The National Energy Board, the national regulatory body, also rejected the proposed development in the Mackenzie valley. Only in the early 1980s was a pipeline built, and then only half-way up the valley, to Norman Wells.

NUNAVUT AND DENENDEH

In 1979, the Aboriginal majority in the legislative assembly of the Northwest Territories endorsed the proposed division of the territories. The government of the Northwest Territories held a plebiscite on the issue in 1982, in which 56 percent of the votes cast favoured division. An Inuit constitutional forum representing Nunavut and a second forum representing the western district, or Denendeh, a northern Athapaskan word meaning "land of the people," were formed to discuss how the territorial division might be accomplished. A major stumbling block became the proposed border between the two jurisdictions. To whom would the Inuvialuit, the Inuit of the western Arctic, adhere?

Despite blood ties with their fellow Inuit in the east, the Inuvialuit decided to keep their economic links with the west. The adherence of the western Arctic, rich in newly discovered oil and gas potential, to Denendeh greatly pleased the Dene and the Métis. The addition of the 2500 Inuvialuit helped raise the Native population of Denendeh in 1982 to near-equality (15 000) with that of the non-Native population (17 000). In 1987, leaders of the two constitutional forums confirmed in Iqaluit the decision to divide the Northwest Territories. Subsequently the Northwest Territories legislative assembly and the federal government approved the territorial division, which occurred on April 1, 1999.

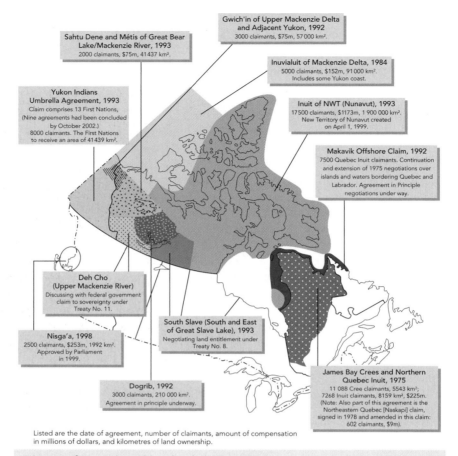

Gwich'in of Upper Mackenzie Delta and Adjacent Yukon, 1992
3000 claimants, $75m, 57 000 km².

Sahtu Dene and Métis of Great Bear Lake/Mackenzie River, 1993
2000 claimants, $75m, 41 437 km².

Inuvialuit of Mackenzie Delta, 1984
5000 claimants, $152m, 91 000 km². Includes some Yukon coast.

Yukon Indians Umbrella Agreement, 1993
Claim comprises 13 First Nations, (Nine agreements had been concluded by October 2002.) 8000 claimants. The First Nations to receive an area of 41 439 km².

Inuit of NWT (Nunavut), 1993
17 500 claimants, $1173m, 1 900 000 km². New Territory of Nunavut created on April 1, 1999.

Makavik Offshore Claim, 1992
7500 Quebec Inuit claimants. Continuation and extension of 1975 negotiations over islands and waters bordering Quebec and Labrador. Agreement in Principle negotiations under way.

Deh Cho (Upper Mackenzie River)
Discussing with federal government claim to sovereignty under Treaty No. 11.

Nisga'a, 1998
2500 claimants, $253m, 1992 km². Approved by Parliament in 1999.

South Slave (South and East of Great Slave Lake), 1993
Negotiating land entitlement under Treaty No. 8.

Dogrib, 1992
3000 claimants, 210 000 km². Agreement in principle underway.

James Bay Crees and Northern Quebec Inuit, 1975
11 088 Cree claimants, 5543 km²; 7268 Inuit claimants, 8159 km², $225m. (Note: Also part of this agreement is the Northeastern Quebec [Naskapi] claim, signed in 1978 and amended in this claim: 602 claimants, $9m).

Listed are the date of agreement, number of claimants, amount of compensation in millions of dollars, and kilometres of land ownership.

Status of several northern land claims in 2000.

Source: Based on *Compass* (November/December 1994): 16. Data from *Arctic Circle* (November/December 1990): 20–21; Department of Indian and Northern Affairs, *Information Sheet*, no. 59 (March 1994). Indian and Northern Affairs Canada, http://www.inac.gc.ca/subject/claims/comp/briem.html (June 15, 1999) and http://www.inac.gc.ca/news/may99/99106bkl.html (June 15, 1999); Northern News Service Online, http://www.nnsl.com/ops/claims.html; Nunavut Planning Commission, http://npc.nunavut.ca/eng/nunavut/general.html.

The population of the Northwest Territories consisted in the late 1990s of approximately 50 000 people, split almost equally into three groups: Inuit and Inuvialuit, First Nations and Métis, and non-Natives. What is remarkable is the speed with which the Aboriginal people have taken control of the political structures. In 1991, the commissioner of the Northwest Territories was a Métis; his deputy commissioner, an Inuk (Inuk is the singular of Inuit); and the government leader, a non-Native. The previous two government leaders were a Métis and a First Nations individual. Many Aboriginal people now fill senior administrative posts. Native self-government, the goal of the southern Aboriginal people, is at least partially a reality in the Northwest Territories, and now in Nunavut as well.

Nunavut might well strengthen Canada's sovereignty in the Arctic, as Canada's claims to the Northwest Passage are based largely on the Inuit's use and occupancy of the area. The voyages through the waters of the Canadian Arctic Archipelago by an American oil tanker in 1969, and by an American icebreaker in 1985, awakened Canadians to the uncertain status of their northern waters. The rapid advance of global warming has led to suggestions that the thinning of the ice cover in the Northwest Passage, if it continues, could make the Passage a viable commercial shipping route.

In the western Arctic in 1984, COPE, the political organization of the Inuvialuit, signed the first comprehensive settlement with the federal government in the Yukon and the Northwest Territories. In return for surrendering their claim to the title of approximately 345 000km^2 of land, the Inuvialuit obtained title to about 90 000 km^2 (an area larger than New Brunswick), including subsurface mineral rights for 13 000 km^2 of this area. They also received $152 million (in 1984 dollars) in financial compensation.

By the terms of a tentative agreement between the federal government and the Council of Yukon Indians that was reached in 1994 after lengthy negotiations, the Yukon's First Nations bands would retain nearly 9 percent of the territory's land mass. In the land-claim settlement, they would also receive approximately $250 million (in 1989 dollars) in cash over a fifteen-year period.

In 1990, the First Nations and Métis of the Mackenzie valley area signed a tentative land-claim agreement. Had both Native groups ratified the agreement, they would have received surface title to an area one-third the size of Alberta and $500 million in cash. Later in the year, however, some individuals rejected what is known as the extinguishment clause in the "agreement-in-principle." Three of the five regional groups believed that the clause required them to give up all treaty and Aboriginal rights, and they consequently refused to ratify the agreement. In late 1990, the federal government announced that it would negotiate new claims with each of the regions in the Native territory separately. By 2003, Parliament had settled three of the five regions' land claims.

In the eastern and central Arctic, the Tungavik Federation of Nunavut and the federal government reached an agreement-in-principle in 1990. Three years later, they signed a land-claim settlement that gave the Inuit absolute ownership of parcels of land totalling approximately 350 000 km^2, a territory roughly one-half the size of the province of Saskatchewan. They also received $580 million for relinquishing their Aboriginal claim to 2 million square kilometres, an area twice the size of the province of Ontario. In 1993, Parliament passed the Nunavut Land Claims Agreement which, in conjunction with the act to create the territory of Nunavut, redrew the map of Canada in April 1999.

Two-thirds of a century ago Aboriginal issues rarely entered into the consciousness of non-Native Canadians. Few Native people lived in cities. Government paid little attention to national resource expansion into northern Native-dominated areas of Canada. Treaty rights received little attention. Canadian history texts began with the Europeans' arrival in North America.

While social and economic inequalities persist for many Aboriginal people, improvements have been made. Aboriginal and treaty rights gained protection in the Canadian Constitution of 1982. The Native population has ceased declining and is now growing at about twice the overall Canadian rate. At universities and colleges the number of Aboriginal students has soared. Aboriginal people have gained a new political consciousness while the attitudes of many non-Native Canadians toward Native peoples have changed markedly.

NOTES

1. Diamond Jenness, *The Indians of Canada* (Ottawa: King's Printer, 1932), p. 264.
2. Marianne O. Nielsen, "Introduction," in Robert A. Silverman and Marianne O. Nielsen, eds., *Aboriginal Peoples and Canadian Criminal Justice* (Toronto: Harcourt Brace, 1994), p. 3.

LINKING TO THE PAST

Aboriginal Links for Canada and the United States
http://www.bloorstreet.com/300block/aborcan.htm

This comprehensive site features hundreds of links to and resources about or by Aboriginal peoples.

The Indian Act
http://laws.justice.gc.ca/en/I-5/

The full text of the current Indian Act from the Department of Justice. Scan through the text to find some of the major revisions made in 1951.

Indian Claims Commission
http://www.indianclaims.ca

Reports, publications, and latest news related to Native claims throughout Canada.

Assembly of First Nations
http://www.afn.ca

Extensive information on many issues affecting First Nations peoples. Go to "Treaties and Lands" for up-to-date information about claims and treaty negotiations.

Royal Commission on Aboriginal Peoples
http://www.ainc-inac.gc.ca/ch/rcap/index_e.html

Highlights from the *Report of the Royal Commission on Aboriginal Peoples*. See also "Forging a New Relationship: Proceedings of the Conference on the Report of the Royal Commission on Aboriginal Peoples: at http://www.misc-iecm.mcgill.ca/EN/publications/cp.html.

Agreements
http://www.ainc-inac.gc.ca/pr/agr/index_e.html

In-depth information on recent treaties, self-government and land-claim agreements, agreements-in-principle and more, from Indian and Northern Affairs Canada.

RELATED READINGS

R. Douglas Francis and Donald B. Smith, eds., *Readings in Canadian History: Post-Confederation*, 6th ed. (Toronto: Nelson Thomson Learning, 2002), contains the following article relevant to this chapter: Tony Hall, "A Note on Canadian Treaties," pp. 474–479.

BIBLIOGRAPHY

Recent surveys of the history of Aboriginal Canada include Olive Patricia Dickason, *Canada's First Nations: A History of Founding Peoples from Earliest Times*, 3rd ed. (Toronto: Oxford University Press, 2002); and Arthur J. Ray, *I Have Lived Here Since the World Began: An Illustrated History of Canada's Native People* (Toronto: Key Porter, 1996). Edward S. Rogers and Donald B. Smith, eds., *Aboriginal Ontario* (Toronto: Dundurn Press, 1994) looks at the history of the First Nations in Ontario.

Studies of Canadian Indian policy include E. Brian Titley, *A Narrow Vision: Duncan Campbell Scott and the Administration of Indian Affairs in Canada* (Vancouver: University of British Columbia Press, 1986); and J.R. Miller, *Skyscrapers Hide the Heavens: A History of Indian–White Relations in Canada*, 3rd ed. (Toronto: University of Toronto Press, 2000). Harold Cardinal, *The Unjust Society: The Tragedy of Canada's Indians* (Edmonton: Hurtig, 1969; and Vancouver: Douglas and McIntyre, 1999), is a Cree's indictment of Canadian Indian policy.

Aboriginal literature is reviewed by Penny Petrone in *Native Literature in Canada: From the Oral Tradition to the Present* (Toronto: Oxford University Press, 1990). On the sensitive question of Indian residential schools see J.R. Miller, *Shingwauk's Vision* (Toronto: University of Toronto Press, 1996); and John S. Milloy, *'A National Crime': The Canadian Government and the Residential School System, 1879 to 1986* (Winnipeg: University of Manitoba Press, 1999).

Four recent studies provide overviews of contemporary conditions for Native people in Canada: James S. Frideres and René R. Gadacz, *Aboriginal Peoples in Canada: Contemporary Conflicts*, 6th ed. (Toronto: Prentice-Hall, 2001); J. Rick Ponting, ed., *First Nations in Canada: Perspectives on Opportunity, Empowerment, and Self-Determination* (Toronto: McGraw-Hill Ryerson, 1997); David Long and Olive Patricia Dickason, eds., *Visions of the Heart,* 2nd ed. (Toronto: Harcourt Canada, 2000); and John Steckley and Bryan D. Cummins, eds., *Full Circle: Canada's First Nations* (Toronto: Prentice Hall, 2001). For recent treatments of contemporary Aboriginal and non-Aboriginal relations in Canada consult Alan C. Cairns, *Citizens Plus: Aboriginal Peoples and the Canadian State* (Vancouver: UBC Press, 2000); and Tom Flanagan, *First Nations? Second Thoughts* (Montreal/Kingston: McGill-Queen's University Press, 2000).

On the Métis, see D. Bruce Sealey and Antoine S. Lussier, *The Métis: Canada's Forgotten People* (Winnipeg: Manitoba Métis Federation Press, 1975), pp. 143–94, and Donald Purich, *The Métis* (Toronto: James Lorimer, 1988). Ethnographic background of the Native peoples of the Yukon and the Northwest Territories is provided in the following volumes of the *Handbook of North American Indians*: vol. 5, *The Arctic*, edited by David Damas (Washington: Smithsonian Institute, 1984) introduces the Inuit; and vol. 6, *The Subarctic*, edited by June Helm (Washington: Smithsonian Institute, 1984) introduces the Dene of the Northwest Territories. For discussions of Nunavut see Donald Purich, *The Inuit and Their Land: The Story of Nunavut* (Toronto: James Lorimer, 1992); R. Quinn Duffy, *The Road to Nunavut* (Montreal/Kingston: McGill-Queen's University Press, 1988); and John Merritt et al., *Nunavut: Political Choices and Manifest Destiny* (Ottawa: Canadian Arctic Resources Committee, 1989).

Overviews of the history of the North include Morris Zaslow, *The Northward Expansion of Canada, 1914–1967* (Toronto: McClelland & Stewart, 1988); and William R. Morrison, *True North: The Yukon and Northwest Territories* (Toronto: Oxford University Press, 1998). Mark Dickerson looks at political developments in the Northwest Territories in *Whose North: Political Change, Political Development and Self-Government in the Northwest Territories* (Vancouver: University of British Columbia Press, 1992). Post–World War II developments are reviewed in Shelagh D. Grant, *Sovereignty or Security: Government Policy in the Canadian North, 1936–1950* (Vancouver: University of British Columbia Press, 1988); and John David Hamilton, *Arctic Revolution: Social Change in the Northwest Territories, 1935–1994* (Toronto: Dundurn Press, 1994).

On Aboriginal politics see J. Rick Ponting, ed., *Arduous Journey: Canadian Indians and Decolonization* (Toronto: McClelland & Stewart, 1986). Material on Aboriginal self-government is available in John H. Hylton, ed., *Aboriginal Self-Government in Canada*, 2nd ed. (Saskatoon: Purich Publishing, 1999); Dan Smith, *The Seventh Fire: The Struggle for Aboriginal Government* (Toronto: Key Porter, 1993); and John Bird, Lorraine Land, and Murray Macadam, eds., *Nation to Nation: Aboriginal Sovereignty and the Future of Canada* (Toronto: Irwin, 2002). For land issues, see William R. Morrison, *A Survey of the History and Claims of the Native Peoples of Northern Canada* (Ottawa: Indian and Northern Affairs Canada, 1983); and Ken Coates, ed., *Aboriginal Land Claims in Canada: A Regional Perspective* (Toronto: Copp Clark Pitman, 1992). On the importance of the Supreme Court of Canada's *Marshall* decision in 1999, see Ken S. Coates, *The Marshall Decision and Native Rights* (Montreal/Kingston: McGill-Queen's University Press, 2000). British Columbia's Nisga'a Treaty is discussed in *The World Is Our Witness: The Historic Journey of the Nisga'a into Canada* (Calgary: Fifth House, 2000). The most complete account of the confrontation at Oka is Geoffrey York and Loreen Pindera, *People of the Pines: The Warriors and the Legacy of Oka* (Toronto: Little, Brown, 1992).

Q uebec underwent an era of rapid change in the years after 1960, as the province evolved into a modern, dynamic, secular society. In many ways, Quebec seemed to become more like other regions of North America. Yet, at the same time, most French-speaking Quebeckers thought it important that their society reinforce its unique linguistic and cultural character.

Most historians argue that the processes of modernization and secularization began well before 1960, during World War II and even earlier. What changed in 1960 was that a new government showed a readiness to make important reforms. An increasingly interventionist Quebec state became a catalyst for change in nearly all sectors of activity, from the economy and education to health and culture. At the same time, just as was the case elsewhere in the western world, many Quebeckers demanded and welcomed change.

What undoubtedly attracted outside attention to Quebec after 1960 was the powerful resurgence of nationalism in the province and the profound implications it had for the rest of Canada. When francophones in Quebec complained of being second-class citizens and sought increased recognition for the French language within the federal government and for the French-speaking minorities outside Quebec, English-speaking Canadians had to respond. When various political movements and parties vied with one another in claiming greater political autonomy for Quebec — and, in some cases, even sought outright independence — Canada's future appeared to be in doubt. In this regard, the aspirations of many Quebeckers appeared threatening.

QUEBEC AFTER WORLD WAR II

During the period 1945–60, Quebec changed in many respects. Quebec's population, like Canada's, increased rapidly, partly because of an influx of immigrants, but most of all due to a sharply increased birth rate. The province also underwent rapid economic growth as investment — much of it foreign — accelerated. The United States not only provided a market, it also supplied development capital for resource industries such as mining. Employment in the principal manufacturing industries also rose significantly, but the major gains in jobs came in the service industries. Thanks to the booming economy, Quebeckers who, like other Canadians, had endured the sacrifices of depression and war now enjoyed greater prosperity.

Traditional ideas and values began to give way. Religious practice declined, particularly in Montreal. Radio and, especially, television introduced new ideas, new norms. As historian Susan Mann explains, "Television brought the world, no longer filtered by press, priest, or politician, into Quebec's kitchens and living rooms."[1] It was incontestably a subversive influence.

Amid these changes, the very conservative Union Nationale government of Maurice Duplessis, supported by traditional elites, emphasized the importance of religious values and of respect for the established order. The Duplessis government, which began an unbroken sixteen-year reign in 1944, favoured private enterprise, encouraged the entry of foreign (largely American) capital, and kept taxes low. It built roads and bridges, especially in election years, and aided small-scale farmers, from whom it derived its firmest electoral support.

Duplessis's policies alienated Quebeckers who were committed to social change. The premier opposed militant union activity because he believed it deterred investment and brought social disorder. As a result, his government designed labour legislation to limit strikes, and even occasionally used the provincial police to protect strikebreakers or break up demonstrations. It set a low minimum wage for non-unionized workers, which affected large numbers of working women and immigrants.

OPPOSITION TO DUPLESSIS

In the 1950s, Duplessis's opponents became increasingly vocal. They included political foes, union leaders, a few members of the clergy, and the newspaper *Le Devoir*, as well as intellectuals such as Pierre Elliott Trudeau. Although all wanted a more liberal, modern Quebec, these critics differed considerably in their views on nationalism. Some, like Trudeau, viewed nationalism as necessarily conservative and reactionary, and resulting only in ethnic conflict. Others, among them journalist André Laurendeau, who later was co-chair of the Royal Commission on Bilingualism and Biculturalism, saw nationalism as a potentially progressive force.

Duplessis's adversaries also attacked the Union Nationale's corrupt political and electoral behaviour. They showed how the party machine shamelessly extorted money from commercial establishments and entrepreneurs throughout the province, and then used it to buy political support so as to ensure re-election. Election day witnessed such abuses as stuffed ballot boxes and police intervention in favour of government candidates.

Progressive elements inside and outside the Roman Catholic church grew restive as the church hierarchy uncritically supported Duplessis in return for subsidies for church schools, hospitals, and social agencies. As well, critics censured the government for "reactionary" attitudes in labour relations, education, and health. Some also claimed that the government's economic-development policies resulted in a virtual giveaway of the province's natural resources to foreigners. Others blamed Duplessis for his obstinate refusal to accept federal money to finance necessary social and educational programs. They also decried the Union Nationale's neglect of urban Quebec, a failure made possible by the government's refusal to revise an outdated

Premier Maurice Duplessis, third from left at the front, at the dedication of Ste-Thérèse Bridge, August 18, 1946. To the right, the Most Rev. Joseph Charbonneau. Church and state co-operated for the mutual benefit of each other.

National Archives of Canada/*The Gazette*/C-53641.

electoral map that blatantly favoured rural areas. And they deplored *le chef's* attacks on the civil liberties of such groups as Jehovah's Witnesses, who were fined and imprisoned for distributing their brochures on the streets.

A Re-evaluation of the Duplessis Era

In their generally harsh assessment of the Duplessis record, critics often ignored what could be considered mitigating circumstances. Patronage, although rife in the Duplessis regime, had been endemic in Canadian political life at all levels of government from the country's birth. The premier's refusal of federal funds for roads, universities, and other programs appeared negative, but how else could he fight Ottawa's intrusions into areas of provincial jurisdiction? Even Pierre Trudeau supported Duplessis's refusal to accept federal grants for higher education. Duplessis did welcome foreign capital, just as his Liberal predecessors had done. But such investment provided jobs and opened up new areas of the province for development. The government's spending policies were admittedly conservative, but they made it possible to keep taxes and debts low.

Even more telling is the fact that the Union Nationale enjoyed very substantial public support, winning four consecutive elections between 1944 and 1956. Even in 1960, a tiny shift of votes would have assured the Union Nationale's re-election. Yet by this time Duplessis, who died in 1959, and Paul Sauvé, his popular, reform-minded successor, who died after scarcely three months in office, were gone, and the once-powerful party appeared a spent force compared with the Liberals, who offered a capable new leader, a dynamic team, and a revitalized program. Perhaps many of those who, in the midst of the Quiet Revolution, viewed the Duplessis era as Quebec's *grande noirceur*, or "Dark Ages," tended to accentuate the sombre realities of the Union Nationale years in order to lend greater credence to their own heady visions and ambitious aspirations.

The Quiet Revolution

 The term "Quiet Revolution" is often used to describe the years 1960–66, during which Liberal Premier Jean Lesage and his *équipe du tonnerre* brought rapid but non-violent change to Quebec. Nevertheless, some observers with a mind to historical continuity point out that the Union Nationale, when it returned to power in 1966, continued the reforms, as did the Liberals under Robert Bourassa after 1970. The Parti Québécois also had an agenda of reform that it implemented in 1976–80. Thus, it might be said that the Quiet Revolution, in spite of pauses, lasted for two decades.

Liberal Reforms

Once in power, the Liberals acted to end electoral corruption. They also cleaned up much of the petty patronage practised by preceding governments. Early in its mandate, the government set up a royal commission to examine Quebec's educational system. Then it established a provincial ministry of education, thus asserting state control over a sector in which the church had hitherto played such a powerful role. Paul Gérin-Lajoie, the minister, reorganized the province's hundreds of school commissions into 55 regional districts. The government built large, "polyvalent" (comprehensive) secondary schools, improved teacher training, revised curricula, and broadened access to educational facilities. The church retreated. In fact, it had little choice, since it simply did not possess the huge financial and human resources that had to be devoted to schooling in the wake of Quebec's postwar population explosion.

Although educational reforms constituted a very important part of the Quiet Revolution, change pervaded all sectors of Quebec society. In 1962, after heated cabinet debate, René Lévesque convinced Lesage to nationalize the province's private electrical power companies and to merge them with the Crown corporation Hydro-Québec. The giant utility company contributed enormously to the province's development over the next two decades. The government also undertook a series of initiatives to promote a more dynamic francophone presence in an economy dominated by capital from outside the province. In the important sector of labour relations, it revised the labour code and, significantly, granted most employees in the public sector the right to strike. Progressive but costly measures in the field of health care included the establishment of a provincial hospitalization insurance plan, one of the Liberals' major electoral promises in 1960. Henceforth Quebeckers could receive hospital care without regard to ability to pay.

QUEBEC–OTTAWA RELATIONS

In his dealings with Ottawa, Lesage adopted a firm autonomist stance. He sought to end conditional subsidies, by which the federal government paid for part of the cost of a program in return for setting its conditions. He also insisted that Ottawa turn over more tax money to Quebec in view of the province's "prior needs." After the Pearson government in Ottawa unveiled its proposals for the Canada Pension Plan in 1963, Lesage successfully responded with a separate plan for Quebec — one that allowed the province to invest the enormous sums of money generated by such a scheme as it saw fit. The Caisse de dépôt et placement du Québec, set up to administer these funds, became Canada's largest investment fund.

The Quiet Revolution altered the face of Quebec dramatically. Sociologist Guy Rocher saw these years as a "cultural transformation," signifying that, beyond the structural reforms, Quebeckers' basic attitudes and values changed significantly.[2] The changes announced the end of what remained of traditional clerical society as the influence of the Roman Catholic church rapidly waned. Talented authors, musicians, and other artists captured the new spirit in their works.

Francophones also acquired a new confidence in themselves that encouraged them to challenge the inequalities they faced. They strongly criticized a Canada in which the federal bureaucracy spoke only English, in which French enjoyed no official recognition in nine provinces, and in which, even in Quebec, French-speakers carried little economic weight. Here indeed were the makings of a new nationalism.

REVOLUTION AND REACTION

Perceptions of the Quiet Revolution have varied considerably. Many in the urban middle class have viewed it as the birth of a modern Quebec, thanks to major reforms carried out in the important sectors of education, political life, the social services, and the economy. A more modern Quebec offered obvious advantages to this group.

By 2000, however, analyses had become more critical, and the almost mythical status given the Quiet Revolution by baby boomers was now contested. Perhaps institutions not linked to the state had suffered too much erosion. Perhaps citizens had become too dependent on an interventionist government. Perhaps the origins of many of the problems which Quebec faced in 2000 could be linked to the failures of the reforms that had been implemented. For example, education had been democratized, but its quality was often judged to be doubtful. The government had intervened vigorously in the economy, but failures had been numerous and costly.

Certainly, in the 1960s, the breathless pace of change upset many more conservative Quebeckers. Disadvantaged citizens in urban areas felt bypassed by the major thrust of the Quiet Revolution, as large-scale spending on education and the rapid growth of the civil service did little for them. In rural Quebec, where hundreds of small schools had been closed and children were being transported long distances by bus to large, impersonal institutions, discontent was rife. After his defeat in 1966, Lesage complained that "education beat us." His biographer, Dale C. Thomson, confirmed that change in this sector "generated more discontent than satisfaction."[3]

The Quiet Revolution engendered big government and bureaucracy, often insensitive to the needs of the individual. Higher spending brought increased taxes. Militant public-sector labour unions made use of their newly acquired right to strike. A small but vocal minority on the left also attacked Lesage, doubting the government's continuing commitment to reform. Radical nationalists viewed Lesage's objective of greater autonomy for the province as insufficient. They favoured separation, with the creation of an independent, more interventionist, French-speaking state.

RETURN OF THE UNION NATIONALE TO POWER

Led by Daniel Johnson, the Union Nationale regained power in 1966, thanks to strong support in rural Quebec and to Lesage's failure to redraw the electoral map. Surprisingly, perhaps, Johnson, and his successor Jean-Jacques Bertrand, who became premier after Johnson's sudden death in September 1968, did not attempt to undo the Liberals' reforms. In the field of education, Johnson applied the recommendations of the royal commission on education and established the Collèges d'enseignement général et professionnel (called CEGEPs), the junior colleges that allowed Quebec students to enrol in occupational programs or to prepare for entrance into the universities. The government also established a fourth French-language university, the public Université du Quebec, which opened campuses in regional centres throughout Quebec.

During the late 1960s, the polarization of Quebec society between left and right over issues such as labour–management relations increased. Strike activity, notably in the public sector, grew dramatically, and, as elsewhere in the western world at this time, protests shook colleges and universities.

The protest movements in Quebec took on a distinct national and cultural hue. Johnson wanted more than linguistic equality for French Canadians. In keeping with Quebec's time-honoured political tradition, he also sought greater autonomy for the province. Pointing out that Quebec, the home of more than 80 percent of French-speaking Canadians, represented one of Canada's two major ethnic communities or "nations," Johnson argued that a new Constitution should recognize this fact through an appropriate division of powers. Ottawa and most of the other provinces appeared willing, though not enthusiastic, to discuss the constitutional issue, but Pierre Trudeau, Canada's prime minister after 1968, warned that he would not allow any reduction of federal authority. To Trudeau, the federal government represented all Canadians — not just English-speaking Canadians — and he believed Ottawa could, and should, act to further linguistic equality across the country.

THE DEBATE OVER LANGUAGE

The Quiet Revolution made conflict over language inevitable in Quebec. Many French-speaking Quebeckers felt that their language did not occupy the position it deserved in the province. While elsewhere in Canada most francophones learned English, the language of the majority, most English-speaking Quebeckers knew little French. The powerful Montreal business establishment included few French Canadians. Many stores in downtown Montreal failed to offer service to customers in French. Commercial signs in Montreal were often only in English.

Quebec's English-speaking community possessed its own institutions, including schools, newspapers, hospitals, churches, and municipal councils. Quebec was the only province where the linguistic minority — in this case, English-speaking — could function entirely in its own language. Moreover, census statistics confirmed that French Canadians in most regions outside Quebec were losing their battle against assimilation. Only in certain areas could French-speakers be assured of getting at least part of their education in French. In addition, the language of the workplace was almost always English.

Since Confederation, Quebec residents had enjoyed the right or privilege of choosing whether their children would be educated in French or English. In practice, however, the great majority of immigrants to Quebec since World War II saw little reason to learn French, and they had enrolled their children in English-language schools to assure their integration into the English-speaking community. Demographers warned that if current trends continued, Montreal would soon have an English-speaking majority. For French-speaking Quebeckers concerned about the survival of their language, "free choice" of the language of education represented a serious threat.

CONFLICT OVER ENGLISH-LANGUAGE SCHOOLS

Many French-speakers wished the government to act in order to ensure that children of non-English origin enrolled in French schools. For its part, the English-speaking community sought the maintenance of free choice of the language of education. The government's legislation, Bill 63, recognized the right of all Quebeckers to enrol their children in English-language schools. The law pleased the non-French population, but it unleashed storms of protest among French-speaking Quebeckers. Language thus became a full-fledged political issue.

A POLARIZED QUEBEC

The 1970s were a difficult period for Quebeckers. Issues such as language, Quebec's future political status, inflation and other economic problems, union unrest, and generational conflict divided the province. In 1970, in the midst of an economic downturn, the Liberals, led by youthful economist Robert Bourassa, regained power.

THE "OCTOBER CRISIS"

The new government soon found itself stumbling from crisis to crisis. Shortly after assuming office, it was confronted with the "October Crisis," as members of a revolutionary fringe group, the Front de libération du Québec (FLQ), kidnapped James Richard Cross, a British trade representative in Montreal, and, five days later, Pierre Laporte, a Quebec cabinet minister. (Laporte was subsequently found murdered.) When Bourassa hesitated and seemed to favour negotiations with the terrorists, Ottawa intervened: first, it agreed to dispatch 8000 heavily armed soldiers to Quebec, to guard public buildings and well-known personalities; then, the following day, at 4 o'clock in the morning, it invoked, for the first time in peacetime, the War Measures Act, which enabled police to arrest more than 500 "suspects" on the mere suspicion of their being sympathetic to the revolutionaries. Nearly all those arrested were eventually released, with no charges being laid against them.

Bourassa appeared equally hesitant in 1971 when, after lengthy discussions on the Constitution, he finally said no to the Victoria Charter, a package of constitutional proposals assembled by the federal government, which included an amending formula and a bill of rights. Hopes for a renewed federalism then dissipated. At the same time, Quebec Liberals faced growing animosity from public-sector unions, whose leaders spoke ominously of their desire to overthrow the government and to replace the capitalist system with socialism. Contract negotiations with the unions led to unruly public-service strikes and even, in 1973, to the arrest and imprisonment of three major union leaders.

BILL 22

Nor could Bourassa avoid dealing with the complex language question. With regard to the language of education, his solution, Bill 22, gave access to English-language schools to children whose mother tongue was English and to those of non-French origin who could pass a language test. It also created enrolment quotas for English-language schools in each school district. In the end, Bill 22 pleased no one. Nationalists complained (rightly, as statistics later showed) that the law would do little to bring immigrants into French-language schools. The English-language community and ethnic groups bitterly denounced the measure as arbitrary and even totalitarian. The issue cost Bourassa support in the election of 1976, which he lost to the Parti Québécois.

Perhaps historians will judge the first Bourassa regime (1970–76) more kindly than did contemporary observers. Bourassa appeared constantly vacillating, but Quebeckers were so sharply polarized on so many issues that major decisions risked alienating large sectors of the electorate. Defenders of the multibillion-dollar James Bay hydro-electric project have argued that its economic advantages have outweighed damage caused to the northern environment and that a substantial financial award compensated for the loss of livelihood sustained by the Cree communities of northern Quebec. Others point to the provincial medicare program, financed in part by federal monies, or the Quebec Charter of Rights and Freedoms, designed to combat discrimination.

THE GROWTH OF NATIONALISM

Quebec nationalism had been intensifying since the late 1960s, with calls for constitutional reform, stricter language legislation in Quebec, and an increased francophone presence in Quebec's economy. Some English-language journalists blamed provincial politicians for undermining Quebeckers' loyalty through their aggressive stance in relations with Ottawa. They also censured French President Charles de Gaulle for the support he appeared to give the cause of independence in his celebrated cry of "Vive le Québec libre!" during a brief speech from the balcony of Montreal's city hall during the Expo 67 celebrations.

While some politicians may have adopted nationalist slogans to gain votes in elections, the real roots of protest went much deeper. Nationalism has been a force in Quebec since at least the early nineteenth century; although its themes varied over time, it was not a new phenomenon in the 1960s.

Contemporary nationalists, however, tended to be members of the new middle class, including teachers,

"Vive la France! Vive le Québec! Vive le Québec libre!" The crowd roared with approval when French President Charles de Gaulle made his famous remark at Montreal's City Hall, July 24, 1967, in support of an independent Quebec.

CP Picture Archive.

civil servants, and journalists. Critics have pointed out that these groups had a vested interest in nationalist causes. A bilingual civil service in Ottawa, for example, would create job openings for francophones. But these nationalists also resented the inferior position that French-speakers occupied in Canada and, to a certain extent, in Quebec itself. Events elsewhere in the world, such as the movements of national liberation in Africa and Asia, reminded many French Canadians of what they perceived to be their own condition. In one poignant autobiographical account, *Nègres blancs d'Amérique* (*White Niggers of America* in English translation), journalist and FLQ theorist Pierre Vallières portrayed French-Canadian workers as cheap labour, as exploited second-class citizens who had no control over their own society and economy.

THE RISE OF THE PARTI QUÉBÉCOIS

In 1967, René Lévesque, dissatisfied with the Liberals' constitutional policies, quit the party; the following year, he founded the Parti Québécois (PQ), which sought to achieve independence for Quebec. Lévesque had the prestige and stature needed to rally the great majority of nationalists.

The rise of the PQ was striking, as party leaders successfully linked nationalism to a variety of social causes, thus enabling the party to build a relatively broad coalition of supporters. Unions, increasingly hostile to the Bourassa government, now came to see a sovereign Quebec as one in which workers would be better treated. Many radical feminists, for their part, saw an independent socialist republic as the key to the liberation of women. This strategy helped the Parti Québécois win an election in 1976 contested by three major parties.

In the heady enthusiasm of the moment, many *péquistes* saw their victory as a vote for independence. Other observers, however, saw the PQ success largely as a vote for good government and against the scandal-ridden Bourassa regime. The PQ had, after all, promised that it would not try to separate Quebec from Canada until the decision was approved in a referendum. Most voters therefore believed that they had voted only for a change in government.

QUEBEC UNDER THE PARTI QUÉBÉCOIS

The new government adopted numerous reformist measures. In order to democratize Quebec politics and prevent powerful interests from "buying" favourable legislation, it overhauled the electoral law to prohibit corporate contributions to political parties. The government also introduced a no-fault system of automobile insurance, covering all personal injuries sustained. It brought in agricultural zoning legislation designed to protect increasingly scarce good farm land, much of which had disappeared due to urban sprawl since World War II. It also supported unions through an anti-strikebreaking law, a move that management bitterly opposed. In 1977 it amended the Quebec Charter of Rights to make Quebec the first Canadian province to protect gays and lesbians from discrimination.

BILL 101

In contrast to Bourassa's vacillation on the language question, the Parti Québécois's stance seemed clear. In 1977, the National Assembly adopted Bill 101, a charter of the French language, which was intended to make Quebec as overwhelmingly French as Ontario was English. This controversial legislation opened English-language schools only to children who had at least one parent educated in English in Quebec. That "objective" criterion was used because of the impossibility of verifying a child's mother tongue, one of the conditions used by Bourassa's Bill 22, to determine admission. French, with a few exceptions, was to become the language of the workplace. Most signs were to be posted in French only. In short, the Parti Québécois hoped to obtain by law for French in Quebec what the "free market" and "free choice" assured English elsewhere in Canada.

The new minority status of Quebec anglophones necessitated often painful adjustments. Anglophones launched successful legal challenges to certain clauses of Bill 101, which weakened the legislation substantially. Many Anglo-Quebeckers, including a large proportion of young adults convinced that they could have a better future elsewhere, left the province. At the same time, a large number of corporate head offices in Montreal, complaining of the language legislation, high taxes, the dangers of separatism, and poor relations with unions, decided to move westward, mainly to Toronto.

Where Social Scientists Disagree

The Origins and Effects of Quebec's Language Legislation

In 1969, the Quebec government began to adopt laws intended to increase the use of French in the province. These laws, the most important aspects of which have affected education, the workplace, and public signage, have provoked passionate debate and intense conflict.

Many social scientists have viewed the linguistic revolution as the result of the realization by the French-speaking majority of its economic inferiority in Quebec. Geographer Eric Waddell points out that, traditionally, French-speaking Quebeckers who wished to function in the world of business had to achieve fluency in English, while most anglophones remained unilingual. Quebec's language laws should thus be seen as attempts to come to terms with the "asymmetrical" nature of French–English relations in Canada. The Canadian and North American context places the French language at a heavy disadvantage in regard to English. Even in Quebec, the English language enjoys a visibility that French does not possess outside Quebec.[1] In marked contrast to Waddell's reasoning, the federal Official Languages Act places all minorities on a theoretically equal footing.

Political scientist Richard Handler also asserts that language laws were "aimed at redressing the economic balance of power within Quebec."[2] Likewise, in a study covering a portion of the 1980s, Marc V. Levine notes the extent of the francophone reconquest of Montreal's economy and concludes that Quebec's language legislation made an important contribution to this dramatic change.[3]

The new and obviously less powerful status of Quebec's anglophones has been the subject of several studies. Many anglophones left Quebec in the 1970s, presumably motivated by political and linguistic fears. In a controversial study, however, sociologist Uli Locher concludes that, even after the adoption of Bill 101 in 1977, anglophones were leaving Quebec primarily because of the lure of greater prosperity in Toronto and the West.[4] Most observers judge that anglophones remaining in Quebec still enjoy far greater rights and privileges than most francophones do elsewhere in Canada. But political scientist Garth Stevenson cautions that Quebec's more generous treatment of its minority cannot be explained solely by the goodwill of the majority. Rather, it is a logical consequence of the demographic balance in Canada and in North America as well as of the vast economic power that anglophones wielded in Quebec until recent times.[5]

Philosopher Charles Taylor attempts to define the basis for the divergent views of anglophones and francophones on the language question. He sees most anglophones, like Americans, putting forth a liberal view of society in which individual rights must take precedence over collective goals. Provisions for bilingualism in federal law can be justified in terms of individual rights: francophones across Canada, at least theoretically, can obtain federal government services in French. Francophones tend to espouse a collective goal: to ensure that there will still be francophones in the next generation. Taylor believes that Quebeckers also share liberal values but that, in order to retain their identity, they distinguish between fundamental liberties, which should never be infringed, and privileges, which are only important.[6]

Many English-speakers decry the very existence of Quebec's language legislation. At the same time, francophones will always feel culturally insecure because of the enormous pressures of the continent's English environment. Because of the emotional nature of the question, it will remain a subject of passionate discussion and an important challenge for Quebec and Canadian society.

[1] Eric Waddell, "State, Language and Society: The Vicissitudes of French in Quebec and Canada," in Alan C. Cairns and Cynthia Williams, eds., *The Politics of Gender, Ethnicity, and Language in Canada* (Toronto: University of Toronto Press, 1986), p. 88.

[2] Richard Handler, *Nationalism and the Politics of Culture in Quebec* (Madison: University of Wisconsin Press, 1988), p. 170.

[3] Marc V. Levine, *The Reconquest of Montreal: Language Policy and Social Change in a Bilingual City* (Philadelphia: Temple University Press, 1990).

[4] Uli Locher, *Les anglophones de Montréal: émigration et évolution des attitudes, 1978–1983* (Québec: Conseil de la langue française, 1988).

[5] Garth Stevenson, *Unfulfilled Union: Canadian Federalism and National Unity*, 3rd ed. (Toronto: Gage, 1989).

[6] Charles Taylor, "Shared and Divergent Values," in Ronald L. Watts and Douglas M. Brown, eds., *Options for a New Canada* (Toronto: University of Toronto Press, 1991), pp. 53–76.

Among the English-speakers who chose to stay in Quebec, bilingualism increased significantly. (Bilingualism outside Quebec, among English-speakers, grew slowly but remained largely an elitist phenomenon.) At the same time, Quebec's "Frenchness" was attenuated by the fact that nearly 40 percent of the majority French-language group reported that they could also speak English. Many Quebeckers whose mother tongue was neither French nor English reported that they were trilingual. Commenting on the census figures of 2001, *The Globe and Mail* suggested that Trudeau's dream of a bilingual Canada might endure only in Quebec.

THE REFERENDUM DEBATE, 1980

Of even greater interest to Canadians than the language question was Quebec's referendum on political sovereignty, which would decide Quebec's — and Canada's — future. In a shrewdly worded question, which implicitly recognized Quebeckers' divided loyalties, the PQ government asked voters for a mandate to negotiate political sovereignty within an economic association with the rest of Canada. In the hope of obtaining majority support, the government appealed both to Quebeckers' desire for change and, by asking voters to give it only the right to *negotiate*, to their more conservative instincts. No unilateral declaration of independence would follow a positive vote. The campaign debate was fierce, dividing families and friends. Claude Ryan, Robert Bourassa's successor as the Quebec Liberal leader, led the *non* forces. Prime Minister Trudeau intervened late in the campaign, promising unspecified constitutional change if Quebeckers voted *non*.

On May 20, 1980, Quebeckers defeated the referendum proposal by a 60–40 margin. While almost all non-French-speaking Quebeckers voted no, the French-speaking population split virtually in half. Analyses of the vote showed that the older age groups, the economically disadvantaged, and those with relatively little education tended to vote *non*. Those in the younger age groups and people with more education and higher incomes more often answered *oui*.

THE 1980s: THE WHEEL TURNS

The mood of the early 1980s in Quebec was pessimistic. The 1981–82 recession dramatically cut employment in the resource and manufacturing industries. Unions suffered membership losses as well as rising unpopularity among a public weary of strikes and agitation. Universities condemned the government's stringent cutbacks in financing.

Nor did the outcome of the constitutional debate cause much rejoicing in Quebec. The federal government's proposals gave Quebec none of the powers that its provincial governments had consistently claimed since 1960. Moreover, Ottawa managed to isolate Quebec by playing it off against the other nine provinces. The proposals became law despite Quebec's objections when Queen Elizabeth II proclaimed the new Constitution on April 17, 1982. Quebec was legally bound by the terms of the document but it lacked moral legitimacy in the province.

The harsh recession of the early 1980s as well as a severe budget crisis forced the Quebec government to reduce services and to increase taxes. Its draconian measures to recover part of the salary increases that had been granted to public service workers alienated the unions. Moreover, the era of large-scale spending and government interventionism had passed as budget deficits increased and a new conservative mood gained strength throughout the western world, including Quebec. Individualism was celebrated as the new cult, and business leaders became its high priests.

NATIONALISM IN DECLINE

Younger Quebeckers now worried more about finding jobs than about championing political causes. As nationalist sentiment weakened, Premier René Lévesque decided to put aside, at least for the foreseeable future, the issue of sovereignty-association, a decision that provoked a dramatic revolt within the party and, in 1985, Lévesque's own resignation. In the elections held shortly afterwards, the party lost power to the Liberals under their resurrected leader, Robert Bourassa.

In the years following the recession of the early 1980s, Quebec's rapid economic growth made it a leader among Canada's provinces. Reassured by the new political stability and by the reduced level of government interference, investment accelerated and business flourished.

While the Bourassa government prided itself in offering competent administration, it failed to exercise leadership with regard to environmental issues. Paper mills, aluminum manufacturing plants, and other industries continued to foul water and air with chemical pollutants, often in flagrant violation of existing regulations. Agricultural wastes, fertilizers, and pesticides polluted the province's rivers. Several incidents involving fires deliberately set in toxic waste and tire dumps dramatized both the dangers of pollution and the government's ecological neglect. The province's environmental record gave Quebeckers, reputed by polls to be among the most environmentally conscious of Canada's citizens, little cause for satisfaction.

THE REVIVAL OF NATIONALISM

Those who had proclaimed nationalism's demise in the early 1980s proved poor prophets. By the end of the decade, both the language issue and Quebec's future links with Canada again became important public topics. The language issue emerged with renewed force in late 1988 over the relatively minor issue of public signs. When the Supreme Court of Canada found Quebec's sign law (which required French-only signs) to be in violation of the freedom of expression provisions of both the federal and the Quebec charters of rights, Bourassa had to act. The Supreme Court had admitted that signs solely in English could be prohibited and that the government could require "the predominant display of the French language." Supporters of French-only signs argued that Quebec needed a French "face" in order to persuade new immigrants to integrate into the francophone community. Bourassa's new law still required French-only signs outdoors, while authorizing bilingual signs within certain stores. Quebec's, and Canada's, anglophones protested vehemently, and three English-speaking ministers resigned from Bourassa's cabinet. Passions cooled over time and, in 1993, the Bourassa government adopted more liberal legislation.

Assessing the overall impact of Quebec's controversial language legislation since the early 1970s is a difficult task. Certainly by the 1990s, Montreal "looked" much more French than it had in 1970. Also, almost all immigrant children were enrolled in French schools, but, in many of these, they constituted an overwhelming majority and had little contact with Quebeckers whose mother tongue was French. Thanks in part to the exodus of many anglophones, more francophones now held upper-level positions in business. More workers earned their living in French, but language legislation did not cover small enterprises, many of whose employees were obliged to work in English. Adversaries of Bill 101 warned that language legislation would hurt economic development and tarnish Quebec's reputation, since English-language media gave abundant publicity to anglophone complaints. But what other solution would have made it possible to promote the use of French energetically without undermining the important, even dominant, role of English in Quebec, particularly in the province's economy?

MEECH LAKE

The constitutional issue followed the linguistic debate. In 1986, the provincial premiers agreed to undertake a "Quebec round" of negotiations, to bring about "Quebec's full and active participation in the Canadian federation" before moving on to other concerns. Quebec put forth five conditions, which included the recognition of the province as a "distinct society" and greater powers with regard to immigration. In June 1987, Prime Minister Brian Mulroney and the ten provincial premiers met in Ottawa and, after arduous all-night negotiations, gave unanimous assent to an accord. Robert Bourassa proclaimed that Quebec could now adhere to the Canadian Constitution "with dignity and honour."

In the months that followed, the federal government and eight provinces, beginning with Quebec, ratified the proposals. Then the accord began to unravel as newly elected premiers in the two remaining provinces, New Brunswick and Manitoba, arguing that they were not bound by their predecessors' signatures, demanded substantial modifications. Subsequently, Newfoundland rescinded its approval. Groups representing women, Native peoples, ethnic associations, and northerners objected that their own concerns had not been addressed. Many Anglo-Canadians, ignoring the often unenviable fate of francophone minorities throughout Canada, said they wanted no part of a "distinct society" that would be free to "oppress" its anglophone minority. Other critics, including former prime minister Pierre Trudeau, argued that the Meech Lake Accord would seriously weaken federal authority.

Protracted negotiations among the premiers did produce an add-on agreement that satisfied some critics. Then, however, a dramatic event took place in the Manitoba legislature: a Cree NDP member, with the support of Native leaders from across Canada, denounced the accord for ignoring the rights of Canada's Aboriginal people and signalled his intention to use the rules of parliamentary procedure to kill it. On June 23, 1990, as the deadline for approval expired, the Meech Lake Accord died.

Most Canadians outside Quebec felt relief at the demise of the accord. In Quebec, however, nationalists, including many federalists, perceived the failure of the agreement as signifying English Canada's refusal to accommodate even the province's minimal concerns. Independence now seemed the only possible choice for those who could not accept the status quo. Several federal members of Parliament from Quebec quit their parties to join a new group, the Bloc Québécois, which favoured Quebec's secession from Canada. To deflect criticism of his government, Robert Bourassa set up a commission to study Quebec's constitutional future, and promised to hold a referendum. Political scientist Vincent Lemieux has argued that Bourassa wished to use the "threat of independence" to elicit new propositions for a reform of Canadian federalism, and thus make it possible to "avoid independence."[4]

CONSTITUTIONAL IMPASSE

The federal government did indeed decide to reopen the constitutional issue. This time, Native peoples, among other groups, played a far more important role in the discussions. Quebec, however, refused to participate in the talks until the final round of negotiations, held in Charlottetown. Quebeckers reacted without enthusiasm to the ensuing agreement. In a referendum held in October 1992, voters in six provinces, including Quebec, rejected the Charlottetown agreement and constitutional negotiations ceased. Sociologist Maurice Pinard pointed out that polls showed a strong majority of Quebeckers felt that the accord offered too little to Quebec; in English Canada, nearly 60 percent of voters felt it gave Quebec too much.[5]

THE REFERENDUM OF 1995

The seeming impossibility of reaching any constitutional agreement with the rest of Canada favoured an increase in nationalist sentiment in Quebec. More importantly, Jean Chrétien, who became Canada's prime minister in 1993, was perceived by even moderate nationalists as rigidly opposed to Quebec's claims for greater autonomy. In that same election, the nationalist Bloc Québécois proved far more popular than Chrétien's Liberals within the province. The return to power of the Parti Québécois in 1994 made a new referendum certain.

In this referendum, held on October 30, 1995, the provincial government asked electors if they wished Quebec to become "sovereign," after having formally offered Canada a new economic and political partnership.

About 200 000 people marched in Montreal's St. Jean Baptiste Day parade, June 24, 1994. The lead banner proclaims, "Next year — My country."

CP Picture Archive (Ryan Remiorz).

The federalist *non* won a razor-thin victory, with only 50.6 percent of the valid ballots cast, in a consultation in which more than 93 percent of eligible voters participated. Bloc Québécois leader Lucien Bouchard's prominent role in the campaign helped explain the strong showing of the *oui*, favoured by well over 60 percent of French-speaking voters. Yet Vincent Lemieux cautioned that, for many electors, a vote for "sovereignty" did not necessarily signify a vote for "independence" and a break with Canada. Anglophones, allophones, and members of First Nations communities supported the *non* option with near unanimity; their behaviour was not surprising, since these groups shared none of the discontent or the aspirations of the francophones.

OTTAWA'S STRATEGY TOWARD QUEBEC

The "love" shown toward Quebec by large numbers of English-speaking Canadians, who invaded Montreal just before the referendum for an enthusiastic pro-Canada demonstration, evaporated rapidly after the vote. Many reacted with bitterness to the outcome of the referendum, feeling that separation was now inevitable and that it was time to prepare to drive a hard bargain with a seceding Quebec that would deprive the province of important parts of its territory. In Ottawa, the Chrétien government sought legal means to block secession. In 1998, in an advisory opinion suffused with Solomon-like wisdom, the Supreme Court of Canada affirmed unanimously that no province enjoyed a legal right to secede unilaterally. If, however, Quebeckers repudiated the existing constitutional order unambiguously in regard to the question asked and to the support received, then all parties had an obligation to negotiate constitutional change in good faith.[6] The Court thus recognized that Quebec's constitutional future was

Relations were sour between Quebec Premier Lucien Bouchard and Canadian Prime Minister Jean Chrétien after the close referendum result in October 1995.

The Globe and Mail, November 1, 2003, Shaun Best/Reuters.

a political question. The Chrétien government then adopted, in 1999, legislation that sought to give Ottawa the right to determine unilaterally the conditions under which it would recognize the result of any future referendum.

Ottawa also sought to increase the federal government's visibility in Quebec. Lucrative contracts went to advertising agencies which were generous donors to the Liberal Party. While the RCMP launched an investigation into allegations of political favouritism and mismanagement of public funds, Prime Minister Chrétien dismissed evidence of impropriety with an appeal to patriotism: maintaining Canadian unity was well worth "the theft of a few million dollars."

Yet the fervour for independence was diminishing in Quebec, at least for the moment. Recognizing this fact, the PQ government stated that no new referendum would be held unless a victory was certain. Sociologists Simon Langlois and Gilles Gagné found an explanation for the decline in the apparent demobilization of the most ardent sovereignists — middle class francophones, 70 percent of whom had supported independence in 1995.[7] As the birth of an independent Quebec seemed to recede into a distant future, this group found little reason to support the Parti Québécois. Concern for health and social services and other issues came to the fore. Still, relations between Ottawa and Quebec remained testy, as Ottawa, now blessed with huge budget surpluses, undertook new initiatives in such fields of provincial jurisdiction as education and health.

CONTEMPORARY QUEBEC

In spite of a buoyant economy, support for the Parti Québécois weakened as voters blamed the government for mismanaging health care, for forcing the amalgamation of cities and suburbs (Montreal expanded to comprise the entire island of Montreal in 2002), and for the stagnation of certain regions of the province. In 2003, believing that change was necessary, they gave a majority of seats to the strongly federalist Liberals, led by Jean Charest, who promised to improve health care, authorize the secession of suburbs from the new cities, and lower taxes. In a series of referenda held in 2004, most of Montreal's wealthier, majority English-speaking suburbs voted to separate from the city.

THE QUEBEC ECONOMY, 1991–2004

Economic recession after 1991 provoked a substantial rise in unemployment. Many jobs in inefficient, formerly tariff-protected industries such as textiles and furniture, which came under considerable competition from imports, simply disappeared.

After mid-1996, however, the provincial economy rebounded. Free trade stimulated exports strongly. The provincial government, for its part, actively sought investments. The disastrous ice storm of January 1998, which deprived 3 million Quebeckers of electricity, some for lengthy periods of time, triggered a period of particularly rapid growth linked to the restoration and upgrading of the provincial electricity grid. By 1999, increased revenues and cuts in services made it possible for the government to eliminate the province's budget deficit and even to lower taxes, thereby earning the approval of bond rating agencies, the business establishment and undoubtedly of taxpayers, but displeasing those who found services less accessible.

After 2000, Montreal underwent exceptional economic expansion, stimulated by growth in such sectors as aeronautics, biotechnology, information technology, pharmaceuticals, and telecommunications. Unemployment levels fell, and Quebeckers' per capita incomes came closer to Ontario levels. According to economist Pierre Fortin, the increasing productivity of the Quebec workforce due to improved technology, research and development, and educational advances, explained the province's improved performance.[8] Yet there were failures. General

Motors closed its huge plant in Boisbriand, north of Montreal, the only automobile plant in the province. And development lagged in many of the province's regions, which suffered substantial out-migration.

POPULATION

Recent demographic trends increased concern for Quebec's future. The 2001 census showed that Quebec was still growing, though at a much slower rate than Ontario, Alberta, and British Columbia. As in other provinces, birth rates remained well below levels necessary for population replacement. Governments attempted to encourage couples to have more children by offering baby bonuses and tax-supported daycare services. As well, migration within Canada hurt Quebec, as more people left the province than entered it. Indeed, higher salaries and better job opportunities in the wealthiest provinces handicapped all of the less favoured provinces. Quebec did put considerable effort into attracting immigrants from abroad, but as a French-speaking province in English-speaking North America, it suffered inevitably from a competitive disadvantage with regard to neighbouring Ontario.

LANGUAGE AND CULTURE IN 2000

A quarter century after the adoption of Bill 101, the French language charter, a large majority of francophones still felt that the situation of French within Quebec was precarious. Increased trade relations with the United States meant that English assumed rising importance for francophones. Reports showed a marked deterioration in the use of French in Montreal, especially among immigrants, who tended to frequent English-language institutions of higher education. For many, English remained the language of social mobility. Many francophones agreed. Enrolment in English-language primary and secondary schools increased after 1992, as francophone children of mixed marriages entered them. Reports showed that many French-speaking high school graduates had poor mastery of the language. Decidedly, the survival of the French language in Quebec would always be under threat.

CULTURE IN AN ERA OF GLOBALIZATION

What effects did globalization, with its disappearing frontiers, have on Quebec culture? Well beyond the borders of Quebec, stage director and playwright Robert Lepage, lyricist Luc Plamondon, film-writer Denys Arcand (who won an Oscar in 2004), and the Cirque du Soleil, a troop of acrobats and other entertainers, gained notoriety. So did such popular singers as Lynda Lemay, Kevin Parent, Pierre Garand, better known by his stage name, Garou, and especially Céline Dion. Although American cultural products, such as the film *Titanic*, attracted Quebeckers quite as much as they fascinated other Canadians, in Quebec the hockey film *Les Boys* ran neck-and-neck with it. For some, globalization was perhaps a threat to Quebec's distinct culture; for others, it obviously presented new opportunities.

At the same time, in modern Quebec's pluralistic society, allophone novelists made important cultural contributions. Not surprisingly, they often emphasized themes linked to the pain of exile and the hopes for a better life in the new land. Italian-born Marco Micone told Quebeckers in a poem, *Speak What*: "We are a hundred peoples come from afar to share your dreams and your winters." Haitian-born Dany Laferrière, Sergio Kokis, born in Brazil, and Abla Farhoud, from Lebanon, are among the voices "from afar" who have enriched contemporary francophone literature.

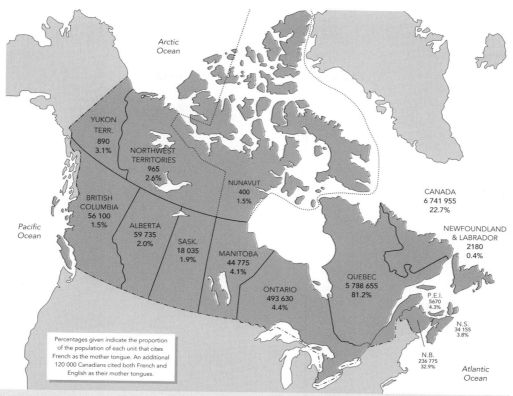

Canada's francophone population, 2001. Note the French-speaking community's strong majority position in Quebec, but minority status (less than 5 percent of the total population) in all other provinces and territories, with the exception of New Brunswick.

Source: Statistics Canada, 2001 Census, *Highlight Tables*, Mother Tongue: Canada, Provinces, Territories.

A Historical Portrait 🌱
☛ Céline Dion and the Global Village

In the 1960s and the 1970s, stars such as Gilles Vigneault, Jean-Pierre Ferland, and Pauline Julien, many of them ardent nationalists, rose to fame in Quebec, although on occasion they performed abroad. Since the 1980s, however, many of Quebec's most talented artists have quite literally gone global, working in Montreal, Toronto, Los Angeles, Paris, London, and elsewhere. Céline Dion epitomized this new tendency.

Dion became a child star in Quebec in the 1980s. In 1984, she sang for Pope John Paul II at Olympic Stadium in Montreal. In 1988, she won first place at the annual Eurovision competition, Europe's Olympics of song contest, held at Dublin and viewed by 600 million telespectators. In 1993, she won Juno awards in Toronto, singing in recently learned English and, in the words of gushing critics, bridging the cultural gap between Canada's "two solitudes." In 1997, she performed two songs for the Academy Awards to an audience that reportedly numbered one billion people. She also picked up two Grammy Awards in New York City. In her acceptance speech, she addressed Quebeckers in French, a gesture that one *Globe and Mail* columnist thought worth more than "a trillion distinct society clauses."

By 2000, Dion, whom *Time* magazine proclaimed a "global diva," had sold more than 130 million albums, with 26 megahits, including "Falling into You" and "Let's Talk About Love." Biographer Barry Grills saw her as building cultural bridges from Quebec to the rest of the planet: she occupied "a huge international territory, while still maintaining a direct connection to the culture where, for her, it all began."[1] Yet Dion asserted, in an interview, "I am very much Americanized." In this regard, she seemed to voice the attraction to the American dream that many Quebeckers have felt throughout their history. In 2002, "Canada's biggest cultural export," as *The Globe and Mail* styled Dion, came out of retirement and released a new English-language album, *A New Day Has Come*; thanks in part to lavish publicity, it immediately became a top hit. A *New York Times* critic hypothesized that Dion's success came from her never being specific: the more general and abstract her message, the

By 1983 Quebec singer Céline Dion was already winning awards. She would go on to become an international diva.
Canadian Press/CP.

more people were able to relate what was said to the particularities of their own experience. Here undoubtedly was globalization in action. Dion then settled in Las Vegas for a three-year engagement worth $100 million, where, from 2003, she performed in an enormous replica of the Roman colosseum specially constructed for her in Caesar's Palace.

---

[1] Barry Grills, *Falling into You: The Story of Céline Dion* (Kingston, ON: Quarry Press, 1997), pp. 9–10.

THE ENVIRONMENT

In the 1990s, the environment became a less popular concern than it had been in the 1980s. Air pollution, originating mostly in Ontario and in the American Midwest, continued to hurt Quebec's lakes and forests, and worsened the problem of urban smog. Environmentalists warned that the province's forests were being cut down at a rate well above their capacity to regenerate. Well-known pop singer Richard Desjardins even produced a film, *L'Erreur boréale*, denouncing what he saw as the collusion between forest companies and the government. Another film, *Bacon*, portrayed the power of the so-called "pig barons." Indeed, farmers cut down large tracts of forest to produce more corn to feed pigs or to obtain land for spreading manure from huge pig farms. After 2000, however, the pendulum began to swing back toward greater concern for environmental degradation. Among other actions, the provincial government announced plans to protect additional portions of Quebec's territory from development.

Although Quebec will remain predominantly French-speaking at least in the foreseeable future, the French language will continue to be spoken by a declining minority outside the province, and by an infinitely smaller minority elsewhere in North America. Canada's commitment to bilingualism and to equal status for its francophone citizens also risks being called into question. Inevitably, the threat of assimilation will continue to weigh heavily upon francophones, and the French-speaking community will have to devote increasing effort to revitalizing its language and culture.

Regardless of the province's constitutional and linguistic evolution, Quebeckers, like other Canadians, will have to find solutions to the problems posed by living in an increasingly pluralistic society. As the dramatic confrontation with the Mohawks at Oka in the summer of 1990 acutely demonstrated, Quebeckers, again like other Canadians, must continue to work for an accommodation with the Native peoples to settle long-standing grievances. Recent steps in this direction include the "Paix des Braves," a new accord signed with the Cree of Northern Quebec designed to deal with Native dissatisfaction with the agreement of 1975. Much energy will have to be directed to combating such social problems as poverty, violence, and a painfully high suicide rate among young males. In addition, all Quebeckers, regardless of language or origin, will have to meet the challenges and pay the price of creating and preserving an environment in which human life can continue to flourish.

NOTES

1. Susan Mann, *The Dream of Nation: A Social and Intellectual History of Quebec* (Montreal/Kingston: McGill-Queen's University Press, 2002, 1982), p. 284.
2. Guy Rocher, *Le Québec en mutation* (Montreal: Hurtubise, 1973), p. 18.
3. Dale C. Thomson, *Jean Lesage and the Quiet Revolution* (Toronto: Macmillan, 1984), p. 309.
4. Vincent Lemieux, "Les partis et l'idée de souveraineté," in Maurice Pinard, Robert Bernier, and Vincent Lemieux, *Un combat inachevé* (Ste-Foy, QC: Presses de l'Université du Québec, 1997), p. 18.
5. Maurice Pinard, "Les fluctuations du mouvement indépendantiste depuis 1980," in Maurice Pinard et al., *Un combat inachevé* (Ste-Foy, QC: Presses de l'Université du Québec, 1997), p. 97.
6. John T. Saywell, *The Lawmakers: Judicial Power and the Shaping of Canadian Federalism* (Toronto: University of Toronto Press, 2002), p. 306.
7. Gilles Gagné and Simon Langlois, *Les raisons fortes: nature et signification de l'appui à la souveraineté du Québec* (Montreal: Presses de l'Université de Montréal, 2002).
8. Pierre Fortin, "L'évolution de l'économie depuis 1960: le Québec a comblé la moitié de son retard sur l'Ontario," *Le Devoir*, March 27, 2000.

LINKING TO THE PAST

The Quiet Revolution
http://www2.marianopolis.edu/quebechistory/events/quiet.htm
A brief account of the Quiet Revolution.

Official Languages
http://www.pch.gc.ca/progs/lo-ol/prov-terr/index_e.cfm
A detailed look at the use of French in each province and territory, from Heritage Canada's Official Languages Support Programs site.

The October Crisis
http://www.cbc.ca/news/indepth/october/
Images, documents, articles, and audio and video clips documenting the October Crisis.

Quebec Elections
http://archives.cbc.ca/300c.asp?IDCat=73&IDDos=651&IDLan=1&IDMenu=73
Video and audio clips related to Quebec elections, from 1960 up to 1998.

The Charter of the French Language
http://www.olf.gouv.qc.ca/english/charter/
Full text of the Charter of the French Language, popularly known as Bill 101.

Quebec Government
http://www.gouv.qc.ca/
The official site of the government of Quebec, with information on the province's culture, society, education, health, institutions, and much more.

RELATED READINGS

The following articles in R. Douglas Francis and Donald B. Smith, eds., *Readings in Canadian History: Post-Confederation*, 6th ed. (Toronto: Nelson Thomson Learning, 2002), deal with topics relevant to this chapter in greater depth: Jacques Rouillard, "The Quiet Revolution: A Turning Point in Quebec's History," pp. 440-53; and Richard Jones, "Politics and the Reinforcement of the French Language in Canada and Quebec, 1960–1986," pp. 453–69.

BIBLIOGRAPHY

Although considerable scholarly material on Quebec exists in English, especially on political and constitutional issues, students wishing to study Quebec society need a reading knowledge of French. Useful general syntheses include Susan Mann, *The Dream of Nation: A Social and Intellectual History of Quebec* (Montreal/Kingston: McGill-Queen's University Press, 2002, 1983); John Dickinson and Brian Young, *A Short History of Quebec* (Montreal/Kingston: McGill-Queen's University Press, 2003); and Paul-André Linteau et al., *Quebec since 1930* (Toronto: James Lorimer, 1991). A dispassionate general interpretation is available in Kenneth McRoberts, *Quebec: Social Change and Political Crisis*, 3rd ed. with a postscript (Toronto: Oxford University Press, 1999). See also David Chennells, *The Politics of Nationalism in Canada: Cultural Conflict since 1760* (Toronto: University of Toronto Press, 2001).

Successive political figures are examined in Conrad Black, *Render Unto Caesar: The Life and Legacy of Maurice Duplessis* (Toronto: Key Porter, 1998); Richard Jones, *Duplessis and the Union Nationale Administration* (Ottawa: Canadian Historical Association, 1983); Dale C. Thomson, *Jean Lesage and the Quiet Revolution* (Toronto: Macmillan, 1984); L. Ian MacDonald, *From Bourassa to Bourassa: Wilderness to Restoration*, 2nd ed. (Montreal/Kingston: McGill-Queen's University Press, 2002); and Graham Fraser, *René Lévesque and the Parti Québécois in Power*, 2nd ed. (Montreal/Kingston: McGill-Queen's University Press, 2002). Studies of constitutional issues include Guy Laforest, *Trudeau and the End of a Canadian Dream* (Montreal/Kingston, McGill-Queen's University Press, 1995); and Alan Cairns, *Charter versus Federalism: The Dilemmas of Constitutional Reform* (Montreal/Kingston: McGill-Queen's University Press, 1992).

Innumerable works exist on the subject of Quebec's independence. For contrasting viewpoints see for example Christian Dufour, *A Canadian Challenge: Le défi québécois* (Lantzville, BC: Oolichan Books, 1990); and Robert A. Young, *The Secession of Quebec and the Future of Canada*, rev. ed. (Montreal/Kingston: McGill-Queen's University Press, 1998). Kenneth McRoberts provides an overview of English-Canadian reaction to Quebec nationalism in *Beyond Quebec: Taking Stock of Canada* (Montreal/Kingston: McGill-Queen's University Press, 1995). In *Misconceiving Canada: The Struggle for National Unity* (Toronto: Oxford University Press, 1997), the same author is highly critical of Pierre Trudeau's policies for national unity.

Analyses of the language question include articles by Richard Jones and William D. Coleman in Michael D. Behiels, ed., *Quebec since 1945: Selected Readings* (Toronto: Copp Clark Pitman, 1987), pp. 223–62. On Quebec's English-speaking minority see Ronald Rudin, *The Forgotten Quebecers: A History of English-Speaking Quebec, 1759–1980* (Quebec: Institut québécois de recherche sur la culture, 1985); and Garth Stevenson, *Community Besieged: The Anglophone Minority and the Politics of Quebec* (Montreal/Kingston: McGill-Queen's University Press, 1999).

The experience of women in Quebec is covered in Micheline Dumont et al., *Quebec Women: A History* (Toronto: Women's Press, 1987). Cultural development is examined in Richard Handler, *Nationalism and the Politics of Culture in Quebec* (Madison: University of Wisconsin Press, 1988). On Quebec society see Simon Langlois et al., *Recent Social Trends in Quebec, 1960–1990* (Montreal/Kingston: McGill-Queen's University Press, 1992). Richard F. Salisbury, *A Homeland for the Cree: Regional Development in James Bay, 1971–1981* (Montreal/Kingston: McGill-Queen's University Press, 1986) is an important analysis of the James Bay hydro-electric project's impact on the Cree.

24

THE ENGLISH-SPEAKING PROVINCES SINCE 1960

TIME LINE

1960 – Louis Robichaud, new premier of New Brunswick, launches Equal Opportunity Program

1962 – Medicare is introduced in Saskatchewan

1969 – The NDP, led by Ed Schreyer, defeats the Conservatives in elections in Manitoba

1970 – Greenpeace founded in Vancouver

1971 – Peter Lougheed's Conservatives defeat Social Credit and form the government in Alberta

1980 – Ottawa launches the National Energy Program, condemned in the West

1985 – The Liberals end a 32-year Conservative reign in Ontario

1986 – Expo 86 held in Vancouver

1991 – The NDP takes power in British Columbia and promises to support "sustainable development" policies

1992 – An explosion at the Westray mine in Nova Scotia kills 26 miners

1995 – The Conservatives led by Mike Harris take power in Ontario and begin to implement the "Common Sense Revolution"

1997 – Hibernia offshore oil platform towed into position 315 km off St. John's, Newfoundland

Opening of the Confederation Bridge linking Prince Edward Island and New Brunswick

1998 – British Columbia concludes treaty with Nisga'a First Nation

2003 – Toronto struck by the deadly SARS virus, then by a general electricity blackout

I n chapters 22 and 23 we looked at the recent history of the Aboriginal peoples and of French-speaking Canada, increasingly concentrated in the province of Quebec. This chapter will survey part of the history of English-speaking Canadians who constitute the majority of the population in nine of Canada's ten provinces. A century ago, the great majority of Canadians whose first language was English could trace their origins to the British Isles. Today, a growing portion of English-speaking Canadians had parents or grandparents who spoke other first languages but who settled in English-speaking Canada where they began the lengthy and often difficult process of integrating into Canadian society, and of transforming it at the same time.

 Before Confederation, groups of immigrants, mainly from Europe, established communities across Canada's territory. In earlier times, geographical separateness and the lack of communication help explain the unique character of each community. Yet even with dramatic improvements in transportation and communication, differences have remained significant. Provincial borders have both reflected and reinforced economic, political, and social distinctiveness. While Quebec underwent its Quiet Revolution after 1960, important changes also transformed all of Canada's majority English-speaking provinces. Not surprisingly, provincial politicians have strongly affirmed the special character and interests of their own provinces. Local media have also argued for greater recognition of regional and provincial concerns, while literature and other cultural forms reflect different local experiences. Strong regional and provincial identities also help explain interregional and federal–provincial friction.

THE ATLANTIC PROVINCES

Canada's four easternmost provinces — Newfoundland and Labrador, Nova Scotia, New Brunswick, and Prince Edward Island — had, in 2001, a combined population that represented just 7.5 percent of Canada's total. Few immigrants settle in this region; indeed, out-migration has often been substantial. There has been little grassroots support for attempts to establish a form of Maritime union in order to increase the Atlantic provinces' bargaining power with the federal government, and the politicians themselves, with their priorities reflecting different ambitions and concerns, have had a vested interest in maintaining the status quo. Yet various programs and bodies have, over the years, assured greater regional co-operation.

PROBLEMS OF THE ATLANTIC ECONOMY

The Atlantic provinces' economies remain relatively undiversified and rely heavily on the primary industries of forestry, mining, agriculture and, although less than in the past because of the decline of fish stocks, fishing. Few manufacturing industries chose to locate in this area, since distances from major markets are substantial and local markets are small. Consequently, unemployment and poverty levels remain relatively high, particularly in rural and outlying areas. In recent years, however, a burgeoning oil and gas industry has assisted the economies of Newfoundland and Nova Scotia while New Brunswick has enjoyed some success in creating service-related jobs. Cities in particular became more prosperous.

Not surprisingly, inhabitants of the Atlantic provinces have ceaselessly decried the country's regional disparities, of which they are the major victims. Since the 1960s, however, Ottawa has recognized the legitimacy of Atlantic complaints, although its numerous policy changes indicate that long-term solutions are elusive. In 1969, for example, the newly established federal Department of Regional Economic Expansion (DREE) began to offer incentives to encourage companies to locate in less-favoured areas of the country, such as the Atlantic provinces. The department spent money on highway construction, schools, and municipal services, and also attracted some new industry. Then, in the early 1980s, the Trudeau government dismantled DREE, feeling that the economic environment was improving. For its part, the Mulroney government created the Atlantic Canada Opportunities Agency, which helped fund businesses in Atlantic Canada. According to economist Robert Finbow, such spending, totalling more than $5 billion between 1970 and 1995, produced "no appreciable closing of the gap between have and have-not provinces as measured by per capita income or unemployment rates."[1] Direct money transfers from Ottawa to individuals, in the form of unemployment insurance, welfare, and other payments did help to boost household incomes.

FEDERAL–ATLANTIC RELATIONS

Historian George Rawlyk has defined Atlantic Canada's attitudes toward the federal government as "ambivalent."[2] Although Confederation has yielded obvious benefits for the Atlantic provinces, most easterners believe that Ottawa's policies have brought far more prosperity to central Canada. Despite perennial manifestations of economic discontent, Atlantic Canadians have generally defended the principle of a strong federal government. Regional discontent has not, in the last century, attempted to find a voice in local separatist movements, mainly because few Atlantic Canadians could argue convincingly that the region would be better off without Canada. Instead, Maritimers sought to promote regional interests either within governing parties or by voting for the main opposition party. Often, they hedged their bets, choosing, in provincial elections, alternative parties to the one in power in Ottawa. In the late 1990s, a significant minority of Atlantic Canadians began to show support for the New Democratic party at both provincial and federal levels, in an attempt to convey dissatisfaction.

NEWFOUNDLAND AND LABRADOR

On May 9, 1997, politicians and business people gathered at Bull Arm, northwest of St. John's, to christen the new Hibernia off-shore oil production platform, which had been built with government and private money at a cost of $6 billion. The festive occasion was marred by a demonstration by hundreds of unemployed fishery workers, protesting against Ottawa's compensation program for the collapsed cod fishery. That event appeared to dramatize the contrast between the Newfoundland of yesterday, a province of low incomes and a slowly dying fishing industry, and the Newfoundland of tomorrow, richer and more developed.

The fishing industry was already in difficulty in the 1950s. Instead of taking the necessary steps to restructure the industry, the federal government extended unemployment insurance coverage to seasonal fishers, a measure that helped increase the number of fishers at a time when the continued health of the industry necessitated significant downsizing. Then, in the early 1970s, Ottawa liberalized unemployment insurance access rules, giving the fishing industry a vested interest in creating a maximum number of short-term jobs that would enable everyone to claim insurance in the off-season. For its part, the provincial government subsidized the building of numerous fish-processing plants, which hired for 10-week periods so that very large numbers of workers would qualify for benefits. Some critics blame the industry's "chronic underdevelopment" on its resistance to technological innovation. More recently, however, Miriam Wright argues that, thanks to government subsidies, modernization did indeed take place, enabling the industry to harvest fish at a level that simply could not be sustained.[3]

Employment in the fishing industry attained a peak in 1988 of 90 000 jobs. Then, in the early 1990s, cod stocks, hitherto thought to be inexhaustible, declined precipitously as a result of overfishing, both domestic and foreign, and possibly, too, because of environmental factors. Destruction of the cod was cited in international scientific literature as a classic example of biological catastrophe. The federal government reacted by imposing a moratorium on catches and then, when fish stocks failed to recover, a virtual closure of the fisheries. At the same time, it launched a compensation plan to eliminate jobs. Shrimp and crab provided a lucrative replacement for a certain number of fishers. Others left Newfoundland. Many in distant outports had only welfare to fall back upon.

ECONOMIC DIVERSIFICATION

Since Confederation in 1949, Newfoundland's governments have sought to favour a more diversified economy. Joey Smallwood, premier from 1949 until 1972, hoped to carry out an industrial revolution to create thousands of new jobs, stem emigration, and drag the province "kicking and screaming into the twentieth century." He encouraged foreign investment and sponsored projects to develop the province's natural resources, such as iron and pulpwood, as well as Labrador's vast hydro-electric potential at Churchill Falls. There were some successes, but many costly failures.

Conservative Premier Brian Peckford's stewardship after 1979 was marked by acrimonious confrontations with the federal government over offshore oil rights and fisheries, with Quebec over electric power sales regulated by a contract that brought immense windfall profits to Hydro-Québec, and with the province's labour unions. Newfoundland's deteriorating economy and rising discontent with the federal Conservatives helped the Liberals regain power in 1989 under Clyde Wells. Wells hoped to transform the province into a flourishing market economy, but his commitment to reform weakened in the face of opposition from within the civil service.

Since the late 1970s, many Newfoundlanders have seen the exploitation of offshore natural resources as the key to creating prosperity. Tragedy marred the start of work in the Hibernia field in 1982 when an exploratory

The Hibernia oil platform is ready to be towed out into the Atlantic Ocean, May 1997. Newfoundlanders hoped that oil production would stimulate the province's economy.

CP Picture Archive/Jonathan Hayward.

drilling rig capsized, killing all 84 crew members. Oil production finally started in late 1997. The provincial government began to reap modest royalties, but critics said that oil wealth hardly flowed beyond St. John's. In addition, the oil industry caused a huge increase in greenhouse-gas emissions, noxious to the environment. Another mega-project, with important economic potential but again not without major environmental risks, involved the exploitation of Inco's huge nickel deposits at Voisey's Bay, in northern Labrador, and the construction of a smelter to refine the ore.

NOVA SCOTIA

Nova Scotia, the most populous and prosperous of the four Atlantic provinces, has the most diversified economy. Tourism provides an important source of income and the province has had considerable success in marketing a traditional, rather folkloric image of itself. Yet primary industries have been the mainstay of the economy, and secondary industry is frequently linked to the processing of primary products. Some areas of the province, particularly Cape Breton Island, have suffered high jobless rates as local industries such as state-subsidized coal mines and steel mills have closed.

Coal-mining had been dirty, difficult, and especially dangerous work. In 1958, for example, the collapse of a tunnel in a deep mine at Springhill caused the deaths of 74 miners. Then, in 1992, a devastating explosion at a mine in Pictou County killed 26 miners. One miner, Shaun Comish, later recalled his fellow workers' constant fears but explained that the men needed a job, any job, to support their families. He also spoke of their hesitancy to unionize in the face of strong company opposition, and of the frequent violations of basic safety regulations, usually with management's knowledge if not at its insistence.

POLITICS AND DEVELOPMENT

Economic issues have generally dominated politics in Nova Scotia. By the mid-1950s, popular discontent with economic stagnation helped bring the Progressive Conservatives, under Robert Stanfield, to power. They improved education and paved roads, but Stanfield's priority was economic development. He created Industrial Estates Limited, with well-known businessman Frank Sobey as its first president, to invest in local enterprises; serious losses, however, notably in stereo equipment and heavy water, followed the investment company's initial successes.

In the 1970s, a Liberal government, aided by federal monies, also planned many development projects, including an oil refinery complex on the Strait of Canso intended to strengthen Nova Scotia's industrial base. But the harsh economic realities of the late 1970s, including substantial increases in hydro-electric power rates, brought the Conservatives, led by John Buchanan, back to power. The new government's anti-union legislation, while embittering relations with labour, helped to create jobs by convincing Michelin Tire, a major employer in the province, to expand production. In addition, the discovery of gas and oil off the Atlantic coast raised hopes for an economic boom that would end "going down the road" in search of jobs. Collapsing oil prices in the mid-1980s, together with the federal government's decision to reduce funding for drilling, delayed these energy projects. In the 1990s, however, the building of the $2 billion Sable Island natural gas pipeline gave a strong boost to the construction industry, and offshore exploration resumed.

Mounting deficits and political scandals tarnished the image of the Conservative government, which was routed in 1993 by the Liberals. They attempted to curb patronage excesses in contract tendering and to initiate reforms in relation to program governance. But their efforts to balance the budget through increased taxes, public-sector wage rollbacks and freezes, and spending cuts provoked, as elsewhere in Canada, considerable popular dissatisfaction. The Conservatives under John Hamm regained power in 1999 while the NDP formed the official opposition. In 2003, as voters complained of inadequate health care and rising automobile insurance rates, Hamm lost his majority but a divided opposition nevertheless enabled him to retain power.

PRINCE EDWARD ISLAND

Prince Edward Island underwent substantial change after World War II, as the traditional "island way of life" increasingly became a myth. Many small farmers, unable to compete because of low potato prices, left the land, though total hectarage in potatoes increased. High energy costs and transportation difficulties also hindered the growth of industry.

Governments responded to changing attitudes. In 1970, the province's Liberal government launched with considerable fanfare a Comprehensive Development Plan for social and economic change and industrial development. Yet little economic diversification actually took place. In the late 1980s, now convinced that development should be based on the province's existing strengths, the government signed agreements with two food-processing giants to build plants on the island and increase the percentage of potatoes being processed in the province.

Many islanders have long feared that pressures from the mainland would destroy Prince Edward Island's way of life. In the late 1980s, for example, they persuaded the provincial government to act in order to make it more difficult for non-residents to purchase land. They also criticized federal plans, supported by the island's tourist industry, to build a "fixed link" across Northumberland Strait to New Brunswick. Ottawa decided to move ahead after 60 percent of islanders voted "yes" to the project in a referendum. The Confederation Bridge, 13 km long, was opened in 1997. That year, tourism increased by 60 percent over the preceding year.

Other economic and social questions also preoccupied Prince Edward Islanders. Voters expressed displeasure with the provincial government's efforts to balance the budget, as civil servants saw their wages cut and rural schools and hospitals closed. Ottawa's move in the late 1990s to reduce benefits for the seasonally unemployed also provoked anger. The provincial Conservative party benefited from this discontent and gained power in 1996. New Premier Pat Binns sought to show his support for small business, judged to be more compatible with the Island's lifestyle, but the province's economy remained closely linked to the potato crop and to tourism.

New Brunswick

Speaking of Atlantic Canada as a whole belies the very real differences among its four provinces. For example, the ethnic and linguistic mix of New Brunswick's population, one-third of which is French-speaking, makes that province distinct. Long at a disadvantage both economically and linguistically, the French-speaking Acadians have sought and, to a considerable extent, achieved greater equality.

In 1968, New Brunswick adopted an Official Languages Act that gave official recognition to linguistic rights. Then, through the 1970s, the provincial government cautiously proclaimed and applied the law's various clauses. Attitudes changed slowly in the face of strong opposition among anglophones to the recognition of francophone rights. In the early 1970s, for example, Acadians confronted Moncton's mayor, Leonard Jones, an adamant opponent of bilingual municipal services. Jones's obstinacy — which students from the Université de Moncton underlined by depositing a severed pig's head on the mayor's doorstep — probably served as a catalyst for the Acadians' struggle.

Since World War II, New Brunswick's governments have sought to stimulate economic development. After 1960, the Liberal government led by Louis Robichaud, the first elected Acadian premier, intervened actively in resource development. When pulp and paper companies failed to use Crown lands they held under long-term lease, the government cancelled their licences and awarded them to other companies. When an American mining company reduced operations in its lead and zinc mine near Bathurst, Robichaud engineered a buyout by Canadian investors, including native son K.C. Irving, who set about building a huge smelter complex.

The Irving family's business interests included 3000 gas stations, trucking and bus lines, shipbuilding, huge forest reserves, paper and saw mills, radio and television stations, and the province's English-language newspapers; these companies employed roughly 25 000 people in New Brunswick. Irving's biographer claimed that "surely no individual in any single Canadian province ... ever held so much raw economic power."[4] Irving hired his own companies to

New Brunswick Premier Louis Robichaud, the province's first elected Acadian premier. His administration in the 1960s built many hospitals, schools, and public buildings.

Provincial Archives of New Brunswick/P57-15.

perform the construction work on the smelter complex, but delays and ballooning costs finally brought the provincial government to allow a takeover by Noranda. Although the mineral industry prospered in the 1960s, it did not have the desired transforming effects on provincial and local economies.

SOCIAL CHANGE IN NEW BRUNSWICK

Social change came rapidly to New Brunswick in the 1960s under Louis Robichaud. His Equal Opportunity program aimed at improving the lot of the province's poorer citizens, often Acadians who lived in rural areas in the north and east; in particular, the government greatly expanded health, social, and educational services. These measures generated fierce opposition among anglophones in the south, who regarded them as proof of a costly Liberal plot to "rob Peter to pay Pierre." A cartoon in one of the Irving newspapers pictured a despotic Robichaud as a modern Louis XIV, with wild eyes, crown askew, and hand clutching a sword threatening his foes. Significantly, in the 1967 election, Robichaud's Liberals lost almost all the predominantly English seats.

NEW BRUNSWICK'S ECONOMY

In the 1970s, Progressive Conservative Premier Richard Hatfield attempted several experiments designed to stimulate New Brunswick's economy and to compensate for the decline of the agricultural sector. One notable industrial venture in which the provincial government invested heavily, the Bricklin automobile project, failed totally. Hatfield came under increasing attack in the 1980s for economic mismanagement as well as for his flamboyant lifestyle (Liberal critics nicknamed him "Disco Dick"). According to biographer Richard Starr, what expanded during the premier's tenure was not the economy, as he had promised, but the government deficit, unemployment, the premier's waistline, and his cabinet. Finally, in 1987, New Brunswick's voters spoke: they elected Liberals in every district in the province.

Job creation and a balanced budget were the new government's priorities. In the early 1990s, expansion in the food-processing industry, new power plants, and more service-related jobs in sectors such as telecommunications helped compensate for employment losses in the forest industry and in federal government services. In particular, the "energizer premier," as one newspaper nicknamed Frank McKenna, proved particularly adroit at attracting telephone call centres to the province, though other provinces accused him of luring away jobs and critics noted that such jobs were generally poorly paid.

McKenna's record and his favourable image as an indefatigable campaigner for change enabled the Liberals to win three consecutive elections. But spending cuts on welfare and health, continued unemployment, and plans to levy tolls on a portion of the Trans-Canada Highway brought much discontent. This climate enabled the Conservatives, under their youthful new leader, Bernard Lord, to win a strong victory at the polls in 1999. Lord nearly lost the election of 2003 as voters showed their unhappiness with the government's failure to block steep increases in the cost of automobile insurance.

ONTARIO

In a country marked by profound economic imbalances, populous Ontario has traditionally been Canada's major "have" region. Half of Canada's new immigrants choose Ontario; indeed, immigration has made Toronto Canada's largest city and transformed it into one of the world's most culturally diverse cities. Toronto has become Canada's financial capital, and also has nearly half the country's head offices. Manufacturing, including 95 percent of the huge automobile and parts industry, is concentrated in southern Ontario, assuring the province relatively low unemployment rates and high per capita incomes.

ECONOMIC DEVELOPMENT

The 1950s and 1960s saw rapid economic expansion in Ontario, stimulated by demand for a wide variety of goods and services. The 1960s saw a massive reshaping of Ontario's education system, as spending tripled. The construction industry prospered thanks to strong demand for housing. Governments at all levels invested heavily in road-building. They also promoted urban transit, sponsored electric-power projects, including nuclear-power plants, and completed work on the St. Lawrence Seaway. Economist Kenneth Rea calls these the "prosperous years."[5] Rea adds that while the Ontario government might take credit for permitting growth to occur and even, on occasion, stimulating it, the motor pushing Ontario's growth was in fact the private sector.

Ontario found the 1970s more difficult as jobs, capital, and people moved west and energy prices skyrocketed. The weakening economy forced the provincial government to act to control public spending. In the field of higher education, the subject of intense public criticism, Queen's Park moved to get, in historian Paul Axelrod's words, "more scholar for the dollar."[6] The severe recession in the automobile industry in the early 1980s also hit Ontario hard. After 1984, however, recovery was rapid. Then, in 1990, recession again descended on the province and

On the 56th floor of the Toronto-Dominion Centre, Toronto, April 1966. Constructed from 1963 to 1969, this building was designed by the German-American architect Mies van der Rohe, and reflected the International Style of architecture. Skyscrapers like this one came to dominate cityscapes from the 1960s onward.

The Globe and Mail/66104-38. Reprinted with permission from *The Globe and Mail*.

unemployment rose dramatically, especially in manufacturing industries, construction, and retail sales. Economists blamed high interest rates, high wage rates, and high prices for commercial real estate. It would take until 1994 for Ontario to recover the jobs lost during the downturn.

Ontario's material success and political power have coloured other Canadians' views of the province. In the past, Westerners and Maritimers suspected central Canada of using Confederation to cement its economic mastery over the rest of the country. Then, in the 1970s, Westerners denounced Ottawa for an oil policy that benefited Ontario, while citizens of less-favoured provinces, ready to "deal with the devil if he had money to invest," as Newfoundland premier Joey Smallwood colourfully put it, criticized the economic nationalism then popular in southern Ontario.

Ontarians held the outsiders' views as largely unjustified, the product of envy, resentment, and frustration. They point out that their taxes pay a large portion of the cost of the equalization grants, unemployment insurance, farm subsidies, and industrial-development projects that the federal government gives poorer regions. Ontario, they insist, has done its share to shoulder the "burden of unity." Indeed, by the 1980s, as political scientists David Cameron and Richard Simeon point out, Ontario had its own grievances to pursue, and its own interests to defend.[7]

Economic expansion proved a mixed blessing. Toronto's high living costs caused increased homelessness and other social problems. Highway congestion worsened as millions of residents of relatively low-density communities beyond Toronto's core relied mainly on their automobiles for travel. Huge swathes of prime agricultural land disappeared beneath shopping malls, suburbs, and industrial parks. Ontario's northern wilderness retreated rapidly as a result of clearcut logging. In the south, natural sites necessary for maintaining biological diversity have been increasingly threatened, and destroyed, as moneyed interests clashed in uneven battle with environmental advocates.

POLITICS IN ONTARIO

Politically, the Progressive Conservatives dominated Ontario throughout the period, until the Liberal victory of 1985. Three premiers in particular made their mark: Leslie Frost, "Old Man Ontario," who co-operated with the federal Liberals in many development projects; John Roberts, a self-described "management man," who oversaw the expansion of the education system in the 1960s; and William Davis, a pragmatic politician who was Trudeau's strongest ally in the patriation of the Canadian Constitution in 1982.

After 1985, Ontario entered an era of political volatility. The government of Liberal Premier David Peterson soon found itself in conflict with Ottawa over free trade with the United States, while its support of Brian Mulroney's Meech Lake Accord undoubtedly cost it voter support. In 1990, the overconfident Liberals lost the election to the NDP, which promised to fight free trade, to make corporations pay their fair share of taxes, and to stiffen pollution controls. Once in power, new Premier Bob Rae cautioned against high expectations of radical change. Yet, in its first budget in 1991, the NDP government opted for a massive deficit in an effort to counteract the deleterious effects of the recession on Ontario's economy. As deficits rose, the Rae government raised taxes and imposed a stringent restraint program designed to control public-sector wages while protecting jobs: employees were to take unpaid holidays, baptized "Rae days." Unions condemned the measures. Employment equity legislation and a law banning the use of replacement workers during strikes displeased business. Popular support for the NDP collapsed, ensuring the government's defeat in 1995 by the Progressive Conservative party led by Mike Harris, who promised to implement a "Common Sense Revolution."

THE "COMMON SENSE REVOLUTION"

Harris cut provincial income taxes substantially yet, thanks to a booming economy, managed to balance the budget by 2000. He also cut spending by decreasing the number of public servants, hospital workers, and teachers, and by reducing welfare payments. These cuts provoked "Days of Action" protests led by organized labour against "Mean Mike" and his policies. The government also took control of education funding, but in turn devolved new responsibilities upon municipalities. It ordered the merger of Metro Toronto's six municipalities, and it also attempted to deregulate the electricity market. These measures provoked some of the most acrimonious debates in the province's history. Business praised the Harris government for restoring competitiveness by lowering taxes, while critics blamed spending cuts for the growth of social inequalities. Indeed, when a contaminated water supply in the town of Walkerton made hundreds of residents sick and resulted in the deaths of seven persons in the summer of 2000, a judicial inquiry laid part of the responsibility on a lack of government controls, due to spending cuts.

In 2002, Harris resigned and was replaced by Ernie Eves, a former finance minister. Then, in elections held in 2003, the Liberals, led by Dalton McGuinty, defeated the Conservatives. Although the Liberals had said they would not raise taxes or electricity rates, they put aside their promises when they discovered, after the election, the existence of a huge budget deficit inherited from the Conservatives.

THE WEST

Since World War II, the region that consists of Manitoba, Saskatchewan, and Alberta has undergone immense change, and the economies of the three provinces have lost much of their former similarity. Oil and gas have replaced agriculture as by far the leading components of the Alberta economy. Agriculture occupies a much greater position in Saskatchewan, while Manitoba boasts a more diversified economy. In the period after 1960, the West's historical sense of powerlessness remained: the region saw itself as a victim of federal policies concerning energy, railway transportation, and agriculture. In recent years, trade relations with central Canada have weakened as all three provinces, and British Columbia, have developed closer ties with the United States.

WESTERN ALIENATION

During the prosperous 1970s, western dissatisfaction grew as the federal government of Prime Minister Pierre Trudeau seemed to give little heed to the region's aspirations. Anger peaked in 1980 when the unpopular Trudeau announced the National Energy Program. The recession of 1981–82 undermined the heady confidence that many westerners had felt during the prosperous 1970s. When Trudeau resigned and when the federal Conservatives won power in 1984 with a strong Prairie contingent, westerners were at first reassured. But soon falling prices for agricultural commodities, oil, and other resources, as well as Ottawa's perceived preoccupation with Quebec, provoked new frustrations.

The meteoric rise of the Reform party after 1987 showed the West's dissatisfaction with the mainstream parties. Proclaiming that "the West wants in," the party condemned the federal government's financial mismanagement, its "welfare-state approach" to meeting social needs, and its commitment to official bilingualism and multiculturalism as well as its immigration policy.

Reform was relaunched in 2000 as the Canadian Alliance but the party's poor showing outside the West in the federal election of 2000 led to increased intraparty strife and the selection of a new leader, Stephen Harper, a former Reform party MP. While continuing to advocate fiscal conservatism, smaller government, and greater autonomy for the provinces, the Alliance also defended Western positions such as opposition to federal gun registration and to environmental controls that might hurt the petroleum industry. At the same time it attempted to widen its geographical and social base by seeking to distance itself from the Reform party's conservative views on abortion, gay rights, and immigration. In 2004, the Progressive Conservative party, with strength in Ontario and the Atlantic provinces, and the western-based Canadian Alliance merged to form a new Conservative party, led by Harper. Elections held in June 2004 enabled the party to increase its representation in Ontario but also underlined the dominant importance of its western base. In addition, francophones saw little reason to give support to the party.

MANITOBA

Manitoba's diversified farming industry occupies a relatively small area in the southwestern portion of the province. Manufacturing is important, while mining and hydro-electricity have undergone considerable development in the north since the mid-1950s. Exploitation of the West's non-agricultural resources at first generated new markets for Winnipeg manufacturers, but the rise of Calgary and Edmonton meant new competition. Winnipeg suffered, too, from the decline of traditional industries such as meat-packing and clothing. Other industries expanded, taking advantage of free trade to increase sales in the United States. In the 1990s, large construction projects also produced economic stimulus, and a low unemployment rate.

Since the 1950s, the Conservatives and the NDP have dominated Manitoba politics. Duff Roblin's Progressive Conservative government of the 1960s proved more progressive than conservative, spending heavily on health, welfare, and education. It also invested heavily in hydroelectric projects such as the huge installations on the Nelson River. Some government-supported private projects failed, however: the Churchill Forest Industries complex at The Pas was halted when the owners disappeared with most of the money. Higher taxes also weakened support for the Conservative government.

In 1969, after building a broad electoral base, popular NDP leader Ed Schreyer succeeded in defeating the Conservatives. In these years of relative prosperity, the Schreyer government spent heavily on public housing and adopted major tax and social reforms. It also launched a second huge hydro-electric development project in the north. Conservative critics denounced the NDP's public automobile-insurance plan, its higher taxes, its investment of public monies in firms of doubtful financial health and, in general, "socialistic" state intervention. When the Conservatives recaptured power in 1977, they proceeded with a program of restraint and lower taxes, but in 1981 cutbacks and the province's dismal economic performance contributed to a return to office of the NDP, led by Howard Pawley.

NDP GOVERNMENT IN MANITOBA

The Pawley government stimulated the province's economy by beginning work on still another hydro megaproject, at Limestone on the Nelson River, and by participating in huge reconstruction projects such as the Core Area Initiative in downtown Winnipeg. By 1987, however, massive tax increases and a restraint program, made necessary by declining federal transfers, gave rise to much discontent.

The question of the linguistic rights of the Franco-Manitoban community also generated fierce debate. In 1971, the Schreyer government had authorized the use of French as a language of instruction in schools, thus restoring a constitutional right taken away in the nationalist frenzy of World War I. Then, in the late 1980s, the Pawley government proposed to extend French-language services. This time, however, the adamant opposition of the Conservatives to new "concessions" forced the government to retreat. After the Conservatives came to power in 1988, they attacked the Meech Lake Accord, perceived as favouring Quebec. They also held the line on taxes, helping them win a third mandate in 1995. Pursuing a neo-conservative agenda, they restructured the delivery of social and health-care services, centralized control over education, and legislated wage rollbacks in the public sector.

Spending cuts as well as increased revenues brought in by a buoyant economy made it possible to eliminate budget deficits. But in 1999, Manitobans, tired of restraint, elected an NDP government led by Gary Doer, a former union leader. Doer reassuringly promised to respect Conservative fiscal policy legislation. In order to limit the power of money in politics, his government acted to end union and corporate contributions to political parties, the second province, after Quebec in 1977, to act in this manner.

SASKATCHEWAN

Neighbouring Saskatchewan's political development has differed substantially from Alberta's. After 1944, the moderately socialist CCF implemented a series of social and economic reforms. Saskatchewan became the first province to enact medicare in 1962. In 1964, the Liberals, led by Ross Thatcher who saw himself as "chosen by God to get rid of these socialists," defeated the CCF (now the NDP). Although they did not dismantle popular CCF reforms, they did work to attract private capital to develop the province's natural resources including potash and pulp and paper.

Denouncing Thatcher's autocratic style and promising a "New Deal for People," the NDP regained power in 1971 and moved to make the provincial government a major player in economic development. It nationalized a large American-owned potash company. It pursued a vigorous exploration and development program in uranium. It established an enterprise that bought large blocks of shares in private companies. Relations between the NDP government of Allan Blakeney and the Trudeau government in Ottawa were frequently strained as both governments struggled over the control of resources and the pricing and taxing of oil, gas, and potash.

SASKATCHEWAN'S ECONOMY

Saskatchewan's booming economy in the 1970s generated increasing revenues, which enabled the Blakeney government to pursue an agenda of "province-building" and to expand health care. Blakeney considered the low living standards of Native peoples to be the province's most serious social problem. Although his government acted to improve conditions in Aboriginal communities in the north, it failed to address the serious social problems of Natives living in the cities.

Agriculture, the province's largest industry, remained subject to violent swings, depending on world wheat prices, export markets, and weather conditions. Low prices for grain and the high costs of technological innovation forced smaller and less efficient farmers to sell their land to larger operators. The Blakeney government hoped to reduce the province's dependence on wheat. But at the same time, in an attempt to stem the decline of the family farm, it set up the Land Bank to provide small farmers with low-cost leased land from the government. Serious administrative problems and wildly fluctuating land prices eventually undermined the bank. Between 1976 and 1996, Saskatchewan lost 14 000 farms. Disused grain elevators, abandoned rail lines and closed hospitals symbolized the sad breakdown of small-town Saskatchewan. In the late 1990s, drought and competition from heavily-subsidized American farmers again brought repeated calls for assistance, eventually heeded by Ottawa, from angry grain farmers.

In 1982, the Progressive Conservatives scored a resounding victory, promising measures to increase the ordinary person's disposable income and particularly to abolish the provincial gasoline tax. As champions of free enterprise, the Conservatives also pursued an aggressive privatization strategy. By the late 1980s, however, an alarming rise in Saskatchewan's budget deficit necessitated substantial cuts in social services and even the re-imposition of a provincial gasoline tax. In addition, political scandals also discredited the government.

Return to Power of the NDP

Popular discontent, particularly rife in urban areas, brought the NDP, now led by Roy Romanow, back to power in 1991. The province's dire financial problems forced the new government to increase sales and income taxes and make large spending cuts, provoking the discontent particularly of public-sector unions, whose members represented a major electoral constituency of the NDP. Impressive economic growth in the early years of the decade, and strong oil and gas prices did, however, strengthen the province's financial health. In 2001, Lorne Calvert succeeded Romanow as premier but had to govern in coalition with provincial Liberals. The Saskatchewan party, a new right-wing party formed from the discredited Conservative party, made significant inroads in rural areas, promising a free-enterprise agenda. A return to deficit financing and accusations of mismanagement appeared to diminish the NDP's popularity, but fears that the opposition Saskatchewan party would privatize public utilities nevertheless enabled the NDP to win a tiny majority of seats in new elections in 2003.

Alberta

Already by the late 1950s, revenues from the sale of oil and gas made it possible for Alberta to spend more money per capita, notably on health and education, than any other province. Then, in the mid-1970s, the sharp increase in international oil prices brought immense new wealth to the province as well as a sense of independence and self-confidence. A bitter crisis in Edmonton–Ottawa relations followed. Strongly influenced by Ontario's pressures to have oil and gas considered "national commodities, belonging to all Canadians," the Trudeau government imposed its National Energy Program, with a "made-in-Canada" oil price that allowed Canadian consumers to pay prices lower than the world price. The producing provinces resented federal price controls, which deprived them of billions of dollars. At one point, the Alberta government reduced the flow of crude oil to the East, and some Alberta automobile bumpers sported stickers belligerently inviting easterners to "freeze in the dark." Alberta also vigorously opposed the Trudeau government's policy of Canadianization of the oil industry, blaming it for the decline in investment in the oil fields.

The expanding oil industry promoted rapid population growth in Alberta as easterners migrated in search of high-paying jobs. Construction boomed in Calgary and Edmonton. Other regions of the province also prospered. Fort McMurray, for example, had only 1200 residents in 1964, when work began on a huge project to extract synthetic crude oil from the Athabasca tar sands. By 1978, when the Syncrude plant opened, the town had a population of 35 000.

Sharply lower oil prices in the mid-1980s checked Alberta's growth and clearly showed the basic fragility of its resource-based economy. Construction on the huge synthetic-oil production and heavy-oil upgrading projects ceased. The jobless rate matched eastern Canadian levels; indeed, many unemployed workers returned to eastern and central Canada. The oil industry urged Ottawa to apply a floor price to provide some stability to the industry. At the same time, Alberta farmers were forced to contend with drought, increasing costs, and declining world grain prices, although huge federal subsidies helped cushion the blow.

ONE-PARTY POLITICS

Politically, Albertans have long favoured one-party dominance. For 36 years, until 1971, they supported Social Credit, as the once-reformist party led by Ernest Manning provided conservative government in a climate of general prosperity fuelled by rising oil revenues. Tensions developed beneath the surface: unions resented labour-relations laws with strong anti-strike provisions, and many Albertans failed to benefit from the new riches. Strongly supported by urban Alberta, a revived Progressive Conservative party led by Calgary lawyer Peter Lougheed won power in 1971 and established a new political dynasty. The immense amounts of oil money flowing into the Alberta treasury greatly assisted the Lougheed government, although it did have to face a resurgence of union militancy during the recession of the early 1980s.

Far higher government expenditures on education, health and welfare services under Lougheed's successor, Don Getty, a former football player, soon led to massive budgetary deficits. Several enterprises in which the Getty government invested money went into bankruptcy. After Getty's resignation in 1992, new leader Ralph Klein, a former mayor of Calgary, successfully warded off Conservative collapse in an election campaign based largely on personality, and then instituted a policy of radical budget cuts to social spending which produced a balanced budget by 1995.

Prime Minister Pierre Trudeau and Alberta Premier Peter Lougheed, 1973, at the Western Economic Opportunities Conference in Calgary. Appearances can be deceiving — despite the cordiality evident in this photograph, animosity existed between the two leaders over the federal government's pricing of Alberta oil and gas.

Herald Collection/Glenbow Archives, Calgary, Canada/NA-2864-23502.

Between 1996 and 2001, Alberta's population increased by more than 10 percent, thanks to an influx of job-seekers from other provinces. Abundant oil revenues enabled the province to reduce income taxes to the lowest levels in Canada, to pay down the provincial debt, and to increase public spending substantially. It also gave large wage increases to health and education personnel, thus putting heavy pressure on neighbouring, less-favoured provinces. In 2001, the popular "King Ralph" won his third and largest majority government. By 2002, Alberta was again spending more per capita on publicly financed programs than any other province.

THE ENVIRONMENT

Economic growth carried a price. Increased logging, together with industrial activity and mining, threatened the last portions of wilderness in the province's northern forests. The provincial government showed scant interest in studying the potentially negative effects of development projects on the environment. Oil and gas production generated huge quantities of greenhouse gases, seen as responsible for climate change. Not surprisingly, Alberta vigorously opposed the federal government's intention to ratify the Kyoto Protocol, which stipulated the reduction of such gases: environmental considerations must not be allowed to threaten the province's thriving economy. Critics noted that energy companies were major contributors to the Conservative party, but polls showed that most Albertans supported their government's position.

BRITISH COLUMBIA

Between 1961 and 2001, British Columbia's population quadrupled to more than 4 million people. Stimulated by the province's rich natural resources, the economy generated high per-capita incomes. Enthusiastic newcomers called it a "lotus land." The province's location on the Pacific Ocean gives it a unique orientation. Indeed, as historian Jean Barman put it, "the more British Columbians looked toward the Pacific Rim, the more the rest of Canada receded into irrelevance."[8] Massive inflows of investment as well as large numbers of new immigrants, mainly from Asia, helped maintain an economic boom. In the late 1990s, however, Asia's faltering economies had a strongly negative impact on British Columbia, precipitating it into recession. Declining prices for raw materials, international competition, and American duties on imports of softwood lumber from Canada compounded the difficulties. Fortunately tourism, the film industry, business services, and high technology industries continued to show promise.

Community Portrait

✦ Clayoquot Sound and the Environmental Movement

The "War in the Woods"

On May 5, 2000, Canadian political leaders met at Clayoquot Sound, on the west coast of Vancouver Island, to unveil a plaque designating this area of great natural beauty as a United Nations biosphere reserve. Henceforth any logging in the area was to be carried out in an environmentally friendly manner. Forestry specialists described the project as the most significant eco-system management experiment in British Columbia's history, and perhaps Canada's.

Traditionally, the forest industry showed little concern for environmental values. Priority went to short-term profit considerations. Then, in the early 1980s, many people began to worry about the accelerating destruction of the earth's last remaining rain-forests, both tropical and temperate. Environmentalists cited biologists who argued that old-growth forests, with deep, multi-layered canopies and centuries of accumulated deadfall on the forest floor harboured an enormous diversity of species whose survival depended on the preserva-tion of such rainforests. Clearcut logging, the method preferred by the forest industry, could not be reconciled with the preserva-tion of biodiversity.

People who were convinced that British Columbia's forestry policies made it "the Brazil of the North" joined the groups inter-ested in wilderness conservation that sprang up. In the late 1980s and early 1990s, envi-ronmentalists actively promoted preserva-tion, notably in the Queen Charlotte Islands.

Clayoquot, an area of some 260 000 ha, was the last major unexploited watershed on Vancouver Island. In 1993, the provincial government, then MacMillan Bloedel's largest shareholder, gave the forestry giant permission to clearcut most of the area's rainforest. Angry environmentalists formed a group, "Friends of Clayoquot Sound," which, in the summer of 1993, waged a "war in the woods," a non-violent campaign of civil disobedience to protest against the government's action. They set up camp in the Black Hole clearcut, an area logged in the 1970s, replanted unsuccessfully four times and now badly eroded. Women were the key organizers of the protest. Fearing that concessions would encourage environmentalists to seek to protect other areas from logging, MacMillan Bloedel obtained an injunction banning demonstrations on company work sites. The government had 900 protestors arrested at the blockades, charged with criminal contempt of court for defying the injunction, and jailed or fined. Friends of Clayoquot continued their campaign, by targeting industrial consumers of British Columbia timber in Europe and threatening boycotts of their products. This tactic proved quite effective, and the battle at Clayoquot achieved international notoriety.

In October 1993, the British Columbia government appointed a panel composed of members of the region's First Nation, the Nuu-chah-nulth, and a team of scientists and technicians. The panel recommended an ecosystem approach that emphasized the maintenance of biological diversity, watershed integrity, and the protection of cultural, scenic, and recreational values. Clearcutting as a method of harvest was to be replaced by a method called "variable-retention," an alternative silvicultural system whereby trees and patches of forest are retained to protect a variety of values and ecosystem components. The government agreed to implement all of the panel's recommendations. MacMillan Bloedel then suspended its clearcutting operations and negotiated with First Nations and environmentalists to find a mutually acceptable approach to some continued logging.

After the Clayoquot campaign, environmentalists won other victories. The provincial government set out a new Forest Practices Code that reduced the maximum size of clearcuts and mandated replanting of harvested areas. British Columbia also moved to place 13 percent of its land base

A clearcut in the Temagami region in northeastern Ontario. The area was a focal point of environmental protests at the end of the 1980s. Today 95 percent of lumber harvesting in Ontario is still done by clearcut.
Courtesy Canadian Parks and Wilderness Society — Wildlands League.

in protected areas, in recognition of its responsibilities in regard to the United Nations Convention on Biological Diversity, which Canada had signed in 1992. Environmental critics asserted however that protected areas were often "rock and ice" where industry had no interest, and that old-growth forests were under-represented. Nor were there any guarantees that a future, more business-oriented government might not roll back environmental protection, or fail to monitor and enforce forest management rules. Indeed, critics have faulted the new Liberal government for acting in precisely this manner.

The initiatives of the environmental movement generated substantial opposition. Compromise between preservationist and economic imperatives seemed impossible. The logging industry accused environmentalists of increasing its costs and diminishing its profits. Forestry workers argued that restrictions on logging would lead to job losses. Some rural communities feared for their very existence. At times

Native peoples and environmentalists differed in their attitudes toward nature. And governments wanted the attendant tax revenues and stumpage fees that the lumber industry provided.

Yet issues were undoubtedly more complex than they first appeared. Was it possible to assign a value in dollars to the maintenance of biodiversity? What would happen to jobs once all old-growth stands were cut? Was reforestation of areas already harvested not a wiser option to assure a sustainable forest industry? Could not other industries such as tourism and recreation offer new potential thanks to wilderness preservation?

The environmental movement's activities brought all those interested in British Columbia's forests, and in forests elsewhere in Canada, to ask these questions, and to seek answers.

Further Readings

Benjamin Cashore, George Hoberg, Michael Howlett, Jeremy Rayner, Jeremy Wilson, *In Search of Sustainability: British Columbia Forest Policy in the 1990s* (Vancouver: UBC Press, 2001).

Jeremy Wilson, *Talk and Log: Wilderness Politics in British Columbia, 1965–96* (Vancouver: UBC Press, 1998).

Since the 1980s, environmentalists and partisans of unfettered economic growth have waged a bitter struggle. Traditional development policy emphasized rapid timber harvesting. Little thought was given to long-term consequences. Indeed, as late as 1980, most logged land was not reforested. The provincial government generally accommodated the industry's wishes. In 1989, for example, Premier Bill Vander Zalm vetoed a cabinet proposal to reduce pulp and paper industry pollutants such as dioxins, declaring: "While I love the environment ... I also love those ... pulp mill workers and someone has to stand up for their jobs." In the 1990s, the NDP government's attempts to develop a more comprehensive approach to forestry practices and conservation provoked substantial opposition from industry and labour.

POLITICAL POLARIZATION IN BRITISH COLUMBIA

British Columbia's political history in the last half-century has been unique. Until recently, two parties with strong Prairie roots but ideologically very different, the Social Credit and the CCF-NDP, controlled the provincial government. In 1952, the Social Credit party, led by W.A.C. Bennett, won a close election by emphasizing the party's role as the new standard-bearer of free enterprise. Bennett governed for the next 20 years, keeping the "socialist hordes" at bay and, as he himself once said, "making policies for the hour."

During the Bennett years, the state played an active role in economic development despite Social Credit's much-vaunted dedication to private enterprise. It assisted large corporations in consolidating their control of the resource sector, by offering them tax concessions, low stumpage rates for timber, and cheap hydroelectricity. It improved highway, maritime, and rail transportation. It nationalized the giant B.C. Electric Company and undertook hydro-electric projects. One of these, the gigantic Peace River Dam, created Williston Lake, the province's largest body of water. Bennett also successfully battled with the federal government in 1961 over sales to the United States of electricity from the Columbia dams, which he favoured.

In 1972, disenchantment with the long-governing Bennett regime favoured the election of the NDP, which promised greater economic and social equality. Under combative leader Dave Barrett, it initiated many controversial reforms — its opponents accused it of "legislating by thunderbolt" — including public automobile insurance and a new innovative labour code. Barrett's reforms, high spending, and new taxes led conservative forces to unite in reaction. Assisted by an economic downturn, this new coalition brought the populist Social Credit party back to power in 1975, under W.R. "Bill" Bennett, W.A.C. Bennett's son.

In the early 1980s, the fall in world market prices for British Columbia's major exports, notably forest products and minerals, pushed the province into a prolonged recession. The government's attempts to curtail spending provoked a fierce confrontation with the public-sector unions, mobilized within "Operation Solidarity," and Social Credit's popularity sank to new lows. But the climate of optimism brought on by Expo 86, which attracted large numbers of visitors, and the "sunshine offensive" of William Vander Zalm, Social Credit's charismatic new leader, enabled the party to win re-election.

Serious conflict-of-interest allegations forced Vander Zalm to resign in 1991. His successor, Rita Johnston, became the first woman in Canada to head a provincial government. In the elections that soon followed, the NDP, led by former Vancouver Mayor Mike Harcourt, took power, promising it would favour moderate, "sustainable development" policies. The province's economy remained strong; its diversification continued, as new service-sector jobs, many related to tourism, more than compensated for the loss of employment in the primary sector. But Harcourt's consensual approach in regard to controversial questions such as the environment, social issues, and labour satisfied few people and indeed made the premier appear weak and indecisive. Higher taxes as well as other measures to control the budget deficit also proved unpopular.

Visitors to Expo 86 in Vancouver are dwarfed by the Expo Centre. Expo generated a mood of optimism in the province's Lower Mainland.

Canadian Press/CP.

Prosperity brought its share of problems. New jobs went principally to the Lower Mainland; resource-based communities in the interior lost jobs and feared for their future. Expensive condominiums sprouted throughout burgeoning Vancouver's city centre, but less prosperous residents struggled to find scarce affordable accommodation, and homelessness increased. In addition, problems of traffic congestion and air pollution threatened to overwhelm the region.

The late 1990s brought hard times. Lost Asian markets, punitive American trade policies, and low prices provoked sawmill closures and job losses. Investment lagged, and average real take-home pay declined. Public spending increased, and so did budget deficits. Critics censured the NDP government as unfriendly to business and blamed environmental regulations for increased industry costs.

In 1996, Glen Clark replaced Harcourt as premier. His style, less consensual, brought him personal blame for what was perceived by many as government incompetence, such as the massive cost overruns of a ferry-construction project, and for poor financial administration, notably in the case of the so-called "fudge-it budgets" in which predicted surpluses turned into large deficits.

In 2001, the Liberals — actually a heterogeneous coalition of conservatives — led by Gordon Campbell, also a former mayor of Vancouver, won a crushing victory over the NDP.

They immediately adopted a popular 25 percent tax cut, thereby provoking a huge increase in the budget deficit. The new government then attacked spending, announcing significant reductions in all areas except education and health-care. It unilaterally rewrote contracts of health and social-service workers, and imposed collective agreements on teachers and nurses. To find more money it raised medical premiums, deregulated university tuition fees, and increased the provincial sales tax. It could also now count on equalization payments from Ottawa, as Canada's eighth have-not province.

BRITISH COLUMBIA–FIRST NATIONS RELATIONS

Government–First Nations relations became an important public policy issue in this period, as the provincial government, reversing a century-old policy, began to participate in the negotiation of treaties. A first agreement, with the Nisga'a of northwestern British Columbia, was concluded in 1998. In 2002, the new Liberal administration held a controversial referendum on treaty-making. A large majority of those who voted wished to limit Aboriginal rights. In any event, under the Constitution of 1982, no province has jurisdiction to determine key issues of title.

Since Confederation, Canada has been an often uneasy association of regions and sub-regions. Differences in geography, culture, language, and population reinforce regionalism, but within English-speaking Canada, economic issues have probably been most significant. The nature of the Canadian economy has been such that the nation's wealth has been concentrated in relatively small areas of the country. Such profound imbalances, though inevitable, create tension.

In the course of debates over the distribution of national wealth and the determination of national policy, the federal government has often played the role of arbiter, to mitigate provincial discontent and regional conflict. No federal budget, however, can be sufficient to satisfy all the demands upon it. And each major federal decision provokes the anger of provinces that, rightly or wrongly, blame Ottawa for being overly attuned to the needs and interests of other provinces and regions.

Canada's history, both early and recent, demonstrates the strength of the provinces and the power of regional interest groups. In this regard, the future will likely resemble the past, and regionalism will thus remain a major challenge to Canadian unity.

NOTES

1. Robert Finbow, "Atlantic Canada: Forgotten Periphery in an Endangered Confederation?" in Kenneth McRoberts, ed., *Beyond Quebec: Taking Stock of Canada* (Montreal/Kingston: McGill-Queen's University Press, 1995), p. 67.
2. G.A. Rawlyk, "The Maritimes and the Problem of the Secession of Quebec, 1967 to 1969," in R.M. Burns, ed., *One Country or Two?* (Montreal/Kingston: McGill-Queen's University Press, 1971), p. 212.
3. Miriam Wright, *A Fishery for Modern Times: The State and the Industrialization of the Newfoundland Fishery, 1934–1968* (Toronto: Oxford University Press, 2001), p. 103.
4. J.E. Belliveau, *Little Louis and the Giant K.C.*, quoted in Rand Dyck, *Provincial Politics in Canada* (Scarborough, ON: Prentice-Hall, 1986), p. 171.
5. K.J. Rea, *The Prosperous Years: The Economic History of Ontario, 1939–75* (Toronto: University of Toronto Press, 1985).
6. Paul Axelrod, *Scholars and Dollars: Politics, Economics, and the Universities of Ontario, 1945–1980* (Toronto: University of Toronto Press, 1982), pp. 141–78.

7. David Cameron and Richard Simeon, "Ontario in Confederation: The Not-so-Friendly Giant," in Graham White, *The Government and Politics of Ontario*, 5th ed. (Toronto: University of Toronto Press, 1997), p. 159.

8. Jean Barman, *The West Beyond the West: A History of British Columbia*, new ed. (Toronto: University of Toronto Press, 1996), p. 351.

LINKING TO THE PAST

Canadian Statistics
http://www.statcan.ca/english/Pgdb/

Statistics on the economy, land, people, and state, from Statistics Canada. Under "People," check out recent statistics on each province's population and growth, education, employment, housing, culture, and much more.

A History of the Northern Cod Fishery
http://collections.ic.gc.ca/cod/

An extensive, illustrated history of the cod fishery in Atlantic Canada. Of special interest for this chapter are the last six sections, which provide information on the destruction of this natural resource and on attempts to rebuild the Atlantic fish stocks.

The Smallwood Years
http://www.heritage.nf.ca/law/prov_gov.html

A brief look at Newfoundland between 1949 and 1972.

Athabasca Oil Sands
http://collections.ic.gc.ca/oil/index1.htm

An introduction to the history, geology, and mining of Athabasca Oil Sands in Alberta.

Friends of Clayoquot Sound
http://www.focs.ca/

This site includes background information on the logging dispute in Clayoquot Sound as well as a detailed, illustrated report.

W.A.C. Bennett
http://sunnyokanagan.com/wacbennett/index.html

A page devoted to W.A.C. Bennett that features an informal biography and numerous photographs, including a reproduction of the Canada Post stamp that bears his likeness.

BIBLIOGRAPHY

Studies of regionalism include Stephen G. Tomblin, *Ottawa and the Outer Provinces: The Challenge of Regional Integration in Canada* (Toronto: James Lorimer, 1995); and R. Harley McGee, *Getting It Right: Regional Development in Canada* (Montreal/Kingston: McGill-Queen's University Press, 1992). Works on provincial politics include Keith Brownsey and Michael Howlett, eds., *The Provincial State in Canada: Politics in the Provinces and Territories* (Peterborough: Broadview Press, 2001), and Rand Dyck, *Provincial Politics in Canada: Towards the Turn of the Century*, 3rd ed. (Toronto: Prentice-Hall, 1996).

The best overview of the Atlantic provinces is E.R. Forbes and D.A. Muise, eds., *The Atlantic Provinces in Confederation* (Toronto: University of Toronto Press, 1993). Miriam Wright, *A Fishery for Modern Times: The State and the Industrialization of the Newfoundland Fishery, 1934–1968* (Toronto: Oxford University Press, 2001), is a useful study of a major economic issue. Economic development issues in New Brunswick are examined in Donald J. Savoie, *Pulling against Gravity: Economic Development in New Brunswick during the McKenna Years* (Montreal/Kingston: McGill-Queen's University Press, 2001). The Acadian community is studied by Richard Wilbur, *The Rise of French New Brunswick* (Halifax: Formac, 1989). The fascinating story of New Brunswick's major business magnate is told in Douglas How and Ralph Costello, *K.C.: The Biography of K.C. Irving* (Toronto: Key Porter, 1993).

An excellent study of federal government intervention in Nova Scotia's economy is James P. Bickerton, *Nova Scotia, Ottawa, and the Politics of Regional Development* (Toronto: University of Toronto Press, 1990). Douglas Baldwin recounts the history of Canada's smallest province in *Land of the Red Soil: A Popular History of Prince Edward Island*, rev. ed. (Charlottetown: Ragweed Press, 1998).

A general survey of Ontario is available in two books by Randall White: *Ontario, 1610–1985: A Political and Economic History* (Toronto: Dundurn Press, 1985), and *Ontario since 1985: A Contemporary History* (Toronto: Eastendbooks, 1998). For studies of Ontario's economy see K.J. Rea, *The Prosperous Years: The Economic History of Ontario, 1939–75* (Toronto: University of Toronto Press, 1985), and Thomas J. Courchene with Colin R. Telmer, *From Heartland to North American Region State: The Social, Fiscal and Federal Evolution of Ontario. An Interpretive Essay* (Toronto: Centre for Public Management, University of Toronto, 1998). On education in Ontario consult R. D. Gidney, *From Hope to Harris. The Reshaping of Ontario's Schools* (Toronto: University of Toronto Press, 1999). Articles on Ontario politics may be found in Graham White, ed., *The Government and Politics of Ontario*, 5th ed. (Toronto: University of Toronto Press, 1997).

On western Canada, Gerald Friesen, *The Canadian Prairies: A History* (Toronto: University of Toronto Press, 1984), provides a highly original synthesis. See also the same author's *River Road: Essays on Manitoba and Prairie History* (Winnipeg: University of Manitoba Press, 1996). An excellent collection of essays focussing on the West is A.W. Rasporich, ed., *The Making of the Modern West: Western Canada since 1945* (Calgary: University of Calgary Press, 1984). On Western regionalism, see Gerald Friesen, *The West: Regional Ambitions, National Debates, Global Age* (Toronto: Penguin books, 1999); and Roger Gibbins and Sonia Arrison, *Western Visions: Perspectives on the West in Canada* (Peterborough, ON: Broadview Press, 1995).

Jim Silver and Jeremy Hull, eds., *The Political Economy of Manitoba* (Regina: Canadian Plains Research Center, University of Regina, 1990), contains articles on many aspects of the province's economy. Howard A. Leeson studies recent politics in *Saskatchewan Politics: Into the Twenty-First Century* (Regina: Canadian Plains Research Center, 2001). On Alberta, Howard and Tamara Palmer's *Alberta: A New History* (Edmonton: Hurtig, 1990) is a useful survey. For material on the province's political history consult Allan Tupper and Roger Gibbins, eds., *Government and Politics in Alberta* (Edmonton: University of Alberta Press, 1992).

Jean Barman, *The West Beyond the West: A History of British Columbia*, rev. ed. (Toronto: University of Toronto Press, 1996); and Hugh Johnson et al., eds., *The Pacific Province: A History of British Columbia* (Vancouver: Douglas & McIntyre, 1996) are general surveys of that province's history. R.K. Carty, ed., *Politics, Policy, and Government in British Columbia* (Vancouver: University of British Columbia Press, 1996), contains many informative articles, notably on the environment. Philip Resnick proposes an interpretation of British Columbia politics in *The Politics of Resentment: British Columbia Regionalism and Canadian Unity* (Vancouver: UBC Press, 2000).

IMMIGRATION AND ETHNICITY

TIME LINE

1947 –	Parliament repeals the Chinese Exclusion Act
1962 –	Racial discrimination is officially ended in Canada's immigration regulations
1966 –	Department of Manpower and Immigration established
1971 –	Ottawa adopts a multiculturalism policy
1986 –	The Employment Equity Act comes into effect
1993 –	Parliament adopts new legislation on immigration
2003 –	Census statistics showed that fully 18.4 percent of Canada's population were immigrants; the country's foreign-born population was second only to Australia's (22 percent)

The history of Canada's immigrants and ethnic minority groups since 1945 involves three closely intertwined elements: the Canadian government's changing immigration policy; Canadians' response to recent newcomers who have made Canada their new home; and the experience of the immigrants themselves. Discussion of the immigrants' experience gives rise to several more specific questions: Where have the immigrants come from, and why? How have they reacted and adapted to their new environment? And what impact have they had on Canadian society?

Members of Canada's non-French non-British ethnic minorities began to question their place in Canadian society, particularly after the mid-1960s, a time when so many other components of Canada's population were also challenging the perceived inequalities of their own status. They naturally expressed serious reservations about the then popular concept of two nations, or two founding peoples, which, while it ignored the existence of the Native peoples, appeared to give special treatment to Canadians of French and British origins. The federal government's multiculturalism policy, announced in 1971, accorded minority ethnic groups an official status they had not enjoyed in the past. It served as recognition of how Canada, in one century, had become a pluralistic society, one in which people of backgrounds other than English or French made up nearly one-third of the total population.

POSTWAR EUROPEAN IMMIGRATION, 1945–1957

In 1946, millions of destitute refugees from war-torn areas of Europe remained crowded in camps, awaiting a permanent haven. Canada felt little responsibility for them. The country had received virtually no immigration during the preceding 15 years. Most Canadians, tired of being told to "do their part," probably agreed that the country had other, more urgent, priorities to attend to. Canada had its own children, as well as its injured soldiers and veterans, to look after. Furthermore, economists worried that the war's end would bring on another depression, as it had immediately after World War I. A wave of new arrivals risked swelling the ranks of the unemployed.

EUROPEAN REFUGEES

Prime Minister William Lyon Mackenzie King sensed Canadians' hesitancy about immigration. He saw little electoral advantage to be gained by opening the country's doors to Europe's homeless. Pressure, however, continued to mount. A few mainly CCF politicians as well as certain religious groups and ethnic associations insisted that Canada had humanitarian obligations toward the unfortunates of Europe. Finally, the Senate Committee on Immigration and Labour recommended that immigration offices be opened in Europe to process as many displaced persons and refugees as the country could absorb.

The Canadian government moved cautiously. The first refugees to arrive in 1946 were some 4000 Polish veterans who had fought with British military units in the war. Hugh Keenleyside, deputy minister of mines and resources (the department that had responsibility for immigration), felt that Canada should admit a few thousand displaced persons immediately. By acting quickly, Canada could obtain the best candidates, improve the country's international image, and encourage other nations to follow suit. In a critical view, John Holmes, an external-affairs officer, later claimed that Canada selected refugees "like good beef cattle, with a preference for strong young men who could do manual labour and would not be encumbered by aging relatives."[1] By the fall of 1948, 40 000 refugees had reached Canadian shores. Although the numbers then began to decrease, about 165 000 refugees had come to Canada by 1953. Many of them, after arrival, applied to bring in their close relatives.

A Historical Portrait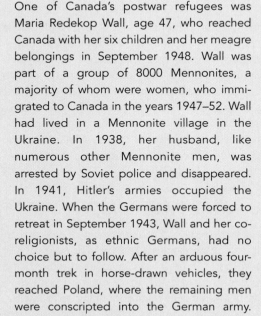

The Immigrant Experience

One of Canada's postwar refugees was Maria Redekop Wall, age 47, who reached Canada with her six children and her meagre belongings in September 1948. Wall was part of a group of 8000 Mennonites, a majority of whom were women, who immigrated to Canada in the years 1947–52. Wall had lived in a Mennonite village in the Ukraine. In 1938, her husband, like numerous other Mennonite men, was arrested by Soviet police and disappeared. In 1941, Hitler's armies occupied the Ukraine. When the Germans were forced to retreat in September 1943, Wall and her co-religionists, as ethnic Germans, had no choice but to follow. After an arduous four-month trek in horse-drawn vehicles, they reached Poland, where the remaining men were conscripted into the German army. With the Soviet advance into Poland in 1944, the Mennonites were again uprooted. Most were taken prisoner by the Soviets; rape and suicides were common. Wall managed to reach a refugee camp in West Germany but spent many anxious months fearing she would be sent back to the USSR. Indeed, at the end of the war, the Red Army did forcibly repatriate thousands of eastern Europeans behind the "iron curtain," often condemning them to prison, persecution, and even death. After spending three years in the camp, Wall was finally chosen to go to Canada. She settled in the Fraser Valley in British Columbia where she bought a berry farm. Adaptation to the new society was not without problems, however, and even within the Mennonite community divergent lifestyles and experiences often strained relations between more conservative Canadian Mennonites and women who had long been forced by extraordinary, and often tragic, circumstances to make decisions and compromises.

This story is told in Marlene Epp, *Women without Men: Mennonite Refugees of the Second World War* (Toronto: University of Toronto Press, 2000).

A number of refugees were well-educated professionals or highly skilled workers. Often, they concealed their training in order to better their chances with Canadian officials, who sought manual labourers. Industries in need of unskilled labour sponsored many of the refugee immigrants, who readily accepted almost any job, salary, and working conditions. Once in Canada, they fulfilled their contractual obligations on farms, in lumber camps, in mines, and often, in the case of women, in domestic service, before moving on to more suitable occupations.

IMMIGRANT LABOUR

Employers frequently exploited new immigrants. One notorious scheme involved Ludger Dionne, an MP and owner of the Dionne Spinning Mill Company at Saint-Georges-de-Beauce, south of Quebec City. In 1947, Dionne obtained government authorization to recruit 100 Polish women for his mill. *Time* reported that he paid them 20 cents an hour; after deductions of $6 a week for board, they were left with $3.60 weekly. Dionne assured parliamentarians that young women from Quebec City did not want to work in the small towns and that his working conditions were better than those in Toronto. For good measure, he also accused his detractors of being propagandists for communism.

Economically, many immigrants progressed rapidly. By 1971, Latvians and Estonians, for example, had incomes that were 25 percent higher than the Canadian average. Political scientist Karl Aun explains this evolution in part by the fact that such groups included unusually large numbers of educational, community, cultural, and political leaders.[2] Yet stories abound like the one about the poor Estonian fisherman who, after settling in southern Ontario, saved as much as possible from the earnings of all family members. Then, with the help of a loan from the Estonian Credit Union, he bought a house with several apartments, continued saving and purchased a second apartment house, moved into the best unit, and eventually sent his children to university.

Historian Franca Iacovetta has described the lives of many poor peasant farmers and rural artisans from southern Italy who settled in Toronto where they faced considerable hardships before they were able to secure a stable life for themselves and their families.[3] Jobs were often dirty, disagreeable, and risky. Iacovetta also examined the personal histories of women refugees from elsewhere in Europe.[4] Each story was unique. Eighteen-year-old Elena Krotz was recruited by Canadian officials in a displaced-persons camp in West Germany. She had fled her native Czechoslovakia when communist authorities sought to arrest her after she participated in a student protest. After staying for a few weeks at a government hostel, Krotz was sent to the home of a farm couple in southwestern Ontario, to work as a servant. She arrived with all her worldly belongings in two tiny bags: a blanket and one change of clothes. A drive to succeed, the encouragement and mutual support of the community, and the relative youth of the newcomers combined to help these immigrants adjust to their new environment.

CANADIAN RESPONSES TO POSTWAR IMMIGRATION

 Since most prospective immigrants to Canada were not refugees, the country needed a general immigration policy. In a much-discussed speech to the House of Commons on May 1, 1947, Prime Minister King attempted to satisfy both supporters and opponents of immigration. He said that Canada would benefit by boosting its population and that immigration would make the country more prosperous and secure. At the same time he put forth the nebulous notion of Canada's "absorptive capacity," promising that the government would "ensure the careful selection and permanent settlement" of only as many immigrants as could "advantageously be absorbed in our national economy." The number admitted could vary from year to year, in an alternating open-door/closed-door approach.

King's comments also reveal Canadian racial attitudes of the era. Responding to those who denounced racial distinctions in immigration policy, the prime minister asserted Canada's right to choose its future citizens. The government did repeal the blatantly discriminatory Chinese exclusion law of 1923. Nevertheless, it continued to apply severe restrictions on Asian immigration since, in King's words, the "massive immigration of Orientals would alter the fundamental composition of the Canadian population" and "give rise to social and economic problems."

Canadians could not agree on how many immigrants the country needed and who should be admitted. Business and financial leaders lobbied for substantial immigration. They argued that a larger population would benefit the economy and yield per-capita savings in areas such as transportation and administration. Ethnic associations and several religious groups also favoured increased immigration.

Many Canadians, however, were reluctant to receive any sizable influx of immigrants. By 1954, only 45 percent of Canadians favoured increased immigration, down from 51 percent in 1947. Many Canadians of British origin feared that immigration would weaken the British element in Canada. Workers often viewed immigrants as competitors willing to work for lower wages. Unions wanted immigrants to be carefully selected and preferably to occupy unattractive jobs in remote regions that Canadians did not want. As the economy began to slow in the late 1950s, a majority of Canadians felt the country was accepting too many immigrants. Senator David Croll, who had been an enthusiastic advocate of higher immigration a decade before, now joked: "If you put pants on a penguin, it could be admitted to this country." After 1957, the new Progressive Conservative government substantially reduced immigration levels.

FRENCH-SPEAKING IMMIGRANTS

As late as 1947, it appeared that if the birth rate of French Canadians remained high, they might one day constitute the largest part of Canada's population. Yet large-scale immigration of non-French-speakers risked undermining the demographic situation of Canada's French-speaking minority. Even in Quebec, francophones often perceived immigrants as a threat because most joined the ranks of the English-speaking minority.

In 1948 the federal government, in hopes of satisfying French-Canadian public opinion, placed French nationals on an equal legal footing with British subjects and American citizens for purposes of entry into Canada. Civil servants, however, immediately subverted the new policy for "security" reasons, arguing that a large proportion of would-be French immigrants might be either communists or former Nazi collaborators.

All told, Ottawa's new policy on French immigration had only a slight effect: between 1946 and 1950, fewer than 5000 French immigrants came to Canada. Although the French authorities did not encourage emigration, prospective immigrants literally besieged Canadian consular offices in Paris. While the Canadian consul in Paris made urgent requests for more staff and more office space, Hugh Keenleyside advised the deputy minister of labour to channel "all efforts in the same direction, that is to say, the encouragement of British immigration to Canada."

Clearly, during this period, the Canadian government preferred British immigrants over all others. In 1955, J.W. Pickersgill, minister of citizenship and immigration, asserted that it was only natural that Canada favour British immigration since it was easier to transplant individuals into "similar soil." Although he viewed the massive influx of new arrivals in 1956–57, 40 percent of whom were British, as "too big for Canada to digest," he added candidly that any attempt to stem the tide of British immigration "would be the finish of the Liberal party in many Anglo-Saxon constituencies."

French immigration did increase in the 1950s and 1960s, before declining again. In the years 1945–80, between one-half and two-thirds of immigrants to Canada were English-speaking, whereas French-speakers numbered only about 3 percent, and bilinguals 4 percent. The remainder, speaking other languages, soon learned English. By 2000, although Canada's major sources of immigrants were no longer European, more than half of new immigrants still spoke English whereas fewer than 10 percent knew French. The census of 2001 showed that immigration was the primary factor in explaining the relative decline of Quebec's population in regard to Canada's total population. Immigration also explained, together with assimilation, why the proportion of francophones in the English-speaking provinces also continued to decline.

AN EVALUATION OF POSTWAR IMMIGRATION POLICY

This first wave of postwar immigration, which brought 1.7 million immigrants to Canada, ended in the late 1950s, when rising unemployment led the Canadian government to reconsider its policy. The year 1957, however, proved a sort of boom before the bust, with 282 000 arrivals — a figure that still paled in comparison with the 400 000 immigrants who came in 1913, when Canada's population was much smaller. Some 37 000 of these new arrivals were mainly young and often highly skilled Hungarians who fled their home-land in 1956 as Soviet armies crushed the Hungarian rev-olution. Among them came the faculty of a Hungarian school of forestry. Transported across Canada on a "freedom train," they were relocated at the University of British Columbia. In general, the resettlement of the Hungarian refugees proceeded smoothly.

Such major movements of people gave rise to myths and half truths. In theory, humanitarian ideals and a sense of international responsibility guided Canadian immigration policy. Canadians believed themselves to be generously offering liberty and opportunity to victims of persecution. In practice, economics usually dictated how many and which immigrants came to Canada. Ottawa sought immigrants possessing certain skills, and initiated bulk labour schemes. Federal authorities directed many immigrants, once in Canada, to farms and to unattractive jobs in remote resource regions. Once they fulfilled their contracts, however, many immigrants soon left for the cities.

Racial bias explains why few immigrants gained entrance from outside Europe and the United States. The introduction of tiny quotas, which remained in effect until 1967, also limited immigration from the Indian sub-continent. In addition, the location of immigration offices and the nature of government promotional literature ensured that the great majority of immigrants came from Britain and the European continent, as well as from the United States.

Jack Pickersgill (right), the federal minister responsible for immigration in the St. Laurent government, greets the dean of the faculty of forestry engineering at the University of Sopron, Hungary, in Montreal, 1957. Some 37 000 young and highly skilled Hungarians, including the entire faculty and student body of this faculty, arrived in Canada during and immediately after the Hungarian uprising of 1956.

Champlain Marcil/National Archives of Canada/PA-147725.

EMIGRATION

During the economic downturn of the late 1950s and early 1960s, immigrants experienced the obverse side of immigration. Disappointed with the lack of opportunities in Canada and embittered by what they considered false promises on Canada's part, many thousands, particularly British, returned home. There they contributed to tarnishing Canada's image, if only temporarily. From the early 1950s to the early 1970s, one in every three or four immigrants to Canada either returned home or moved to the United States.

Even more worrisome to many Canadians was the movement southward of 800 000 native-born Canadians in the period 1952–71. Perhaps one-tenth of this group consisted of profes-sionals or managers — the much-publicized "brain drain." Historian Arthur Lower conjectured that this loss of talent helped keep Canada "in that state of low water which has always been the object of the Yankee's good-natured scorn."[5] After a temporary reversal of the brain drain in the 1960s and early 1970s, at the time of the Vietnam War and race riots in the United States, the movement to the South resumed in the late 1970s and 1980s. The problem worsened in the 1990s. In certain years, the number of nurses and physicians who emigrated represented the equivalent of about one-half of the number of graduates from Canada's nursing and medical schools. Many engineers, scientists, teachers, and managerial workers also joined the trek south, attracted to the United States by the prospect of better working conditions and higher salaries and, perhaps, by southern sunshine. The cost to Canada was substantial, as emigrants took with them skills they had developed in largely publicly financed postsecondary schools.

THE IMMIGRANT EXPERIENCE SINCE THE 1960S

Due to an economic slowdown, the Diefenbaker years (1957–63) witnessed a slump in immigration. Unions expressed fears that immigrants risked taking Canadian workers' jobs. Most MPs were at best indifferent. Even Diefenbaker, despite favourable public pronouncements in speeches aimed at ethnic groups and despite his own non-French non-British origins, appeared to have little interest in the question.

Sometimes immigration made sensational headlines. The press reported numerous cases of foreign seamen who jumped ship in Canadian waters and then hurriedly married Canadian women in order to remain in Canada. Large-scale illegal Chinese immigration also appeared to overwhelm the government. Ottawa promised to grant amnesty to most illegals who would come forth and declare themselves (many thousands did), but illegal immigration rings continued to operate.

The Conservatives introduced new regulations in 1962 that ended the use of race and national origin as reasons for exclusion from Canada. The old discriminatory provisions appeared unacceptable in an era that discredited racism. In 1960, Diefenbaker had proudly presented the Canadian Bill of Rights, which rejected discrimination by reason of race, national origin, colour, religion, or sex. Economic factors also contributed to the reversal of the former policy: Canada could no longer obtain the labour it needed from the "old countries." For a time, southern Europe supplanted Britain and northern Europe as the area of origin of most immigrants to Canada. Then, immigration diminished from these countries, too, and Canada turned its attention toward Asia and the Caribbean.

A NEW WAVE OF IMMIGRANTS

Assisted by the return of economic prosperity in the early 1960s, the Pearson government (1963–68) instituted structural changes designed to increase immigration. In 1966, it established the Department of Manpower and Immigration to relate immigration to the needs of the labour market, while the Department of the Secretary of State obtained responsibility for the integration of immigrants into Canadian society.

New immigration regulations set up a points system for selecting independent immigrants. Criteria included education and training, personal qualities, occupational demand, and age and linguistic capacity. Sponsored dependants and, particularly, non-dependent relatives now found it more difficult to gain admittance. The government also set up the independent Immigration Appeal Board, which was almost immediately overwhelmed with appeals from alleged "visitors" who had applied to stay but had been refused and ordered deported.

The gradual elimination of racial discrimination from Canada's immigration policy, the decline of European sources of immigrants, and the expansion of the network of immigration offices around the world transformed the face of Canadian immigration. In 1966, for example, 87 percent of immigrants were of European origin; only four years later, 50 percent came from other regions. The West Indies, Haiti, Guyana, India, Hong Kong, the Philippines, and Indochina all figured among the major suppliers of immigrants in the 1970s and 1980s. By the 1990s, Sri Lanka and Taiwan had replaced the Caribbean nations as major homelands of arriving immigrants. In the early 2000s, China, India, Pakistan, the Philippines and South Korea, all in Asia, were the most important source countries. Visible ethnic and racial minorities increasingly became part of Canada's social fabric. In 2001, such minorities made up more than 13 percent of the country's population (a figure expected to surpass 20 percent by 2016), and 35 percent of the populations of Vancouver and Toronto. For example, the number of Canadians of Chinese origin increased from 60 000 to nearly 350 000 between 1961 and 1986, and then to 1 million by 2001.

IMMIGRANT SETTLEMENT

The new immigrants did not spread out evenly across the country. Since 1945, about 60 percent of all immigrants have settled in Ontario, especially southern Ontario. Good employment opportunities and the region's prosperous image attracted them, as did well-established ethnic communities with religious centres, clubs, welfare organizations, newspapers, and other services. Quebec, with one-quarter of Canada's population, has usually received fewer than 15 percent of new arrivals — about the same proportion as British Columbia. Alberta, especially during oil booms, also attracted many immigrants.

In all regions, immigrants settled mainly in major metropolitan areas. As many as one-half chose Toronto: by 2001 that city had become North America's most ethnically diverse city and possibly the world's. Vancouver and Montreal also attracted large numbers of immigrants. Big-city Canada thus became much more cosmopolitan.

The Haim Abenhaim family, Sephardic Jewish immigrants from Morocco, arriving in Montreal, 1960. In the early 1970s, immigrants from developing countries began to come to Canada in significant numbers.

Canadian Jewish Congress National Archives/PC 2/1/7 A.4.

ADAPTATION

Most immigrants from developing countries found their new life in Canada a considerable material improvement over the past. In any case, political conditions prevented many immigrants from returning home, even if they so desired. They did, however, face a much greater cultural shock than did earlier British and European immigrants. Provincial governments and community associations have, to an extent, attempted to assist the new arrivals. Mutual aid and support among families have also been important. Still, it has often been difficult to find jobs to match past occupational experience, especially in times of economic slowdown.

Immigrants also faced the upsetting necessity of coming to terms with Canadian customs. A study of South Asians (people from India, Pakistan, Bangladesh, and Sri Lanka) showed that "only a small proportion" of homeland cultural practices survive the settlement process. Culinary habits and cultural celebrations tend to be maintained in those cities where immigrant groups are sufficiently numerous, but it is more difficult to retain religious practices: Hindu parents, for example, often find that children know far more about Christianity than they do about Hinduism. Historian Hugh Johnson recorded the story of Tara Singh Bains, a Punjabi who arrived in Vancouver in 1953. The now-elderly Bains, a man of strong religious convictions, told Johnson he deplored what he saw as the erosion of spiritual values among members of his community. Bains testified, "Materialism has created so many doorways to attract human thinking towards luxury, enjoyment, and selfishness..."[6]

IMMIGRANTS AS A PERCENTAGE OF TOTAL POPULATIONS OF CENSUS METROPOLITAN AREAS, 2001

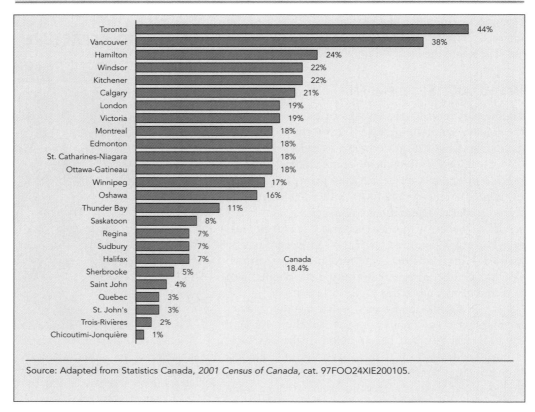

Source: Adapted from Statistics Canada, *2001 Census of Canada*, cat. 97FOO24XIE200105.

Furthermore, the clash between contemporary Canadian values and mores and accepted values and attitudes in the country of origin has frequently caused painful problems for immigrants. For example, the close interaction of the extended family, common in many cultures and providing an extensive support system, has gradually disappeared in North America, where the functional unit is now the nuclear family. The role of women in the family, particularly in southern European and South Asian cultures, has generally been defined very rigidly; male authority generally goes unchallenged, and male financial supremacy backs up that authority. Contact with Canadian mores in this regard has often provoked conflict within the immigrant family. Parental authority has also weakened in the context of Canada's much more permissive society. The generation gap between immigrant parents and their children has often deepened into a gulf as children become Canadianized through the schools, television, and contacts with friends.

DISCRIMINATION

Many immigrants, especially members of visible minorities, suffered discrimination in Canada. In the 1970s and 1980s, the media gave wide publicity to numerous instances in which Sikhs were attacked and their turbans forcibly removed. Blacks were frequently harassed or physically assaulted. In Montreal, a taxi company fired its Haitian drivers, claiming that it was losing

Sod-turning for Edmonton's Hindu Centre, 1976.

Provincial Archives of Alberta.

business to companies that employed only white drivers. (Haitians responded by buying the city's second-largest taxi company.) Incidents of police shootings of young black people in Montreal and Toronto sparked widespread demands for inquiries into alleged racism in police forces.

Historian Stanley Barrett's research on a suburban Toronto community in the early 1990s showed the existence of widespread racism against visible minorities. He suggested that South Asians saw racism as inevitable, and sought to defend themselves by fostering strong links with their own ethnic communities. African Canadians, more in contact with the "white" community, often felt bitterness and anger in the face of what they perceived as rejection by their neighbours. Barrett also found strong negative attitudes toward French Canadians, who were seen as "intent on taking over and ruining the country."[7]

Most complaints about discrimination have concerned employment and housing. One survey showed that three-quarters of West Indians judged employment discrimination in Toronto to be "very serious." Surveys in eleven other Canadian cities repeated the same finding. In 2002, census figures showed that income gaps between immigrants and other Canadians were widening; the Canadian Labour Congress cited racism as a major factor. Although provincial human-rights commissions did receive numerous complaints of discrimination, many victims failed to report incidents, believing that nothing would be done or, worse, fearing retaliation. Human-rights defence groups have criticized the courts for their slowness and their leniency, and have denounced existing laws for their lack of severity.

The Employment Equity Act of 1986 helped bring about a striking increase in the representation of visible minorities in private companies regulated by federal statute, such as banks and transport companies. But, in a period of personnel reductions in the federal civil service, Ottawa was slow to improve its own poor hiring record.

"Established" Canadians have had mixed reactions to the new arrivals from the developing nations. Religious and civic groups have strongly urged the admission of refugees, such as the Indochinese "boat people" in the late 1970s and refugees from Kosovo in 1999. Yet the general population has shown substantial opposition to increased immigration in general, and to immigration from developing countries in particular. Various studies have shown that many Canadians dislike immigrants' speaking their home languages in public or wearing traditional dress. They tend to see immigrants as ignorant of Canadian cultural practices and unwilling to "act like Canadians," and they have expressed discomfort with the changes in Canadian society that have been brought about by immigration.

The arrival in Canada, particularly in Vancouver, of a relatively large number of wealthy Chinese immigrants from Hong Kong in the late 1980s provoked considerable reaction. Government and business leaders appreciated the large financial investments a number of newcomers made. But some Canadian residents criticized what they perceived as ostentatious displays of wealth, such as the construction of "monster homes." Reacting to a number of unpleasant incidents, Vancouver's first Chinese-Canadian city councillor complained, "The Chinese are damned if they're poor and damned if they're rich." British Columbia's lieutenant governor, Chinese-Canadian David Lam, attempted to calm tensions, recommending that newcomers become more involved in the community and that older residents turn a blind eye to pretentious houses.

IMMIGRATION IN RECENT YEARS

The deep recession of the early 1980s again caused immigration to decline. Economic problems contributed to an anti-immigrant backlash, as many Canadians saw immigrants as competitors for scarce jobs or believed they were crowding the welfare rolls.

Research carried out by two York University sociologists has indicated that "the objective evidence does not support the view that the relation between immigration and unemployment is a major problem."[8] Most other studies concur, demonstrating that immigrants do not increase unemployment among indigenous workers but rather help to create a larger, more flexible, and more adaptable labour force. Immigrants often work at jobs that Canadians cannot or will not do. Moreover, through their need for housing, food, clothing, and other consumer goods, immigrants increase the size of the domestic market and thereby assist in boosting growth. Still, it appears that Third World immigrants in the independent immigrant category, despite high education levels, usually earn less than other immigrants and often work in jobs for which they are overqualified. Many find it difficult to have diplomas and other credentials recognized.

Yet the image of immigrants lined up outside employment offices in times of recession has surely influenced public opinion far more than have sociological studies. Thus, from 1982, the government felt it necessary, in view of Canada's economic problems, to revise each year's quotas downward, according to its vague predictions of what the economy could bear. Immigration declined to its lowest levels in more than two decades. The government did, however, facilitate the entry into Canada, after 1986, of several thousand "business-class" immigrants — wealthy entrepreneurs, especially from Hong Kong. These individuals agreed to invest their capital in Canada, set up businesses, and thus create jobs for Canadians.

In the late 1980s, Ottawa gradually raised the ceiling on immigration from 100 000 to 200 000. But taking into account annual emigration of at least 50 000, the net immigration figure was substantially lower. Then, in 1990, the federal government announced further increases in immigration — a politically risky decision as the economy slowed and as certain groups, such as the Reform party, attacked immigration and multiculturalism policies. In fact, an average of nearly 220 000 immigrants were admitted to Canada each year during the period

LEADING SOURCE COUNTRIES OF IMMIGRANTS, SELECTED YEARS

1960	1976	1984	1991–96	2001
Italy	Britain	Vietnam	Hong Kong	China
Britain	United States	Hong Kong	China	India
United States	Hong Kong	United States	India	Pakistan
Germany	Jamaica	India	Philippines	Philippines
Netherlands	Lebanon	Britain	Sri Lanka	South Korea
Portugal	India	Poland	Poland	United States
Greece	Philippines	Philippines	Taiwan	Iran
France	Portugal	El Salvador	Vietnam	Romania
Poland	Italy	Jamaica	United States	Sri Lanka
Austria	Guyana	China	Britain	Britain

Source: Employment and Immigration Canada, Immigration Statistics, various years.

1992–1999. From 2000, annual levels increased slightly. Most immigrants now came from Asia; after the cession of Hong Kong to China in 1997, China replaced the former British colony as Canada's major source of immigrants, while India placed second.

In the early 1990s, fewer than 40 percent of immigrants belonged to the so-called "economic class" in which one family member, the principal applicant, was seen as a potential investor in the Canadian economy or assessed for skills deemed in demand in Canada. Fully 75 percent of immigrants had belonged to this class in 1968. By far the great majority of immigrants admitted to Canada now belonged to the other two categories of "family class" (that is, close relatives of Canadian residents) and refugees. In response to critics, who thought that immigration should be more closely linked to economic needs, Ottawa sought to give greater emphasis to the economic class of immigrants. New rules for economic migrants set out in 2002 favoured educated applicants with work experience and a confirmed job offer, people judged to be adaptable and to have "flexible and transferable skills" for the "knowledge economy."

Regardless of the number of immigrants admitted, many Canadians expressed the view that Canada accepts too many immigrants. Some cited the deleterious effects on the environment and on living conditions of rapid population growth, fuelled largely by immigration, particularly in southern Ontario and in British Columbia's Lower Mainland. Others worried that immigration favoured the emergence of new social problems, such as a violent gang culture. At the same time, other observers of Canadian immigration policy, including immigration officials and demographers, warned that, because of current low fertility rates, Canada's population would begin to contract in the medium term without very substantial increases in immigration. Some middle-aged Canadians began to worry about who would pay for their old-age pensions and future health care, and urged the government to bring in more immigrant taxpayers. As Canada's work force aged, business appealed for more skilled workers to alleviate worrying labour shortages.

REFUGEES

Much of the criticism directed at federal immigration policy in the 1980s and 1990s has concerned refugees. Across the world, millions of human beings became refugees, fleeing war and persecution in their own lands. Canada could not be immune to such mass movements.

Humanitarian and refugee-advocacy groups as well as ethnic communities favouring more immigration from their home countries judged Canada's refugee quotas to be unreasonably low. They also denounced the government's cumbersome procedures for studying the cases of refugee-status claimants, resulting in backlogs which grew larger each year.

According to reports, public opinion became less sympathetic to the cause of refugees. Many critics were undoubtedly influenced by the large numbers of would-be immigrants who entered Canada illegally — so-called "queue jumpers" — and who claimed refugee status, but whose reasons for emigrating from their countries of origin seemed to be primarily economic. Indeed, the "hearing" that virtually all refugee-status claimants now requested — an unforeseen consequence of earlier legislation — became, according to historian Gerald Dirks, "a routine channel for evading the normal admission requirements and getting easy access to Canada."[9] In 1986, the dramatic arrival of a large group of Tamil immigrants from Sri Lanka on the shores of Newfoundland and, the following year, of a group of Sikhs from India on the coast of Nova Scotia, was sufficient proof for many Canadians that Ottawa had lost control over entry into the country.

Public pressure led the Mulroney government to act against illegal immigration in 1988, by which time government efforts to clear the huge backlog of some 125 000 refugee-status claimants had become hopelessly bogged down. The number of new claimants declined. New legislation in 1993 limited the right of rejected applicants to appeal, resulting in a further drop in the number of claimants arriving in Canada. Through the 1990s, the acceptance rate of refugee claimants declined from about 75 percent to about 50 percent. Refugee lawyers blamed "compassion fatigue": panel members, they said, were becoming hardened to stories of abuse and persecution. Religious and ethnic groups feared that the measures also discouraged true political refugees. Government spokespersons countered that Canada still remained far more open to refugees than did other western countries.

The terrorist attacks of September 11, 2001, in the United States brought new and tighter immigration rules, which took effect in 2003. In response to American accusations that Canada admitted too many refugees without proper security vetting, Canada decided to turn back claimants arriving at Canadian land borders and invited them to seek asylum to the United States, whose rules were reputedly more restrictive. Critics maintained that henceforth more refugees would seek to enter Canada illegally, in order to make their claim from inside Canada.

MULTICULTURALISM

Canadians have often taken pride in the image of their country as a "cultural mosaic" (or a "tossed salad," in one writer's words), rather than as an American-style "melting pot." Official policy no longer favours rapid assimilation, and social scientists prefer to speak instead of integration or of acculturation. In the 1960s, observers began to speak of the emergence of a "third force," consisting of Canadians of neither French nor British descent.

In October 1971, Prime Minister Trudeau told the House of Commons that the government "accepts the contention of other cultural communities that they, too, are essential elements in Canada and deserve government assistance in order to contribute to regional and national life in ways that derive from their heritages." Multiculturalism — but not multilingualism — was to be encouraged. The Constitution of 1982 gave additional, though somewhat vague, protection to multiculturalism. Then, in 1988, a revised Multiculturalism Act provided new funds for promoting cultures and reducing discrimination.

Politicians understood the potential electoral benefits of recognizing the contributions of ethnic groups. Also, the Trudeau government hoped that recognition of multiculturalism would attenuate existing hostility toward bilingualism and biculturalism and that it would appeal to

Hockey legend Willie O'Ree, the first African-Canadian player in the NHL, chats with children at the Harmony Brunch in East Preston, Nova Scotia, held to commemorate the International Day for the Elimination of Racial Discrimination.

Nova Scotia Human Rights Commission.

English-Canadian nationalists who wanted a distinct Canadian identity. Yet probably most Canadians, including the British, the French, and the "lukewarm white ethnics" from northern and western Europe, found multiculturalism meaningless. As time went on, impatience with the whole concept grew, especially when governments agreed to provide funding.

By the mid-1980s, the federal government was investing modestly in multiculturalism, funding ethnic day-care centres, heritage-language classes, cultural festivals, and conferences and providing grants for the preparation of histories of the major Canadian ethnic groups. Money was made available to complete the revitalization of Vancouver's Chinatown and to transform this ethnic neighbourhood into a shining symbol of Canada's new multicultural nature and, at the same time, a valuable tourist attraction. (By 2000, however, Vancouver's Chinatown was in decline; it had also lost its exclusiveness as new Chinatowns grew up in suburbs such as Richmond.)

Several provincial governments also contributed financially to support multicultural policy. The Ontario government, for example, used its Wintario lottery funding program to create a research institute, the Multicultural History Society of Ontario. Many school boards set up courses in non-official languages. In Edmonton, for example, immersion schooling could be had in Arabic, Chinese, Hebrew, Ukrainian, and German. Such policies have practical relevance: already by the late 1980s, English was *not* the mother tongue of 50 percent of the children enrolled in Toronto public schools nor of 40 percent of those enrolled in Vancouver schools.

Where Social Scientists Disagree

➣ Evaluating Canada's Multicultural Policy

The arrival in Canada of large numbers of immigrants, first from Europe and, since the late 1960s, from the Caribbean, Latin America, Asia, and Africa, has immensely diversified Canada's population. Until the 1950s, governments espoused a policy of rapid assimilation of newcomers into the "Canadian mainstream." As interest in the rights of minorities grew throughout the western world during the 1960s, immigrant groups sought government intervention to help them conserve at least part of their ethnic heritage. In response, Ottawa elaborated, in 1971, a somewhat vague multicultural policy. Since then, governments and public agencies at all levels have launched programs favouring the retention of national cultures.

Official federal policy views multiculturalism as "a powerful bonding agent" that "helps unite us and identify us, while at the same time allowing every element of our society to retain its own characteristics and cultural heritage."[1] Observers have generally been somewhat suspicious of these stated intentions. In 1988, for example, Howard Palmer described federal policy as, at least in part, an attempt to win the ethnic vote in urban Ontario and to temper western Canada's rising opposition to the policy of bilingualism.[2]

Regardless of the inevitable political considerations underlying the policy, has multiculturalism been worth pursuing? Yes, thinks Norman Buchignani, who feels that federal policy has helped groups such as the South Asians feel "comfortable about being South Asian and Canadian at the same

time."[3] He also views multicultural policy as heightening awareness among native-born Canadians of the new communities that have recently established themselves in their midst. More critically, Lance W. Roberts and Rodney A. Clifton argue that the policy at least has symbolic value, permitting members of ethnic groups to "participate and benefit as members of a complex industrial society while retaining the sense that they belong to a smaller, more intimate community."[4]

Other observers express doubt. C. Michael Lanphier and Anthony H. Richmond argue that it is probably impossible to reconcile equality of opportunity and integration with "the maintenance of separate identities and cultural pluralism."[5] Gilles Paquet agrees. He sees multiculturalism as having heightened the belief among "other" Canadians that they do not have to adapt their mores while, at the same time, the "dominant cultures" have remained dominant: "The gap between expectations and realities has generated much ... frustration."[6] Peter S. Li and B. Singh Bolaria hold a similar opinion. For them, multiculturalism is "the failure of an illusion, not of a policy."[7] The illusion is that a cultural solution, such as multiculturalism, could solve problems such as ethnic inequality and racial discrimination, whose roots are political and economic. (Perhaps such criticisms explain why, in the 1980s, government multicultural programs broadened their involvement in race relations.) For his part, novelist Neil Bissoondath, who refuses the role of "ethnic" which would have him labelled an "East Indian-Trinidadian-

Canadian-Quebecker," argues in a controversial book that the policy of official multiculturalism, by encouraging immigrants to focus on "There," the ancestral homeland, rather than on "Here," the new homeland, actually highlights the differences that divide Canadians rather than the similarities that unite them.[8]

Regardless of the disagreements, Robert A. Harney, a student of the Italian community in particular, saw merit in simply pursuing the debate. Multiculturalism, he said, was part of Canada's eternal search to define itself. "Survival lies in traveling toward an identity, and we will all be better served if that traveling itself remains our identity."[9]

---

[1] *Multiculturalism ... Being Canadian* (Ottawa: Secretary of State for Multiculturalism, 1987), p. 9.

[2] Jean R. Burnet with Howard Palmer, *"Coming Canadians": An Introduction to a History of Canada's Peoples* (Toronto: McClelland & Stewart, 1988), p. 176.

[3] Norman Buchignani and Doreen M. Indra with Sam Srivastiva, *Continuous Journey: A Social History of South Asians in Canada* (Toronto: McClelland & Stewart, 1985), p. 227.

[4] Lance W. Roberts and Rodney Clifton, "Multiculturalism in Canada: A Sociological Perspective," in Peter S. Li, ed., *Race and Ethnic Relations in Canada* (Toronto: Oxford University Press, 1990), p. 133.

[5] C. Michael Lanphier and Anthony H. Richmond, "Multiculturalism and Identity in 'Canada outside Quebec,'" in Kenneth McRoberts, ed., *Beyond Quebec: Taking Stock of Canada* (Montreal/Kingston: McGill-Queen's University Press, 1995), p. 314.

[6] Gilles Paquet, "Political Philosophy of Multiculturalism," in J.W. Berry and J.A. Laponce, eds., *Ethnicity and Culture in Canada: The Research Landscape* (Toronto: University of Toronto Press, 1994), p. 63.

[7] Peter S. Li and B. Singh Bolaria, *Racial Minorities in Multicultural Canada* (Toronto: Garamond Press, 1983), introduction.

[8] Neil Bissoondath, *Selling Illusions: The Cult of Multiculturalism in Canada*, rev. ed. (Toronto: Penguin Canada, 2002), p. 222.

[9] Robert A. Harney, "'So Great a Heritage as Ours': Immigration and the Survival of Canadian Policy," in *Daedelus* 117 (Fall 1988), p. 93.

The federal government's support of ethnic diversity has given rise to the question of who really speaks for the ethnic communities and, thus, of which associations the government ought to support. Twenty organizations, for example, now represent Edmontonians of various Asian origins. In Vancouver, the well-established Chinese Benevolent Association has on occasion feuded with newer, more activist, organizations, such as the Chinese Cultural Centre, over various local issues, in particular a plan to build a freeway through Chinatown. In Toronto, West Indians have a multitude of often-competing organizations whose membership is determined by island of origin.

 Indeed, the ethnic communities themselves have questioned whether the federal and provincial governments fund the right programs, or whether they have preferred short-term, highly visible manifestations of what has been labelled "ethnic exotica." Perhaps rather than keeping immigrants "singing and dancing and talking their own language," as one journalist put it, the federal government should address "real" problems such as ethnic inequality in the Canadian labour market. Certain groups such as the Ukrainians have vigorously proposed the recognition of minority-language rights. Other students of multiculturalism doubt that English–French dualism and ethnocultural pluralism can really be reconciled, or that the vastly diverse multicultural third force has the power to assure changes in the traditional bases of Canadian society. Agreement on such issues currently appears impossible.

NON-OFFICIAL LANGUAGES

Heritage-language programs emphasize retention of the mother tongue and are seen to have moral and psychological value. However, immigrants and their offspring, in order to integrate into Canadian society, have had to learn English or, in Quebec, to a lesser degree, French. Although such groups as the Portuguese, the Greeks, and the Chinese have had considerable success in retaining the language of the country of origin, assimilative trends generally become more pronounced over time and the retention of non-official languages diminishes sharply. As ethnolinguist Joshua Fishman put it, "for 95 percent of the third generation, the language of the cradle is the language of the streets."[10]

Barely 15 percent of Ukrainian Canadians, for example, speak Ukrainian as a home language, and intermarriage has hastened the pace of assimilation. Of Toronto's half-million-strong Italian community, historian Robert Harney estimated in 1984 that only a minority (belonging generally to the original immigrant generation) were "active in Italian institutions."[11] In his opinion, large numbers of Italians have deliberately broken their ethnic links and taken refuge in "Anglo conformity" because of the prejudice they have faced. Studies suggest strongly that linguistic assimilation leads to destruction of the cohesive ethnic community. While the prognosis for linguistic survival appears bleak for older ethnic communities from Europe, the number of Canadians speaking such languages as Chinese, Spanish, Punjabi, Tagalog, and Arabic is increasing rapidly as immigration rejuvenates these groups.

THE IMPACT OF IMMIGRATION

Immigrants have had an immeasurable impact on Canada's economic, political, social, and cultural life. The contributions of entrepreneurs such as the Reichmann brothers (born in Austria and Hungary), Thomas Bata and Stephen Roman (both born in the former Czechoslovakia), and David Lam (from Hong Kong), of Montreal publisher Alain Stanké (born in Lithuania), of journalists Peter Newman (born in Austria) and Adrienne Clarkson (born in Hong Kong and appointed governor general of Canada in 1999) are noteworthy. Film director Atom Egoyan was born in Cairo, Egypt, of Armenian refugee parents, who settled in Victoria, British Columbia in 1963. The young Egoyan at first renounced his ethnic roots but later, as a university student, sought to reconnect with them, as his film *Ararat*, bearing on the Turkish massacre and deportation of as many as one million Armenians in 1915, attests.

Since the late 1970s the number of non-British, non-French writers in Canada has grown substantially and Canadian literature has become increasing diversified. Indeed, Canada became part of the literary global village as many novels written by new Canadians featured settings that often had little to do with Canada. Austin Clarke, born in Barbados, set *The Polished Hoe*, his ninth novel, a poignant account of injustice, on an imaginary West Indian island in the 1950s. Indian-born Rohinton Mistry used Bombay as his setting for *Such a Long Journey* and *Family Matters*, while Michael Ondaatje, from Sri Lanka, set *The English Patient* in Tuscany, Italy, in the closing moments of World War II. In business, in the arts, in politics, indeed in virtually all spheres of activity, the Canada of 2000 reflected the increasing presence of the Asians, Latin Americans, West Indians, Europeans, and other immigrants who had settled in the country in earlier years.

Immigrants have brought new political questions to the fore in such areas as education and social policy, and the ethnic vote has become significant in many constituencies. Immigration has also enabled urban Canada to acquire a much more diverse and vibrant cultural life. Demographically, immigration has boosted Canada's population significantly: from 1981 to 1986, net immigration represented one-fifth of the country's population growth; from 1991 to

TOP TEN COUNTRIES OF BIRTH FOR RECENT IMMIGRANTS AND ALL IMMIGRANTS, 2001

RECENT IMMIGRANTS[1]	NUMBER	%
1. P.R. of China	197 360	10.8
2. India	156 120	8.5
3. Philippines	122 010	6.7
4. Hong Kong	118 385	6.5
5. Sri Lanka	62 590	3.4
6. Pakistan	57 990	3.2
7. Taiwan	53 755	2.9
8. United States	51 440	2.8
9. Iran	47 080	2.6
10. Poland	43 370	2.4
Subtotal	910 100	49.8
All other countries[2]	920 580	50.3
TOTAL	1 830 680	100.1

[1] Immigrants counted in 2001 and who came to Canada between 1991 and 2001

[2] Major "other" countries include the former Yugoslavia, Poland, United Kingdom, South Korea, Vietnam, Romania, and Russia

ALL IMMIGRANTS[3]	NUMBER	%
1. United Kingdom	605 955	11.1
2. P.R. of China	322 825	6.1
3. Italy	315 455	5.8
4. India	314 690	5.8
5. United States	237 920	4.4
6. Hong Kong	235 620	4.3
7. Philippines	232 670	4.3
8. Poland	180 415	3.3
9. Germany	174 070	3.2
10. Portugal	153 535	2.8
Subtotal	2 783 195	51.1
All other countries	2 665 285	48.9
TOTAL	5 448 480	100.0

[3] All people counted in 2001 not born in Canada

Source: Adapted from Statistics Canada, *2001 Census of Canada*, cat. 97F0009XCB01002 and 97F0009XCB01003.

1996, more than one-half; and from 1996 to 2001, fully two-thirds. With immigration, the importance of both the British and the French components of the population has declined, while, from a linguistic point of view, the fact that the great majority of immigrants eventually adopt English as their new language has contributed to weakening the relative position of Canada's francophone population and increasing that community's fears for survival.

Immigration brought much of the blue-collar labour that Canada needed for large-scale industrial and resource development in the 1950s. Immigration also provided many of the country's skilled workers and professionals. In the 1960s, for example, hundreds of American university professors entered the country, permitting the rapid expansion of the Canadian university system but also setting the stage for the nationalist outcry against American domination in the early 1970s. Bringing in educated immigrants helped ease the pressure on Canada's already overburdened educational system. Ironically, for a country that has often complained of suffering a brain drain to the United States, Canada has been criticized by some developing countries for attracting the highly qualified people that those developing nations so desperately need to keep at home.

Immigration will surely remain a much-discussed issue. There is little prospect that Canadians can ever agree on how many immigrants the country needs, how many refugees it should welcome, where immigrants should come from, and what role they should play in Canadian society. Nevertheless, there can be no doubt that, because of immigration, the Canada of the first years of the twenty-first century is a much more diverse land than the country that emerged from World War II.

NOTES

1. John W. Holmes, *The Shaping of Peace: Canada and the Search for World Order 1943–1957*, vol. 1 (Toronto: University of Toronto Press, 1979), p. 101.

2. Karl Aun, *The Political Refugees: A History of the Estonians in Canada* (Toronto: McClelland & Stewart, 1985).

3. Franca Iacovetta, *Such Hardworking People: Italian Immigrants in Postwar Toronto* (Montreal/Kingston: McGill-Queen's University Press, 1992).

4. Franca Iacovetta, "Remaking Their Lives," in Joy Parr, ed., *A Diversity of Women: Ontario, 1945–1980* (Toronto: University of Toronto Press, 1995), pp. 135–67.

5. Quoted in Christina McCall Newman, "The Canadian Americans," *Maclean's*, July 27, 1963, p. 10.

6. Hugh Johnson, *The Four Quarters of the Night: The Life Journey of an Emigrant Sikh* (Montreal/Kingston: McGill-Queen's University Press, 1995), p. 227.

7. Stanley R. Barrett, *Paradise: Class, Commuters, and Ethnicity in Rural Ontario* (Toronto: University of Toronto Press, 1994), p. 235.

8. Quoted in Henry Aubin, "Do Immigrants Steal Jobs or Create New Ones?" *The Gazette* (Montreal), January 10, 1985.

9. Gerald E. Dirks, *Controversy and Complexity: Canadian Immigration Policy During the 1980s* (Montreal/Kingston: McGill-Queen's University Press, 1995), pp. 79–80.

10. Quoted in Robert Harney, "'So Great a Heritage as Ours': Immigration and the Survival of the Canadian Policy," *Daedelus* 117 (Fall 1988): 83.

11. Quoted in Margot Gibb-Clark, "'Italian Community's a Myth,' Historian Says," *The Globe and Mail*, October 20, 1984, p. 14.

LINKING TO THE PAST

Mennonites in Canada
http://collections.ic.gc.ca/encyclopedia/

An online encyclopedia of Mennonites in Canada.

Immigrant Voices
http://www.canadianhistory.ca/iv/

An overview of immigration patterns and issues related to immigration to Canada, from Confederation to the present.

The Canadian Bill of Rights
http://laws.justice.gc.ca/en/C-12.3/index.html

The full text of the Canadian Bill of Rights, from the Department of Justice.

Multiculturalism
http://www.pch.gc.ca/multi/index_e.cfm

Government information on the policy of multiculturalism and the operation of the Canadian Multiculturalism Act.

Canada's Ethnocultural Portrait: The Changing Mosaic
http://www12.statcan.ca/english/census01/products/analytic/companion/etoimm/contents.cfm

Detailed statistical information on Canada's ethnic, linguistic, and cultural groups and communities from the 2001 census.

Canada at the Millennium: A Transcultural Society
http://collections.ic.gc.ca/heirloom_series/volume7/volume7.htm

An illustrated account of the contributions to Canadian society of immigrants from fifty nations.

RELATED READINGS

The following article in R. Douglas Francis and Donald B. Smith, eds., *Readings in Canadian History: Post-Confederation*, 6th ed. (Toronto: Nelson Thomson Learning, 2002), relates to a topic in this chapter: Will Kymlicka, "The Merits of Multiculturalism," pp. 480–89.

BIBLIOGRAPHY

For comprehensive overviews of Canada's immigration policy, see Ninette Kelley and Michael Trebilcock, *The Making of the Mosaic: A History of Canadian Immigration Policy* (Toronto: University of Toronto Press, 1998; and Donald H. Avery, *Reluctant Host: Canada's Response to Immigrant Workers, 1896–1994* (Toronto: McClelland & Stewart, 1995). Controversial questions are examined in Peter S. Li, *Destination Canada: Immigration Debates and Issues* (Toronto: Oxford University Press, 2003); Daniel Stoffman, *Who Gets In: What's Wrong with Canada's Immigration Policy — And How to Fix It* (Toronto: Macfarlane Walter & Ross, 2002); and Reg Whitaker, *Double Standard: The Secret History of Canadian Immigration* (Toronto: Lester & Orpen Dennys, 1987). Immigrant adjustment is studied in Shiva S. Halli and Leo Driedger, eds., *Immigrant Canada: Demographic, Economic, and Social Challenges* (Toronto: University of Toronto Press, 1999). The scholarly review *Canadian Ethnic Studies* contains a wealth of material on the various facets of the immigrant experience.

Among the many publications on ethnicity see Peter S. Li, ed., *Race and Ethnic Relations in Canada*, 2nd ed. (Toronto: Oxford University Press, 1999); and Augie Fleras and Jean Leonard Elliott, *Unequal Relations: An Introduction to Race, Ethnic and Aboriginal Dynamics in Canada*, 3rd ed. (Scarborough, ON: Prentice Hall Allyn Bacon, 1999). Informative essays on all immigrant groups may be found in Paul Robert Magocsi, ed., *Encyclopedia of Canada's Peoples* (Toronto: Multicultural History Society of Ontario and University of Toronto Press, 1999). An ongoing series, "Canada's Ethnic Groups," published by the Canadian Historical Association with the support of the Canadian government's multiculturalism program, provides useful syntheses of immigrant experience in Canada. The "Generations: A History of Canada's Peoples" series, published by McClelland and Stewart in conjunction with the Multiculturalism Directorate, contains book-length studies of many immigrant groups. The introductory volume to the series is Jean R. Burnet with Howard Palmer, *"Coming Canadians": An Introduction to a History of Canada's Peoples* (Toronto: McClelland & Stewart, 1988).

Howard Palmer and Tamara Palmer, eds., *Peoples of Alberta: Portraits of Cultural Diversity* (Saskatoon: Western Producer Prairie Books, 1985) is a good overview of one province's ethnocultural groups. The Chinese experience in Canada is examined in Peter S. Li, *The Chinese in Canada*, 2nd ed. (Toronto: Oxford University Press, 1998). Studies of Italian immigrants include Nicholas DeMaria Harney, *Eh Paesan!: Being Italian in Toronto* (Toronto: University of Toronto Press, 1998); and Franca Iacovetta, *Such Hardworking People: Italian Immigrants in Postwar Toronto* (Montreal/Kingston: McGill-Queen's University Press, 1992). On Portuguese immigrants, see Carlos Teixeira and Victor M. P. Da Rosa, eds., *The Portuguese in Canada* (Toronto: University of Toronto Press, 2000). Scholarly works on the Jewish community include Robert J. Brym, William Shaffir, and Morton Weinfeld, eds., *The Jews in Canada* (Toronto: Oxford University Press, 1993); and Alan T. Davies, *Antisemitism in Canada: History and Interpretation* (Waterloo, ON: Wilfrid Laurier University Press, 1992).

On multiculturalism, see Richard J. F. Day, *Multiculturalism and the History of Canadian Diversity* (Toronto: University of Toronto Press, 2000); and Augie Fleras and Jean Leonard Elliott, *Engaging Diversity: Multiculturalism in Canada*, 2nd ed. (Toronto: Nelson Thomson Learning, 2002). Vigorous critiques of this policy may be found in Reginald Bibby, *Mosaic Madness: The Poverty and Potential of Life in Canada* (Toronto: Stoddart, 1990); and Neil Bissoondath, *Selling Illusions: The Cult of Multiculturalism in Canada*, rev. ed. (Toronto: Penguin Canada, 2002). Studies on racism and discrimination include Evelyn Kallen, *Ethnicity and Human Rights in Canada*, 2nd ed. (Toronto: Oxford University Press, 1995); Frances Henry et al., *The Colour of Democracy: Racism in Canadian Society*, 2nd ed. (Toronto: Harcourt Brace, 2000); and Leo Driedger and Shiva S. Halli, *Race and Racism: Canada's Challenge* (Montreal/Kingston: McGill-Queen's University Press, 2000).

CONTEMPORARY CANADA

TIME LINE

1972 – Team Canada defeats the Soviet hockey team

National Action Committee on the Status of Women established

1976 – Montreal hosts the Twenty-First Olympic Games

1981 – Terry Fox dies of cancer after running halfway across Canada

1982 – Proclamation of the new Canadian Constitution

1988 – The Free Trade Agreement signed between Canada and the United States

The Winter Olympics held in Calgary

1989 – 14 women students slain at l'École Polytechnique in Montreal; Parliament later commemorated this tragic event by instituting the National Day of Remembrance and Action on Violence Against Women

1991 – Canadian troops participate in the Gulf War

1994 – The North American Free Trade Agreement (NAFTA) comes into existence

2001 – Terrorist attacks on New York City and Washington, D.C.

2002 – Canada ratifies the Kyoto Protocol

2003 – Canada refuses to participate in the American-led war in Iraq

The era of rapid change and experimentation, begun in the 1960s, continued through the 1970s and even beyond. Women, Native peoples, gays and lesbians, and ethnic and other minorities sought recognition of their rights. In the late 1980s and 1990s, these groups made effective use of the Charter of Rights and Freedoms, adopted in 1982, to bring governments to revise laws and policies in their favour. Public opinion gradually accepted these changes that were transforming Canadian society. Environmental groups also became more active, showing that more Canadians were coming to appreciate the harmful effects of unregulated economic growth on their environment.

Immense technological change came to the world, and to Canada, in these years. In the early 1980s, the first personal computers entered Canadian homes. Ten years later, the internet began to link Canadians and the rest of the world ever more closely. The computer age enabled companies and governments to process data with speeds and efficiency unimaginable scarcely a few years earlier. It also brought new and serious challenges to citizens' rights to privacy.

Yet in some ways, more conservative attitudes and values asserted themselves after 1980. Economic difficulties contributed to fostering more individualistic preoccupations. At the same time, overstrained public finances dictated cuts in government expenditures and rising taxes. In such circumstances there was little money for new social programs. When governments promised to lower taxes to make reductions in services more acceptable, they then had to cut programs even further to finance such tax cuts.

Prime Ministers Pierre Trudeau and Brian Mulroney succeeded in convincing Canadians to give them solid mandates, but for both rising discontent made it increasingly difficult to maintain a workable political consensus. Questions concerning the economy, relations between the provinces and Ottawa, trade and other links with the United States, and social issues divided Canadians. Voters showed more volatility, as old political loyalties broke down. After 1993, a prosperous economy and a divided and regionalized opposition favoured the Liberal government of Jean Chrétien. The arrival, after 1998, of the first budgetary surpluses in more than a quarter century paved the way for a more activist government.

RISING PRICES

For most of the contemporary period, Canadians' major concern has been the economy. From the early 1970s until the mid-1980s, rising prices in particular worried them. In some years, the cost of food went up by more than 10 percent. Sharply rising housing costs in cities such as Vancouver, Toronto, and Ottawa pushed younger Canadians out of the housing market.

Politicians blamed outside forces for these substantial price increases. World food prices moved sharply upward in response to greater demand. Oil prices rose substantially, too. Motorists complained bitterly. But they also abandoned their roomy, high-powered American automobiles in favour of smaller, more efficient, imported vehicles, mostly from Japan.

Nevertheless, domestic causes of inflation also existed. Unions were accused of making unrealistically high wage demands that forced companies to raise their prices. In turn, labour blamed rising prices on excessive corporate profits. Inflation conditioned individuals to expect more inflation and to demand bigger wage increases. This behaviour, though understandable, ensured that the problem persisted.

THE TRUDEAU GOVERNMENT

The wave of Trudeaumania on which Pierre Elliott Trudeau had ridden to power in 1968 had, by 1972, been transformed into a swelling tide of Trudeauphobia, as the seemingly modest Trudeau of 1968, who had said that he wanted to "dialogue" with Canadians, became an arrogant, remote, temperamental personality. Questions of policy influenced electors as well. A backlash against bilingualism and "French power" cost the Liberals many votes. The government's apparent inability to handle economic and social issues — not only inflation, but also unemployment, welfare, strikes, and high taxes — also galvanized voter disaffection.

Following the election of 1972, which the Liberals nearly lost, the Trudeau government worked to win back voter approval. It greatly increased public spending on social programs and indexed income-tax brackets and exemptions to the cost of living in order to protect taxpayers from inflation. (These measures had catastrophic effects on government finances.) To win support in populous central Canada, the government promised to keep oil prices (then increasing rapidly) at levels substantially below world levels — a policy that naturally infuriated the oil-producing western provinces. Then, in 1975, the Liberals adopted a wage and price freeze. These controls, which affected the public sector and large private companies, lasted three years. The rate of increase in prices did slow, but it took more than controls and guidelines to defeat inflation.

By 1970, many Canadians, particularly in industrialized southern Ontario, were expressing concern for the high degree of foreign (especially American) ownership of the Canadian economy. Some urged large-scale nationalization of foreign-owned businesses and resources, or at least a gradual buying back of large enterprises. Others believed that actual ownership mattered little if Ottawa exercised stronger control over giant foreign-owned corporations operating in the country. Although the Trudeau government set up an agency to screen takeovers, American investment in Canada did not noticeably decline.

By the late 1970s, with Canada again in a severe inflationary crisis, the business community in particular worried about the foundering economy and the rapidly rising federal deficit, which the government financed by borrowing heavily, even at historically high interest rates. Regional discontent increased, too. The West, in particular, complained that Trudeau paid little heed to its concerns. With the notable exception of Quebec, the Trudeau consensus largely broke apart, with the result that the Progressive Conservatives, under their new leader, Joe Clark, a federal MP from Alberta, won a fragile mandate in the election of 1979.

CONSERVATIVE INTERLUDE

The energy question precipitated the collapse of Clark's brief government and a return to power of the Liberals. Promoting a policy of "short-term pain for long-term gain," Clark's finance minister announced a new excise tax on gasoline designed to bring billions of dollars into the federal treasury in order to attack the rising deficit. Defeated in the House of Commons, the government resigned. During the ensuing election campaign, Trudeau promised to revoke the immensely unpopular tax. (After gaining power, he then imposed new gasoline taxes.)

THE END OF THE TRUDEAU ERA, 1980–1984

Trudeau's final mandate proved difficult. The prime minister immediately launched the National Energy Program (NEP) to Canadianize the petroleum industry by reducing the role of American oil companies in Canada. Western Canada denounced Ottawa's move to appropriate a greater share of huge oil revenues for itself. The federal government responded that too great a transfer of wealth to one province would upset the equilibrium of Confederation. Ottawa's initiative proved ill-timed. Just as it spent billions of dollars purchasing foreign oil companies and assisting exploration by Canadian companies, oil prices crashed dramatically.

Trudeau also went forward with a plan to "patriate" the Constitution and particularly to insert within it a Charter of Rights and Freedoms and an amending formula by which the United

Kingdom's consent would no longer be necessary for constitutional changes. Although most Canadians outside Quebec approved of Trudeau's initiative, Quebec refused to sign the agreement. Thus, the province that since 1960 had been most insistent on the need for constitutional change was not a party to the reformed Constitution.

Women's groups won the inclusion in the Charter of an article affirming the equality of male and female persons. The Native peoples' associations succeeded in their efforts to entrench Aboriginal and treaty rights. But the Charter recognized only existing rights, and left these undefined.

Most Canadians were, however, primarily interested in bread-and-butter issues. When a recession hit Canada in 1981–82, they blamed Ottawa for mismanagement of the economy. The recession resulted in part from government monetary policy, particularly high interest rates, designed to dampen inflationary pressures. It also stemmed from worldwide overproduction in the resource industries, in agriculture, and in secondary manufacturing. The daily press offered a sombre litany of factory closings, layoffs, and cutbacks. Finally, the constantly unfavourable polls convinced Trudeau that he should resign.

The signing of the Canadian Constitution by Her Majesty Queen Elizabeth II, April 1982. Prime Minister Trudeau looks on. The new Constitution ended the British Parliament's power to amend the British North America (BNA) Act, and also included a Charter of Rights and Freedoms.

Bob Cooper/National Archives of Canada/PA-140705.

TRUDEAU'S RECORD

The Trudeau years were replete with paradoxes. Trudeau championed the trusty Liberal theme of national unity at each election. Yet, during his term in office, the country faced the most serious threats to its existence that it had ever confronted, especially from Quebec and the western provinces. Trudeau had also pushed for the inclusion of a Charter of Rights in the Constitution, insisting on the need to defend Canadians' political liberties. Yet, during the FLQ crisis of October 1970, his government invoked the War Measures Act and thereby effectively suspended civil liberties, enabling the police to arrest hundreds of individuals and to hold them incommunicado for several days, without ever laying charges against most of them.

Trudeau frequently denounced the dangers of nationalism, especially French-Canadian and Quebec nationalism, but his legislation controlling foreign investment, as well as his National Energy Program of 1980, convinced Americans that he was a strident nationalist. Furthermore, his government adopted the Official Languages Act in 1969 in an effort to ensure greater equality for French-speaking Canadians by making government services more widely available in French. While slow progress made French Canadians despair of ever attaining genuine equality, many English-speaking Canadians complained that they were now the victims of unfair treatment.

Trudeau had long spoken of the need to build a "just society," but what role were women to play in bringing such a society about? During the first Trudeau mandate (1968–72), the House of Commons had only one female member. Feminists complained that parties showed no interest in working to recruit promising female candidates. Society's changing attitudes did bring a slow improvement. Yet even by the 1990s, most women involved in political activity continued, in political scientist Sylvia Bashevkin's words, to "toe the lines" and to fill "conventional maintenance roles."[1]

In foreign affairs, Trudeau rejected Canada's traditional role as a "helpful fixer" in favour of a policy based on national self-interest. Certainly the sale of arms to military dictatorships during his tenure showed the precedence commercial interests took over human rights. Nonetheless, Canada did increase its developmental assistance to Third World nations significantly.

THE CHARTER AND BILINGUALISM

By the time of Trudeau's death in September 2000, Canadians believed the Charter of Rights and Freedoms to be his greatest legacy, a defining element of the Canadian identity. Certainly Charter decisions changed the face of Canada, by upholding minority and individual rights. At times, critics accused judges of acting as social engineers who usurped the power of elected legislators. From the early 1990s, however, the courts assumed a more deferential stance toward parliamentarians and law enforcement.

Trudeau's dream of a bilingual Canada at first enthused many Canadians, particularly French-speakers who aspired to linguistic equality. Yet, by 2000, although English-language study was mandatory in Quebec, second-language instruction remained optional in several English-speaking provinces. Outside Quebec, many federal offices designated as bilingual were unable to offer service in French. Air Canada consistently flouted language laws with impunity. The census of 2001 showed that, while the number of French-speaking Quebecers able to converse in English increased to over 40 percent, English-speaking Canadians outside Quebec became less bilingual. In addition, in spite of federal assistance to French-language minorities outside Quebec, the decline through rapid assimilation of these groups continued. Except in Quebec and New Brunswick, the overwhelming weight of English appeared to compromise hopes for a bilingual Canada.

THE PROGRESSIVE CONSERVATIVES IN POWER

The Canada of the mid-1980s differed greatly from that of the 1970s. As in the United States, a conservative mood prevailed. For many Canadians, Liberal support of state intervention and of the federal government's strategic role in the economy now signified unacceptably high levels of government spending, rising taxes, and government interference. The Conservatives' praise for free enterprise and their vision of a more decentralized Canada, a "community of communities," appeared more appropriate. In elections held in 1984, Canadians showed they wanted change by giving the Conservatives a huge majority of seats.

As a sign of the times, a new group of entrepreneurs kindled popular interest. Among them were the Bronfmans, whose corporate empire included 152 companies, with assets of $120 billion in 1988; Albert and Paul Reichmann, who built a vast real-estate and resource empire, much of which crashed down with the collapse of property values after 1990; Galen Weston, who succeeded in the 1980s and 1990s in turning around the seemingly moribund Loblaws supermarket chain and in making it into the industry leader; and Pierre Péladeau, of Quebecor in Montreal, whose holdings grew from a tiny periodical, bought in 1950 with a loan of $1500, to a $450 million newspaper and printing empire.

THE FIRST MULRONEY GOVERNMENT

Although business welcomed the new Conservative government, its appeal was much wider. Brian Mulroney, a businessman chosen as leader to replace Joe Clark, had promised an "era of national reconciliation," notably in federal–provincial relations. Mulroney appeased the West by dismantling the National Energy Program; he satisfied Nova Scotia and Newfoundland by yielding them control of offshore mineral resources; and he pleased the Quebec government by promising to negotiate Quebec's acceptance of the Constitution of 1982.

The strong economic recovery also aided the Conservatives. Unemployment fell. A sharp decline in the inflation rate brought interest rates down, making it possible again for businesses and consumers to borrow. The omens appeared favourable for the construction of a new political consensus among Canadians.

The Conservatives had blamed the Liberals for Canada's poor relations with the United States. Announcing that Canada was again "open for business," the Mulroney government sought to encourage foreign investment. In the course of Mulroney's two mandates, Canada–U.S. relations were to undergo, as historian John Herd Thompson put it, "a revolutionary shift toward ideological and political convergence and a remarkable accommodation on a wide range of divisive issues."[2]

The Conservative honeymoon proved brief. The Mulroney government's frequent bouts with scandal soon hurt its public image. Regionalism rose phoenix-like out of the country's flagrantly unequal economic recovery. While southern Ontario basked in virtually full employment, Quebec and the Atlantic provinces faced continued high jobless rates. In addition, the decline of oil and resource prices, coinciding with a severe farm crisis, hurt the economies of the western provinces.

Prime Minister Brian Mulroney greets American President Ronald Reagan on his arrival for the "Shamrock Summit" at Quebec City, 1985, during which both leaders made much of their Irish origins. Mulroney hailed the summit as the inauguration of a new positive era in Canadian–American relations.

CP Picture Archive (Paul Chiasson).

THE FEDERAL DEFICIT

Mulroney also found it difficult to reduce his government's huge budgetary deficit. As the national debt grew, Ottawa had to devote about one-quarter of its revenues simply to paying the interest on its borrowings. Mulroney promised "unyielding determination" to eradicate the deficit. Yet, in spite of the government's valiant stands, the political necessity of maintaining federal expenditures hampered plans to control spending.

When Ottawa reduced grants to the provinces, provincial governments accused it of pushing its deficit on them. Ordinary Canadians, especially the worried middle classes, prevailed upon the government to reaffirm its somewhat wavering faith in the universality of social programs such as old-age pensions. Labour and the poorer provinces rallied to the defence of the much-maligned unemployment-insurance program. Ottawa clearly understood the political risks of effecting drastic cuts in spending. Rather than reducing expenses, the government found it easier to raise income and sales taxes substantially, and to continue to borrow.

THE GREAT FREE-TRADE DEBATE

The conclusion of a comprehensive trade agreement with the United States became the Mulroney government's most passionately debated initiative during its first mandate.

Canada has always sought wide access to foreign markets for its exports, while simultaneously using tariffs to reduce imports to protect Canadian jobs in industries unable to withstand competition from abroad. When multilateral trade negotiations discredited protective tariffs, Canada, like many other countries, erected a host of non-tariff barriers such as quotas in an effort to impede the entry of cheap imports of goods such as clothing and footwear. The downward slide of the Canadian dollar after 1976 helped less productive Canadians compete in foreign markets. It also meant that imports cost more.

As trade increased with the United States, Canada insistently proclaimed its belief in diversification. Nevertheless, the numerous "Team Canada" trade missions to Asia, Europe and Latin America, organized by Ottawa, failed to have any fundamental impact. Indeed by 1985, fully 80 percent of Canada's exports went to the United States, and 70 percent of its imports originated there.

Prime Minister Brian Mulroney now argued in favour of even closer trade relations with the Americans. He asserted that a free-trade agreement with the United States would create jobs. Increased sales of goods in that market would also diminish Canada's burgeoning balance of payments deficit in relation to the flow of investment income, tourism, services, and interest payments to foreign lenders to finance the growing mountain of federal debt. Many sectors of the business community favoured free trade. Polls showed that, in the early stages of the debate, a solid majority of Canadians backed it, too. Consumers were generally convinced that free trade would bring lower prices.

As the debate heated up, public support for free trade cooled. American protectionist measures weakened Canadian enthusiasm, though at the same time they seemed to make some form of agreement even more urgent. Labour unions, farmers, the churches, the federal New Democratic and Liberal parties, and several businesses warned that free trade would cost thousands of jobs. They argued that American companies might close their higher cost branch plants in Canada and serve the Canadian market from their more cost-efficient American bases. Anti-free traders further warned that a deal could endanger Canada's more generous social programs. It even risked jeopardizing Canada's political sovereignty.

THE CANADA–U.S. FREE-TRADE AGREEMENT

 Arduous negotiations culminated in an accord in 1987. By its terms, tariffs would end gradually, and Canada would gain enhanced access to most sectors of the American market. To resolve trade disputes, the agreement created a binational review panel that would simply ensure that each country's trade agencies made their decisions on the basis of existing law. (The United States would later make frequent use of this measure to block or penalize imports from Canada.) In future, Canada could no longer bar most American takeovers of Canadian industries. Moreover, although Canada gained unrestricted access for energy exports to the United States, the deal also secured American access to Canadian supplies even in times of shortages. But Canada did obtain exemptions for its agricultural products sold through marketing boards and its threatened cultural enterprises. Negotiators left the delicate issue of trade-distorting subsidies, given by governments to favour agriculture and certain industries, to later discussion.

By refusing to accept the accord, the Liberal-dominated Senate forced an election in late 1988. Discussion of free trade became the major issue. The Conservative victory, though with a substantially reduced majority, ensured ratification of the agreement in early 1989. As plant closures brought steep job losses in 1989 and 1990, the labour movement blamed free trade. Other observers placed the responsibility on high interest rates, a rising Canadian dollar, a relative decline in productivity, and a deteriorating international economic situation. The Conservative government pushed on. Shortly after the election, it agreed to sign a new treaty with the United States and Mexico forming a North American free trade zone.

THE COLLAPSE OF CONSENSUS

The re-election of the Conservative government in 1988 soon brought about leadership changes in the two opposition parties. The NDP chose Audrey McLaughlin to succeed Ed Broadbent; she thus became the first woman to lead a federal political party. Jean Chrétien, who had occupied several cabinet posts under Trudeau, easily won the Liberal leadership, though his support in Quebec was weak due in part to his perceived insensitivity to Quebec's exclusion from the constitutional agreement of 1982.

After the election of 1988, popular discontent with the Conservatives grew rapidly. Scandals implicating cabinet ministers tarnished the government's image. Better-off Canadians complained when the government "clawed back" their family allowances and old-age pensions. The government's decision to replace the hidden manufacturers' sales tax with a fully visible goods and services tax (GST) of 7 percent, from January 1991, provoked vehement opposition. The deepening crisis in public finances limited the government's ability to respond to the demands placed on it. High interest rates and much increased unemployment brought on by the harsh recession of 1990–91, particularly in the central provinces, only compounded the prevailing discontent.

Many Canadians outside Quebec blamed Mulroney for the constitutional fiasco of the Meech Lake Accord, designed to bring Quebec to give its assent to the Constitution of 1982. Within Quebec, support for sovereignty bounded upward. For their part, western Canadians saw the Mulroney government as overly attuned to the interests of central Canada; the meteoric rise in popularity of the Reform party provided evidence of a powerful wave of discontent.

The Conservatives tried again to achieve an agreement on constitutional reforms in 1991–92. This time, wide consultations took place before the federal, provincial, and territorial first ministers and the heads of Native organizations met at Charlottetown in 1992 and agreed on proposals that attempted to respond to a host of agendas for change, including Senate reform and Aboriginal self-government. A referendum held in October 1992 saw the voters of six provinces, including Quebec, reject the agreement. Constitutional change appeared dead.

ELECTION OF 1993

The federal election of 1993 revealed the importance of Canada's regional divisions. The Progressive Conservatives, now led by Kim Campbell, Canada's first woman prime minister, met with a defeat of precedent-setting proportions: only two of their candidates were elected. The Liberals won a majority, thanks in large part to Ontario. Quebec voters preferred to give their support to a party committed to Quebec's independence, the Bloc Québécois, which became the official opposition in Parliament. Close behind came the West-based Reform party. Reform supporters urged greater fiscal responsibility for governments. They also tended to reject the welfare state, multiculturalism, official bilingualism, full gender equality, aboriginal self-government, and civil rights for homosexuals. Finally, the unpopularity of provincial NDP governments in Ontario and British Columbia contributed heavily to that party's dismal performance.

THE CHRÉTIEN GOVERNMENT

Once in power, the new Liberal government accepted most of the Conservative policies it had denounced. It did not repeal the GST. After severely criticizing free trade during the election campaign, it adopted the North American Free Trade Agreement (NAFTA) with the United

Canadian peacekeepers, part of the large Canadian force in Bosnia in 1998.

Department of National Defence.

States and Mexico. To control spending, it froze civil servants' wages, and it continued to cut unemployment benefits and tighten eligibility rules, provoking strong reaction among groups of workers concerned, particularly in eastern Canada. At the same time, it transferred into its general revenue fund most of the surplus that the unemployment insurance fund now accumulated because of high premiums. Steep reductions in defence spending made it necessary to cut short several peacekeeping missions for lack of soldiers and equipment. Canada's international reputation suffered. The government also made very substantial cuts in grants to the provinces for health, education, and social welfare.

POLITICAL SUCCESS, ADMINISTRATIVE FAILURES

When Chrétien left office in 2003, and was succeeded by Paul Martin, a former finance minister, his political successes were evident. He had won three elections — 1993, 1997, and 2000 — each time with a majority of seats and about 40 percent of the votes. The opposition he faced in Parliament remained divided and regionalized. Voter support for both the NDP, on the left, and for the Bloc Québécois dwindled. On the right, two parties divided conservative support. The Progressive Conservatives attempted to regain lost popularity. The Western-based Reform party, even reconstituted as the Canadian Alliance, failed to expand its influence beyond the West. More moderate Canadians preferred the centralist Liberals, particularly in Ontario, where the majority of Liberal seats were situated. Only in 2003 did the two conservative parties agree to unite to form a new Conservative party. In elections held in 2004, the party did gain seats in Ontario although Liberal support remained strong in the province. In neighbouring Quebec, however, anger in the face of scandals dating from the Chrétien era resulted in a huge surge in support for the Bloc Québécois and helped prevent the Martin government from obtaining a majority of the seats in Parliament.

A lengthy list of costly administrative failures and mismanagement of public monies provoked substantial criticism of the Liberal government. In addition, the government and even the prime minister were faulted for questionable ethics and political patronage. Yet voters proved ready to pardon Liberal faults. Certainly a prosperous economy helped the party retain power. But the Liberal government could also boast of having finally brought order to government finances. Thanks to spending cuts and especially to increased revenues from high taxation rates and economic growth, the federal budget finally registered a surplus in 1998. Additional surpluses enabled Ottawa to reduce income taxes, and to begin to pay down accumulated debt.

DECLINE OF THE WELFARE STATE

Many people regretted the decline of the universal welfare state of the 1970s. A widespread consensus on collective responsibility and shared risk no longer existed, they said. They blamed deficits not on social spending but rather on the decreases in corporate taxation instituted by the Conservatives and maintained by the Liberals. For policy critic and activist Maude Barlow, the Liberal government had become "the political agent of big business interests."

Canadians agreed perhaps reluctantly that certain entitlement programs should be transformed in order to target benefits increasingly to specific groups of needy and vulnerable individuals, such as low-income parents. But for a large majority, universal publicly funded health care was sacred, a defining feature of Canada which distinguished it from the United States, where health care, largely in private hands, was expensive and often inefficient and coverage blatantly unequal. In the early 1980s, increasing hospital user fees and extra billing by doctors led to fears that access to public health care was threatened. Canadians applauded the Canada Health Act, adopted by Parliament in 1984, which penalized such practices. Then, in the 1990s, as some provinces sought to increase the role of the private sector in an effort to curtail sharply expanding health costs, the governing Liberals assured anxious citizens that there would be no two-tier public-private system.

And yet the health system was obviously in a state of crisis. Popular dissatisfaction mounted as hospital waiting lists for diagnostic tests and surgery lengthened, hospital emergency wards were overwhelmed, drug costs soared, services were disinsured, and shortages of professional personnel developed. Asked by the federal government to report on the health-care system, Roy Romanow, a former provincial premier, urged in 2002 that the public health-care system be retained, reinforced, and expanded. Ottawa agreed to inject substantial new funds into the program, but sought to hold provinces accountable for the manner in which they spent federal monies. Many doubted that the system was financially sustainable in the long term, and they feared that health care funding risked crowding out spending in other important areas such as education and the environment.

CANADIAN–AMERICAN RELATIONS

In the 1990s and early 2000s, Canada's exports to the United States increased substantially, stimulated by free trade and a depreciating Canadian dollar. Huge quantities of Albertan oil and gas flowed south. Several provinces exported electricity. The automotive industry in southern Ontario exported most of its production. Foreign ownership rose. Critics contended that Canada had become dangerously dependent upon the United States. Mel Hurtig, a tireless advocate of an independent Canada, titled a new book "the vanishing country."

GLOBALIZATION

Although Canadians generally supported trade liberalization, many also agreed with critics across the world (including Canadian author Naomi Klein whose book, *No Logo*, became an international best seller) who asserted that the new economic order, propelled by technological innovation, stripped governments of their sovereign powers. In their view, governments were abdicating control to market forces through privatization, deregulation, and expenditure reduction. Increased global competition risked favouring reduced standards, resulting in increased poverty, diminished government services, weaker labour laws, swamped local cultures, and fewer environmental controls. Globalization, they argued, entailed more golden arches and branded clothing and footwear. The real needs of citizens would be ignored. Canadian nongovernmental organizations played an important role in opposing globalization, mainly at international conferences where world trade and investment issues were discussed.

TERRORISM

The terrorist attacks in the United States on September 11, 2001, which resulted in the loss of some 3000 lives, had profound effects on Canada. Ottawa's response was far-reaching and multifaceted. It improved aviation and airport security, and invested heavily in increased border security. It announced more spending on police and intelligence agencies. An anti-terrorism bill gave new powers of investigation and detention to law-enforcement authorities. Civil libertarians denounced certain of its provisions.

Canada also moved beyond its traditional role of peacekeeping when it agreed in 2002 to deploy combat troops to Afghanistan to serve under American control. However, when American and British troops invaded Iraq in 2003 without the authorization of the United Nations, the Canadian government refused to participate. While the great majority of French-speaking Canadians opposed war, English-speaking Canada was divided over the issue. The business community in particular feared that Canada's position would cause the Americans to launch new trade offensives against Canada. However, Ottawa did agree to send more troops to Afghanistan.

DEMOGRAPHY

In 2004, Canadians numbered 31.5 million, about 10 million more than in 1971. High levels of immigration, not births, explained much of the growth, which was substantially more rapid than that of most European countries or Japan. Provinces whose population continued to expand rapidly, particularly Alberta, Ontario, and British Columbia, were those whose vigorous economies attracted newcomers both from abroad and from other Canadian provinces.

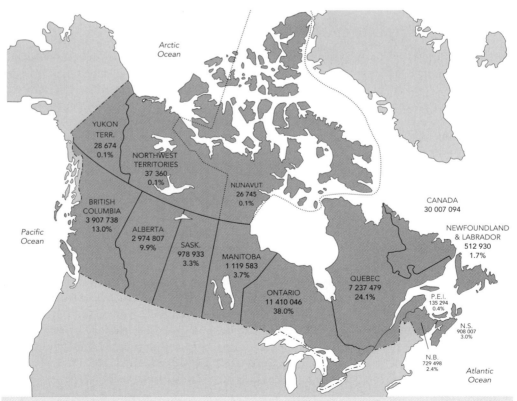

Distribution of Canada's Population by Province and Territory, 2001.

Source: Statistics Canada, *2001 Census*, "Population and Dwelling Counts."

Urban Canada continued to grow after 1970, but many rural areas and centres based on the exploitation of resources lost population. By 2001, more than one-half of Canada's population inhabited just four large metropolitan areas: Toronto and the Golden Horseshoe area around the western end of Lake Ontario; Montreal; Vancouver and the Lower Mainland; and the Calgary–Edmonton corridor.

THE BIRTH RATE

By 1970, couples no longer had enough children to replace themselves. By the mid-1980s, the average Canadian family had shrunk to include a mere 1.6 children. Many women simply postponed having children. But sociologists noted an increase in "yuppie-style" marriages they called "dinks" — dual-income, no kids — as many couples found it difficult to juggle children and careers. After 1970, recourse to new birth-control methods became more frequent. For example, thousands of men and women underwent voluntary sterilization. The number of abortions also increased.

The issue of abortion began to provoke passionate debate in Canada in the 1960s. Under a law adopted by Parliament in 1969, abortions remained illegal except when continued pregnancy threatened a woman's life or health. Discontented with the arbitrariness of the law, women's groups mobilized to demand the decriminalization of abortion. Finally, in 1988, the Supreme Court of Canada found the abortion law to be unconstitutional. Although the Mulroney government attempted to recriminalize abortion in a new bill in 1990, the Senate defeated the measure.

 As birth rates plummeted and advances in medicine enabled people to live longer, Canadian society began to age rapidly. The baby boomers, for their part, embarked on a collective midlife crisis in the 1990s. In quest of their youth, some male boomers turned to Viagra and hair dye, while female boomers bought cosmetics to iron out the wrinkles. The "flower power" of the 1960s and 1970s yielded to "grey power," forcing politicians to heed the concerns of seniors. Not surprisingly, more conservative attitudes asserted themselves. Education, emphasized so strongly in the 1960s and 1970s as the baby boomers passed through the system, had to share much of the attention (and the funding) with health care, pension reform, and other issues of particular interest to older Canadians.

The revolution in family patterns, begun in the late 1960s, continued into the 1980s and 1990s. Divorces became even more frequent, particularly after 1985, when new legislation made "marital breakdown," evidenced by a year or more of separation or by adultery or cruelty, the only grounds for divorce. Common-law unions gained in popularity, especially among younger Canadians. Governments moved to adapt legislation to this trend.

GAYS AND LESBIANS

 Gays and lesbians increasingly worked for self-affirmation and liberation after 1970. They denounced what they viewed as police harassment and repression, and demanded better protection from "gay-bashing" and other forms of violence. They rallied to such cries as "Out of the Closets and into the Streets," and "Gay is Just as Good as Straight." Gay groups pursued agendas of political and social activism. Gay and lesbian associations were established in the workplace. Television began to portray homosexuals in less stereotypical terms, and by 2000 gay roles in television series were common. Canada's first Gay Pride celebration was staged discreetly in Toronto in 1972. A quarter century later, 750 000 people attended a Gay Pride parade in that city, more than in any other North American city. Although Canadians showed greater tolerance, gays hastened to point out that tolerance did not mean acceptance.

Gay community activists in Toronto, protesting a speech by right-wing family values advocate Anita Bryant, 1978.

Archives of Ontario/C193-3-0-3167, 78285-20, AO5290.

DISCRIMINATION BANNED

Gays also sought legal protection from discrimination, and recognition for same-sex couples. Laws changed slowly, and opposition, particularly from conservative religious groups, was substantial. In 1977, Quebec became the first province to prohibit discrimination by reason of sexual orientation. In 1999, a verdict of the Supreme Court of Canada compelled Alberta, the last province, to act.

In 1995 the Supreme Court of Canada ruled that the Charter of Rights and Freedoms prohibited discrimination against gays and lesbians. A series of court challenges established that gay couples possessed many of the rights and duties of married couples, and laws were rewritten to reflect this in such areas as spousal support, pension rights, adoption, and medical decision-making. In 1997, British Columbia became the first province to amend laws to extend legal recognition to same-sex relationships. More recently, some provincial courts have ruled that federal laws defining marriage as the union of one man and one woman violate the Charter's equality provisions. The federal government announced that it would obtain an opinion from the Supreme Court before deciding this contentious issue.

THE CHANGING ROLE OF WOMEN

After 1970, relations between the sexes underwent a fundamental transformation. By 2000, though the goal of full equality was still far from being achieved, the male-dominated society of a generation earlier had been substantially eroded. Women worked within a multitude of organizations, and promoted a variety of visions, to bring about these changes.

INSTITUTIONALIZED FEMINISM

When the government failed to act quickly on the recommendations of the Royal Commission on the Status of Women, women established, in 1972, the National Action Committee on the Status of Women, an umbrella organization now embracing 600 widely disparate associations representing 5 million members. Growing pressure brought Prime Minister Pierre Trudeau to appoint a minister responsible for the status of women and to establish the Canadian Advisory Council on the Status of Women. Most provinces appointed similar councils. Quebec's Conseil du statut de la femme, equipped with funds for research, produced a detailed plan for change, *Égalité et indépendance*. Women's groups organized a multitude of conferences and workshops during 1975, the year the United Nations decreed to be International Women's Year.

In part, the home became the battleground for equality of the sexes. Change came slowly, and child care continued to be mainly women's work. A federal government poster published during International Women's Year extolled the homemaker's virtues by linking "women's" jobs in the home to prestigious occupations: nurse, teacher, accountant, chef. Women criticized the publicity for failing to mention a homemaker's less-prestigious occupations: janitor, launderer, dishwasher, waitress, taxi driver, and maid.

The 1980s brought to the fore one very sombre element, hitherto seldom discussed openly: violence against women. Reports showed that as many as 10 percent of wives suffered beatings and noted that the numbers appeared to be increasing. In response, Ottawa announced major funding initiatives. Local women's groups opened shelters to assist homeless and battered women. They also set up rape-crisis centres, fought for laws restricting pornography, and organized assistance for Native women, immigrant and refugee women, and women on welfare.

Editorial staff of *Chatelaine*, 1972. Traditionally a homemakers' magazine, *Chatelaine* switched its emphasis to women's issues in the 1970s.

Courtesy of *Chatelaine* © Maclean Hunter Publishing Ltd.

WOMEN IN THE WORK FORCE

In the 1970s, union membership grew far more quickly among females than it did among males, and unions started to pay greater heed to women's needs. In one case, women backed by the United Steel Workers filed a complaint for discrimination with the Ontario Human Rights Commission, to force Stelco to hire women for production jobs at its plant in Hamilton. The commission's verdict was favourable, and Stelco began hiring women for these well-paid jobs. In Quebec, women's committees succeeded in convincing their unions to adopt policies on child care, maternity benefits, equal pay for work of equal value, job safety, sexual harassment, and discrimination. The myth of female docility evaporated rapidly as women-dominated organizations such as nurses' unions waged bitter, sometimes illegal, strikes against what they judged to be unsatisfactory working conditions. Although women remained underrepresented in union executives, particularly in international unions, they began to play a greater role, as symbolized by the election in 1975 of Grace Hartman as president of the Canadian Union of Public Employees (CUPE), Canada's largest union, and in 1986 of Shirley Carr as head of the Canadian Labour Congress. Yet the majority of women still worked in difficult-to-organize sectors such as banks, restaurants, offices, and retail stores. They often worked part-time as well.

Working outside the home necessitated better daycare facilities, and governments moved to make such care more affordable and available. Quebec, for example, set up a system of publicly-supported centres where parents paid just $5 a day per child. Across Canada, there were far more families with pre-school children than there were spaces in licensed daycare centres.

By the 1970s, the principle of equal pay for men and women performing the same task had gained wide recognition. Yet, in the 1980s, the average woman's wage remained at approximately 65 percent of the average man's. Although women's lesser work experience and the generally lower educational levels of older women explained part of this difference, the continued concentration of women in low-paying occupations appeared to be the principal factor.

EMPLOYMENT EQUITY

In 1984, the federal Commission on Equality in Employment recommended employment-equity programs, to be implemented through affirmative action. Ottawa responded by requiring employers under federal jurisdiction, such as banks and national transportation companies, to give women and minorities better job opportunities. It also made affirmative-action plans mandatory for all firms doing business with the government.

The notion of equal pay for work of equal value, or pay equity, became the battleground of the 1990s, as women argued that they were generally paid less than men for jobs requiring similar skills, effort, responsibility, and educational levels, and entailing similar working conditions. Ottawa and some provinces instituted pay-equity laws, which forced employers to compare the value of the work being done in their male- and female-dominated work categories and then to increase the wages of any women who, according to the results of the comparisons, were being underpaid.

The growing conservatism of the 1990s and early 2000s had implications for women. In Ontario, for example, the Harris government, which took office in 1995, repealed certain elements of the province's pay-equity legislation. Women judged that government budget cuts in health and welfare and the struggle against poverty hit them disproportionately. Still, there was progress toward greater equality. Statistics Canada reported that the gap between higher men's pay and lower women's pay decreased substantially between 1985 and 1995. By 2000, women occupied about one-third of managerial positions, usually on lower rungs, but only 10 percent of corporate directors were women. Half of the doctors and dentists were women, and nearly half of the new lawyers and accountants. Not surprisingly, women experienced increased levels of stress and even depression as they attempted to hold down jobs while raising families.

Challenges for Labour

While the claims of women moved forward rapidly in the late twentieth century, those of labour encountered serious obstacles. The numerous strikes in the public sector during the 1970s alienated public opinion. Taxpayers quickly realized that they would have to foot the bill for what many viewed as excessive government generosity. Moreover, most Canadian workers did not belong to unions. They, as well as many workers affiliated to small organizations, resented the attempts of the most powerful unions to secure a greater share of the national wealth for their members. Canada acquired a negative image for the frequency of its strike activity.

The 1980s and 1990s brought new challenges. A more conservative public approved governments that moved to limit strikes, freeze or cut wages, and reduce the number of employees. Private-sector unions fared no better. Many high-paying manufacturing jobs disappeared as companies "rationalized" their operations. New contracts often imposed wage rollbacks, or pegged wages to profitability, or brought a reduced pay scale for new employees. Recessions undermined the bargaining power of unions and thus severely limited the number of work stoppages. Unions themselves were often torn by internal strife.

Recruitment increased in the late 1990s, reversing a downward trend, thanks in part to an improving economy. By 2002, about one-third of Canadian workers were unionized. Labour attempted to reinvent itself, and to appeal to employees who now sought stress relief, schedules that did not disrupt family life, and greater control over their careers. Unions sought new members where they could find them. The United Steelworkers, for example, diversified into call centres, telemarketing, data processing, and other new-technology domains. Still, unions often raided each other in the search for new members.

Cultural Concerns

After 1970, university expansion slowed. Student enrolments increased more modestly, although the proportion of women grew rapidly. By 2000, women full-time students were far more numerous than men in university bachelor's and master's degree programs, although engineering, applied science, and mathematics faculties still represented a largely male domain. A crisis in university financing appeared during the 1980s and early 1990s, as deficit-ridden provinces forced universities to accept real cuts in spending. Significantly, not one new university opened its doors in Canada between 1980 and 1994. Most provinces also imposed higher tuition fees and turned enthusiastically to corporate benefactors for additional financing. The late 1990s did see some public reinvestment in universities; in particular, the federal government, now laden with budget surpluses, invested heavily in research and funded large numbers of university chairs.

Contemporary Religion

Immigration from Asia diversified Canada's religious face, as sizable communities of Muslims, Buddhists, and Hindus became established. For most Canadians, however, the emphasis on individuality meant that religion became largely a personal matter. Canadians moved away from religions based on theology and denominational identification, and toward a view of religion as an inspiration for moral and ethical behaviour. The great majority said they still expected to turn to organized religion for rites such as baptisms, weddings, and funerals but, with the notable

New religious groups in Canada. A photo taken on Ste. Catherine Street, Montreal, May 1, 1993. Religion has become both more personal and highly diversified. Sociologist Reginald Bibby claims that Canadians now want "religion 'à la carte,' preferring to pick and choose ... from religious smorgasbords."

Photograph by Michel Brunelle.

exception of members of smaller Protestant conservative and evangelical churches, they attached diminishing importance to regular attendance at worship services. While two Canadians in three attended weekly religious services in 1946, only one in five did so in 2001. Sociologist Reginald Bibby, a long-time observer of Canadian religious behaviour, judged that Canadians now wanted "religion 'à la carte,' preferring to pick and choose beliefs, practices, programs, and professional services from increasingly diversified religious smorgasbords."[3] At the same time, he viewed most churches as simply unable to "sell their product effectively."

HEALTH

In the health-conscious 1970s and 1980s, many Canadians devoted long hours to exercise: they walked, they cycled, they swam, they jogged, and they gardened, sometimes relentlessly. When they tired of strenuous activity, they played Trivial Pursuit, invented by two Montrealers; it became the most popular board game of the 1980s. Or they learned to cook using the microwave ovens that entered a large majority of their homes in the course of the decade. They also enjoyed interactive games such as Nintendo on their home computers. And they watched more television, with more channels (for which they paid more money).

Increasingly mindful of the risks of cancer and heart disease, Canadians began to heed appeals to eat less salt, sugar, and fat, and to consume more vegetables, fruit, and whole grains. The number of tobacco smokers declined. Those who did smoke paid more taxes and saw their packages covered with grisly health warnings showing black lungs, infected gums and, in an appeal to men, limp cigarettes.

The rapid spread of the deadly AIDS (Acquired Immune Deficiency Syndrome) virus after 1980 finally brought health authorities to launch campaigns promoting "safe sex" or abstinence.

At first the disease hit gays, because of risky sexual practices. Then it spread among drug users, hemophiliacs, blood transfusion recipients, and heterosexuals. By 2000 the disease had killed more than 15 000 Canadians, but medical advances were helping to prolong the lives of those afflicted.

With the spread of the internet in the 1990s, a whole new world opened. Sedentary Canadians spent long hours in front of their computer screens discovering the world. Participation in sports dropped sharply. Preventive health measures seemed less popular. Rather than eat broccoli and tofu and drink fruit juices and low-fat milk, more people preferred the fare of the fast-food restaurants: triple hamburgers with cheese, large fries, and a large drink. Not surprisingly, by 2000, one-half of the adult population and one-third of children were over-weight. A serious health crisis seemed in the making.

SPORTS

Spectator sports dominated popular culture. Athletes basked in glory as long as they scored goals, hit runs, or won races on the slopes in the winter and on the speedways in the summer, and as long as they avoided the steroids that proved to be widely used in certain field sports. Hockey enjoyed immense interest, but it now had to share the spotlight with football, baseball, and, increasingly, basketball. The Blue Jays baseball team in Toronto, which began playing in 1977, became the most financially successful enterprise in any sport and went on to win the World Series in 1992 and 1993.

Hockey underwent an important expansion in the 1970s as the National Hockey League took in several franchises from the failed World Hockey Association. Although most players were Canadian, most new teams were American, and American directors made the important decisions. Wayne Gretzky, undoubtedly the sport's major revelation of this era, attained the crowning glory of being pictured on the cover of *Time*. As players' salaries soared, teams found survival more difficult in small Canadian markets. The Canadian public strongly disapproved proposals for government assistance to millionaire players and owners. Some owners then sought to sell their teams to larger American markets. The Quebec Nordiques, for example, were transferred to Denver where they promptly won the Stanley Cup.

In the late 1960s, Ottawa discovered the importance of sport as an instrument for promoting national unity and yielding political capital. It then began investing heavily in high-performance sports in order to produce more medal-winners in international competitions. The Canada–Soviet hockey series in 1972 showed that the return on such investments could be considerable. Watched by the largest Canadian television audience on record until that time, Team Canada won the series in the last seconds of the dramatic final encounter. One ecstatic Canadian university president suggested that the series probably did more to create a Canadian identity than ten years of Canada Council fellowships.

OLYMPIC GAMES

Montreal hosted the summer Olympic Games in 1976, the first time that this prestigious international gathering took place in Canada. (In 1988, Calgary was the site of the winter Olympics.) Provincial and municipal taxpayers were uneasy at the prospect of new budget deficits, but Montreal mayor Jean Drapeau assured them there was no more possibility of incurring a deficit than there was of his becoming pregnant. After the Olympic lottery, Olympic coins, Olympic stamps, and other promotional paraphernalia failed to prevent a massive deficit, delighted cartoonists drew sketches of a pregnant mayor.

Canadian women's hockey team, with team coach Danièle Sauvageau (in the centre) just after winning the women's gold medal at the Salt Lake City Olympics.

Canadian Press/COA/Mike Redwood.

The winter Olympics held in Salt Lake City in 2002 provided Canadians with much satisfaction. When figure skaters Jamie Salé and David Pelletier failed to win first place because of a bribed judge, the resulting outcry forced Olympic officials to reconsider the result, and to award a gold medal to the Canadian couple. Speedskaters Catriona Le May Doan and Marc Gagnon also rose to the challenge and secured gold medals. Both Canadian women's and men's hockey teams won first place by triumphing over American teams. Canadians felt good, and passionately Canadian. They celebrated enthusiastically in the streets, they waved flags, and they vowed, "We're not going to be pushed around by the Americans any more." Globalization had not struck down nationalism. General Motors, describing itself as the Canadian Olympic team's proudest sponsor, had full-page Maple Leaf flags printed in newspapers, advising readers to post them in any window "to show how proud you are of our women's and men's national hockey teams." A consultant in sport policy called Canadian successes an emotional high-water mark for a generation. Pelletier and Salé then went on to grace cereal boxes, while proudly patriotic Canadian hockey stars returned to their mostly American teams where they were paid, of course, in American dollars.

CULTURAL DEVELOPMENT

In the nationalist climate of the 1970s, cultural development came to be inextricably linked to the affirmation of national identity. For many English-speaking Canadians, the danger to survival came increasingly from the United States, mainly because many other Canadians avidly consumed that country's cultural products.

After 1970, the Americanization of Canadian broadcasting in English continued apace, although Canadian cultural industries did enjoy some protection through regulatory barriers.

These determined, for example, how much non-Canadian programming could be broadcast on Canadian television stations. Then cable television enabled almost all Canadians to gain access to the major U.S. networks. The arrival of satellite dish services in the late 1990s made protection in this area virtually impossible.

Statistics showed the extent of foreign domination of Canada's cultural industries. By 1990, for example, foreign-owned publishers had acquired 80 percent of Canada's book market. Nearly 85 percent of record sales were foreign, as were 80 percent of magazines sold in Canada. When Canada moved to protect Canadian magazine publishers in 1998, the United States immediately threatened economic reprisals. In movie theatres, Canadian films had less than 5 percent of screen time, although a growing number of American producers, subsidized by the Canadian government, filmed in Toronto and Vancouver, considered a "Hollywood North." Yet some critics insisted that while Canadians consumed and borrowed American cultural products, they also reconstituted them and imprinted them with Canadian values. Sometimes they even sold them back to the Americans. In this way, cultural anthropologist Frank Manning maintained, "the beaver can, and does, bite back," although Manning was uncertain whether the bite was serious or only a playful nip.[4]

Ottawa also provided subsidies for artists in all fields and funded cultural infrastructures. In spite of reduced funding, the CBC continued to affirm its objective of preserving and enriching Canadianism. The National Film Board (NFB), another important publicly supported institution, produced numerous high-quality documentaries, a field in which it excelled. The Canadian Film Development Corporation, later Telefilm Canada, gave financial backing to several critical successes, among them Peter Carter's *The Rowdyman* and Gilles Carle's *La vraie nature de Bernadette*. After the mid-1980s, it shifted its emphasis toward television production.

The years 1985–2003 saw the production of several notable Canadian feature films. David Cronenberg's *Dead Ringers* proved a financial success, while several films by Atom Egoyan, among them *Speaking Parts* and *Exotica*, earned him an international reputation. Don McKellar's first feature-length film, *Last Night*, in which he mocks presumably Canadian virtues such as politeness and the welfare state, won a prize at the Cannes Festival. But Canadian films in English generally played to small audiences. Most did not have the glossy production values of American successes, and modest budgets meant modest promotion and modest distribution.

Quebec films represented close to 70 percent of Canada's entire feature-film industry; they were the most successful in competing with American films. In 2002, a Quebec film, *Séraphin: Un homme et son péché*, an adaptation of a well-known novel by Claude-Henri Grignon, became the biggest blockbuster in Quebec's film history; more than one million Quebecers flocked to theatres to shed a tear for the long-suffering Donalda, victim of her miserly husband. The film was set in St. Adèle, a village in the Laurentians north of Montreal, in the 1890s when landless pioneers were colonizing the region's poor farmlands.

Alanis Morissette

CP Picture Archive/Andrew Wallace.

Canadian television had notable successes, too. The 1990s saw the production by Radio-Canada of the series *Lance et compte*, centred on the professional and love lives of a group of hockey players; it proved an astounding success, attracting nearly half of the total French-language viewing public. The miniseries *Anne* and *Road to Avonlea*, based on Lucy Maud Montgomery's perennially and internationally popular novel, *Anne of Green Gables*, enchanted millions of nightly viewers in 1999. The "Anne industry" also attracted hundreds of thousands of foreign tourists, many of them from Japan, to Anne's supposed homestead in Prince Edward Island. In music, such groups as the Philosopher Kings, Tragically Hip, and Barenaked Ladies carried off numerous awards, while such singers as Céline Dion, Alanis Morissette, Shania Twain, and Kevin Parent gained widespread notoriety.

CANADIAN LITERATURE

After 1970, there were more Canadian writers and they wrote more. The growth of universities, as well as increased government funding and a larger population, help explain this significant growth. International acclaim gave many writers publicity, and established their reputations abroad as much as within Canada.

Literature mirrored Canadians' preoccupations, attitudes, and aspirations. Nationalist themes, for example, recurred frequently in novels in both English and French Canada, particularly during the 1970s. Many literary works explored the experience of minority groups such as Native peoples and immigrants. For example, Joy Kogawa, in *Obasan*, poignantly evoked the fate of Japanese Canadians during World War II, while Acadian author Antonine Maillet painted a new image of Acadia and its people in her works. Other novels explored lesbian or gay themes. Historical settings were also common. *Les filles de Caleb*, Arlette Cousture's novel about the life of a family in the Mauricie region of Quebec a century ago, inspired a long-lasting television series.

Some writers set their works in small towns with closed societies. An example was Deptford, the scene of a powerful trilogy of novels by Robertson Davies featuring vivid central characters. Others dwelt upon the realities of urban living. Quebec playwright Michel Tremblay's works have featured a wide variety of Montrealers, including elegant upper-class ladies, drag queens, country singers, and very ordinary mortals from the working-class neighbourhoods he knew as a boy. Canadian literature also underlines the important role that regions have played in Canadian life. Atlantic writer David Adams Richards wrote of poverty and pride in north-eastern New Brunswick in *The Coming of Winter* and *Blood Ties*, while W.O. Mitchell's *Roses Are Difficult Here* chronicled a year in the life of an Alberta foothills town called Shelby.

More recently, an increasing number of Canadian authors have written for international audiences. Margaret Atwood's novels saw phenomenal sales abroad. *The Blind Assassin*, which won the prestigious British Booker Prize in 2000, told the story of a woman growing up in a small Ontario town before World War I. In 2002, three of the finalists for the Booker prize, Yann Martel, Carol Shields, and Rohinton Mistry, were Canadian authors; Martel was awarded the prize. In the words of one critic, foreign attention proved a wonderful reinforcement for "neurotically insecure Canadians." Here, perhaps, was the globalization of Canadian culture.

SOCIAL ISSUES

Poverty remained a serious problem despite what was, generally, a growing economy. Governments revamped social programs such as aid to families and pensions to seniors, taking away payments from higher-income Canadians but increasing assistance to the poorest. At the same time, spending cuts pushed Canadians on social assistance below low-income cutoff lines. The poor failed to come any closer to the rich in terms of income. Marital breakdown, together with the trend to reject the institution of marriage, resulted in large numbers of single-parent families, most of them headed by women. Many of these families had very low incomes. One critic captured the dilemma of many poor parents in the title of a book, *Pay the Rent or Feed the Kids*.

As unemployment grew during the recession of 1990, rising demand overwhelmed food banks in urban areas. Canadian cities also saw the emergence of a homeless class that included refugees, people with mental and physical disabilities, Native people, single mothers with children, youth, and substance abusers. Increasingly, provincial spending cuts to welfare and social housing were seen as primary causes of homelessness.

CRIME

Rising crime rates became a serious social concern in the 1970s and 1980s. Many offences were drug-related. Although violent crime nearly doubled in the 1980s, rates for murder and armed robbery remained far lower than in the United States. Crime rates in Canada varied from one province to another, but they tended to increase steadily from east to west. In the 1990s, however, crime rates dropped steadily, as the cohort of young Canadians decreased in size. Tragically, suicides were seven times more common than murders. Across Canada suicide prevention groups were set up to assist distressed persons.

THE ENVIRONMENT

Environmental issues gained increasing visibility after 1970 as Canadians discovered the negative aftermath of the unbridled, almost unregulated, development of past decades. They also learned that environmental issues were global in nature: the "greenhouse effect," the depletion of the ozone layer, the pollution of air and water, and the destruction of tropical and temperate rain forests all involved worldwide responsibility, and solutions required international cooperation. During the 1980s and 1990s, Canada signed several multilateral agreements on the environment, notably those concerning climate change and biological diversity.

More importantly, many Canadians came to see themselves, and perhaps especially others, as part of the problem. An expanding and wealthier population oriented toward consumption produced large quantities of wastes. It also made unsustainable demands upon natural resources. The burning of fossil fuels to heat homes, to run automobiles, and to drive industries fouled the air; most scientists agreed that it also favoured climate change through the so-called "greenhouse gases" it produced. As numerous lakes and streams of the Canadian Shield became lifeless and as the surrounding vegetation showed increasing evidence of damage, Canadians realized the devastating effects of acid rain. Many industries also spewed chemical effluents into both air and water. Agricultural methods, such as straightening streams and small watercourses, contributed to the erosion of topsoil and, through the abundant use of pesticides, herbicides, and fertilisers, to the pollution of water. Farmers and property developers drained ecologically sensitive wetlands for agricultural or residential purposes, logging companies prepared to harvest the country's last old-growth stands of timber, and untouched wilderness receded still further north.

No easy solutions existed. Concerned citizens set up associations to publicize environmental dangers or to propose solutions. Some groups, such as the World Wildlife Fund, had international ramifications. Other groups were Canadian creations. Greenpeace itself, a well-known multinational environmental lobby, had its origins in Vancouver.

GOVERNMENTS AND THE ENVIRONMENT

Public pressure brought governments to take an interest in the environment. They established standards for clean air and clean water, and set up agencies to monitor compliance. They also provided for environmental assessments of important projects such as the construction of dams. In the late 1990s, however, provincial governments gave priority to eliminating deficits and reducing taxes. They found it politically easier to cut environmental spending than health care. With lower budgets, governments often failed to apply their own laws and to monitor compliance. In a report in 2002, the federal environmental commissioner concluded that Ottawa was not respecting its international obligations regarding sustainable development.

Disposal of the millions of tonnes of wastes that Canadians produced annually proved increasingly onerous. In the early 1970s, landfill sites replaced open garbage dumps, but rural residents strenuously resisted having these sites in their "back yards." With the aid of provincial subsidies, municipal governments gradually instituted recycling programs for glass, metals, paper, and plastics. The problem of storing or eliminating toxic wastes proved particularly controversial.

The battle for cleaner air and water involved tradeoffs. Pulp and paper mills polluted rivers and smelters poisoned the air, but they also provided jobs and revenues. When provincial governments attempted to impose costly pollution controls, companies often resisted and threatened to shut down operations. Controlling air and water pollution meant difficult and prolonged negotiations with the United States, whose industries were major polluters of Canada's water and air.

Conflicting economic and environmental preoccupations were also in evidence in regard to the problem of preserving biological diversity. Although Canada created new national parks and marine conservation areas, many natural regions still had few or no protected areas. Worse, forestry, mining, and agriculture and recreational activities in areas adjacent to existing parks as well as within them caused increased ecological stress on the parks themselves.

THE KYOTO PROTOCOL

The major struggle pitting environmental considerations against economic development in the late 1990s and early 2000s concerned Canada's plans to ratify the international pact on the reduction of greenhouse gases signed in Kyoto, Japan in 1997. The pact was based on the theory that such gases caused climate change which would result in dangerous levels of global warming and a greater incidence of extreme weather. While Canadians debated the merits of reducing emissions of greenhouse gases, emissions increased substantially.

As time passed, opposition to Kyoto mounted. The refusal of the United States to ratify the protocol raised concerns about Canada's competitiveness with its major economic partner. Alberta, in particular, led the charge against Kyoto, fearful that ratification would hurt its petroleum and gas sector. Industry asserted that compliance would cost jobs and investment, and launched a heavy advertising campaign, especially in Ontario. Ottawa finally ratified the treaty in 2002 but there was as yet no broad national agreement on a strategy to meet Canada's obligations.

Since 1867, Canada has evolved into an increasingly complex society. The nation's population diversified ethnically and culturally in the nineteenth and, more rapidly, in the twentieth century. Material progress and improved living conditions, though by no means continuous, were generally apparent; their attendant costs, both human and environmental, were at first less apparent, except to their immediate victims. After 1960, however, Canadians in general came to realize that high living standards and consumer choices often entailed environmental degrada-

A Canada goose stands on railway tracks as a plant belches smoke in Hamilton, Ontario. In 2002, the Canadian Parliament ratified the Kyoto protocol designed to limit the growth of greenhouse gases deemed responsible for climate change.

CP Picture Archive/Kevin Frayer.

tion. The role of the state increased greatly, especially after 1930, when governments came to play a role in virtually every aspect of human existence. Associations of all types proliferated as Canadians sought to counter the powerlessness of the individual acting alone.

Although Canada has undergone immense change, in many respects the basic themes of the country's early history remain operative today. In 1867, four major groups made up Canada's population — the Native peoples, French-speaking Canadians, English-speaking Canadians, and immigrants; today, the same four groups are evident, although not in the same proportion as in 1867. Canada in 1867 was a nation of regions; despite modern transportation and the communications revolution, it remains so today — indeed, to such an extent that doubts have often abounded about the survival of existing political arrangements. By the 1880s, federal–provincial affairs had become acrimonious; more than a century later, conflict continued to pervade intergovernmental contacts. French–English relations were the source of bitter controversy in the nineteenth century; intercultural relations have continued to generate passionate debate in the twentieth. Relations with the Native peoples were an important preoccupation in the nineteenth century as European settlement expanded westward; during the second half of the twentieth century, Aboriginal rights became a complex but very present public-policy question.

In 1867, British and American influences weighed heavily on the new nation; today, the impact of the United States on Canada — culturally, politically, and economically — is in many ways far more weighty. Finally, despite the coming of the welfare state, flagrant social inequalities distinguish Canadians from one another, much as they did in the past. Reductions in government spending for social services may well increase these inequalities. Constant change, but equally apparent continuity — these are the two themes that reflect the past as the inhabitants of the northern half of North America enter the twenty-first century.

NOTES

1. Sylvia Bashevkin, *Toeing the Lines: Women and Party Politics in English Canada*, 2nd ed. (Toronto: Oxford University Press, 1993), p. vi.
2. John Herd Thompson and Stephen J. Randall, *Canada and the United States: Ambivalent Allies*, 3rd ed. (Montreal/Kingston: McGill-Queen's University Press, 2002), p. 274.
3. Reginald Bibby, *Mosaic Madness: The Poverty and Potential of Life in Canada* (Toronto: Stoddart, 1990), p. 84.
4. David H. Flaherty and Frank E. Manning, eds., *The Beaver Bites Back? American Popular Culture in Canada* (Montreal/Kingston: McGill-Queen's University Press, 1993), p. 4.

LINKING TO THE PAST

Canadian Charter of Rights and Freedoms
http://laws.justice.gc.ca/en/charter/

The full text of the Charter of Rights and Freedoms.

The North American Free Trade Agreement
http://www.sice.oas.org/trade/nafta/naftatce.asp

The full text of the North American Free Trade Agreement.

Canada's Seniors at a Glance
http://www.hc-sc.gc.ca/seniors-aines/pubs/seniors_at_glance/poster1_e.html

Facts and statistics on Canada's aging population, including life expectancy, income, expenditures, living arrangements, and health.

Canadian Lesbian and Gay Archives
http://www.clga.ca/

The online component of the archives includes chronologies, essays, articles, and biographies of accomplished gay and lesbian Canadians.

Status of Women Canada
http://www.swc-cfc.gc.ca/

Gender equality, economic issues, and policy research are among the topics explored on this site from Status of Women Canada, the federal government's department charged with promoting gender equality and the full participation of women in the economic, social, cultural, and political life of the country.

Greenpeace Canada
http://www.greenpeace.ca/

The official site of Greenpeace, founded in Vancouver in 1971.

BIBLIOGRAPHY

Bibliographical material on contemporary Canadian history is abundant; only a sampling of works can be given here. On economic issues consult Kenneth Norrie and Doug Owram, *A History of the Canadian Economy*, 3rd ed. (Toronto: Nelson Thomson, 2002); and Michael Hart, *A Trading Nation: Canadian Trade*

Policy from Colonialism to Globalization (Vancouver: UBC Press, 2002). Critical studies of Canadian–American economic relations include Stephen Clarkson's two works, *Canada and the Reagan Challenge*, 2nd ed. (Toronto: James Lorimer, 1985), and *Uncle Sam and Us: Globalization, Neoconservatism, and the Canadian State* (Toronto: University of Toronto Press, 2002). Concerning the free-trade debate see Marc Gold and David Leyton-Brown, eds., *Trade-Offs on Free Trade: The Canada–U.S. Free Trade Agreement* (Toronto: Carswell, 1988).

Writings on the environment include Chad Gaffield and Pam Gaffield, eds., *Consuming Canada: Readings in Environmental History* (Toronto: Copp Clark, 1995); Kathryn Harrison, *Passing the Buck: Federalism and Canadian Environmental Policy* (Vancouver: University of British Columbia Press, 1996); Judith I. McKenzie, *Environmental Politics in Canada: Managing the Commons into the Twenty-First Century* (Toronto: Oxford, 2002); and Mark Jaccard, John Nyboer and Bryn Sadownik, *The Cost of Climate Policy* (Vancouver: UBC Press, 2002).

Political parties are examined in Hugh G. Thorburn and Alain Whitehorn, eds., *Party Politics in Canada*, 8th ed. (Toronto: Prentice-Hall, 2001). An excellent account of the Trudeau years may be found in Stephen Clarkson and Christina McCall, *Trudeau and Our Times*, vol. 1, *The Magnificent Obsession*; vol. 2, *The Heroic Delusion* (Toronto: McClelland & Stewart, 1990, 1994). For a critical dissection of the Mulroney government see Brooke Jeffrey, *Breaking Faith: The Mulroney Legacy of Deceit, Destruction and Disunity* (Toronto: Key Porter, 1992). On Jean Chrétien see Jeffrey Simpson, *The Friendly Dictatorship*, rev. ed. (Toronto: McClelland and Stewart, 2002). Studies of the Canadian left include Alan Whitehorn, *Canadian Socialism: Essays on the CCF–NDP* (Toronto: Oxford University Press, 1992).

Useful works on federal–provincial relations include David Milne, *Tug of War: Ottawa and the Provinces under Trudeau and Mulroney* (Toronto: James Lorimer, 1986); and Garth Stevenson, *Unfulfilled Union: Canadian Federalism and National Unity*, 3rd ed. (Toronto: Gage, 1989). Keith Banting and Richard Simeon, eds., *And No One Cheered: Federalism, Democracy and the Constitution Act* (Toronto: Methuen, 1983) presents a highly critical analysis of patriation.

Among surveys of Canada's international relations see John English and Norman Hillmer, *Making a Difference? Canada's Foreign Policy in a Changing World Order* (Toronto: Lester, 1992); Thomas F. Keating, *Canada in World Order: The Multilateralist Tradition in Canadian Foreign Policy*, 2nd ed. (Toronto: Oxford University Press, 2001); J.L. Granatstein and Robert Bothwell, *Pirouette: Pierre Trudeau and Canadian Foreign Policy* (Toronto: University of Toronto Press, 1990); Nelson Michaud and Kim Richard Nossal, eds., *Diplomatic Departures: The Conservative Era in Canadian Foreign Policy* (Vancouver: UBC Press, 2001); and John Herd Thompson and Stephen J. Randall, *Canada and the United States: Ambivalent Allies*, 3rd ed. (Montreal/Kingston: McGill-Queen's University Press, 2002).

The history of women in Canada is covered in Alison Prentice et al., *Canadian Women: A History*, 2nd ed. (Toronto: Harcourt Brace, 1996). Labour history is examined in Bryan D. Palmer, *Working-Class Experience: Rethinking the History of Canadian Labour, 1800–1991*, 2nd ed. (Toronto: McClelland & Stewart, 1992). On higher education see Paul Axelrod, *Values in Conflict: The University, the Marketplace, and the Trials of Liberal Education* (Montreal/Kingston: McGill-Queen's University Press, 2002). David H. Flaherty and Frank E. Manning, eds., *The Beaver Bites Back? American Popular Culture in Canada* (Montreal/Kingston: McGill-Queen's University Press, 1993), defines originality in Canadian culture. On one aspect of the development of Canadian culture see Ted Magder, *Canada's Hollywood: The Canadian State and Feature Films* (Toronto: University of Toronto Press, 1993).

Colin Howell, *Blood, Sweat, and Cheers: Sport and the Making of Modern Canada* (Toronto: University of Toronto Press, 2001), is an informative study of sports history. Reginald W. Bibby analyzes contemporary religion in *Restless Gods: The Renaissance of Religion in Canada* (Toronto: Stoddart, 2002). On gays and lesbians see Gary Kinsman, *The Regulation of Desire: Homo and Hetero Sexualities*, 2nd ed. (Montreal: Black Rose Books, 1996); and Tom Warner, *Never Going Back: A History of Queer Activism in Canada* (Toronto: University of Toronto Press, 2002).

The evolution of Canada's welfare state is discussed in Raymond Blake and Jeff Keshen, eds., *Social Welfare Policy in Canada: Historical Readings* (Toronto: Copp Clark, 1995); and James J. Rice and Michael J. Prince, *Changing Politics of Canadian Social Policy* (Toronto: University of Toronto Press, 2000). Health care issues are discussed in C. David Naylor, ed., *Canadian Health Care and the State: A Century of Evolution* (Montreal/Kingston: McGill-Queen's University Press, 1992). On housing, consult John R. Miron, ed., *House, Home, and Community: Progress in Housing Canadians* (Montreal/Kingston: McGill-Queen's University Press, 1993).

Canadian Prime Ministers Since Confederation

Sir John Alexander Macdonald
Conservative, 1867–73, 1878–91

Alexander Mackenzie
Liberal, 1873–78

Sir John Joseph Caldwell Abbott
Conservative, 1891–92

Sir John Sparrow David Thompson
Conservative, 1892–94

Sir Mackenzie Bowell
Conservative, 1894–96

Sir Charles Tupper
Conservative, 1896

Sir Wilfrid Laurier
Liberal, 1896–1911

Sir Robert Laird Borden
Conservative and Unionist, 1911–20

Arthur Meighen
Unionist and Conservative, 1920–21
Conservative, 1926

William Lyon Mackenzie King
Liberal, 1921–26, 1926–30, 1935–48

Richard Bedford Bennett
Conservative, 1930–35

Louis Stephen St. Laurent
Liberal, 1948–57

John George Diefenbaker
Progressive Conservative, 1957–63

Lester Bowles Pearson
Liberal, 1963–68

Pierre Elliott Trudeau
Liberal, 1968–79, 1980–84

Charles Joseph Clark
Progressive Conservative, 1979–80

John Napier Turner
Liberal, 1984

Martin Brian Mulroney
Progressive Conservative, 1984–93

Kim Campbell
Progressive Conservative, 1993

Jean Chrétien
Liberal, 1993–2003

Paul Martin
Liberal, 2003–

Index